EXPLORING MID-MICHIGAN

EXPLORING MID-MICHIGAN

A GUIDE TO FLINT, THE SAGINAW VALLEY, AND THE THUMB

Edited by Mary Jo Kietzman and Paul M. Gifford

MICHIGAN STATE UNIVERSITY PRESS | *East Lansing*

Michigan State University Press
East Lansing, Michigan 48823-5245

Library of Congress Cataloging-in-Publication Data
Names: Kietzman, Mary Jo editor | Gifford, Paul M. editor
Title: Exploring mid-Michigan : a guide to Flint, the Saginaw Valley, and the Thumb /
edited by Mary Jo Kietzman and Paul M. Gifford.
Description: East Lansing : Michigan State University Press, 2026. | Includes bibliographical references.
Identifiers: LCCN 2026001292 | ISBN 9781611865776 paperback | ISBN 9781609178314 |
ISBN 9781628955811 | ISBN 9781611865790 hardcover
Subjects: LCSH: Flint (Mich.)—Description and travel | Saginaw River Valley (Mich.)—Description and travel |
Lower Peninsula (Mich.)—Description and travel | LCGFT: Guidebooks
Classification: LCC F574.F62 E97 2026
LC record available at https://lccn.loc.gov/2026001292

Cover design by David Drummond
Cover art is "Saginaw Michigan skyline along the banks of the Saginaw River"

Visit Michigan State University Press at *www.msupress.org*

CONTENTS

PART IV. Tours

PREFACE

I learned about the Federal Writers' Project (FWP) state guides around the time I walked the length of the St. Clair River, preparing to teach a First-Year Experience as part of a cohort of classes that explored "Borders and Crossings." Immersion in the history and culture of an unfamiliar Michigan microregion that grew around and in the islands in the St. Clair River delta was a powerful self-educational experience. I wanted to help other people have a similar immersive experience in Flint and the Saginaw Valley. I purchased the 1941 *Michigan: A Guide to the Wolverine State* and found it still useful after many years. Would it be possible to get a group of writers together, recreate the FWP process and together produce a regional guide? I decided to give it the old college try and hoped the process and our starting point—the Saginaw River and its watershed—would produce a new, more holistic vision for it.

A grant from the Michigan Humanities Council was my cue to assemble a team composed of colleagues, former students, and new connections from around the region. I used the grant money to pay young writers for their travel and writing (in the spirit of the Works Progress Administration), helping them gain professional experience and have some adventures.

Flint's tainted water supply was still on everyone's minds at the start of the project, but a focus on rivers and the greater watershed promised to take us somewhere new, beyond our troubled city's limits. Local history, by its nature, whether written by antiquarians, genealogists, or academics, tends to be just that—local. It focuses on a particular place, defined by political boundaries (city, village, township, county) and ignores the places that surround it. People who live in one place likely know little about places outside their own stomping grounds. This lack of familiarity extends to people with differing political views. White and Black people often fear each other's environments. City people think rural areas are playgrounds. Country folks view cities as dangerous. If we harbor any hope to advance our country, then, we need to get beyond our little comfort zones and explore outside them. We traveled the region for four years and were surprised by how much more connected things were in the past, before the automobile, redlining, the highway system, deindustrialization, and new technologies split places and people apart. Hope grew that our work might suggest ways to mend some of those broken links or, at the very least, make local people more curious about places they don't know or avoid.

Initially, we sent individual writers out to cover various topics and locales. We started with the idea that our guide would be a book of "tours." They submitted drafts, which contained valuable information, experiences, and perspectives, but as the book took shape, the editors recognized that the tour format didn't always work and that more research was needed. We reshaped draft writing for consistency of style and approach, while preserving individual voices. This process came to more closely resemble that of the FWP, in which a staff of editors and writers wrote from field notes and interviews collected by other paid writers.

We thought long and hard about whether and how to cite sources. We carefully researched every essay, profile, route, and tour and fact-checked stories we heard and read online and in county histories. But we decided not to load the text and burden the reader with heavy academic footnotes. Some sources are named in the text, others suggested, but all can be found in the comprehensive bibliography.

The project began in June 2021—the same month two U.S. congressional representatives introduced a bill to start a new FWP. Nothing came of that idea. But our group initiative produced the book you hold in your hand, which we hope you'll take on the road and use. What the guide lacks in reviews of restaurants and hotels is made up by its deep insights into the people and places that travelers might encounter. There are real journeys detailed here as well as suggestions for intellectual journeys: Topics, questions, events and issues, heretofore unrecognized, are raised so that ambitious readers and researchers might explore them.

Though we did not have a federal government or even a foundation underwriting this work, we had the steady advocacy of Ken Sylvester, director of the Office of Research at the University of Michigan–Flint, who also provided funds to supplement coverage of publication costs along with Theodore Rippey, dean of the College of Arts, Sciences, and Education. Their financial support kept the cost of the book low enough to be an affordable resource for the people of our region and a model for people in other communities, in and out of the Rust Belt, especially those that are troubled or overlooked.

ACKNOWLEDGMENTS

Research for this guide was an excuse for lots of road trips, daily walks, and canoe trips, but the best part of it all was having a good reason to call up and sit down with local people for casual talks and more formal interviews. From them I've learned about farming, German history and heritage, Black communities in Bay City and Port Huron, restoration of wetlands, toxicology, trains, and so much more.

I am most grateful to Tom Trombley, of the Castle Museum, and Sam Fitzpatrick, formerly of Bay County Historical Museum, and the volunteers at every local museum who generously shared their time and stories with us. Their knowledge is the backbone of this collection. They include Kim Ankley (Capac Community Historical Museum), Doug Deming (Sportsman's Haven in Sebewaing), Janet Gaith (Liken Museum in Sebewaing), Peggy Hellwig (Elkton Area Historical Society), Grai Joseph (Lapeer County Historical Society), Dan Kirshman (Steam Railroading Institute in Owosso), Gregory Lawrence (Cobblestone Museum), Lori Murawske (Frank Murphy Memorial Museum), Robert and Elaine Phillips (Deckerville Museum), Ann Ransford (Roethke House Museum), Steven Schulze (Pigeon Historical Museum), Scott Waller (Grand Blanc Historical Society), Gary Watt (Vassar Historical Museum), Cindy Willson (Millington-Arbela Historical Society), and Robin Zurek (Log Cabin Museum in Bad Axe). Thanks, too, to the volunteers at the other museums, in Bridgeport, Columbiaville, Mayville, North Branch, Otisville, and Watrousville.

Special thanks to Nancy Schuette for inviting Paul and me to visit her small dairy farm and for several long chats at her kitchen table. Other farming-educators include Dale Edgington, Laura DeLind, Noah Dutcher, Ginny Knagg, Pat McCarron, Wes Reinbold, and Roger Weiss. Eric Dunton, Shiawassee Refuge wildlife biologist, and Lisa L. Williams spent hours sharing their experiences working on issues related to restoration of the Shiawassee Flats and watershed pollution issues. Ann Kennedy invited me to spend the day at Eccles School, one of several active one-rooms in Huron County. Ralph Arellano (Flint), Anita Ashford (Port Huron), Jason Bias (Bancroft), Amy Cox (Marlette), Jacqui Gilbert (Ubly), Dan Haubenstricker (Frankenmuth), Krista Heiser (Millington/Fostoria), David McDonald (Bad Axe), Alex Mixter (Saginaw), Glen Morningstar (Hemlock), Darold Newton (Bay City), Carl Osentoski (Port Austin), and Kaye Sims (Kingston) gave generously of themselves to ensure that their communities were accurately represented.

Tom Huggler took me pheasant hunting, shared his writing, and thoughtfully answered every emailed question; Todd Shorkey, pilot of the *Princess Wenonah*, shared his knowledge of shipping; Myles Willard shared his research and time to teach me about Murphy Lake; and William Wright offered his wisdom from a life in and around Saginaw Bay. I am grateful to all the pastors who allowed me to visit their congregations, especially those on Flint's East Side: Burnetta Driver, Sister Christina Frey, Shelley Lassiter, Tommy McDoniel, and the late Betty Rogers. Jim Glasco, too, must be mentioned for sharing Calvarymen CDs, coffee, and inspired conversation. Thanks too to Sherry Hayden and Mike Keeler for a verbal and physical tour of Pierce Park. Family and friends of colleagues and students were generous with information: Joanie Childs, Harold Ford, Delma Jackson, Don Lierman, Bre Moore, Megan Moore, Linda Schwaderer, and Joshua Shank. Librarians who have been particularly helpful are Callum Carr (University of Michigan–Flint), Michael Madden (Flint Public Library), Grant Shaw (Hoyt Library), Rachel Stock (Sloan Museum), and Matthew Wolverton (University of Michigan–Flint).

INTRODUCTION

This book is neither the kind of guide that advertises sites nor a Pure Michigan commercial. It is rather an attempt to produce a guide like those written by the Federal Writers' Project (FWP) between 1937 and 1941. The FWP was a branch of Roosevelt's Works Progress Administration (WPA), a jobs program that helped Americans weather the storm of the Great Depression. WPA workers built bridges, dams, roads, and airports, while creative types, employed by the FWP, traveled back roads, visited libraries and museums, collected oral histories, and took photographs that were edited into volumes that held a mirror up to the people of each state. *Michigan: A Guide to the Wolverine State* was published in 1941, when automobile tourism was coming into its own.

Our guide focuses on a region that was the industrial-agricultural heart of Michigan that has beaten irregularly for the last three decades. The ten counties covered in the volume have lost almost everything they could lose: population, industries, small farms, natural resources, and clean water. But loss is not our focus; it is, after all, the habit of the world to fall apart. What we have seen in traveling the region and hope to make known is the staying power of the land and people, the people who arrived from far away, dug in their heels, gripped their tools, worked, and are now reworking the natural, human, and social landscapes around them. In our improvised, amateur, homespun epic, you'll encounter some pretty big characters, heroes in their own spheres of influence: lumberjacks, foundry workers, labor activists, utopian dreamers, missionaries, judges, natives who refuse to move, preachers in unlikely places, artists who paint street scenes, and poets who celebrate the child's desire to sink down in a mossy quagmire and come back a bird, or, with luck, a lion. We need these people, past and present, with their stories, ideas, and dreams, and they are here collected for you, so you can climb up on their shoulders and see all the way to Saginaw Bay and beyond.

A contributor to the 1941 guide thought optimistically that the easy-come, easy-go, take-as-much-as-you-want days were over. Well, history proved him wrong: Avarice, pride, and opportunism did not go out of style. The challenges facing people in mid-Michigan today are not so very different from those our civic ancestors faced: to humanize workplaces, be better stewards of natural resources, break up monocultures, and empower the rank and file. Size and numbers may measure success of an industry, city, university, or farm in the short term, but anything sustainable depends on the quality and depth of relationships—to the land and to one's neighbors. First things first: We must get to know both.

All of us, whether homegrown or transplanted, are summoned to the higher calling of learning as much as we can about the place we live in. Michael Evanoff gives us a powerful clue for approaching the task creatively. At the end of his St. John Street neighborhood memoir, he remembers times walking in Kearsley Park (on Flint's East Side), courting the girl he would marry, and making willow whistles. Evanoff's family immigrated to Flint from Macedonia when he was a young boy, and he grew up in the "international village" around the Buick factory. He did well in Flint schools, graduated from the University of Michigan School of Law, and eventually moved his family to the suburbs. Though his suburban lots had streams and plenty of willows, "for some reason, [he] never made another willow whistle." But he held onto the memory of the one he made in Flint and how it enabled him to rise like a lark over the dingy city.

Flint, birthplace of General Motors and the United Auto Workers (UAW), is the epicenter of this regional guide. The factories closed and took with them almost eighty-thousand jobs. Then crack cocaine, arson, violent crime followed, and just when things began to settle down, Flint had a water crisis. The world saw in Flint a human face unable to cover things up. Today, C. S. Mott's "model city" is every academic's case study for U-pick "urban" pathology. Disease narratives are important for exposing toxic conditions, but they isolate Flint, making the city vulnerable to ongoing exploitation. By restoring Flint to its regional context, we position it in a geographical community of cities that share a river system that drains highly productive land. We have never not had machines in the garden here. Migrants from Missouri and Mississippi as well as immigrants from Mexico and Macedonia were drawn to its urban-rural mix, and many hybrid forms of life emerged, including the occupational category of shop worker–farmer. Hybridization is the engine of evolution—as important as the thumb is to the hand—and local people who today continue integrating neighborhoods, fostering kids, teaching humanities, rotating crops, and experimenting with restorative agricultural methods ought to see their work of mixing and mingling for what it is: a creative force that offers a powerfully attractive alternative to living, thinking, producing, and consuming in discrete bubbles.

Watershed loosely determines the area covered in this guide. The Saginaw River Valley is the state's largest watershed in area, covering 8,700 square miles. Shaped like a butterfly facing the bay, its left wing reaches up almost to Houghton Lake, and its right wing brushes the north side of Pontiac. Its major rivers (Shiawassee, Tittabawassee, Flint, and Cass) combine in an enormous marshland that was once an ancient lake bottom. Cities were built on the high ground along riverbanks that slope into floodplains, edged with glacial moraines that are full of field, cobble, and pudding stones, which settlers picked up and worked into vernacular farmhouses and foundations. These four major rivers loosely define the regional boundaries. Because the Cass River rises out of a peat bog in the eastern Thumb (as does the Black River), we've included the whole peninsula in the study area.

Watershed is also a good model for thinking about community, because it is a system of relationships—between water and land, natural and manmade orders, as well as the different cities and towns connected by the rivers and tributaries. Abundantly fluid, our valley's first water problem was that there was too much of it. Surveyor General of the Northwest Territory Edward Tiffin, whose 1815 report describes swampy lakes and marshes interspersed by sandy ridges, could see no incentive for white settlers to move in. But move in they did, attracted by the "green gold" of the pines and the river system that promised easy transport of logs to Saginaw. There was the added incentive of cheap land after the Swamp Acts of 1849 and 1850 returned marshy lands to the states, which one could purchase for 50 cents to $1.50 an acre on the condition they be "improved." At that time, improvement meant making them suitable for farming, which required drainage. In the ancient "land between the rivers" of the Fertile Crescent, it was thought that the gods dug the canals and dredged the rivers. In the Saginaw Valley, that task was accomplished by settlers, who diked the spreading rivers, ditched the fields, and established drain commissions that formalized cooperative relationships between farmers. That work literally took a village.

Two hundred years of settlement and many watershed moments later, most of us realize that there are serious consequences for misusing natural resources. Drainage caused a host of other problems. Clear-cutting the forests was a bad idea. Unregulated hunting and fishing led to species' extinction. Putting thousands of trees and ships, chemicals, and waste in the rivers—any of them—caused irreparable damage to the environment and human health. Saginaw provides a case in point. The city's tap water, drawn from the river, tasted like chemicals for years, forcing residents to rely on hand pumps that drew water from wells. It wasn't until 1947, when the Army Corps of Engineers came to the Saginaw River Valley to address the flooding problem, that polluters across the watershed were identified and the public began to understand that watershed is, in a real sense, communal: My water is your water is our water is their water. Dumping in Flint, Chesaning, Lapeer, and Midland on tributaries had contaminated the Saginaw River, and the only solution was to build the Whitestone pipeline, completed in 1949, which brought water from Lake Huron. When, in 2014, city and state officials made the "cost effective" decision to switch Flint from Detroit water to Flint River water, no mention was made of Saginaw's decades-long water crisis.

Watershed vision gives us the big picture, the whole butterfly. Thinking comparatively helps us see the paths we might take, assess alternatives, develop shared resources, and borrow strategies from sister cities. Flint and Midland offer case studies of prosperous company towns with very different workforces. Saginaw has always had a wider array of industries, including foundries that drew large numbers of Black and brown workers and a history of segregated neighborhoods, urban renewal, and inner-city decay similar to that of Flint. Bay City's lumber-era red light district on Water Street is still drawing visitors to a restored waterfront for tall ships, a four-day annual fireworks festival, and boat cruises. All our cities were lumber towns, and Saginaw and Flint tightened links during the automotive era, but the connections were not just on the corporate level. Flint, Saginaw, and Bay City had working-class traditions that began with the Knights of Labor and the German Workingmen's Association, instrumental in organizing the Ten Hours or No Sawdust strike of 1885. In rural worlds, the Patrons of Husbandry and other farm advocacy groups supported the interests of farmers against corporate entities. All of these groups were, in a sense, forerunners of the UAW, which became a major force for change after Flint workers occupied factories for forty-four days in 1936–1937 to demand recognition of their union. Our region also had a number of colonies and intentional communities that provide case studies for the ways successful communities are established. When we know our neighbors, we can always go next door to borrow that cup of sugar, necessary tool, or pinch of wisdom. Going next door is the best way to heal histories of racial discrimination and segregation that have created donut cities with empty centers surrounded by mostly white suburbs and towns.

In writing our guidebook, we stayed relatively faithful to the structure of the 1941 original. "Part I: The General Background" contains essays on topics such as geography, archaeology, Native American history, migration and immigration, industry, race, and literature. "Part II: Cities" contains profiles, supplemented with experientially scaled pieces that explore particular neighborhoods, sites, and histories to break through prejudices about race, class, and beauty and blight. "Part III: Rural Locales" moves through the rural counties, including a swath of land settled by Germans, and a discussion of farming, and "Part IV: Thumb Tours" details four driving tours across the Thumb to special destinations like Shay Lake (a resort developed in the 1950s for Black city dwellers), the ancient petroglyphs, and unique ecosystems like Minden Bog. Some of the tours link places by geography or biogeography: the towns in the German belt, coastal wetlands, and agricultural lands. We conclude with a long section on regional ecology that details the change in progress from the great drying of the settlement period (when drainage was the norm) to the rewatering and protection of peat-producing wetlands that include marshes, bogs, swamps, and prairie fens. This section includes a list of recommended day trips and river paddles. The guide aims to enlarge the imagined home range of local readers, map out new areas for further study, and model a way of doing public history and public humanities that sees the unseen, prioritizes human connection, and requires teamwork to accomplish.

The FWP guides may be our North Star, but we also have two local muses: Ishdonquit ("Passing Cloud")—known locally as "Indian Dave"—an Ojibwe man who continued to live a traditional life, tracing and retracing the paths of his group's range, into the twentieth century and Bill Orling, an amateur painter, who documented the St. John Street neighborhood, even as bulldozers demolished it. Bill drove a truck for Flint schools but every day after work, he would head to the neighborhood to sketch. In a journal he kept, Bill wrote, "I look southwest at all the empty houses and know that real soon they will be gone. Kaput. At first, I avoided this being my duty, but no longer. Every bit of my spare time must be spent drawing street scenes."

Modern technology may have disabled native abilities. But the lives of Ishdonquit and Bill Orling remind us that we can reclaim them by moving around and getting to know the resources of our own watershed. If you follow their lead and take the hints found in these pages, Michigan's state motto, *Si quaeris peninsulam amoenam circumspice*, will become not just some old Latin words on a shield but a direction for your future: "If you seek a pleasant peninsula, look around you."

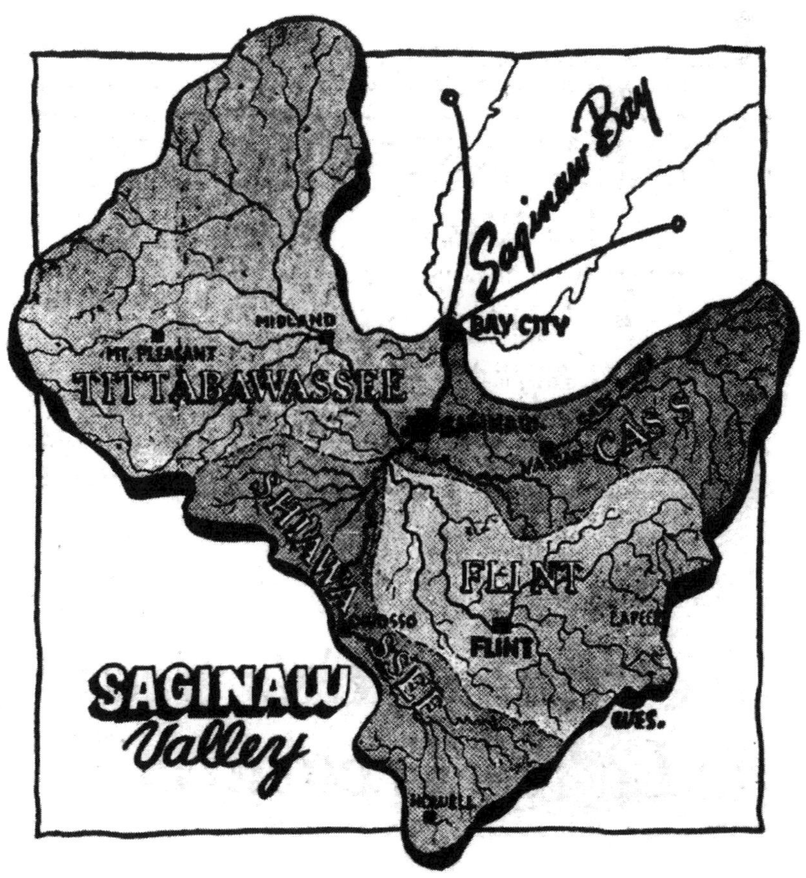

Saginaw Valley "Butterfly." Like the insect, the watershed is also capable of transformation.

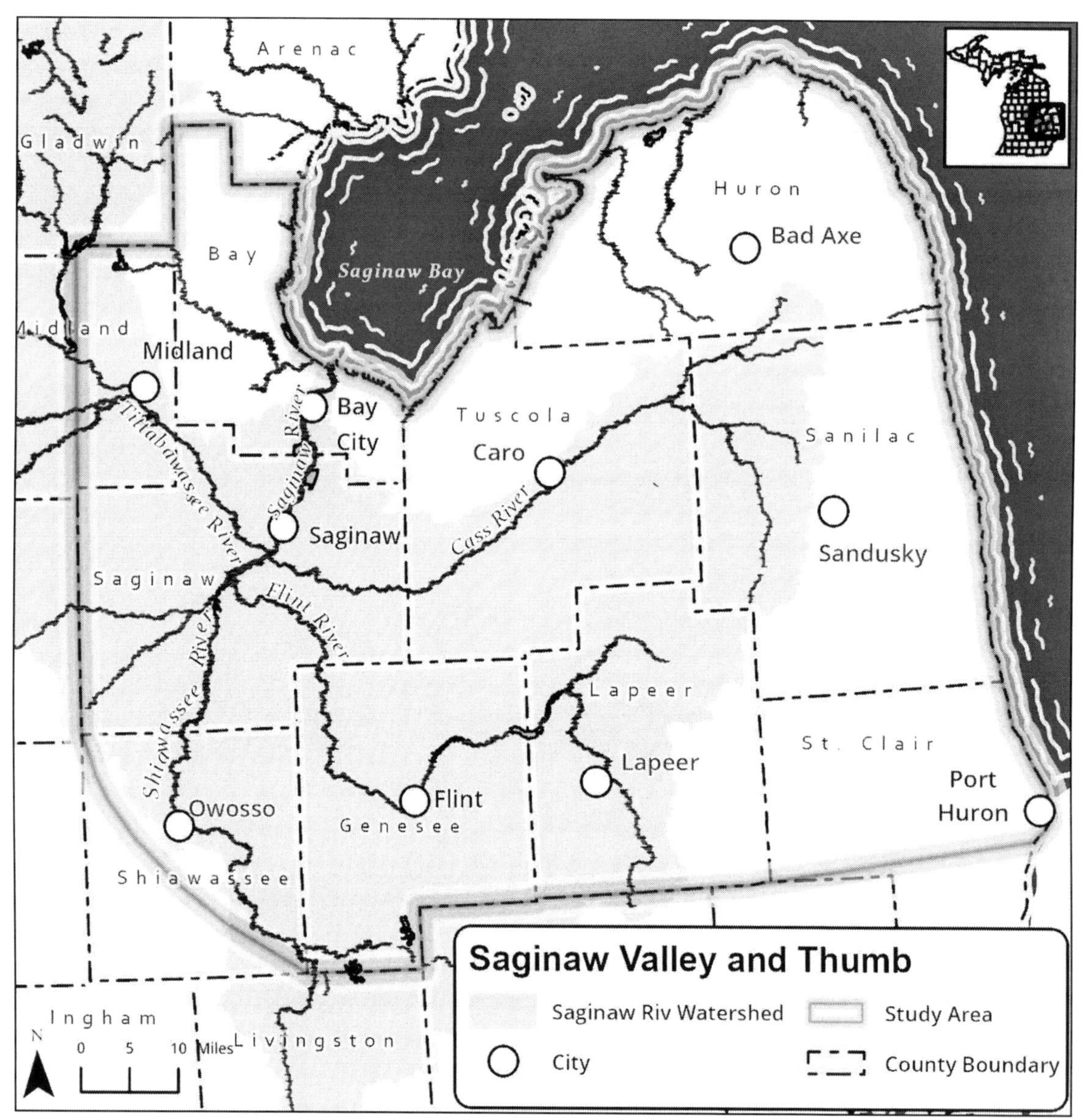

Saginaw Valley and Thumb. UNIVERSITY OF MICHIGAN–FLINT GIS CENTER.

PART I

THE GENERAL BACKGROUND

NATURAL SETTING

Martin M. Kaufman

In 1993, 1,600 runners lined up to ascend Pike's Peak in Colorado. I was one of those runners. Just before the start, a man next to me asked where I was from. "Michigan," I said. He responded: "Oh, you're a flatlander." Was he implying I had my work cut out for me, or was there a bit of regional arrogance from someone who thought mountainous terrain was more interesting than "flat land"? Maybe both—or it could have just been an observation. *Bang!* went the starter's pistol. No time to provide an adequate response. Until now.

Perception of landscapes is shaped by one's current location and experience. Michigan looks flat when viewed on a relief map of the United States—especially if you have never been here. Driving through Michigan, however, changes your perspective. If you enter Michigan from the south, you soon notice many hills, punctuated by lakes, wetlands, and forest stands. You pass trucks hauling gravel and see signs for ski slopes. Your conclusion of this being a flat is starting to unravel. It is not flat. What happened here?

There are hills in Michigan because glaciers deposited material. This small bit of knowledge may prompt us to ask why some of these hills exhibit concentric patterns. Their forms tell a story. If we observe the soil in the hill, and find it a mix of textures (sand, silt, clay, gravel), the hill is likely the result of glacial deposition. In order to deposit this diamicton (unsorted glacial sediment), the glacier had to slow down or stop. And the size and shape of the hill may give us insight into the direction of the glacial retreat and its duration.

Let's dig a little deeper. In Michigan, you can drill a sixty-foot well, and within that relatively short distance find two different types of clay, gravel, and sand. When you are done drilling, you look up and see forest stands with nearly as many tree species as the entire continent of Europe. In any direction we can see wide variety of spatial forms, such as inland lakes, wetlands, rivers, plains, and forests, underlain by different processes.

There are also power lines, dams, pipelines, roads, and the rest of the human-built environment sitting on top or buried beneath the natural landscape. People make imprints on the earth, but it is not a one-way street. Geography translates literally into "earth" (*geo-*) and "writing" (*graphos*). A landscape, therefore, is the product of human-environment interaction, how a society behaves toward nature expresses its culture, guides the modifications of landscapes, and feeds back to the culture in a continuing cycle.

Our journey starts with an overview of the region's geology, soils, climate, and vegetation. Next, we ratchet through different geographic scales by following nature's organization of water by watersheds. Water defines Michigan through the state's shape and traverses a complex cultural, economic, and political spectrum. This spectrum spans from the solace water has always provided in terms of its quantity, quality, and accessibility to the injustices produced by the Flint water crisis. The journey ends with a reflection on where we are.

The Layering of Earth and Michigan

The rocks beneath us tell the story. Five hundred million years ago, during the Paleozoic era, North America was covered by a shallow sea, and variable sea levels led to dozens of retreats and advances (transgressions) of the sea across the Great Lakes region. Some of the seas were warm and clear, with a high density of shelled creatures, while other seas were muddy and took in fine silts and decayed vegetation from low-lying land. When desert conditions existed, the seas became excessively salty and supported little life, or they were brackish with gypsum, sulfide, and chloride minerals. There were even periods when the sea became a huge shallow swamp sporting a lot of vegetation.

Each sea left its records in the sediments piled and spread on its floor. Through compaction and cementation, the sediments transformed into rock, during the process of lithification. Compaction occurs as the weight of the overlying material increases, forces the grains closer together, reduces pore space, and then eliminates some of the contained water. This eliminated water often carries minerals in solution, and these minerals later precipitate as new minerals within the pore spaces. This activity causes the individual particles to bind together (cementation).

Building the Michigan Basin was a long-term construction project. The floor of each sea became the container (basin) of its successor, making each new sea smaller. Eventually, Michigan's basin filled with a nested pattern of shallow bowl-shaped rock formations. These bowls were made of rocks reflecting the wide variations in depositional environments Michigan experienced over millions of years. There are layers of sandstone, limestone, shale, rock salt, and gypsum as well as mixtures between these rock types, such as shaley limestones and limey sandstones. The formations differ in thickness and extent, but they all slope from their edges to the center of the basin.

The basin covers all of Michigan's Lower Peninsula and the eastern half of the Upper Peninsula to an extent of approximately 80,000 square miles (180,000 square kilometers). Sedimentary rocks in the basin attain a maximum thickness of 16,000 feet (4,848 meters). Although we know what is in the basin, we do not know why the basin exists. Perhaps rocks lying beneath the basin were subjected to tectonic forces, such as tension, which would tug on the crust, thin it, and create a depression; or the basin may have been a byproduct of the forces building the Appalachian Mountains. The debate is ongoing.

It is good to know your neighbors. The basin is bounded from the northwest to the northeast by the Canadian Shield, which is a region of exposed Precambrian rocks lying within the stable 2.7-billion-year-old continental crust called the craton. Some of these very old rocks are visible as outcrops in the Upper Peninsula of Michigan. Structural arches, which are elongated uplifts in the crust, border the basin to the southwest and southeast. Overall, there is a moderate elevation change throughout the region, from a low point of 333 feet above sea level in St. Clair County to the high point of 1,033 feet above sea level in Genesee County. Though later covered by glacial deposits and largely out of sight, the rocks of the Michigan Basin have played a significant role in the past and present of the east-central Michigan region.

Grindstones, a Thumb, and Groundwater

Lake Huron, like all the Great Lakes, can get testy. In 1834, Captain Aaron Peer was looking for a place to shelter his schooner *Rip Van Winkle* from a storm. Near the tip of the Thumb, he found a natural harbor west of the Pointe Aux Barques lighthouse. Once ashore, the crew came across huge flat rocks lying on the shore and within the forest. These rocks were special formations called "grindstones" within the Marshall sandstone formation. Grindstone has a grit finer than sandstone and is well suited as a sharpening stone. From the 1830s until the 1910s, when carborundum made them obsolete, Grindstone City produced the premier grinding wheels in the United States.

Marshall sandstone has played other roles in the region's development. For one, it stood up to the glaciers to create Michigan's iconic Thumb. When glacial ice was moving southward through Lake Huron, it contacted the Marshall sandstone. As this is one of the hardest rocks in the Lower Peninsula and is positioned near the surface of the northern Thumb, the glaciers could not scrape it away. The rock split the advancing ice into one tongue going south toward Port Huron and another lobe flowing westward into the peninsula, carving out Saginaw Bay.

An important aquifer (water-bearing rock) also lies within the Marshall sandstone. How can a relatively dense rock contain water? Sandstone retains only a small part of the pore space present before lithification, which greatly reduced the primary pore space. Secondary openings, such as joints and fractures along with bedding planes, contain and transmit most of the groundwater in sandstone. Bedding planes are the horizontal spaces between layers of sedimentary rock. Almost one-half of

Michigan homes receive their water from aquifers, with higher percentages found in rural areas, such as the Thumb and most of the other counties within east-central Michigan. Many farms in the region also irrigate their crops with water from the Marshall sandstone aquifer.

Glaciation and Great Lakes

Six advances and retreats of glacial ice scoured Michigan during the Pleistocene Epoch 2.4 million years ago. This activity created the Great Lakes and left the state covered with glacial sediments to an average depth of three hundred feet. The overwhelming majority of the surface landforms we now see in Lower Michigan are from the last glacial period, called the Wisconsinan, which lasted between seventy-five thousand and ten thousand years ago.

During the Wisconsinan, the Laurentide ice sheet readvanced southward across the region of the present Great Lakes. Deeper valleys served as natural conduits for ice flow, and these depressions resulted in several large lobes moving forward under the control of the river courses. The Lake Michigan lobe followed the valley in which the basin of Lake Michigan was created. Without stopping to admire its work, this lobe continued southward beyond the site of Chicago to form the extension referred to as the Illinois lobe.

A second important ice front, the Huron-Erie lobe, followed valleys to sculpt the basins of Lakes Huron and Erie. The elliptical shape of the rock strata in the Michigan Basin controlled the location of Lake Huron's western shoreline and produced its curved shape (with the mentioned exception of the Thumb). Another overachiever was a smaller third lobe called the Saginaw. This lobe was pushed out from the Huron-Erie extension into the basin of Lake Saginaw. As this ice mass moved southward, it crept gradually out of the Saginaw drainage depression and onto the upland where it spread out as a relatively thin sheet, which eventually extended into the valley of the Kankakee River in northern Indiana.

Glacial Landscapes

Most of Michigan, including the east-central region, is covered by glacial deposition. Landforms resulting from deposition originated from the meltwaters or directly from the ice. Water-laid materials are called "outwash" and consist of sorted and stratified deposits. Deposits from flowing water sort due to contact with a frictional surface such as the ground or when they reach a slower body of water.

Ice-laid glacial landforms include drumlins and moraine systems. Drumlins are elongated, teardrop-shaped hills of rock, sand, and gravel that formed under moving

Moraines in East Central Michigan.
WILLIAM R. FARRAND AND ROBERT W. KELLEY, *THE GLACIAL LAKES AROUND MICHIGAN* (1988).

glacier ice. None exist within east-central Michigan. Moraine systems, however, are a prominent landscape feature across Lower Michigan, including the east-central region. When the ice front of the glaciers stalled, melting ice dumped its load of rock waste. Forward-moving ice also added material. These deposits built ridges of hummocky hills (small knolls or mounds under twenty-five meters in height) made of variably sized, unsorted rocks. Along this ice front, ground-up rock debris was deposited at every successive stop. These belts of rolling or rugged hills are termed "end moraines."

In east-central Michigan, the most significant moraine is the Port Huron. As the ice in the Thumb melted away, the Huron and Saginaw lobes separated along a northeast-to-southwest axis. Sediments were deposited in the growing area between them. At the end of those lobes, long moraines were formed, including the Port Huron moraine, extending in a U-shape from Port Huron to Bad Axe to Cass City.

In 1861, surveyors George W. Pack and Rudolph Papst found an old axe at the spot that ultimately gave its name to the city of Bad Axe. They also would have noticed the till plains (or ground moraines) often filling in the spaces between the hilly end moraines. These large, flat or gently sloping areas contain unsorted deposited material from a melting glacier. In some areas, these depositions can be hundreds of feet thick. The soils are often fertile, consisting of clay and sandy loams capable of supporting a wide variety of crops. Interspersed within these ice-laid deposits are wetlands, lakes, and depressions, which add to the diversity of east-central Michigan's landscape.

In contrast to these unsorted ice-laid deposits, there is outwash, which consists of sorted and stratified deposits created from glacial meltwater. In east-central Michigan, eskers and kettle lakes are two of the visible ice-laid glacial deposits. Eskers are sinuous ridges of outwash materials, flanked by slopes composed of ice-contact sediments. They are formed by glacial debris deposited within ice-bounded channels. Eskers are found in Genesee, Lapeer, Tuscola, and Sanilac Counties. The Hogbacks area, straddling Genesee and Lapeer Counties, is a combined esker and moraine complex, with wetlands and lakes between the glacial ridges. Hiking trails lead through dense forest. Just one more example of dull flat land.

Kettle lakes form when a block of ice breaks off from a glacier. While the glacier continued to melt, soil, rocks, and gravel filled the area around the block of ice. After the block of ice melted, all the surrounding debris fell into the hole, creating the kettle type basin. When this basin filled with water, it became a "kettle lake." Irregular shapes and significant depth characterize kettle lakes. Curvy Otter Lake in Lapeer County is a kettle lake, with a depth reaching almost 150 feet. In southern Genesee County, the finger-like Lobdell Lake attains a depth of 78 feet.

The Lake Plain, Soils, and Crops

Many parts of Michigan were covered by water during the retreat of the Wisconsinan ice sheet. Under the weight of the massive ice, the land sloped toward the ice margin, and water ponded between the high ice sheet and the higher lands to its south. These lakes arising from the trapped meltwater are "proglacial," meaning they occur in front of the glacier.

Some of these lakes hung around for thousands of years, and eventually drained. Beneath these lakes, flat and expansive glacio-lacustrine plains developed. Saginaw Bay on Lake Huron was once much higher and extended inland, and the former bottom of this intrusive body of water now makes up the glacio-lacustrine plains encircling Saginaw Bay. These lands appear flat, with areas of heavy clay interspersed by stretches of water-washed sand and gravel from the former lake beaches. One exception occurs on the western side of the Thumb, where retreating glaciers deposited their sediment loads directly into lakes, forming moraines on top of the old lake plain. This creates significant relief, which is visible south of Bay Port along M-25, east of Sebewaing.

Because of repeated inundation, however, most topographic features in the Saginaw Lowlands are subtle. These features include remnants of the proglacial lakes, such as shorelines, sandy ridges, and sandy beaches. There are also numerous vegetated inland sand dunes, most dating to the period immediately after the postglacial lakes had.

The majority of the soils in the Saginaw Lowlands evolved from the silt loam and silty clay loam sediments deposited within the deep pools of the proglacial lakes. Many of these sediments are very dense in the subsoil and inhibit infiltration. Because these soils coexist with a high water table, the soils in this region are often wet. In contrast, dry, sandy soils characterize a few areas, especially those occupied by dunes, glacial outwash, or stretches of the Cass River Valley in Tuscola and Saginaw Counties. More than 75 percent of the soils in the region lack adequate drainage.

Within east-central Michigan, local land use reflects this glacial geology. Prior to European settlement, the vegetation was characterized by hardwood and conifer swamps, grassland, and, to a lesser extent, peat bogs. Large areas were drained and converted into row-crop agriculture, where the major cash crops are field beans, potatoes (especially in Bay County), sugar beets, corn, and wheat. Subsurface drain tiles and deep drainage ditches manage the excess soil moisture. Other significant crops include oats and forages used for livestock feed. Toward the interior of the Thumb, the soils derive from glacial moraines and outwash and are therefore more diverse and well-drained. These soils support a diverse land cover, including some intact forests, while offering a similar crop palette. Dairy farms are a common sight throughout the entire region.

Several geographic factors account for this type of agriculture: the level, generally highly productive soils (when drained); the nearby markets, which favor dairy and poultry; the presence of four sugar beet processing plants in the region; the length of growing season, which ranges from 130 to 160 days; and the Lake Huron–moderated temperatures favoring dry field bean production.

Climate

The climate of the upper Midwest region, including Michigan, is chiefly governed by latitude, continental location, large-scale circulation patterns, and the Great Lakes. Our winter and transitional season day-to-day and week-to-week weather patterns are generally controlled by the position and configuration of the polar jet stream. During summer, the invasions of warm, humid air exert the most influence.

Wind within the mid-latitudes (23.5°N/S to 66.5°N/S) generally flows from west to east. These westerly winds bring into east-central Michigan four types of different air masses from three different source regions: (1) northwestern Canada (continental polar), (2) Gulf of Mexico and southern United States (maritime tropical), (3) Hudson Bay and northeastern Canada (continental polar), and (4) northern Rockies and Pacific Northwest (maritime polar). Occasionally, airflow originates from the western Atlantic or southwestern United States. These air masses create a climate classified as humid continental, with warm summers and cold winters and a relatively even distribution of precipitation throughout the year.

In east-central Michigan, the average annual temperatures range between 30°F during January to 82°F in July. Annual precipitation in the form of rain varies only slightly, between thirty-two and thirty-four inches. Snowfall demonstrates a bit more variability, ranging from thirty-seven inches at Port Huron to sixty-seven inches per year at Port Austin. This range of snowfall indicates the presence of some "lake-effect" snow in the Thumb. Lake-effect precipitation is common in Michigan, but prevailing westerly winds make it less frequent in the Thumb.

Temperature enhancements also occur. Urban areas tend to be warmer than the surrounding countryside. This phenomenon is called the "urban heat island," and it arises when vegetation is replaced by asphalt and concrete for roads, buildings, and other structures. Flint is the only city in the region with the size and density to generate a heat island.

Vegetation

Associations between tree species and glacial topography developed in Michigan after the glaciers retreated. Although much of the forests in east-central Michigan have been removed, some of the original patterns remain. In well-drained, loamy soils within the rolling terrain of ground moraines, we find stands of oak, beech, sugar maple, and hickory. Loamy soils exhibit a near balance of clay, silt, and sandy particles. Ash trees used to be part of this mix, but the emerald ash borer has decimated them.

Within the poorly drained, less sloping areas of ground moraines, we see elm and sugar maples. The wet soils of the more poorly drained clay soils found in the Saginaw Lake Plain gave rise to red maples, elms, willows, alder, and ash. Conifers, especially white pine, dominate the sand areas within the lake plain. Birch, poplars, and white cedar thrive within areas of second growth, especially the forested areas of Sanilac County destroyed by massive fires in 1871 and 1881. Another distinct feature found here is oak openings. These formations consist of a fire-dependent savanna community, dominated by oaks and characterized by a graminoid (grass-like) ground layer of species. Lake plain oak openings occur on the sand ridges, level sandplains, or adjacent depressions. Open conditions were maintained by frequent fires and in depressions by seasonal flooding.

Many species of grasses and shrubs inhabit the region. Bluejoint grass is common throughout North America and resides in the moist to wet soils in lake plains and intermoraine depressions. Alongside you can find dogwoods, blueberries, leatherleaf, wiregrass, and mosses.

Watersheds

John Wesley Powell, scientist, explorer, and an early director of the U.S. Geological Survey, put it best when he said a watershed is "that area of land, a bounded hydrologic system, within which all living things are inextricably linked by their common water course and where, as humans settled, simple logic demanded that they become part of a community." Powell spoke these words in the late nineteenth century. Since then, population has increased dramatically, and more people have become part of the watershed community. This increase in population within a finite hydrologic system has created new and increasingly complex human-environment interactions. For example, water shortages are increasing in frequency (California); floods are becoming more expensive (everywhere); and a significant amount of our water infrastructure is aging and failing with sometimes disastrous consequences (Flint Water Crisis and the Edenville dam failure of 2020).

With water, there is an integrated functional hierarchy accompanying its spatial hierarchy. The smallest wetland provides habitat for organisms, a headwater stream hosts the breeding grounds for endangered fish species, the larger rivers deliver water for agriculture, and Lake Huron takes in their inputs and offers places to swim, sail, fish, and paddle. Pollute the small wetland, and the adjacent groundwater degrades. Over time, some of this contamination makes its way into a stream, placing additional pressure on the endangered fish species. Moving up the hierarchy, farms tapping into the larger streams for an irrigation source are now watering their crops from streams transporting contamination. Some of the irrigated water runs off, reaches groundwater, and flows into Lake Huron, along with the contamination remaining in the larger stream. Meanwhile, some of the fish and their food supplies in the streams die. The ability to enjoy Lake Huron taking this all in diminishes. The paradox of watersheds is they are mostly land, with water making up only a small fraction of their total surface area. This reality creates the need to manage land properly to protect the water.

An Area of Concern

The United States and Canada created the Areas of Concern (AOC) Program in 1987 under the Great Lakes Water Quality Agreement. Forty-three Great Lakes sites with environmental damage were designated as AOCs in need of restoration, fourteen of them in Michigan, including a significant portion of the Saginaw Bay watershed.

Environmental problems in this watershed include contaminated sediments, degraded fisheries, loss of significant recreational values, nonpoint source discharges, combined sewer overflows, sanitary sewer overflows, and industrial sources of dioxins and polychlorinated biphenyls (PCBs). Illegal discharges from facilities owned by General Motors and Dow Chemical were responsible for the dioxins and PCBs. These cases have been litigated, and the settlements reached specified remedial measures, but the effects will linger for decades.

Because of the functional and spatial hierarchies of water, negligence, indifference, and mismanagement in a few locations can affect large areas. The Saginaw Bay watershed encompasses most of the east-central region. It is Michigan's largest watershed (8,709 square miles), spreads across twenty-two counties, and drains 15 percent of Michigan's total land area. It supports the largest contiguous freshwater coastal wetland system in the United States, and the Saginaw is one of the few navigable rivers in Michigan.

Geo- and -Graphy

Pollution of the environment is one imprint made by people on the landscape. Economists define pollution as an "externality," meaning it represents an unwelcome cost to a third party (in this case the public). In a similar vein, much of the built environment in the United States does not serve the public well. The status of our roads, bridges, dams, rail infrastructure, and water pipes is dismal, which is well documented by the quadrennial reports from the American Society of Civil Engineers. Problems in the built environment translate into negative impacts on the natural environment. Our "geo-" and "-graphy" (earth writing) is out of whack, which makes it certainly worth investigating.

The Built Environment

Part of the mismatch between constructed landscapes and the natural environment relates to time. Nature works within physical laws, and these laws affect the duration of a physical system's work. For example, glacial ice takes ten to twenty years to develop, because that duration is required to create the pressure necessary to squeeze the air out of the snow and transform it into ice. Conversely, in agriculture, much research focuses on finding ways to grow crops faster, and with higher yields. Why do we need more food sooner? In the United States, 30–40 percent of food is wasted every year. Rushing to get things done stresses the natural landscape, creates unwanted feedback in our natural systems, and is often not necessary.

Time and Space Convergence

When approaching east-central Michigan by car, a familiar built landscape unfolds—one all too common. Large electrical wires appear, highways widen, and cell towers appear on the horizon. These are forms of infrastructure designed to speed up travel, communication, and power transmission.

Geographers refer to this phenomenon as "time-space convergence." The internet has made the world smaller, and texting somebody in Japan is now easy. In addition, fast trains (yet to appear in the United States) connect major cities, and you can video call your brother and sister in San Diego. Unfortunately, the impact of this technology has been to separate people from the environment. Too often, it is only through the windshield of a car that people experience the outside world.

Where We Are

What can you do in east-central Michigan? How can you find your place? By making a couple of stops. The first stop is just north of the Blue Water Bridge in Port Huron. Stand outside of the car and look at Lake Huron. When its beauty has completely awed you, imagine it is 1855 and an escaped slave from a southern plantation is crossing into Canada near the very ground you stand on. After the war, his or her family may have settled in Saginaw, along with many other ex-slaves from Canada. Once again, look back at the lake and note the curvature of the shoreline, a product of Michigan's basin and the glacial architects. Then let your mind drift again, to several thousand years ago, when the Paleo people were shaping chert found around Saginaw Bay for their hunting weapons. Chert breaks by mechanical means and along irregular planes, so a thorough understanding of the rock's physical properties was required.

Next, proceed to Marlette, in the center of Michigan's Thumb. Immigrants from Ontario first settled this area in 1855 looking for timber and fertile soil. They found both. On your left is a cornfield, and to your right a field of soybeans. Sanilac County, where Marlette is situated, leads the state in acreage planted for both crops. Walk to the edge of the cornfield, scoop up some soil, and dampen it a bit if it is dry. A field hand test can give you a good approximation of the type of soil it is. In this area the soil is probably loam, which took thousands of years to form after the glaciers receded. Is it hilly nearby? You may be on a moraine, and the soil you just picked up evolved from the material directly deposited by a glacier roughly ten thousand to thirteen thousand years ago.

Wipe your hands and continue on to Flint. Take any exit and find a neighborhood. Park, and walk to the center of the street. Five to seven feet below the concrete is a twelve-inch cast iron water main pipe, which delivers drinking water to the homes on the block. These pipes are now almost one hundred years old and at the end of their lifespan. Not seen, but often heard, as they are rupturing at a rate of almost one per day. This is a common problem not confined to Flint. Turn and face the houses. Another smaller pipe, called a service line, delivers water from the main into each house. In the United States, between seven and ten million of these pipes contain lead. Maybe a child in the house you are looking at drank lead-contaminated water. Your mind races back to the late 1800s. In 1890, the Massachusetts State Board of Health advised the state's cities and towns to avoid the use of lead pipes. One published bibliography in 1943 listed more than one hundred articles and reports in

English on lead poisoning from drinking water. Despite these warnings, lead pipes are still used to transmit water.

The threads of the past are now woven with those of today. We can stand anywhere in east-central Michigan and envision different periods of time and extents of space and begin to think about how to improve our future. No place stands alone. It is adjacent to another and connected to its past. This is where we are.

AN ARCHAEOLOGICAL JOURNEY

Beverley A. Smith

Somewhere in our collective consciousness, residing deeper for some than for others, is the realization that this land was once the homeland of Indigenous families, communities, and nations. We know that terrible things happened to the Native people of our region in the recent past, but those details are largely suppressed or even justified as we consider our privilege in living in this rich and beautiful place. Perhaps we have wondered, though, about the story of our region before farms, neighborhoods, roads, industries, towns, and cities appeared and wish to envision the landscapes and the people who lived here before the colonial enterprise when our ancestors from Europe, Africa, and elsewhere settled here, bringing a very different way of life and drastic changes to the environment.

The story of the precolonial history of our region is complex, dynamic, and elusive. Most of us know this history only from museum exhibits, where pottery and stone tools document the past or where dioramas display figures with long black hair and dressed in buckskin clothing engaging in everyday activities like fishing or farming in an effort to portray an earlier way of life. But there is so much more to know.

This narrative is a journey through time describing the past cultures and lifeways of Michigan's First Nations, but it also incorporates aspects of my own journey of discovery as an archaeologist working in the region at some of the most important sites in the Saginaw Basin. The practice of archaeology—locating and excavating sites and analyzing the material remains left by people of the past—is a scientific enterprise that leaves room for the humanistic interpretive imagination. Excavation itself is a destructive exercise because, once disturbed, it can never be put back. Like any science, archaeology is governed by strict ethical principles and should never be undertaken cavalierly.

As with any scholarly enterprise, this narrative depends on the legacy of many passionate and curious scholars who, beginning in the early twentieth century, undertook a daunting task: to make sense of the thousands of artifacts being excavated from archaeological sites in the region. They did not simply describe these artifacts, such as projectile points, bone and antler tools, and pottery shards, which all seemed to have been made or decorated in myriad shapes, sizes, and design elements. These early scholars organized them in time, creating a chronology of change; in space, by creating maps of site distribution; and as assemblages, associations of types and styles of artifacts across time and space. To these early citizen-scholars in our region, especially Fred Dustin, Wilbert Hinsdale, and many others, we owe a great debt.

Later in the twentieth century, with the emergence of radiocarbon dating, environmental reconstruction, flotation (fine-scale screening), and myriad applications of other techniques appropriated from the hard sciences, archaeology has become a respected academic discipline. However, the role of avocational (nonprofessional) archaeologists continues to be critically important and we can all participate in the practice and interpretation of archaeology through organizations like the Michigan Archaeological Society. Founded in 1924 and incorporated in 1954, the society holds regional monthly meetings to inform us all about recent discoveries and interpretations through presentations, workshops, and community outreach. Most recently, archaeologists recognize and welcome the important role of the descendant community—contemporary Indigenous people who care deeply about their ancestors and their past and work to protect sites and repatriate their ancestors.

The Saginaw Basin, formerly referred to as the Saginaw Valley, roughly incorporates the land from Midland, south to Lansing and east to Lapeer, extending north into the Thumb, covering an area of about seven thousand square miles. There are more than four thousand archaeological sites recorded in this region, with almost 1,500 sites known in Saginaw County alone, which has the highest density of archaeological sites in the state. This region is also home to the earliest evidence of Michigan's residents.

When the glacier that covered our region fifteen thousand years ago began to melt and retreat northward to form today's polar ice cap, the early meltwater became dammed up, forming the massive glacial Lake Algonquin. The land was a tundra-like environment, interspersed with spruce forests supporting animals that would very soon become extinct, such as mammoths and mastodons, and species that would follow the lichen of the tundra northward, such as caribou.

Michigan's earliest people enter our region as early as fourteen thousand years ago and several sites document their presence for the next four thousand years. These early occupants, called "Paleo-Indians," made large, chipped stone fluted projectile points that were hafted to spears to hunt caribou and quite likely mammoths and mastodons, whose remains may possess cut marks and other evidence of butchering at some localities. The earliest sites in Michigan form a line, roughly along the I-75 corridor, from Macomb to Midland Counties, with arguably the most informative site being the Gainey site, now under a housing development in Grand Blanc. Our knowledge about Paleo people suffers from a lack of preservation at sites where remains of plant use, houses, and other features of life have long since decayed. These fragile sites are difficult to identify, ethereal in their footprint, and profound, because they document an ancient adaptation to a very different environment.

Over the next few thousand years, glacial Lake Algonquin found several outlets, and the water drained with a vengeance. Around ten thousand years ago, Lake Huron was actually two lake basins, known as Lake Stanley, separated by a land feature known as the Amberly Ridge, where recent underwater archaeology claims to reveal the presence of stone hunting blinds that may have been used to intercept migrating caribou. Pollen cores documenting plant life indicate that by about eight thousand years ago, the mixed hardwood forest supported animal populations in an environment that would look very familiar to us today. This environment was, however, frequently inundated by rising lake levels during the Nipissing stage. Early and Middle Archaic sites, until about 6,500 years ago, were rare in the archaeological record. Some sites were likely swept away, but alluvial sediments also deeply buried and protected other sites of this period.

When I came to Michigan for graduate school in the 1980s, I excavated at a site that caused quite a stir. The Weber I site was discovered when a new bridge was to be built over the Cass River near Frankenmuth and deeply buried deposits revealed, for the first time, a living floor with preserved animal and plant remains as well as hearths and artifacts dating to the Middle Archaic. We found evidence of a pattern of life that would endure for the next several thousand years—small encampments of people hunting white-tailed deer, collecting nuts and fruits and, from the rivers, turtles, small aquatic animals, and fish. An upper level, closer to the surface, dated to the Late Archaic, documented a continuation of this way of life at this spot.

Research intensified in the 1990s, as many archaeologists explored and modeled the nature of life in the Archaic period. We came to appreciate the critical role of the dendritic (tree-like) configuration of the major rivers in our region, the Shiawassee, Tittabawassee, Cass, and Flint Rivers, which converge at the city of Saginaw, forming the Saginaw River that empties into Saginaw Bay. These rivers provided important sources of food to the hunting and gathering way of life, but they were also the early highways along which families moved seasonally, spending the warm season near the shore of the bay, and moving inland to winter along the upland margins of the basin. We have located sites near Chesaning, discovered in survey for a modern natural gas pipeline, that represent these cold season sites and date from the Middle Archaic through to the fifteenth century.

From six thousand years ago, the Saginaw Basin was a very popular place to live. In the Late Archaic, we find not only living sites but burial sites, where ancestors took their final journey in graves with finely made artifacts, often sprinkled with red ocher, a natural, bright-red pigment used as paint, perhaps symbolizing blood. Late Archaic artifacts reflect exceedingly fine craftsmanship, such as polished stone weights, bannerstones, and birdstones, which were attached to atlatls (spear-throwers), providing deadly accuracy for hunting deer. Together with nuts, plants, and animals of the rivers, resources were bountiful, and the large number of sites indicate that the region supported an increasing and thriving population.

A source of a specific type of stone, called chert or flint, is necessary for making chipped stone projectile points, and Bay Port chert is found locally around Saginaw

Bay and on the Charity Islands. By the Late Archaic, however, we also see the evidence of extensive trade networks, particularly for copper, which was traded into the region from ancient mines in the Upper Peninsula. New products and ideas were also coming in from the south. By the end of the Archaic period, the tropical cultigen squash is adopted and pottery is a radical new technology. This is the Woodland period. After a few hundred years of experimentation, making some rather poor-quality pottery in the Early Woodland, the region again experiences a cultural florescence, including some rather surprising innovations and ideas.

In the Middle Woodland period, beginning about two thousand years ago, people continued to follow their traditional ways, but external cultural forces and environmental changes make this period very interesting and prosperous. Lake Algoma refers to a small rise in the water levels in Lake Huron, but it was enough to flood the confluence of the major rivers, resulting in a massive wetland, now the city of Saginaw. Wetlands support a very high biomass of plants and animals that were widely used by hunter-gatherers, and one of the largest sites in the region took advantage of the Shiawassee Embayment—the wetlands. The Schultz site is among the earliest professionally excavated sites in our region, but this extensive work had left important questions. Archaeologists usually refrain from excavating an entire site, because it is recognized that new technologies and methodologies can bring important insights. In the 1990s, archaeologists returned to the Schultz site to employ fine-scale recovery (using window screen rather than previous quarter inch screen) to "wash the dirt away," capturing remains of tiny seeds and fish bone. As a result, we could document that fish and many wetland plants were very important, including *manomin* (wild rice). We had always suspected that it had a much broader range (it is now confined to lakes west of Lake Michigan), and now we had the evidence.

Ideas from more southerly regions were also impacting people at that time. One surprising discovery was the likely domestication of a local weedy plant, *Chenopodium*, which commonly grows in the area today (a related species from South America is enjoyed today as quinoa). We must reject the notion that plant domestication occurred in only a few emergent "civilizations" in the world and recognize that experimentation with plant characteristics by controlling their reproduction was "invented" and sometimes later rejected in many times and places, including the Saginaw Basin—farming is a lot of work when you don't have to do it. The large populations of the Middle Woodland, however, appear to have seen the benefit of the additional work of cultivating not only squash but also *Chenopodium*.

The Middle Woodland is famous in eastern North American archaeology for the development of a highly sophisticated cultural tradition, called Hopewell, centered in Ohio and Illinois. Elaborate burials in mounds, a thriving artistic tradition of carving pipes, hammering copper, making pottery, and a vast exchange network importing shark teeth, grizzly bear teeth, mica, and copper, all tied, it seems, to a new spiritual belief system. At the Schultz site is a large, circular earthwork that likely played a role in Hopewell-influenced ceremonial events. The Schultz site remains one of my favorite sites, because our work added so much to the understanding of Middle Woodland life on the margins of the Hopewell core in Ohio and Illinois.

Pottery is now an everyday item in local life, and good sources of clay are found on the riverbanks in the basin. Archaeologists love pottery, because it preserves well, breaks easily, and reflects changes in technology and style. A common way of making pottery or a shared design motif can reflect social and cultural relationships across time and space. Burned remains on the interior of a pot, called "crud," can be chemically analyzed to determine foods cooked in it. This is the source of the earliest evidence of maize, also originally from Mesoamerica, in the Great Lakes region, beginning almost two thousand years ago.

In some regions to the east, west, and south of our region, maize becomes a staple crop, and nations who relied on it settled into permanent, year-round villages often protected with a palisade. Here, however, it didn't assume such importance. Maize is present in archaeological sites in the Late Woodland, beginning about 1,500 years ago, but was never adopted as a major food source. The people of the Saginaw Basin continued to hunt, fish, and collect wild plants, moving seasonally as they had always done; such was the natural bounty of our region.

Indigenous history has been told and retold over the millennia through stories, parables, and symbols, rather than as a written record. Archaeologists have long recognized that "oral history" is powerful and effective as lessons of the past are conferred upon each generation. In our region, a spiritually powerful locality has been preserved that provides a lens into the symbols that inspired such history—*Ezhibiigaadek Asin* (written on stone), also known as the Sanilac Petroglyphs. Petroglyphs are rare sites and at Sanilac, Late Woodland people carved images into a soft rock, giving us a window into that elusive aspect of the past.

The arrival of the French and later the British to the Great Lakes, beginning in the early seventeenth century, brought profound changes to Indigenous people. Despite European propensity to write down their observations, the early historic period in our region is particularly poorly documented. The Indigenous nations are recorded on early maps as the *Atsistaehronons* or *Nation du Feu* (Fire Nation) and were probably several nations later named in the historic period as the Sauk, Fox, Mascouten, Potawatomi, Ottawa, and others. All are encapsulated in the identity of Anishinaabeg/Anishinaabek, the "true people" speaking Algonquian languages. According to historians at the Ziibiwing Center for Anishinabe Culture and Lifeways, thirty-four tribes have Aboriginal land claims to Genesee County under the 1807, 1819, and 1837 treaties with the United States, including the most recent Native nation to enter the Saginaw Basin from the east, the Black River–Swan Creek Mississauga Ojibwe around the end of the eighteenth century. From sparce references from the seventeenth through the nineteenth centuries, disparaging descriptions of local Indigenous people as "sullen," "lazy," and of course "violent" are the frequent tropes born out of ignorance or agendas to appropriate land for their own purposes. Trade, disease, warfare, diaspora, and treaties transformed life, dispossessing Indigenous people from their land and, by the end of the nineteenth century, their culture, religion, and language through forced assimilation, most profoundly illustrated by the tragedy of the Indian industrial boarding schools. The Mount Pleasant school finally closed in 1933.

Burial sites, where ancestors begin their journey to the afterlife, are large and important localities throughout the Woodland period, as with earlier periods, and are places of great consternation for the descendant community in our area today. The excavation and curation of ancestral remains and their artifacts was conducted with impunity by earlier archaeologists, creating great stress between scientists and the descendant community. With the passage of federal legislation known as Native American Grave Protection and Repatriation Act in 1990, Indigenous people in Michigan began to petition museums and educational institutions to regain these remains for repatriation and reburial. It was in this contentious climate that the Stone Street Ancestral Burial Ground was discovered in downtown Flint in 2008.

Located just to the east of Atwood Stadium, we discovered that this late nineteenth-century neighborhood had been built on a Woodland period burial ground. When the old houses were razed and large foundations were dug for new houses, human skeletal remains and their associated funerary objects were disinterred and left lying on large mounds of dirt intermixed with rubbish from the nineteenth and twentieth centuries. The Saginaw Chippewa Indian Tribe of Michigan council asked museum professionals at the Ziibiwing Center for Anishinabe Culture and Lifeways to reclaim these ancestors for reburial. While some thought these back dirt piles should be bulldozed back into the foundation pits, others did not wish to see their ancestors reburied with the artifacts from the more recent occupants, and I was asked to direct the project to separate the Woodland period ancestors from the "Eurotrash," so the ancestors could be reburied in cleansed earth. From 2010 to 2013, thanks to tribal workers, together with student and community volunteers, we screened seventy-six thousand cubic feet of dirt and reclaimed a minimum of 110 individuals, ranging in age from infant to mostly elders. The bones told us that, apart from cavities and osteoarthritis, people were generally healthy and strong, consuming a mixed diet of wild foods and some maize. The idea that these remains resulted from a "battle" was dispelled when we could find no evidence of violence, such as arrowheads in the bone. We also recovered artifacts that helped to date the burial ground, including pottery, stone tools, and copper. The most exotic of these items were large pendants made from *Busycon* (conch-like) shells imported from the southeastern coastal waters. I often wonder about the many people across the continent who exchanged these exotic shells as they made their way to Flint to be included in burials at Stone Street more than one thousand years ago.

The Stone Street Recovery and Reburial Project was an important archaeological endeavor for all who participated. I hope it represents the future of archaeology in our region. We learned about the strong ties between the ancestors and contemporary communities, ties that are spiritual and real and deserve our respect. As Natives and non-Natives toiled in the hot sun, smudged for cleansing, feasted, laughed, and loved those three long summers, we came to a rather profound realization: This terrible desecration of ancestors had brought about a reconciliation between people and communities who would otherwise have never met and became lifelong friends and colleagues. We learned that with trust, respect, and hard work, we can right the wrongs of the past and the present—this is the profound gift of these ancestors.

THE INDIGENOUS PEOPLE AFTER SETTLEMENT

Paul M. Gifford

The Indigenous people living in our region at the time of white settlement called themselves Anishinaabe (plural: Anishinaabek or Anishinaabeg). Outsiders identified these independent bands, by their common language and culture, as Ojibwe or Chippewa. Treaties defined most as members of the Saginaw Band of Chippewas, with some also as members of the Swan Creek and Black River Bands. Their language is part of the Algonquian family, which includes Ottawa, Potawatomi, Sac (Sauk), Fox, and other groups. Suffering extreme trauma after white contact and American domination, many nevertheless managed to remain in the area, in contrast to groups in other areas of the United States, where treaties and armies forced Indigenous peoples to move to western territories, to Canada, or to reservations. In this region, many who survived the initial period of white settlement found refuge in the reservations in Isabella County created in 1855, but others remained on the land on which their ancestors had lived. This article is an attempt to trace the history of the Anishinaabeg who stayed in this region outside reservations.

Archaeology suggests that following a long period of continuous occupation until about 1200 or 1300, the Saginaw Valley became a temporary, transient place for hunter-gatherers. They fished for sturgeon and pike and hunted elk, deer, bear, and small mammals like beaver and muskrat, as well as geese, turkey, and grouse. Women planted corn, squash, and beans. Some scholars have speculated that a tribal confederacy of the Cree and Ojibwe may have existed before breaking up. In any case, tribal names varied and tribes fought and reformed.

Traditions that William R. McCormick collected from elderly Indians as early as 1834 and first published in Thomas and Galatian's *Indian and Pioneer History of Saginaw County* (1866), but also supported by Mary Sagatoo (quoting Nau-qua-chic-a-ming), have been so widely repeated that they have become "fact," although scholars like David Edmunds and Joseph L. Peyser have expressed doubt, because the culture of the Sac and Fox in Wisconsin in the early seventeenth century more resembled that of the prairie tribes of Illinois and Iowa than the woodland tribes of Michigan. With this caveat, this story describes how the Sacs occupied much of Michigan at one time, with the Ojibwe living on Lake Superior and the Potawatomi in the southern part of the state. This tribe was frequently at war with its neighbors in Michigan and Ontario. A council, with representatives of the Ojibwe, Potawatomi, Menominee, Ottawa, and Iroquois, met at Mackinac Island and declared war on the Sacs. A large number of Ojibwe and others then came down in canoes and attacked the main village of Sacs on the west side of Saginaw River, known as Sac-haw-ning ("the place of the Sacs," according to McCormick, although the more widely accepted etymology is Sag-ong, "the place of the outlet") as well as other nearby settlements. The Sacs retreated by crossing the river to a place called Skull Island, where they suffered a further defeat. Skull Island was in the 1870s identified as being twelve miles below Saginaw City and the "next island above Stone's Island." Other battles were fought near the Flint River, near what is now Flushing and the city of Flint, on the Cass River, near what is now Bridgeport, and on the Tittabawassee River, the opponents coming from the Detroit River area. The few Sacs who survived then left the region for Wisconsin, ultimately forming the Sac and Fox tribe. These events happened before the arrival of the Europeans to North America.

The arrival of the French at Quebec in 1608 and the Dutch at Albany in 1621 had a profound effect on the people living in the Great Lakes region. The French and Dutch competed for influence, resulting in the French establishing trading posts deep in the interior, while the Dutch dealt with the Iroquois Confederacy at what is now Albany. Soon the Native demand for and access to European products, such as knives, kitchen utensils, and blankets, caused the Iroquois to enlarge their hunting grounds by attacking other tribes, both Algonquian and Iroquoian, in Ontario, Ohio, and Michigan. The bitter fight between the Iroquois, using firearms and metal weapons, and the interior peoples, with stone and wooden tools, created what Richard White considers communities of refugees living around the Great Lakes in the mid-seventeenth century, at the time of their first encounter with French traders and missionaries. Louis-Armand de Lom d'Arce de Lahontan's 1688 map shows an abandoned settlement of Sakis at the interior of Saginaw Bay (Baye du Sakinan), supporting the view that Iroquoian aggression in the 1640s and 1650s had emptied the population of eastern Michigan.

The Indians at first regarded the French as spirits (*manido*), according to White, but through trade with them that included arms, the governor at Quebec eventually empowered the Algonquian peoples enough that by 1700, the French-Indian alliance was able to push the Iroquoian peoples back. From this period, especially after the founding of Detroit in 1701, the Indians in the Great Lakes and the French traders and missionaries created what White calls a "middle ground," where the Indians recognized the French not as spirits but as mediators of conflicts between tribes. Lahontan's 1688 map shows the Saginaw River basin as a beaver hunting ground for tribes friendly to the French, indicating that by that time, some Indians had entered the region at least seasonally. Certainly enough had come permanently by about 1750 that one fur trader established a post. This was Jean-Baptiste Brillant dit Beaulieu, whose wife Itagisse was believed to be a close relative of Neome, chief of the Fisher Band, which in the 1830s resided in Grand Blanc Township. Beaulieu (or "Bolieu," as spelled in the 1860 Michigan Supreme Court case that describes this) married about 1750 and died in Detroit in 1781, so his post, which did not last long, must have existed under the French regime.

The British succeeded the Dutch at Albany in 1664 and began to challenge France for control of the fur trade. The Seven Years' War (or French and Indian War), from 1754 to 1760 and concluded by the Treaty of Paris in 1763, upset the "middle ground." In 1763, Pontiac, an Ottawa chief living near Detroit, led an organized effort against the newly victorious British. Their policies, which—unlike the French—included withholding gunpowder and ammunition, indicated both an arrogant dislike of Indians as well as an intention to take over the entire country rather than just the outposts themselves. This offended many, including not only the Indians but the French around Detroit and along the Mississippi as well. British troops eventually subdued Pontiac's Indian forces by the end of the decade. During the American Revolution, Michigan Indians supported the British and Loyalist side, since they knew that the colonial population wanted to eventually settle on their lands. The Treaty of Paris in 1783 left Michigan under American control, although British forces controlled Detroit until 1796. Anthony Wayne, commanding a force of about three thousand, defeated an Indian army at the Battle of Fallen Timbers in 1794. This led to the Treaty of Greenville in 1795, in which the confederacy of Indian tribes (including the Shawnee, Delaware, Ojibwe, Ottawa, and others) ceded two-thirds of what became the state of Ohio to the United States.

The United States now barely controlled the isolated settlements at Detroit and Mackinac. To assert control of the border region against threats by the British, federal leadership wanted to promote American settlement. President Thomas Jefferson assigned Governor William Hull to acquire land in Michigan from the Indians. Although the tribes did not want to sell and had preferred the British, the Saginaw Band, Black River Band, and Swan Creek Band (the latter two living in what is now St. Clair County) sold about five million acres in southeastern Michigan (including Flint and some of the region described in this book) to the United States in the Treaty of Detroit of 1807. The treaty allowed the Indians to continue to live on unsold federal land in their traditional manner.

During the years before the War of 1812, the Shawnee Prophet in Indiana and his brother, Tecumseh, led a campaign to unite the indigenous peoples in the Midwest to reject Americans and return to the old ways. Despite Tecumseh's charisma and effectiveness, the War of 1812 (in which most Indians supported the British, given that they knew that most settlers were Americans) meant further losses. Tecumseh died at the Battle of Thames in 1813, and many Indians fled to Walpole Island and other places in Ontario. Demoralized British troops abandoned Detroit, and after ratification of the Treaty of Ghent in 1815, the United States was firmly in control of

Detroit and Michigan. The Indians suffered losses so great that, in this region, they never again fought the Americans.

Former military officer Lewis Cass came to the Michigan Territory as governor in 1813, charged with the task of establishing American control and influencing the Indians to cede land. As well as fixing the boundaries between what became Canada and the United States, the war caused the fur trade to be split between British and American companies. Cass expected pro-American traders like Jacob Smith, who had established trading posts on the Clinton River and then the Flint River, and Louis Campau, whose post was on the Saginaw River, to use their influence on local Indian bands to agree to give up land.

At a gathering at Saginaw (a marker at the intersection of Court and Hamilton Streets indicates the location) in September 1819, Cass negotiated with leaders of the various bands in the region in public councils and private meetings. Cass found that the Indians fiercely opposed Secretary of War John Calhoun's position to exchange their land for land west of the Mississippi, preferring to receive smaller reservations in Michigan. The Americans held the upper hand, however, by virtue of their victory in the War of 1812. In addition, the Indians trusted Jacob Smith and Louis Campau, who also acted as agents of the Americans. Three leaders—Neome, chief of the Flint River band; Kish-kaw-ko ("The Crow"), whose band was located near what is now Zilwaukee, including Crow Island, where his reserve would be located; and the young but eloquent O-ge-maw-ke-ke-to, whose band lived at the forks of the Tittabawassee (and for whom Ogemaw County was named)—spoke at the first council. O-ge-maw-ke-ke-to asked for peace but refused to relinquish any land, remarking that he preferred the British, who did not want to take their land, to the Americans. However, the large quantity of whiskey that Cass and Campau had brought distracted Kish-kaw-ko and other opponents from active discussion. After two more public councils and numerous private meetings, with the Americans agreeing to grant reservations on the Flint River to individuals (including Jacob Smith's white children under their "Indian" names), as well as other provisions, the natives ceded sixteen million acres to the United States. In return, the Indians would receive annual payments of one thousand silver dollars, the services of a blacksmith with livestock (to help them farm), the right to hunt and fish on the land that remained federal property, as well as various reserves. The treaty (covering all the land in our area except a portion in the southeastern area that was covered by the 1807 treaty) went into effect in 1820.

Settlers trickled into the Michigan Territory during the following decade, although the number remained small, even after the opening of the Erie Canal in 1825. For the Indians, life continued in a cycle since they had entered this region. Small bands, consisting of perhaps fifty individuals, planted corn, potatoes, turnips, beans, and sometimes squash, pumpkins, and melons in one spot, often an oak opening, and then in the fall moved upriver to the heads of streams, constructing wigwams in areas where they hunted and fished. Toward winter, they floated in their canoes downriver to heavily forested sites, where they hunted and trapped. In late winter they tapped maple trees and produced large quantities of sugar and then returned to their corn fields, beginning the cycle again. They traded pelts and skins, as well as sugar and honey, with traders at stationary posts, as they had for more than 150 years, now principally for whiskey and tobacco.

The 1830s posed extreme challenges for the Anishinaabe in the region. Two epidemics, cholera in 1834 and smallpox in 1837, killed perhaps a third or more of them. The Saginaw Chippewa in the latter year totaled 993. Entire bands died of the dreaded disease. Trader Benjamin O. Williams related how he visited the settlement at Chesaning and found only one elderly woman alive. In addition, the first wave of white settlers came in 1836, many to southern Genesee and Lapeer Counties, disrupting traditional hunting. The economic crisis of 1837 affected credit generally and Indian traders specifically. Pioneer reminiscences frequently describe the Indians' hunger and alcoholism and their begging for food. The fur trade era had now come to a complete end.

Federal policy toward Indians meanwhile advocated their removal to land further west. In treaties made in 1836, 1837, and 1838, the Ojibwe sold reservations they had received in the earlier treaties. Led by their chief, Esh-ton-a-quot, two bands of the Swan Creek and Black River tribe (which together numbered 360 in 1837) exchanged their Michigan land for land in Kansas. However, most members of these two tribes, as well as all the Saginaw Chippewa, refused to leave. In 1841, some joined the Wesleyan mission across the border at Sarnia. Although most did eventually settle on the reservations that were created in Isabella County in the 1850s (as well as the Saganing Reservation on the Bay-Arenac county line and across the border on Walpole Island), several bands managed to stay somewhat intact near their traditional hunting grounds, using annuity payments to purchase federal land.

Some retained their traditional religion, but most came under the influence of missionaries, Methodist and Lutheran. This was caused by the cultural crisis, hunger, and the need to fight the temptations of alcohol and to find trustworthy protectors. Methodists had been very successful as frontier circuit riders since the American Revolution, but Lutherans were at a disadvantage, as they came from Germany and had to learn to speak English and needed to adapt to American circumstances. This was perhaps the reason for the Methodists' success and the Lutherans' failure. Nevertheless, Indians wavered between conversion and rejection. In 1852, Oliver H. Perry, a hunter from Cleveland, witnessed an annual "hunting pow-wow" in Indian Fields Township (Tuscola County), that went on for three days and nights, attended by other "heathen" Indians from Sebewaing and Quanicassee, with "drum beating, screetching & yelling all night," enabled by five gallons of whiskey. Lutheran missionary Johann Strieter witnessed a pow-wow, probably at Shebahyonk (near Sebewaing), which the chief, Nau-qua-chic-a-ming, explained as a thanksgiving to *gichi-manidoo* (the great spirit). While the chief nestled a jug of liquor in his arms, two men stood inside a staked-off area, one beating a double-headed drum made of a hollow log, the other shaking a gourd rattle. A man and a woman, both covered with pelts, began to dance, each thrusting to the other in turn a pelt with the call "*Hui*!" and jumping into the area, followed by others.

Edward R. Baierlein came from Germany to Frankentrost in 1848 and lived with the band led by chief Pay-mos-e-gay (*Bemassikeh* in Baierlein's spelling) for six years. In 1839, the chief had purchased land on the Pine River in Bethany Township, Gratiot County. Baierlein learned their language, translated Luther's catechism and, importantly for us, wrote a vivid account of an early cross-cultural experience that reveals Indian beliefs on several points. Sensitive to both their difficulties but also to their pride in a distinctive way of life, the missionary did not suggest the possibility of building log houses or of clearing land to farm until he had lived with them and observed their suffering and winter starvation for four years. Even then, he noted that they felt that farming, indeed anything the white man regarded as work, was beneath their dignity. "He sees himself equal with the deer, bear, and buffalo," wrote Baierlein, "They do not work, yet they live. Why should he work? He lives free in the forest, and that is what he wants to do till he falls down and dies, just like the animals." Yet the Indians seemed to enjoy visiting the missionary in his log house, which was also a school and a place to share religious discussions. This group of Indians, with one German missionary and his wife, gathered around one of the first Christmas trees in Michigan in 1846. "Forty Indians came," noted Baierlein, none of whom had accepted Christ, but "a loud 'ah' came from all sides, as they saw the brightly lighted tree before them, full of fruit, in the middle of the winter." Pay-mos-e-gay exclaimed that he had never found a tree like that in all his forests. Sadly, this communal life ended when Baierlein accepted a reassignment in 1853, and his successor could not understand the Indians' point of view and so could not relate to them. The mission ended in 1853, and the band moved to reservations in Isabella County, where, as the youth had some education, they obtained jobs in the reservation administration.

George Bradley (1810–1871), who was based in Flint from 1845 to 1853, was the chief Methodist missionary in this region. He established missions in the 1840s on the Flint River in Taymouth Township, Saginaw County; at Janesville Station, on the Kawkawlin River in Bangor Township, Bay County (now known as Ogaukawning Church); and at Nepessing, also called Bradley's Chapel, in Lapeer County. Methodist policy was to encourage the Indians or its Missionary Society to purchase land on which to build churches and schools. By 1854, the first and third missions, with the addition of one on a branch of the Saginaw River called Hamlin or Wahb-zeeb-ne-kah-ning, comprised one circuit, while Janesville and five other missions further north and west made up another circuit.

Bradley advocated for a reservation in Michigan, with allotments by family. This resulted in the Treaty of Detroit, made in 1855, which gave approximately six townships in Isabella County and the Saganing Reservation near Saginaw Bay (on

Ogaukawning Church in Kawkawlin, built in 1847. PHOTOGRAPH BY AUTHOR.

the Bay-Arenac county line) to the Saginaw Chippewa. The race for Michigan pine had begun, and speculators coveted Isabella County's extensive pinelands. A further treaty, made in 1864, attempted to secure rights to the reservations. Most of the local Indians left the area and moved after 1855 to the reservations in Isabella County.

At the time of the 1855 treaty, the Saginaw Chippewa consisted of twelve bands, while the members of the Swan Creek and Black River tribe who remained in Michigan had consolidated into one band. Individual members of these bands were listed in an annuity payment roll made in 1854. Larry M. Wyckoff's research identifies each band and describes land purchases made both by members and by missionaries on their behalf. As early as 1835, some chiefs had made purchases of federal land in order to avoid removal, and members lived on those tracts while continuing to hunt on unsold land. Methodist missionaries first purchased land in 1847. Most of the Saginaw Chippewa bands that existed in 1854 were associated with Methodist missions. Some removed themselves to Isabella County reservations in 1855 or soon thereafter, including the Pine River Band in Gratiot County; the Swan Creek Band in Swan Creek Township, Saginaw County; and a band that had been living near what is now North Branch, Lapeer County. Some of the bands from the Swan Creek and Black River tribe, which lived on the Black River in Worth Township, Sanilac County, and on the Belle River, in Riley Township, St. Clair County, also left during this period. But remarkably, other bands remained on lands that their chiefs had purchased and even on lands owned by white people. These communities retained their structures as bands to some degree, but members also left and joined other communities.

In the period from 1855 to 1920, the largest community was at Pewanogowink, on the west bank of the Flint River in Taymouth Township, Saginaw County. Saw-gaw-che-way-o-say (Thomas Dutton, d. 1865) had been a member of the band that in 1819 was located at the southern end of the Pewanogowink Reservation, under the leadership of Neome. He purchased eighty acres in section 21 in 1851, near land that had been purchased by Man-que-to-gunia and Ma-os-e-be-nacy in 1845 and by George Bradley for the Missionary Society of the Methodist Episcopal Church. This community built a church, cemetery, and schoolhouse. In 1854, the annual report of the Missionary Society called the school "flourishing" and the church "prospering." The 1870 census lists about seventy Indians in this neighborhood. The 1877 *Atlas of Saginaw County* shows over four hundred acres held by Indians, with approximately twenty households in the community. Fifty-three Indians lived there in 1900 and thirty-five in 1930. Daniel Wheaton (Ash-she-ton-qua-ba) (c. 1828–1911), a Methodist preacher, was an influential local leader in his day. Remarkably, a small community resides there today, more than 150 years after the first purchase, and the cemetery remains in use.

Another community lived in St. Charles Township, Saginaw County. Members of the Shiawassee band, which in 1854 consisted of thirty-three individuals, purchased lands in St. Charles Township, Saginaw County, near the Shiawassee River, in 1853 and 1854. In 1860, the number of people was ninety-eight, and in 1870, it was fifty-four. In 1877, according to the *Atlas of Saginaw County*, they remained there as owners. An Indian church was in existence on section 26 (West Birch Run Road) in 1916. In 1930, the census listed thirty-seven Indians in this township.

Nau-qua-chic-a-ming (Nauck-che-gaw-me, Nauck-chic-qua-ming, Noc-a-chick-a-me, Nage-Dschikamik, "middle of the lake") (d. 1874), probably the best-known local chief, resided on the Big Rock reservation on the Shiawassee River (modern Chesaning) in the 1830s. Due to rumors that the federal government planned to remove all Indians from the state, his band moved to Canada but, in 1845, returned and bought land near the mouth of the Shebeon Creek (north of Sebewaing). In that year, three German missionaries came to the band, built a one-and-a-half-story frame house, a log church, and a stable and began teaching the children. Although the missionaries became frustrated with the practical difficulties of their mission as

Nau-qua-chic-a-ming, chief of the Cheboyganing River band, with son and grandson on horseback, c. 1870. MOSES B. HESS SCRAPBOOK V, BOX 1, HESS FAMILY PAPERS, 1774–1936, BENTLEY HISTORICAL LIBRARY, UNIVERSITY OF MICHIGAN.

well as competition from the Methodists, they were optimistic about the prospect of the band's conversion.

At the beginning of 1854, the band planned to join the Pine River Band in Gratiot County, to which the missionary Edward R. Baierlein had been attached, following the maple sugar season. But an American trader, fearful of the loss of their business due to the move, convinced the band that more than half of the pastors were frauds, that the Bible was full of lies, and that they would be forced into servitude. Suddenly they rejected Christianity. Some moved to Canada, while others joined the chief, who bought land on the Cheyboyganing River in Buena Vista Township, Saginaw County.

Other tribal members purchased nearby tracts between 1859 and 1864, so that in 1891, about a hundred lived in this community.

Although Nau-qua-chic-a-ming's band rejected the religious teachings of the Lutheran missionaries, it accepted secular instruction in reading, writing, and arithmetic. Frank Squanda (1859–1904), who had taught at the Oscoda Indian school, was a successful farmer, able to negotiate between cultures. He spoke German as well as English and played the violin. Roselynn Ederer's book *Indiantown* describes how the Squanda stayed in the area, while others gradually left, having sold land for nonpayment of taxes. Some descendants still live in the area, their Indian ancestors having married Germans.

A substantial community, made up of members of the Swan Creek and Black River tribes who refused to remove themselves to the west, formed around Lake Nepessing in Lapeer County. Peter Chatfield (Wab-ka-kah) (1874–1948) related that his great-grandfather, Peny-go-wish, left St. Clair County and moved to St. Anne Island, which is next to Walpole Island. The latter's son Pay-me-quo-ung (William Chatfield) (c. 1815–1864) moved his band to Lake Nepessing. The chief purchased land in the northwest corner of Elba Township in 1846, and George Bradley and the Methodist church purchased nearby land in 1848 and 1850. Bradley established a church, cemetery, and school. The buildings, long abandoned, still stood in 1914. The band moved to Isabella County after 1855, where Pay-me-quo-ung's son, William Chatfield (Wa-wa-sum) (1841–1904), lived when he enlisted in 1861 to fight in the Civil War. Chatfield returned to the area and bought a forty-one-acre farm in Oregon Township that bordered Pleasant Lake. This became home to other members of the band, which today is recalled by Indian Road, which runs nearby. His children attended the Mount Pleasant Indian School, and his son Peter also attended the school at Carlisle, Pennsylvania. Peter was well known in the area, playing on the Lapeer baseball team and coaching the high school's football team, as well as playing in the Walpole Island band. Despite his apparently successful adaptation to white culture, he hated how settlers had trampled on his family's dignity. In a letter he wrote in 1937, he deplored how white men had plowed up a graveyard one-half mile east of Elba on M-21, where his grandfather was buried.

When white settlers began coming to Genesee County, the Fisher Band lived near Copneconic and Loon (formerly Squaw) Lakes in Fenton Township. In 1835, Kaw-gay-ge-zhick (Robert Fisher) bought eighty acres in section 27 of Mundy Township, a little north of those lakes. Between 1847 and 1850, other members bought land totaling 120 acres in sections 9 and 10 of neighboring Gaines Township. The 1860 census counted forty-seven Indians in Gaines Township, and by 1873, David Fisher (Wahbaness) (c. 1811–1884), son of Kaw-gay-ge-zhick, owned the Gaines Township land. This bordered the large tract of land that Henry Howland Crapo owned and developed. Members of this band lived on this land and were employed as laborers on the Crapo farm well into the twentieth century. Descendants live in the area today.

In the early 2000s, the Swartz Creek Historical Society led an effort to restore this cemetery, which is on private property.

Near the oxbow of the Cass River at Wahjamega, in Indianfields Township, just south of Caro, another community developed. Mark Joshua (Mash-kee-yosh) (who may have been identical with Maish-ke-aw-she, listed as a member of the Nepessing Band in 1854) was one of a few Indians who returned to this vicinity, where they had lived earlier. He had been converted in Canada fifty years before his death in 1892 by Peter Jones, an Indian preacher. Others joined them, and by 1880, a small community of thirty-two lived in that township on land owned by lumber baron Charles Montague and was still there around 1905. Descendants still live in the Caro area.

Finally, in what might be considered a "spillover" from the reservation in Saganing, which is largely in Arenac County, a sizable community lived in Pinconning Township, Bay County. The Saginaw Bay, which at one time provided excellent fishing, gave sustenance to this community.

Several of the men enlisted as soldiers during the Civil War, and for the few who survived and lived among white people, their status as veterans and membership in the Grand Army of the Republic engendered respect among the settler community. Federal policy in this period sought to make farmers of the Indians and to assimilate them into white culture and allowed the largely Methodist missionaries to help accomplish this. Many of the children in this region went to the Mount Pleasant Indian School, which operated from 1893 to 1933. But the sad truth is that few were inclined to become farmers. Most men got by on incidental labor on farms, as fishermen, and as hunting and fishing guides. Women did beadwork and sold baskets. Alcoholism continued to cause health problems, even if it numbed the pain of life.

Individual Indians who lived off the reservation in our region continued to speak their language, fish, and trap muskrats and turtles. Camp meetings lasting as long as three weeks drew them to the churches at Taymouth and elsewhere, providing occasions for solidarity and personal renewal. They began to accept a role as distinctive members of the larger communities in which they lived.

In the years after the forests had been cut and when farms had been established, white people in Tuscola County (and neighboring Lapeer and Saginaw Counties) recognized a familiar man who appeared regularly in towns like Fostoria, Millington, and elsewhere. His name was Ish-don-quit, but they knew him as Indian Dave. He died in 1909 at an elderly age. According to stories about him collected many years later by Dorothy Stott Dinsmore and Anne Hallock, he was present at the Treaty of Saginaw and his first wife and children died in the smallpox epidemic of 1837. In 1866, during the controversy over the placement of the Tuscola County seat, he took the county books upstream from Vassar to Caro in a canoe. He lived in a traditional nomadic manner in a wigwam, although he also spent time in the settlements at Taymouth and Indianfields Townships. His significance to the white community seems to have been that he represented a survival of his people, despite the onslaught

Ishdonquit (Indian Dave), died 1906. MILLINGTON ARBELA HISTORICAL SOCIETY.

of settlement. He supported himself by making bows and arrows and rustic tables; examples of his work are held by the Millington-Arbela Historical Society, the Montrose Depot Museum, and the Mayville Historical Museum. In 1979, there was a campaign to erect a historical marker to honor him, which now stands in the Wisner Cemetery, where he was buried.

Perhaps this was the reason that Frank Squanda invited "everyone" to a picnic in 1896 at Indiantown, Buena Vista Township, featuring games, a cornet band, and dance music. Squanda announced that it would resemble Buffalo Bill's Wild West Show, with Indian singing. The much larger Indian community on Walpole Island (across from Algonac, St. Clair County) began in 1898 an annual fair (called a

War dance performed at Indian Fair, Walpole Island, Ontario, c. 1910.
AUTHOR'S COLLECTION.

"pow-wow" starting in the 1950s), featuring a parade, "war dances," games, and band tournament. Excursion steamers brought crowds from Detroit to this event, at which they bought souvenirs and took part in the entertainment. Although the indigenous population in the region was too small to support an event much larger than the Buena Vista Township picnic, which did not last long, these events indicate that a new period had begun.

Popular culture, influenced originally by Buffalo Bill's Wild West Show, created a new, if artificial, interest in American Indians. Modern pow-wows developed from such public events as the Walpole Island Indian Fair. Plains-style headdresses and dances became part of these events. Some felt a need to conform to these popular images. George Cook (1917–1974), a Flint native and descendant of the Fisher Band, for example, called himself "Chief white Bird," wore a feathered Plains headdress, and, in the 1960s, operated a souvenir store at Houghton Lake. Cook did not qualify as a tribal member, as only one-eighth of his ancestry was Indigenous, but he advocated for the tribe in other ways.

Federal Indian policy, starting in the 1960s, began to promote self-determination. A major change came to the Saginaw Chippewa when it began gaming operations in 1981, first with bingo, then expanding to card games and slot machines and finally with the construction of the Soaring Eagle Casino in 1996 and the Saganing Eagles Landing Casino in 2008. Profits exceeded the tribal government's wildest expectations and created capital to allow it to build schools, a cultural center, and social service facilities. In 1985, the tribe approved a revision to its constitution, largely to define eligibility and membership. This required that members have a minimum of 25 percent Indian ancestry. Further policies encouraged residence on the reservation in Isabella County. Membership requirements, which determine shares of the considerable profits from gaming, have caused controversy among descendants. But regardless of official tribal policy, descendants of the Saginaw and Black River and Swan Creek Chippewa living in this region remain proud of their identity and ancestry. Their families have withstood trauma for almost two hundred years yet still endure.

MIGRATION AND IMMIGRATION

Paul M. Gifford

Migrants and immigrants to our region came at different times in response to different economic activity. Economic depressions (as in the 1890s, in the 1930s, and in the period after 1980) caused people to leave, while economic booms drew people here. Some came as immigrants from Europe and later from Asia, but most came overland from other parts of the United States and Canada. Today, census categories (white, African American, Hispanic, Native American, and Asian and Pacific Islander) tell incomplete stories—the reality, of course, is more complex.

Rather than listing every group that might have had a member in this region, this essay looks only at those groups large enough to have created communities here, indicated by the existence of religious and social organizations. The first movement began in the 1830s and continued until about 1890, with migrants and immigrants looking to transform forests into farmland. The pine boom in the northern part of this region, which lasted from the 1850s until about 1890, created a new demand for labor, attracting men to work in the woods and at mills in the cities. Then a new crop, sugar beets, introduced around 1900, caused the sugar companies to recruit foreign-born families and individuals. Finally, and most importantly, the development of the automobile industry after 1910 drew on both local migration and migration from other parts of the United States and Canada as well as Europe and Asia.

During the era of the fur trade, which ended about 1840, the Indigenous population was the host population, and the few newcomers who entered the region did so as traders, needing to adapt by learning the Indigenous language, accepting names given to them, and sometimes taking wives and thus becoming part of the communities. These newcomers include men like Jacob Smith, born in Quebec of German parentage, who in about 1810 set up a trading post on the Flint River, and Louis Campau, a Detroit native, who in 1816 established a trading post at Saginaw, in competition with Smith. Elsewhere in the region, descendants of the French (and French Indian) families who had settled in the Detroit River region in the eighteenth century found their way here.

Small numbers of Yankees from New England and New York made their way to Detroit, largely as military officers, professionals, and merchants, after 1800. The first steamboat, *Walk-in-the-Water*, made its maiden voyage in 1817 from Buffalo to Detroit. The Erie Canal's completion in 1825 did not yet result in a flood of migrants to Michigan, because land in western New York was still available. By the time of Alexis de Tocqueville's 1831 trip from Detroit to Saginaw, there were only a tiny number of settlers north of Pontiac, and, as Tocqueville discovered, recent settlers were avoiding the Saginaw Valley.

However, in 1836, a rush began. One group came from Genesee County, New York, and named the new county in Michigan, created in 1836, after their old home. Settlement in Shiawassee, Lapeer, and St. Clair Counties followed soon afterward. They bought tracts in the southern tiers of townships in those counties and spread into Saginaw and Tuscola Counties. By 1850, about forty thousand people lived in our region, about one-third of whom were born in New York. Though frequently called by historians "New Englanders," the vast majority came from the state of New York, especially from the western part of the state. Although the bulk of their ancestry came from English Puritans who settled in New England during the seventeenth century, other forebears included immigrants from Holland and Germany who settled in the Hudson and Mohawk Valleys, and Scotch Irish from New Hampshire and Maine. Very few came from the cultural hearths of Pennsylvania and the Chesapeake.

These pioneers, having been brought up in frontier conditions, expected to continue living as they had for generations: clearing forests, burning stumps, planting wheat, and building houses and roads, and creating the Jeffersonian ideal of communities of yeoman farmers. Some barely had the resources to buy forty acres of federal land at $1.25 per acre. Others were wealthy capitalists, scouting out the best tracts for purchase and then holding on to them for later sale. The more entrepreneurial among them platted towns and opened stores and hotels. Millers built grist mills and sawmills along rivers, forming the first industries. Methodist, Baptist, Presbyterian, and Episcopal churches soon followed, along with country schools and eventually private academies. Settlers from New York continued to move to this region until after the Civil War. The New York-born population in the region reached 36,739 in 1870 and 39,751 in 1880. By 1900, as pioneers died off, the number had declined to 26,138.

Anglo-Canadians, meaning English (or at least non-French) speakers mostly from Ontario, composed the next group of migrants. Michigan, especially Detroit and the eastern counties toward Lake Huron, was the natural extension of westward migration from Ontario, since the land and climate in northern Ontario were unsuitable for agriculture. Although Canadian births created high numbers of what the census called "foreign-stock" residents in our region, most of the early population of Ontario had its roots in migration from New York and other states, first by Loyalists in the 1780s and later by others seeking land on the northern shore of Lake Ontario and in the Niagara frontier. One 1812 estimate indicated that 80 percent of Ontario's population was born in or descended from people who lived in the United States. After 1820, organized efforts, including landlord-assisted schemes and discounted

Harry Dunn

I once did know a charming boy, whose
name was Harry Dunn.
His father was a farmer in the county of Odun.
They had everything 'twas needed, a home
and good land,
But he only wished to have a time in the
woods of Michigan.

One morning Harry started for Bay City, hired
out to the lumbering crew,
And the next place he found himself was in
the woods of Pinconning.
He worked for three long months, ofttimes he
would write home,
Saying the winter will soon be over and when
the spring comes, I'll return.

One morning Harry, he arose, on his face he
wore no smile.
He called his chum outside the door, whose
name being Charlie Tile,
Saying, "Charlie, I had a dreadful dream,
which filled my heart with woe.
There's something soon to tell me that home
we ought to go."

But Charles, he only laughed at him, which
pleased him for a time,
Having said on to Charlie, "It's time to fall
the pine."
They walked up until about ten o'clock all on
that fateful day,
But a hanging limb fell down on him and killed
him where he lay.

His comrades gathered round him and drug
the limb away.
I was standing close beside of him, those
words I heard him say,
Saying, "Comrades, now I'm dying, my hour
will soon right come.
See the Lord, in his great mercy, look on my
friends at home."

In two or three days after, Harry's coffin was
sent home.
To maintain all of his honor, of poor, poor
Harry Dunn.
When his mother saw the coffin, she fell down
like a stone.
They picked her up, but her heart was broke
when Harry, he returned.

Likewise his poor old father didn't seem to
wear no smile.
But in two or three months after, they buried
the poor old man.
In two or three months after, they buried the
poor old man.
So you'll see what occurs o'er in the woods
of Michigan.

Come all you jolly lumberin' boys wherever
that you be,
I would have you pay attention and listen
unto me.
Don't leave your poor old parents, stay home
if you can,
But if you're forced to leave your home, don't
lumber in Michigan.

As sung by Lon Louks (1881–1961), of Bad Axe, and recorded by Karl Byarski, 1950s.

passage, brought new immigrants from Ireland (the majority of whom at first were Protestant), England, and Scotland. The earliest migrants from Ontario thus tended to share an ancestry similar to those of Yankees, while those coming later in the nineteenth century tended to reflect this Irish, English, and Scottish background.

In our ten-county region, the number of people born in Canada was 21,881 in 1870; 59,035 in 1880; and 58,522 in 1900. The strongest period of immigration was between the end of the Civil War and the 1890s. Although a minority in Genesee and Shiawassee Counties, Canadians dominated in the rest of the region, especially in Huron, Sanilac, and St. Clair Counties. In 1880, 68 percent of the population of Sanilac County, 52.1 percent of Huron County, and 33.4 percent of St. Clair County was born in Canada, among the highest proportions of Canadian-born inhabitants in any county in the United States.

German immigration to the region began in 1845 with the establishment of the Franconian Lutheran colonies, starting with Frankenmuth. As this is covered elsewhere, we will mention here only some of the German communities outside that "belt." Detroit attracted many Germans beginning in the 1830s. Some later sought farms, which accounts for the communities, for example, in St. Clair County, particularly in Casco Township, where St. Paul's Lutheran Church was established in the community of Peters in 1858, in Marine City in 1857, as well as Capac in 1870 and Port Huron in 1871. Germans from Detroit bought land in the hills of Hadley Township, Lapeer County, where they founded a church in 1860. After the Civil War, the State of Michigan actively pursued German immigrants by appointing a commissioner, M. H. Allardt, to recruit them. Allardt successfully convinced a group in Dresden, the capital of Saxony, that had organized as a cooperative for emigration, to settle in Michigan. The colony purchased ten thousand acres of land largely burned by the 1871 forest fire from lumber baron Eber B. Ward in Delaware Township (west of Forestville), Sanilac County, and between 1872 and 1876 over eighty families settled there. Catholics, mainly from southwestern Germany, began settling in Maple Grove Township, Saginaw County, in the 1850s and 1860s, creating a parish in 1883 and later a school. Germans, both Catholic and Lutheran, came from Canada and established a community in Sherman Township, Huron County, after the Civil War. The number of German-born in the region reached its maximum (twenty-seven thousand) in 1890, after which it declined. A small number of war brides and refugees came after World War II.

The earliest English-born to settle in the region probably came via New York, as from 1850 to 1870 the largest number of this group lived in Genesee County. Elsewhere, in the more Canadian counties, such as Bay, Huron, and St. Clair, the English came as part of the migration from Canada. This "invisible" group, which joined existing churches rather than founding their own, blended rapidly into the English-speaking community. Numbering 6,144 in 1870, this group increased to over 10,000 in 1890, probably reflecting the migration from Canada during this period.

Immigrants from Ireland included both Catholics and Protestants. Census numbers do not distinguish between the two, but it is likely that most of those who came from New York were Catholic, while some of those who came as part of the post–Civil War migration from Canada were Protestant. The first Irish Catholics to come to the region settled among the French in southeastern St. Clair County and, starting in the 1830s, in Genesee County. The mother church in Genesee County, St. Michael's, began as a mission in 1843. Elsewhere in the region, English-speaking Catholic churches tended to form in the years after the Civil War, as in Saginaw (a mission in 1841, parish in 1866), Port Sanilac (mission 1854, parish 1863), Lapeer (1868), and Caro (1879). Many of the Potato Famine–era immigrants worked as migrant laborers constructing railroads, and it took some time for them to become permanent residents of these communities. In 1870, Irish-born numbered 7,427; the number increased to 8,610 ten years later but decreased to 5,421 in 1900. They were scattered throughout the region, with the largest number in St. Clair County, followed by Saginaw and Genesee Counties. Some Irish became farmers, and they purchased land throughout the region. Concentrations and communities did develop. Enough had settled in Mount Morris Township by 1865 that they petitioned for a Catholic church, construction for which began in 1868. The largest community, however, was in two neighboring townships in St. Clair County, Emmett and Kenockee Townships (set off from Clyde Township and organized in 1850 and 1855 respectively), due in part to the efforts of land agent Patrick Kennedy. Emmett Township was named for Robert Emmet (1778–1803), the Irish Republican, and the village of Emmett was incorporated in 1883. Father Lawrence Kilroy established a log church in the community of Anchorville in 1853, which, although at considerable distance, served the Irish settlers of the area and in 1867 was given charge of the parishes at Kenockee and Columbus. Kenockee Cemetery is the only reminder of the original church, which became Our Lady of Mount Carmel parish, located in the village of Emmett.

Nationalism ran high among Irish Catholics, leading many who had settled first in Canada after the cheaper passage to Halifax or Quebec to leave the British-dominated country and come to the United States. The Fenian Brotherhood gained wide support among Irish American Civil War veterans, who planned to invade Canada. The circle of Fenians in Port Huron was led by the remarkable brothers, lawyers O'Brien and William F. Atkinson, and the latter commanded a brigade in the unsuccessful invasion of Canada at Malone, New York, in 1870.

Protestant Irish, coming from Canada, bought farms in the region but did not establish a strong imprint. One organization that had much influence in Ontario, especially rural Ontario, was the Orange Order, an anti-Catholic, Unionist fraternal organization. In 1893, the Michigan legislature authorized the incorporation of the Loyal Orange Institution after revisions that made it avoid political activity and activity against any religious group. By this time, the order tended to identify more as Canadian and less as Irish. Local lodges of this organization existed in Port Huron, Flint, Saginaw, Bay City, Yale, Clio, Akron, Marlette, Cass City, Bad Axe, and elsewhere. Internal division in the mid-1920s, however, led to its decline.

French Canadians came to Michigan, mainly from Quebec, following the Civil War. In 1900, there were 6,156 Canadian-born of French background in this region.

Almost two-thirds of that number lived in Bay and Saginaw Counties, most in the cities of Bay City and Saginaw. French-speaking Catholic parishes were established in Bay City (1867 and 1895) and Saginaw (1893). French newspapers were published in Bay City between 1878 and 1904. Many of the men worked in the woods during the winter and, in the off-season, worked in mills in Saginaw and Bay City. Some also bought farms in Huron County, particularly in Lincoln and Meade Townships. French Canadians popularized square dances and associated music among Polish immigrants, who as fellow Catholics socialized with them in church halls.

Poles coming from Canada settled in Paris Township, Huron County, by 1856, one of the first Polish settlements in the United States. They were the vanguard of the first wave of Polish emigration, coming from the part of Poland occupied by Prussia, where they strongly resisted the official Germanization (and Lutheran) policy. As an example, dances at Polish weddings in the Thumb always began (following the bridal dance) with the bride and groom dancing to the tune of the banned national anthem, *Mazurek Dąbrowskiego*. The settlement of Poles increased to the point that by 1900, there were almost four thousand Polish natives in the region. The largest concentration was in Bay City, where Poles began to settle about 1870, finding work in the sawmills and lumber camps; in the 1885 strike, one representative noted that the Poles were the lowest paid workers. There were two Polish-language Catholic churches in Bay City (founded in 1874 and 1906), one in Saginaw (1887), and two in Huron County, at Parisville and Kinde (1903).

By 1900, lumber companies had cut the forest and families occupied all the good farmland. The major cities in the region were Saginaw (pop. 42,345) and Bay City (27,628), which were Michigan's third and fourth largest cities. Flint's population (13,193) was less than that of Port Huron (19,158). If further immigration and migration to the region was to take place, it would be to the cities. The automobile industry subsequently changed the equation, and Flint became the leading city. But before we get there, we need to look at the consequences of the introduction of a new crop.

Unlike other crops, sugar beets required constant attention, and farmers soon understood that sugar beets required labor of an industrial nature. To meet the demand for labor, sugar companies looked nationally to find workers. Farmers in Nebraska had been raising sugar beets since the late 1880s, and companies there had been recruiting ethnic Germans from the Volga River region of Russia. Michigan sugar companies regarded them, with their work ethic and large families (including children, who could do some of the work without the backbreaking task involved in stooping), as ideal workers, and in 1901, the first chartered train from Nebraska brought these "Russian" workers to Michigan. This became an annual event, and by 1907, the annual "pilgrimage" (as one local journalist called it) amounted to over a thousand people. By the 1910s, Volga Germans were coming to the region directly from Russia. They worked on farms in many parts of the region, such as around Akron

Laborers work in sugar beet field near Bay City, c. 1905. AUTHOR'S COLLECTION.

and Fairgrove, in Tuscola County, in Sanilac County, and in Saginaw County. They also established communities in Saginaw, Flint, and Port Huron. In Flint, they lived near the First Reformed Church on Gillespie Street, and in Port Huron near St. Paul's Evangelical Lutheran Church on 14th Street and Wells. In Saginaw and elsewhere, they joined existing German-language churches, but they also formed a social club, the Wolga Club, which still exists. In 1920, there were 2,274 Russian natives whose mother tongue was German living in the region. Some of the "Hungarian" beet weeders were Germans from the Banat region in what is now Serbia and Romania (known as Danube Swabians), including some brought to Caro from Cincinnati on a special train in 1912.

The other immigrant group originally recruited from Nebraska (but also from Wisconsin) was Czechs, mainly from Moravia. They settled in Shiawassee County, western Genesee County, and Saginaw County, due to contracts the Owosso Sugar Company made with local farmers. Some large farms, like the Crapo Farm in Swartz Creek, employed many Czech laborers as sugar beet workers. As a result, many of them bought farms in the area in addition to working in the automobile factories in Flint. There were enough to form a Czech-speaking Catholic parish and a social club, the Friendship Club, which sponsored dances, plays, and card games. In Owosso, local Czechs formed a branch of the Západní Česko Bratrská Jednota in 1916. Even if the language has not survived, local Czech-Americans have preserved other aspects of their culture. Accordions and brass bands play polkas at rural dances (local farmer

Bedrick Smeage's band, with Mexican American singer Hilario Cantu, recorded for RCA Victor in the 1940s), and for many years, a weekly polka show was broadcast on WOSO. An Owosso bakery, Kolache Kitchen, features the Czech pastry *koláče*. In 1920, there were 1,559 Czech speakers in the region, nearly all in Shiawassee, Saginaw, and Genesee Counties.

The sugar companies also recruited many recent immigrants living in various cities, including Cleveland, Toledo, Wyandotte, Detroit, and elsewhere. These were primarily Poles and Hungarians. The Poles tended to come from Russian-occupied Poland, unlike the earlier immigrants to Bay City and the Thumb, who had come from Prussia. In 1909, a Vassar newspaper noted the return of the various immigrant groups to their homes in Detroit, Wyandotte, and Toledo, where in the winter months, they would work in the factories, shipyards, and railroads. Hungarians were part of this mix, having been brought by sugar companies to the region by 1904.

Individual Jews, mainly from Germany, came to the region in the nineteenth century, mostly as peddlers or dry-goods merchants. Enough had settled in Bay City to form a congregation in 1878. Later immigrants organized further congregations in that booming lumber town, and in 1907, its Jewish population was estimated at nine hundred. The massive Jewish emigration from eastern European in the late nineteenth and early twentieth centuries caused new communities to form in Flint and Saginaw. In 1917, the Jewish population of Bay City and Saginaw was estimated at 1,000, while that of Flint was 385. The religious congregations that formed were B'nai Israel (1890) and Beth El (1903) in Saginaw and Congregation Beth Israel (1925) and Temple Beth El (1935) in Flint. Rather than working in automobile shops, immigrant Jews tended to be independent business owners. The earliest immigrants in Bay City worked mainly as fruit or junk peddlers, traveling on wagons in rural areas and with pushcarts within the city. In Flint, many located their businesses near the Buick factory. The decline of the region has unfortunately caused congregations in Saginaw and Bay City to close and merge.

Immigrants from Arabic-speaking countries came to the region as early as the 1880s, largely as peddlers. They included members of the Druze community from Lebanon, Orthodox Christians from Palestine, and Maronite Catholics from Lebanon. Most of the community in Flint were independent, neighborhood grocers. There was a concentration of "Syrians" on Parkhill, off Industrial Avenue, but in 1920, most lived above their stores, which were scattered around the city. Kamol and Michael Hamady first came to the region in 1907 to work in sugar beets on their relative's farm in Tuscola County but went to Flint and eventually ran the city's largest grocery chain. In the 1970s, Muslims from Syria and elsewhere (largely professionals) settled in Flint and Saginaw and organized mosques.

The outbreak of war in 1914 led to a cutoff of travel across the Atlantic and of the supply of labor for the sugar beet crop. The sugar companies responded by recruiting workers, largely Mexican natives, through contractors in San Antonio, Texas. The

Housing for Mexican farm laborers, probably at Prairie Farm, Albee Township, Saginaw County, 1941. COURTESY OF THE LIBRARY OF CONGRESS.

Mexican Revolution (1910–1920) had caused a large number of refugees to flee to that state, creating a substantial pool of laborers willing to travel for work. The first group came to Michigan in 1915, and gradually more came, so that by 1927, 75 percent of the beet laborers in the state were from Mexico. As with the European beet workers, Mexicans brought their entire families to work in the fields, which allowed their employers to evade child labor laws.

Over the years, as farmers introduced newer varieties of sugar beets, insecticides, and new machinery, beets needed less weeding and thus fewer laborers. Labor shortages during World War II were answered in 1942 by the Bracero Program, which allowed Mexicans (in addition to German POWs in 1945 and in a brief, unsuccessful attempt, Puerto Ricans) to work on short-term contracts. The Bracero Program continued until 1964, but by that time, sugar beet farming was largely mechanized and needed few laborers. Other crops (pickling cucumbers and strawberries) also attracted laborers from Texas and Mexico.

Of course, Mexicans began working in the automobile plants soon after they first arrived in the region. In 1920 there were 129 Mexican-born individuals in Saginaw and 96 in Flint. The number in the ten-county region increased to 1,005 in 1940 and 1,228 in 1950. The city of Saginaw had the largest population of Mexicans, most concentrated in the city's northeastern section. Unfortunately, changes in gathering census data has made it somewhat difficult to analyze the growth of the Mexican American population. From 1960 to 1970, the Mexico-born population in Saginaw declined from 2,759 to 2,195 and in Flint increased from 687 to 957. Much of the Mexican American population must have been born in the United States, because the number of individuals who identified themselves as "Hispanic" increased steadily from 1990 to 2010 and in numbers far larger than the early Mexican-born population would suggest. In Saginaw County, the Hispanic population grew from 11,105 in 1990 to 15,573 in 2010, and in Genesee County, from 6,391 in 1990 to 12,983. Today, some undocumented Mexicans may be found working in construction, in restaurants, and as agricultural laborers, largely living under the official radar as a "floating," unstable population. Lacking barrios, descendants of the earlier migrants are well integrated into the general population. At the same time, however, the increase in Hispanic political power has caused Mexican Americans in Saginaw and Flint to create institutions that resist this integration and assimilation by promoting Spanish-language instruction and cultural events. These include the Mexican American Council in Saginaw and the Latinx Technology and Community Center in Flint.

Although the first foreign-born to work in the new Flint automobile plants undoubtedly included those who came from the sugar beet fields, the news about jobs there drew people from immigrant communities around the United States. A survey by the Archdiocese of Detroit revealed that there were 240 Polish families in Flint by 1910. That year, Poles, under the leadership of Father John B. Hewelt, organized All Saints Catholic on Industrial Avenue. The church established a cemetery in 1913 and a school that offered instruction in Polish in 1914, with a building on Addison and Maines Streets. By 1920, Flint's Polish-born population reached 1,474. In 1938, seven Polish organizations organized a nonprofit corporation, Dom Polski, and built a hall on North Saginaw Street that hosted meetings, political rallies, and social events. Locals regarded the Polish neighborhood as bounded approximately by Industrial Avenue, Saginaw Street, Stewart Avenue, and Pasadena Avenue.

Hungarians also came first to Genesee County as sugar beet workers, although later migrants left coal fields in Pennsylvania and Ohio and industrial sites elsewhere. Their numbers ranked a close second to Poles in terms of foreign-born inhabitants. In 1930, there were 1,254 people in Flint who reported "Magyar" as their mother tongue. Hungarians lived in the St. John Street neighborhood, east of the Buick factory, and, like other immigrants from eastern Europe in this period, tended to work in the Buick foundry. To serve Hungarian speakers, Hungarian Baptist (1916), Hungarian Reformed (1917), and St. Joseph's Roman Catholic Church (1922) were founded. George Simon's orchestra played "Gypsy" music, and the Hungarian American Culture Club, a restaurant, served customers until the 1960s. In a campaign

Assyrian immigrants pose in costumes after play at Fairview School, Flint, 1933.
MARTHA JOSEPH FILE, GENESEE HISTORICAL COLLECTIONS CENTER, UNIVERSITY OF MICHIGAN–FLINT.

led by Susie Puskas, the community brought many refugees from the 1956 uprising in Hungary to Flint.

The third largest immigrant group that lived near the Buick factory was from Italy. Italians came to the area first as railroad laborers and as workers in the coal mines in Saginaw and St. Charles. There were enough Italians in Saginaw by 1913 to organize Our Lady of Mount Carmel parish. Although the number of Italian-born in Flint surpassed that of Saginaw by 1920 (482 in Flint, 395 in Saginaw), Flint's Italians never had their own parish, but the Sons of Italy hall on North Street acted as a community center.

Persecution sent Assyrians, members of the ancient Nestorian branch of Christianity, from northwestern Iran, via Chicago, to Flint in the 1910s. Soon the community in Flint became the fourth largest in the United States. They worked mainly at Buick and lived in the St. John Street district and East Side, organizing a church and cemetery by 1930. Melchizedek Z. Bacchus, an Assyrian Pentecostal preacher, wrote and published a Syriac translation of *Pilgrim's Progress* in 1931. There were about two hundred Persian-born individuals in Flint in 1930.

The auto boom brought many other foreigners to the region. These include myriad nationalities under what Americans called "Slavish" (Slovak, Rusyn, Lemko, Ukrainian), as well as Russians, Croatians, and Macedonians (Bulgarians). Many came from Pennsylvania mines. Eastern European Slavs organized St. Michael's Byzantine Rite Catholic Church (and cemetery) in 1917 as well as a Slovak-speaking Catholic parish, Most Blessed Sacrament (1928). Russians and Ukrainians formed St. Nicholas Russian Orthodox church by 1918, but Macedonians and other Orthodox immigrants also joined it. Rather than working for General Motors, however, Macedonians and Greeks tended to run independent businesses, especially "family" and "Coney Island" restaurants throughout the area. A Greek Orthodox church was organized in 1920.

Many people from England and Scotland came to Flint, especially after World War I. The economic situation in Europe was bad, and high unemployment in places like Glasgow and Newcastle caused many skilled machinists to seek work in the automobile plants. In 1920, the number of English-born people living in Flint amounted to 1,573 and those born in Scotland numbered 500. These groups increased the number of Episcopal and Presbyterian churches in the city. English natives organized a lodge of the Sons of St. George in 1911 (it ended in 1955), while Scots formed a lodge of the Order of Scottish Clans in 1915. The Flint Scottish Pipe Band, still in existence, was created in 1916. The Flint Scots House, on East Kearsley Street, was formed in 1948, where monthly dances were still held in 1964. In 1940, Genesee County had 2,786 people born in England and 1,109 in Scotland. A similar growth in immigrants from Germany also resulted from economic dislocation in Germany, and Swedish machinists also came. Unlike the Eastern Europeans who lived near the Buick factory, these immigrants blended into the native white population with ease.

Flint's huge population growth during the 1910s largely resulted from domestic migration rather than immigration from abroad. Most of the migrants were poor, with little chance of accumulating capital sufficient to buy farms. Many men had worked by the day, whether as miners, part of threshing crews, railroad laborers, or lumberjacks. The largest group came from within Michigan. The beginning of the automobile boom coincided with the end of the logging era, for one thing. Farming on marginal, cutover land sold by the lumber companies was a fruitless endeavor, leading many to leave. Many young men simply left farms in better agricultural regions (in Michigan as well as the neighboring states of Ohio, Indiana, and Illinois) and went to Flint to find work.

Perhaps the most distinctive group of white migrants came from an area centered on the Missouri Boot Heel, in the far southeastern part of the state, including neighboring parts of Arkansas, Tennessee, and Kentucky. The migration began in 1916, and by 1920, 1,235 Missouri natives lived in Flint (ten years earlier, there had been only 83). By 1930, the number had increased to 6,544, ranking a distant second to Michigan natives (84,178) but ahead of those born in Ohio (5,041).

African Americans moved to the region before 1840. In that year, the census counted eleven in the region (nine in Genesee and two in Lapeer Counties). Although the state had inherited the Northwest Ordinance's law against enfranchising Black men, Michigan's 1837 constitution prohibited slavery (reflecting the strong antislavery opinions of its settlers), but conditions before the Civil War, especially after the Fugitive Slave Act (1850), made settlement on the American side of the Canadian border unstable. The end of the Civil War, however, improved political and social conditions for African Americans, and the relatively better economic conditions caused many to come from Canada, like Isaac D. Williams, an escaped slave from Virginia who had worked as a laborer for the Great Western Railway in Ontario before coming to East Saginaw in 1868, where he published his reminiscences in 1885. Small communities formed in Flint, Saginaw, and Bay City. In each city, churches became the centers of the communities, serving educational and political as well as religious needs. In Flint, two churches, Quinn Chapel African Methodist Episcopal Church (founded in 1875) and Mount Olive Baptist Church (1910), served their members. Saginaw had Bethel African Methodist Episcopal Church (1867) and Zion Baptist Church (1868).

Both communities in Flint and Saginaw lived in residential areas somewhat segregated from the rest of the population. In Flint, the community was concentrated south of the central city, around 11th Street and Pine Street, east of Saginaw Street. Occupations varied but for men included being a janitor, doing "odd jobs," and working as a teamster. Women worked as laundresses, dressmakers, and household servants. Saginaw's community was more dispersed, mostly living scattered on the east side, although a smaller number lived on the west side. Occupations were like those of Flint. Coal mining developed in Saginaw in the 1890s, and following recruiting efforts in the Appalachian coalfields, many came from there to work in the coal mines. Numbers, however, remained small until World War I. In 1900, there was a total of 1,118 African Americans in the region, almost all in Saginaw, Flint, and Bay City. In 1910, the "Negro" population (combining Black and mulatto people) of Flint was 397; of Saginaw, 314; and Bay City, 160. Much of the population was born in Michigan, and many had originally come from the South on the Underground Railroad, settled in Canada, and later moved to Michigan.

Then, during World War I, a labor shortage caused Flint to witness a sudden influx of African Americans from the South. In 1920, there were 1,701 African Americans in Flint. In addition to the older neighborhood, a new one had emerged in the North End, east of the Buick factory, on Michigan Avenue and on streets leading toward St. John Street. By 1930, Flint had a Black population of 5,725.

Saginaw's Black population grew from 328 in 1920 to almost 3,000 in 1930, much of this growth happening between 1927 and 1930. Chevrolet Division Grey

Iron Foundry was the chief employer of these migrants. The older, established community lived on the West Side, while the new industrial migrants settled in the northeastern part of the city. Saginaw native Willie McKether makes the point that the migrants during this period, having left the South with its more severe legal and social restrictions, did not complain about the segregation and restrictions they encountered in the North.

In both Saginaw and Flint, Black residents experienced housing segregation, limited employment opportunities, and exclusion from downtown businesses. Until the late 1950s, newspapers included ads for houses that announced they were intended for "colored" people. Downtown stores and eateries discouraged sales to African Americans. Nevertheless, they saw improved social as well as economic conditions.

World War II created a new demand for workers, and many African Americans flocked to Flint and Saginaw. The Black population in Flint more than doubled between 1940 and 1950, from 6,599 to 14,043. Before the war, Georgia had produced more than its share of the population would predict, but now Arkansas, followed by Mississippi, became the leading source. Although a comprehensive study has not been made, it is likely that chain migration from places like Rison, Arkansas, resulted in entire kinship networks moving to Flint. The Black population in Flint reached 36,553 in 1960 and continued to grow, reaching 60,338 in 1970. Even after General Motors began to decline in the 1970s, it increased to 78,804 in 1980. At this point, the size of the community became large enough that it no longer was a minority community, and by 1990, it was almost half the population.

In Saginaw, the African American population also grew rapidly during the 1940s and 1950s. In 1950, the size had more than doubled in the previous ten years, from 3,315 (1940) to 8,671. It almost doubled again by 1960 (16,550) and continued to grow through migration until 1970, when the population reached 22,288. After 1980, the population reached a plateau (27,555) and actually declined after 1990, when the population hit its maximum (28,046). But the white population declined after 1950, severely so after 1970, so that Saginaw's Black population became a majority by 2010.

Following World War II, numerous displaced persons (Ukrainians, Jews, and others) came to Flint to work in the factories, as did Hungarians after the failed 1956 revolution there. These newcomers joined existing communities. In the 1980s, the Jewish community in Flint sponsored many Jewish immigrants fleeing the Soviet Union, although most left in subsequent years. However, the big change resulted from the changes brought by the Immigration Act of 1965, which ended the quota system and allowed potential immigrants to come from hitherto restricted countries, like India, China, and elsewhere in Asia and Latin America. In addition, immigrants with skills in fields such as medicine received preferential treatment in admission.

With the array of medical insurance benefits available to members of the United Auto Workers, hospitals and clinics in Flint and Saginaw expanded. Many medically trained immigrants sought residencies in Flint and Saginaw and subsequently opened practices. Others went to underserved small towns in the region. Today, many clinics and offices are staffed by immigrant physicians with the help of native nurses and receptionists.

Although the region contains natives of China, Vietnam (including Hmong), the Philippines, and Korea, the largest number of Asians is from South Asia (India and Pakistan). Most live in the wealthier suburban areas of Flint (Grand Blanc and Flint Townships) and Saginaw. Over five hundred Pakistanis live in Grand Blanc Township, and Indians are scattered among the two townships. Recently, Sikhs (originally coming from New York City) have been moving into the Flint and Saginaw areas, mostly buying liquor stores and gas stations. Immigrants from these areas have established mosques, Korean Presbyterian churches, Hindu temples (in Flint and Saginaw), and a Sikh gurudwara (in Flint), all in suburban locations.

THE AUTOMOBILE INDUSTRY

Ted McClelland

By the end of the 1870s, pine upriver was so depleted that Flint's lumber kings began casting about for a new industry to save the town from economic devastation. In 1882, Begole, Fox and Company's sawmill transformed itself into the Flint Wagon Works. Wagons required a lot of hardwood (mainly oak), and Flint sawmills had plenty of oak. William A. Paterson had been, in 1869, the first to establish a carriage making and repair shop, though strictly for a local market. William F. Stewart started a business making buggy bodies and woodwork in 1881. But it was William Crapo "Billy" Durant, who purchased a patent for a road cart with an improved suspension and, with J. Dallas Dort, organized the Flint Road Cart Company and made Flint ready to manufacture automobiles. Durant had a knack for selling and making deals and soon contracted with Paterson to manufacture his product with an annual production of fifty thousand vehicles. Manufacturers of more specialized products, like the Imperial Wheel Company, Flint Axle Works, and Flint Varnish Works, followed.

So renowned was Flint for putting rural America on two or four wheels that in 1901, the city fathers erected a series of wrought-iron arches over Saginaw Street, spelling out, in white lettering, "VEHICLE CITY." Flint was now the second-largest producer (after South Bend, Indiana, home of Studebaker) of wagons and carriages in the country. But there was a feeling that if Flint wanted to maintain its preeminent position in the transportation business, it ought to start looking into this new vehicle rolling out of shops and garages throughout Michigan: the horseless carriage. By the turn of the century, Detroit's Henry Ford and Lansing's Ransom Eli Olds had already designed the cars that would bear their respective names.

James Whiting, manager of the Flint Wagon Works, convinced his employer to buy the Buick Motor Company for $10,000 and move it from Detroit to Flint. To run Buick, Whiting appealed to Durant. Setting up shop in the Flint Wagon Works, Buick built forty cars that first year. By 1906, Buick had outgrown the Wagon Works and moved into a three-story plant on an old, oak-covered tract known as the Hamilton farm, along a new street appropriately named Industrial Avenue.

In 1908, Durant merged Buick with Oldsmobile to form General Motors (GM), which would one day become the world's largest industrial concern. The ambitious Durant quickly acquired a third auto company, located in Pontiac; then, feeling he had to add a Detroit automaker to his portfolio, he paid $3.5 million for the Cadillac

The Buick complex, c. 1930. WINCHELL/DAVY COLLECTION, GENESEE HISTORICAL COLLECTIONS CENTER, UNIVERSITY OF MICHIGAN–FLINT LIBRARY.

Motor Company. The Vehicle City, which had begun the first decade of the twentieth century with a single hand-assembled motorcar, was by its end the second city of the new industry, behind only Detroit. In 1910, one out of every six automobiles sold in the United States was a Buick—a total of 30,525 cars. The demand for Buicks meant a demand for workers to build Buicks. Flint's population tripled between 1900 and 1910, and in 1914, Flint was the fastest-growing city in the United States. After Durant lost control of General Motors, when it went into debt during an economic downturn, he started a new company, Chevrolet Motor Company, at the old Flint Wagon Works. Chevrolets were built in a complex along the Flint River (it was nicknamed "Chevy in the Hole," either because it lay in a depression along the river or because it was a hellhole—probably both). Buicks were built in the North End. Two Fisher Body plants supplied bodies to both.

Saginaw's lumbering history also made it an ideal spot for automaking. Saginaw had wealthy investors, still flush with lumber fortunes. It had railroads. It lay along a mighty river. And it was close to Flint. In the GM universe, Saginaw was a vassal city to the company's capital. It never developed an automobile of its own, despite several attempts in the early twentieth century (the Rainier Touring Car and the Argo Electric are long forgotten), and it was never home to an assembly plant. Instead, Saginaw produced parts that were shipped to the assembly lines in Flint, thirty miles to the south, and Detroit, one hundred miles away. Saginaw Steering Gear, which would eventually produce steering columns for most GM cars, was founded in 1906. The Malleable Iron Plant and the Grey Iron Foundry, which poured castings for engine blocks, opened in the late 1910s. A plant that started out making crankshafts eventually built transmissions. Saginaw contributed to General Motors one piece at a time.

Following the success of the 1936–1937 Sit-Down Strike and GM's recognition of the United Auto Workers (UAW), the union was the first element in a forty-year run of prosperity that would make Michigan's autoworkers the highest-paid industrial employees in the world. The other was World War II. The war lifted the entire nation out of the Great Depression, but it was especially a boom time for Flint and Saginaw, returning their factories to levels of productivity not seen since the 1920s. In Flint, Buick turned out steel cartridge cases, tank power trains, 20mm shell bodies, Hellcat tank destroyers and mounts for anti-aircraft guns. Fisher Body built Sherman tanks, M-10 tank destroyers, M-36 sluggers, and M-26 Pershing tanks. AC Spark Plug provided sixty million spark plugs for airplanes. Defense contracts pushed Flint's industrial employment to 43,640, then a record high. Saginaw played an essential role as part of the Arsenal of Democracy. Malleable Iron made track blocks for tanks and trigger housings for rifles and machine guns using a lightweight Armasteel developed at the plant. Grey Iron poured magnesium for airplane engines. Steering Gear built .30 caliber air-cooled Browning machine guns.

The outcome of the war was even better for the auto industry than the war itself. As the only major nation that had not been bombed flat, the United States emerged as the world's sole industrial superpower. In the 1950s, more than 90 percent of the cars driven in the United States were built by General Motors, Ford, or Chrysler. GM alone built half, and the company could not build them fast enough to satisfy the citizens of a victorious nation looking to treat themselves to comfort and speed after a decade and a half of economic depression and wartime deprivation. In Saginaw, engineers at Steering Gear were perfecting an innovation that would define luxury in postwar American automobiles: a hydraulic steering wheel, better known as power steering. Power steering was so popular that Steering Gear built another plant and hired an additional 1,500 workers to satisfy the demand. By 1957, power steering was installed in all Cadillacs, 88 percent of Oldsmobiles, 70 percent of Buicks, 55 percent of Pontiacs, but only 28 percent of plebeian Chevrolets. In those years, Grey Iron was the world's largest grey iron foundry, with six thousand workers pouring four thousand tons of iron a day. When GM produced its fifty-millionth car, in 1954, it featured Saginaw-made parts from bumper to bumper. From Grey Iron came engine castings, inlet manifold castings, and cylinder head castings; from Malleable Iron, steering gear housings, front wheel hubs, and differential cases; and from Steering Gear, steering gear assemblies and power steering boosters. A later innovation from

Steering Gear was the collapsible steering column, a safety innovation first installed in GM cars in the 1960s.

In 1958, Flint observed GM's fiftieth anniversary with parades, pageants, and a nationally broadcast television special depicting the city as emblematic of the nation's postwar prosperity. The parade drew three hundred thousand people to the city's downtown. Flint had burgeoned into a city of nearly two hundred thousand people—one-third employed in the auto industry—and it owed all its wealth and growth to General Motors. The 1960s were even better. Vietnam was the perfect little war for General Motors: The company received $426 million in defense contracts in 1964. By 1967, that figure had increased to $776 million. In 1965, the corporation sold 7,278,000 automobiles, with net sales of $20.7 billion, both company records. Its 409,000 hourly workers averaged $3.74 per hour—substantially above that reported for all U.S. manufacturing employees by the Bureau of Labor Statistics. This was when gasoline cost 31 cents a gallon, and a new house averaged $21,500.

Life had never been better for the American autoworker. The national unemployment rate did not exceed 4 percent in any of the forty-eight months between 1966 and 1969. After a sixty-seven-day strike in 1970, the United Auto Workers won two long-coveted perks: "30 and Out," which guaranteed autoworkers the right to retire after thirty years of service, at age fifty-eight, on a full pension, and an annual cost-of-living raise. In 1973, after a brief strike against Chrysler, the UAW won even more generous perks: a dental plan, a longer holiday break between Christmas and New Year's Eve and the opportunity to retire on a full pension after thirty years of service at any age. "The union got to a point where we ran out of things to negotiate for," a participant in the 1970 strike said. "What more could we ask for? We had a good wage, we had good health care, we had a good pension. Everything was there."

Less than two weeks after the Chrysler strike was settled, everything began to unravel for the American auto industry and the American autoworker. The 1973 Yom Kippur War resulted in King Faisal of Saudi Arabia declaring a retaliatory embargo. As gasoline prices jumped from 39 cents a gallon in 1973 to 55 cents in 1974, Americans suddenly stopped buying American cars. The percentage of disposable income spent on new cars dropped from 4.8 percent to 3.8 percent—the lowest since the Korean War—and a lot of the purchases were fuel-efficient Fiats, Hondas, and Volkswagens, which were less expensive to fill than street yachts like the Lincoln Continental and Chrysler New Yorker. The Big Three found themselves in a bind, which they soon figured out how to make worse. GM, Ford, and Chrysler didn't want to build small cars, because only huge cars provided the profits necessary to pay the wages and benefits they had just lavished on their workers.

The Arab oil embargo was the beginning of the end for Saginaw's Grey Iron, Nodular Iron, and Malleable Iron foundries. As consumers demanded smaller, lighter, more fuel-efficient cars, GM began casting engine blocks out of aluminum rather than iron. The foundry had never been a pleasant place to work. It was hot, grimy, and exhausting, but it provided a good living to 6,800 autoworkers.

In 1986, GM announced the closing of Nodular Iron, which cost 1,747 workers their jobs. Malleable Iron closed in 2004 and was demolished in 2010. Grey Iron changed its name to Saginaw Metal Casting Operations; today, fewer than five hundred workers pour aluminum castings, the plant having abandoned iron in 2005. As GM's foundry, Saginaw smoked and steamed during the era of big American iron: the Oldsmobile Toronado, the Cadillac Eldorado, the Chevrolet Bel-Air. With the coming of the Chevette, the Cruze, and the Volt, its output dwindled. The smaller, four- and six-cylinder engines needed less castings, parts could be made from aluminum, and front-wheel drive technology required fewer parts.

After the economy recovered from the Arab oil embargo recession, so did GM—for a while. GM employment in Flint peaked in 1978, at 76,933 workers. As late as 1980, Flint still had the highest median wage for workers under thirty-five in the country thanks to union contracts that allowed new hires to start at the same rate as their more experienced coworkers. "The state of GM in 1977, it was hot," said David Vizard, a former autoworker who was hired as the *Flint Journal*'s labor reporter that year. "The biggest problem in the plants was absenteeism. They were working around the clock. Three shifts. Even if you didn't show up for work, they let it go for a long time. You got warnings, you got screamed at, but they needed people. Especially if you had experience. That robotic exercise of working on the line, it's a very hard thing to maintain for a long period of time."

Then, in the early 1980s, came another oil shock and another recession, which had their roots in the disruption of the oil supply caused by the Iranian Revolution and the anti-inflationary interest rates set by President Jimmy Carter. Americans could not afford the gas to fill a big car or the loan to buy it. Carter's successor, Ronald Reagan, refused to loosen the money supply until inflation declined. Car sales hit a twenty-year low. In the fall of 1982, the national unemployment rate was 10.8 percent, the highest since the Great Depression. In Saginaw, nearly eight thousand workers were laid off. In Flint, the unemployment rate was 25 percent. GM laid off workers at plants all over Genesee County.

Local 599, which represented Buick workers, had the largest membership in the entire UAW. Its monthly newspaper, *The Headlight*, began a "Hard Times" page, featuring articles on topics like debt, economic forecasts, and depression. Don Spillman wrote in January 1982 that his "members will survive because they are plenty tough. . . . We all hope the overinflated salary of GM President Roger Smith is cut more than just a little bit so as to reflect he is as serious about saving the Corporation as well as the UAW is." Smith, of course, was the Roger of *Roger & Me*, which became the highest-grossing documentary film of all time. Its director and star was Michael Moore, the son of an AC Spark Plug worker and a muckraking local journalist, whose alternative newspaper, the *Michigan Voice*, had long railed against the community's tax abatements for General Motors. Moore framed his movie as a quest to persuade Smith to spend a day with laid-off autoworkers in Flint. He wanted the GM chairman to understand the human cost of what Moore believed was a greedy corporate betrayal of the city that had given birth to General Motors and loyally provided the labor that helped it become the world's largest corporation.

GM never recovered from the decade between the Arab oil embargo and the recession of 1982. In 1970, the company produced 45 percent of all vehicles sold in the United States, while foreign manufacturers produced 7 percent. Today, foreign auto companies produce half, while GM makes only 20 percent. Flint and Saginaw never recovered, either. As the birthplace of General Motors, Flint was a one-horse town, entirely dependent on its largest employer for its identity and its livelihood. The 1980s were the beginning of what Flintstones call "the pull out": GM's slow, steady disinvestment in its hometown. The city was gripped with a sense of desperation and betrayal.

Buick City was supposed to be Flint's salvation. In the mid-1970s, GM executives told Local 599 President Al Christner that the company was fed up with high absenteeism, insubordinate employees who slashed foremen's tires, stacks of grievances, and semiannual strike threats. Flint had a culture of labor-management conflict dating back to the Sit-Down Strike. The union, to save jobs, adopted the Quality of Work Life program, an attempt to end grievances and strikes by giving the guy on the line more say in how the plant was run. Workers could shut down the line, adjust machine settings, reject raw materials—all decisions that had once been reserved for foremen. Absenteeism, which hurt quality more than any other infraction, was cut to 2 percent in plants that adopted Quality of Work Life. Grievances—and the time-consuming hearings necessary to settle them—almost disappeared, because, one worker said, "you could settle a lot more issues with the plant manager."

The success of the Quality of Work Life program, plus the desire to emulate Japan's "just-in-time" manufacturing process, convinced GM to build a new super-plant on the site of Buick Assembly. Buick City was supposed to be GM's version of a Toyota plant: an eight-factory, 235-acre, $280 million complex in the North End of Flint. GM wanted to break down work classifications by assigning assemblers to six-person teams, in which every member could do every job. The company also wanted just-in-time delivery of parts, instead of stockpiling materials in the plant. The Japanese had assembly lines delivering parts to the assembly line and robots welding seams and painting bodies.

Buick City resulted in the closure of Fisher Body Plant One in 1985. Instead of building bodies on the South Side of Flint and trucking them to the North End, which wasted gasoline, manpower, and time, GM would build the entire car in one location, which would save hundreds of dollars per vehicle. Not only did Fisher One's closing result in the loss of 2,550 jobs, it was seen as symbolic of GM's disinvestment from Flint, since the Sit-Down Strike had begun there. After the plant was sold to a Detroit developer, a few surviving Sit-Downers picketed in protest, believing GM was exacting belated revenge for the strike.

Buick City opened in September 1985. With twenty-eight thousand workers drawn from factories all over Flint, the plant was supposed to represent the city's recovery from the recession. This hive became the birthing chamber of the LeSabre, a compact, front-wheel drive sedan at the bottom of the Buick status ladder. Buick City did a great job producing LeSabres. From the time the complex opened, the LeSabre was one of J. D. Power and Associates' highest-ranked automobiles for quality and reliability. There was no problem with Buick City.

The problem was with Buick. It was a car that filled the parking lots of public golf courses at 11 o'clock on Wednesday morning. It was the car your retired high school principal drove to church. Gasoline cost less than a dollar a gallon in the 1990s. Young drivers who had once begun the Buick-to-the-grave cycle in a LeSabre were now buying sport utility vehicles. In Buick City's first decade, GM lost another ten points of market share, falling from 40 to 30.7 percent. Christner was voted out of Local 599's presidency by workers who were angry about the concessions of the early 1980s and thought the Quality of Work Life program "was just another management scheme to eliminate jobs," as one member put it. He was eventually succeeded by Dave Yettaw, a Vietnam vet who took the local back to its militant roots, appearing at Flint City Council meetings to protest the company's tax abatements. Only a dozen years after it opened, GM decided to shut down Buick City, moving production of the LeSabre to its plants in Hamtramck and Lake Orion, Michigan.

In an attempt to save the plant, the UAW had taken out ads in *The Wall Street Journal* and *Inventor's Business Daily* in November 1997, publishing a company memo that ranked Buick City second in quality of GM's nineteen North American plants. It was of no use. General Motors had scheduled the Flint autoworker for extinction. Once Buick City closed, the count would stand at twenty thousand—less than one-quarter of the population just twenty years before. GM also disassembled Chevy in the Hole, its riverfront Chevrolet complex, a process completed in 2004. The company's largest remaining plant is Flint Assembly (formerly GM Truck and Bus), which is in Flint Township, not Flint proper.

Buick City sat empty for fifteen years, until RACER Trust, the quasi-governmental agency that took over GM's abandoned properties after the company filed for Chapter 11 bankruptcy proceedings in 2009, finally knocked down the last remaining buildings. In the meantime, B's Bar and Grill and the United Van Club, the shoprat taverns across Industrial Avenue from the plant gates, closed their taps. Trees burst through the shop floor. Deer began capering among grasses as thick as savanna, and the surrounding North End neighborhood became so depopulated that a couple built a memorial to the victims of 9/11 on corner lots they purchased from the city for a few hundred bucks apiece. Chevy in the Hole is now the site of Chevy Commons, a 140-acre state park planted with such native species as wild lupine, black-eyed Susan, showy goldenrod, ironweed, red osier dogwood, elderberry, and tamarack. Where there was once an auto plant, there is now a playground, a meadow, a walking trail on an old railbed, and a river overlook.

There are still auto plants in Flint and Saginaw, but manufacturing is no longer the number one employer in either city. Flint's auto industry employment is down to 5,500, less than a tenth of what it was in the late 1970s. Saginaw's peaked in 1979, at 26,100. Now only a few hundred workers remain in Saginaw Metal Casting Operations. The steering gear plant, which has been known as Nexteer Automotive since GM sold it to China's Pacific Motors, employs more than 4,500. Those declines are consistent with GM's overall decline in hourly employment—from 511,000 in the 1970s to 50,000 today—as a result of automation and loss of market share. The jobs that remain are not as good as the ones that left: in 2021 GM held a job fair to hire temporary workers at a parts processing center in Burton. The pay: $16.67 an hour.

In both Flint and Saginaw, losing jobs has meant losing people. Flint, once Michigan's second-largest city, with a population of nearly 200,000, is down to 81,000 after the 2020 census. Saginaw has also lost more than half its population, declining from 98,265 in 1960 to 48,115. GM built both cities as the third act of an industrial drama that ran from lumber to carriages to cars. Now both cities are looking for a fourth.

THE RISE AND FALL OF BUICK CITY

Thomas F. Adams

I was destined to be a shop rat. Both of my grandfathers, my father, my brother and sister, and most of my aunts, uncles, and cousins labored in General Motors (GM) plants. In 1976, Buick employed over eighteen thousand hourly workers. I became one of them.

The two-mile long Buick complex was a city within a city, with over one hundred buildings covering 8.7 million square feet of floor space on 310 acres. Railcars and trucks delivered raw materials to a place where twenty thousand men and women toiled everyday within the factories, shops, laboratories, studios, and offices to produce every component and assembled them into complete automobiles. Buick Manufacturing had its own engineering facility, foundry, forge, railroad, hospital, trucking fleet, police force, and fire department. More than seventy miles of conveyors connected the various operations. That revered collection of factories will forever hold the title of "the Buick" in the minds of workers.

Buick City built its last car in 1999, and the rest of the Buick complex ceased operations a few years later. This is a tale of the rise and fall of Buick City from the perspective of ordinary workers whose labor made it all possible.

Casimir Wolos, my maternal grandfather, immigrated from Poland to Flint, where he hired into the Buick foundry, Factory 70. He crossed the Atlantic with all his possessions in an oak-strapped sea trunk, arriving in New York the same year Buick's Factory 70 began producing iron. He settled long enough in New Jersey to marry Josephine Bogolska, but soon after Josephine give birth to their first child, the young family joined the thousands of immigrants who migrated to Flint, Detroit, and other industrial cities.

Flint was a boomtown in the early twentieth century. The Wolos family moved to Tilden Street, at the heart of the Polish enclave created when Poles moved from the St. John Street neighborhood to the area around the newly built All Saints Catholic Church on Industrial Avenue. All Saints, the Dom Polski building on Saginaw Street, and the White Eagle (one of many shop bars that lined Industrial Avenue, which announced its presence with the odor of urine for blocks) were community institutions, where Poles blended with the local working-class cohort to become Americans.

The neighborhood was shaped by foundry culture, with the presence of prostitutes on payday producing a circus atmosphere. The 50 Grand, a raunchy stripper bar, was located on the north end of Industrial Avenue, where Buick workers could cash paychecks and immediately spend them on "entertainment." Later, endless blocks of vacant shops, storefront churches, liquor stores, taverns, and strip joints became the legacy of 1960s and 1970s white flight. After the wave of deindustrialization in the 1980s, Flint earned the dubious distinction of being among the top ten cities in the country for highest number of strip joints per capita.

But during Casimir's time, like the shift change at Buick, men still poured from church after Sunday mass and flowed into local pubs. Casimir, a gregarious storyteller and skilled card player, often treated his mates to drinks at the Eagle, regaled them with stories, or played his violin carried from Poland. The neighborhood was safe and prosperous. He built two houses on Tilden Street and owned a commercial building. He lost one of the houses and the commercial building during the Great Depression but never accepted public assistance. He called Tilden Street home for the rest of his life.

A pension and healthcare benefits were the rewards of a career in the shop, but cancer and black lung disease were the penalties of foundry work. Black lung is associated with coal miners, but the foundry's toxic cocktail of core-binding chemicals, pulverized sea coal, and asbestos had the same effect as years of inhaling coal dust. The foundry closed in 1980, but black lung continued killing workers for decades afterward. The "25 and Out" retirement contract provision for foundry workers was not a reward; it was simply an acknowledgment of the violence done to their bodies.

My grandfather, who tossed coins to the swirl of children around him on his walk home when he won at cards, was diagnosed with cancer, but it was black lung that killed him. Doctors wanted to do surgery to remove the cancer, but the black lung made him too weak to survive the procedure. Still, despite everything, Casimir died grateful to be an American.

This was the shop.

As a child, I always wondered what it was like in "the shop," where my father spent all his time. The veil of mystery lifted when I hired into Factory 31, the Buick axle plant in 1976. Factory work was drudgery. It was filthy, poisonous, and mind-numbing. The gloom of the heat-treat department smothered the afternoon sunshine. My job consisted of plucking three-foot long steel axle tubes from a conveyor and stacking them in a steel tub, engulfed the entire time by vaporized cutting oil and the thunder from surrounding machinery. The floor trembled from the massive presses located across the street in Buick's main stamping plant, Factory 12. My partner, a new hire, fed the tubes into the machine that spit them out on my end. We ran more than three thousand tubes during our shift—twice as many as the other two shifts combined.

We were allowed to drink from a water fountain or use the bathroom only during designated breaks.

This, too, was the shop.

Management expected workers to leave their brain at the door and follow orders. Some bosses routinely exploited new hires who had not yet achieved ninety days seniority, because they could fire them any time and work them harder than everyone else. Nature, however, waits for no one. One day, before reaching the ninety-day mark, I signaled to my partner to stop loading the machine, then ran up the two flights of stairs to the closest restroom located in the overhead structural steel. The sound of steel tubes dropping off my empty workstation into a steel tub soon echoed through the department.

When I came back, the boss was waiting for me. "I should fire you!"

"Okay, fire me," I agreed. "I'm not shitting my pants to keep this job." But my partner and I ran twice the parts as anybody else, so the boss left us alone for the rest of the shift. It was my first taste of GM management by fear. I've been a union activist ever since.

One of the other new hires operating a mechanized welder intuitively reached in to adjust a misaligned part just as the welding tips lowered. It welded through her hand, nearly severing it. Production halted briefly—just long enough to send her to the Buick hospital, clean up the mess, and reset the machinery. Production, after all, was always management's first priority.

The welding machine was my job until I crossed Division Street and was hired onto skilled trades as an industrial truck repair apprentice. With my new position, I moved across the road and into the foundry.

Built in 1927, Factory 70 was the most advanced gray iron foundry in the world. Instead of shoveling sand from piles on the floor as was the custom, Factory 70 workers poured sand from hoppers directly over the machinery. Electric-powered ladles and conveyors transported the molten iron. Declaring the Buick foundry "light, airy and cool," the business press claimed that the extensive ventilation system prevented the gloom, confusion, and stifling heat found in other foundries. Industry observers declared Factory 70 the safest metal castings plant in the country—possibly the world.

In 1972, 2,200 workers produced 1,500 tons of iron castings a day. The foundry covered over 810,000 square feet of floor space that included a pattern shop, core room, melting area, casting room, and finishing room. It was a spectacle of sparks and thunderous machinery. Hot iron pouring lines ran along one side. On the opposite side, hot metal cranes traveled along overhead monorails, delivering molten iron from the cupolas in the bowels of the foundry.

My foreman stood barely five feet from his boots to the top of his hard hat. He owned the LeSabre Lounge, a honky-tonk bar located on Dort Highway named after a popular Buick model. It was popular with both workers and bosses. He talked constantly as he escorted me to the supply crib. Explosions and screaming machinery punctuated the "orientation," which boiled down to "Your journeyman is really your boss. I assign overtime on Monday and hand out paychecks on Friday. Otherwise, don't bother me!"

Welcome to the Foundry!

We dodged the spray of molten iron, sparks, and smoke that engulfed the bespectacled men on the pouring line. While waiting at the crib window I studied the display of naked women that adorned the cabinets and countertops. The crib attendant offered me a pull from his whiskey as he regaled me with heroic tales of the Knights of the Ku Klux Klan. My foundry orientation complete, I was welcomed unconditionally into the rank and file.

The foundry was called the dumping ground of the Buick—misfits, outcasts, and outlaws. Three shootings occurred in Buick plants, including the foundry, the year I hired in. A gunfight erupted on the shop floor between two men fighting over a woman. No one was injured, but all three were fired. The men returned to the foundry after doing time in prison. One of them later threatened to blow Leo Dolehanty's brains out for standing shoulder to shoulder with the plant superintendent while watching workers leave the plant early.

The sand shovelers were probably the toughest department in the foundry. Shovelers grew marijuana on the roof, ran a numbers operation, sold pot, beer, and liquor. Once, a newly assigned boss named Lyle told the shovelers things were going to change now that he was in charge. The shovelers' leader laughed at him and spit in his face. A couple hours into the shift, the shakeout was mysteriously clogged with sand and iron production stopped. Sand cores and iron castings rained on the boss from the catwalks. Someone slashed his tires and the convertible top to his Corvette. That was followed by a brick through the windshield and death threats. A nervous breakdown ended Lyle's bossing days.

He wasn't the only one who was a target of direct action. The notorious foreman, nicknamed "Rat" (because he resembled Mickey Rat, the underground comic book character), sowed chaos and conflict as he prowled the overhead catwalks, spying on workers and searching out napping janitors. Someone laid a trap for Rat, placing cardboard over a hole cut into the walkway. Rat stepped onto the cardboard, fell through the hole, and plummeted to the concrete floor below. The accident left him with a permanent limp and ended his patrols on the catwalks. Another abusive foreman nearly lost a foot when someone filled his boot with molten iron. Foundry workers were a direct sort of people.

Conflicts between laborers and supervisors, foremen, and "management" like Lyle and Rat were not limited to the foundry. They were, in fact, part of the fuel

Two workers pour molten iron at Buick foundry, 1940. THE SLOAN MUSEUM ARCHIVES PHOTOGRAPH COLLECTION, SLOAN MUSEUM ARCHIVES.

that fed the growth of the union from the Sit-Down Strike on. Seasoned truck repairmen like Elmer Krebsbach, hardened by island hopping across the South Pacific during Second World War, regarded management as contemptuously as he had regarded the Japanese. The reprimand on his violation record was a badge of honor. He'd called a foreman an "asshole" and a "prick" for outsourcing repairs to 17 Garage. Outsourcing meant a cut in pay, which was unforgiveable. Retaliation took the form of "work-to-rule"—a kind of slow-moving strike where everyone followed the rules to the letter but accomplished little. The action shut down foundry production. Management stopped sending repairs to 17 Garage and withdrew Elmer's penalty. Production resumed. The reprimand remained as a symbol of victory and solidarity.

Solidarity of the "work-to-rule" type was an important part of foundry culture that extended across race lines, or at least more so than was the case in other factories. When James "Cap" Wheeler was hired into the Buick foundry in 1955, skilled trades and management were completely white. Cap and other Black workers ran into a gauntlet of catcalls and racist insults hurled by white workers every time he walked through Factory 11 to get from the parking lot to the foundry and were ordered to stay out of their areas. Complaints to management and the union failed to stop the assaults, so Wheeler returned with eighty or ninety foundrymen to settle the matter. Fistfights and beatings put an end to the harassment. Afterward, Black workers walked through the plant unmolested.

Eighty percent of the foundry workforce were Black. The harsh environment was a potent unifier among the rank and file. "In the foundry," Cap Wheeler explained to me in an interview, "we all got along—whites and Blacks would stick up for each other because at the end of the day when everyone headed to the showers, they were all black!"

Cap became active in the union as soon as he arrived on the shop floor. But the union was itself often not very unified—it had many factions with their own priorities, divided into caucuses. Cap joined Al Christner's Solidarity Caucus, because the group in power, Rank and File Caucus, had rules that barred low-seniority workers, who were typically Black, from running for union office. When Cap hired in, Black applicants were the last hired and Black workers were the first fired. There were no Black employees in skilled trades—Buick would not hire them, and the union was not pressuring management to do so.

The first meeting of the Solidarity Caucus was held at the Dom Polski Hall, because the local leadership denied any opposition group use of the union hall. Dom Polski, however, turned out to be a one-time meeting place. When the Black members joined the rest of the Solidarity members in the basement for drinks, the bartender refused to serve them. Everyone walked out—never to return. Solidarity.

Cap walked entire departments off the job to protest excessive penalties, overtime, or unsafe conditions. Sometimes a department would empty out spontaneously when management fired someone. "We would walk them out and hide on the roof for as long as it took to get what we wanted," Cap explained. "When the guys in the union hall found out what was going on they would call us in and give us hell, but we didn't care."

Outside the foundry, in Buick engineering (the prestigious Factory 78), things could be even more divided along race, gender, and class lines. Engineering management congratulated themselves for being so progressive for hiring Black people and women into the experimental trades (after being forced to do so by policy changes), but new Black hires were taken to an off-site interview. Things weren't easier for women workers, who suffered every kind of sexual harassment known to man, so it's no wonder they accounted for one-quarter of the union in 1974 and half the rank and file by 2007.

Elitist attitudes were on full display when I hired into engineering as an experimental twelve-volt electrician after leaving truck repair. After a month on the job, my supervisor called me into his office to applaud my work performance and admitted management had me on "secret probation," because some of the test mechanics were upset. They couldn't understand how some outsider foundry rat managed to get one of the prized jobs in engineering that rightfully belonged to one of them. They denigrated my character to my boss—thus I was placed on secret probation. Confused, I asked my boss to show me where "secret probation" was in the contract. He never mentioned it again.

I did not know it at the time, but back when I crossed Division Street to work in the foundry, the entire Buick complex was at a crossroads. Working seven days per week, twelve hours per day, Buick seemed to be on fire, but tough times were just ahead. GM already planned to close Factory 70 and considered the same fate for Buick Final Assembly.

With political and economic turmoil, aggressive foreign competition, inept management, and a disgruntled workforce, Buick was on the chopping block. The Arab oil embargo of 1973 crushed Buick sales, leaving unsold inventories to pile up. Buick shed workers, as GM surrendered the small car market to Japanese imports. In the first two and a half months of 1974, car production halted, and twelve thousand workers hit the streets.

Al Christner, president of United Auto Workers (UAW) Local 599, learned that GM planned to close the Buick foundry and possibly Final Assembly. If that wasn't enough, Flint faced the prospect of losing the entire Buick complex and eighteen thousand well-paying working-class jobs. At that time, the foundry was fifty years old, and some plants associated with Final Assembly were more than seventy years old. At best, they would require updating to be competitive. Not only that, but Buick workers also had a militant reputation, and management considered foundry workers in particular a lost cause. Angry workers filed hundreds of grievances every month, prompting Christner to send letters to management threatening work stoppages. In short, this did not seem like the time or place for a successful reinvention.

Christner, Local 599 president from 1971 to 1984, had a reputation as a tough bargainer and fierce advocate for the workers. Raised on a farm, a child of the Great Depression, Christner hired into the Buick in 1948. The cultural change from farm to factory life shocked him. "I came from a farm where we didn't treat our animals as dirty and nasty as bosses did workers," he remembered. He was an unlikely disciple of cooperation with management, but without radical action, he knew the Buick would cease to exist.

Christner invited Buick personnel director Bill Rowland to the union hall to discuss plans to save Buick. They set aside historic disputes and devised a plan to convert Factory 70 into a modern torque converter facility: Factory 81. They convinced GM's board of directors and sold the plan to skeptical workers at a Halloween party, where, dressed as devils, the men took off their masks and shook hands, in a performance that signaled the new relationship between labor and management.

The Factory 81 concept was based on Quality of Work Life (QWL), a philosophy of labor-management relations based on cooperation, rather than conflict. Labor and management leaders set aside their disagreements and separated out troublemakers on both sides. Management's gamble that Factory 81, which would be the sole producer of torque converters for GM's next generation of front-wheel-drive vehicles, paid off, in part because of committeeman Leo Dolehanty's worker education programs, which included GED preparation, training videos for each new piece of machinery, a computer lab, and the first computer-assisted design (CAD) program at the Buick. The success of the program gave Buick a reprieve. Instead of closing Final Assembly, the corporation accepted the proposal, presented by Rowland, Christner, and City of Flint officials, to create the Buick City project, modeled after Japan's Toyota City.

Despite these successes, the charm of QWL eventually wore off when old habits reemerged. Abusive management and toxic union politics crept into the system. Mutual respect gave way to distrust when management used QWL to control workers instead of empowering them. As a result, workers in 1984 voted four local union presidents out of office because of their support for QWL, including Christner, who arguably saved the entire Buick complex.

Even before things soured, change is rarely positive for all parties involved. When Factory 81 was fully operational, truck repair required fewer workers. I was relegated to grease monkey on third shift while the plant retooled from rear-wheel to front-wheel drive production. Eight months later, I resigned from truck repair and hired into Buick engineering as an electrician.

But before I did that, I met Dave Yettaw. A highly regarded committeeman, he had risen through the leadership ranks in Local 599 politics to become Local 599 president, where he became a key figure in the fate of Buick City. Like Cap, Christner, and many others, Yettaw got involved in the UAW because of an abusive boss and poor union representation from "shyster" committeemen. He was elected committeeman in 1972 and immediately ran afoul of the powerful Unity Caucus. Eventually, Yettaw recognized that he would have to join Unity and become caucus chairman to move up.

Like many of the 599 rank and file, Yettaw considered QWL a scam by management to get the union to ignore the contract. In many ways he was right. At the 1986 UAW Constitutional Convention, which he attended as a delegate, he recalled there were all kinds of leaflets and stuff being passed out:

> I was taking literature from everyone. There are people there from the far Right, the NRA, and there's people there from the far left. There's the Socialists and there's Communists and Trotskyists. I took some literature of Jerry Tucker's New Directions. And I'll never forget this Sergeant at Arms. He doesn't know me, and I don't know him. And he says, "You aren't taking that Communist literature, are you?" And I said, "Well I don't know Region 5—I didn't even know these people." And he said, "Yeah, you see that guy's picture right there (pointing to the man's picture)? I said, "Yeah." He said, "Well that's Jerry Tucker,

> and he's married to that nigger Aunt Jemima." And I thought, Jesus Christ! I said, "You're a Sergeant at Arms? I don't care if the guy's wife is polka dot, that's his business!"

He then witnessed a violent attack on members of the New Directions Movement (NDM; a reform movement that advocated a return to the UAW's founding principles) by Administrative Caucus guys who slugged a woman from Tucker's Region 5, and felt he knew now "what these people [were]." The Administration Caucus had controlled the International UAW since 1946 and had banned Victor Reuther (one of the UAW's founding members) for supporting the New Directions. Yettaw always admired the Reuthers, so after returning to Flint, he left Unity and joined the NDM.

After that, politics at UAW Local 599 became even more toxic. Unity Caucus was infuriated by Yettaw's defection to NDM. The UAW administration compared NDM to the Communist Party and considered Yettaw as a traitor to the UAW. After a contentious election, Yettaw was elected president and the lone NDM member in the Local 599 leadership—everyone else belonged to Unity Caucus.

Roger Smith, GM chairman from 1981 to 1990, who thought labor costs were too high and was obsessed with reducing the number of workers, also instigated a Renaissance plan for GM that involved factory renovations, purchasing tech firms, and launching the Saturn Corporation. Buick City was one facet of Smith's plan to restore GM's glory days, and to be fair, it did breathe new life into a dying factory, temporarily. The Buick City project was a new way to manufacture automobiles with bodies built on site, which meant investing $280 million to renovate Final Assembly. Innovative manufacturing techniques, including increased mechanization of labor, temporarily catapulted Buick to the top of the industry. Buick City was Smith's shining example of the factory of the future, run by robots, computers, and a few contented teams of workers. Although Buick City's startup was initially plagued with technical problems—the robots were painting each other instead of cars and installing windshields into the back seats—the problems were eventually worked out, and Buick City built the highest quality cars in the world.

However, labor-management cooperation turned into conflict at Buick City, just as it had at Factory 81. Managers became less interested in the team concept or quality control issues than the quantity shipped out the door. One manager outlawed stopping the line to prevent defects. He became the stuff of Buick City legend, when workers stopped the line because there was a problem with the car hoods. He flew into a rage, jumped onto the hood of a nearby car, and jumped on it until an imprint of the air cleaner appeared in the sheet metal. Then he declared, "Now that's a bad hood. Everything else is going out the door. Fixing it is the job of the dealerships."

The larger controversy, however, that ended Buick City involved an expansion project of the Buick City body shop. Dave Yettaw participated in a groundbreaking ceremony with management in 1995 to create a "flex body shop." The new body shop would allow for multiple vehicle platforms to be built at Buick City instead of just one, guaranteeing Buick City's viability for decades into the future. Construction was already underway when committeeman Kenny Scott led a political rally on the shop floor of Buick City at the same moment GM executives were touring the plant. With between fifty and one hundred workers present, Scott demanded that management give a bigger role to the in-house construction department, Factory 25, despite the fact that major renovations to factories had generally been done by contractors, as the nature of the construction was beyond its capabilities. The production line stopped during the rally, which management considered a wildcat strike. They threatened to fire Scott and everyone who participated in the rally.

Why did Scott do it? The answer, as it often was in the union, was politics. Local 599 was in the midst of an election campaign for delegates to the upcoming UAW Constitutional Convention. Scott was running for delegate, so he joined with Herb Brandon, the skilled trades shop committeeman representing Factory 25, to gain votes from skilled trades workers. According to Dick Danjin, former aide to UAW President Stephen Yokich, the stunt was orchestrated by UAW leadership. Scott followed orders when he led the political rally in Buick City in the presence of GM executives. Yokich intended to crush his opposition in Local 599, including Dave Yettaw, by destroying Buick City.

An angry Buick director of labor relations called Yettaw, demanding to know what was going on at Buick City. It was the first Yettaw had heard of it. GM headquarters halted and eventually canceled the flex body shop project, ending any possibility that Buick City would get a new product after the current production run. The Unity and Administration Caucuses mounted a misinformation program that blamed Yettaw for the cancelation of the flex body shop. The two caucuses joined with the local Chamber of Commerce, the *Flint Journal*, and the mayor of Flint to deny him a fourth term. The unlikely coalition warned workers if they reelected Yettaw, Buick City would close. The smear campaign succeeded. The membership voted Yettaw out in 1996. GM announced the closing of Buick City six months later.

The Buick was greatly diminished when General Motors celebrated its centennial. In fact, it was no longer called Buick; it was now known as Powertrain North. Powertrain consisted of Factory 36 (the engine plant) and the ghost of the old Buick foundry, a piston manufacturing operation located in Factory 81. Factory 36 built its last engine and closed its doors in 2008, exactly one hundred years after Billy Durant organized General Motors.

The City of Flint did everything it could to accommodate GM in order to create and maintain Buick City and other GM facilities around the city. It gave GM hundreds of millions of dollars in tax abatements for every aspect of GM's operations, including fill dirt, shrubs, trees, doors, hardware, frames, paint, drywall, tile floor for the executive garage, parabolic lighting, and "toilet room interior accessories." City officials didn't want to annoy the corporate bosses for fear they would pull up stakes and leave. The State of Michigan even offered GM a last-minute, $165 million incentive package to keep Buick City open. It failed.

As the last car snaked its way through Buick City on June 29, 1999, the bosses handed out commemorative "Top Quality Awards" as the workstations fell silent. Management staged a photo op replacing the last car built, a Pontiac Bonneville, with a Buick surrounded by a crowd of beaming smiles and applause. Pablo Lopez, lifelong union activist, asked the plant manager, "Why are you smiling?"

GM ended Buick City production, along with the hopes and dreams of thousands of its workers and people associated with the operation of the plant. Workers who were not ready to retire became "GM gypsies," scattering up and down I-75 and across the country. Salaried workers at all levels saw their careers at GM evaporate. Some employees lost livelihoods, healthcare, and pensions. The disruption and chaos caused in local communities and individual lives is impossible to overstate.

I retired from General Motors in 2006 and went on to exercise my contractual benefits to complete master's and PhD degrees in history at Michigan State University. Job well done; thank you; goodbye!

RACE AND FLINT'S WATER CRISIS

Katrinell Davis

There's a thin line between Black and white life in Flint—and a whole lot of history. Flint's racial divide dates back to the Federal Homeowners Loan Corporation and Federal Housing Authority's use of racially restrictive property appraisals and covenants between the 1920s and 1940s that denied home loans to Black people, especially outside of predominately Black neighborhoods, confining them, prior to the open housing referendum in 1968, to ghettos.

In 2022, after decades of economic downturn and white flight, the thin line remains somewhere northwest of downtown Flint. Take a leisurely drive north on Flint's red-brick Saginaw Street, and you'll see a landscape of boarded up businesses and empty spaces. People living here face a hand-to-mouth daily struggle and tormenting contrasts. Here there are empty houses without running water or electricity; over there in neighborhoods, on both East and West Sides, are Tudor Revival homes with manicured lawns. Communities of poor Black people squat in abandoned houses around Hamilton and Martin Luther King Avenues, while those living in the College Cultural neighborhood can live untouched by the city's problems. Privileged neighborhoods were among the first to receive infrastructure support following the water crisis.

Although some homes in predominately white and affluent neighborhoods like Mott Park have deteriorated in recent years, much of the public space and amenities in these neighborhoods, including a soccer field, a playground, and a tennis court, have been preserved due to the collective wealth and action of concerned residents, who, in some cases, have written successful grants to improve the appearance of their neighborhoods. Just around the corner from an affluent neighborhood you might find a neighborhood garden operated by a multiracial coalition of citizens also attempting to devise equitable and sustainable solutions to the challenges of living in a bankrupt city. Residents of all racial and ethnic groups play crucial roles maintaining neighborhood stability. In addition to keeping up their yards, some residents help protect their neighborhoods from danger by joining collective efforts to chase squatters and criminals away.

At the same time, Flint residents—many of whom embrace the moniker of "Flintstones"—have had bigger worries than the aesthetic, economic, and communal challenges confronting the area. They have had to advocate for affordable and safe water to counter decisions made over decades that have degraded the city's water infrastructure. Federal laws, such as the recently passed Infrastructure Investment and Jobs Act (IIJA), could have helped the Flint neighborhoods that were not part of the city's recent pipeline replacement program. President Joseph Biden pledged to eliminate lead service lines and expand access to clean drinking water systems within schools, daycare centers, and homes across the nation via the IIJA, a $55 billion–plus infrastructure investment. The bill also allocated over $21 million to clean up Superfund and brownfield sites that contribute to elevated toxic exposure among children who live close to these profoundly polluted areas.

Accordingly, in December 2021, the Biden administration proposed the Lead Pipe and Paint Action Plan (LPPAP), which supports infrastructure investments by involving over ten federal agencies in efforts to replace lead pipes within the next decade. This plan requires federal agencies to prioritize lead pipe replacement efforts in underserved communities, while implementing new regulatory procedures designed to protect high-risk communities from lead in drinking water. The LPPAP also establishes a cabinet-level partnership tasked with improving lead remediation in schools and daycare centers that includes the Department of Education, the Environmental Protection Agency (EPA), Department of Health and Human Services, and the Department of Agriculture. The fate of this proposal depends on the outcome of the 2024 presidential election.

Efforts to address lead contamination are timely and necessary, but implementation of such policies can be undermined by administrative constraints and biases that influence how water protection laws are monitored and regulated. We note this regulatory blind spot, because in reality, the battles that communities fight against lead contamination are also shaped by the long-standing practice of privileging profit over people. Residents of Flint can tell you all you need to know about the ways their experiences were ignored during the water crisis, and that is a fight that is far from finished.

The Origins of the Water Crisis

Flint's water crisis was triggered by the State of Michigan's decision to balance its budget on the backs of "disadvantaged" communities. This began in the early 2000s, when the state opted to abandon the long-standing practice of sharing sales tax revenues with municipalities. Localities had long depended on such revenue sharing to cover the costs of essential services. Once the inevitable crisis followed, instead of proactively tackling the fiscal challenges it had helped create with technical assistance or targeted intervention programs, Michigan leaders used the recently enacted emergency manager law (1990) to take control of the local finances of various cities (all of them with Black majorities) throughout the state.

Since 2002, Flint has had four emergency managers, all empowered to make significant decisions on the city's behalf. The last two, Darnell Earley and Gerald Ambrose, faced criminal charges stemming from their involvement with the city's water crisis. Earley, appointed as state overseer in September 2013, is best known for switching the city's water supply source in April 2014. Flint had been contracting with Detroit's municipal system for its water. But Earley, citing budgetary constraints, backed a scheme to draw water from the badly polluted Flint River—despite it being abundantly clear that Flint's outdated water treatment plant could not manage the bacteria and other waterborne contaminants that would be unleashed on Flint's residents.

It must be noted that, at least five years before this action, the Michigan Department of Environmental Quality (MDEQ) had disinvested from many Safe Drinking Water Act requirements that it considered "non-health-related" and "temporary." These included requiring water service providers to conduct Lead and Copper Rule compliance testing and notifying consumers when contaminants were found. Adding insult to injury, the MDEQ failed to require the city to take steps to control corrosion in its water distribution system after the water source switch, which was a decision that allowed lead to leach from Flint's pipes and soon unleashed a cascading disaster.

Federal and state bureaucracies had known about elevated lead levels in Flint's water. They opted to ignore the consistent pleas from residents about health ailments caused by the brown, foul-smelling water flowing from their faucets. Flint residents did not begin to see positive changes until independent researchers in late 2015—eighteen months after the water source switch—verified the level of contamination that was now in Flint's water supply. Repairs to Flint's water distribution system did not begin until Flint residents settled a lawsuit, filed against the City of Flint and the State of Michigan.

The city, according to the settlement, was required to replace lead service lines at homes with active water accounts as of March 28, 2017. At that time, only 10,836 homes with lead and galvanized steel service lines were eligible for excavation. This is less than 20 percent of the homes in the city and just over a third of the twenty-nine thousand metered homes supplied by city water lines. The parties settled at about the time when the state opted to discontinue free bottled water distribution to city residents. Lawyers for Flint residents have been back in court five times requesting that the city finish the job, which remains incomplete. In May 2024, Michigan state officials agreed to take over the project and vowed to finish it by August 2025.

In March 2023, the state settled with Flint residents for $626 million, compensating primarily lead-exposed minors (e.g., kids with blood lead levels from

0.1 micrograms per deciliter [mcg/dL] to 10.0 mcg/dL and above) compensating primarily lead-exposed minors (kids with .1 mg/dL to highest BLL), legionnaire's victims, as well as some business owners. It was the largest civil settlement in Michigan history—a victory for Flint, eclipsed by several things: the elaborate paperwork and documentation required to file a claim, the $1,000 cap on adult claims, and the fact that the state dropped criminal charges against then-Governor Rick Snyder (who Flintstones know was responsible).

The Impact of the Water Crisis

The water crisis continues to take a toll. Although it is no longer in the news headlines and has been swept under the rug on the national level, the consequences of the water crisis are still being felt by many Flint residents. From rising rates of health complications to the daily struggle to obtain clean water, the contamination of such a vital resource has diminished the quality of life for many Flint residents—for far too long.

While some residents are proactively attempting to do what they can, they are aware that the systemic problems that caused the crisis persist along with the consequences. Brian Larkin, a Flint native and urban city planner, thinks that the water crisis was created by a lack of state and federal investment in the city in addition to the habitual mismanagement of Flint's infrastructure. As he put it: "One of the key things that comes out in any discussion about the Flint water crisis is the state of Michigan's emergency manager laws, and it comes up because the decisions that led to the switching of the water sources happened under the leadership of emergency management."

This mismanagement of Flint's water, according to Larkin, was "born out of a municipal finance, financial crisis, a city that has experienced the decrease in population and decrease in the employer base." He characterizes the water crisis as a "tipping point" caused by the mismanagement of Flint's infrastructure and municipal services.

Concerned with blighted space, Larkin believes that one essential step to moving Flint forward is for residents to be better connected to, and represented by, state and local environmental regulatory agencies. Trust, he says, can be strengthened through an improved relationship and communication between residents and these institutions. As he put it, "We have to improve our relationships with our environmental agencies [and] enhance communications in the decision-making process." Though the settlement between the state, city, and Flint's residents as necessary. At the same time, he believes that it is an inadequate remedy because it was not designed to fix the systemic problems plaguing the city. "We have to come up with better systems," says Larkin; but many Flintstones despair of having a real voice.

Former Flint City Council member Monica Galloway reinforces Larkin's position, stating, "I'm not saying that lead isn't a problem, but it's not *the* problem." She mentioned that negligence at so many levels has only aggravated problems and allowed them to go unchecked for far too long. “First of all, we were poisoned,” explained Galloway. “We know we’ve been dealing with lead for years, but this wasn’t that; this was negligent.” According to her, state officials from the MDEQ and EPA had placed Flint residents on the back burner for years due to the assumption that the community was “not worth going out on the limb for.” Due to this history of disrespecting and undervaluing residents, she noted that the first measure that would move Flint beyond the water crisis and toward restoration was financial relief for residents. Expensive water bills have been a burden for Flint’s predominately working-class and poor residents. Considering that the water was unsafe to use, let alone consume, Galloway notes that Flint residents are owed money. Alongside relief efforts, Galloway speaks to the problem of public trust in the water system and government oversight: “When you’ve experienced trauma, the mind doesn’t trust that what you’re saying is true. Even if the water might be good, the mind says, ‘Ah, you fooled me once, I can’t let you [fool me again].’”

Looking Past the Crisis to the Future

In many neighborhoods—especially on the northwest side of downtown Flint—no one needed to receive an official notification about issues with the water. The problems, according to numerous accounts by residents, were obvious. While discussing how he discovered the water crisis, Ali Cleaves, a local youth leader and coach, recalls seeing “a stream where water was coming, and it was staining the concrete in the areas. . . . It was real rusty looking. It was turning the sidewalks red.” According to this long-term Flint resident, it was a sure sign that something was wrong with Flint’s water supply.

Cleaves views the water crisis as a reality check for Flint, one that reveals how little officials value the well-being of the community. As someone who has worked with youth for years, Cleaves emphasizes the importance of pouring resources into Flint’s youth in the aftermath of the water crisis. Resources and community support will inspire and mobilize them. As he put it: “I kind of feel like I was destined to do this, to work with young people . . . giving back to the community and hoping they can feed off of the energy that I can bring that’s gonna assist them in career success.”

He also voices frustrations with too many things being left to the residents—the people who were wronged—to manage or correct past mistakes. And local citizens have yet to see what responsibility public officials will be forced to acknowledge regarding their criminal actions against the Flint community. In Cleaves’s opinion, “They need to pay. There needs to be not just criminal charges brought up to people, but they need to be convicted. They need to serve some time.”

Paul Herring Sr. agrees but prefers a grassroots perspective and encourages citizens to take it upon themselves to improve their community, rather than waiting for the government officials that they don't trust. "Many people in Flint feel they're owed," he explains, "I don't care what they owe me." He thinks Flint residents need to shift focus from feeling owed to focusing on what is owed to the children of the community who desire a bright future despite what happened to the city. Instead of feeling like a payout is owed, we need to collect the funds to rebuild Flint's water plant. By taking an initiative of this kind, Herring believes, Flint could move past the water crisis without having a "chip on its shoulder" that would ultimately stunt its potential growth.

He also encourages Flint residents to take advantage of plans to improve the city. While many view government officials' plans to turn Flint into a "college town" or "tourist attraction" as a way for them to strip it of its culture (and displace its Black and brown residents), Herring views this as an opportunity for residents to think ahead and use those city plans to their advantage, acknowledging that money must be invested on these endeavors and systems need to be created to make this vision a reality.

Race and the Water Crisis

There is no doubt that race matters in Flint. It matters everywhere social groups compete for resources and power. And it will continue to matter until the structural factors that maintain power imbalances and resource inequalities are adequately addressed. For example, due in part to where they live in the city, Black children in Flint are more likely to be exposed to lead than white children. In addition, Black children are more likely to reside in conditions that make them more vulnerable to lead poisoning, such as residing in pre-1978 homes and lead-emitting commercial facilities. Black children are also less likely to receive follow-up care after being identified as lead exposed than similarly situated white children. Children also need equal access to quality preventive pediatric care—no matter where they live. When inequitable conditions are in place, unacceptable disparities emerge.

While race matters, class also matters. We mention this because problems facing most folks in Flint are profoundly shaped by resource disparities and the structural circumstances that undermine access to necessary essential services. As demonstrated by the experiences shared by Flint residents, we cannot conclude that Black folks got the worse from the water crisis. The reality is that Black and white residents alike were compelled to fight for water justice in Flint because polluted water compromised and claimed both Black and white lives across the city.

Still, the claim that Flint was susceptible to the conditions that caused this crisis—because of its identity as a poor Black city—is valid. Forged primarily by white flight (driven by measures designed to ensure residential segregation and racial banishment), the socioeconomic well-being of residents of majority Black cities and towns usually draws the short end of the stick in the game of racial capitalism and competition for essential services. Compared to the affluent and mostly white suburbs that ring Flint, majority Black Flint has resource-starved schools, ill-equipped community agencies, and poor neighborhood upkeep and emergency services.

Flint is not the first or only predominately Black city to be heavily burdened by depopulation and long-term municipal debt. Such factors undermine a city's capacity to make federally mandated repairs to key assets like water systems and leaves them vulnerable to EPA fines. Cities like Flint are also victims of predatory municipal finance stakeholders (aka "poverty pimps"), whose unrestrained greed—as richly exposed in the case of Flint—turn an essential service crisis into a wealth-stripping and a life-threatening public health disaster.

REGIONAL LITERATURE

William David Barillas

If you're from Mid-Michigan, or live there, or visit there, or just imagine it from afar, literature about the place can help you perceive it with greater depth and sense of dimension. "First we have to see, be taught to see," poet William Carlos Williams once wrote. "We have to be taught to see *here*, because here is everywhere, related to everywhere else. Of only one thing, relative to a work of art, can we be sure: it was bred of a place. It comes from an application of the senses to that place, a music." In poetry and prose, one can hear that music. A reader can appreciate the rhythms and melodies of lives lived in a place, in one particular part of the world.

Rather than a history of Mid-Michigan's literature, the following is a discussion of a few works of prose and poetry. I gesture toward chronology and historical development, but breeze by through centuries and decades past in favor of more recent titles. One need not read these works in any particular order. I suggest picking up books I mention as one might pick up stones in a Michigan field, attracted by their shape and beauty, before wondering what tectonic and glacial forces dropped them there. I'll mention additional books in passing and suggest where to look for more writing set in the Saginaw Valley and Michigan's Thumb.

Mid-Michigan literature begins with the Native American oral tradition. The main tribes of Michigan, the Ojibwe, Odawa, and Potawatomi, are part of a larger group of North American tribes called the Anishinaabe. Some Anishinaabe stories involve Nanabozho, the culture hero and trickster figure. One story concerns a flood that overtakes the world, leaving Nanabozho afloat on a raft with a group of animals. A version by Fred Ettawageshik appears in *The Art of Tradition: Sacred Music, Dance, and Myth of Michigan's Anishinaabe, 1946–1955* (2009), edited by Michael D. McNally and from sources curated by Fred Ettawageshik, Jane Ettawageshik, and Gertrude Prokosch Kurath. Other books featuring the flood story include *Tales of Nanabozho* (1963) by Dorothy M. Reid; *Nanabozho, Giver of Life* (1987), edited by Alethea K. Helbig; *Ojibwe Narratives of Charles and Charlotte Kawbawgam and Jacques LePique, 1893–1895* (1994), edited by Arthur P. Bourgeois; and both *Ojibway Heritage* (1976) and *The Manitous: The Spiritual World of the Ojibwey* (1995) by Basil Johnston.

Documents from the pioneer era include Alexis de Tocqueville's writings about his trip to Flint and Saginaw in 1831. Tocqueville (1805–1859), a French aristocrat, came to the United States in 1831 to study prison reform but was more interested in American culture and government. The resulting book, *Democracy in America* (1835–1840), remains one of the most insightful studies of American society. Of particular interest here are Tocqueville's travel notes and the book that resulted from his time in Michigan. His notebooks, published in *Journey to America* (1959), translated by George Lawrence and edited by J. P. Mayer, appeal to our contemporary taste for concise, descriptive prose. Journal entries on the trip from Detroit to Saginaw appear on pages 134 to 143. Tocqueville later drew on these passages while writing *A Fortnight in the Wilderness* (1860), the narrative of his trip to Michigan.

Tocqueville begins his account by explaining how he and his companion, Gustave de Beaumont, sought to experience untamed landscapes and encounter Native Americans living similarly to their ancestors. Michigan was in a fervor of land speculation, leading the travelers to believe that no one would understand their interest in touring not to chase after some financial scheme but simply to see the country for themselves. While outlining the circumstances and worldview of the pioneers, Tocqueville also contemplates the wild Michigan forests, whose imminent destruction he mourns. He admires the Ojibwe who traded with him and Beaumont and helped them on their way. Flint then consisted of a few houses and John Todd's tavern, where the travelers were greeted by a black bear on a chain. In Saginaw, then just a village in the wilderness, they visited the store of Gardner D. Williams, a trader with the American Fur Company who later served in state government and as mayor of Saginaw.

Tocqueville's accounts can be supplemented by Beaumont's writings. Beaumont's letter of August 2, 1831, to Ernest de Chabrol recounts the Michigan journey. It can be found in *Alexis de Tocqueville and Gustave de Beaumont in America: Their Friendship and their Travels* (2010), edited by Olivier Zunz and translated by Arthur Goldhammer. Beaumont incorporated the trip, with rapturous descriptions of the Saginaw forest, into his novel *Marie, or Slavery in the United States* (1835; trans. 1958). *Marie* is a hybrid text combining a romantic melodrama about interracial lovers with sociological analysis of racism in Jacksonian America.

Late in the nineteenth century and into the twentieth, the last surviving pioneers recorded their experiences and gathered documents in books like the forty volumes of the *Michigan Pioneer and Historical Collections* (1874–1929). These may be read online along with county histories like *History of Genesee County, Michigan: With Illustrations and Biographical Sketches of Its Prominent Men and Pioneers* (1879) by Franklin Ellis, and *History of Genesee County, Michigan: Her People, Industries and Institutions* (1916) by Edwin Orin Wood.

At least one such book was published about each county, featuring biographies of local settlers, descriptions of landscapes, archaeology, town histories, maps, and illustrations of prominent homes and farms. One features the improbably long title *Indian and Pioneer History of the Saginaw Valley, with Histories of East Saginaw, Saginaw City, and Bay City, from Their Earliest Settlements, also Pioneer Directory and Business Advertiser for 1866 and 1867* (1866), edited by James M. Thomas and A. B. Galatian.

The volume is worth seeking out for Charles P. Avery's essay, "Treaty of Saginaw of 1819," a narrative that includes Ojibwe leader O-ge-maw-ke-ke-to's eloquent retort to General Lewis Cass during the negotiations. Thomas and Galatian also include William McCormick's "Battle of Skull Island," an attempt to substantiate oral histories of massacres of the Sauk people, from whom the Saginaw region received its name, by Ojibwe warriors in the seventeenth century.

From the frontier period Michigan passed into the logging era, the heyday of the family farm, and ultimately industrialization. Flint's carriage factories provided the basis for the automotive industry, with General Motors being founded in Flint in 1908. Social changes wrought by the transition from agrarianism to industrialism came swiftly. Writers documented this shift, contemplating its social, psychological, and ecological impacts.

Two farm novels set in Mid-Michigan have literary qualities that commend them to contemporary readers: *Years of Eden* (1951) and *What End But Love* (1959) by Gordon Webber (1912–1986), who grew up on a farm near Linden. *Years of Eden* touches on events in the life of a boy on the farm and in the nearby town. *What End But Love*, which fictionalizes Linden as "Basswood" (another name for the linden tree), deals with a farm family reuniting in 1934.

One novel of urban-industrial life in Mid-Michigan was written by Catherine Brody (b. Catherine Borodovko, 1900–1962). Brody gained national attention with her syndicated column "What Happens When a Girl Goes Job-Hunting," which involved working for a week at different jobs in twenty cities. Her experiences in Michigan led her to write *Nobody Starves* (1932), about a young couple whose lives go from bad to worse, first in Detroit and then in Flint, during the Great Depression. Their suffering stems from the fact that they do not join in the labor struggle but rather cling to the American myth of individual effort and reward. Brody's novel garnered praise from literary lights such as Sinclair Lewis and John Dos Passos.

A later novel set in Flint, *The Car Thief* (1972) by Theodore Weesner (1935–2015), has enduring literary merit. Weesner fictionalized his experience as a troubled teenager in the 1950s. The central character, Alex, steals cars not for profit but out of boredom and alienation, driving around the Flint area and then abandoning the vehicles. Place names ground the action, with the first chapter featuring Flint's Chevrolet Avenue and Court Street and the town of Shiawassee, with references to Flushing, Grand Blanc, and other locales. What most distinguishes this novel is Weesner's pacing and style, which allow readers to "experience" Alex's perceptions. Critic Roger Sale describes Weesner's prose as "wonderful . . . , sharp, pointed, locking us into each moment, suspending us from all other possible moments, giving us a sense that something is going to happen soon." *The Car Thief* has garnered a reputation as an artful, underappreciated late twentieth-century classic.

Weesner's other novels include *Winning the City* (1990), in which a teenager loses his rightful place on a Flint city league basketball team when a factory supervisor arranges to have his sons play. The protagonist, Dale, responds to this injustice by joining a team made up of other boys from white, Southern migrant families. Weesner also published *Children's Hearts* (1992), a collection of Flint stories, some of which were folded into *The Car Thief*. All of Weesner's writing reflects his working-class background, regardless of setting.

Since 1980, deindustrialization has led to economic decline, population loss, and urban decay in cities like Buffalo, Detroit, and Flint. In response, writers have developed a new genre, Rust Belt literature. Most of this writing consists of journalism and creative nonfiction. A strong work of fiction, however, appeared in 2022: *Chevy in the Hole* by Kelsey Ronan (b. 1986), a novel of working-class life by a writer from Flint.

Chevy in the Hole tells of Gus, a young man who returns to Flint after overdosing in Detroit. While trying to get his life together, Gus meets Monae, an activist who works at a local museum. The novel centers on their relationship, which progresses shakily due to their differences: He's white, she's Black; He's self-absorbed and insecure, she's idealistic and hard-working. Their efforts to create a better life together coincide with a vision of Flint rising into a new landscape of self-sufficiency and community engagement. Gus glimpses this possible future when he hears of urban farming and trees being planted in Chevy in the Hole, the former site of a massive Chevrolet factory.

Ronan's sense of place is evident in local references, like the weather ball atop Citizens Bank, Michigan School for the Deaf, AutoWorld, and Buick City. She establishes historical context by incorporating events such as the 1937 Sit-Down Strike, the 1953 Beecher tornado, and the wild 1967 postconcert party at which Keith Moon of The Who drove a Lincoln Continental into the pool at the Holiday Inn on Bristol Road. This historical backdrop frames the novel's present, as the main characters navigate challenges posed by the 2014 Flint water crisis.

Of course, not all good writing is grounded in geographical specificities. Consider the fiction that Charles Baxter (b. 1947) has set in the fictional town of Five Oaks, Michigan. A native of Minnesota, Baxter lived in Michigan for nearly twenty-five years. He spent one year teaching high school in Pinconning, so Five Oaks might stand for the town in Bay County. But local references are scarce in these narratives, making the setting more of a generalized small-town Midwest than Mid-Michigan. Baxter's wheelhouse is not cultural geography but character development, narrative structure, and prose style. He is that rare bird, a literary author whose often exquisite writing is accessible and pleasurable to a wide readership.

Baxter's Five Oaks novels are *First Light* (1987), *Shadow Play* (1993), and *Saul and Patsy* (2003). He is particularly good at contrasting ordinary, well-adjusted people with exceptional individuals, outsiders, and the outlandish—as in *First Light*, about an auto salesman and his sister, an astrophysicist. In *Shadow Play*, the misdirected good intentions of Wyatt, assistant city manager, conflict with his wife's interest in magic, his mother's mental illness, and his aunt's proselytizing for an indifferent God.

Saul and Patsy plays a high school teacher, a Jewish transplant from the East Coast, against a mentally troubled student.

Baxter has also written Five Oaks stories that contrast the ordinary with the strange. Perhaps the best example is Baxter's story "Gryphon," which appeared in his 1985 collection *Through the Safety Net*. The story involves a fourth grader whose teacher takes sick. The substitute is an eccentric woman who spurns the curriculum in favor of increasingly bizarre lectures. "Gryphon" has become a contemporary classic, a story that people recommend to friends and that teachers find will provoke class discussion. The story has occasioned teaching guides and scholarly articles and was adapted for television in 1988.

Those interested in finding more Mid-Michigan fiction should consult *Michigan in Literature* (1992) by Clarence Andrews, who provides book summaries and an index that includes Flint, Saginaw, and other places. Robert Beasecker also indexes place names in *Michigan in the Novel, 1816–1996: An Annotated Bibliography* (1998), which appeared in an expanded online edition in 2013. That edition can be accessed on an open access platform of Grand Valley State University, along with *Michigan in the Novel, 2012–2016: A Five-Year Checklist* (2019). The print version of Beasecker's book, like Andrews's *Michigan in Literature*, can also be consulted online, like many other books mentioned in this essay.

A few recent Mid-Michigan novels bear listing here: *American Poet* by Jeff Vande Zande (2012), set in Saginaw; *Dewey Defeats Truman* (2013) by Thomas Mallon, set in Owosso; and *Swarm Theory* (2016) by Christine Maul Rice, *The Streets Have No King* (2017) by JaQuavis Coleman, *Motown Man* (2020) by Bob Campbell, and *Your Silent Face* (2021) by Tim Lane, all set in Flint. R. S. Deeren's *Enough to Lose* (2023), a collection of short stories set in rural Tuscola County, in the Thumb region, was named a Michigan Notable Book.

Like novels and short stories, memoirs can also map the experience of place. One Mid-Michigan memoir with strong literary qualities and psychological insight is *A Situation in Flushing* (1965) by Edmund G. Love (1912–1990). Love tells of his childhood in Flushing, a town in Genesee County, in a time when people still lived much as they had in the nineteenth century, with hand pumps, gas lamps, horse-drawn carriages, and steam trains. Love vividly portrays townspeople like his grandfather, a prosperous owner of lumberyards and president of the village council. His mother, according to Love, was the first woman in Flushing to go to college; his father, a once-promising professional baseball player, owned the town's first automobile. Love captures a moment in American life just before technological changes ended the relative isolation and slow pace of small-town life. Love also published *Hanging On, Or, How to Get Through a Depression and Enjoy Life* (1972), about his experiences in Flint and Ann Arbor during the Great Depression.

The Last Farmer: An American Memoir (1988) by Howard Kohn (b. 1947) was a finalist for the Pulitzer Prize. Kohn's father worked the family's farm in Beaver

Township, Bay County for forty years, employing the same methods as had his father and grandfather. Kohn returns on visits, having left in the 1960s, lived elsewhere, and become a successful writer. Generational conflict yields to understanding as Kohn does chores, contemplates the landscape, and finds that his devotion to journalism draws on his father's German Lutheran work ethic and sense of propriety.

An outstanding example of Rust Belt nonfiction is *Rivethead: Tales from the Assembly Line* (1991) by Ben Hamper (b. 1955). Hamper grew up in Flint's Civic Park neighborhood, the oldest of eight siblings with a devout Catholic mother and an alcoholic father. He spent the 1980s working at the Chevrolet plant on Van Slyke Road, where he and his coworkers coped with stress by drinking and being rowdy at work. For a time, Hamper was something of a celebrity, appearing on national television and in his friend Michael Moore's film *Roger & Me*. The book, which deals with Hamper's early life as well as his time as an autoworker, is marked by clever phrasing and a knowing, cynical humor.

In *Teardown: Memoir of a Vanishing City* (2013), Gordon Young (b. 1966) shares narratives of people living amid empty lots and abandoned buildings, as well as politicians, bankers, ministers, students, and others. He provides historical context for Flint's struggles, from the city's settlement through its mid-twentieth-century zenith and then downsizing, disinvestment, and deindustrialization. *Teardown* stands with *Rivethead* and *Roger & Me* in a growing canon of texts about Flint's troubles.

Personal perspectives on the Flint water crisis are provided by Mona Hanna-Attisha (b. 1976), a Flint doctor who advocated for her city, in *What the Eyes Don't See: A Story of Crisis, Resistance, and Hope in an American City* (2018) and David Hardin (b. 1956), who volunteered with the Red Cross to provide water, in *Standpipe: Delivering Water in Flint* (2021). Hardin's memoir was published by Belt Publishing, whose list features a series called City Anthologies that includes *Happy Anyway: A Flint Anthology* (2016), edited by Scott Atkinson.

Other recent Mid-Michigan memoirs include *First Years: A Farm Boy Faces the Future* (2021) by Ed Demerly (b. 1941), about the author's youth on a dairy farm in Bennington Township, Shiawassee County. His colleague at Henry Ford College in Detroit, Rick Bailey (b. 1952), wrote *Tumbling Up: A Memoir—The Freeland Years* (2021). Bailey grew up in Freeland in Saginaw County. Jon Scieszka (b. 1954), known for illustrated children's books like *The Stinky Cheese Man and Other Fairly Stupid Tales* (1992), published *Knucklehead: Tall Tales and Almost True Stories of Growing Up* (2008). *Knucklehead* provides vignettes of Scieszka's childhood in 1950s Flint, full of humor and boyish misbehavior.

Marylin E. Atkins (b. 1946) wrote *The Triumph of Rosemary* (2017), an account of her difficult but inspiring life. Born to an Italian American teenager and a married Black man, Atkins was adopted by a white couple in Saginaw. She later studied at Saginaw Valley State University and the University of Detroit Mercy Law School, becoming an attorney and then a judge in Detroit. More recently, John Ribner (b.

1970) published *Wasted Youth: A Flint Punk Rock Memoir* (2020), which deals with intraband conflict, dicey concert venues, urban violence, and family dysfunction. More recently, Jan Worth-Nelson (b. 1949) received strong reviews for *That's My Moon Over Court Street: Dispatches from a Life in Flint* (2023), a collection of short essays about people, places, and experiences originally written for *East Village Magazine.*

Discussion of poetry from Michigan invariably begins with Theodore Roethke (1908–1963), the state's most celebrated poet. Saginaw-born and bred, Roethke wrote brilliantly both in closed forms and free verse. His work broke from the impersonality of modernism, embracing instead a psychological and spiritual emphasis that influenced Sylvia Plath, Galway Kinnell, and many other poets. Although he lived most of his adult life outside Michigan, teaching poetry writing at colleges, Roethke's early life in Mid-Michigan remained a central subject of his work.

Roethke was born into a family of German immigrants who operated a florist business on Gratiot Avenue in Saginaw. Their property included twenty-five acres under glass, where Roethke's father, Otto, grew roses and other flowers. As a child, the future poet contributed to the family business by completing chores around the greenhouses. Otto, a Teutonic perfectionist, "planted flowers as if he hated them," Roethke remembered in his poem "Otto." Roethke both admired and feared his father, who was impatient with his sensitive, bookish son.

Otto's death of cancer just before Roethke turned fifteen was the most consequential event in the poet's life. After graduating from Arthur Hill High School and the University of Michigan, Roethke went on to a career that saw him win the Pulitzer Prize, the National Book Award, and other honors. But bipolar disorder, compounded by alcoholism, led to mental breakdowns such as the episode in 1935 that caused him to lose a teaching position at Michigan State University. Roethke associated his mental illness with a quest for spiritual transcendence, in which his father's death figured as a primal loss. In one early poem, "The Premonition," he remembers sensing his father's mortality as they walked in the woods. "On the Road to Woodlawn" recalls his father's burial at Saginaw's Oakwood Cemetery. The loss so pervades Roethke's poetry that one notes its shadow even in poems on other subjects. The renowned villanelle "The Waking," for example, with its uplifting paradoxes like "I wake to sleep" and "What falls away is always, and is near," hints at grief when we consider that what "fell away" from the poet was his father, and with him, the poet's childhood.

Roethke's second book, *The Lost Son and Other Poems* (1948), contains poems that address Saginaw and his childhood there. These include the "greenhouse poems," such as "Root Cellar" and "Big Wind," which evoke the plants, buildings, people, and work associated with the floral operation. Roethke dwells not only on flowers but also on the compost, worms, and roots that underlie everything that blooms and that provide symbols for the unconscious mind. The greenhouses, Roethke wrote in his essay "An American Poet Introduces Himself and His Poems," were "both heaven and hell, a kind of tropics created in the savage climate of Michigan, where austere German Americans turned their love of order and their terrifying efficiency into something truly beautiful."

Other Roethke poems include "Highway: Michigan," a description of autoworkers in rush-hour traffic. The poem's original title, "Dixie Highway: Michigan," specifies the setting in or near Saginaw. The much anthologized "My Papa's Waltz," about Roethke's father roughhousing with him when he was about five years old, takes place in the kitchen of their Saginaw home. The six long poems that make up the "North American Sequence" in Roethke's last book, *The Far Field* (1964), mostly contemplate landscapes of the Pacific Northwest (the poet lived in Seattle during the last decade and a half of his life, teaching at the University of Washington). But these poems often turn to Michigan. One section of "Meditation at Oyster River" speaks of "a Michigan brook" and the Tittabawassee River in spring. In the book's title poem, Roethke describes an area on his family's property where he watched birds and "learned of the eternal." The sequence ends with "The Rose," which shifts from the Pacific coast to a memory of his father lifting him above the roses in one of the greenhouses.

In the late poem "The Saginaw Song," Roethke roasts both his hometown and himself. He namechecks Swan Creek, Hemlock Road, and his friend Burrows Morley, takes shots at the ladies' guild and local bartenders, then gets serious with stanzas about his parents. In addition to *The Collected Poems of Theodore Roethke* (1975), readers interested in Roethke's Mid-Michigan should seek Allan Seager's biography *The Glass House: The Life of Theodore Roethke* (1968). Seager includes otherwise uncollected writings in which Roethke speaks of his youth. Also see three essays in *On Poetry and Craft: Selected Prose of Theodore Roethke* (2001): "Some Self-Analysis," "An American Poet Introduces Himself and His Poems," and "Theodore Roethke." The last essay includes the following lament: "I mean almost nothing . . . to the people of my own state, to the man on the street—and desire that regard most passionately." Roethke would be gratified to know of those in Mid-Michigan acting to change that: poetry lovers, teachers, and the Friends of Theodore Roethke Foundation, founded by Anne Ransford, which has preserved the Roethke house as a museum and community center.

One poet who took a cue from Roethke is Gary Gildner (b. 1938). "I like to see people in poems," Gildner wrote in 1970, "or their presence strongly felt, as in Roethke's 'Root Cellar.' People and things and movement." Some of Gildner's poetry deals with his childhood in Mid-Michigan. When he was six, his family moved to Flint from West Branch. Housing was scarce so they briefly lived in a converted garage across the street from Bendle High School, before moving to a house on Buder Street then, years later, to a house near Maple Road. Gildner's life revolved around family, church, and school (he attended St. Mary's Cathedral School and Holy Redeemer High).

Gildner's Michigan poems make memories of quotidian events poignant and meaningful. His first book *First Practice* (1969) features poems about Gildner's childhood in Flint, with "Under the Hose" referring to Thread Lake Park and the pool there and "Stadium Poem" describing a moment at Holy Redeemer High School stadium. *Nails* (1975) begins with "The House on Buder Street," a catalog of events shared with family, neighbors, and friends, and "After World War II," about a family drive around town. The title poem recalls his father building the house near Maple Road; "They Have Turned the Church Where I Ate God" enumerates memories of Holy Redeemer Church.

Catholicism and Gildner's childhood parish also figure in poems like "The Picnic" from *The Runner* (1978), "1952" from *Cleaning a Rainbow* (2007), and "Coming Clean" from *Digging for Indians* (1971). The last book also includes "My Mother Writes" and "Heart Attack," about his parents' lives in Flint, years after he left. In "I Call My Mother," from *Bunker in the Parsley Fields* (1997), Gildner's widowed mother mentions that a good friend of his, Eddie Hill, who appeared in "The House on Buder Street," has died.

Patricia Hooper (b. 1941), like Roethke, was born and raised in Saginaw and attended Arthur Hill High School. As a student at the University of Michigan in 1960, she met Roethke when she received a Hopwood Award and he was giving the Hopwood lecture. In October 1961, *Poetry* magazine published her long poem "The Stone Boy," which finds her visiting her former home on Mason Street in Saginaw. "At the Rifle River" from *Separate Flights* (2016) describes sighting a bald eagle in a wild area just north of Saginaw Bay. Poems set in Saginaw include the title poem of *At the Corner of the Eye* (1997) and "Reunion," from the same book. "The World Book," from *Aristotle's Garden* (2004), captures an early memory of an encyclopedia saleswoman visiting her home.

Danny Rendleman (b. 1945) was born in Flint and lived there through his fifties, teaching at the University of Michigan–Flint and anchoring the local poetry scene. His poetry has appeared in many journals, and in his books *Signals to the Blind* (1972), *The Winter Rooms* (1975), *Asylum* (1977), *Skilled Trades* (1989), *Victrola* (1994), *The Middle West* (1995), *Stepping into the River Once* (2005), and *Continuo* (2014). Much of Rendleman's work is contemplative; when he turns to autobiographical subjects, he includes few place names. The title poem of *Skilled Trades*, for example, introduces a lament about his autoworker father by describing a family photo and only later mentions two Flint area taverns. "The Blue Handkerchief," from the same book, portrays his eldest brother. Though Rendleman does not name Russell Avenue, the street on which his family's lived, he evokes the setting as encountered years later. He also remembers his brother's 1956 Buick, which symbolizes an equivocal manliness and sorrow over the passage of time.

The automobile motif appears in a number of Rendleman's poems, marking their origins in the Vehicle City. In "Tremor," from *The Middle West*, Rendleman recalls "the '57 Chevy my Dad / bought me . . . / a hard-top with dual exhausts," conveying the cruising culture of the early 1960s, when he "would wait at Walli's Drive-In / for Donald Barber to show up / in his old man's Oldsmobile." An ambulance appears in "Getting My Father Out," set at his parents' house in Flint, where the speaker waits for the attendants to remove his father's body. *The Middle West* also features "Cheese Lines, Flint, Michigan," Rendleman's most specific evocation of "Flint, a city / as hard and abrupt as its quick bitten name."

Al Hellus (1958–2008) acted as a poetry booster in Saginaw, sponsoring poetry slams and an annual one-day public reading of Roethke's *Collected Poems*. His poetry appears in three chapbooks, *A Vision of Corrected History with Breakfast* (1995), *Alternative Baseball and Other Poems* (1997), and *Legend of the Turnips* and a book, *How Much of Your Heart Is Left* (2008). *Songs of Saginaw* (1999), a chapbook Hellus published with Marc Beaudin, takes its title from Roethke's "Song of Saginaw." Also of note is Hellus's elegy "at roethke's grave."

Denise Miller (b. 1970) wrote *Core* (2015), which includes poems adapted from oral histories of two men who worked at the Saginaw Malleable Iron foundry. Their testimonies were among those collected by Michelle S. Johnson from Black and Mexican American people who migrated to Saginaw. Monica Rico (b. 1979), also of Saginaw, took an MFA in creative writing at the University of Michigan and has published extensively in literary journals. The poems in her book *Pinion* (2023) trace family history, beginning with her Mexican-born grandfather coming to Saginaw in the 1930s for employment in General Motors foundries.

The poetry of Sarah Carson (b. 1984) treats working-class life in Flint with empathy, frankness, and a quiet, dark humor. Along with three chapbooks, she has published the books *Poems in Which You Die* (2014), *Buick City* (2015), and *How to Baptize a Child in Flint, Michigan* (2022). Jonah Mixon-Webster (b. 1988), also Flint-born and raised, has published *Stereo(TYPE)* (2018), a book of performance and concrete poetry expressing its author's perspective as a Black gay man and intellectual. One section presents poetic narratives of the Flint water crisis. In his first book *Carbon Footprint* (2020), Donny Winter (b. 1988) of Midland, poet, educator, and activist, speaks of growing up gay in rural Michigan. His second book, *Feats of Alchemy* (2021), is a work of science fiction in verse.

In conclusion, we read literature of place, like that which portrays Mid-Michigan, to connect with local experience, landscape, and heritage. Theodore Roethke exemplifies this connection, drawing inspiration from his Saginaw upbringing to write poems that resonate with readers worldwide. His poetry lends credence to Williams's observation that "here is everywhere, related to everywhere else." By embracing both local voices and writing from other traditions, we appreciate literature not as an either-or choice but as a complementary exploration. This inclusive approach promotes an understanding of cultural nuances transcending geographical boundaries, expressed in diverse writings that can broaden our perspectives on the world.

PART II

CITIES

FLINT AND GENESEE COUNTY

Profile

Flint, Michigan (pop. 81,108), covering thirty-one square miles on the Flint River, is the twelfth largest city in the state, with a population that is 56 percent Black and 33 percent in poverty. For most of the twentieth century, Flint was identified as "Vehicle City," a name that referred to its history of carriage and auto manufacture. When General Motors (GM) closed Fisher Body, Delphi (formerly AC Spark Plug), Chevrolet, and Buick City between 1987 and 2008, it sealed Flint's postindustrial fate. By the late 1990s, downtown was a row of empty and boarded up storefronts, and the city became known mostly for its economic and social problems, culminating in 2014 in the Flint Water Crisis. Flint Assembly, at Van Slyke and Bristol Roads, the larger of the two factories that remain, is the anchor for a viable South Side neighborhood with a functioning school. Factory and school—remnants of the two things that made Flint almost a utopia for working-class Americans.

Most of the factories and associated industrial shops are gone, as are most of the schools (the district once had over thirty elementary schools but today has only four). Despite heavy losses, Flint has assets: invested people who built and continue to build Flint (the legacy foundation and the people who live in and love their city) and neighborhoods where people come to stay like College Cultural, Woodcroft Estates, Mott Park, Fenton Road, and large swathes of north and northwest Flint. Even those districts that have lost the most (businesses, people, schools) have blocks of affordable single-family homes, neighborhood organizations, and green spaces. Nevertheless, Flint's negative reputation has the staying power of a nasty virus, and that is why we need a general and generous review of the city's history. Historian Andrew Highsmith's *Demolition Means Progress* (2016) has come to shape the most recent stories about Flint. That narrative, which primarily focuses on racial segregation, is important, but we sidestep it here in order to offer a bigger temporal and spatial picture and different stories, elicited by things seen and people encountered in real-time explorations.

Nineteenth-century Flint was the center of a largely agricultural region. Its residents were the county's merchants, bankers, mill owners, and ministers, whose "society" was punctuated by libraries, literary societies, lectures, and social customs (such as New Year's visits) that aped that of New York City. Industry (sawmills and a woolen mill) attracted workers, but they did not create the same working-class culture of the sort that developed in Saginaw and Bay City. This began to change as the carriage factories grew in importance after the start of the century, with the growth of labor unions and a local Socialist Party. An even more profound change happened with the success of the automobile factories in the 1910s.

The kind of skilled labor done by carriage workers gave way to repetitive, mindless assembly-line work. Men, often with little education, came to Flint from regions that had been lumbered out or where farms were not profitable. The city's population grew at an astonishing rate while developers and carpenters created block after block of small houses surrounded by yards. As the neighborhoods multiplied, so did schools, as well as other community organizations like churches and lodge halls. The Great Depression caused workers to leave Flint, but as economic conditions started to improve, Flint autoworkers organized a strike, successfully stopping the assembly lines by occupying factories for forty-four days, which forced General Motors to recognize the United Auto Workers (UAW).

The Sit-Down Strike (1936–1937) became a beacon for a prodemocracy movement that began in 2011 to contest the state's assignment of an emergency manager to Flint, and it continues to inspire residents in their struggle for clean water. The Water Crisis (2014–2016) amplified voices that found a unifying refrain in the slogan "Flint Lives Matter." Suddenly, if you lived in Flint, you were strong, had grit, and were part of a generations-old myth of popular resistance. The reconnection to labor history may have been the biggest gain for Flint residents who waited for all the water lines to be replaced, for reparations, and for someone to admit wrongdoing.

Where are the working-class people of Flint today? Staying in the neighborhoods, fishing the river, going to their churches, working in shops in the industrial fringe, eating in one of the remaining coney islands or neighborhood restaurants like Luigi's, El Potrero, or Cantonese Buffet. They make it downtown when there is a car show, a motorcycle rally, or the demolition of a building they relied on to anchor their work and social lives—such as that of Fisher Body, AC Spark Plug, and the Industrial Mutual Association (IMA) Auditorium. A remnant of the blue-collared flock turned out the day they tried to demolish the IMA Auditorium.

The Industrial Mutual Association grew out of an insurance organization for carriage workers founded by J. Dallas Dort in 1901 that provided compensation to families in the event of a worker's injury or death. The landmark edifice had been incorporated into the design of AutoWorld (the failed theme park in operation from 1984 to 1986), and city planners wanted to remove all evidence of that expensive blunder. But few who showed up to watch the morning of February 23, 1997, mentioned AutoWorld, since they were busy remembering milestones celebrated at the IMA, such as proms, graduations, New Years' Eve dances, concerts, circuses, and a wrestling match when the Sheik bit off Dick the Bruiser's ear. After a thunderous explosion, the cloud of opaque smoke cleared over rubble and whispers became shouts of joy: the IMA Auditorium was still standing! It didn't matter that bulldozers would dismantle the ruin in coming days. For the time being, nothing could kill their building; nothing could kill them.

Creative destruction lubricates the turning wheel of capitalism, and downtown Flint has been under construction for close to fifty years. The public has learned to be angry when Black communities are wrecked for highways and "urban renewal," but most still sigh hopelessly when parts of Flint's public history are sold to private interests, including the old City Market and Oak Park. Few know that the Masonic Temple that had a popular and inexpensive basement dining room is now going to be developed as a venue by a private interest.

Ruin of First Reformed Church, later Muhammed's Mosque No. 53 and finally Flint Masjid, Gillespie Street, Flint. PHOTOGRAPH BY AUTHOR.

Flint's peoples' history can still be read, however, in the tracts of workers' houses from the 1910s and 1920s and ruins, like the church on the corner of Gillespie and Buick Streets in the North End, perched on a knoll in waist-high grass. It was originally built by Russian Germans who got jobs in the factories after leaving the sugar beet fields. After their descendants dispersed in the 1960s and African Americans moved to the neighborhood, the church became a Nation of Islam mosque, but it has been empty now for two decades. Despite the outsized burning match and the word "entropy" in the sanctuary, this is a quiet place where you can feel the current of community life with all its comings and goings. Painted pigeons on the church's weathered exterior walls add to the feeling that we are all part of an ongoing mass migration. Go inside and listen for the cries of a city past, passing, and to come: It is up to Flint's people to dream a new city that is just for everyone.

Flint Is Established

Genesee County was once covered with oak-hickory and maple-beech forest. The first rush of white settlers, mostly from the Genesee Country in western New York, began in 1836. But the family of Rufus Stevens came to Grand Blanc as early as 1823 or 1824. His son Sherman Stevens recalled overpaying for a dead cow carcass, which he used as wolf bait; he trapped seven and claimed the bounty payments. When the family began to plow their land, they broke the yoke, and to get an augur, they traveled to the nearest "hardware store"—Jacob Smith's trading post at Flint River—where a large group of Indians had congregated to trade for whiskey. Smith is regarded as Flint's first white settler, followed by another Indian trader, John Todd, who ran a tavern from 1830 to 1836 where Saginaw Street meets the river.

After statehood, it was not long before newspapers advertised land for sale, attracting speculators and settlers. Henry Howland Crapo (1804–1869), a clerk in New Bedford, Massachusetts, was one such person. Already an established businessman, Crapo sent his only son, William, to scout out available pinelands. William was pointed toward the Driggs tract, a twelve-thousand-acre parcel in Lapeer County on the Flint River. In his journal, William described seeing the "regiment of great white pine trees," twelve to thirteen feet in circumference and forty to fifty feet high, as "we drove our sleigh among the trees for miles without obstruction."

The prospects looked good, and Crapo, using a loan from an investor whose wealth came from whaling and foreign trade, paid $150,000 in cash for the tract. When he came to Michigan in December 1852 to see it for himself, he concluded that he had paid too much and that the seller had misrepresented the value of the tract. Finding it was too late to harvest timber that winter and impossible to run logs to Saginaw because of the rapids at Flushing, Crapo nevertheless took control and embraced the challenges that lay ahead. He went back to New Bedford, journeyed to Maine to learn the ins and outs of running a sawmill, and convinced a Maine man to run his mill on the Flint River. Very soon he realized that it would be impossible to run his new venture from a distance, so at the age of fifty-one he moved his family to Flint.

Though he had never anticipated living in Flint, he was not scared away by the unpaved main street—Saginaw Street (part of the old Indian trail, which had been made a military road to Fort Saginaw in 1820)—or the fact that the businesses and saloons were little more than shacks or that shingles served as currency. Henry Crapo was all in. To handle the volume of logs that needed cutting, he purchased a second mill on the north bank of the river and eventually financed construction of a railroad line connecting Flint to Holly, making the transport of lumber to Detroit much easier. Like others who would follow, he became a politician and booster as well as a businessman. He served as governor for two terms (1864–1868), and in 1860 he purchased swampy land in Gaines Township, twelve miles west of Flint, to demonstrate that Michigan's wetlands could become productive through ditching and draining. Eventually, he developed a large farm where he raised a prize herd of Hereford cattle—the first in the state. Indians in the vicinity, known as the Fisher band, claimed trapping rights, which Crapo did not dispute, and he enclosed and dedicated their burial ground. Descendants of this band never left the area. Though other enterprising men followed Crapo—notably, his grandson, William Crapo "Billy" Durant, founder of General Motors—few stayed as directly involved in their enterprises or were as fond of the land and took as many risks as Henry Crapo.

Was Flint a "hick town"? That is what Charles Stewart Mott (1875–1973) called it in 1905, when Billy Durant first made him the offer to relocate his wheel, hub, and axle manufacturing firm from Utica, New York. Since Crapo's time, Flint had a core group of businessmen who ran sawmills, planing mills, and other firms that worked with hardwood after the pine was depleted; these businessmen were Alexander McFarlan (owner of the oldest mill on the Flint), William Atwood, Josiah Begole, David Fox, and George Walker. Flint also had flouring and chemical mills, salt works, Oren Stone's woolen mill, and the Flint Gas-Light Company.

Flint's professional and commercial class was keenly interested in education and culture. Its wives incorporated the first Ladies' Library Association in Michigan in 1851, becoming one of the first circulating libraries in Michigan. Lawyer Edward H. Thomson, whom the State of Michigan sent to Stuttgart, Germany, to promote immigration, built a large Shakespeare collection (which the University of Michigan bought after his death) and enjoyed a wide reputation as a lecturer on the Bard. Avon Street and the Shakespeare Club (founded in 1888) are two surviving relics of Thomson's influence. M. Louise Thayer (1813–1880), a lawyer's wife, had a reputation as a poet; her epic poem *Wilfred: Or the First Year of War* (1865) was the first published literary work by a Flint author.

Nineteenth-century prosperity has left its mark in other ways. Immigrant James Hurley, who had initially walked to Flint with one dollar in his pocket and made good

Workers at Chevrolet, 1916. ROY MILLOY COLLECTION, GENESEE HISTORICAL COLLECTIONS CENTER, UNIVERSITY OF MICHIGAN–FLINT LIBRARY.

with a lumber and coal yard and soap works, left $12,000 to every church in town, regardless of denomination, as well as the land and initial endowment for Hurley Hospital, which opened in 1908. Some of the surviving houses include the Robert J. Whaley House, built before 1873 (624 E. Kearsley St., open regularly) and Stockton House at Spring Grove (Ann Arbor St., open for tours). Other privately owned nineteenth-century houses can be found on Church and Grand Traverse Streets south of the Flint River and on East Street east of the downtown area. The Carriage Town Historic District, northwest of downtown, was established in 1982 by a citizens' group in order to preserve the nineteenth-century houses. Three churches date from this era: St. Paul's Episcopal Church (1872) and First Presbyterian Church (1885), nearly opposite each other on Saginaw Street, and Court Street Methodist Church (1888–1889), on Court Street at Church Street.

Flint Becomes the "Vehicle City"

Flint's great boom began in a series of investment decisions made by prominent local businessmen. In the first years of the twentieth century, there were four wagon and carriage works in Flint: James Whiting's Flint Wagon Works, the W. A. Patterson Company, the W. F. Stewart Company, and the Flint Road Cart Company of Billy Durant and Dallas Dort, which became the second-largest manufacturer of wagons and carriages in the country. Two restored buildings on Water Street remain as memorials to the carriage industry: Factory One (today owned by GM), originally part of Stone's Woolen Mills that was leased by Durant's and Dort's company, which now houses an archival collection relating to automotive and Flint history as well as a collection of automobiles, and the Durant-Dort Carriage Company office building, originally built in 1896 and restored in 1975. Whiting's firm got the money together to buy Buick Motor Company, located in Detroit, and eventually Billy Durant, because of his connection to family money and local investors, took over managerial control of the firm and made plans for mass production. Durant then convinced Charles Stewart Mott and William Doolittle, owners of Weston-Mott, to move to Flint, which they did in 1906.

The industrial boom brought headaches to city leaders. Every possible lot within the city limits filled up with houses. In 1908, developers built the first housing subdivision north of the old city, Oak Park, between North Saginaw Street and Industrial Avenue. Others followed, so that by 1920, most of the modern city from downtown north to Pierson Road was platted and built up. Population tripled between 1900 and 1910 (from 13,103 to 38,550) and more than doubled between 1910 and 1916 (to an estimate of 79,373). A city plan, presented in 1920, called for an expansion of rail facilities and highways in order to relieve congestion, as well as parks to provide recreational facilities.

Engineering the Model City

General Motors was so successful that by 1911 Mott sold Weston-Mott, having become sole owner when his partner died after only two years in Flint. Mott took his payment in GM stock and a guaranteed place on its board of directors. He was, however, thinking about moving back to New York state, possibly because his wife Ethel suffered from depression and spent long periods of time in New York with her family. Mott biographer Edward Renehan writes that "there were rumors of infidelity on C. S.'s part during this period (1911–1912)." Ethel turned to Christian Science and tried to get well in order to play a role in her husband's life, but her "demons"—feelings of depression, anxiety, and worthlessness—returned. She died in a freak accident—falling from a second-story window at Applewood (the family's home in Flint)—on the morning of June 6, 1924. C. S. Mott was in Detroit at the time. There was no investigation and no mention in the *Flint Journal* of her death.

At the time of his wife's death, Mott had already recommitted to Flint, and what renewed his interest in the city was the election of Flint's first Socialist mayor, viewed as a major threat by Flint elites. The contest between capitalism and socialism in the highly ideological election of 1912 launched Mott's career as local politician and model-city builder.

Socialists began to organize in Flint just after the turn of the century, when economic activities remained diversified, personalized, and clearly under local control. Although wagon and carriage making was the town's biggest industry by 1900, cigar making and agricultural processing and services also held important places in the growing economy. When carriages began to be mass produced, workers fought to establish a local of the Carriage and Wagon Workers Union—to no avail. They were highly skilled men, used to working on one vehicle at a time, who could see that de-skilling made them dispensable. Imagine the insecurity they felt during the transition to building automobiles on a rudimentary assembly line. These changes eroded machinists' independence and focused the attention on class relations for the first time. To make things even more tense, an overextended GM suffered a financial crisis in 1910 and had to be bailed out by eastern bankers. In the upheaval, Durant temporarily lost control of the company, and "the Buick" shut down completely that summer, throwing thousands of automobile workers on the street. Flint's boomtown optimism vanished.

Sensing an opportunity to win over workers, Socialist Party organizers pushed hard, ran regular meetings, and printed a weekly paper called *Flint Flashes: The Voice of the Exploited Worker*. All this work paid off when Flint citizens in 1911 elected John C. Menton, a cigar maker and longtime union member, to be their mayor. Once in office, local Socialists tried to create a truly ambitious reform program. Mayor Menton appointed a twenty-five-member commission that included representatives from all the city's crafts and professions. He investigated corruption at the Flint city water works and cracked down on "blind pigs" (unlicensed drinking establishments). Other initiatives were clearly prolabor: establishing a citywide eight-hour-day, expanding parks, opening schools at night for dayshift workers, and constructing a labor temple to hold union meetings and other activities. Finally, in an effort to humanize the Flint police, Menton appointed George Artis, a Black carpenter, as police commissioner. This nomination shocked Flint's establishment; the *Flint Journal* reported that a majority of the alderman "do not propose to have other than a white man holding public office in Flint." Socialism was condemned in the press battle as atheistic, un-American, and destructive of family values.

City business and industrial leaders urged Mott the millionaire to run against Menton the Socialist. They formed the Independent Citizens Party that stressed the need to run a city on a "business system" and felt that workers' complaints and demands were annoying "side issues" that threatened to scare off capital and industry. "Towns without capital," wrote the editor of the conservative *Flint Arrow* (quoted in Richard W. Judd's *Socialist Cities*), "are dead towns, and dead towns are hardest of all upon labor." Mott won the mayoral election in 1912 and again in 1913 and 1918, by stressing businesslike efficiency; and his greatest accomplishment, according to historian Ronald Edsforth, was "to normalize the assumption that businessmen alone had the responsibility for directing economic and social development, and on the need to exclude independent-minded working people from public decisions affecting these matters." Three significant buildings, where movers and shakers in that era congregated, remain, although they remain private, are the Masonic Temple (755 S. Saginaw St.), built in 1909 and closed in 2018; the Elks Lodge building (142 W. Second St.), built in 1913 in the Renaissance Revival style, private since 1973; and the Hotel Durant (607 E. Second Ave.), completed in 1920 and in operation until 1973, now an apartment building.

Being mayor woke Mott up to his desire to "fix" Flint's social problems, and he began by building neighborhoods to organize, as expressed in the foundation's apologia, *Foundation for Living*, the "masses of people who brought with them problems and differences which were to result in social chaos for years to come." General Motors formed the Modern Housing Corporation in 1919, which built Civic Park, Mott Park, and Chevrolet Park subdivisions that tended to isolate the white, native, and middle-class worker from the "foreign" and "Negro districts" common to industrial cities of the period.

Mott had started a foundation in 1926, two years after the death of his wife Ethel, who had adjured him in private letters to consider "poor souls that hardly see daylight between work and worry." His first foray into social programming was community education, an idea brought to his attention by Frank Manley, a physical education teacher at Martin School and Mott's tennis partner during the summer of 1935. Boys' clubs, Manley thought, might solve Martin's delinquency problem, and schools, if kept open after hours, could function as clubs. It is worth noting that former Mayor Menton, had proposed opening a free night school in the North End. Mott embraced the idea. Labor unrest was in the air: Franklin D. Roosevelt, in his 1934 stump speech at Atwood Stadium, adjured bosses to treat workers better, so increasing public access to education would be good for his image and could quiet the buzz in the streets for an autoworkers' union. Mott funded a pilot project in five schools, and before long all forty public schools were running a full program of classes, workshops, and social and recreational events. In addition to the Mott Foundation's support of community education through annual support of the Flint Public Schools, the foundation supported the YMCA, YWCA, Big Brothers, and many other social programs; paid sociologists to study the social dynamics of racial minorities, migrants, and factory workers' children; and, in later years, developed recreational areas near Flint, like Mott Lake, For-Mar Nature Preserve and Arboretum, and Holloway Reservoir. But Mott forever after touted the community schools program as the cornerstone of his "model city," which he encouraged the nation to emulate.

In 1947–1948, Mott experimented with extending the program to Fairview, the school that served the St. John Street neighborhood (originally considered Flint's "foreign" district, but which by then was 92 percent black). Elizabeth Welch had been principal of Fairview for decades, and she had run the school along the lines of the settlement house established by Jane Addams in Chicago, keeping it open in the evenings, where adults could learn English, be taught citizenship requirements, and learn how to make financial transactions and how to get along better at work. There were similarities between Welch's and Mott's approaches but also striking differences. For instance, Mott decided that broken homes contributed to delinquency and wrote a letter to the GM board of directors asking them not to hire mothers of "maladjusted" children under fourteen unless permitted by social workers. His intention to "break down the barrier between home and school" extended the reach of corporate control. Mothers on the list had to get a letter signed by a social agency saying work would not harm their children.

Mott Foundation programs in Flint undoubtedly enriched lives that revolved around factory shifts, but they also came under criticism. Local UAW official Norman Bully felt that the Mott Foundation was an "anti-union organization" and blamed Mott for the formation of the Plant City Committee to run civic organizations and programming in ways that disempowered citizen efforts and worker solidarity. In 1964, a Black group accused the Mott people of using community schools to perpetuate segregation; and in 1966, four Flint NAACP (National Association for the Advancement of Colored People) members handed copies of a letter to a thousand educators brought to Flint for a community education workshop in which they claimed that the Mott program promoted the "white father image," which "succeeds in suppressing and keeping the Negro in his place." It is difficult to reconcile Mott's two faces. On the one hand, he was Mr. Flint, the good neighbor, who lived at Applewood (a relatively modest mansion), drove a Corvair, smoked a pipe, and pitched in to rebuild houses after the Beecher tornado. On the other, in an interview with Studs Terkel, he directly compared looters during the 1967 Detroit riots to the Sit-Down strikers: "When you have people breaking into stores, and you have police and the National Guard with things loaded, and they don't stop those people—it's terrible. It's an absolute duplicate of the Thirties, with the sit-down strikes."

The scope of Mott's investments may open a new window on his personality. In the years he was developing and promoting the community schools project, he was also diversifying into agribusiness in the mucklands in Florida. A 1939 travel brochure to the company town of Clewiston—home of the U.S. Sugar Corporation—suggests parallels to Michigan: a massive inland lake, swampy but fertile flat land, ideal for growing cane (not beets) that could be refined into sugar. Mott purchased the bankrupt Southern Sugar Company on the south shore of Lake Okeechobee and continued developing small plantation villages, one called "Harlem," for Black cane workers. Mott held a majority of the company stock but stayed behind the scenes, giving his associate, Clarence R. Bitting, the job of promoting the company and making the enterprise profitable. Bitting authorized the construction of new research

"Good neighbor" C. S. Mott helps with reconstruction following Beecher tornado, 1953. THE SLOAN MUSEUM ARCHIVES PHOTOGRAPH COLLECTION, SLOAN MUSEUM ARCHIVES.

facilities, hired engineers and technologists, and gained federal support for corporate sugar-growing efforts in the Everglades. But getting adequate laborers was a problem. While Black workers were recruited from Georgia and Alabama, they didn't want to stay: The conditions, the pay—the whole situation—was not what they had been promised, yet foremen kept them working with blackjacks and rifles. The federal government indicted the company and four of its employees in November 1942 for conspiracy to enslave, and the testimony of over thirty men revealed a pattern of false promises and forced labor. The indictment was ultimately quashed on a technicality relating to the makeup of the grand jury. U.S. Sugar also argued that as a corporation, it could not be held accountable to laws made for individuals. Nevertheless, the FBI investigation evidently scared the company into changing its labor practices. U.S. Sugar never again recruited native Black people, instead importing cane cutters from the British West Indies. The case is discussed in Alec Wilkinson's book, *Big Sugar: Seasons in the Cane Fields of Florida* (1989).

The U.S. Sugar website credits Mott as its visionary progenitor, and the Mott Foundation and the Mott Children's Health Center together are still majority shareholders. Sugar money flows back into Flint to fund projects in impoverished Black neighborhoods, which is an awfully ironic closed loop. The most recent newsworthy story involving the Motts' Florida business involves the contamination of Lake Okeechobee's water supply, which was happening while the contamination of Flint's water was drawing national attention. No one connected the dots.

People in Clewiston are grateful to U.S. Sugar for the pool, the country club, and all the cultural amenities—the same attitude commonly expressed in Flint. And no doubt Mott sincerely wanted to give back to the city that had given him so much. After community schools, higher education became his top priority. Mott gave the land behind his Kearsley Street residence to Flint Junior College. Then in 1950 he offered $1 million toward a building for a four-year college, if Flint citizens supported the proposal, which they did. In the mid-1950s Mott joined with other local philanthropists to launch the College and Cultural Development, that envisioned a campus of museums, auditoriums, and theaters, as well as junior and "senior" colleges. The senior college, begun in 1956, was the Flint College of the University of Michigan. Five years later, with discussion of expansion to a four-year program, the Mott Foundation, in 1965, committed over $2 million to enlarge the existing building. But the new state constitution, enacted in 1963, ended branch campuses, requiring new colleges to become autonomous. In 1965, newly elected governor George Romney attempted to enforce the new constitution. Mott resisted and, having already promised to give money to the University of Michigan for a children's hospital in Ann Arbor, gained the support of University of Michigan's administration. Governor Romney relented; Mott referred the issue to a committee; and the University of Michigan–Flint was born in 1971.

Flint Grows

Apart from Mott's plans, Flint began to change fundamentally at the time of World War II. The Depression had forced many Flint autoworkers to return to farms or elsewhere, but the economy improved enough later in the decade to allow the Sit-Down Strike to unionize employees and gradually improve conditions in the factories. The real boost came from wartime government contracts. Women and migrants filled the demand for labor, while a military officer managed production and suppressed labor problems.

After the war, the economy boomed, as the factories attempted to satisfy the increasing demand for automobiles. The UAW's strikes in 1945 and 1950 led to raises in wages. Builders created new housing developments, most of them in outer areas within the city limits, in order to alleviate the shortage caused by depression and war. Black people from the South came in increasing numbers, encouraged at first

Flint Cultural Center

One of Flint's gems is the Flint Cultural Center, just east of downtown. This campus incorporates schools, museums, and theaters, drawing regular visitors from the region. These include not only buses carrying kids, but homeschooling parents bringing theirs. Originally a level oak opening (look for the large trees surviving from that era), the site became Henry H. Crapo's "near farm" and, in 1880, home to the Oak Grove Sanitarium. The Flint Board of Education bought some of the site in 1920, and the old sanitarium housed Flint Junior College, while Flint Central High School was built in 1922. Automotive pioneers J. Dallas Dort, who owned much of the land nearby, north of Kearsley Street, and C. S. Mott bought a sixty-five-acre tract in 1916.

Postwar prosperity encouraged Flint's residents to want their children to enjoy more fulfilling lives than their parents had. In 1949, they voted to support a bond issue for a college, the condition upon which Mott offered a million dollars. Mott gave two-thirds of his land to the Flint Board of Education, and new buildings for the junior college started going up in 1954.

It was *Flint Journal* editor Michael Gorman, however, who promoted idea of a cultural center, starting in 1954. He twisted the arms of influential Flint citizens whose wealth was both old and new to contribute, and contribute they did, in a collaborative way that encouraged many to have a stake in the project. New buildings soon arose.

The leading destination is the Flint Institute of Arts. Founded in 1928 as a community art school, it quickly broadened its mission to teach art through exhibitions and programming. The collection has grown to 9,700 objects, with strengths in American and European painting, sculpture, decorative arts, and works on paper. A 2018 addition exhibits art glass and features a "hot shop" to demonstrate glassmaking. The museum also contains an art library, movie theater, and café.

The Flint Institute of Music is responsible for a community music school (the Flint School of Performing Arts), with instruction in instrumental and vocal music, dance, and theater; the Whiting Auditorium, which is a venue for the Flint Symphony Orchestra and other performers; and the Flint Repertory Theatre, which produces plays held in the Bower Theater and Elgood Theatre. The main building is called the J. Dallas Dort Music Center. Built in 1971, it replaced an earlier house, in which the carriage manufacturer and man most responsible for the early twentieth-century development of the city lived, incorporating the design of the older house.

Two of the original 1950s projects are the Sloan Museum of Discovery and Longway Planetarium. The Sloan, named for long-time GM chairman Alfred P. Sloan Jr., began with the collection of artifacts originally assembled by the Genesee County Historical Society. Local history is incorporated into the complex, as is the early vehicle gallery, but new installations (added during the recent renovation) feature installations to interest children in science and technology. This orientation is not new; the iconic turquoise dome in which the planetarium's shows are held reminds us of the shock Americans felt after the launch of Sputnik in 1957. It is the largest in Michigan, offering classes on the solar system and laser shows. Its Spitz Model B planetarium projector is able to produce 3,083 stars in their proper relative brightness.

Applewood (1400 E. Kearsley St.) was the home of C. S. and Ruth Mott until their deaths. The elegant, perhaps understated, Jacobean Revival house, designed by Mott's brother-in-law Herbert E. Davis, was completed in 1917. The fifty-two-acre property includes a formal garden, an apple orchard, and outbuildings that originally supported a working, although hobby, farm. The name reflects the long association of Mott's ancestors with apple growing and cider and vinegar manufacturing. Ruth Mott Foundation offices occupy the upper floors of the house. The house and grounds are open to the public on weekends from May to October.

The most recent addition is the Flint Cultural Center Academy, opened in 2019, a charter school for grades one through eight. Its philosophy uses the assets of the Cultural Center institutions. Also on the campus, but technically not part of the administrative structure that runs the rest of the Cultural Center, is the Gloria Coles Flint Public Library, at the corner of Kearsley and Crapo Streets.

---

by President Roosevelt's executive order prohibiting racial discrimination in wartime industries, as well as the demand for workers, but redlining and custom forced them to find housing in one of two segregated districts. General Motors built new factories on the outskirts: Ternstedt, on Coldwater Road, and Flint Truck and Bus, on Van Slyke Road. By 1956, local UAW membership reached over seventy-two thousand members. The economic boom permitted *Flint Journal* editor Michael Gorman to press local donors to contribute to a new cultural center.

Flint's Black population, which in 1940 was a small minority (4 percent of the total), more than doubled by 1950 and grew exponentially through the 1950s and 1960s, growing in absolute numbers even into the 1980s. This growth changed the nature of the Black community, from that of a small, isolated population living in two out-of-the-way neighborhoods, to one with considerable political power. These changes came about in part because the UAW encouraged Black autoworkers to involve themselves in local politics. A new era began with the election of Floyd McCree in 1966 as mayor (although under the weak mayor charter) and, in a referendum held on February 20, 1968, the defeat, by a margin of only forty-three votes, of an attempt to rescind an open housing ordinance that the city commission had passed the previous October. Although Flint largely avoided the arson and shootings experienced in the Detroit riots of 1967, white fear increased, and, as Black people began to move into neighborhoods west of North Saginaw Street, white flight toward Flushing and other suburbs began.

Downtown Revitalization

While C. S. Mott was actively running the foundation, city planning was outside the scope of its purpose, and it remained so after his son C. S. Harding Mott (1906–1989) became president in 1965. Within a few years, this changed. Harding Mott, then the foundation's business manager and vice president, with influential local bankers and merchants, had organized the Greater Flint Downtown Corporation in 1956.

This group felt an urgent need to improve business (due in part to the growth of neighborhood shopping centers), or else the members' properties would decline in value and the city would lose revenue. Its efforts came to fruition in 1964, when Montgomery-Ward built a store (since converted to the McCree Courts and Human Services Building) on Saginaw Street. In 1970, Harding and others formed a new nonprofit, the Flint Area Conference, Inc. (FACI), with a membership similar to that of the earlier Greater Flint Downtown Corporation. Harding was determined to make Flint a "people magnet" once again, and to do that he became a builder, unlike his father, who preferred to repurpose. FACI's initial goals were to develop an automotive hall of fame, an enlarged, new airport, and a plan for the downtown. The initial idea was to place the hall of fame on an island to be constructed in the Flint River with a new interstate, I-475, drawing some of the I-75 traffic out of Detroit into downtown Flint along thoroughfares passing through urban neighborhoods cleared of blight.

Moving the University of Michigan–Flint campus downtown was another facet of Harding's vision for a vibrant new Flint. In 1970, the Mott Foundation granted the University of Michigan $1.1 million to purchase land south of Court Street and Lapeer Road for expansion, needed because of the demographic explosion that was affecting colleges everywhere. Harding Mott, however, wanted the university downtown and pitched the idea to new chancellor, William Moran, who agreed. The proposal was formalized in FACI's 1972 plan that presented a downtown campus as a "people generator" that would help stimulate downtown activity. Following planning studies, the university began to demolish buildings and in 1974 constructed a classroom-office building, facilitated by a $2 million Mott Foundation grant.

The third piece of the development trifecta was to develop the river. The Mott Foundation gave substantial grants to the City of Flint for the St. John Industrial Park and riverfront project, as well as for the Doyle urban renewal project (which produced the Doyle-Ryder school and ultimately the River Place townhouses and high-rise apartment building on the north side of the river). It also granted FACI $1.5 million for the Riverfront Center and $250,000 for a study of the automotive hall of fame, now called AutoWorld. These major financial investments in city planning required a new philosophy, articulated in the Mott Foundation annual report of 1976, which announced its intention to end the over $4 million annual support for the Flint Board of Education. It was an odd or opportune moment, depending on one's social views, to pull the plug on the schools that were strife-ridden and struggling to integrate. All but a few of them stand in ruins today; and the only things growing are the blue spruce trees in their yards, planted as posthumous memorials to the elder Mott's vision.

After 1976, the Mott Foundation looked beyond Flint, awarding grants to a wide range of projects, both in the United States and elsewhere. Throughout the 1980s, though, millions were spent in Flint on projects designed to improve the look of downtown and to attract visitors: Riverbank Park (1979); the Hyatt Regency Hotel

(1981); River Village, with townhouses, a high-rise apartment building, and a small retail area (1982). AutoWorld, the educational indoor theme park that was the core of these redevelopment projects, opened in 1984 but was bankrupt by 1986 and ridiculed in Michael Moore's hit film *Roger & Me*. The Mott Foundation also developed Windmill Place (1982) and the Water Street Pavilion (1985), a festival marketplace with high-end retailers, which closed in 1989.

Although AutoWorld's failure was the most blatant of all these projects, the sad reality is that most eventually failed. Writing in 1992, University of Michigan–Flint professors George Lord and Albert Price criticized the idea that the city had to be a "growth machine," which they thought was "irrational and inappropriate" in an era of national deindustrialization. The Hyatt Regency Hotel is a case study for the way overbuilding exacerbates urban problems. The hotel cycled through two more owners before it was sold to a conservative Christian organization. The Institute in the Basic Life Principles, of Hinsdale, Illinois, paid $6.5 million in cash for it and converted it to the Riverfront Character Inn and Convention Center. It held a few seminars that promoted the philosophy of the organization's founder, Bill Gotthard, and housed an "accelerated college program" for homeschooled students. But by 2005 the Character Inn was in trouble. In 2009 its owners sold it to the Crim Fitness Foundation with a $20 million grant from the Mott Foundation. Finally, in 2016 it was given to the University of Michigan–Flint, the same fate that befell other failed projects. Currently the Riverfront Center Residence Hall, it houses the university's School of Management, a student dormitory far from full, with large classrooms rarely used in an era of online education. The university broke ground in June 2024 for a new building to house the College of Innovation and Technology.

In the 1990s, as activity at the old industrial sites was dead or dying, Flint's leaders recognized that the city needed to take on a new identity. Enrollment at the University of Michigan–Flint and at Engineering and Management Institute (renamed Kettering University in 1998) was strong, leading some to see the city's future as a college town. Third Avenue was renamed University Avenue. William S. White, the Mott Foundation's new president, used foundation money to enable the construction of the new building named for him on the former site of AutoWorld. Ownership of most of the downtown buildings created as redevelopment projects in the 1970s and 1980s was transferred to the University of Michigan.

The Mott Foundation's attitude toward downtown redevelopment changed in 1999, when local politicians incorporated a nonprofit, Uptown Reinvestment Corporation. The Genesee County Focus Council had felt a need to consolidate plans in order to request money from the state or Mott Foundation. Over the following four years, the foundation granted it more than a million dollars to develop a revitalization plan and redevelopment strategy. The plan was to find private developers to buy unused downtown buildings and convert them to restaurants, stores, and offices, with loft apartments on the upper floors. The Community Foundation

The Crim

Come to the streets to the east of downtown Flint almost any sunny morning and you will see groups of runners and walkers. These suburbanites converge to enjoy exercising together in a way that in the 1960s, people would have thought strange. The annual event that brought that change is the Crim Festival of Races, which happens every August, when thousands of runners and walkers of all stripes take part.

Its namesake founder, Bobby Crim, came from the Missouri Boot Heel as a nineteen-year-old in 1950 to work at Buick. After military service, he graduated from college and became a high school teacher in Davison, teaching government. This led to his becoming a state representative in 1967 and speaker of the Michigan House from 1975 to 1982.

Crim began road racing in 1968 in an effort to lose weight, and his hobby coincided with a new health trend, "jogging," that took off in the early 1970s. He organized a ten-mile road race in 1977 in Flint that would benefit the Special Olympics. Each year the number of participants grew. The organizers formed a nonprofit in 1985 and added further groups. An 8K race and a 5K "family walk" were introduced, as well as evening concerts and carnival rides; in 1992 the name of the event became the Crim Festival of Races. Today it draws as many as sixty thousand people from across the country and globe.

The Crim Fitness Foundation, with offices at the YMCA building, promotes physical training programs, obesity prevention, and improving access to physical activity in addition to the annual festival. The Crim Festival has developed into Flint's biggest expression of civic voluntarism, involving individuals and groups who come in order to support it.

---

of Greater Flint provided grants for facade improvements. The Mott Foundation transferred title of the commercial buildings it owned on the east side of South Saginaw Street to Uptown Reinvestment Corporation. These moves benefited the same construction company that had done most of the earlier work on the failed projects, as well as local elites, who, as Laura Jordan writes, restored "their own capital accumulation and prestige formerly damaged by deindustrialization," arguably "at the expense of the working class," who, as Lord and Price found, do not typically favor growth ideology.

In addition to the Saginaw Street projects, the Mott Foundation in 2014 engineered the reuse of the former Flint Journal office and press buildings by locating Michigan State University's College of Human Medicine's Flint programs in the two buildings, establishing the Hurley Children's Clinic and creating the Flint Farmers' Market (after closing the Flint City Market), now owned by the Mott Foundation and managed by Uptown, in the area between the buildings. The foundation calls this development the "Health and Wellness District." The implosion in 2013 of the nineteen-story Genesee Towers building (built in 1968) leaves the Mott Foundation Building as Flint's last remaining skyscraper, a symbol of the economic power that controls the fate of the city. How far that control extends is beginning to be critically examined by journalists like Jordan Chariton, who has argued that the foundation handpicked the emergency managers who approved the sequence of decisions (including signing onto the proposal for a new water system) that led to using the Flint River as a source of drinking water for the city. Some faculty at the University of Michigan–Flint note that the Mott Foundation, through targeted major gifts, is changing the university's direction away from broad-based liberal arts and sciences to something closer to a polytechnical school, with programs that develop the skills of future workers for the new chip and battery factories they hope will come to the megasites like the controversial one in Mundy Township, south of Flint, almost two square miles in size.

Steven Dandaneau identified and critiqued Flint's culture of dependency on GM and its legacy foundation in 1996, and since then the economy has not improved. Flint has lost fifty thousand people since 2000, and its shrinking tax base limits what the city government can do, so the foundation has covered everything from grass cutting and garbage collection to building a free daycare center and doling out cash payments to pregnant mothers. Many Flint people say that they don't want a bailout by the rulers of this "kingdom"; they want accountability. Even more, they want to be respected as free agents.

"Agency" can refer to a government department or, more philosophically, the capacity to act. The word "foundation" is similar: It is an endowed organization that funds charitable causes but also the groundwork on which something is raised. Agencies and organizations can be helpful, but the essence of community is the groundwork of person-to-person relationships that citizens build. When word hit the streets in 2013 that Uptown had a plan to move the Flint City Market, opponents organized a petition drive, held noisy community meetings, wrote letters to editors, and held protests. Their voices were ignored, and the market was moved anyway; and then came the Water Crisis—a direct result of the suppression of local democracy. Flint residents complained for a full year before they got the attention of officials or the media, and retrospective analyses agree that ignoring peoples' suffering was the biggest crime of all. The Shorenstein Center on Media, Politics, and Public Policy charged the national media with negligence, claiming that they presented Flint residents not as agents of political activism but, overwhelmingly, as a beaten down, powerless, almost feckless population.

Politics

Although the role of the Mott Foundation in Flint's development is certainly important, we cannot forget that the city's government retains some agency. The charter that was adopted in 1979, bringing back the strong mayor with city council

Statue City

Something art-related (but not connected to the mural project) is happening in downtown Flint, noticeable because there is so little foot traffic. The population of statues is increasing, driven by the desire for equity in representation. These statues run the gamut from predictable to pretty weird.

The statues began during the bicentennial when a group of Polish American veterans campaigned to honor Revolutionary soldier Casimir Pulaski, and they did so with a granite sculpture that rests unobtrusively in Riverfront Park, now part of the University of Michigan–Flint campus, on the north side of the Flint River, near Harrison Street. The statues might have formed an ethnic enclave if only the impressive bronze statue of Mahatma Gandhi, sculpted by Ashok Gudigar of Bangalore and paid for by an immigrant Birmingham physician, had not taken center stage in University of Michigan–Flint's Willson Park in 2010, which is Governor Henry H. Crapo's old backyard.

Statues of Billy Durant and Dallas Dort by Derek Wernher. PHOTOGRAPH BY AUTHOR.

In 1988, about the time Michael Moore released *Roger & Me*, the city of Flint found a more subtle way to remind GM not to abandon its birthplace. The city commissioned Derek Wernher of Metamora in 1988 to sculpt a bronze statue of William Crapo Durant, which was placed at street level at the foot of the pedestrian bridge at the corner of Water and Lyon Streets. Durant's business partner J. Dallas Dort joined the site in 1992. The two figures look out on Water Street, with a restored industrial building on one side and a restored office building on the other, both ancestors of the General Motors Corporation.

The success of Back to the Bricks, begun by a group of old car enthusiasts in 2005 as an extension of the Woodward Dream Cruise, led organizers to propose some way to memorialize early auto pioneers. Self-taught sculptor and Flint native Joe Rundell, a retired GM skilled tradesman, took the challenge. Joe was a skilled engraver of guns but had only dabbled in sculpture. He offered to create the first one—David Buick—free of charge. The Back to the Bricks directors liked what they saw, and before long, with the help of local businesses, more were on the way.

The organization created the GM Automotive Pioneer Statue Plaza, near the sidewalk on Saginaw Street between Kearsley and First Streets, in 2013, soon adding Rundell's bronze statues of Louis Chevrolet, Albert Champion, Billy Durant, and C. S. Mott, while those of other auto pioneers, like Walter Chrysler and Charles Nash, as well as "Rosie the Riveter" and a *Flint Journal* carrier, grace the baggage carousels at Bishop International Airport. Further Rundell sculptures include another one of Mott (near the entrance to the Mott Memorial Library at Mott Community College), Bobby Crim (near the entrance of University of Michigan–Flint's Riverfront Center), Ford dealer Otto Graff (southeast corner of Court and Saginaw), and the first African American mayor of Flint, Floyd McCree, in front of the Flint Municipal Center. In addition, the city hall has five busts of prominent Flint women, also by Rundell, as well as two autoworkers, sculpted by Suzanne Johnson of Grand Blanc, standing on the front lawn.

We may see more. Mayor Sheldon Neeley, with the St. John Street Historical Committee, plans to create a park on West Boulevard Drive along the Flint River near the Utah Dam and has secured partial funding for it. The plan calls for ten or eleven statues of African Americans to be placed along a pathway, together with other amenities such as a playground, barbecue grills, and picnic tables.

---

form of government that ran the city before the adoption in 1929 of city manager with weak mayor system, has provided avenues of influence from ambitious people from different parts of the city.

Flint may have had the Don before the nation had the Donald. Don Williamson, one of the most colorful and controversial mayors, served as mayor from 2003 until 2009. He was a successful businessman who made his fortune with a number of auto-related businesses. Like Donald Trump, he turned down his mayoral salary, and worked for $1 a year, and like Trump, he often played loose and fast with the rules of both business and government. Williamson was convicted and served three years in prison for several business scams in the early 1960s. Like Trump, Williamson's tenure as mayor generated both strong support for him and strong opposition to him.

He ran for mayor twice, losing badly in 1991 and 1995, before being elected in 2003, after Woodrow Stanley was recalled. He won his first full term, defeating state representative Floyd Clack, and then winning a second term in 2007 over Dayne Walling. In 2008, Williamson faced a recall himself, but chose to resign, citing health issues, in early 2009. His time in office was highlighted by his brash and colorful personality, with him being accused of giving out cash to voters through his auto dealership, showing up at city construction sites with a trademark red-white-and-blue hard hat, and visiting crime scenes with his "Don-Mobile" topped with loudspeakers. During his time in office, he often came into conflict with the Flint City Council, once describing them "as valuable as puke on a brand new carpet."

Because of Flint's financial problems, during the first decade of the twenty-first century, the State of Michigan brought in a series of mayors and emergency managers leading Flint in an often confusing timeline. Flint's financial problems were caused in large part by a dramatic decline in revenue. Between 2006 and 2012, property taxes revenue declined by 33 percent, income tax revenue by 39 percent and, most significantly, state revenue sharing declined by 61 percent. State laws allowed the State of Michigan to take over local governments that were facing a financial crisis and exercise wide-ranging powers that would override the elected officials.

In 2002, the city was facing a $30 million deficit, and Governor John Engler appointed Ed Kurtz emergency manager, who reduced the deficit by closing facilities, cutting pensions, and raising water rates. But just a few years later, in 2011, Governor Rick Snyder again declared a financial emergency and named Michael Brown as emergency manager. He cut expenses by eliminating the pay for the mayor and city council, laying off city officials and closing offices. In response, protests and legal challenges arose over the emergency managers and their wide-ranging powers. During this time, Flint was governed by a series of elected and unelected leaders, which often raised doubts about who actually was in charge. The Water Crisis in 2014 exacerbated this question, and in April 2015, the emergency manager was replaced by a Receivership Transition Advisory Board until Karen Weaver was elected later that year. Sheldon Neeley replaced Weaver by a narrow vote in 2019.

As Flint changed mayors and tried to recall several of them, the city council emerged as an even more contentious and divisive body. In recent years, council meetings have often gone on for eight or ten hours, or more, after much bickering over parliamentary rules, racial division, and personal insults. In the forefront of the division was First Ward councilman Eric Mays, a longtime community activist who was frequently expelled from meetings and once was led out in handcuffs by the police after his disruptive behavior. On one occasion, he was caught pawning a city-issued computer at a local pawn shop and on another occasion had his council wages garnished to pay the costs of a frivolous lawsuit he filed against the city and other council members. Yet Mays was known to respond well to his constituents and was regularly reelected by substantial majorities and, in 2021, was chosen as council president.

While Flint's water issues seem to be on the road to resolution, the city faces many critical issues in the years to come. Among them are financial issues resulting from a loss of its tax base while legacy costs mount; governmental civility; economic growth; racial challenges; crime; and out-county division, driven by race, economics, and crime. In the end, the city of Flint will face its new challenges as it faced its past ones. From its earliest years, Flint has been a city of conflict and contradictions, of struggle and success, of hope and heartbreak, and it may continue to be that in the future.

Points of Interest

The **Mott Foundation Building** (S. Saginaw St. at 1st St.) is an Art Deco sixteen-story structure built in 1930 that has stood as an iconic landmark ever since. When the Genesee Towers building next door was imploded in 2013, this building again became the city's tallest.

Capitol Theatre (140 E. Second St.), a vaudeville and movie theater with commercial spaces built in 1926, was recently restored and is used as a performing arts venue. The ceiling is painted to evoke a night-sky blue and has constellation patterns on it, now restored with LED lighting.

MW Gallery (815 S. Saginaw St.), a recent addition to downtown development, is a gallery, founded by C. S. Mott's daughter, Maryanne Mott, and her late husband Herman Warsh, which regularly displays works by African American artists that depict the African diaspora. The gallery is part of the monthly art walk in downtown Flint and also lends its works to other institutions.

Buckham Gallery (121 W. Second St.) is a nonprofit art gallery, established in 1984. It features exhibitions of artists in many forms, hosts the monthly Artwalk, and holds literary events as well.

Riverbank Park, nicknamed "the Peoples' Park" when it opened in 1979, is a landmark of modernist landscape design. Lawrence Halprin & Associates, an internationally acclaimed landscape architecture firm, created this one-third mile linear park that straddles the river in the city center as an integral part of a flood control project undertaken with the U.S. Army Corps of Engineers.

Powers Catholic High School and Michigan School for the Deaf (1505 W. Court St.) sit on a twenty-acre parcel of land donated by Colonel Thomas Stockton. Another prominent Flint citizen, Edward Thomson—lawyer and Shakespeare collector—proposed the bill in the state legislature to create the Michigan Asylum for Educating the Deaf and Dumb and Blind. There's a perfectly preserved Superintendent's Cottage (built in 1888–1889) on the grounds. The school opened in February 1854 and educated up to 250 students. The students were taught manual trades to give them employment upon graduation: printing, boot and shoe making, cabinet making, and sewing. There is a sizable deaf community in Flint, probably because of the presence of the school. There's a new school on the grounds and a nearby church. Powers moved to this site in 2013, occupying what originally was Fay Hall, part of the School for the Deaf, built in 1913.

Flint River Trail is a twenty-seven-mile long paved bicycle trail that follows both sides of the Flint River, stretching from University of Michigan–Flint north, across Dort Highway, past the water tower, and into the Mott Recreation Area. It passes through urban, rural, and suburban landscapes, with scenic views, and opportunities for animal sightings. A good starting point is the parking lot for Genesee County Habitat for Humanity's ReStore (101 Burton St.).

Pierce Park Nature Preserve, the land for which was donated to the city by realtor John L. Pierce in 1941, took until 1965 to become the city's fourth municipal golf course. It was open and lit 24/7 to accommodate all the shifts of shop workers. In 2012, Flint's emergency manager closed the course. Green blight set in, and the process of invasive species moving in and crowding out natives began. Fast forward to the COVID-19 pandemic shutdown of 2020, and national groups like the Michigan Department of Natural Resources and Ducks Unlimited. Above all, its mission is to engage the community in ecological protection, recreation, and enjoyment. Today the park is a preserve, with 3.3 miles of nature trails, a pollinator garden, and meadows, with plans to restore a wetland along Gilkey Creek and an urban forest.

Neighborhoods

Don't neglect the neighborhoods—once densely populated, the residential blanket is now full of holes and green spaces. If you stay in your car, things can look dangerous—"zombified" even—but on foot, you see that there are many people who

---

Among Children

Philip Levine

I walk among the rows of bowed heads—
the children are sleeping through fourth
grade
so as to be ready for what is ahead,
the monumental boredom of junior high
and the rush forward tearing their wings
loose and turning their eyes forever inward.
These are the children of Flint, their fathers
work at the spark plug factory or truck
bottled water in five-gallon sea-blue jugs
to the widows of the suburbs. You can see
already how their backs have thickened,
how their small hands, soiled by pig iron,
leap and stutter even in dreams. I would like
to sit down among them and read slowly
from the Book of Job until the windows
pale and the teacher rises out of a milky sea
of industrial scum, her gowns streaming
with light, her foolish words transformed
into song, I would like to arm each one
with a quiver of arrows so that they might
rush like wind there where no battle rages
shouting among the trumpets, Ha! Ha!
How dear the gift of laughter in the face
of the eight-hour day, the cold winter mornings
without coffee and oranges, the long lines
of mothers in old coats waiting silently
where the gates have closed. Ten years ago
I went among these same children, just born,
in the bright ward of the Sacred Heart and
leaned
down to hear their breaths delivered that
day,
burning with joy. There was such wonder
in their sleep, such purpose in their eyes
closed against autumn, in their damp heads
blurred with the hair of ponds, and not one
turned against me or the light, not one
said, I am sick, I am tired, I will go home,
not one complained or drifted alone,
unloved, on the hardest day of their lives.
Eleven years from now they will become
the men and women of Flint or Paradise,
the majors of a minor town, and I
will be gone into smoke or memory,
so I bow to them here and whisper
all I know, all I will never know.

---

and local activists Mike Keeler and Sherry Hyden, in walks from their home through the old golf course, noticed the proliferation of buckthorn and the loss of native milkweed. Before long, they connected with the College Cultural Neighborhood Association and others to found a nonprofit, which has cobbled together small grants from several local foundations as well as state and national groups like the Michigan Department of Natural Resources and Ducks Unlimited. Above all, its mission is to engage the community in ecological protection, recreation, and enjoyment. Today the park is a preserve, with 3.3 miles of nature trails, a pollinator garden, and meadows, with plans to restore a wetland along Gilkey Creek and an urban forest.

Neighborhoods

Don't neglect the neighborhoods—once densely populated, the residential blanket is now full of holes and green spaces. If you stay in your car, things can look dangerous—"zombified" even—but on foot, you see that there are many people who persist in place like backyard lilacs that can't quit blooming; they are caretakers, sitting on porches, watching kids play in dusty yards. They are curious and will ask you what you are doing if you take a picture. Intergenerational poverty is the outsider's explanation for the stationaries, those said to be "stuck in Flint," but if you ask residents, most will tell you that Flint is home. "I am just like a tree that is planted by the water and I'm not being moved," one North End resident told interviewer Delma Jackson.

Besides the stationaries, there are newcomers and homecomers seeking refuge from the rat race in the kingdom of cheap houses where hard edges are softened by moss. Walking helps you notice hopeful signs, and it says to residents, "I'm here, interested, open to meeting." "Hello" is all it takes for the stranger to stop being a stranger. Because it is rare to see walkers in the neighborhoods, people are curious. A person in a skeleton T-shirt, wearing all black and white, pulling a wagon piled with belongings in plastic bags, crossed a street. She moved in close enough for me to notice the square jaw and facial hair. "I saw you taking a picture of that sign, so I thought you were lost." No, I'm not lost, but thanks for being concerned. By the way, I like your outfit. "Just trying to help people find inner peace." If you get out of your car and walk the neighborhoods, you will quickly realize that there is nothing to fear; every person has something to say if you are willing to stop and listen.

The North End

Flint's North End developed around the Buick factory. Located between Hamilton and Stewart Avenues, it was once the largest automobile factory in the world until Henry Ford opened the River Rouge complex in 1928. Immigrants from eastern and southern Europe and Black people who came to Flint in the 1910s and 1920s made St. John Street an "international village," in the words of Michael Evanoff, whose Macedonian family moved from Cleveland in 1925. By today's standards, the St. John Street neighborhood would have been the worst place to live—a compact industrial enclave between the river and the Buick factory, with the foundry at the center, creating clouds of smoke that carried sooty rain that coated cars and darkened curtains. Yet people who lived here had work, camaraderie, businesses, social and political clubs (the Bulgarian hall held Communist Party meetings; the Ukrainian hall on Mississippi Street hosted many affairs for the Black community), as well as schools, churches, and civic halls. No one says that this community was totally without prejudice, but with thirty-four ethnicities, most people were "different."

By 1916, there were numerous factories that made components for Buick, including Weston-Mott, Flint Varnish Works, Champion Ignition Company, Michigan Motor Castings, W. F. Stewart Company, and the Commonwealth Power Company. Thousands of men worked in these plants and needed homes. Soon after 1900, Durant-Dort executives planned a subdivision near the factory and, by 1916, had developed Oak Park, one of the most thickly populated sections of the city. Real estate advertisements from the 1920s gush about the elegance to be had in homes on Stockdale, Dupont, and Detroit Streets, with porches, fireplaces, breakfast nooks, cove ceilings, French doors, entrance halls, and other features. Welch Boulevard was a location where the buyer could expect a larger, better built, more finely equipped and comfortably arranged home than average. North of downtown, on Detroit (now Martin Luther King Jr.) and Saginaw Streets, were grand homes, theaters, a ballroom, and, in the late 1930s, Billy Durant's bowling alley, which was his last and most humble business venture.

The Black Community Grows

Until they married and had their own families, Black workers lived in barracks or, more often, in boarding houses owned by Hungarians, Italians, and other foreign-born residents. Henry Clark remembered Black people and Poles living in the same houses on different floors in the early to mid-1920s: "They did fine for a long time," but "in time, they became prejudiced against the blacks as the other whites and they gave the Polish men better jobs, too." Eventually, Clark bought a house on Gillespie Street in a neighborhood of Russian Germans, but when the Depression hit and factories laid off workers, he could no longer make payments.

During the 1920s, new churches formed, helping to stabilize the community, including Galilee Baptist Church (1921), Shiloh Baptist Church (1922), and Canaan Baptist Church in the North End. Leadership in the community was provided by two doctors, John W. Moore and J. Leonidas Leach. The latter for many years was head of the local chapter of the National Association for the Advancement of Colored People (NAACP), organized in 1918. Dr. Leach led the effort to build a three-story community building (called the "Flint Community Building") on Dewey, just west of Industrial Avenue, which was dedicated in 1922. The building housed barber shops, shower baths, a billiard hall, lodge rooms, a dormitory, and dancing and skating floors. Unfortunately, only ten years later the building was beyond repair, and the economic conditions of the Depression caused its sale.

People today feel nostalgia for the old St. John Street neighborhood, whether as the international village with its racial mix or the later ghetto, where Black people were self-sufficient. "Black people owned things. You had little side stores, clubs, and I'll never forget on Hickory Street, a gentleman, Mr. Moore—he had a store—blacks had all kinds of businesses," remembered a participant in a recent neighborhood oral history. William Orling, who grew up on Mott Avenue, just north of St. John Street, painted Moore's store and wrote on the back of the painting: "They lived in the back of the store. After they closed for the evening, if you had to have something and went to the back of the store and knocked on their door, they'd open the store up. Everyone there thought the world of Mr. and Mrs. Moore." Mr. Orling's body of work, now on display at the Gloria Coles Flint Public Library, preserves the look and feel of the lost neighborhood.

During World War II, Black people came north in greater numbers. C. S. Mott, through Flint's Recreation Department, funded the construction of a community center in 1945 at 3420 St. John Street, which featured speakers, arts and crafts, sports, dramatics, and musical programs. The school district hired its first Black teachers that year. In the shops, foundry solidarity and union politics created Black leaders who, when they ran for public office, were able to make changes that would forever alter Flint's social landscape. Before the 1937 strike, some Black people, like Henry Clark, Prince Combs, and Combs's wife Leola, took Roy Reuther's classes at the Pengelly Building that groomed them for leadership roles. In the union hall, everyone called each other "brother," and Black men participated fully with white men. Civil rights activism was a natural next step, and union brothers boycotted local establishments like bars and bowling alleys that refused to serve Black people.

Henry Clark was elected to the original fifteen-man committee before the Sit-Down Strike and eventually became the first union steward at Buick. Roger Townsend served in 1943 on UAW Local 599's executive committee and in 1952 was elected to the Michigan Legislature, serving until 1964. Nathaniel Turner and Edgar Holt helped organize the Foundry Council at Buick. Turner was elected to the Genesee County Board of Supervisors in 1952 and ran unsuccessfully in 1956 for First Ward commissioner. Fred Tucker, formerly the financial secretary of Local 599, was elected in 1959 to the Genesee County Board of Supervisors. Holt, whose left-wing background made running for political office impossible, headed the Flint branch of the NAACP beginning in 1957 and managed Floyd McCree's unsuccessful campaigns for commissioner from the Third Ward in 1954 and 1956 as well as his first successful run in 1958. McCree made national news in 1966 when he was elected mayor.

By this time, the Black population of Flint had almost quadrupled its 1950 number and increased that of 1960 by 57 percent. The city's white population, which had increased each decade until 1960, dropped 15 percent between 1960 and 1970. The North End Black neighborhood had by this time expanded past the St. John Street district northward along North and Selby Streets, west to the Polish neighborhood between Industrial Avenue and Saginaw Street, and southwest through the Oak Park subdivision. Black-owned businesses served a local clientele, but North End jazz clubs like Chez Paree, 50 Grand, the Motor City, and the Minor Key thrilled white youth, allowing racial mixing not possible elsewhere in Flint.

The 1960 city plan called for the complete redevelopment of the St. John Street area, arguing that 40 percent of its housing was dilapidated and that the neighborhood was severely overcrowded. For the planners, "redevelopment" meant the complete demolition of all buildings and the creation of an industrial park. The Model Cities program, which intended to correct the top-down planning of earlier programs, created an elected community council, which started meeting in 1968, and in 1969, it voted to approve the land use plan and relocation and acquisition plan. Nevertheless, about a hundred St. John Street residents signed a petition opposing the plan, and a feasibility study, funded by the Mott Foundation, revealed that about 40 percent did not want to move. In 1970, the city began to spend federal grants to pay for the plan.

The St. John Street renewal area accounted for 1,050 families and 416 individuals, of whom 96 percent were Black. Only small numbers were able to purchase or rent housing in the private market, while 93 percent were going to public housing. The Flint Housing Commission, established in 1964, built five housing projects by 1970, mostly low-rise apartments, scattered throughout the city. Of these, only River Park, near Carpenter Road, west of the Flint River, was in the likely trajectory of migrants from St. John Street. Section 8 houses built elsewhere could accommodate others. Nothing remains of the St. John Street neighborhood today. The industrial park never attracted many businesses, and the St. John Street Community Center became the Flint police academy for a time but was later sold.

As the Black population moved west, Catholics, clustered in the North End, moved out of Flint. St. Agnes, built in 1928, lost most of its congregation to white flight in the 1970s and 1980s and is now closed. Powers Catholic High School, which had just opened on West Carpenter Road in 1970, eventually relocated in 2013 to the renovated Michigan School for the Deaf.

Once St. John Street was demolished and residents dispersed throughout the North End, the Flint River became the new boundary line between Black and white Flint. Poverty and disinvestment remained. Of the three wards north of the river, the Third Ward has been hardest hit. Median income is $24,000, and 50 percent of the

"Barbecue Steve," who sells barbecue and soul food on the street. DRAWING BY CONNOR TINNIN.

population live in poverty. There are no open schools in this ward, and 25 percent of the population do not have a high school diploma.

On the north-south avenues of Saginaw Street and Martin Luther King Avenue, what businesses there are stand out against a landscape of blight: party stores, pawn shops, a couple of night clubs, Saginaw Bargain Lot, barber and beauty shops, stores selling homemade soaps and lotions, and barbecue joints like World's Best BBQ (at the intersection of Saginaw and Pierson Streets) and Big Baby's. The main business strip, with fast food and chain pharmacies, has moved west to Clio Road.

Ubuntu and Ujamaa

The Water Crisis mobilized the North End community. Black entrepreneurs began to come back to North Saginaw Street, bringing skills, ideas, and hope for change. Moses West, a former Army ranger from Texas, donated an atmospheric water

Feed Five Thousand

Artist Relford

I grew up in the Pierson Road 'hood on the North Side of Flint, and when I came up in the '80s and '90s, getting to know streets like Sherman, Gracelawn, Home, Marengo, and Mott, it was 90 percent African American. Most families were on food stamps and welfare.

I always walked to school down Gracelawn, littered with trash, drug needles, used condoms, and liquor bottles. One morning still stands out. Police sirens were going off and the firefighters were getting off their truck to put out a fire. Through the commotion, there was a person laying on the ground covered up in cardboard boxes; others were coming out of abandoned houses to watch the fire, looking like they needed food, water, clean clothing, and medical attention. Homeless people all around, coming out of hiding to watch another house burn down.

I never asked my mother why people lived on the street, but I decided on the spot that I wasn't going to let that happen to me. For a while, things were okay. Although most of us didn't have fathers, we had a father figure in our athletic director, Mr. Otis Spann (RIP). He was also school dance DJ on the ones and twos and a deacon at Shiloh Missionary Baptist Church on Leith Street. Life experiences and realities that Mr. Spann tried to warn us about hit hard during the 1990s, when gangbanging took us in all directions, in and out of legal trouble.

In one sense, we were lucky. Flint rappers like M. C. Breed, the Dayton Family, Top Authority, and Ready for the World brought what they were doing in the streets to the mic: It was like we had our own Motown right here in Flint. A deep rap hook, "Things Ain't What They Should Be," got me through my hard times; and I wasn't alone—rap music was therapy for all of us struggling with drugs, guns, and the death of homies.

Parents and elders, even those with good plant jobs, were having hard times, too. Drug habits landed many of them on the street. The first person I watched become homeless used to drive through the 'hood in his old-school car, decked out in a sharp suit, alligator shoes, and lots of gold chains and rings. Two years later he was on the streets, renting out that same Bonneville to the neighborhood dealer in exchange for drugs.

Then what I thought would never happen to me did: I was sent to prison for a drug offense, lost ten years of my life, and when I got out, came back in Flint to put my life together. I'd gotten a job as a paralegal but when layoffs came, last hired was first fired. I couldn't pay my bills, though I tried everything from reaching out to churches, asking family members for loans, and trying to find side work. Before I knew it, I was living out of my car, spending the night at rest stops outside the city (as long as I had money for gas), and dealing with embarrassment and shame of feeling like a total failure. Eventually, I would get it together, but not before I was shot in some kind of vendetta situation that, to this day, I don't understand. That experience woke me up.

I knew I had to be part of the solution to problems that were mine but so much bigger than me. I liked to cook and so I started a meal program called "Feed Five Thousand" inspired by Matthew 14:13, in which Jesus feeds a crowd of five thousand with only five loaves and two fishes. I also wrote my story, published it, and began to share it with men and women in the shelters around Flint. Half the battle is removing the stigma and the shame. If we build the courage to show vulnerability in public, our tragedies can build up the community.

machine to the community, and LaToya Ruby Frazier worked with local women Shea Cobb and Amber Hassan to produce a photographic record, *Flint is Family in Three Acts*.

Art shines a light on the strengths of people in the neighborhoods, but those people still need to eat. Party stores are hubs, crowded on weekends with people buying lottery tickets and liquor but also food: chicken, burgers, ribs, chops, hot dogs, and catfish—essentials in what has been called a food desert. After a long wait, change is coming. Fresh Start Hutchinson Neighborhood Market, opened in 2020 on North Saginaw Street, funded by city, state, the Mott Foundation, and brownfield tax credits. The North Flint Food Market Cooperative broke ground on Clio Road at Pierson Road in 2021 with the help of grants from the State of Michigan and the Mott Foundation and opened in November 2025. Longing for a self-standing and self-governing African American community can be heard in the Zulu and Swahili words *ubuntu* and *ujamaa*, used in yellow, red, and green Pan-African marketing. In Flint's North End and across the city, emphasis is being given to networking and developing Black leadership along new models. Pastor Sherman McCathern's Ubuntu Village in the Urban Renaissance Center (Civic Park) may have been the first to deploy this African model. Nonprofits like Communities First, Inc., which repurposes old schools and public buildings, also run workshops to help families save money, keep property, and develop intergenerational wealth. Institutions that are part of the Flint Cultural Center are underwriting events for a month-long celebration of Juneteenth to draw Black residents to the Sloan Museum and the Flint Institute of Arts with exhibits by and about people who look like them.

Some industrial redevelopment has happened in recent years. The Lear Corporation took over the former Buick Engineering site. Nearby, the massive Buick City complex finally closed in 2010. After some years, an outside developer, Ashley Capital, bought the site and created its first structure, the Flint Commerce Center, in 2024. There are also inviting new neighborhoods: Metawanee Hills, a cluster of duplexes and single-family homes built on a hill north of Eleventh Street, as well as Smith Village, with both multifamily and single-family units north of Fifth Avenue, both offering mixed-income options. Deeper into the North End, around Moore Street, Catholic Charities has broken ground on Sacred Heart Veterans Village, a community of tiny homes designed to alleviate some of the pain for a segment of Flint's unhoused population. Although the population continues to decline, it's a good sign that the infrastructure is being built to support positive change.

Points of Interest

Ophelia Bonner Park (south of Gracelawn Cemetery, access on North St.) is twenty-six acres of rolling land and beautiful trees, a remnant of the oak openings that covered what is now Flint.

Max Brandon Park (Martin Luther King, Jr. Ave. and Dupont St.), once called Dewey Woods after the original landowner and later Forest Park, is unusual for being a large (107-acre) and beautiful oak-hickory forest. The park has been restored and has walking and running trails, a wetland, a playground, and lots of educational signage.

Flint Lake Park (between Pierson Ave. and Stewart), formerly an amusement park (1921–1961), is now a quiet oasis with an interesting urban legend attached. Due to several drownings, some residents believe that the devil resides in the lake. The naturalistic explanation is that an underground river has sucked down trees and peat, cattails and kids, but some believe that the sucking mud at one end is the gateway to the underworld.

"Junkyard Alley" (N. Dort Highway, from Leith to the railroad overpass near Pierson) describes numerous junkyards that dot both sides of this stretch of highway. Scrap metal dealers, most of them Jewish immigrants, began to congregate here around 1940, led by Abe Natchez's Industrial Iron and Metal Company. By the early 1960s, there were at least a dozen used auto parts businesses.

Doyle-Ryder Community Education Center (1040 N. Saginaw St.) began as Doyle school, built in 1902, which was the northernmost school in Flint before the automobile era. When it was refurbished in 1974, it became Doyle-Ryder. At that time, there was a Doyle urban renewal project that replaced an aging neighborhood with Windmill Place—a four-building complex with businesses, offices, and a food court. Now that is gone, too. If you walk through River Village Apartments, you can still see windmills.

University Park Estates was a housing project, started in 1999, that built 150 homes in the $150,000–$200,000 price range that sold out as soon as they were built. This subdivision offered middle-class families a suburban environment in the city.

Berston Field House (3300 N. Saginaw St.) opened in 1923, and it has been the backdrop for the development of the city's top boxing and basketball talent as well as an important symbol for race in the city's history. It was the first community center to allow Black residents to use its facilities and programs, although some point out that the pool had different swimming times for Black and white people.

First Reformed Church, later the Nation of Islam Mosque (Gillespie Street at Buick St.) was originally built as a church for Russian German immigrants who came to Michigan to pick sugar beets and eventually to Flint for work in the factories. It later housed the Nation of Islam Muhammad's Mosque of Islam #53 became the mainstream Flint Masjid in 2000. The graffito inside was done by British artists as part of the Flint Public Art Project.

The East Side

The East Side sits between the old sites of Buick and AC Spark Plug, and its residents have always been working class with a "do-it-yourself" attitude. It developed during Flint's first boom—streets were platted in 1909—when people lived in tents, shacks, even piano boxes along the river, and real estate became a big business. Billy Durant said his company would take on five thousand men if there were houses to put them in; the city issued over 1,200 permits for houses in 1914 but needed thousands more. Lots sold with $500 worth of building materials and the expectation that buyers would frame and roof their own houses. Local lumberyards flourished. Lewis Ready-Cut (a Bay City kit house firm) opened an office on Saginaw Street and advertised in the *Flint Journal.* Recognizable Lewis cottages (of two and four rooms), four-squares, and bungalows are all over the East Side, priced between $200 and $1,000. The fancier ones have Craftsman features: heavy trim, wide eaves, and dormers. These simple workers' houses enabled blue-collar families to own their own homes, and their inviting porches and shared driveways encourage sociability and cooperation. Detached garages (now a thing of the past) doubled as living quarters for extended family and are still plentiful here.

By 1920, Kearsley Park—the central bead in Flint's emerald necklace—was ready for use, and by 1928, the neighborhood was full, with everyone working. A sampling of occupations from the 1400 block of Jane Street from 1947 shows that the majority were factory workers at Buick (machine operators, tool grinders, and one office worker) and AC Spark Plug (stock chasers and assemblers), but there were also assemblers who worked at Chevrolet and Fisher Body; one woman worked at Marvel Carburetor. Other neighbors worked at McDonald Dairy, the Pere Marquette Railroad, James Lumber, and Flint Screw Products Company. There was a restaurant owner, a cobbler, and an embalmer.

People who lived on the East Side were a mix of nationalities and ethnicities: Assyrians, Mexicans, and Hungarians crossed the river from the overcrowded St. John Street neighborhood; migrants from rural Michigan and other adjacent states; recruits from Arkansas, Missouri, and Tennessee. The sons of East Side families, educated at Walker and Homedale Schools, grew up to be U.S. congressmen and senators (Dale and Dan Kildee and Don Riegle), esteemed educators (David Blight, a Yale historian of the Civil War), and local leaders (Gary Fisher). There was a rich human humus here that nourished two or three generations, so long as "Generous Motors" kept the presses stamping and hedged peoples' lives with regular paychecks.

Once the plants closed and the business districts on Lewis and Franklin died, the bottom fell out, and security gave way to precarity. "Our parents were left to scavenge for scraps of jobs and stand in long welfare lines," writes Melissa Richardson, who remembers buying beer and cigarettes with food stamps at Heddy's Market on Franklin Street, in an essay anthologized in *Happy Anyway*. Since then, there has

Four-square Craftsman and two typical workers' cottages on East Side.
PHOTOGRAPH BY AUTHOR.

been one reason after another to leave: crack, drive-by shootings, arson, bad water, no schools, and food deserts.

But the workers' houses remain, standing together black-eyed, die-hard, charred, tattooed, and dignified. Some are salvageable; others are in ruins. But even ruins, if appreciated, can be the portal to a second, more internal world: Our eye is drawn to the place where a facade has fallen away, where what should have remained hidden is exposed, where the opaque becomes accessible. Ruins train our imaginations and are much more than "blight," which is the generalized term enabling large-scale destruction. The Genesee County Land Bank, brainchild of East Side son Dan Kildee, repossesses tax-delinquent properties to restore and resell. In fact, only a handful of houses are restored annually while hundreds are demolished. "Green innovation districts" is the new euphemism for the old "urban renewal," but both entail bulldozing whole chapters of the local architectural record.

Couldn't we let the old houses stand for seed? Advertise them as "partially built," and watch how their unfinished state activates agency? Baltimore reinstated a homesteading program in 2024 that worked in 1973: houses for a dollar, with guaranteed low-interest construction loans. Were the university, for instance, to inventory Flint's workers' cottages (as is being done in Chicago), this might renew the appeal of small-scale living and help locate the "missing middle" of the housing market. Repairing Flint's existing "tiny houses" would draw more creatives like Tim, from Iowa, who came here to live off disability so he could spend days composing music and ministering to neighbors with "partial profiles." Edith Montana, a forty-ish content creator and polytheist, bought a house with $4,000 of Facebook donations and now has an extra lot ($25), two ponds, a wood stove, and seventeen cats and can't say enough about the hospitality of her neighbors.

Former East Siders who moved away are coming back; life here was good enough to try to recreate. Christine bought her grandmother's big white house on Kearsley Park Boulevard to keep it in the family. "In that room [she points to the front corner of the house], is my grandpappy's piano. He started a church out of a tent in Burton. Every Christmas there were like fifty of us in there. I can't let that go." Cheryl and her husband Keith have their own house on Indiana Street, but, when Cheryl's mother died, they kept her house on the river and use it as a getaway, visiting twice daily to feed ducks and geese. Rene Petersen and her extended family own several houses in a block on Lewis. Every December, they fill the empty lots with glowing plastic Santas, Marys, Josephs, elves, snowmen and reindeer. "It's been pretty depressing down here in the last ten years. But if just one person riding that city bus feels a little better when they pass us, it's worth it."

Folk Expressions

The impulse to assemble persists long after the factory whistle blew for the last shift change. You read it in the writing on the walls here: "I was stabbed / Need prayers," "RIP Grandpa, RIP Tank," "Gone but Not Forgotten," "All these Drinks and Drugs No Longer Help," "God is Dead." Flat misery, if it can pick itself up and make something with what it found on the ground, discovers a new purpose; a tire becomes a garden planter, bowling balls become fencepost toppers, bathtubs become grottoes for the Blessed Mother, and a concrete goose gets a new hand-crocheted outfit that makes the grandkids giggle and the husband happier. A house isn't home without an American flag—even if it has to be painted on a shipping pallet and there isn't room enough to fit all the stars.

People on the East Side have place-based imaginations. One shopworker, who lived on the corner of Minnesota and Kansas Streets, marked his lot with a homemade street that renamed the intersection "Kansas" and "Kansas," because "there's no place like home." He plowed his lot with a full-size John Deere and kept bees; and though the garage couldn't accommodate a cow, he painted one on plywood. Gypsy Jack, who worked at Buick, created a Wild West Museum on Davison Road and welcomed kids coming from Homedale School who were awed by his basement jail, covered wagon, and Western paraphernalia. The house is empty and decaying now but branded with the words "Wild Wild Midwest" on its eastern wall—the masterpiece of all East Side house museums.

Small Churches

If imagination is one of the neighborhood's strengths, religion is the other. There are main denomination churches (Methodist, Episcopal, and Catholic) on the major arteries, but deep in the "state" streets crossed with those named for somebody's mother (Mabel, Belle, and Jane) are twelve tiny churches, not much bigger than workers' cottages, but marked as different with a cross or a scary Bible verse. All comers are hugged, fed, taught, forgiven, and known by women pastors, as adept at meeting many different needs as these buildings have been in their hundred-year lives.

The Lighthouse (1657 Mabel)—a bright white frame building trimmed in Mother-of-God blue—was a Pentecostal church in 1918 and a Baptist church in the 1950s but was used as a grocery store during the Depression. Echoes of Faith Holiness Church (corner of Jane and Olive Streets) was Homedale Baptist Mission (1916), then the Reorganized Church of the Latter-Day Saints (1922), an Orange Order temple (1959), and then a church again. Always Hope Ministries (1502 Mabel) was a church in the 1920s and then an Odd Fellows' Hall. The Pentecostal Temple Church (1658 Delaware) was Nicholas Romley's grocery store. Our Saviour Apostolic (1502 Bennett St.) was, in the 1920s, a Pilgrim Holiness Church.

Scholars of religion stress the important role Pentecostalism played in the agrarian labor movement in places like the Mississippi Delta and the Missouri Boot Heel, enabling poor people to create new moral communities to defend those most vulnerable in a rapidly industrializing society. Pastor Betty Rogers said the same thing more memorably in her own idiom, "We aren't like those other churches that make you feel like you're at a funeral. The difference here is that we have life and you have liberty to praise the Lord, to enjoy yourself, to love and encourage one another." A native Mississippian, she led and fed her congregation at Echoes of Faith on Jane Street for thirty-seven years. The first day I visited, Cathy (a regular) welcomed me warmly: "It's just a little country church." People stood and sang a capella from handwritten song sheets, and Betty expected them to turn the pages of their Bibles to follow her preaching, because it was important they know "it's God talking, not just me." A full dinner—turkey, chicken, or lasagna warmed up in the small basement kitchen—followed every Sunday service. When she first came up from Mississippi, Betty lived in the basement of the church, eventually inheriting a tiny house next door from an elderly neighbor. She knew her sheep by name and prayed for each one out loud: "Lord, please send David a nice little house where he can live happily with his dog." She also prayed for Donald Trump—after the January 6th insurrection—and for the mission of Jimmy Swaggart.

Services in East Side Black churches like Our Saviour Apostolic are similar, but the people are dressed up and the emotional volume is cranked way up. Sister Tilman, in a blue satin sheath with white heels, purrs into the mic: "Oh, I feel good today. God has been so good to me." She stirs up the crowd by itemizing all the reasons she's got to be blue: "My nephew is being cremated, but I am happy! He ain't the first to die. God said a tree lives and a tree dies. My sister got cancer, but I am happy! I don't know what's happening in my own family. Don't know what's going on in my own body. What I know is that I love the Lord."

The music, preaching style, and idiom differ church to church, but all have down-to-earth people, homemade liturgies, and the common message that, despite our brokenness, the Holy Ghost will lift our burdens, remove our shackles, and free us to shout, dance, and be our own true selves.

St. Mary's Catholic Church, now a "Mission," is one of three on Franklin Street. A committed group of nuns—the Sisters of God's Love—are responsible for planning and running a range of essential services: food pantry; support groups; Thursday adoration and rosary; and monthly eucharistic processions. The church is home to the Mary Mother of Flint icon (2600 N. Franklin St.), painted for the Water Crisis, which depicts an African American Mary standing on the banks of the Flint River, blessing water brought to her by children. "People needed a figure they could trust," said the former Pope of Flint, Father Tom Firestone. A reproduction of the icon has been placed in a lightbox, so Mary visibly beams maternal compassion at the intersection of Franklin and Dakota Streets near the drive-thru Mini Mart and Fli-In Wheels motorcycle club.

Points of Interest

Kearsley Park was one of the jewels of the 1920 Nolen city plan that advocated converting wetlands surrounding downtown into parks, and it was and is a gathering place for pageants, political and union rallies, and, most recently, a squatter camp during the Water Crisis. An annual tradition, the "Burning of the Greens" (used Christmas trees) ran from 1953 to the early 1970s, when the city passed an air pollution control ordinance.

Latinx Technology & Community Center (2101 Lewis St.) was established in 2001. It meets the needs of Flint's Hispanic community with Spanish- and English-as-a-second-language classes, as well as tutoring and youth programs, as well as an Early Childhood Center.

Asbury Farms (headquarters at 1653 Davison Rd.) is the brainchild of a Methodist pastor; there are seventeen hoop houses in full production (along Jane St.) with ten of them winterized for cold crops. The food raised supplies the neighborhood hubs and is dispensed through programs like Hurley Hospital's Food Farmacy.

Assyrian Church of the East (3112 Lewis St.) was the first Aramaic-speaking church in North America. Persecution drove members of the Nestorian branch of Christianity from places in northwest Iran to Flint after World War I. The community in Flint became the fourth largest in the United States. They worked mainly at Buick.

AC Spark Plug site (corner of Davison Rd. and Dort Hwy.) was the site of the plant that Albert Champion started on Industrial Avenue in 1907. Champion was persuaded by Carl Bergmans, a Belgian tile artist, to use his spark plug kilns to manufacture art tile. Flint Faience and Tile Company (1921–1933) employed 1,800 people as the Depression set in. Tile murals graced mansions, GM headquarters, colleges, hospitals, and schools. For local examples, see tiles around the altar at St. Matthew's Church (701 Church St.), on the Spanish-style Halo Burger building (800 S. Saginaw St.), and on Garfield School (301 E. McClellan St.; closed in 2010).

The West Side

Changes to the way we work, live, and imagine ourselves have made it harder for Americans today to fathom, let alone participate in, collective action. We are proud of our personal achievements and experiences and don't like thinking about work that makes us automatons. But any collective action requires some loss of individual identity if we are to act with and for others. The famous Flint Sit-Down Strike began at Chevy in the Hole (near the Flint River) and Fisher Body (on South Saginaw Street). Down in the hole, men understood things as muscular events rather than through words and abstractions. Decisions were taken as workers collapsed due to the heat and speed of the assembly line or as they watched police gather to storm the factory. When the strike was settled, joy erupted in a spontaneous street party, the likes of which Flint has never since seen.

General Motors demolished the factories it closed in Flint, but you can still walk through the site where the Sit-Down Strike happened if you park at Tenacity Brewing on Grand Traverse and head into Chevy Commons—labor's holy ground, reimagined as a state park. To many Flintstones, $30 million for a park sounds a little too much like AutoWorld. For years, the city dumped yard waste on the concrete shop floor cracked by sturdy weeds. Sometime around 2013, signs appeared, saying things like "Reclaiming Chevy in the Hole" and "Phyloremediation in Progress." A cap was installed over the toxic ground and twenty feet of soil thrown on top of it, seeded with grasses and wildflowers—"native plants." Greening the brownfield is an improvement, but it also enforces forgetting. The path of resistance, by contrast, involves remembering the place as it was when men worked here.

General Motors Sit-Down Strike

By 1936, the country had been in an economic depression for seven years. Autoworkers' pay had dropped by about half, while foremen used fear and intimidation to discipline and drive workers. The assembly line ran so fast that men had to urinate on the job, and if it malfunctioned, they lost money, because they were paid by piece rather than hours worked. When it dawned on them that they were no more than slaves, they became radicals.

Pulling off a major strike against the world's largest corporation required months of dedicated union organizing. The workers had lost trust in the American Federation of Labor that promised a strike in 1934 but failed to follow through, but mass firings, blacklists, and shop-floor informers made them wary of signing on to a new union. Wyndham Mortimer and Robert Travis, Communist organizers, arrived in Flint during the summer of 1936 to organize for the fledgling UAW. They spent months holding secret meetings in basements talking to the men about how collective action was the only way to improve their lives. By the time six hundred men signed on to the union in Fisher 1, they were chomping at the bit to strike. Organizers had hoped to hold off until the new labor-friendly governor, Frank Murphy, took office on January 1, 1937, but when men saw company goons loading industrial dies (patterns

Sit-Down Strike, Flint, 1937. GENESEE HISTORICAL COLLECTIONS CENTER, UNIVERSITY OF MICHIGAN–FLINT.

for auto parts) onto railcars, the wait was over. "Stop the train, there's a strike on," an autoworker yelled to a compliant engineer. One by one the men turned off the machines and sat down.

The sit-down was a nonviolent, but militant, tactic that had been used in the late nineteenth century by the Industrial Workers of the World and other progressive unions. The Reuther brothers, who were in Flint to train and guide local men and women, built on the tactic with their understanding of Gandhi's nonviolent direct-action movement in India. Sit-downs were performative declarations—exercises in free expression—different from the strike picket line, where the company could continue to operate by employing strikebreakers. GM filed a trespassing complaint, which the courts generally upheld, but this time, Judge Edward Black refused to evict the strikers immediately. This gave the UAW time to organize and attempt to negotiate.

The first plant to strike was Fisher Plant No. 1 (South Saginaw), but the strike spread to Fisher 2 in the Chevrolet complex and eventually to Chevrolet 4, though the strikers created a rumor that 9 was the target. Work stoppage at Chevy 4, along with the earlier Battle of Bulls' Run that led Governor Murphy to send the National Guard to keep the peace in Flint, forced GM to acknowledge the UAW.

The strike had been a community-wide action that included sympathetic workers in plants not on strike as well as the wives and girlfriends of strikers. Genora Johnson, wife of Kermit Johnson, the striker who planned the taking of Plant 4, organized a Women's Auxiliary of five hundred to six hundred members and an Emergency Brigade that confronted police, blocking the Plant 4 entrance with their bodies. Ella Coleman, who worked in food service, remembered walking from Chevrolet to Fisher carrying meals to different shops on strike, including the bus company and Standard Cotton Products—"It was cold; but it was nice, too. We didn't mind."

The victory had a ripple effect throughout the region: Strikes in Saginaw, Zilwaukee, and Detroit followed. In 1937, there were 477 sit-downs across the nation and half of them took place in Detroit. Labor relations have changed. Over the last twenty years (2004–2023) across America, the annual average for major work stoppages is seventeen, according to the Bureau of Labor Statistics, though that figure is on the rise.

In a city with a large number of recently erected statues, the Sitdowners Memorial Park (originally dedicated in 2002, behind UAW Region 1-D offices at 1940 W. Atherton) is the most effective. It contains statues depicting strikers sitting in car seats, a granite revolving globe, and a tribute to women, with a memorial depicting actions of the Women's Brigade. The historical marker on the Chevrolet Avenue Bridge where strikers battled police is slight evidence of what Flint people accomplished here; it is dwarfed by Kettering University, an institution that has cleared the shop bars, banks, strip clubs, and houses that once lined Glenwood and Chevrolet Avenues, erasing all evidence of working-class culture.

Planned Neighborhoods and How We Live Now

Beyond Chevy in the Hole, in the neighborhoods of Flint's west side, you can see evidence of the way welfare capitalism controlled the city's development by segregating and controlling the masses. Between 1900 and 1920, Flint's population grew from thirteen thousand to ninety-one thousand, and businessmen stepped in to address the housing crisis, as sociologist John Ihlder advised them to do in a 1916 essay. Flint's largest planned neighborhood was Civic Park, located two miles north of the Chevrolet plant. Building began before World War I by a group of businessmen, but after the war, GM's Modern Housing Corporation took over, building 950 houses in 1918–1919. They did it by creating a veritable city on the site with a narrow-gauge railroad, several sawmills, and ninety-six bunkhouses for the 4,600 construction workers.

Civic Park was imagined as an enclave for "the aristocracy of labor"—which meant the skilled work force. Deeds stipulated occupants had to be "wholly of the white or Caucasian race" and could not keep livestock, sell liquor, or construct outdoor cesspools or privies on their properties. Prospective buyers could choose between twenty-eight different house designs, but the signature one was Dutch Colonial: two stories, gambrel roof line, and a slate roof. An elementary school, community center, deep oak forest of Bassett Park (2251 Forest Hill Ave.), and business district made this a very desirable neighborhood designed as a garden suburb.

Civic Park integrated quickly in the 1970s. Despite a historic district designation and a community-wide effort, supported by grant money and nonprofit bureaucracy, the neighborhood declined. Today, one-third of the properties are vacant and only 41 percent of those still standing are in "good" shape. Any big plans for neighborhood uplift depend on foundation grants: The Urban Renaissance Center, centered in Joy Tabernacle in the restored Community Presbyterian Church (1927), and St. Luke's N.E.W. Life Center are the biggest recipients. Historical signage installed in 2023 is designed to encourage walking tours.

The Modern Housing Corporation continued building houses for GM employees throughout the 1920s in Flint and Pontiac, Michigan, and Janesville, Wisconsin. In Mott Park, south of Civic Park, builders replicated the Dutch Colonials with slate roofs on Cadillac, Bagley, Monteith, and Joliet Streets. But they also built many large and small brick Tudors and other architecturally distinctive homes on Nolen Drive and Dougherty Place, streets with views of the actual Mott Park and golf course—the second municipal course in the city (1925).

Woodcroft Estates, otherwise known as "the GM mansions," is a neighborhood platted in the 1920s to help elites avoid "undesirable encroachment" by other elements—"foreign or Negro." Bankers and real estate men who purchased a three-hundred-acre parcel above Swartz Creek platted three-acre lots and required purchasers to submit architectural plans for approval before building. Two large stone gates on Miller Road usher you down Parkside Drive or Westwood Parkway, differentiating those who belonged from those who didn't. The boys on the "Little Missouri" basketball team in Theodore Weesner's novel *Winning the City* are aware that "two low-life rednecks is about all they'll put up with on that side of Miller Road" where "just about everybody . . . is rich as hell."

Planned neighborhoods for different classes of white people encouraged working people to trade shop-floor solidarity for participation in a consumer-oriented lifestyle. The open housing referendum ended the unofficial segregation enforced through real estate practices, but it didn't effectively integrate neighborhoods, because middle-class white people simply abandoned their slate-roofed colonials. It took deindustrialization and poverty to mix things up on Flint's west side, which is now integrated and, in some areas, run-down. Arson fires have thinned out streets of small houses, marginal stores, empty schools, and unkempt lots. Try to see them not as blight but as openings for life.

Corunna Road

Corunna Road, for instance, is full of such openings, unpretentious places that don't worry about their image. The neighborhoods off this major thoroughfare were built for shopworkers at Chevy in the Hole when it skyrocketed in 1915–1916, and they are still populated with working-class people of all races. Gone are the open-all-night coney islands, but there are still independent businesses like Bubbles and Bows—a pet groomer, painted pink with black paw prints, full of cigarette smoke but also gentle people used to handling difficult animals. Kamil has run his Middle Eastern market for thirty years, after doing his "apprenticeship" at the Bread Basket down the street. Kamil takes customers' orders for meat and drives to the halal butchers in Detroit twice a week for *kefteh*, lamb, chicken, beef, breads, and fresh produce. There is Donlan's Fish Market and Seoul Market, the only Asian market north of the Detroit area. The African Herb Store has had nineteen years on the corner of Corunna and Ballenger. Holy Land Bakery opened three years ago and is run by two sisters from Bethlehem. Business is great—"Thanks God!" says Mesa, who has the best English of the five women who cook, laugh, and throw bread in the oven five days a week. Further west is the Dive Shop that gives scuba lessons on site and arranges diving trips to Lake Huron and the St. Clair River to explore shipwrecks. The nearby Economy Motel, owned and operated by a family from Gujarat, houses "regulars" who have few options for shelter. Older, affordable, commercial buildings are plentiful along Flint's run-down avenues—Corunna, Ballenger, and Dort—enabling newcomers to try things and residents to try new things, too. On the roads where you see pawn shops, and check cashing, and used tire businesses, keep your eyes peeled for Mimi's Cuban Café or Brothers Brunch House. There's even a new hip-hop dance studio—Fli-City—on Corunna and Downey, behind the bright jungle-themed mural. No obvious advertising, just a black mailbox on the avenue with decal letters that spell out "Vertical Ambition."

Mother Flint

Madame World wears acrylics and trusts Shein and Temu. Madame World wishes on dandelions and zooms down the hill on a bike, hair ablaze in the sunlight. Madame World also enjoys a chilled can of beer and some junk food on summer evenings. Sometimes you'll catch her walking down the street, skinny frame and loud voice and all that attitude. Other times, you'll hear her call you from across the street as if you were her grandchild: "Hi, baby, how you doin' today?"ther times still, she will come to class completely barren of life, all of her mother's loving fingers and lullabies smoked out of her hair, entrapped into a missing poster at Walmart.

We no longer ask her how she is. Instead, we listen to her mumble: She's on her way, my mother. Have you seen her? It wasn't an overdose. He was murdered, I'm telling you. My son was murdered! I have the money, just wait. Just wait. I'm not feeling good at all, man. I just want to see my kids!

There are times when you feel rushed just thinking about her. During those times, she does everything in a hurry, out of breath: speaking, smiling, tying shoes, looking for money in a purse that's far too bulky, looking through a box of food for cheese that her kids would love. Our Madame World gets chased around by the Real Madame World a lot in these streets. Perhaps that's why her footsteps get so quiet, so familiar, when she skeletons her way across that abandoned lot. All that weed growing so happily out of the broken pavement, all those cigarette butts, Hot Cheeto packets. All those birds up above, all that sweetly murmuring River Flint.

Her house is holed and boarded, but the crickets from the nearby tree chirp their nectar just the same. That breeze still flounders through her street, gleefully like a contentedly drunken man or like a child on the first morning of summer vacation. And her porch slouches in the middle like a mother's lap long tired from the weight of kids, and if you are brave enough to peep inside, you'll see the gleam of Christmas lights in July, a bloom of flowers in the yard, a swing. Some hope. Some humming.

Go to her house. Sit quietly beside her on the porch as a storm breaks. It is the habit of the world to fall apart. Watch our Madame World hummingly bring out the sewing kit, the milk bottle, the gardening tools, and whatever other instruments are necessary. Watch her patch the world back up.

Points of Interest

Kettering University (University Ave. at Chevrolet Ave.), founded in 1919 and known as General Motors Institute for many years until divested by GM in 1982, was named in 1998 for inventor and industrialist Charles Kettering. Known for cooperative education, it specializes in engineering and management.

Happy Hollow was once a park, with a main entrance off Hammerberg Road, across from the Flint Tennis Club sign. An asphalt path runs into the distance with I-69 on one side and the Michigan School for the Deaf (now Powers High School) on the other. Cement sidewalks indicate a paper neighborhood, planned but abandoned before it could be built. Once used by Girl Scout and summer playground groups, later proposals for Happy Hollow never went anywhere. Today, it is owned by the Mott Foundation, which plans to donate it to the state as part of Chevy Commons State Park.

Glenwood Cemetery (Court St. east of Bradley Ave.) was created in 1879 as part of the "rural" cemetery movement, which advocated a landscaped, park-like design. This scenic cemetery, with winding paths, preserves a ravine that divides it into two halves, full of the graves and mausoleums of the families of Flint's industrial and business leaders.

Spring Grove is a 2.2-acre wetland on West Second St. that was restored by a neighborhood effort and is identifiable by twin silos originally built to store materials for concrete production. Environmental Protection Agency brownfield funds paid to remove the concrete slab that covered a natural spring, flowing at five gallons per minute. Volunteers from the nearby GM Tool and Die, as well as neighbors who love the spot, mow grass, stock the pond with fish, and have even brought in sand to make a tiny beach for local kids.

The South Side

Wednesday night is the most essential moment of the week for the Golden Leaf Club (1522 Harrison St.). Officially called "Open-Mic Night," but sometimes unofficially "Funk Night," this is when black Caddies, Dodge Chargers and battered Chevies pack the empty lots. It is when a multiracial, multiclass, multigenerational crowd converges upon the round Formica tables flanking the Golden Leaf's small stage to hear dizzy distortion dripping from the heavy speakers. Wednesday nights in the summer, the energy spills out into the streets: BBQ drums smoke on every corner, surrounded by lawn chairs and impromptu parties in all the empty lots, with folks waiting for the live band to start playing from the stage behind the club. South Side Wednesday nights are the place to be if you want to taste real life in Flint.

What is most remarkable about the Golden Leaf Club, especially in a city that has witnessed so many changes, is that it directly connects to the early, pre–Great Migration Black neighborhood of Flint. It first received a liquor license in 1935, but the two-story concrete-block building in which it is located was originally built about 1912 for an earlier Black organization, the Maple Leaf Club (so named because many of the members were natives of Canada). Political clubs were a prominent feature of local politics in this period, and the Maple Leaf Club, which organized in 1910 and formally incorporated in the following year, was headed by Thomas L. Kelley, a Black man who had served as deputy sheriff for seven years. Kelley and the other organizers, we can presume, opposed the state's local-option prohibition law, under

Golden Leaf Club.
PHOTOGRAPH BY AUTHOR.

which Genesee County residents voted to make the county dry in 1909. The club's political position no doubt put it at odds with much of the rest of the local Black community, dominated as it was by Baptist and Methodist preachers. In the ensuing years, police targeted the club numerous times for liquor violations. In 1922, for example, an irate resident complained to the *Flint Journal* about "notorious resorts" like the Maple Leaf Club, Paddy Ryan's Place, and the Alcazar Club, as well as the "drugstores" owned by William McKeighan (a controversial politician known for his connections to Detroit's Purple Gang). During the years of national Prohibition, the club was run as a barber shop and pool hall. Finally, in 1936, the police closed it as a "nuisance."

By this time, as new "beer gardens" were opening up in Flint, a flamboyant Black numbers "banker" and restaurateur, Magnus Clark, had moved to Flint from Detroit, where he had run a restaurant called the Cotton Club. Clark and Roy VanDyne, a Black lawyer, operated the Golden Leaf Club in addition to their own practice and businesses, which for Clark was a barbecue restaurant on St. John Street. Clark, called the "mayor of Brownsville," hosted boxer Joe Louis in his visits to Flint. In the late 1930s, the Golden Leaf Club was the backdrop for the weekly gossip column in the *Flint Brownsville News*, making it seem like the hottest place in town.

This energy, this liveliness, contrasts markedly with the quiet emptiness just across the street. Standing on the front porch of the Golden Leaf and looking out across Harrison Avenue, one confronts four acres of grassy field. Beyond the narrow parkway curb, there are no trees here, just a shaggy mass of knee-high grass riven by the occasional muddy rut, formerly the site of Clark School. Built in 1912 and originally racially integrated, its enrollment became almost entirely Black; the school was shuttered in 1971. It was finally demolished in 2014.

These three locations—the Golden Leaf Club, the site of Clark Elementary, and the expressway—compress the history, tragedy, and triumph of one of Flint's most remarkable neighborhoods into a symbol-laden tableau. When redlining and racist housing covenants kept Black Flint residents apart from their white neighbors, they built their own communities on Flint's South and North Sides. After Flint's open housing ordinance was enacted, the heart of these neighborhoods had already been stricken by disinvestment, and shortly thereafter they were largely demolished for the interstates.

Flint's original Black neighborhood was established between Thread Lake and downtown Flint in the early 1900s. The neighborhood was initially integrated, both racially and economically, and many of Flint's first Black businesses were established here, such as Walker's department store, Brooks confectionary, and Raymond's barber shop.

Adjacent neighborhoods, such as Woodside to the north, were bound by housing covenants prohibiting nonwhites from purchasing houses. Thus, upwardly mobile whites in Floral Park were able to move to more affluent neighborhoods when they

Peter and Scotia Jacquette in front of their sandwich shop, Flint, 1933.

PETER JACQUETTE PAPERS, GENESEE HISTORICAL COLLECTIONS CENTER, UNIVERSITY OF MICHIGAN–FLINT.

could afford it, and as a result, Floral Park became predominantly Black. Nevertheless, the South Side Black neighborhood was more prosperous than its counterpart, the St. John Street neighborhood on the North Side. Residents felt that life was good: "We were happy, we had our own little neighborhood, we had our playground and our church activities," Ruth Scott, who grew up there in the 1930s, told an interviewer. Malcolm X (then Malcolm Little) rented a room from Delia Williams at 1411 Liberty Street for a couple of months at the end of 1942. He worked as a janitor at AC Spark Plug, saving for a move to New York City, where he would be introduced to the Nation of Islam.

The integrity of the South Side was disrupted by the construction of a four-level stack interchange constructed between 1973 and 1974, which took out a dozen blocks of Floral Park and other nearby subdivisions. More demolition followed to make room for I-69 east and I-475 south. The NAACP initially supported the expressway extensions, anticipating both the passage of the open housing ordinance and the construction of affordable housing for displaced residents. Many residents were instead moved into public housing units, and the impacted neighborhoods declined.

The Flint Housing Commission was established by the city in 1964 to meet the needs of the three thousand families relocated due to the expressway expansions. Howard Estates at 1928 Howard Avenue is a ninety-six-unit public housing complex that opened in July 1968 and was built on the site of the old Women's Hospital, which organized in 1919 and, in 1923, moved into an old house on six acres at 1900 Lapeer Street.

The interstate extension cut off the South Side's connection to downtown. What remained of Floral Park declined, while the more recently developed subdivisions to the east also struggled. Two decades into the new millennium, the fragmented South Side Black neighborhoods continue to shrink, but sites like the Golden Leaf Club and the area's many parks and churches continue to speak to the area's rich history, its complex present, and its uncertain future.

Black Bottom is the neighborhood called Beachdale in official land records. It occupies a peninsular basin west and south of Saginaw Street, framed by the railroad and the meandering Thread Creek. Clustered bungalows, spread over eight residential streets, are hidden away behind the strip of commercial buildings. Golden Leaf manager Lottie Reid was seven or eight years old when her family moved into the neighborhood around 1955. Its residents were predominantly white at the time (mostly migrants from the Missouri Boot Heel). "I called it 'Black Bottom' because it didn't have any street lights and it would get real dark there at night." Reid remembers a close-knit community where it seemed everyone had a garden and a fruit tree of some kind in their yard, and people shopped at Foster's grocery store at the corner of Barton and Beach. She added there were just nine Black children who attended nearby Lincoln School (now the International Academy) and later McKinley Junior High. By the time Richard Johnson's family moved to the neighborhood in 1961, the enclave was well underway to becoming a mostly a Black community. As far as the origins of the Black Bottom moniker, Johnson said: "Being young, I just inherited the name."

The Southside Reunion, held every August at Brennan Park, feels like a multigenerational tailgate, where fond memories along with beer and barbecue are shared among the "family." The term "South Side" is a holdover from the days when Flint's Black residents defined their identities based on geography: "North Side or South Side?" You were either one of us or one of them. The division was handed down by great-grandparents, grandparents, and parents, who lived in the neighborhoods where the city's first Black dwellers resided. South Siders were naive and stuck up; Northsiders the streetwise rogues. Or so it went.

Points of Interest

Quinn Chapel African Methodist Episcopal Church (2101 Lippincott Blvd.), founded in 1875, is Flint's first Black church by thirty-five years. The church began as a prayer service at the house of Nancy West. The following year, under the leadership of Rev. John Ferguson, the congregation moved into a frame building on Seventh Street. Services at the present location were first celebrated on Christmas Day in 1961.

Mount Olive Missionary Baptist Church (424 Kennelworth Ave.) dates its origins to 1907 and remains an active congregation. Services were first held in the former Arbeiter Hall (the local branch of a German American labor organization, which also hosted political meetings supporting Socialist Mayor John C. Menton and others) on Ninth Street.

Christ the King Catholic Church (1811 Seymour Ave.). This parish was established as a spiritual home for Black Catholics by Father Norman DuKette (1890–1980). Mass was celebrated in the homes of parishioners and at rented facilities from 1929 to 1946, when the first church was built on Clifford Street. That church was demolished in 1969 as part of the I-475 construction but moved to its current perch on Seymour Avenue in 1972. The current building was dedicated in 2002. DuKette himself was an imposing figure whose example continues to inspire parishioners, who recommended him for sainthood in 1980. In 1926, DuKette became the first Black priest to be ordained by the Archdiocese of Detroit and founded St. Benedict the Moor parish. The bishop reassigned him to Flint after he was shot by a Detroit policeman for no clear reason. In Flint, Christ the King had no established parish; DuKette gathered a congregation through connections he made while working in the shop. According to Vickie Larsen, historian for Christ the King, he preferred factory work because it let him meet prospective parishioners. By the time renovations began on a Clifford Street residence to convert it into a church, DuKette had gathered one hundred families, most of whom were converts. He was honored in 1975 by the Black Catholic Clergy Caucus as the oldest living Black priest in the United States. His grave occupies a place of honor at Old Calvary Cemetery.

Thread Lake was created when Thread Creek was dammed as a millpond by 1834 for the first gristmill in the area. Its history as a recreational destination began in 1898, when Abram Peer, who had moved to Burton Township in 1879, bought land on the lake, recognizing its recreational potential. After clearing brush, he built a pavilion and created a wooded, park-like area for picnics, outdoor meetings, and reunions. A July 4th celebration in 1898 kicked off the summer with a reading of the Declaration of Independence, and in August, the African Methodist Episcopal Church held a three-day camp meeting. In 1890 a Pioneer Society picnic, usually held in Fenton on Long Lake, took place on Thread Lake; these gatherings were the way the past was remembered, and before the society disbanded, its members formed the Genesee Historical Society. Peer sold a portion of his land to the city in 1910 for Thread Lake Park, and the city built a dance pavilion and playground equipment. When the Detroit Urban Railroad extended the Flint line down Saginaw Street to Peer Avenue, development was guaranteed, and Lakeside Amusement Park, featuring a sixty-five-foot roller coaster and carousel, opened in 1913 and operated until 1935. Today, Thread Lake feels tucked away from the rest of the city, serene and bucolic. It is a pleasant place to kayak or canoe, especially in the early spring before the lily pads thicken in the shallows and carp start jumping. The park remains popular for fishing and can be accessed by Thread Lake Park at the southern end of Howard Avenue or McKinley Park at the end of Collingwood Parkway.

Little Missouri

Midcentury Flint had a reputation for being full of "hillbillies," but most white Southerners weren't from Appalachia, as is often thought. They came from the Boot Heel of Missouri and neighboring Arkansas and Tennessee, which explains why people called a large swath of the south end (between S. Saginaw Street and Fenton Road, south of Hemphill) and across the city limits into Burton "Little Missouri." If you ask on the street about that place, most people will shrug; but ask in Donna's Donuts on Bristol or Bernie's Market on Atherton, and they'll tell you you're in it. Stop by MasterCraft, aka Bob's Bait and Tackle (4194 Fenton Rd.), to see a curious backwoods scene emerge out of the dusky darkness—glass-eyed creatures gathered around a wood stove: bison, red fox, turkeys, black bear, with many mounted ducks, squirrels, a muskrat mid-chew poised on a log, and fish squirming as if just caught. Randy Kilbreath has preserved the woodland creatures of fifty years ago, when Fenton Road was still a dirt road that led Flint's workers to lakes where the business class had summer cottages. Randy learned the basics of taxidermy from a Missouri connection and taught himself the finer points, starting a profitable sideline to a bait, tackle, and sporting goods store that had two locations in Little Missouri and Fenton.

In the early days, Flint employers recruited in the Missouri Boot Heel—the extreme southeastern part of the state wedged between Tennessee and Arkansas. The region was also called "Swampeast" Missouri, because the land is a floodplain covered with cypress. Logging and draining created rich farmland, worked by sharecroppers who grew and harvested "King Cotton" for large farm owners. Hoeing or "chopping" cotton was hard, hot work, so it is not surprising that when recruiters first appeared in places like Kennett, Dexter, Malden, and Poplar Bluff, they hit paydirt. Men couldn't get out of the cotton fields and cypress swamps fast enough. The Mason Motor Company placed the first ad in the *Dunklin Democrat*, August 25, 1916, offering 25 cents a day, a ten-hour workday and the reassurance that "one hundred boys from Dunklin County [were] already in Flint."

Migrants came up to Flint in droves on buses provided by the corporation. For decades the *Flint Journal* ran ads from persons looking to share rides to Southeast Missouri, Arkansas, and the Ozarks. The northbound buses would drop them at "Chevrolet Corners" (corner of W. Kearsley and Asylum Streets), where the Chevrolet employment office was located. Across the street was Oscar Martin's pool hall, called the Cotton Club, where they congregated before and after work. In 1937, a scandal broke about GM selling jobs to the Missourians. According to UAW official Norman Bully, Floyd Corcoran, the Chevrolet employment manager, "ran the bus companies. He ran the ads. He sold jobs. So, Chevrolet is 85 percent hillbilly." Management preferred hiring greenhorns from the South who never heard of making $3 or $4 a day, rather than local "troublemakers." James Humphrey, himself a Missouri native and Sit-Down striker, noted that the plan "backfired on 'em": "Southerners are good, solid union. Damn Right." Some were even instigators like Gilbert Rose, a union organizer, from Dexter, Missouri, who went down to GM headquarters in Detroit before the strike with a letter listing workers' grievances: "I told 'em I was chargin' them with violation of the proclamation of freedom that Lincoln signed because I was a slave."

There were two waves of migrants—in the 1920s and from 1940 through the 1950s. At first, the migrants thought of Flint as a temporary place to make big money and then to return South, and many did continue to farm in Missouri during the summer and work in Flint during the winter. Over time, however, a permanent community formed in the city and on its fringes. Coming from an impoverished area into an urban environment in a northern city, migrants told interviewers that they preferred to live and work with people from their region. There was a vein of Southerners along the river where the Chevrolet Plants 2, 4, and 10 extended into lower downtown and south along Swartz and Thread Creeks and into the urban fringe down Fenton Road and Saginaw Street.

Houses are small but unique, since many were built by shopworkers themselves with many additions for extended families. Chicken coop, tool shed, or shack (garage) offered a place for Grandma or for young marrieds. Living in homes on the urban-rural fringe meant going without indoor plumbing. There were hundreds of outhouses in around Hemphill Road and on both sides of Fenton Road and South Saginaw Street; some people used them as late as the 1960s, and one family on West Schumacher had a well with a bucket until the early 1980s. In the 1940s and 1950s, subdivisions were built specifically for shop workers; a good example is Fentonlawn subdivision, a ten-block neighborhood around Whittemore and Parkland. Author Theodore Weesner, whose father was from Missouri, wrote about the neighborhood in his novel *Winning the City*, commenting that "Little Missouri hillbillies retained a code of independence and pride that had many keeping neat yards" and vegetable gardens. Even today, many of the streets are dirt, and wild turkeys wander the neighborhood fringes.

Standard Cotton Products (now a brownfield at 2701 Camden St.) was a factory in the heart of Little Missouri, owned by Jewish entrepreneur Ellis Warren, that employed mostly Southerners. It started out manufacturing bedding, but, by the 1930s, was making pressed cotton pads sewn to burlap for floor cushions and upholstery for GM vehicles. Workers described the shop as having the atmosphere of a Southern cotton mill: low wages, long hours, and an unhealthy environment. When the autoworkers struck in 1936, the men at Standard Cotton followed. Strikers remembered that they "had a lot of fun in there" and amused themselves, "listening to the radio, reading, playing cards, putting on talent shows, and playing guitars and harmonicas they brought from home." Many songs came out of the Sit-Down Strike, and Standard Cotton had one of their own, a battle song set to the tune of the hillbilly song "I Was Born Four Thousand Years Ago":

> Oh, the cotton factory is a low-paid place,
> And the cotton is staring you in the face.
> When you ask for more pay
> They would only turn away,
> For they think you can live and work this way.
> We worked fourteen hours a day.
> But the Standard Cotton's going to change its way.
> We've been working in the dust,
> Now the machines are going to rust,
> If the company don't settle up with us.

Music was central to the group identity of these migrants. It grew out of Baptist and Pentecostal services, as well as frequent revival meetings and singing conventions.

By reminding them of shared beliefs, it preserved culture and enabled them to face the challenges of a new environment. Within church congregations, smaller groups of three to five members ministered to the community through performance, recording, and touring. Gospel quartets, duos, and soloists were plentiful in Flint, and those associated specifically with Little Missouri included the Calvarymen, Chansonaires, Templeaires, Gospel Singing Byrds, Elrods, Burt and Muriel Poole, and Beth Ann Albrecht. Bernice Byrd explains her journey on the back cover of *Shall I Tell You? (From the Heart)*: "I was born in Risco, Missouri, in 1928, in a little humble share-cropper's house. My folks were hard working people and never had much of this world's goods. But I was handed down a heritage worth far more than silver or gold and that heritage was that I was taught the right from wrong and how to build on a firm foundation, the Lord Jesus Christ." Everything changed for these migrants—geography, climate, way of life, and the society around them—but the music reassured them that Jesus, the blood, and the promises were constant, giving their lives continuity, fellowship, and an outlet for their feelings.

Bluegrass legend and banjo player Wade Mainer came to Flint in 1953 with an evangelist to get away from the old boys and booze of the country music scene in North Carolina, where he had been a star on the radio. He lived with a good-sized family in a shack until he got a house built and got a job at Chevrolet. "I didn't have experience. On the form, I put down 'singer' and 'worked in a sawmill.' They didn't even check me out. I know the Lord had his hand in it." Mainer stopped playing banjo until evangelist and singer Molly O'Day convinced him to get that banjo out again, but after resuming playing, he limited himself to gospel and played only in church settings. Mel Hammon, who came to Flint from Paragould, Arkansas, in the late 1940s, played the fiddle at events at local schools sponsored by a group that he founded, the Michigan Bluegrass Association, and was featured at the 1987 Festival of American Folklife in Washington, DC, along with his son and brother.

Jim Glasco, the original bass singer for the Calvarymen (organized in 1955), was cutting hair two mornings a week at the Ainsworth barber shop on Fenton Road until very recently. "I come in for the people," he says, and has many regulars that frequent the shop. He is quick to affirm that singing is his ministry and that a spiritual awakening redirected him from pursuing a career in country music. Jim's family were cotton farmers from Piggott, Arkansas, where Jim recalls "blacks and whites got along well—better than up here, because everybody was struggling." His father Lloyd came up in the 1920s, participated in the Sit-Down Strike, and worked at Fisher 1 for thirty-four years, hooking heavy coils to an overhead conveyor belt. Jim was entrepreneurial. In addition to his performing career, he ran a religious bookstore on the corner of Belsay and Lapeer Roads and started a travel agency that took fans on tours of England and Europe (much like Marv Herzog, the accordion player from Frankenmuth).

As the years went by, "Little Missouri" became a place tag used disparagingly to signify an undesirable, blighted neighborhood with, in Weesner's words, "dirty little kids," "hillbillies" who "never get anywhere in this world," crappy houses ("but what d'ya expect for $1,000 down?"), and a "coffee and cigarette atmosphere." But those who grew up there are deeply loyal to one another and to the place—even as they acknowledge its ugliness. "Burton is never going to look really nice because it's got a lot of those little houses," wrote a journalist in 1978. "By today's standards, it probably was poorly planned." Mailboxes still lean between narrow dirt drives and small squat homes, lending a rural flavor to parts of the area, which is fitting for a population proud of saying they are "half-city, half-country."

Points of Interest

Fisher Body Administration Building (4098 S. Saginaw St.) was built in 1925 and is the sole survivor of the complex originally the site of the Durant Motor Company, then purchased by Fisher Body Corporation, which became a GM subsidiary. Workers at Fisher 1 built car bodies for the Buick. Fisher 1 was the first factory to shut down in the 1936–1937 Sit-Down Strike, and it was the first factory to be demolished in 1988. The Great Lakes Technology Center, erected on the site in 1989, briefly housed several significant GM entities, but the last tenants to occupy it left in 2007.

South Flint Plaza (South Saginaw St. at Atherton Rd.) opened in 1955 with an enormous 365,000 sq. ft. of commercial space. Some new businesses have recently begun to occupy the formerly empty spaces. Across Atherton Road is Top Hat Auto Wash with its gem of a sign.

GM Flint Assembly (3100 Van Slyke Rd.), GM's longest operating plant in Flint (since 1947), currently employs five thousand workers. Also here are Flint Engine Operations and Flint Metal Center, which employ hundreds more.

Flint's Suburbs

For most of the nineteenth and well into the twentieth centuries, Genesee County was dominated by Flint. Flint's stupendous growth meant that by 1920, the city's population was 73 percent of the entire county. But Flint's share of the county's population began to decrease as early as 1930, and by 2020, it made up only 20 percent. Smaller towns—mainly Fenton and Flushing—had their own industries and functioned as markets for surrounding farmers; their transformation into suburbs over time was more organic than the notion of "white flight" suggests. White flight explains what happened from the late 1960s, when middle-class whites began to separate themselves into homogeneous communities cut off from the city that drew their parents and grandparents for work. That story continues into the present. As Flint declined, those with means gravitated south toward Grand Blanc and, more recently, Fenton, where houses like residential box stores line up on shores of three lakes, where, in the past, Natives congregated, pioneers picnicked, and marl was mined. There is nothing natural about this world any longer; all its fine details are designed to say something about the occupants' status. Closer to Flint, older suburbs are decaying and suburban poverty is on the rise in Beecher, Mount Morris, Montrose, Clio, and Genesee.

Already by 1916, with the factories booming and housing in short supply, Edwin O. Wood, in his *History of Genesee County*, described Clio as a suburban option with lower-priced houses. He commented that there were between 300 and 400 residents of the northern settlements, Clio and Mount Morris, who commuted to Flint factories for work, besides 1,500 living in Saginaw and 1,200 in Bay City. The interurban railroad connected the cities and smaller towns and villages of the entire region, enabling men to commute. As housing construction in Flint increased, however, more shop workers moved into the city.

Neighborhoods began to sprawl in the 1920s, as car ownership increased and roads improved, and a small number of subdivisions outside the city developed at this time. These were in Burton Township, off Saginaw Street south of the city, in Genesee and Mount Morris Townships, off Saginaw Street north of the city, and a few in Flint Township, west of the city. Already by 1940, there were 10,909 people in Burton Township, and by 1960, its population (29,700) nearly reached its 2000 peak of 30,308. Genesee Township's major growth happened during the 1950s and reached its peak of 25,589 in 1970. Similarly, Mount Morris Township peaked in 1970 at 29,349. Much housing within the Flint city limits was constructed after World War II, so that by the 1960s, there was little vacant land left. Developers went further afield to build their subdivisions in incorporated satellite towns like Fenton, Davison, and Grand Blanc, which met Federal Housing Authority (FHA) requirements for water and sewerage. Farmers sold off roadside lots to individuals all around Genesee County, and Flint autoworkers moved to places like Millington, Otter Lake, Columbiaville, Holly, and Otisville. The whole economy of greater Flint was constructed around easy mobility.

The booming economy attracted African Americans from the South throughout this period, but they were forced into segregated neighborhoods. The planning of I-475 resulted in the destruction of the two oldest Black neighborhoods and divided up the white East Side. Already by 1967, when the city enacted an open housing ordinance, Black residents had begun to move out of these neighborhoods, especially in the North End. This led to white flight, especially toward Flushing. Neighborhoods where Black and white kids had played together in this period of transition in the late 1960s and early 1970s became all Black as families left, leaving behind older, often widowed, white women. Between 1960 and 1970, Flushing's population increased by 91 percent and Grand Blanc's by 228 percent. Much the same level of growth occurred in Davison.

The events of 1967, on the local as well as national level, brought forth a period of cultural change, upsetting what people had thought of as stability and progress. In the political sphere, Black activists like Flint's Edgar Holt now needed to identify as "Black Power" advocates in order to find audiences. Many working-class whites supported George Wallace in the 1968 presidential election, with Genesee County giving him 15 percent of the vote, well above the statewide 10 percent. Federal housing programs were a problematic solution that created new kinds of ghettos. "Tension" was the watchword in the city schools that culminated in the 1972 Pontiac bus bombing, an event that rocked the Flint community, as well as the suicide of Paul Cabell, the Black vice principal of Beecher High School. Sadly, white people resisted the process of integration, and communities stabilized only after massive population transfers.

Residential segregation was the tool white people used to effectively subvert the U.S. Supreme Court's decision in *Brown v. Board of Education*. The NAACP tried with some success to argue that Detroit schools would never achieve integration due to white flight. Both Federal District Court and the U.S. Court of Appeals agreed, and in 1970, Judge Stephen Roth (a Hungarian American product of Flint's St. John Street neighborhood) ordered a new plan for integration that included fifty-three of eighty-five surrounding, mostly white, school districts. But in 1974, the U.S. Supreme Court, packed with four new Nixon appointees, overturned the lower courts' decisions by a single vote in *Milliken v. Bradley*, which secured the suburbs as white enclaves.

Since the 1980s, Americans have accepted an individualized conception of life, with no thought given to the loss of an integrated community or at least the enlivening diversity of city life. In our region, those trends have led to the heaviest development in the southern suburbs of Fenton Township, Davison Township, and especially in Grand Blanc Township—all communities near major freeways (I-75, I-69, and US-23). Commuters now travel from Grand Blanc and Davison to Oakland County, Fenton, Ann Arbor, and places in between. "Our nation, I fear," wrote Thurgood Marshall in his dissenting opinion in *Milliken v. Bradley*, "will be ill served by the court's refusal to remedy separate and unequal education, for unless our children begin to learn together, there is little hope that our people will ever learn to live together and understand one another."

Beecher

Covering five and a half square miles in parts of Mount Morris and Genesee Townships, the Beecher School District developed into a suburb in the 1930s to meet Flint's housing shortage. By the time the GM Ternstedt plant was opened on Coldwater Road in 1953 to manufacture body hardware, Beecher looked like most working-class neighborhoods within the city, with tiny houses fairly close together. Today, Beecher looks marginal, with a small business district and school at the intersection of Saginaw Street and Coldwater Road. This small place has, however, been in the national spotlight for a natural disaster—the 1953 Beecher tornado—and two tragic gun deaths: the 1972 suicide of a Black assistant principal; and the shooting in 2000 of a six-year-old girl by a classmate.

Beecher was a rural place from its founding in the 1830s up until 1915 when real estate developers bought farmland up and down Saginaw Road to plat the earliest subdivisions, notably Crestline (Carpenter and Saginaw) and Northgate (Cass, Cornell, Yale, and Princeton Streets). Beecher appealed to migrants coming to Flint for its open space, lower taxes, and loose zoning regulations, which gave them the freedom to keep a garden and chickens. Residents built a high school in 1933, and in 1938, voters made the area a metropolitan district, but the majority believed less government was best government and so did not press for amenities like sewer and water service.

The independence and strength of Beecherites was tested in the aftermath of the tenth deadliest storm (with 116 local fatalities) in America's history. Those who saw the cloud coming rushed to basements if they had them, but over half of Beecher's new houses did not. Some took off in cars; others barely had time to throw themselves into a ditch, lay atop their children or hide anywhere they could. Survivors said the noise was like being under a trestle with two freight trains going over your head. "Perhaps the most striking thing about the immediate response," remarked sociologists William H. Form and Sigmund Nosow in their study *Community in Disaster*, was what Beecherites did for themselves and one another in the "rainy darkness without electric power, without special equipment or outside aid." Victims helped neighbors, digging bodies out of rubble, applying tourniquets, calming the hysterical, and taking those who had lost family under their wings. Neighbors watched the wrecked houses of other neighbors to prevent looting before the National Guard arrived to do that job. Despite concern that more tornadoes would form, Beecherites made stretchers and transported people to Hurley Hospital, the Industrial Mutual Association Auditorium, and the Ternstedt plant, where temporary emergency units were set up.

President Dwight D. Eisenhower declared Beecher a national disaster area, and aid organizations rushed to assist, but the ability of victims to marshal their own resources was remarkable. Beecher residents contributed $14,000 and local businesses handed out tools to help in the rescue efforts, while restaurants and stores emptied their shelves to feed the victims and rescuers. The Beecher volunteer fire department was open around the clock, providing all kinds of assistance, and the pastor of St. Francis of Assisi Catholic Church initiated a building bee called "Operation Tornado," with volunteers from all walks of life, including Charles Stewart Mott, construction companies, and UAW locals across the city.

Just as devastating was the period between 1968 and 1972, when certain administrative decisions stressed the school and community. By 1960, Beecher was 10 percent Black; integration had been happening gradually and without issue. Problems arose in 1968, when a majority of low-income houses, provided by the Department of Housing and Urban Development's Section 235 and 236 programs, became concentrated in Beecher and Northwest Flint. These programs were supposed to help poor and minority families become homeowners and integrate them across the spectrum of suburban communities.

School Superintendent Randall Coates wrote to Lansing repeatedly, pointing to the injustice of concentrating cheaply built houses for poor Black people in one area. He testified in a 1970 lawsuit against a builder and tried to explain that overcrowded schools would necessitate half-day sessions. Taxpayers, especially white families, would leave, and the result would be "not a good environment for integration." Some white people tried to help Beecher integrate, like Danny Sain, a UAW leader, and his wife Doris, who started the interracial group Common Concern and met with their neighbors. Superintendent Coates took one more important step in August 1970, when he appointed the first Black administrator, Paul Cabell, to the office of vice principal for the specific purpose of easing racial tensions.

Despite the nearly impossible task of disciplining a thousand-person school, Cabell was well liked and effective. But all three national media outlets—*The New York Times*, *Life*, and *Ebony*—that covered his suicide on February 24, 1972, addressed his struggle with self-styled "radical" teacher George Moss. Theirs was a battle of competing ideologies. Cabell followed Martin Luther King's belief in cooperation, integration, and nonviolence, while Moss was clearly an antiestablishment proponent of Black militancy. The contest climaxed when a note passed in class that contained a racial slur inflamed the anger of Black students. Administrators called an assembly to regain control, but students shouted Cabell down, calling for George Moss to speak, instead of "Uncle Tom."

In a three-page suicide note, addressed "For Beecher," Cabell made the opening declaration: "I consider myself to be a black man," as if it was uppermost in his mind to contradict someone else's consideration of him. He went on to say that he was "weary of fighting insensitive trainers, also known as teachers," signaling that he understood what he was up against in the contest with Moss: "I cannot allow myself to turn against what I knew to be right," but "on the other hand I cannot turn nor will I turn against my own people." Cabell's note named names, but for the sake of community unity, they were suppressed. George Moss tried to strip Cabell's martyrdom of its obvious meaning: "As long as a black commits suicide they think he's some kind of schizophrenic jerk," but others felt differently. An African American former Mott Fellow who was working on a doctoral degree alongside Cabell at the

University of Michigan, in a letter to the *Flint Journal*, wrote: "We can't make it without Whitey, black brother, and he's permanently entwined with us—the 'troublesome presence.' His better world is thwarted if he doesn't make it with us. He is the genesis of our problems, but only in togetherness can we realize a solution to this social and economic madness that blankets us."

In the week after the tragedy, Michigan Civil Rights Commission representative Olive Beasley attended two meetings between school personnel and Black parents. She described the meetings as unproductive "disasters" with high levels of "emotionalism" and no effective adult leadership. The proposed interracial citizens' committee fell on its face when just a few people volunteered to participate. White residents panicked and left Beecher and North Flint quickly.

Between 1970 and 1980, the number of white residents in Flint declined from 138,065 to 89,470. Their fears were ramped up by malicious blockbusting real estate agents of both races. Areas like Manley Park in northwest Flint went from being middle-class white to totally Black within just four years. This was heartbreaking for middle-class Black people who wanted badly to live in a mixed environment, because they had noticed that the schools were better in such places. Rosaline Brown remembered that as soon as she moved into Manley Park in 1973 with the "beautiful idea" of raising her children in an interracial setting, "For Sale" signs began to appear in neighbors' yards. Between 1960 and 1980, the nearby St. Agnes Catholic Parish lost eight hundred families, who left as Black people moved into the cheap houses built quickly in the neighborhoods along Pierson Road and Saginaw Street in the late 1960s.

The Beecher area seems to have stabilized somewhat, although 32 percent of residents today live in poverty. There is a memorial to the tornado disaster on the southwest corner of Saginaw Street and Coldwater Road that lists the names of the dead and describes the event. Opposite the memorial is Beecher High School. Shuttered for twenty years, it is set to reopen in 2026 after an $18 million renovation, with funds contributed by the Mott Foundation and other local philanthropists. Buell Elementary, where six-year-old Kayla Rolland was shot by a classmate on February 29, 2000, was demolished, and there is no memorial for her. A drive through the neighborhoods shows them to be integrated when taken as a whole. The houses are poor but well cared for, and there is street life. Sections have the rural feel that could in 2023 draw newcomers as it did in 1920—if white suburbanites could entertain the beautiful idea that a mixed racial environment would be a healthier place for children to grow up.

Mount Morris and Clio

Mount Morris is a city (pop. 3,170) and township (pop. 20,016), named for Mount Morris in western New York. Because the pioneers were advocates of temperance, the community was first known as the "Coldwater Settlement," from which Coldwater Road takes its name. The township was formed in 1855 and the village was incorporated in 1867. The Pere Marquette Railroad connected the community to Flint and Saginaw and, later, the interurban line did so as well.

The city of Mount Morris, with a business district on Saginaw Street, retains a small-town feel, with trains that run through downtown regularly. Of note here are the First Methodist Church (with origins in meetings held in the 1830s) and St. Mary's Roman Catholic Church. The latter, established in 1868, originally served a small, rural Irish community, and the building, built in 1903, is the oldest Catholic church edifice in the county.

Commercial development at the intersection of Clio Road and Pierson began in 1957 with the opening of a Hamady supermarket. More businesses sprouted up along Clio Road, but unfortunately, the commercial area has declined since the 1990s, and the former Hallwood Plaza is largely empty.

The character of the northern outer suburbs has shifted with Flint's fortunes. Clio (pop. 2,517) was a farming community and railroad town that gradually came to feel like a bedroom community for the factory town. The railroad, interurban lines, and regular bus service were all used by residents to commute to AC Spark Plug, Buick, and Chevrolet. Clio has a relatively prosperous feel, with many downtown businesses. The Musical Tent drew crowds every summer from 1954 with a full orchestra at every performance and stars from New York and Hollywood performing in operas, musicals, and plays. The Musical Tent became the Clio Area Amphitheater, still providing entertainment on summer evenings in Clio City Park (N. Mill St.). The park follows along Pine Run and has a walking trail and skateboard park. The Clio Depot Museum preserves local and railroad history.

Montrose

Montrose Township's early settlers from New York included John Farquharson, a Scottish native, who in 1846 named the region for a city in Scotland, hoping to attract further Scottish settlers. The first mill, on Woodruff's Creek, was built in 1849 by James Sisco, described as a "colored" man by Edwin Wood, although census records identify him as white. Montrose was incorporated as a village in 1899 and as a city in 1980. The area is mostly agricultural, and a nearby blueberry farm is the source of the annual Blueberry Festival. The Montrose Historical & Telephone Pioneer Museum (144 E. Hickory St.), in the old depot, has, besides artifacts related to local history, an unusual and comprehensive collection of telephones, originally created by the owner of the local telephone exchange.

Flushing

Flushing (city pop., 8,411; township pop., 10,701) developed as a settlement in the 1830s, owing its existence to the Flint River, which turns northward here to flow toward Saginaw Bay. The rapids at Flushing made it an ideal mill town, and Connecticut-born brothers Charles and James Seymour, who had lived first at Flushing, New York, eventually bought eighteen thousand acres, dammed the river, and built a sawmill and grist mill. By 1839, a wooden bridge had been built over the Flint River where the Main Street Bridge crosses today. In the following decades, more land-hungry farmers arrived, bringing entrepreneurs with them. The city supported three hotels, two opera houses, blacksmiths, wagon makers, a foundry that made plows, a clay pit (downriver) and a sandstone and shale quarry (upriver). The best example of Flushing stone, quarried from the riverbanks where the golf course is presently, can be seen in St. Paul's Episcopal Church in Flint. Flushing Riverview Trail, completed in 2005, offers incredible views of the river from bluffs. The trail starts in a parking lot of Bueche's Food World.

Thomas Ludwell Lee Brent (1784–1845) was a unique character who settled in Flushing during the pioneer period. A member of an elite Virginia planter family, he spent twenty years as secretary of the American legations in Madrid and Lisbon. When Andrew Jackson's new Secretary of State Robert Forsyth in 1834 thwarted Brent's desire to find another post, he and his Spanish wife, daughter, and son remained in Europe. But then, rather than returning to a genteel life in Virginia, Brent chose to embark upon an idealistic project in the wilds of Michigan, for which he had little preparation. This decision, made by a cultured man who had spent most of his adult life at the Spanish and Portuguese courts, must have been influenced by a strong opposition to slavery and perhaps by Alexis de Tocqueville himself, whose *Democracy in America* appeared in 1835. In any case, he bought federal land in Michigan through an agent and came directly with his family from Europe to New York in 1837 and then directly to Detroit. Brent purchased over twenty thousand acres in Genesee, Saginaw, Lapeer, and St. Clair Counties, but he soon lacked sufficient cash to pay his taxes. He hired men to clear the forest and to construct a sawmill, paying them in land.

Slowly realizing he wasn't cut out for the hard work of pioneering, Brent nevertheless chose to live in the style to which he was accustomed. He built a mansion, called "Rosemont," which included a music room with a piano, where he probably played duets on the flute with his wife or daughter. His wine cellar must have been the only one in the county. In 1844, he wrote to his friend Dolley Madison (widow of President James Madison) that he had abandoned hopes of obtaining another diplomatic post and was "resolved to try to resign ourselves to our hard fate in these woods . . . that we may be enabled sooner than we expected to sell out our small estate here, and emerge from the deep recess of these forests, and roam free from the shackles of office." Brent died the following year. The house was razed in 1965, but Brent's kingdom of "Barcelonia" is now accessible to all as Flushing Township Nature Park (8301 McKinley Rd.), with a kayak launch and two miles of walking trails through forest alternating with wet prairie.

From the half-century separating the arrival of the Seymour brothers to Flushing's incorporation, the village grew slowly. The seismic event in Flushing's history was the arrival of the Cincinnati, Saginaw, and Mackinaw Line (soon absorbed into the Grand Trunk Railroad) in 1888 and the construction of a depot near the intersection of Main Street and Seymour Road. The new rail line, with its myriad and daily connections, spurred faster development in Flushing and made larger cities like Saginaw and Bay City more accessible.

Flushing's growth paralleled that of Flint: From 1900 to 1950 the population more than doubled, from 900 to 2,226. This growth continued into the postwar era to the point that the city ran out of water, which then had to be trucked in from Flint. In 1954, voters approved a community water system, after which fifty-nine new homes were erected in and around the village. The FHA threatened to redline certain Flushing subdivisions until sewer lines were built, after which forty-one new housing permits were issued in the mid-1950s. The movement of people out of Flint seriously crowded Flushing's schools, and by 1958, the high school principal suspended admissions. Flushing's three schools, among the most overcrowded in the country with a 34:1 student-teacher ratio, were not unique: In Mount Morris and Beecher districts, for instance, the ratios were 50:1 and 44:1 respectively.

By the 1960s, Flushing was one of the most popular destinations for white families fleeing Flint, especially neighborhoods in North Flint. The Flushing Historical Society, formed in 1973, tackled various projects, notably restoration of the depot, preserving the village ambience of the town, visible in the Main Street Historic District with a whole range of architectural styles. This, in turn, has kept real estate prices high and the community even whiter than Grand Blanc or Davison. Flushing Area Historical Society and Museum (431 W. Main St.), in the old depot, contains memorabilia and files concerning Flushing.

Flint Township

To the west of the city of Flint lies Flint Charter Township (pop. 31,447). Like the rest of the area, it was settled in the 1830s and 1840s, and it remained a farming community into the 1920s. In the southwestern part of the township, an unincorporated community at the corner of Miller Road and Linden Road was called Otterburn. Bishop International Airport began when in 1928 banker Arthur G. Bishop offered the City of Flint a farm at the corner of Bristol and Torrey Roads for development as an airport. The city later annexed it. Development and enlargement continued, and today the airport ranks as the third busiest in Michigan. Developers built the Genesee Valley Mall at Miller and Linden Roads in 1970, leading to commercial development on Miller Road and north on Linden Road and the disappearance of stores in downtown Flint. Flint Charter Township in 2020 was 31 percent Black, most living in the northern part of the township. Most of the township lies in the Carman-Ainsworth School District.

Swartz Creek

Swartz Creek (pop. 5,838) is a suburb to the southwest of Flint, lying on Miller Road. Originally the place was called "Miller's Settlement," and the two-thousand-acre

Gatepost tile from Crapo Farm made by Flint Faience and Tile Company, c. 1928.
GENESEE HISTORICAL COLLECTIONS CENTER, UNIVERSITY OF MICHIGAN–FLINT LIBRARY.

Crapo Farm dominated the area. Introduction of the sugar beet led to Czechs coming to the area in the 1910s. With the sale of Crapo Farm in 1955, subdivisions grew, and in 1958, Swartz Creek was incorporated as a city, taking pieces of Flint, Gaines, and Clayton Townships.

Grand Blanc

Grand Blanc (city: 8,091; charter township: 39,846) is the name of the oldest township in Genesee County as well as an incorporated city. The name ("Great White") seems to have its origin in the French Algonquin patois that once passed as a lingua franca, referring to a chief of a local band whose features indicated his European ancestry, and the pioneer settlers pronounced it in the French manner. The area was first settled by Jacob Stevens in 1823, and his son Rufus later established a mill on the dammed Thread Creek. The first permanent settlers were the Perrys, and their influence and impact remain to this day. Before the City of Grand Blanc was carved from the township and incorporated in 1930, there were hamlets known as Grand Blanc Center (at Saginaw and Perry Roads) and Gibsonville or Whigville, near Hill Road and Saginaw Street.

Industry came first to this agricultural community during World War II, when the Fisher Tank Arsenal began rolling out tanks and tank destroyers before the roof of the building was even finished. In 1942, seven new neighborhoods were developed to house workers, with another six added by the end of the decade. The Sherman and later Pershing tank and the Wolverine tank destroyer were the main products, with over nineteen thousand being manufactured until 1945. Although Fisher Body was always behind the production in the plant, the building was expanded and sold to the Buick Motor Division in 1950. Fisher Body then operated it between 1951 and 1955, producing 4,200 Patton tanks for the Korean War effort. It then operated as a metal stamping plant. Unfortunately, as General Motors declined, the use of the Grand Blanc facility also decreased. By 2013, the GM Weld Tool Center, as it had been known since 2002, shut down. GM plant closures are one of the many things that tie Grand Blanc to Flint, despite the effort of some suburbanites to deny the close relation.

Grand Blanc was one of many suburban communities to reject the "New Flint" plan in 1958. The plan would have annexed Grand Blanc and Mount Morris, and Grand Blanc, Genesee, and Burton Townships, as well as parts of Flint, Mount Morris, Mundy, Vienna, and Thetford Townships, to create a sixty-two-square mile metropolitan area with one government and one school system. Secessionists argued that they had moved to get away from Flint and wanted to manage their own issues without the involvement of big government and a big corporation. Historian Andrew Highsmith implies that race was the unspoken reason many left, and while possible, it was a decade before the enactment of Flint's open housing law. More likely it was a direct result of technological achievement and affluence: factory workers were making higher wages in the 1950s and were also buying hunting cabins, boats, and snowmobiles; a suburban home was part of that middle-class package. As Black people spread into formerly white neighborhoods through the 1970s, however, realtors began to use "good schools" as a main selling point for homes in Grand Blanc.

Grand Blanc's school district was the first (1903–1904) in the county to consolidate its rural schools, and today it is the second largest in the state. The current, modern Grand Blanc High School is an impressive rectangular landmark on the corner of Holly Road and South Saginaw Street with over 2,500 students and not nearly enough teachers. Nevertheless, students report that the demographic distribution is "perfect," with students of all races coming from Flint through the Schools of Choice program. In 2021–2022 the district was 64.7 percent non-Hispanic white and 17.5 percent Black. Beyond the school, many young people feel isolated and constrained in a community that is not walkable or safely bikeable. "Car-dependent cities like mine," remarks future city planner Kalyn Woznicki, "put a price on every experience. Each time you go out, you need to spend money on gas and spend money wherever you go to socialize. There are no places for young people to gather anymore."

The city looks new and busy. Big-box stores are disguised behind monumental facades, while new ethnic businesses—Yemeni coffee shops and Thai restaurants—pop up and join the mix of older eateries. Although more or less economically and ethnically a one-layer city, there is some migration of middle-class Black people and Asian immigrants settling here, because it is close to the new Ascension Genesys Hospital as well as the tech companies in Oakland County.

The conspicuous consumption in Flint's southern fringe can almost make you forget the poverty in Flint. Like it or not, though, these communities are connected, and there needs to be more, not less, regional thinking. Basil Zimmer's New Flint idea may not have been the answer, but neither is obliviousness to regional problems. Things in the landscape that offer continuity between one place and another (the former GM plant at 10800 South Saginaw St.) as well as things that connect the present with the past are important to identify, if only for the reflection they enable and opportunities they may open. Examples of the latter include the First Baptist Church of Grand Blanc (6106 S. Saginaw St.), the oldest church building in Genesee County, founded in 1833 and built in 1851; the Perry/McGrath Historical Park (5078 Perry Road); the Grand Blanc Heritage Museum (203 3 E. Grand Blanc Road); and Thread Creek Farm (east of Dort Highway, across the railroad tracks and Thread Creek). Occupied and run by Virginia Evatt Knag, a sixth-generation descendant of pioneer Jonathan Davison, the farm is run on principles of community supported agriculture.

Goodrich

Goodrich (pop. 2,022) is a village in Atlas Township, in the far southeastern corner of Genesee County. Today, along with other communities in the southern part of the county like Fenton and Grand Blanc, the area is one of the most prosperous. Named for the Goodrich family—brothers Moses and Enos purchased over a thousand acres here in 1835, then brought other relatives—the community served the surrounding agricultural area for many years. Although farming is still carried on in Atlas Township, suburbanization is well under way here, especially along the shores of Lake Shinanguag, with larger and ever more luxurious homes appearing. The atmosphere is bucolic, thanks to the run-down farm buildings offsetting the heavy stone lake houses. The unincorporated community of Atlas, at the corner of Gale and Perry Roads, retains a nineteenth-century feel, having been founded in 1831 by Norman Davison and originally named Davisonville. Goodrich was a stop on the interurban railroad between 1900 and 1931, linking Flint and Detroit via Oxford. With cars leaving every half hour, the electric railway encouraged local travel, opened markets for dairy farmers who shipped out milk on it, and delivered patients to the Goodrich General Hospital. Opened by local doctor Amos Wheelock in 1916, the hospital operated until 1961 and was succeeded by Wheelock Memorial Hospital, in operation from 1964 to 1997, when it joined Genesys as a hospice. The Ladies' Library Association established a library in 1877. The building remains in its original condition, awaiting restoration. Unusual for its size, there are two eighteen-hole golf courses in Atlas Township and Goodrich. The Atlas Valley Country Club, on Perry Road, was founded in 1912 as the Flint Golf Club by golfing enthusiasts from Flint, like J. Dallas Dort and others. The club moved to a site near Thread Lake in Flint in 1918 and the course acquired its present name in 1938. The Goodrich Country Club opened in 1972 with an eighteen-hole course.

Burton

Burton (pop. 29,715) lies to the east of Flint and consisted of farms for much of its history. Prior to urbanization, the township had only an unincorporated community around the corner of Belsay and Lapeer Roads, and the first subdivisions were off South Saginaw and Fenton Road in an area called "Little Missouri." Autoworkers built many of the houses themselves on lots they purchased. Burton's character changed when I-69 stimulated commercial development, first at Center Road and Court Street with the opening in 1968 of the Eastland (after 1986 known as Courtland Center) Mall. Meijer Thrifty Acres built the first big-box store in 1973 on Center Road near Atherton Road, causing further development, even as GM employment began to decline. Burton incorporated as a city in 1972 but, reflecting its history as a development of urban sprawl and interstate highways, lacks a center. Largely a residential community, with light industry, Burton has four school districts (Bendle, Atherton, Bentley, and Kearsley) and For-Mar Nature Preserve and Arboretum (2142 N. Genesee Rd.), a former dairy farm that, instead of being developed, is rewilding. Martha Merkley, who with her late husband, Forbes, raised a world champion Holstein cow here in the 1940s, gave the property to the Genesee County Parks and Recreation Department in 1970. The animals were this childless couple's family, and their devotion to each other and to this place is remembered in the name For-Mar, which has become what Martha hoped it would be: "A green oasis in a sea of subdivisions."

Davison

Davison (city: 5,173 pop.; township: 20,434). Seelyeville was the original name of the settlement in the Black Creek basin established by a handful of families who ventured here from Saratoga County, New York, in 1836. The settlement was incorporated as a village, named Davison in honor of Norman Davison, a judge from nearby Atlas Township, and developed an array of businesses necessary for a farming community. When, in 1908, ninety automobiles arrived in the village, shipped from Flint, the five-mile distance closed fast.

Davison became a city in 1939 with a population of 1,300, and by 1970, the population was 5,259. Platting of subdivisions began in the late 1940s. The first was developed on what was originally a racetrack, called Rosemoor Park, which operated from 1895 to 1943, with horses and later cars. The park closed in 1943, and the owner sold the land for development of what Andrew Highsmith calls a "whites only" subdivision. Houses in Rosemore Park and other 1950s subdivisions were of a postwar, Levittown nature: small, quaint nine-hundred-square-foot boxes, but with greater distance from city "problems," such as noise, close neighbors, outdoor cooking smells, trash burning, and the like. Racial mixing would eventually be perceived by most white people as an urban problem, but in 1950 African Americans were still just a minority in Flint (8–10 percent).

White people were lured into 1950s suburban developments by FHA-approved mortgages, a phrase splashed all over newspaper want ads, which meant buyers would be guaranteed urban amenities in a pastoral setting. But Davison's rapid growth led to a sewage disposal problem. In 1951, a $200,000 treatment plant was built but was overloaded within three years. The suburban sewage problem was eventually resolved with a system that sent the wastewater of twelve small suburban communities back to Flint for processing. This later became the Genesee County Sanitary Sewer District Number 1. While Flint processed their waste, the suburbs were demanding separate identities.

Davison's old downtown is tucked away, with Main Street running parallel to M-15, east of the railroad tracks, although it still hosts small businesses. The more bustling area is the strip on State Road north of I-69. There are shops, a park—Robert Williams Nature and Historical Learning Center (10069 Atherton Rd.)—and a bike trail in Jack Abernathy Park, all worth checking out. What you won't see is a statue to Michael Moore—the city's most famous son, who was a thorn in the side of this community beginning in 1972, when he was elected to the school board during his senior year of high school. Although he grew up to criticize Davison's homogeneity and prejudices, its insularity gave him the confidence to start a newspaper in fifth grade and, later, the encouragement to think freely enough to become a serious culture critic with a national platform. About the time when the Mott Foundation was pulling out of Flint Community Schools, Moore, an Eagle Scout, developed the idea for the "Freedom School," where adults in the community would teach young people skills (crocheting, auto mechanics, carpentry, etc.). He also began a hotline that answered questions about addiction, pregnancy, counseling—the sort of issues young people found difficult to discuss with their parents. Eventually he started alternative newspapers published under a series of names (*Free to Be*, *Flint Voice*, and *Michigan Voice*). His modus operandi was exposing injustice, and his main target was General Motors for the receipt of enormous tax abatements from the city. He appeared at the GM seventy-fifth anniversary parade carrying a sign, "All the world loves a charade."

Davison Township is growing, as its remaining farmland is sold to high-end developers, creating exclusive subdivisions with names like Rivershyre and Crossings at Copper Ridge. The land rolls and upscale homes look out on wetlands, preserved but contained.

Fenton

The southeast section of Genesee County consists of hills and rolling terrain dotted with lakes created by receding glaciers. These lands, extending south of Davison and Grand Blanc into Fenton and Holly and westward to Linden, Byron, and Argentine are drained by the Shiawassee River. On surveys and maps dating from 1860, the forest type in this section is labeled "oak openings," and clusters of oak are still visible, notably at Fenton and Maple Roads, and at Linden County Park on the southern shore of Lake Byram.

Fenton (city pop. 12,050; charter township pop. 16,843) historically has been the second-largest settlement in Genesee County. Situated near three large lakes—Lake Fenton, Lake Ponemah, and Silver Lake—it has witnessed different eras: first serving as a market for the surrounding agricultural community with local industries; then as a Flint recreational location and suburb; and more recently, together with nearby Holly and Linden, as a residential area for commuters within the greater Detroit–Ann Arbor sprawl. Fenton, which lies on the Shiawassee River, began when Clark Dibble, who, like other early white settlers, came to sell whiskey to the Indians. He built a sawmill in 1834 and the settlement became known as Dibbleville. In 1837, investors William

Steamer *City of Flint* on Lake Fenton, c. 1900. FENTON HISTORICAL SOCIETY.

M. Fenton and Robert LeRoy came to the nascent town and rapidly transformed it at the time when New Yorkers were coming to the area in droves. Fenton built a hotel, bought and sold land, and the two platted Fentonville in 1837. In 1863 the village of Fenton was incorporated.

Fenton attracted small industries, such as a woolen mill, a foundry, and factories producing wooden products, including picture frames. A. J. Phillips and Company organized in 1889 to manufacture wood products. Phillips employed as many as two hundred workers to make snow shovels, ironing boards, clothes racks, and screen doors. Competition from the Continental Screen Door Company of Owosso forced the Fenton company to close its factory in 1913. Its founder, who died in 1904, left his personal office building to the city, which now houses the A. J. Phillips Fenton Museum (310 S. LeRoy St.), operated by the Fenton Historical Society. Phillips and his children also built houses next to each other on West Shiawassee Avenue. The museum houses many artifacts, including many original items from the Phillips family and company.

The lakes north and west of Fenton, lying in Fenton Township, were long enjoyed by people from Flint and Detroit. The annual Genesee County pioneer picnics were held at McCann's Grove on a point at the north end of Lake Fenton (until the 1930s known as Long Lake). Cottages and hotels on the lake at one time could be reached by horse-drawn trolleys, taking passengers from the depot, and Case's Island in the lake was home to numerous cottages. At the turn of the twentieth century, two excursion boats, the *City of Flint* and the *City of Fenton*, plied the lake. As elsewhere in Michigan, summer cottages after 1960 became year-round houses, and today the lakes are surrounded by expensive homes. The former recreational destination is now closed to all but residents.

In 1960, US-23 was completed, connecting Fenton to Flint and Ann Arbor and points north and south. By that time, developers had built new subdivisions that attracted people who worked in Flint, and the new highway shortened the drive. In 1964 the village incorporated itself as a city, annexing land north and west of the village boundaries. City planners began an urban renewal program. Although a stretch of downtown was placed on the National Register of Historic Places in 1974, voters chose to demolish it the next year. In more recent years, the city's park, on the Shiawassee River, has developed into a popular destination. Among Fenton's notable buildings is the Fenton Hotel. Just west of the city is Silver Lake Park, a county park with a crowded beach. The city's population grew until it stabilized at 8,284 in 1970. Then a second period of growth after 2000 caused the population to increase to over 12,000 in 2020.

Linden

To the west of Fenton, on one of the arms of Lake Ponemah, lies the village of Linden (pop. 4,124). Its most notable feature is the Linden Mill, built in 1871. It operated as a water-powered gristmill until 1956, when it became home to a library and museum, the Linden Mills Historical Society Museum. Currently inactive, the mill and millpond, now a park, offers a bucolic view. The Linden Hotel, an old business, operates as a bar and restaurant. Nearby Pine Lake and Byram Lake were surrounded by farms, orchards, and a few cottages until the mid-1950s when Flint workers began moving out of the city. Jane Elder, head of the Sierra Club Midwest, grew up on Pine Lake. Her father, who worked at AC Spark Plug and lived with his parents on Rankin Street in Flint's north end, moved the family out into what his daughter remembers as a landscape of fading orchards, old pastures, wood lots, and a blue gem of a lake tucked into a glacially carved bowl. The developer of Pine Lake's eastern shore platted lots and dug foundations, and workers built their own houses. Modest homemade houses stand out in what has become an overbuilt shoreline. Sewers and water treatment facilities came to these lakeside communities by the mid to late 1970s, but even treated water, returned to the Shiawassee River and eventually

Saginaw Bay, adds bacteria and nutrients that cloud the water and encourage the growth of bacteria and nuisance muck.

Northeastern Genesee County

North and east of Flint is Genesee Charter Township (pop. 20,581), which, like the other suburban townships, was, for most of its history, rural. The Flint River ran through it, and it was dammed in 1969, creating Mott Lake and the Mott Recreation Area. The Flint River Trail along Mott Lake begins in Genesee Veterans Park (6507 N. Genesee Rd.). Reuben McCreery built a sawmill and platted the town of Geneseeville in 1858. The unincorporated village exists today as Genesee and still bears nineteenth-century traces, like Greek Revival houses and the Methodist church. Most of the suburban development has taken place in the Genesee Road–Coldwater Road area.

Northeast of Genesee is the town of Otisville (pop. 819), the most outlying "suburb" of Flint that offers fewer subdivisions and seems much more pastoral. Forest Township was originally covered with white pine, and a lumber boom was underway after William Francis Otis, of Cleveland, purchased tracts of land and a sawmill in 1852 and, through a resident manager, operated it until all the pine in the township was cut. Otis platted the village in 1863 but never settled here. Some small industries, such as a foundry and a broom handle factory, followed. Stop by the Otisville Museum of Area History (122 E. Main St.) to check out, among other items, the antlers of an eastern elk, found at the bottom of nearby Picnic Lake, a portrait of William Francis Otis, and some enormous pine tree cross sections. For locals, Otisville is a hub with a library, a few restaurants, and even a gym on the main street.

Southeast of Genesee, along Carpenter Road (the northern boundary of Flint), are neighborhoods with a high concentration of Black residents. An interracial citizens' group, United for Action, protested the siting of dirty industries here in the 1990s, notably the Genesee Power Station (a wood-burning incinerator). Ultimately, they couldn't stop the power plant from being built, though they did block other potentially toxic industries like a tire-burning facility. But in the wake of the Flint Water Crisis, when an asphalt plant was located in the same census tract, citizens were outraged and labeled the move yet another instance of environmental racism. Despite reassurances from the Michigan Department of Environment, Great Lakes, and Energy, local people feel that yet again the quality of life in a Black neighborhood is less important than in white areas.

Historical Crossroads Village and Huckleberry Railroad (6140 N. Bray Rd.) began with an impetus to save two historic structures on the east side of Flint that were going to be demolished for new highways and urban renewal programs: the Buzzell House—a Greek Revival, the oldest house in Flint—on East Court Street and the

Wisner barn on Lapeer Road. In 1969, the Mott Foundation gave 208 acres on the shore of Mott Lake as a site for a historic "crossroads community" to the Genesee Parks and Recreation Commission. The village opened as a living history museum in 1976 for the Bicentennial. Over the years, thirty-four structures from around the region have been moved to the village, including a mill from Atlas, a bank from Vassar, a brick office block from Fenton, and a country church from Cohoctah. While our actual communities were growing further and further apart in terms of class and lifeways, their castaways were forming a conglomerate that gives the feel of a rural village in the nineteenth century. There are a number of vintage rides and an operational railway offering visitors forty-minute rides drawn by both steam and diesel locomotives.

Genesee County is rich in parks (more than eleven thousand acres of land and water), and one you don't want to miss—unique for its stands of white pine and hemlock and Works Progress Administration (WPA) stamp—is Richfield County Park (6322 North Irish Rd., Davison). WPA workers built the five warming shelters (the largest seating three hundred) with fieldstones and massive tree trunk supports. Multiple fireplaces in each shelter vent through central chimneys, and these shelters can be rented by the public. The Flint River is accessible down a grand fieldstone staircase or a "trees and rocks and trail" configuration that was common to WPA and Civilian Conservation Corps designs. The vintage suspension bridge over the Flint River is the park's landmark whether you are walking over the river on it or paddling under it. The park includes a canoe and kayak launch, trails, playscapes, and a Motocross BMX trail.

SAGINAW

Profile

Located between the confluence of four major tributaries and the bay, Saginaw was ideally situated to become a hub of commerce and industrial activity. Once the leading city in our region and third largest in Michigan, the casual visitor can see Saginaw's history in the contrasting architectural landscapes of the city's two halves, hugging opposite riverbanks. While the West Side's neighborhoods and local business districts remain viable and intact, the East Side, full of vacant lots resulting from demolition of commercial buildings and houses, struggles. It took over fifty years for the two separate cities of Saginaw City and East Saginaw to become one community through legislation that, in 1889, called for one city hall, one school board, and several more bridges across the river. Over time, the two communities grew apart because of racial difference (with East Saginaw developing large communities of Black and Mexican residents); but the tide has turned slowly over the last thirty years. At present there is a strong push for reconnection.

Vestiges of the cities' cosmopolitan aspirations remain on both sides of the river in the Gothic churches, wood and stone mansions, and grand public buildings—none grander than the post office, originally opened in 1898. The lumber boom had peaked and the two halves merged by the time U.S. Treasury architect William M. Aiken created a building that combined elements of a fortress and French château and ornamented the "castle" with details of local flora and fauna and a donkey gargoyle, memorializing the lost world Tocqueville visited, with Chippewa Indians, elk, bear, beaver, and French Canadian fur traders. When the city considered demolishing it for a larger post office in the 1930s, a citizen committee urged replacement. Today, the sized-up replica holds the collections of the Castle Museum of Saginaw History (500 Federal Ave.). A county museum millage only passed if the collections were housed in the castle, a clear signal that this building is the cornerstone of the city's identity.

Though the castle was saved and the neighboring Richardsonian Romanesque Hoyt Library (505 Janes Ave.) preserved, many other monumental buildings on the East Side were abandoned in the rush of progress, capitalism, and fears of racial unrest. Yet even in more battered sections of the East Side, grand buildings stand,

Castle Museum of Saginaw History, Saginaw. COURTESY OF THE LIBRARY OF CONGRESS, CAROL M. HIGHSMITH ARCHIVE.

lifting their eloquent decay above the banality of new construction. These ruins are a treasure, because they hold the past secure, helping us imagine alternatives.

History

There were thirty-one inhabitants in Saginaw when Alexis de Tocqueville and Gustave de Beaumont visited the settlement in 1831. The two French visitors had come up the Saginaw Trail through thick woods that gave way to vast prairie and a river "nearly as large as the Seine at Paris." The scene left an "enduring impression on our souls," he writes, describing the *bois-brûlé* (Métis, or French Indian) paddling them across the river in bright moonlight while singing a French song, horses breasting the gentle current, the looming primeval forest. Even then he could see that "in but few years these impenetrable forests will have fallen and the noise of civilization and of industry will break the silence of the Saginaw."

"Saginaw Forest (Indian Guide)," sketch by Gustave de Beaumont, 1831. SECOND BEAUMONT SKETCHBOOK, ALEXIS DE TOCQUEVILLE COLLECTION, BEINECKE RARE BOOK AND MANUSCRIPT LIBRARY, YALE UNIVERSITY.

Norman Little, buried in Brady Hill Cemetery, is the man generally considered to have been the first city builder. A native of Avon, New York, his father Charles Little had traveled to Saginaw in 1822 and bought land on the west bank of the river where a fort had just opened. That fort would close within the year, due to the extreme sickness of the troops, brought on, they thought, by river flooding, stagnant water and unwholesome vapors. Early settlers called the fever and chills "ague"; we know it as malaria, spread by mosquitoes. Tocqueville describes how swarms of mosquitoes drove him out of the settlement after only two days. The swampy and buggy conditions of the area deterred settlement temporarily.

Norman Little returned in 1836, determined to complete his father's vision, and founded Saginaw City. He had flooded eastern land offices with bright-red posters, advertising Saginaw's ideal location on a navigable river just twenty miles from the bay, surrounded by forests, fed by four major tributaries and other streams that reached nine hundred miles inland. After his initial purchases of land on both banks, Little had a lighthouse built at the river mouth and arranged a contract for a

Norman Little's wildcat Bank of Saginaw issued this three-dollar bill in 1837.
AUTHOR'S COLLECTION.

canal that would connect the Saginaw with the Maple River and eventually with the Grand River. If a water route to Lake Michigan could be secured, Saginaw would rival Chicago. Very little was dug and even less remains of Norman Little's vision, but there is a canal remnant visible from a bridge on Raucholz Road (1/4 mi. north of the Brant Rd. intersection), southwest of St. Charles.

The early part of 1837 was a flush time for Michigan when it entered the union in January. The 1840 census counted 920 people in Saginaw County. Little built a bank and began printing bills ornamented with pictures of canal boats and steamers. Cash flowed, wages were high, paper was traded for gold, but the bank got carried away with its paper money, as perhaps Little had with his paper town. He had built an enormous hotel, the Webster House, anticipating a rush of settlers. The only thing backing Little's wildcat currency was his ability to sell land in the new city, as the bank did not have the assets or the capital. In the financial panic at the end of 1837, Saginaw and other paper cities across the region collapsed. The state canceled Little's canal contract, many settlers left down the Saginaw Trail, and Little—bankrupt—sold what remained and returned to New York.

Faith in his idea helped Little persevere through enormous setbacks. During the five-year economic slump, he worked to sell the Saginaw idea to investors. By emphasizing the potential lumber resources in the valley and dwindling supplies in the East, Little secured the support of New York City merchant James Hoyt and his son Jesse. Representing Hoyt's company, Norman Little returned to Michigan, only to find that the city he had begun to build on the west bank was priced beyond his reach. Undeterred, he took a different tack. Hoyt and Company would develop the less desirable, low and swampy land on the east bank of the river. Hoyt and Little purchased a mile-long tract of about twenty-four thousand acres and began to develop it, with a big sawmill in Buena Vista Township. Hoyt knew that connection was everything, and the sawmill's first big work was to saw the boards for the Genesee Plank Road to Flint and a second plank road east to Tuscola. East Saginaw's aggressive boosters created a competition between the two cities that spurred development, and ultimately East Saginaw became the more important of the two because of Hoyt's investments, including railroad lines to and through the city, the first railroad bridge at the end of Genesee Street that landed on the west bank miles above Saginaw City, and a shipyard, where men built lumber barges that would be equipped with sails and pulled by steamboats to yards in Detroit, Buffalo, Tonawanda, and Albany. By 1870, Michigan was the largest supplier of lumber to eastern cities.

The Lumber Boom

Saginaw's industrial roots were literally in the forests around it. Eastern white pines, some as tall as 175 feet with trunks seven feet thick, were to Tocqueville's imagination a "living palace built for man," destined to fall before ambitious entrepreneurs. The frontier moved westward from depleted eastern forests, dragging the entire lumber culture with it to Michigan. A few crude sawmills appeared in the Saginaw Basin in the 1830s, but the boom didn't happen until after the Civil War, when anyone with money to invest opened a sawmill or boom company. For their part, the "shanty boys" sacrificed comfort and risked their lives, felling trees and breaking jams while (as they joked in the song "Michigan-I-O") suffering board that "dogs would laugh at" and "bed" in "the snow," though they thought they had "landed safe in Saginaw."

The needs of sawmills and logging camps caused merchants like Anton Schmitz, who operated a hardware store built on stilts over a bayou, to expand. By 1863, Schmitz took on a partner, George Morley, who would eventually buy him out. Over time, Morley Brothers grew into a Saginaw institution, with an enormous wholesale hardware business on North Washington, ambitious window displays, and a thick catalog. The Saginaw store was divided into departments—a novelty in 1881. Other important businessmen were German Jewish clothing merchants, Little Jake Seligman and Max Heavenrich, and the master craftsman Englehardt Feige, who started Feige's Interiors in 1854, building cabinets and furniture.

In 1882—the peak of the lumber boom—the twenty-mile stretch of river between Saginaw and Bay City was one continuous pile of lumber, cut by 60 mills—110 if you count those in Bay City and Essexville. When the wind blew right, sailors on Saginaw Bay could smell the pine resin and sawdust from the mills. While books like the 1881 *History of Saginaw County* celebrated the enormous numbers of board feet cut and shingles produced, no local voices were there to speak in defense of the

Shanty Boy Monroe

It was on the twenty-ninth of April in the springtime of the year,
Our logs were piled up mountains high, we could not keep them clear.
Their foreman said, "Brave boys, turn out! With hearts devoid of fear,
We will break those jams at Gary's Rock, and for Gagetown we will steer."

Now some of them were willing, while others they were not,
To break those jams on Sunday, they thought they hadn't ought.
But six of our brave Canadian boys did volunteer to go,
To break those jams on Gary's Rock with their foreman, young Monroe.

They had not rolled off many logs, till they heard his clear voice say:
"I'll have you boys be on your guard, for the jam will soon give way."
Scarcely had those words been spoken, till the jam did give and go,
It carried off those six brave boys and their foreman, young Monroe.

When the rest of their companions this sad news came to hear,
In search of their dead comrades to the river straight did steer.
Some of their mangled bodies, a-floating down did go,
While crushed and bleeding near the bank lay that of young Monroe.

They took him from his watery grave, brushed back his raven hair;
There was one fair form among them, a girl from Saginaw town,
The riverman's true friend, whose moans and cries rose to the skies
For her own true love had drowned.

The wages of her own true love the boss to her did pay,
The shanty boys made up for her a generous purse next day.
Fair Clara was a noble girl, the riverman's true friend.
She, with her widowed mother dear, lived at the river's bend.

Fair Clara did not long survive, her heart broke with grief,
And scarcely two months had vanished, till her heart did give and go,
And her last request was granted, to be laid by young Monroe.

The shanty boys cleared off the woods, and the lovers there laid low,
It was the handsome Clara Vernon and her true love, Jack Monroe.

Come all of you bold shanty boys, I'll bid you come and see,
Those manmade mounds, so greenly kept beneath the hemlock tree,
Carried the day and the date of that sad, sad fate of their foreman, young Monroe.

Sung by Ray Hoffmeyer, of Atlanta, Michigan, 1976, recorded by Paul Gifford.

---

trees. Bernhard Fernow, a German-born pioneer of forest management, warned of the harm done to the general welfare of the nation by clear-cutting, and in his first publication after becoming head of U.S. Department of Agriculture's Division of

Forestry, he challenged the claim made by Michigan's lumbermen that there was timber to last a thousand years. Predictions had grossly missed the mark, and one thousand years of timber disappeared in thirty. Even so, lumbermen were slow to support any forestry legislation. When in 1888 Arthur Hill—a Saginaw baron—was invited to speak at Michigan's first forestry convention (spearheaded by University of Michigan academics), he spoke only of the need to enlist the cooperation of the railroads in preventing forest fires. From our vantage point, the silver lining might be hard to see, but the lumber barons did build schools, hospitals, auditoriums, and training centers.

Lumber had its spillover industries: shingles, staves, and, of course, salt, which became such big business that a village south of East Saginaw was even named Salina. Brine was pumped and salt produced by boiling it in vats heated by sawdust fires. Brine drillers in Sebewaing hit a vein of coal in 1890, and John C. Liken started the Saginaw Bay Coal Company. The new resource gave everyone hope that Saginaw's prosperity would continue. Lumbermen like Arthur Barnard used capital from lumber to excavate mineshafts all around the Saginaw region southwest to St. Charles, and they laid out little cities below the earth. This dangerous work required specialized skills, so workers were recruited from Ohio, West Virginia, and Pennsylvania mines—immigrants (especially Italians) and African Americans among them. The industry peaked by 1907 in Saginaw County. Union contracts, machinery, flooding, and the coal's poor quality caused many mines to close by that date, and the last, near St. Charles, shut down in 1952. You can still see a coal mine ruin on land now owned by the Shiawassee National Wildlife Refuge if you follow the Woodland Trail (access from parking lot at 5050 Stroebel Rd.).

In the thirty-year period of post-lumber economic adjustment, many of the lumber barons invested in coal and sugar beets but recognized a need for manufacturing. The Merchant and Manufacturers Association, established in 1906, would be central to Saginaw's industrial reinvention, raising money for land purchases that would induce new enterprises to relocate to Saginaw. Between 1910 and 1919, due partially to World War I, Saginaw's labor force grew by about ten thousand. Shops took advantage of the remaining stands of hardwood, making carriages, wagons, cabinets, pianos, and even rulers. The Saginaw Clay Manufacturing Company, located at South Jefferson and Rust, established in 1894, mined clay near Flushing and shipped it by rail to Saginaw to be manufactured into bricks for paving streets, buildings, and homes. Historian Jeremy Kilar notes that by 1910, thirty-six corporations had been supported by this group, including two that would be key to Saginaw's twentieth-century industrial might: Jackson-Church and Wilcox (Jacox, later Saginaw Steering Gear, a division of General Motors) and Valley Grey Iron (Chevrolet Grey Iron Foundry). Lumber barons like Arthur D. Eddy, William B. Mershon, Arthur Hill, and Wellington Burt continued to support the Merchant and Manufacturers Association, which created a foundation for a second economic rise during the auto boom.

Germans

Industry and jobs drew people to the valley, but immigrants themselves brought customs, values, and new forms of social life that added greatly to the community. Germans began to arrive in the decade after the financial crisis, and their immense energy for organizing civic life was a model for Anglo-Americans. The first Franconians, who established Frankenmuth in 1845 and three other rural colonies, preferred a degree of separation from Americans. But soon afterward came refugees from the political events of 1848 who had more education and professional skills. The "48ers" sought to enjoy the privileges life afforded in a democracy, such as free expression and free association. Small groups of German immigrants began to organize cultural, athletic, musical, and educational societies in both East Saginaw and Saginaw City. The Liederkranz Singing Society, established in 1855, met in the shop of Volusin Bude, an architect and builder who designed the Germania School. A German Masonic lodge was organized in 1854. With the purchase of a city block bounded by Lapeer, Third, Fourth, and Tuscola Streets in 1856, the Germania Club, which began as a turnverein, its members at first performing gymnastic exercises outdoors, then built a gymnasium and later other facilities. The organization's constitution established some practical rules: members would use the more personal form of address (*du*, not *Sie*), wear black-red-gold emblems to display democratic feeling, and moderate their drinking.

From its humble beginnings, the club grew, especially after the Civil War, acquiring a massive library of German books, supporting an orchestra and men's and women's choruses; a dramatic and literary section; and a kindergarten, a gymnasium, and bowling alleys. It sponsored singing festivals featuring choruses from German organizations in other cities. A high point was the production in 1886 of an opera, *Joseph in Egypt* by Étienne Mehul, complete with professional soloists and orchestra and the Germania chorus. The club welcomed non-Germans to participate in their parties, concerts, and shows. A similar club, the Teutonia, opened in Saginaw City in 1858.

The Germania organization sold its 1877 building and in 1970 moved to a site in southwest Saginaw. At that point it was mainly a golf club. A decline in membership, however, forced its sale in 2011. The only historic German building in the old neighborhood today is St. Mark's German Evangelical Church (1901; since 2001: Living Water Ministries, Church of God in Christ), at 924 Lapeer Street.

Working-class Germans also formed their own death-benefit society, the Arbeiter-Verein (originally established in Germany in 1863 to advance the interests of the working class toward socialism). This organization's halls provided spaces for social and political events. The hall in East Saginaw opened in 1869 and that in Saginaw City in 1871. On Saginaw's West Side, the community was located near the intersection of Court and Fayette Streets. The Arbeiter Unterstützungs Verein, then an organization with a local membership of over a thousand members (with an equal number on the East Side), built a hall at Adams and Oakley in 1913. The organization folded in the 1930s, and today the hall belongs to the Veterans of Foreign Wars.

An Auto Town

Machine shops and foundries that made sawmill equipment in the nineteenth century retooled in the twentieth to manufacture gears and parts for Flint's auto industry. The Jackson-Church-Wilcox Company produced the Jacox steering gear, which proved superior to Buick's wobbly mechanism, and Flint's Billy Durant knew a good thing when he saw it. He purchased the company in 1909, promoting Melvin L. Wilcox to be general manager of the Buick plant in Flint, while his son Merrill Wilcox was made general manager of the plant in Saginaw. By 1921 this plant was manufacturing two thousand gears daily.

Durant saw the potential for joining forces with plants in Saginaw. He bought the Rainier factory, which had not been able to make an affordable luxury model, and continued experimenting in that vein, producing the Marquette (1909–1912) and the Peninsular (1912–1913) before he finally called it quits and used the factory to make mortar shells during World War I.

The Saginaw gearbox was the invention that sustained manufacture in the city for generations. It would go through many updates and be built under different names—Saginaw Products, Saginaw Steering Gear, and later Delphi and Nexteer. In 1919, GM purchased Saginaw Malleable Iron foundry, which by 1949 was the largest malleable iron plant in the world, and the corporation's new Saginaw Products Division now included the former Jackson-Church-Wilcox Company, the Malleable Iron foundry (which in 1930 became Saginaw Steering Gear), the Grey Iron Foundry Company (built in 1919), and the former Michigan Crankshaft Company (later Saginaw Metal Casting Operations). Saginaw had five main plants within the city limits—two on the West Side and three on the East Side.

The River

As cities and industries grew across the watershed, Saginaw's drinking water became unpalatable. A new water purification plant was dedicated in 1929, but the chemical taste persisted in city water, as did residents' use of local pumps. The 1947 flood brought the Army Corps of Engineers to Saginaw for a public hearing at which twenty-one counties reported on their pollution and flood and water supply problems. Dow Chemical admitted it was a polluter but had plans to "lick the problem." The

Children using water pump, Saginaw, c.1925. CASTLE MUSEUM OF SAGINAW HISTORY.

work-around for Dow was the Whitestone pipeline, finished in 1949, that brought Lake Huron water to Midland and Saginaw.

As in all places, the Depression hit Saginaw hard, although Mayor George Phoenix was sympathetic to the plight of the poor. He protected the squatter camp of tarpaper shacks ("Phoenixville") south of the Court Street bridge and allowed colonies of houseboats, an outgrowth of the wanigans (cooking rafts) of the lumber era, to anchor in the bayous around Ojibway Island. For the most part, Saginawians tolerated the "river people," regarding them as independent-minded "gypsies"; and families were rescued when their homes were broken up by ice flows or other accidents. Police crackdowns occurred mainly during Prohibition, when river people were making and selling moonshine. Houseboats began to die out in the 1960s, when people accused residents of dumping sewage into the river. In 1976, the city cleared out the last of the "river bog slums" to create Wickes Park.

Sailboats, sloops, and schooners had been built in Saginaw since the 1850s, and, as the river was dredged and widened for logging operations, shipyards became busier and more profitable. In 1868, there were an estimated eighty-six vessels per day traveling up or down the Saginaw River. Steamers and passenger liners traveled from Alpena to Detroit with stops in Bay City and Saginaw. Flat-bottomed sidewheelers with comfortable accommodations, like the *Metropolis* and *Wellington Burt*, made frequent trips along the river and excursions to points on Saginaw Bay.

Piers and docking facilities were also improved in an effort to make Saginaw a major inland port. General Motors and Dow bought tracts of land along the river, and docks, piers, and terminals were built to import shipments of pig iron and export scrap metal, as well as limestone, grain, beans, and chemicals. In the years leading up to the opening of the St. Lawrence Seaway in 1959, people saw the river as key to Saginaw's future growth—a highway to national and world markets. In 1958, the Saginaw Grain Company shipped one thousand tons of navy beans from the Carrollton dock near the Sixth Street bridge to Rotterdam, and farmers and industrialists expected to see bigger profits from skyrocketing cargo tonnage. That never happened. To dock in Saginaw, ships had to take a one-hundred-mile detour from the Lake Huron shipping lane and negotiate a shallow bay and turnaround basins in a relatively narrow river. The bay entrance could be widened and channels dredged, but that picture became complicated when in the 1970s new environmental regulations required careful disposal of potentially contaminated sediments. When industries began to close in the 1990s, Saginaw had nothing to fill the ship holds that emptied at its docks. At that time, boosters circled back to Norman Little's canal idea and regretted that the waterway had not been built.

Between 2014 and 2016, river shipping hit its lowest level in decades, but more recent seasons have seen improvement. There were 171 ships on the Saginaw in 2023—a far cry from the 86 per day, but there are still sixteen docks at Essexville, Bay City, Zilwaukee, Saginaw, and Buena Vista that receive bulk products—sand, gravel, rock salt, coal, cement "clinker," calcium chloride, and other materials. Most of the ships are "self-unloaders" that use a long boom and conveyor belts to take material from the hold and drop it into huge piles on the sites near the river's edge or hoses that fill receiving silos. Recently, international ships have been at Saginaw docks unloading wind turbine components, and we may see more green energy components in the years ahead.

Recreation on the river has always found a way to thrive. As Saginaw's population grew, the Union Street Railway, which electrified Saginaw's streetcars in 1889, built Riverside Park in 1894 to guarantee Sunday riders. The park, located at the foot of Michigan Avenue where the Tittabawassee flows into the Saginaw River, had a

People enjoying themselves with guitars, mandolins, and beer on houseboats on the Saginaw River, c. 1905. CASTLE MUSEUM OF SAGINAW HISTORY.

dance pavilion, amusements, boat rentals, and concessions, along with a tent city and a summer houseboat colony. The park lasted until 1937, falling victim to the change brought on by the automobile and the Great Depression. Today, new park lands are popping up all along the waterways. Green Point is part of the Shiawassee National Wildlife Refuge, and the old Germania Club golf links are in the process of being restored to wetlands. The newest park in Saginaw County is the Saginaw River Headwaters Recreation Area, developed by the State of Michigan on the site of the old Saginaw Malleable Iron plant, which closed in 2007.

Divided Lives

The ethnic and racial composition in Saginaw changed with fluctuations in its economy. When people speak of the "old neighborhood," they often mean the northeast section of the city, dominated by the Potter Street Station (501 Potter St.), built as a passenger depot for the Flint and Pere Marquette Railroad in 1881 and used until 1950. It was close to the river, near what would become the site of Grey Iron, and an easy walk downtown. In the early decades of the twentieth century, Irish and Polish railroad workers lived in small houses and intermarried at St. Joseph's Church on Sixth Street. Mexicans and African Americans began to move into the neighborhood in the 1920s to work in the nearby foundry. The neighborhood around the Potter Street Station was, like that of St. John Street in Flint, an international village that enabled racial and ethnic minorities the chance to open businesses and build networks.

The Great Depression caused tensions, relieved only by repatriating hundreds of Mexicans so that there would be more work for native whites. However, farmers quickly found out that native whites didn't want to weed beet fields: "A city man will take one look at a beet field and walk away," said one. By 1938, just six years after hundreds were sent "home"—"somewhere south of the Rio Grande"—the sugar companies started advertising for a return of the hardworking Mexican and Tejano agricultural laborers. Once back in our region, they returned to field work but increasingly moved into the foundries and factories as well as business ventures. On Potter Street, near the train station, there was a tailor shop, two restaurants, and a pool hall that were owned by Mexicans.

After World War II, as the First Ward became solidly Black and brown, white ethnics, especially Poles, left St. Joseph's parish and moved into neighborhoods in the southeast, around Hess Avenue. St. Casimir's was the main Polish church in that neighborhood and still holds masses today and runs the Bishop Rey Academy next door. Residents worked at Lufkin Rule, the Heinz and Hausbeck pickle factories, and Saginaw Metal Casting, or they took a bus to Grey Iron or carpooled to Dow in Midland. The Hispanics in the First Ward joined organizations like the Mexican Civic Union (1945) that opposed discrimination and, later, the American GI Forum, which began as a veterans' advocacy group but ultimately engaged in the struggle for civil rights.

The communities on both sides of the river became increasingly divided in the twentieth century. White residents left the East Side, fearful of the growing numbers of Black and Hispanic residents as well as the strife that bubbled up in the late 1960s—an inevitable reaction to racial injustice. For the Black community, what followed was devastating: an apocalyptic epidemic of crack cocaine that created addicts and drug lords. The East Side emptied, while working-class communities in Carrollton and Zilwaukee, linked by the Sixth Street bridge, grew quickly. Even though crime has dropped dramatically, the city has not yet recovered from the perception that East Saginaw is dangerous. Incidents like the abduction, rape, and murder of a white girl by two Black teens in 1997 set things back. At a parole hearing, the convicted man apologized for actions that led to "fears and uncertainties" and encouraged criminal behavior in the neighborhoods, instead of "building a better Saginaw."

Change for the Better

Saginaw began to focus on historic preservation in the 1970s and 1980s, with the creation of Heritage Square Historic District and the Old Saginaw City (now known as Old Town Saginaw) District, both on the west side of the river. The East Side has monumental public buildings, as well as stunning Gilded Age mansions in varying stages of decay, especially on Jefferson Avenue.

The East Side became the focus of urban renewal, and, tragically, its story contains the same plot elements as that of Flint's Black neighborhoods: redlining, highway construction, white flight, crime, and demolition. In 1988, the neighborhoods around Potter Street Station had a lot of broken glass and weeds, but there were Black-owned businesses still holding on. But the City of Saginaw aggressively pursued state and federal funds for blight removal that became available in the 1990s and early 2000s. Congressman Dan Kildee spearheaded the land bank idea in both Genesee and Saginaw Counties, so that sparsely populated sections of the city could become "clean and green" through demolition. If a house of significance was in the zone, it could not be sold, even if there was a buyer interested in restoring it. By 2009, 35 percent of the houses in the area south of Grey Iron were gone, but the new problem of vacant land was here to stay.

Saving the station was one of many ideas floated over the years for projects that would "fix" this deindustrializing city. Other ideas included a "Saginaw Sawmill" lumber camp theme park (which died when investigators discovered that the site was seriously contaminated), a twin-tower downtown office building, and a NASA consortium on Ojibway Island. The field of healthcare is the largest employer today in Saginaw. Recent developments include a campus of Central Michigan University's College of Medicine, located near Covenant Medical Center. These days most Saginawians embrace the idea of slow growth, steady business, and community cooperation to develop shared resources.

"I don't use the word 'decline,'" notes Tom Trombley of the Castle Museum. "I prefer 'change,'" underlining the way the Goodridge Brothers' (African American photographers) used a special rotating Cirkut camera to capture panoramic views of Saginaw's triumphs but also its tragedies, like the great fire of 1893 that burned up thirty-some blocks. Tragedy was just one part of an ever changing, always unfinished city.

When asked what's "cool" about Saginaw, during the Jennifer Granholm "Cool Cities" campaign, one resident spoke about the beauty of the river view, the twinkling lights of the farther shore. Resident input for the 2022 city plan highlighted how important Saginawians believe it is to connect the neighborhoods with nonmotorized paths and to develop the riverfront. People talk about walkability, but to make that happen, we need a shift in public perception as much as new infrastructure. As in Flint, residents need to overcome the idea that walking the city is dangerous.

A devastating flood in downtown Saginaw, at corner of Jefferson and E. Genesee, 1904. CASTLE MUSEUM OF SAGINAW HISTORY.

Shaping Their Community: Black Americans in East Saginaw

At the time that Black people appeared for the first time in the census in 1860, East Saginaw had observed its first decade. The intersection of Genesee and Washington, then as now, served as the heart of the growing community. The stately brick, four-story edifice of the Bancroft House, built in 1859, sat at the southwest corner. Dirt roads were hemmed in by wood plank sidewalks, and modest structures lined the streets. Steamers filled the river. Mills dotted the banks, churning their sawblades and belching pollutants and sawdust into the air. As the city developed, Black residents participated in its civic and economic life, helping to create a vibrant space even as they faced discrimination.

The first official record of Black people residing in either of the Saginaws is the 1860 census, where census takers recorded a total of thirty-seven people of color, with only one family on the west side. They were written down as cooks, washers, barbers, housekeepers, and notably, real estate owners. By 1864, prospects from the

Washington and Genesee intersection changed due to the opening of the Genesee Bridge. Black residents made their first community-building moves, establishing the Bethel A.M.E. Church in 1867 and the Zion Baptist Church in 1868.

One of the most prominent African Americans to settle in East Saginaw in the early years was William Quincy Atwood (1838–1910), who arrived in 1863. Atwood was born in Alabama, son of a wealthy planter and his enslaved mistress. His father's will gave him a substantial inheritance, which legally he could receive only by going to the nearest free state, Ohio. After financial failure in California, Atwood returned to Ohio and shortly thereafter traveled to East Saginaw and decided to settle. He speculated in land and opened his own sawmill, making him one of the wealthiest men in the Saginaw Valley and one of the wealthiest Black men in the state. At the time of his death, his estate was worth $103,000.

Another prominent family, the Goodridge family—two brothers, William and Wallace, and sister, Mary—settled in East Saginaw in 1863. Glenalvin, their oldest brother, had established himself as a respected and talented photographer in York, Pennsylvania, but had been falsely accused of rape by a white woman and imprisoned. Their father secured a pardon for Glenalvin, and the pair joined the rest of the family in 1865. The brothers reestablished the photography studio they had left behind in York. Glenalvin, who had contracted tuberculosis in prison, was not able to fully restart his career, succumbing to his illness.

William and Wallace Goodridge carried on. Their first studio was in the Crouse block on the northeast corner of Genesee and Washington. They rented studio space on the third floor where they could make use of skylights. During their time in that studio, the Goodridges witnessed progress just outside as the dirt roads became paved with Nicholson pavement in 1868, a method of closely setting wood blocks to create a hard, relatively smooth surface. Their photographic work documented the changes in Saginaw as it metamorphosed from lumber town to industrial city. After the building was lost to fire in 1872, the Goodridges opened a new studio, two blocks down Washington Avenue.

Both Atwood and the Goodridges engaged in issues facing the Black community. They, along with other prominent Black community members, organized and participated in debating societies where they considered the concerns of the community and how to improve conditions. On two separate occasions, through the Goodridges' connections and Atwood's financing, they brought famed civil rights activist Frederick Douglass to speak. An active Republican, Atwood served as a state delegate to the 1888 national convention and two more times as delegate-at-large.

Shortly after the turn of the century, the Bancroft House had grown from a modest building to a new six-story, *L*-shaped building with 237 rooms and a rooftop garden. The improved Bancroft held a grand opening in August 1916. Already by that time, the streets were paved with bricks, and electric cables crisscrossed overhead. Electric trolley cars ran along the busy streets, their tracks embedded in the center. People came to shop at Morley, its state-of-the-art building gracing Washington Avenue (it would expand by 1922), or perhaps J. C. Penney, which opened a store in 1920. By 1925, the Second National Bank building soared to twelve stories across the street from the Bancroft. The Hoyt Building, constructed after the fire in 1872, changed hands in 1889 and was thereafter known as the Eddy Building.

Throughout the twentieth century more people of color migrated to Saginaw, recruited by GM for their foundries, and the river became a boundary demarking the predominately white west side and the increasingly Black and brown East Side, making them distinctive places, rather than a truly blended city. As General Motors expanded, so did Saginaw's total population, and the African American population skyrocketed from 328 in 1920 to 3,315 in 1940. GM recruitment for its foundries was the major factor. The *Saginaw News* noted with pride in 1934 that the Grey Iron Foundry was the largest in the world.

Residence choices were not organic but rather caused by a number of interlocking factors. According to interviews with Grey Iron workers, most of those recruited knew someone who had already made the journey to Saginaw, such as a family member or a former neighbor. The new recruits could stay with those families or friends. Most did not have their own transportation and therefore opted to work closest to where they could live, which was the northeast side, known by its political designation as the First Ward, situated north of Genesee and Washington. It contained a mix of foreign-born whites and nonwhites.

As more Black people moved to the area, white people began to move out. GM required a large labor force near its foundry, and Saginaw's white population wanted to keep Black people confined to the East Side. Coupled with lending practices and realtor intervention to create a systemic racial separation in neighborhoods, the First Ward became predominately Black by 1940. Black people stayed mostly to the north of Potter Street and the railroad tracks, just to the north of the heart of downtown. When postwar industrial growth brought more people to Saginaw, the lines blurred, as African Americans pressed southward.

Some people opted to find other employment rather than work in the foundries. They were limited to the service industry, and even then, many still faced a racial hierarchy. For example, the Bancroft Hotel would hire African Americans, but the hotel would not welcome them as patrons. Their Black employees were required to only enter the property from the rear, and they were relegated to jobs such as dishwashers, elevator operators, and stockers.

Despite the diversity of the east side, there were many businesses that would not serve Black customers. Interviewees told anthropologist Willie McKether that popular places like Home Dairy, Triants, S. S. Kresge, and Woolworth's either would not serve them at all or would only serve them via takeout from the back. They were also not welcome in entertainment venues such as skating rinks and bowling alleys.

As the Black population increased, so too did attempts to restrict Black life and movement, particularly in housing. White residents actively attempted to use the city government to support their desire for segregation. In 1926, a group of over one thousand residents brought a petition to the council in hopes of placing legal residential restrictions on Black people and Mexican Americans. Two more attempts followed, both unsuccessful. As the Black population expanded, white residents began to claim they did not feel safe going out, especially at night. They also claimed their African American neighbors were dirty and compared them to animals. Although the city refused to act on demands for restrictive ordinances, the city also did not respond to counter efforts by the Black community to create support for the community. In 1929, the council denied a petition from the Saginaw branch of the NAACP to appoint a social worker to help with housing and other social problems. Through lack of housing availability and lack of opportunity to move outside of the First Ward, white residents of Saginaw still created the segregation they had sought through the failed ordinances. Because there were not enough houses, the homes that existed were cut into multiple dwelling units. Those units were rented to Black people by mostly white landlords. Despite limitations, Black people of East Saginaw still actively took part in their community. They owned businesses that would cater to their needs when white-owned businesses would not. They responded to hotels barring service by opening their homes.

Those returning after World War II found a bustling downtown. Disembarking at Potter Street Station, one could still walk a few blocks to Genesee, where businesses lined the street. In any direction one could see stores, restaurants, and theaters. As people came and went, cars now jammed the roadways, and the electric trolleys were now a thing of the past.

The bustling streets showed evidence of progress, and Black Saginawians, especially those returning from military service, were ready to see change in social and political aspects of life as well. There was a noticeable uptick in political participation and involvement in the United Auto Workers (UAW) after the war. There were firsts, too: the first Black teacher hired by Saginaw Schools (Margaret Haithco in 1946), first Black firefighter (William S. Hurt Sr. in 1947), and the first Black president of a UAW local (Harry W. Browne in 1947). African Americans first appeared on the political stage when Rev. Cornelius Monroe ran unsuccessfully for city council on a housing reform platform. These firsts opened new pathways for Black Saginawians, seeming to promise a new day coming when they could tackle the community issues of concern to them.

Community clubs were important outlets for expression and collaboration. The Frontier Club of Saginaw, founded in 1954 as a local branch of a national community improvement organization, brought nationally recognized Black leaders as speakers and provided leadership for direct action against discrimination. In the 1950s and

1960s, the group organized mass sit-ins at restaurants that refused to serve Black patrons. Karen Betts-Browne recalled when groups in the early 1960s would gather at a selected white-owned restaurant on Genesee before their Tuesday Frontier Club meetings in an attempt to be served. She said that there were times they would sit well into the night with no service.

Housing remained a flashpoint through the decades. Between 1950 and 1960, the Black population almost doubled, from 8,608 to 16,550, while the city's population grew by just 5.8 percent. It should not be surprising that this population boom, combined with restricted housing for Black people, led to strife.

Lawyer Henry Marsh and his wife Ruth arrived in 1954. He became involved in clubs and organizations very quickly, including the Junior Chamber of Commerce, which was by invitation only. Marsh remained vocal about issues of discrimination in service industries and housing. Black people including Marsh were refused mortgages and bought homes on land contracts or had to have white friends make "straw" purchases for them.

The Michigan Civil Rights Commission, after a 1966 investigation, issued a scathing report on the state of housing in Saginaw and made recommendations that included a comprehensive ordinance prohibiting discrimination in housing. The city responded with its own Citizens' Advisory Committee, which sought ways forward through community conversations and nonbinding agreements. Rather than working with the city to craft such an ordinance, the Citizens' Advisory Committee, through the Chamber of Commerce, instead worked with the local Board of Realtors, consulting with the local NAACP branch, to craft a nondiscrimination policy. This could have had significant impact, because realtors played a part in limiting options for Black home buyers. The Chamber of Commerce downplayed the nonbinding nature of the policy.

People knew the city's housing crisis would certainly get worse, because the east and north sides of Saginaw would soon be irrevocably changed by a new interstate bypass that would cut through the heart of the Black community on the east side before crossing the river. The Michigan Civil Rights Commission argued that the interstate bypass project, known euphemistically as "urban renewal," would exacerbate housing problems. The people displaced by the project would have nowhere to go due to the housing shortage.

As a housing crisis percolated, Black people were making moves to break the color barrier of the city council: Harry Browne ran multiple unsuccessful campaigns through the 1950s until Henry Marsh finally succeeded in 1961. Marsh had cultivated a network of support from white business leaders through the Junior Chamber of Commerce and received more votes than any single candidate, which by custom should have made him mayor. Though the Black community was beyond ready for a political voice, Marsh did not think Saginaw was quite ready for a Black mayor, and he did not push for the custom. Four years later, Marsh was reelected, again with the most votes, and this time he did insist. However, the council selected James Stenglein by just one vote. Two years later, in 1967, Henry Marsh finally became the first Black mayor of Saginaw and one of the first Black mayors in the nation.

While Marsh maneuvered in political waters, Saginaw's Black population had run out of patience. In 1966, a group of disaffected Black young adults began United Power, an organization to address the issues facing the community. Early leaders of this group included Alfred Loveless and Arthur "Art" Smith. Art Smith wrote in the *Saginaw Afro-Herald* that the group's "main interest is black people—more specifically, grass-roots black people with no voice, no freedom, no means, less money and very little hope." The fledgling organization felt their elders were no longer taking enough direct action. United Power was not enamored with Henry Marsh, because they felt he was too willing to capitulate to the white community.

Just three months after Marsh was elected mayor, the city faced civil unrest. What began in June as a group of youth seeking better recreation facilities erupted into a full demonstration in July 1967. Young Black leaders, including Loveless, led protesters in a sit-down at the busy intersection of Washington and Genesee during rush hour, effectively grinding traffic to a halt. At a meeting with Marsh, they demanded an open housing ordinance, the elimination of slum housing, recognition of grassroots leaders, improved recreation, education, and work opportunities. The sit-in transformed into unrest, as splinter groups ran down streets, breaking windows and vandalizing the city. Fears of a massive riot, like that in Detroit, stoked panic. The police opened fire on a group gathered at a house on Lapeer and Sixth Streets, injuring several, none fatally. In response to the unrest, after the city calmed, Marsh appointed 220 members to a newly organized Committee of Concern to address the underlying issues in Saginaw.

Sit-in demonstration at the corner of Washington and Genesee, July 1967.

The committee worked to address housing, jobs, public accommodation, and schools, and it recommended an open housing ordinance.

While the protesters demonstrated and the subsequent Committee of Concern began its work, the federal government finalized its urban renewal project plan, the I-675 corridor. The bypass would bring traffic quickly in and out of the bustling city, and more importantly, it would also create a route around the Zilwaukee Bridge, a drawbridge that frequently brought cars to a standstill on I-75. Having another route would alleviate the interstate traffic and prevent traffic jams on busy weekends. The Department of Transportation never considered an alternate through Saginaw other than one that bisected the predominately Black community. By the time of the protests, no one had yet been displaced, but it was looming.

People from the impacted community spoke out at hearings, but it was clear the government and the city were determined to move forward. From the city's perspective, it was a cheaper way to get a needed bridge built across the Saginaw River. In these hearings, those who were going to be displaced and have their neighborhoods torn apart were left with few assurances. The main factor for the city's planning department was that there would be no loss of tax revenue, because the lack of options for the displaced people would cause them to remain in the area. The engineering report stated that construction would commence in 1967 or 1968.

I-675 cut through the northeast side of Saginaw before crossing the river and looping northward. It divided neighborhoods and school districts. It created a physical wall between sections of town. No longer could one look up the block from Genesee and Washington and see businesses along the corridor. It is now hard to see beyond the overpass.

City Council passed the open housing ordinance in 1968. The ordinance succeeded in expanding places where Black people could buy homes. However, the reaction of the white population was to simply move farther out to the townships west of Saginaw. The result is that Black people live in more places on both sides of the river than their early confinement to the northeast side, but Saginaw remains deeply segregated.

Deindustrialization affected Saginaw greatly. GM reduced its plants and sold off parts of its company. Jobs moved overseas. Eventually, Saginaw Malleable closed and Grey Iron shrunk, effectively abandoning the East Side. White people had already begun the process of moving further away from East Saginaw, once it officially desegregated, and were lured by the suburban sprawl to the north and west of the city. Industry and other amenities sprang up in these growing communities, and soon, in no small part due to the swiftly moving I-675, the townships grew in people and financial revenue. Meanwhile the city's resources dwindled, because many major businesses also left downtown Saginaw, abandoning the buildings and transforming long, bustling streets into quiet, empty pass-throughs. Some of the businesses closed. Others left for the greener pastures of the new Fashion Square Mall in fast-growing Saginaw Township.

The tax base went with them, and the revenues that once built East Saginaw into a city to be envied dried up. The city fell into disrepair, and abandoned buildings deteriorated to the point they could not be saved. The flagship Morley Building, which had graced the busy thoroughfare of Washington Avenue for so many decades, was razed in 1981.

Loss of job stability led to loss of social stability as well. As the city grappled with job and income loss, young residents turned to street gangs, and the east side of Saginaw faced territorial divisions and violence.

Manufacturing is no longer the top employment sector in Saginaw. Automotive jobs that once dominated the employment landscape still account for many jobs but far fewer than before. The city is working to revitalize the downtown region again and might be able to do so with a new medical "diamond." The healthcare industry has grown in recent years, becoming the top employment sector.

Today, when one stands at the intersection of Genesee and Washington, many edifices are still there. The Bancroft now houses luxury apartments. The (now Huntington) bank and the Eddy buildings still stand sentinel. Traffic zips through. While far too many storefronts remain empty, waiting for new owners to see their potential, signs of hope remain.

The Look for America Tour on STARS Route 7

The traveler in Paul Simon's famous song "America" starts out in Saginaw and "walked off to look for America." He hitchhiked for four days, boarded a Greyhound in Pittsburgh, and wound up counting the cars on the New Jersey Turnpike. But there is an easier way to find America. Just hop on and ride a STARS (Saginaw Transit Authority Regional Services) bus for an hour—you'll get oriented to the city's layout and meet people you wouldn't bump into any other way. Technology connects to things we choose, but what about all the people and things we never thought of? Riding the bus gives the world and other people a chance to choose us.

American cities up until the 1950s were rich in public transportation. Horse-drawn and electric trolleys took people around their city, while the interurban electric railroad ran hourly service to Bay City, Flint, and surrounding towns. Today there is just the bus, which many use to get to work, shop for food, and access social services.

Though you may not need to ride the bus, it can be a relief to leave the car. For a dollar a ride, you'll have an experience. As you take a seat, greet your fellow passengers. You may be a surprise to them. Saginaw residents don't think of their town as a tourist destination, but here you are.

This Route 7 tour begins and ends at the Rosa Parks Central Transfer Plaza in downtown Saginaw. On December 1, 1955, Rosa Parks was arrested for refusing to give up her seat for a white passenger on a Montgomery, Alabama, bus. That inspired the Montgomery bus boycott and helped energize America's civil rights movement.

Route 7 leaves the Plaza going west on Johnson Street. The large building on your right is the Dow Event Center, formerly the Saginaw Civic Center. On April 25, 1977, seven thousand eager fans packed Wendler Arena, the left part of the building, to see and hear Elvis Presley. Mail-in ticket payments had been received from another two thousand people that the arena could not hold. Elvis wanted to do something about that, so he returned to Saginaw on May 3. Just fifteen weeks after his second sold-out Saginaw appearance, Elvis died at his home, Graceland.

Next is the Temple Theater, a grand movie palace originally built for the Elf Khurafeh Shriners in 1927. The theater, restored to the peak of its glory, gives Saginaw a beautiful venue for live events and cinematic adventures. With an organ console that rises from beneath the floor, the Temple offers modern audiences a unique entertainment experience.

In the next block, on your right, is Huntington Bank. Built in 1925, it was Saginaw's tallest building for years. The magnificent first-floor banking hall is a must-see.

The Bancroft Hotel, at the corner of Washington and Genesee, is a six-story building that in 1916 replaced the original four-story hotel, built in 1859. President William Howard Taft stayed here when he visited Saginaw. Now it is Bancroft Luxury Apartments, with commercial space on the first floor. The red brick Lee Commons, built in 1888, was the home of lumber baron Charles Lee, next door to his sawmill. Since 2011, the city has worked with dedicated citizens to clean it up and raise funds for its restoration, saving it from demolition. Today, it is a public space for microbusinesses, nonprofits, workshops, and meetings. The vision for Lee Commons is to be a front door to Saginaw, welcoming visitors to the city's riverfront. The home's last resident is remembered for keeping a pet leopard.

Just past the main Post Office is Saginaw's City Hall, built in 1937 on the same site where its predecessor was erected after competing cities on opposite riverbanks merged in 1889.

Shortly after City Hall, note the red-brick Holy Family Church. A replica of Michelangelo's famous statue, the *Pietà*, is next to the church, offering a spot for quiet contemplation. The parish was founded in 1893, and this building was begun in 1916. It survived the recent wave of church closings and consolidations and is one of fifty-six parishes in the Diocese of Saginaw.

The bus passes through an area of the city called the Grove; the land along South Washington for a half mile south of city hall was divided into large lots during the 1860s. Wealthy Saginaw families built elegant homes on many of these lots. Over the years, homes in the Grove have been converted to commercial or office uses. The Montague Inn (1581 S. Washington Ave.), an elegant seventeen-room bed and breakfast with banquet facilities, is a Georgian Revival house originally built for Robert and Edwina Montague between 1929 and 1933.

After the bus turns on Ezra Rust Drive, look to the right for the Japanese Tea House (527 Rust) and Cultural Center, a gift to Saginaw from its sister city,

Tokushima, Japan. Construction here began with a lovely Japanese garden, opened in 1971, followed by "one of the most authentic tea houses in North America." The garden's Zen aesthetic depends on a careful arrangement of elements, so that each separate thing stands alone but in friendly relationship with the other elements. The garden, like Saginaw itself, is a constellation of things partially hidden or tucked away, waiting for contemplative visitors.

To the left, across from the Tea House, note Saginaw's Waterworks Building, a Neo-Gothic showpiece of art and engineering, completed in 1929. Daily, this facility treats millions of gallons of water, piped sixty miles from Lake Huron's Whitestone Point, serving many Saginaw County communities. The foyer includes paintings by Saginaw artist William John Von Schipmann, one depicting the 1819 Treaty of Saginaw, the other Green Point. The artist included the ruined cabin of Gabriel Lajeunesse, the beloved Acadian sought by Evangeline, heroine of Longfellow's famous epic poem, published in 1847: "Far to the north . . . in the Michigan forests, Gabriel had his lodge by the banks of the Saginaw River . . . When over weary ways . . . she had attained . . . the depths of the Michigan forests, found she the hunter's lodge deserted and fallen to ruin!"

Past the Waterworks, you can see Lake Linton on the right, and Ojibway Island beyond the lake. The island was once just a high spot in a marsh. However, dredging Lake Linton provided material to build it up. Ojibway Island is a popular park and the launch site for Saginaw's Fourth of July fireworks. An outdoor stage hosts concerts during the summer. The 1819 treaty reserved 640 acres along the Saginaw River, including Ojibway Island, for James Riley, son of a translator for the treaty negotiations.

The bus turns left onto Fordney Street. Watch for a playground made of crayons. Behind Crayola Park, it looks like a giant kid had some fun with the big crayons, coloring the silos on the opposite bank of the river. This is "Shine, Bright Saginaw," the second-largest mural in the United States, with over 1.6 acres of painted surface, covering the old bean elevator. Completed in June 2024, it is the biggest work ever painted by Spanish muralist Okuda San Miguel, working with a team of Saginaw artists.

After Crayola Park, look on the left for a two-story white house—the Cushway House. Built in 1844 by Benjamin and Adelaide Cushway (Cauchois) inside the remains of Fort Saginaw on the west side of the river, it is Saginaw's oldest surviving structure. The Cushways came to Saginaw in 1833, when Benjamin was named blacksmith for the Ojibwe, as provided by the 1819 treaty. The house has been moved twice, once in 1869 to the corner of Fayette and Perry Streets, and again in 2001, across the river to its present site.

On the right side of the bus, look for the Saginaw YMCA. In the mid-1960s, the Y's gym was the Saturday night venue for the "Y-A-Go-Go" dances, organized by Saginaw radio disk jockeys Bob Dyer and Dick Fabian. In the fall of 1965, they booked a little-known duo called Simon and Garfunkel for a February 1966 gig. Shortly after the booking, Simon and Garfunkel's "Sound of Silence" rocketed to number one on the Billboard charts. Years later, Dyer recalled a phone call with Simon: "I asked Paul Simon if they were still charging the $1,250 we paid them to play, and he said they were getting about four times that much—then. When asked why he hadn't pulled out, he said he had to see what a city named Saginaw looked like." Apparently, he liked it; he wrote "America" while he was here.

In 2010, "America" lyrics appeared on vacant buildings and out-of-the-way places all over the city, the work of Saginaw artist Eric Schantz, who had returned after moving away. He said, "'America' had become a homesick song for Saginawians. People left to go find their America, to pursue their American dream. And when they left, they never really came back, 'cause there wasn't really much to come back to."

After passing the Y and crossing Rust Street, look to the right to see the Saginaw River. You may see people fishing from the riverbanks, from small boats, or through the ice in the wintertime. These may not be the "Saginaw fishermen" Lefty Frizzell sang about in his 1964 hit "Saginaw, Michigan," but they enjoy the benefits of years of work and millions of dollars invested to clean up the waters of the Saginaw. The recovery of fish, like perch and walleye, brings people from all over the Midwest to fish in the Saginaw River, even here in the city.

A half mile from the YMCA, Fordney Street ends, and the bus makes several turns on streets that were part of the former village of Salina. That name highlighted the discovery of salt brine far below the ground here. Wells were drilled and enterprising sawmill owners used bark and wood waste from lumber production to boil off water from the brine producing salt. By 1880, much of the salt sold in the United States came from Saginaw Valley sawmills, making them very profitable.

A few blocks after turning on Washington, look left into Forest Lawn Cemetery for a one-story yellow brick building with a green tile roof. In 1881, the City of East Saginaw bought ninety-seven acres to begin Forest Lawn, because Brady Hill, the oldest cemetery, was running out of space. After the 1889 merger of East Saginaw and Saginaw City, the City of Saginaw built this structure as the office for Forest Lawn and a trolley station for the Washington Avenue streetcar line, a forerunner of today's STARS Route 7.

Just past Forest Lawn, Washington splits. The bus passes Countryview Townhomes and weaves its way through mixed-race, working-class neighborhoods, making its last outbound stop at Bridgton Place. You might have noticed residential density pick up as we got further south. People who wanted newer housing moved south from East Saginaw, some to multifamily housing projects.

As the bus rumbles back toward the city, it's worth noting that this part of Washington Road is reputed to follow the Saginaw Trail that brought Tocqueville and Beaumont to Saginaw in 1831.

Returning to Salina, we see late-nineteenth-century houses and the Kosciusko Club. This was formerly a Polish neighborhood, and many residents worked at Hausbeck Pickles and Peppers, now in the white factory-warehouse on Hess Avenue. It's been in business for one hundred years and is going strong as a supplier of pickles to chains like Burger King and Subway. Die-hard pickle fans can still buy their pickles at Jack's Fruit Markets in Saginaw and Bay City.

The bus returns to Washington Avenue. Farther along, you can see the Children's Zoo (1730 South Washington) and the adjoining Hoyt Park, given to East Saginaw by New York lumberman Jesse Hoyt. From 1892 to 2000, the lower area of Hoyt Park was flooded each winter, and Saginaw boasted one of America's largest ice rinks. That fell victim to twenty-first-century budget cuts, but skating has been revived, thanks to volunteers.

Saginaw's oldest "surviving" gas station sits alone next to a big grassy space. Muralist Eric Schantz painted it as a preservation strategy: If it's public art, people won't mind it there. Nearby vacant spaces and new medical buildings are on land that was the site of the Mitts and Merrill foundry and machine shop.

St. Mary's Hospital began in 1874 when four nuns arrived in response to a request from the priest at St. Mary's Church. Many of their early patients were lumber workers who bought health insurance from the hospital for $5 per year. St. Mary's is also notable for being the birthplace of Stevland Hardaway Judkins, born here on May 13, 1950, better known as Stevie Wonder.

As the Route 7 bus returns to the Rosa Parks Transfer Plaza and as you look back on all you've seen through the bus windows and heard from your fellow passengers, ask yourself: Does "Michigan seem like a dream to [you] now?" When you get some time, listen again to Paul Simon's "America," and consider what it was about Saginaw that inspired that song. Although time, trade, and technology have been rough on this factory town, Saginawians still go to work every day, say their prayers, sing their songs, and strive to build a better world. Buses are an important part of the social infrastructure—which refers to all the people, places, and institutions that foster cohesion and support. Ride them any chance you get in every city you visit that has public transportation.

The Theodore Roethke Home Museum

The Theodore Roethke Home Museum (1805 Gratiot Ave.) is the birthplace of Theodore "Ted" Roethke (1908–1963), a Pulitzer Prize–winning poet considered by many critics to be one of the greatest poets of the twentieth century. Roethke's boyhood home stayed in the family, belonging first to his father, then his mother, and then his sister, June, an English teacher in the Saginaw Public Schools. The more regal fieldstone house next to it was owned by Roethke's uncle. When the properties became available, they were purchased by the Friends of Theodore Roethke Foundation, which subsequently turned the home into a museum and hope to host visiting writers and provide outreach for community literacy and mental health.

During Roethke's youth, his father Otto and uncle owned a thriving greenhouse business started by his grandfather Wilhelm, who had been forester to the German Chancellor Otto von Bismarck before immigrating in 1873. At that time, property in the Tittabawassee floodplain was cheap, and Wilhelm bought a lot of it. At its height, the firm had twenty-five acres of greenhouses within the city limits, three retail outlets, fields for growing oats to feed the delivery horses, and a small game preserve where Otto experimented with raising pheasants and partridges. Ted pulled weeds, gathered moss, and delivered flowers.

Although the home and property were dear to the poet, Roethke's childhood was not without hardship. His poetry suggests that his father was a complicated man, driven by his work in the greenhouses and unable to get over a quarrel with his brother Charles over company finances. Stubborn men, they continued to run the business but otherwise refused to communicate.

When Theodore was a young teen, his father was diagnosed with terminal cancer. The man withered, was soon bedridden, and spent his last days on a second-floor screened-in porch (forever after one of Roethke's favorite writing spots), writhing in a pain that morphine could no longer ease. The same year his father died, Uncle Charles killed himself, and these losses forced Theodore to grow up very quickly.

Although Roethke went to the University of Michigan, where he earned bachelor's and master's degrees in English, and eventually Harvard for further graduate studies in English, he would remain connected to Saginaw. The home at 1805 Gratiot Avenue was a haven when struggles with mental illness forced him to return; and his mother was an anchor that enabled his writing.

Roethke's first book of poems, *Open House*, came out in 1941, and while the book was well received, a number of critics noted that the poems, though technically proficient, were too reliant on the work of other poets. To make poems that were more his own, he went home to Saginaw in 1946, with Guggenheim Fellowship money, to the physical house as well as the scraggly mucky landscapes filled with low lives—"The small! The small!"—that he heard "singing clear." Roethke began to experiment with poems that were more sensuous in nature and less overtly intellectual. To write these poems, he drew on memories associated with his father's greenhouse world. On a BBC broadcast in July 1953, Roethke recalled: "As a child, I had several worlds to live in, which I felt were mine. One favorite place was a swampy corner of the game sanctuary where herons always nested." Another was a far field, of about twenty-two acres, fronted with poplars where oats were also grown for the draft horses. Roethke's biographer Allan Seager notes that the word "field" occurs as often as any noun in Roethke's work and runs through his work as a symbol of eternity and even perhaps the blank page.

While on his fellowship, Roethke wrote the bulk of the poems that would become his groundbreaking second book, *The Lost Son and Other Poems* (1948). The book included a section referred to as the "greenhouse poems," in which he explored the images, sounds, and odors of his youth, including a summer job working at Dailey's Pickles. Critic Ian Hamilton called Roethke's greenhouse poems "among the best things he wrote." Michael Harrington argued that Roethke truly found his own voice and central themes in *The Lost Son*, and one could argue that Roethke's blossoming was predicated by his return to Saginaw. Memories of his youth would be a taproot for Roethke for the rest of his life.

Roethke returned to the house numerous times throughout his life, almost always with the intention of doing more writing. His final, posthumous return to Saginaw would come after a fatal heart attack at the age of fifty-five. His ashes were interred at Saginaw's Oakwood Cemetery. Cemeteries were a familiar place to Roethke, a florist's son. As a boy, he delivered many bouquets to funerals, learning early that death is part of life. But the traumatic losses of uncle and father in adolescence left him reeling and longing for the godlike gardener who could "fan life into wilted sweet-peas with his hat, / Or stand all night watering roses, his feet blue in rubber boots." Only the seasonal cycle could calm the terror of that early brush with death: In one poem he compares the winter light passing over the surviving bones and dry seed-crowns to the way his own inspiration surveys and illuminates.

It would be easy to drive past 1805 Gratiot and not give much thought to it. It's in a part of Saginaw where many houses of a similar size stand along the road. However, this home has a history one can feel, the same history and echoes that Roethke was seeking when he returned. Should you call to get a tour, you will see that they have Roethke's actual childhood bed, the one he stands on in his poem "Otto" to overlook his father's "fields of glass." Take a moment and wander the grounds that the Friends of Theodore Roethke Foundation has so generously preserved. Close your eyes and imagine the greenhouses teeming with life. Listen for Otto making his late-night winter journeys from the house to the greenhouse's boiler, which needed to be attended throughout the winter to protect the flowers from the cold. If you're quiet, you might hear the scratch of Roethke's pen against paper, as he works diligently on another poem sprung slowly from Saginaw's fertile ground.

Points of Interest

Saginaw Art Museum (1126 N. Michigan Ave.), operating since 1947, houses a respectable permanent collection of European and American painting, watercolors, and sculpture, and features special exhibits that address community diversity and the natural world.

The Saginaw Song

Theodore Roethke

In Saginaw, in Saginaw,
The wind blows up your feet,
When the ladies' guild puts on a feed,
There's beans on every plate,
And if you eat more than you should,
Destruction is complete.

Out Hemlock Way there is a stream
That some have called Swan Creek;
The turtles have bloodsucker sores,
And mossy filthy feet;
The bottoms of migrating ducks
Come off it much less neat.

In Saginaw, in Saginaw,
Bartenders think no ill;
But they've ways of indicating when
You are not acting well:
They throw you through the front plate glass
And then send you the bill.

The Morleys and the Burrows are
The aristocracy;
A likely thing for they're no worse
Than the likes of you or me,—
A picture window's one you can't
Raise up when you would pee.

In Shaginaw, in Shaginaw
I went to Shunday Shule;
The only thing I ever learned
Was called the Golden Rhule,—
But that's enough for any man
What's not a proper fool.

I took the pledge cards on my bike;
I helped out with the books;
The stingy members when they signed
Made with their stingy looks,—
The largest contributors came
From the town's biggest crooks.

In Saginaw, in Saginaw,
There's never a household fart,
For if it did occur,
It would blow the place apart,—
I met a woman who could break wind
And she is my sweet-heart.

O, I'm the genius of the world,—
Of that you can be sure,
But alas, alack, and me achin' back,
I'm often a drunken boor;
But when I die—and that won't be soon—
I'll sing with dear Tom Moore,
With that lovely man, Tom Moore.

Coda:
My father never used a stick,
He slapped me with his hand;
He was a Prussian through and through
And knew how to command;
I ran behind him every day
He walked our greenhouse land.

I saw a figure in a cloud,
A child upon her breast,
And it was O, my mother O,
And she was half-undressed,
All women, O, are beautiful
When they are half-undressed.

Schuch Hotel (301 N. Hamilton) formerly a tavern, was established in 1863; it is now vacant.

Saginaw Valley Railway Museum (900 Maple St.) is a teaching institution for railroad history and technology housed in the Pere Marquette Railway depot, restored in 1907.

Backwater Burbs

The satellite towns around Saginaw—Zilwaukee, Bridgeport, and St. Charles—sit on "100-year" floodplains, meaning that there is a 30 percent chance of flooding over the life of a thirty-year mortgage. Major floods occurred in 1986, when the Saginaw River rose over its sandbagged walls, and in 2020, when the upper Tittabawassee broke through two dams and flooded the entire county. Even in years with average precipitation, swollen tributaries overflow into already rain-soaked flatlands, turning yards into lakes.

Zilwaukee (pop. 1,521) is a town overshadowed by the bridge that stole its name but worth visiting for the atmosphere and ancient watering hole, the Expressway Bar. There is also a bait shop, fishing pavilion, boat launch as well as aggregate and cement yards with regular barge traffic.

Smitten with the loveliness of the wet prairie's bluejoint grass and wildflower bedecked banks, Daniel Fitzhugh bought land on both sides of the river in 1835. Settlement and development did not begin, however, until two brothers, Daniel and Solomon Johnson, Quakers from Orange County, New York, came to the valley in 1847. They didn't have excess capital but had big plans for a river town they imagined as the terminus for Saginaw River trade, since they thought the sandbar at Carrollton would prevent larger lake vessels from passing further upriver. They named the settlement Zilwaukie (Zilwaukee) to lure prospective German settlers and encourage them to envision it as a new Milwaukee.

The Johnson brothers built a sawmill and used it to cut Cass River "cork" pine into planks for a road to Saginaw City, five miles away. Then they built a wharf and a warehouse to encourage ship traffic; the brothers even projected a bank and printed currency that was never used. By 1858, they were bankrupt, unable to compete with the money Jesse Hoyt was pouring into the development of East Saginaw.

The township had five settlements that grew up around sawmills and salt works, including Wellington Burt's company town of Melbourne. But Zilwaukee was the only one of the five to endure. In 1923, Consumers Power built a steam-generating power plant north of the village and added an enormous coal-burning steam turbine plant four years later that would be the industrial mainstay of the community for many years.

The four-lane bascule drawbridge, which opened in 1960, proved inadequate to handle increases in vehicle traffic and shipping. The bridge had to be opened multiple times a day, resulting in massive traffic backups, especially in summer. Many solutions were proposed, including a tunnel under the river, but, after the dust settled, a bridge—concrete, not steel—was deemed the best and cheapest option. The new Zilwaukee Bridge, completed in December 1987, consists of two bridges side by side and is one-and-a-half miles long, with a 125-foot clearance over the shipping canal. It continues to mark for many Michiganders the location where "up north" begins.

Though obviously convenient for drivers, it is less clear that the Zilwaukee Bridge has been good for the economic health of communities in the Saginaw Valley. If the design had given drivers a glimpse of the tantalizing Crow Island marshes, that alone would have drawn visitors. As it is, the concrete walls act as blinders. There is a tiny sign on the northbound approach that points toward Zilwaukee, but few take the suggestion. Motorists speed up and over the marshy ecotones where worlds meet and mesh. For a view of the marshes, drive along Westervelt or bike the 6.2-mile Bay-Zil Rail Trail. There is parking at the north end of it on Hotchkiss Road and it begins just north of Koch Road in Zilwaukee.

Bridgeport (township pop. 9,949) is an unincorporated village on the Cass River in Bridgeport Charter Township, first platted in 1836. Most visitors see it as a group of franchises and motels on Dixie Highway off I-75. The focal point of the old village center is the State Street Historic Bridge, where the Cass makes a sharp bend. The town's original name was Cass Bend, until Lilly Cook built a wooden floating bridge and pronounced it "Bridgeport." Until 2002, the current iron bridge, built in 1906, was the only bridge over the Cass in the vicinity. It was limited to pedestrians in 1958 and afterwards thought of as just something from the old days. But, as one of only six surviving multi-span through-truss highway bridges left in the state, townspeople worked to restore it and make it the centerpiece of the Cass River Trailhead Park. An old gas station where Dixie Highway curved with the river, closed for forty years but still standing, was also restored for use as a restroom facility at the trailhead. The nearby Cass River Park and canoe launch adds to the feel of a rewilding river corridor. The Bridgeport Historical Village Museum (6190 Dixie Highway), south of the park, includes the Bridgeport Town Hall (1896) and the Greek Revival Hannay House (1853). The museum has an interesting collection of Paleo-Indian artifacts collected from the area and tools and other artifacts from a community that had four brickyards.

Past and present sit next to each other in Bridgeport (as they do in nearby Birch Run). Without the old stuff, the town would be like any other place in America—an aneurysm on a main artery. What is needed is a sign that reads "Welcome to Bridgeport: Gateway to the Shiawassee National Wildlife Refuge." That might give drivers headed up north a reason to take a short detour.

St. Charles (pop. 2,054) is a village southwest of Saginaw. Today, most residents commute to Saginaw or Midland for work, but in the past, the town boomed as a center for lumber and coal. It boasts a small but distinctive downtown, with an old hotel and church. St. Charles was incorporated in 1853 and for several decades was home to lumber, lath, and shingle mills. In 1896, nearby coal deposits were discovered, and for forty years, the two mines brought prosperity to the community. St. Charles advertises itself as the "Gateway to the Shiawassee Flats," as duck hunters who flock to the nearby Shiawassee River State Game Area bring business to the town. The St. Charles Historical Museum has exhibits on the area's lumbering and coal mining. The Bad River runs through town, providing a pleasant backdrop for the rail trail that runs to Saginaw. Ringwood Forest (Ring Rd.) is one of the earliest forest plantations in Michigan, established in 1883 by William Lee Ring, whose father lumbered the area in the 1860s. Trails along the South Branch of the Bad River and an alley of spruce trees are highlights. Given to the University of Michigan in 1930, it is now part of Saginaw County Parks.

Chesaning (pop. 2,456) is a city on M-57, south of St. Charles, on the Shiawassee River. It retains its Algonquian name (*kichesening*, "big rock") as two large limestone rocks, left behind as retreating glaciers moved north, formed landmarks here. In the 1830s and earlier, it was the seasonal residence of an Ojibwe band. At the time of the Treaty of Saginaw, Nau-qua-chic-a-ming, later chief of the Cheboyganing Band, was a young father with two children living with this band. The first white settlers came here in 1841, and a sawmill was built the following year. The town grew as the center of a fertile agricultural region with a large gristmill. In the twentieth century, the major employers were a drain tile company, a meat packer, and the Roycraft Coach Company that manufactured trailers from 1936 into the 1950s. Several large houses grace the main street that date from the lumber era. Today, the main growth industry is marijuana, with outdoor farms and several retail stores in town.

Chesaning was the first community in our region to use its riverfront as a tourist attraction. From 1937 to 2013, the community organized the Chesaning Showboat—a float made to look like a Mississippi riverboat. Entertainment in the early years followed a minstrel show format, with local singers, dancers, comedians, and a chorus. After the war, Chesaning commanded bigger names; Jerry Van Dyke, Pat Boone, Phyllis Diller, Jim Nabors, Lawrence Welk Show stars, the Beach Boys, Marie Osmond, and Crystal Gayle appeared in the 1970s and 1980s. By 1988, spectators were calling out minstrel show routines and ethnic jokes as offensive. To draw audiences in the new millennium, the town tried and failed to reimagine Showboat as a music festival. Seniors who came on buses were irritated with all the young people who took their music standing up and blocked the view. Fashions change, and Showboat ended, but while it lasted, it was a signature community project. The Saginaw County Fair (11350 Peet Rd.), held annually since 1914, moved here in 2002 after the fairgrounds in Saginaw closed. The Chesaning Area Historical Museum (602 W. Broad St.) is a community-closet-type museum with photo albums from the Showboat era.

Since the 1960s, suburban growth from Saginaw has occurred mainly to the west and northwest, especially in Saginaw Township, in addition to the area created by the colleges. The Tri-Cities identity (for Saginaw, Bay City, and Midland) was even more firmly established when Delta College and Saginaw Valley State University (SVSU) were created in the early 1960s. Both campuses were located on former farmland, that of Delta College off Mackinaw Road, between Delta and Hotchkiss Road, in Frankenlust Township (Bay County), and that of SVSU off Bay Road, between Pierce and Freeland Roads, in Kochville Township (Saginaw County), with a new post office, University Center, created for both. Leland I. Doan, Dow Chemical's president and son-in-law of the company's founder, provided the impetus, beginning in 1955, for the school's establishment. Bay City Junior College, which was founded in 1920, became Delta College in 1961. Saginaw Valley College began as a private liberal arts college in 1963, then became a state school in 1965, and Saginaw Valley State University in 1987. Delta College also offers classes at its facilities in downtown Bay City, with a bright-orange planetarium (100 Center Ave.), Saginaw, and Midland. SVSU's campus includes the Marshall M. Fredericks Sculpture Museum, containing over two hundred models of the late Birmingham sculptor's monumental works.

Along the Tittabawassee River's right bank runs Midland Road, which goes by Freeland (pop. 7,630), an inauspicious town in an agricultural area merging with suburbia. On the northeastern side of the road, just southeast of Family Baptist Church, is an abandoned cemetery with a few marble stones standing and others under the grass, in need of attention. Buried here are pioneers who settled here as early as 1835, like members of the Braley family, who came with a wagon from western Massachusetts, bringing the first wagon and plow to the area. Also are members of the McCarty and Hackett families, who came from Ireland. The burial ground is a graveyard restoration waiting to happen, to preserve traces of history in the landscape.

BAY CITY

Profile

Bay City (pop. 32,661), lying three miles upstream from the point where the Saginaw River enters Saginaw Bay, was once dotted with seasonal Ojibwe settlements concentrated on the west bank of the Saginaw River and along the nearby Kawkawlin River, between undisturbed mounds of an earlier people. Settlers mistook these mounds for natural elevations, and when they dug into them for a brewery foundation, they discovered copper and silver artifacts. By that time, Bay City was a booming lumber town with thirty-three sawmills and piles of lumber on each side of the river, ready to be loaded onto ships, to build other cities. Mill hands, shanty boys, and dockwollopers packed into Water Street saloons, until a denuded valley silenced the saws, and the days of using sawdust as fuel to heat up the boiling kettles of brine ended. People hunkered down in their enclaves until those who had money reinvested it into other industries: coal, boats, railroad cranes, kit houses, and sugar beets—the first agricultural industry in the valley.

Bay City today is reimagining itself as a livable small city. More racially homogeneous than Saginaw or Flint, Bay City's urban center is stable, frequented by tourists in the summer months, as are the unblighted neighborhoods on both the east and west banks. The river cuts through the center of the city and is its focal attraction. Its banks and middle grounds have paths for walking and biking, and the downstream Crow Island marshes are a paradise for fishermen and paddlers. Boats fill the river in the summer and colorful shanties dot the frozen river in winter. Bridge tenders man stations on the four bascule drawbridges, lifting the metal leaves so that freighters can pass under them, carrying limestone, iron ore pellets, coal, and agricultural fertilizers to Zilwaukee and Carrollton. Commercial traffic has declined since the high-water mark in 2000, when there were four hundred annual passages of lake boats.

There are traces of the lumber era in the historic downtown blocks on both sides that date from the 1870s and 1880s, with prominent stone churches and public buildings on the east and old warehouses with a Gothic Revival library on the west. Walk or drive down Center Avenue for a jaw-dropping look at the monumental and curiously ornamented mansions built by lumber barons and their families.

Bay City Hall. BAY COUNTY HISTORICAL SOCIETY.

The Polish neighborhood in the South End may not be as lively as it once was, but it still boasts churches, restaurants, bars, and a Polish League of American Veterans hall. Euclid and Wilder Roads in West Bay City have the predictable franchises without suburban overdevelopment, but there are surprises, like the Saginaw River Marine Historical Society (4101 Wilder Rd.), housed in the former Bay City Mall. The museum collects artifacts, art, and ephemera related to the Saginaw Bay with an emphasis on the 650-plus vessels built in the area.

River mouths are places of much activity, and Bay City's location has always made it attractive. The Indigenous people relied on surrounding marshlands to provide fish and game as well as wild rice, and they built wigwams on the elevated pine and oak groves on the west bank. When Detroit French came to the region, they, too, built homes close to the river (hence the sobriquet "Muskrat" French), and lived by trapping, fishing, and acting as liaisons between the Native people and fur traders. Muskrat was served as a Lenten delicacy in Michigan river towns from Downriver Detroit to Monroe and in Bay City, Linwood, and Pinconning. The last establishment to dish up that delicacy in Bay City was the Green Hut on Columbus Avenue, advertising muskrat on Friday nights through 1962.

History

A Detroit Frenchmen, Leon Trombley, came north on the Saginaw Trail through miles of wet prairie in 1831 to work as an agricultural land agent and, as the Treaty of Saginaw provided, to teach the Indigenous people to farm. Considered to be the first settler, he built a log cabin on the east bank of the river, near the foot of modern-day Fourth Street, that was replaced eventually by a Greek Revival house. The Trombley House was restored and moved in 1981 by barge to its current site near the south entrance to Veteran's Memorial Park (901 John F. Kennedy Dr.). Trombley quickly realized that Indians did not want to farm, as they would gather furs but ignore the potato crop. He returned to Detroit in 1835, two years before the smallpox outbreak devastated the Native population, causing the survivors to sell their reserved lands on the west bank. Settlers like Albert Miller registered this loss in the passing of landmarks like the Lone Tree, isolated in prairie along the river between Portsmouth and Bay City, which was the constant perch of a white owl. This tree marked the burial place of Ke-wah-ke-won, a chief who promised on his death bed that the Great Spirit would watch over his people. Floods of 1838 killed the tree, but the white owl still kept its vigil until William McCormick shot it on a hunting expedition in 1842.

James Fraser, a Scotsman who recruited other countrymen and capitalists, was one of the first to see the potential of the lumber industry here. Fraser built sawmills at Kawkawlin (1844), at the foot of Sixth Street (1845), and on McKinley Street (1847). Fraser convinced James G. Birney (1792–1857)—a nationally known abolitionist, former Kentucky slaveowner, and presidential candidate of the Liberty Party in 1840 and 1844—to move to Bay City. With James Fitzhugh, a New York financier, the three men reorganized the Lower Saginaw Land Company (1842) and led the effort to turn a village into the metropolis of the North. Birney, the spiritual leader of the community, lent books to neighbors, championed the causes of temperance and Indigenous rights, and led the first Presbyterian congregation in the city. Although he retired to the East Coast in 1855, his son, James G. Birney Jr., arrived in town the

Sage and McGraw's "monster" sawmill, Bay City, 1880s. BAY COUNTY HISTORICAL SOCIETY.

following year and had a hand in changing the name of Lower Saginaw to Bay City, which incorporated in 1859, joining the separate villages of Portsmouth and Lower Saginaw.

Significant population growth on the west side of the river began in 1863, when Henry W. Sage, with his business partner John McGraw, built a sawmill and a town on a tract of 116 acres on the west side of the river, around Midland Street. Sage, living in Brooklyn, had amassed a small fortune from his freight yard near Ithaca, New York (with access to the Erie Canal), and a mill and lumber yard in Albany, New York. He had been buying pine lands throughout Michigan since his first visit to the Saginaw Valley in 1847, so when he and partner McGraw built what was reputed to be the largest sawmill in the world, he had plenty of timber land from which to draw. The mill at peak production in 1870 cut over thirty-four million linear feet of lumber. Sage and McGraw's town, initially called Lake City but later renamed Wenona (after the mother in Henry Wadsworth Longfellow's *The Song of Hiawatha*), had a store, a warehouse, a brick office building, a boarding house, tenement apartment, and twenty-three individual dwellings. Within four years, Wenona was a promising city of 1,200 residents. Sage opposed public improvements, such as sewers, and funded the campaigns of political candidates who would protect his interests.

The only vestige of Sage's company town is the sawmill office, a rather severe vernacular building (now a private residence at 214 S. Arbor St.) that once dominated the shacks and cottages of Beutel Row, named for the old cannery. Sage's 1884 gift to the people of the city is more accessible: The cost of the Sage Library (100 E. Midland St.) is engraved on its cornerstone to publicize the lumber baron's benevolence. Rumor had it, however, that 25 cents was deducted from the pay of every mill worker to offset the cost of the gift. The library, designed by Cornell University's first architecture professor, is a monumental structure that mixes the styles of French Château with Ruskin Gothic. A niche in the front of the building houses a statue of the Lady of Learning, missing an arm (a weird reminder of the hazards of mill work), and on the lawn is a cast-iron fountain, depicting the rape of Leda by a god who took the form of a swan.

Ethnic Groups

The lumber boom attracted migrants. Besides numerous Anglo-Canadians and Americans, Bay City's ethnic groups included French Canadians, Germans, Irish, British, Poles, and Swedes. The French Canadians settled in Dolsenville, or "Frenchtown," as it came to be known, near the eastern side of the river mouth around Woodside Avenue and the Banks area across the river. St. Joseph's Catholic Church remained French-speaking until the 1920s. Once the mills closed, the French turned to fishing for work. Many German immigrants from the Frankenlust area southwest of the city were employed in the salt works at Salzburg, on the west side; but in Bay City itself, there was a lively German community with Catholic and Lutheran churches, singing societies, and a newspaper. Poles settled on the south side after 1870. They organized two Catholic churches and had a newspaper, *Polski Sztandar*.

After the Civil War, Black people began to move from Canada into the United States; in 1870 Bay City had a community of about fifty. Cornelius Edwoods (1860–1952) was a well-known citizen and respected printer of *The Bay City Tribune*. Virginia-born James Baker, a barber, collaborated with brothers Henry and William Susand from Berlin, Ontario, on a patent to improve a sawmill dog, a device for holding lumber while it was being cut; his son, Oscar W. Baker (1879–1952), became a prominent lawyer, despite an accident that resulted in the amputation of his lower left leg. Baker was the president of the Freedman's Progress Commission, which in 1915 organized an exhibition in Chicago and compiled the *Michigan Manual of Freedmen's Progress*, seeking to change public perception of Black men and women by celebrating their many accomplishments during the previous fifty years of freedom. The community grew during the mid-twentieth century, beginning in the 1940s, with spurts in the 1960s and 1990s. Today, the population remains around 3 percent, with an additional 2 percent listed in the census as mixed race.

Bay City's Jews (the second-largest community in Michigan after Detroit) arrived from Germany, Poland, and Russia during the 1870s, settled on the east side of the river along Twelfth Street (now Columbus Avenue) and started out as peddlers, first by pack and later by horse and wagon, bringing produce and construction supplies to lumber camps and rural areas around the Thumb in exchange for scrap, which they sold in Bay City salvage yards. Two synagogues opened in the 1880s, and the building that housed the Temple of Abraham Synagogue (corner of Jackson and Tenth Sts.), founded in 1914, still stands.

The German and Flemish population in Bay City may also account for the popularity of raising and racing homing pigeons. Both Bay City and Saginaw had "homing clubs" that were established in the 1930s and began to hold races within Michigan but also as far away as Indiana. Michael Glynn, a member of the Bay City Pigeon Fanciers Club, reports that when he was growing up there was a loft "on every block" in Bay City but hardly any pigeon people in Midland, where he was born. The Germans and Poles "raised and showed, raced, flew rollers and tipplers and raised them for food." Other nationalities—Irish and Russian—were known to keep and raise them, but it was an especially strong way to express cultural solidarity among Flemish, Germans, and Poles.

Labor Struggles

Bay City was the center of popular agitation for workers' rights in the "Ten Hours or No Sawdust" strike of 1885. The strike began on July 9, when workers left the mills, after learning that their pay was being cut without a reduction in work hours. They wanted a ten-hour day at an eleven-hour pay rate. Governor Russell A. Alger, who had lumber interests in Saginaw, sent in the state militia to regain control, but a reporter for the *Detroit Free Press* wrote on July 16 that troops were unnecessary, describing the holiday ambience pervading Bay City, calling it a "knapsack picnic." The strike brass band serenaded crowds at the armory, and there was a dress parade on Center Avenue attended by five thousand people.

Poles and Germans were the backbone of the strike, which effectively unified workers across ethnic lines. Daniel C. Blinn, editor of Bay City's *Labor Vindicator* and a member of the Knights of Labor, rejected the mill owners' desire to deal with workers as individuals and came very close to viewing the labor dispute as a problem of class: "Let the millmen feed their own horses; let their wives cook their own meals. . . . Let all persons who labor quit and see how they can get along without labor." The Knights of Labor (the largest and most important labor union in nineteenth-century America) enjoyed success, with three thousand of Bay City's seven thousand mill hands as members, organized into fifteen local assemblies, including a "Black" assembly. The Knights provided relief for strikers' families, offered to mediate with the mill owners, supported the festivities when the strikers walked, and took barges to Saginaw to join forces with the striking "dockwollopers" (longshoremen).

Although many elected officials supported the organization, the might of the lumber machine proved to be too much, forcing laborers to go back to work with a cut in pay. Nevertheless, the strike was significant, because the local community had stood with labor against exploitation by the lumber barons. Today, a historical marker in Wenona Park provides details about the strike.

Paul Bunyan

Working men continued to find camaraderie and solidarity in the bars and brothels of the Hell's Half Mile red-light district on Water Street. Every May, after lumber harvesting season was over and the logs were safely sorted into holding booms, the lumberjacks, or "shanty boys," as they were called, with wads of bills and some sporting red sashes tied around their waists to brighten grubby work clothes, hit river towns like Bay City for good times. "What timber beasts howled for came in whalebone corsets and little brown jugs," writes Laurence Rogers, who believes the local French Canadian lumberjack Joe Fournier, said to have had enormous hands and two rows of teeth, was the local hero who inspired Saginaw Valley's own cache of Paul Bunyan stories. Joe was murdered at the Third Street dock on a November night in 1876 by a stonemason, who hit him on the head with a mallet. Bay City had a reputation for having the wildest saloons and gambling dens, some of which had trapdoors to drop drunken lumberjacks with empty pockets into the river. Local writers were the first popularizers of Bunyan legends. Oscoda newspaperman James MacGillivray, who first heard tales of Paul Bunyan in a lumber camp on the Au Sable River when he was thirteen, was the first author to publish a Paul Bunyan story, "The Round River Drive," when he did so in 1910. James Stevens spent years in the Saginaw Valley collecting these stories, which gave him material for five Paul Bunyan books, the first of which appeared in 1927. Paul Bunyan became a household name during the Great Depression, when people needed food, work, and hope. New problems caused people to fall back on old solutions, and just as Paul helped woodsmen face their daily dangers by subjecting terror to ridicule, the symbol of American size, strength, and ingenuity inspired the different heroics of 1930s Americans.

Industries

By the late nineteenth century, Bay City was one of the busiest ports on Lake Huron. The river was deepened and widened and wharves were constructed. During the 1880s, four thousand vessels cleared the port annually. During peak season, twelve large ships came into town daily, with passengers as well as freight, coming from Saginaw, Detroit, Cleveland, and Toledo. Steamers left for Saginaw every two hours,

Tugboat pulling timber barge on Saginaw River, Bay City, 1890s. BAY COUNTY HISTORICAL SOCIETY.

and others for Port Austin, Au Gres, Tawas, and Au Sable. The *Wellington R. Burt*, named for Saginaw's wealthiest lumbermen, steamed daily between the cities. Despite railroads, shipping remained an important means of transportation.

Railroads were slow to come to Bay City, as shipping was adequate to get lumber to market and bring a return on investment. That changed, however, once East Saginaw was connected to Flint in 1862, and a twelve-mile stretch was completed between Bay City and East Saginaw. The villages on the west side soon got the Lansing, Jackson, and Saginaw Railroad to extend from Saginaw. This soon became Michigan Central, with further connections, which greatly helped to add value to Henry W. Sage's timberlands in the interior. The Pere Marquette Depot was built in 1904 in downtown Bay City along North Madison Avenue. By 1964, the last train had departed from this depot.

The age of lumber was over as fast as it had begun. By the 1880s, there were no tracts of pine left in the Saginaw Valley. Lumber companies had purchased lands further north and developed rail connections to bring logs to Bay City. Companies also rafted logs from Canadian mills on Georgian Bay across Lake Huron, until a Canadian duty on exported logs enacted in 1894 put an end to that.

Fortunately, the economic boom was not solely based on timber extraction, because the salt industry was closely connected. Leftover wood and sawdust from the mills heated the brine that was then turned into salt, and later a cleaner method of using steam from the mills was adopted. Most of the salt produced in Michigan came from the Saginaw Valley, and it was shipped around the country as well as used to preserve fish. By 1868, Bay City had ten salt operations, but the end of the lumber industry also ended salt production.

Indigenous people as well as the early settlers found excellent fishing in Saginaw Bay, with plentiful sturgeon, and a commercial fishing industry arose. James Fraser established a cooperage in the 1840s to make barrels to hold salted fish. Large loads of fish went to New York, Detroit, Cleveland, Cincinnati, and even farther south. Ice shanties, then and now, can be seen dotted along the waterways. The Banks area would be covered with nets or seines used to trap fish and haul them ashore. By the early twentieth century, commercial fishing had begun to decline and was all but gone by the 1950s.

Shipbuilding in Bay City was also closely connected with the lumber industry. Smaller shipyards started in the 1850s and 1860s, and by the 1870s and 1880s the shipyards of Frank Wheeler and James Davidson were building some of the largest ships on the Great Lakes. Davidson stuck to wood, building tugboats and some of the largest lumber barges and bulk freighters in his yard, much of which is now Kantzler Arboretum and Veteran's Memorial Park. A platform overlooking the river maps the former shipyard and ship graveyard under the river, from which a rudder was salvaged and installed as a memorial. In the 1880s, Wheeler started to build steel-hull ships, and his large yard in West Bay City (now the site of Wheeler's Landing Marina) employed nearly 1,400 workers. The company prospered until the early twentieth century.

After the boom in industry and population that came and went with lumber, Bay City lost 10 percent of its population between 1884 and 1900. With the exceptions of Sage Library and elaborate mansions, little remains of the barons' legacies in town. Many of them were absentee owners, who made enormous profits but did not reinvest in the region. Nevertheless, it was capital from lumbering that brought in the sugar beet industry. Local lumberman Nathan B. Bradley, in response to the offer of the State of Michigan bounty, led a campaign to create the Michigan Sugar Company in Essexville, with Bradley and Thomas Cranage as executives. The building in which the plant was located still stands in Essexville. Local capital also created the Bay City Sugar Company and the West Bay City Sugar Company, both later bought by Michigan Sugar. Today one of the largest employers in Bay County, the company's mill can be seen towering above the southwest corner of the city on South Euclid Avenue. It has just opened a molasses desugarization facility, allowing molasses to be further refined to produce more sugar without planting more acres of beets.

New industries were slow to emerge but eventually did. Holes were drilled around Bay City (Center Ave.) in search of coal, and prospectors had some luck, but coal was about to be eclipsed by diesel, natural gas, and home heating oil. More lasting success came when companies, responding to local needs, invented labor-saving equipment.

Launch of bulk freighter hull from Defoe shipyard, 1952–1953. BAY COUNTY HISTORICAL SOCIETY.

Bay City Dredging Works, for instance, manufactured a wide range of land-dredging machines like the walking dredge (1916) used to ditch wetlands as far away as the Florida Everglades. Traditional industries like shipbuilding and lumber mills made the very smart move of figuring out how to mass produce kit boats and kit houses.

Bay City's large-scale boatyards were still operating at the beginning of the twentieth century, but it was clear that the age of wooden ships was ending. Something new was on the horizon, though: the phenomenon of weekending, which made leisure time a regular part of peoples' lives. Those with time and money for cottages also wanted personal watercraft. Clifford Brooks got the idea to make "knock-down" boats and sell the patterns and materials as kits. In 1904, after a brief period of experimentation, he began selling precut, mail-order boats nationwide and was so successful that local high school principal Harry Defoe wanted in on the action. He quit his job to start a rival kit-boat company, Defoe Boat and Motor Works, in 1905.

Defoe would go on to build luxury yachts after World War I at his final location on Woodside Avenue, rum-runner chaser boats during Prohibition, and patrol craft used by the U.S. Navy and Coast Guard during World War II to escort supply ships from Canada to Britain during the Battle of the Atlantic. His ingenious rollover method both increased the time in which ships were built and proved to be safer for shipyard workers. Defoe even built large lake boats, including the *Ojibway*, the last lake boat built on the river in 1952 and sold for scrap in 2022. The business carried on with Defoe's sons at the helm before closing in the 1970s, leaving Gougeon Brothers as one of few boat builders in the area.

The knock-down boat phenomenon inspired William and Otto Sovereign to transfer the technology to home building. If one could machine the parts and pieces of a boat, why not a house? They founded Aladdin Homes in 1906, two years before better-known Sears and Roebuck began selling house kits, and was so successful that by the end of 1913, the company had shipped 2,400 kits, and in their peak year, 1917, shipped 3,200 kits. The company remained in business until 1982.

Aladdin used Lewis Manufacturing Company, founded in 1895 and known for a range of lumber products, to mill the housing pieces. Aladdin's massive success led Lewis's president, Adna Lewis, to plunge into the national market with their own kit house catalog with 105 different models in a wide range of prices. The catalog showed evidence of its prior seven-year association with Aladdin in its sophisticated marketing techniques and similarities between several of the models. Lewis (its kit division being renamed Liberty Homes in 1925) was in business until 1973. International Mill and Timber did the same between 1916 to 1971, using the trademark "Sterling Homes." These Bay City companies helped Flint through the house famine of its second boom, when houses couldn't be built fast enough. In a three-year period, surviving records show that of the 163 kits the Lewis Manufacturing Company manufactured and mailed to Michigan addresses, 84 went to customers in Flint.

The population of Bay City grew little until World War II increased industrial activity, giving Bay City another big boom with the North American Chemical Company, which purchased the old McGraw mill site and became one of the largest employers until 1927; Industrial Brownhoist, which employed many thousands until its close in 1983 (later cleared for the site of Uptown Bay City), manufacturing rail-mounted wrecking cranes; Bay City Dredgeworks, located on Center Avenue (currently the site of Bay Cast), which continued to build mechanical shovels and dredging machines until 1960; and the Defoe shipyard, begun in 1905.

General Motors has been in operation in Bay City since the 1920s. Louis Chevrolet and William C. Durant bought a site on Woodside Avenue in 1916 and added it to Chevrolet in 1918, providing engine parts. The site had been the home of the National Truck Company, operated by Henry B. Smith originally, starting in 1892, as a bicycle manufacturer. Eventually it became Bay City GM Powertrain. Electric

Auto-Lite Company was brought to Bay City's west side from Toledo and opened as Prestolite, remaining in business through the 1980s, making electrical parts for automobiles. The old Union Truck plant was purchased by Dow Chemical Company, which also added two more plants to Bay City.

Remaking Bay City

By midcentury, Bay City had surpassed its lumber era population and was reaching around fifty-three thousand—its peak population. Postwar housing demand led to expansion outside the city. Bay City was again prosperous, with safe neighborhoods, secure manufacturing jobs, parks, and a family-oriented atmosphere. By the 1970s and 1980s, however, the restructuring of the auto industry and the closure of other large manufacturers put thousands out of work. The Bay City GM plant employed nearly four thousand workers in the 1970s but just under five hundred today. In 1990, the population dropped below forty thousand, for the first time since the lumber era, and today, it hovers around thirty-two thousand. Signs that manufacturing may rebound include a decision by a Korean semiconductor firm, SK Siltron, to locate its second Mid-Michigan plant in Bay City to manufacture silicone wafers for electric vehicles.

Bay City also experienced a series of urban renewal projects throughout the 1970s—particularly in the first and ninth wards, with the construction of the Independence Bridge, the BayTown neighborhood, Maplewood Manor, Maplewood Park, and the Liberty Bridge. The Independence Bridge replaced the aging Belinda Street bridge, allowing for industries to remain in the city and for quick access to new shopping districts in Bangor Township and the highways located to the west of the city. Other areas of the city saw urban renewal projects as well, such as the Bradley House and Smith Manor. Three historic districts were established in this period: Midland Street, Downtown Bay City, and Center Avenue, with hundreds of historically significant homes, churches, a school, and a cemetery.

The 1980s was a time of transition for all the cities in our region. Down in a trough between waves, each of them reached for a lifeline, and when a native daughter had just become a major pop celebrity, it's understandable that the mayor, with a homecoming concert in mind, would offer her the "keys to the city." Pop icon Madonna became Bay City's next big thing. She was born in Bay City's Mercy Hospital (now the Bradley House, a senior living apartment). Her grandmother, Elsie Fortin, lived in the Banks area on the west side, where she raised her daughter, the singer's mother, Madonna Louise Fortin Ciccone. Though her parents lived in Pontiac, after her mother died and father remarried, Madonna Jr. spent summers with her grandmother in Bay City. Once she reached celebrity status, Madonna and her hometown were what you

Ore boat unloading at Essexville. PHOTOGRAPH BY TODD SHORKEY.

might call star-crossed: Her star rose while the city's fell, causing more than a few Bay Citians to court her favor. Refusing three different offers to accept a city key, finally, when she was being inducted into the Rock & Roll Hall of Fame, she named Bay City as her one and only hometown.

But that hasn't put an end to speculation about what exactly Madonna meant when she described it as a "smelly little town" on national television and later explained publicly that she didn't intend to be mean. In fact, admitted a city official, the air pollution from the gas refinery and nearby sugar beet plant was so bad the Environmental Protection Agency forced the industries to pay penalties to families with homes in the Banks area. To explore this local obsession with Madonna, a good starting point is the new *Birthplace of Madonna* mural on the city market wall along Adams Street, the Michigan Rock and Roll Legends Hall of Fame at the Bay County Historical Society, where, if you time it right, you might even catch a screening of Zach Neumeyer's 2021 film *Smelly Little Town*.

Bay City developers were wise enough not to put all their eggs in the Madonna basket but recognized early that the city's location and natural features are its best and most stable assets. River development began in 2004 with the Waterfall Park project, with a focal fountain and seating in a park overlooking the river, with access to the dock where the *Princess Wenonah* boards for seasonal river tours. Renovations to Wenonah Park and bandshell followed, and areas along the river were connected in the late 1990s by a ten-mile paved pathway, the Bay County Riverwalk/Rail Trail. A good place to begin the trail is the parking lot near the Trombley House. Trail highlights include the Kantzler Arboretum and the Middle Grounds (a two-mile island in the middle of the Saginaw River) with boardwalk, crooked bridge, access to the Bay City Rowing Club, and Bigelow Park at the northern end. More recently, Uptown Bay City, a new district of town filled with condos, restaurants, walkable areas, and retailers, sits on what was the location of Industrial Brownhoist.

People seventy years ago would not have thought to come to Bay City to rent kayaks, ride peddle trolleys on a bar crawl, or mountain bike in the Sugar Trails on the Middle Grounds. Perhaps visitors and residents in seventy years, when city planners finally realize that recycling is the way to economic as well as environmental health, will be riding electric trolleys and taking houseboat vacations. During shipping season, freighters coast through regularly to deposit loads at docks in Carrollton and Zilwaukee and provide continuity with the industrial past. However, they share the river with paddlers and pleasure craft, and all of these can be seen gliding and drifting together under a sky popping and fizzling with fireworks at the annual Fourth of July celebration. Independence Day is such a huge thing here that houses have installed fireworks decks for ease of viewing. There really is no better place to celebrate freedom than on the water of the lower Saginaw as it winds slowly bayward toward horizons no longer obstructed by the sad monotony of milled timber. The land is free, and regrowth is happening here.

St. Stanislaus Kostka Church

At the beginning of summer, the blue sky extends above the church like an unbroken ceiling. White gulls with black-tipped wings and herons fly with ease over the two 175-foot-tall brick spires, each topped with Latin crosses of fading gold. St. Stanislaus Kostka church, with its parish center, rectory, school, and parking lot, takes up an entire city block. The school, completed in 1910, closed in 2011 and is slowly falling into genteel disrepair.

A large digital sign stands at the corner of Van Buren and Kosciuszko Avenue between two pale brick pillars, displaying mass times and other events that are happening at the church. Above the digital sign is a banner that reads "Our Lady of Czestochowa." In fact, this is the name of a parish that includes the two churches operating in Bay City's South End, which has historically been the locus of Bay City's Polish quarter: St. Stanislaus Kostka Church and St. Hyacinth's Church.

To the northwest of the church entrance is a vibrantly painted statue of Mary, the Mother of God, adorned in her bright sky-blue robe. A short, well-worn dirt path leads through a bunching of flowers and roses to this statue, where church members have prayed for her to intercede for them. Below are plaques honoring parishioners who fought and lost their lives during World Wars I and II. Between the statue of Mary and the church is a flagpole with an American flag flapping gently in the wind.

In Bay City, as in cities across the country, it was common for immigrants to build their own churches so that mass or services could be spoken in their mother tongues. Before they had a church of their own, Bay City Poles attended mass at St. James Church on Monroe Street with Father Xavier Szulak. In 1874, Ludwig Danielewski (1845–1903), considered the first Polish colonist, suggested that they build their own church. Months later, in July 1874, the first version of the St. Stanislaus Kostka church was proposed. Both the original wooden church (1874) and the later Gothic brick church (1892) were designed by Leverett Anson Pratt, the renowned architect of Bay City who was responsible for designing and constructing many of the city's finest buildings.

Christen Seward is a Bay City native and sixth-generation Polish American. Her great-great-great grandfather, John Zielinski Sr., moved to Bay City from Poland in 1882; his son, John Jr., worked as a carpenter during renovations to the church in 1939. "The story goes," she remarks, "that Aunt Mary Ann didn't have meat on the table for that entire year because of the expense it cost their family. The boys ate first, and then the girls. When he finished the job, he went to collect payment for the work he'd done, but Father asked him if he would consider it as his donation to the church, and he agreed to that."

Stories of early Polish Americans making personal sacrifices for the sake of building and maintaining their churches, like the one told by Seward, are not uncommon. When construction began on the brick church in 1890, each parishioner was asked to donate $60 toward the $60,000 building. This feat is especially incredible considering that many of the Polish immigrants were newly emancipated peasants from small villages, where they had dwelled in thatched-roof houses with mostly dirt floors. It makes the church building a particularly impressive achievement.

The Polish neighborhood was located south of Columbus Avenue (some say Seventeenth Street) and east of the river. "This was the edge of the city where, in the early days, people could have a garden and a cow. Most Poles who settled in Bay City were farmers, so even though they worked in sawmills and later factories, they did some farming, right in here in the city. In the neighborhood we stayed close and lived close. All my aunts and uncles lived either across the street or around the corner." Closeness to the church and the school, which taught Polish language and Polish history through the 1950s, was very important.

The parish was the social organ of the community, holding religious festivals and Polish weddings. Bishop Kenneth Povish, who had earlier been St. Stan's parish priest, remarked at the occasion of the church's centennial in 1974 that "if the walls of old Pulaski Hall could talk, they could tell a fascinating story about insurance societies, banquets, dramatic performances, veterans' meetings, parties, concerts by singing groups, lecture platforms, and a host of other events that kept people together, brightened their lives, and molded them into useful citizens."

In 1974, Poles still made up a quarter of Bay City's population and were the largest ethnic group, still concentrated in the South End. Why did this community stay together for over a century when other Polish neighborhoods in other cities fragmented? A likely reason is the racial homogeneity of the city. With no big influx of African Americans, there was no fear of instability, so the white population stayed put.

You won't hear Polish spoken on the street or even in the church as you once did, but walk in Jack's Meats or Krysiak House Restaurant or attend the annual St. Stan's Festival, and all the foods and sounds are there: sausage, *pierogi*, *gołąbki*, polka music, and dancing. In the home, important traditions involve special meals associated with religious feasts. *Wigilia* is the traditional Christmas Eve supper, which begins when the first star lights the sky and the family gathers for the breaking of the *opłatek*—a thin, unleavened wafer stamped with figures of the Christ child, Mary, and the angels. Easter is equally important, and there is a harvest festival in mid-October. All festivities involve mass, followed by dinner and dancing. Passing such important traditions onto the next generation is regarded as very important in this community, as is involvement with the parish. As the third and fourth generations marry non-Poles and even non-Catholics and come under the spell of consumer culture, the elders worry about the survival of these traditions.

Points of Interest

Saginaw Rear Range Light, the first lighthouse on the Saginaw River, built 2,300 feet from the mouth, was completed in 1839. Dow Chemical owns and is restoring the land and the lighthouse, with the cooperation of local nonprofits.

Bay-Zil Bike Trail (Hotchkiss Rd. access) is the beginning of the 6.2-mile bike trail to Zilwaukee. Plenty of locals walk the half mile to the Dutch Creek bridge, which offers good fishing and great views of the marshes and waterways that flow to and from the Saginaw River. Kramer's grocery store (3536 Hotchkiss Rd.) is still selling homemade sausage as it has done since 1893. Make sure you admire the folk-art bird house made from local stones.

USS *Edson* and Saginaw Valley Naval Ship Museum (1680 Martin St.) offers tours of a decommissioned Vietnam-era navy destroyer.

St. Laurent Brothers Candy & Nut House (1101 N. Water St.) has offered nuts, chocolate, and candy since 1904.

Bay City Hall, an iconic Richardsonian Romanesque building, designed by local architects Leverett A. Pratt and Walter Koeppe, was finished in the 1890s. The clock tower is worth a visit for panoramic views of the city and river.

Bay County Historical Society (321 Washington Ave.) has an extensive research library and several permanent exhibits on the history of the city and its function as a port. The museum is also home to the Michigan Rock and Roll Legends Hall of Fame.

Masonic Temple (corner of Madison Ave. and Sixth St.) dates from 1891. Designed by local architects Leverett A. Pratt and Walter Koeppe, the building was monumental with its arches, columns, and onion domes. A fire in 1903 destroyed the roofline and damaged the building severely, yet its Moorish character is still visible in the geometric design of its terra cotta tiles. Currently, the building houses A Community Center for the Arts.

First Presbyterian Church (805 Center Ave.) is a Romanesque church built in 1892, designed by Leverett A. Pratt and Walter Koeppe. The heavy granite pedestals contrast with an interior worship space that is round and light.

Trinity Episcopal Church (911 Center Ave.) is a Gothic Revival church built in 1887 of Sandusky limestone and trimmed with Berea sandstone. Arched windows and stone tracery catch the eye; the central window, in richly colored glass, was made in Munich and paid for by lumberman Thomas Cranage and his wife in memory of their daughter Sarah Pitts Cranage.

Temple Israel (2300 Center Ave.) was designed by Alden Dow and constructed in 1960.

Tobico Marsh

If people were completely good, they would not experience the calm joy felt in solitude while surrounded by a hardwood forest, an unfurling throng of ferns, or a marsh's varied landscapes. This same joy would come to them in the midst of their cities, and for some, it does. But for many city dwellers and suburbanites, a morning or afternoon ramble in nature helps them remember who they are. Tobico Marsh, located between Bay City and Linwood, is an ideal place for recreation and recovery, because it takes us back to the kinds of coastal wetlands that were once abundant along the Great Lakes and are now rare. We are privileged to enjoy this nearly two-thousand-acre remnant, designated a National Natural Landmark in 1976 because of its large size, relatively undisturbed condition, and variety of aquatic plant life.

From the intersection of Euclid Avenue and State Park Drive, continue north, following signs to Tobico. You pass the Chickadee Nature Trail (0.45 mi.) that winds through a lakeplain prairie—a landscape unique to Saginaw Bay, the St. Clair River Delta, and the Lake Erie marshes. Sand deposits and thin mineral soils support a patchwork of different natural communities that live side by side—wetland woods, wet meadows, cattail marshes, and oak savanna prairies.

There are two main options for walks with no chance of losing your way: the Tobico Marsh Big Loop, a 2.8-mile trail that takes you northwest through many different ecosystems, and a shorter loop that leads to the 1.25-mile Frank N. Anderson Trail, through the marsh, over the lake, and to the Saginaw Bay Visitors Center. From there, you can circle the lagoon. If you have a kayak, paddling is an option in the lagoon or the open water of the marsh.

If you walk through the interpretive shelter and continue to follow the wide trail, you will be heading north on the Big Loop trail. One-quarter mile and one mile in, there are observation towers that take you forty feet into the canopy, where you may see such birds as the sparrow, vireo, black-capped chickadee, and pileated woodpecker and small mammals such as black and fox squirrels, chipmunks, raccoons, and opossums. In the summer, you may glimpse swans in the Tobico Lake from the heightened vantage points.

All seasons are beautiful here. In winter, while walking the Big Loop trail, one is surrounded by the tall grey pillars of leafless maples and oaks. On late afternoons in January, before the sun sets, rays of sunlight stripe the blankets of dazzling snow. But in summer, the marshland and hardwood forest are a cacophony of sounds: the whining buzz of mosquitoes, the raspy music of late summer cicadas, the melodious chirping of birds, and distant quacking and honking of ducks and geese. Light filters down onto the sand and dirt walking trail through the overlapping leaves of beech trees. The world is emerald green—as if the forest itself, teeming with life, is a gemstone.

The entire Tobico Marsh was once under water. On certain sections of the Big Loop, you will notice a shift in the trail's elevation and an excess of sand. These are intersecting sand ridges that are former shorelines where land ended and an older Lake Huron began. In the evening during springtime, as you are rounding the northernmost part of the Big Loop Trail, you will hear a surprisingly loud sound: thousands of frogs ribbitting in a chorus that vibrates the air without ceasing. Their cumulative voice sounds like a consciously composed song, resounding somewhere between the chirp of a cricket and the tweet of a bird, yet it comes from small marshland amphibians, the leopard frogs. Despite being mostly unobservable from the path, you can hear them as though you were standing directly in front of a wind ensemble playing steadily in the midst of the forest. This northernmost section is also the best place to watch the sun setting from within the Big Loop Trail. As the trail continues west, it passes through an oak barren savanna, where a sprawling undergrowth of ferns and grasses grows between the old oaks. Deer bed down at night on grasses and underbrush.

The word "Tobico" is derived from the Ojibwe word Pe-to-be-goong, which means "the little lake by the big lake." Tobico Lake, which is the largest inland lake in Bay

County, was once a shallow water bay that was attached to Saginaw Bay. As the longshore current moved sand parallel to the shoreline over the course of hundreds of years, the little lake became completely sealed off from the big lake by a sand deposit, called a sand spit. Today, that strip of land is lined with houses along Killarney Beach Road.

In 1839, John Mullet, a federal surveyor, noted the many pine trees that were three to seven feet in diameter. As you walk the trails, you will notice that there are hardly any trees that have trunks that size and those trees with the largest trunks are not coniferous pines, but deciduous oak and maple trees, because the old-growth pine forest was logged between 1847 and 1861. The forest surrounding you, as you walk the Big Loop Trail, has grown back since that time. After the pine had been extracted, money made and mansions built, the lumber era receded, as the glaciers did eighteen thousand years earlier. At that point, the owners of Tobico Marsh, known locally as "the eddies," had no further use for the land, until a group of their fellow lumbermen purchased it to establish the Tobico Hunt Club.

The club's eight founding members, William B. Mershon, Arnold Boutell, Clark Ring, George Morley, C. M. Greenway, William L. Hutchins, Guy Garber, and Frank Anderson, used the marshland for hunting and other recreational activities. Members were only allowed to hunt ducks two days a week from September 15 through November 10. Despite these strict limitations, they shot a wide variety of ducks, predominantly mallards, black ducks, and teal.

Eventually many of the original members of Tobico Hunt Club passed away, and the two surviving members, Frank N. Anderson and Guy Garber, no longer enjoyed their hunting excursions into the marsh. It became "too easy," Anderson remarked. During the club's seventy years, the Tobico Marsh largely recovered from the effects of logging, and in 1957, Anderson and Garber sold the property to the state for $40,000 (a pittance) to preserve the biodiversity of habitat needed to sustain the myriad species of waterfowl and wildlife.

If you head north from the parking lot on the walking trail for a quarter mile, you arrive at the Frank N. Anderson Nature Trail. Following that paved trail east, away from the forest, you cross the southern portion of Tobico Lake on a boardwalk, where you pass two observation decks. On a clear evening in summer, this pathway is also an excellent place to watch the sunset transform the sky and clouds into shades of purple, yellow, orange, red, and blue—all reflected in the lake's clear water. Nature's painting is bordered by the expansive rods of native cattails, where numerous muskrats live and red-winged blackbird's nest.

If you walk further east on the paved trail across the lake, you come to an intersection. To the left (north), the trail dead-ends after a brief walk; to the right (south), you can walk for three-quarters of a mile on the trail, built over the old road bed of the Detroit and Mackinac Railway, and arrive at the Saginaw Bay Visitor Center at the Bay City State Park, founded as the Jennison Nature Center in 1950 and renovated in 2023. Make sure you see the taxidermy of Michigan's only documented wolverine, which lived in Minden Bog in the middle of the Thumb until 2010.

Tobico Marsh is not a remote northern landscape by any means, and no matter how silent it becomes, you can always hear the faint din of cars speeding down the nearby M-13 highway. Like the greater Saginaw Valley, Tobico was ravaged by the greed of a few, but it was also saved by a few sportsmen turned environmentalists, realizing that to sustain the sport they loved, waterfowl needed a healthy home. The Greek word for "home" is *oikos*, the root of the word "ecosystem"—the intricately linked community of organisms (including ourselves) that survives in the aftermath of massive resource extraction and landscape manipulation. We ensure our survival if we let the forest and the marsh teach us how to weave a world—and the first step is to spend enough time and attention to find something fascinating, whether it's a bird, rock, duck, or cattail. Then see how it moves, how it appears to be made, how it relates to the lives around it. If you do this, then you will have begun a way that helps you have deeper experiences wherever you are.

Kawkawlin, Linwood, Pinconning

Before I-75 was completed, M-13 (South Huron Road) was the main route in the eastern part of the state to northern Michigan. After World War II, affluent Michiganders in the booming cities were ready to enjoy life. They bought hunting cabins, cottages, fishing boats, and other recreational toys and took their families to Tawas and other towns along the Huron coastline. This was the beginning of the "up north" getaway. The car trip was so popular that resort hotels and beach communities closer to cities, in places like the St. Clair Flats or even Bay City's Wenona Beach, closed down. Meanwhile, on main roads like M-13, businesses catering to tourists opened. You can still see Deer Acres Fun Park (closed permanently) with a gauntlet of concrete toy soldiers lined up along the road and a turquoise castle entryway. The Turkey Roost opened in 1955 and is still serving "Thanksgiving Everyday," minus the caged turkeys out front. Frank's Great Outdoors opened in 1945 and appears to be thriving, as do the three cheese shops in Pinconning. If you stay on I-75, you miss all of this, as well as the side roads giving access to the bay and the lovely Nayanquing Point State Wildlife Refuge (1570 N. Tower Beach Rd.) as well as Bay County Pinconning Park (3041 East Pinconning Rd.), with miles of boardwalk, sandy beach, and views on a clear day across the bay to the tip of the Thumb; this is also an RV park with log cabins to rent as well as kayaks. To access this park at a quieter more northerly point, drive to the end of Cody Estey Road (off M-13). There is a parking lot, and you can follow the sand spit south between rows of oaks. A boardwalk through the marsh is also an option.

Kawkawlin Township (pop. 4,419), named for the river that flows through, today is largely a residential suburb of Bay City, with houses along both sides of the river. An Indigenous community formed around a Methodist mission that was established here in 1847, and the original building still stands. A state historical marker recognizes the Ogaukawning Church (Euclid Road at Hidden Road), still under Indian control. The town's traditional business section or "village" is located next to South Huron Road and stands near the site of a water-powered sawmill, built by James Fraser and Cromwell Barney in 1845. Oren A. Ballou, a Rhode Island manufacturer, bought Fraser's interests in 1857, and his son Dexter managed it and became a partner. Frederick A. Kaiser, a German immigrant, first worked for Fraser and then developed salt works and sawmills and a railroad linking Kawkawlin with Pinconning. Many of the mill employees bought land and developed farms after draining the land. Among others, Germans from Illinois moved to the area around 1905.

Linwood is an unincorporated community, claiming to be the Walleye Capital of Michigan, that straddles the borders of Kawkawlin and Fraser Townships. It was settled in the 1870s and 1880s following the growth of the Michigan Central Railroad and the establishment of a sawmill. French-speaking settlers, coming from Macomb County and from southwestern Ontario, found the marshy land near Saginaw Bay to be much like home. They were joined by French Canadians from Bay City who had originally come from Quebec. The settlers farmed, trapped, and fished in the bay. They organized St. Anne's Church in 1889. There is a local history museum in a small, restored icehouse. Although commercial fishing is long gone, there is a large marina with adjacent campground and cabin rentals. People today make a living serving as fishing guides, running charter boats, and running businesses like bars and taxidermy shops.

Pinconning (pop. 1,204) lies further north along M-13. This city's name comes from the river that flows through it and is said to derive from the Ojibwe *o-pin-nic-con-ning*, meaning "potato place." Most Michiganders know the name as part of Pinconning cheese, which is, however, unknown outside the state. After most of the timber was cut, farms grew. Cheesemaker Daniel Horn, a Russian German immigrant, came here from Wisconsin in 1915 and produced a variety of Colby cheese that could age. His daughters' families and others ran cheese businesses, which proved a smart way to attract the increasing traffic on US-23. The food giant Kraft operated a cheese factory here from 1936 to 1993, producing commercial varieties of cheddar, Colby, and Havarti. Today, Pinconning cheese is made by cheesemakers in Wisconsin, although Williams Cheese Company in nearby Linwood is still active.

Pinconning, like any other place, is not so void of interest that we have to beat an orderly retreat into the past to find something to say about it. Spend time checking out the farms, the petting zoo, and drive out to the lake. There is a trail that runs atop a sand ridge between the blue bay and a cattail marsh, where the cottonwoods make their watery sounds and you can sit in their shade facing lakeward, where there will be white herons, or landward to watch the bird life in the marsh. When you read poet Charles Baxter's "Midwestern Poetics," remember that he lived and taught school in Pinconning and found enough inspiration to set three novels in this place.

Women's Work

We will never know exactly what gave Annie Edson Taylor the idea of going over Niagara Falls in a barrel. She arrived in Bay City in 1898 from Auburn, New York, with the intention of teaching dancing, rented an establishment on Water Street, and, after just three years, had no students and needed money. It was the end of the lumber era, and many of the monied people moved on. What could she do?

Maybe the old lumber floating in the Saginaw River gave her the idea for a daredevil plunge, or maybe it was her own imagination tracing the river's movement from Lake Huron down the St. Clair River, Detroit River, across Lake Erie to the Niagara River and the inevitable Niagara Falls. Local reporting focused on the barrel—five-foot-tall, constructed out of Kentucky oak by the West Bay City Cooperage Company—that would make or break her.

On October 24, 1901—her sixty-third birthday—Taylor was tucked into the barrel and cut loose in the Niagara River near Goat Island, going over the falls, yet she survived the 167-foot drop. But her dastardly manager Frank Russell dashed whatever hopes she had of earning enough fame and wealth from this stunt to redeem a mortgage on a ranch in Texas. After she survived the falls, he booked lecture shows for her in towns around Michigan and the Midwest, and she appeared, two weeks later in a vacant store on Water Street with her "famous barrel and the cat that made the trial trip" to speak of her experiences. Russell, blatantly sexist and ageist, upstaged her at every turn, telling the press two months later that she was last seen in Buffalo talking about pawning her coat to get something to eat. Annie passed away in 1921 and is buried in the Oakwood Cemetery in Niagara Falls, New York. History pertaining to her story can be read on a plaque on the fence at the Third Street Waterfall Park downtown.

Two educated, middle-class women, Myra Seely Parsons and Mary Cabay Sagatoo, wound up in northern Bay County towns in the 1870s and worked quite intentionally to build their communities. Myra Seely's family had moved from Onondaga County, New York, to East Saginaw in 1867 to join relatives who were already involved in lumbering and land-buying ventures. Her father opened a store in East Saginaw, and Myra grew up in a comfortable environment, with books, a piano, and fashionable clothes. She kept in touch with a young man from home, Mahlon Parsons, who came west eight years later, settled in Kawkawlin, and worked as the general overseer for a lumber company. Eventually he and Myra married, and the couple bought one thousand acres of land (helped by investments provided by both sets of parents) in the Linwood area. This sizable purchase signaled that this energetic pair wanted to start a farm and raise a family but also build a community. Myra sacrificed much for this work and clearly imagined it in terms of their joint project in the "forest primevle [*sic*]," a phrase from Longfellow's poem, "Evangeline."

Myra and Mahlon must have seemed to be "lords of the manor," with their ownership and control of one thousand acres, but they did not act the part. Instead of profiting, they gave generously. To the French-speaking community, they gave the land for St. Anne's Church, school, and cemetery. They built, stocked, and ran a general store; Mahlon filled in as postmaster and eventually justice of the peace; and they donated land for the Linwood public school. No matter how destitute a local man was, Mahlon made sure he voted, even if it meant paying his train fare to Bay City. Myra bore and raised seven children, kept a large apiary, and searched for new markets for the family's farm products but was always intensely involved in the community beyond her family. She knew the ins and outs of school operation (books, teachers, erasers) as well as the struggles of farm hands and shell-shocked Civil War veterans like Mr. Mains. Myra and Mahlon built him a shack where he could live out his life on the beach while being fed and cared for by the family. Women like Myra in small towns like Linwood, who took time to learn medicinal cures, set bones, pick potato bugs off plants, deal with swarms of bees, cook the fish caught and flesh trapped or shot locally for work bees and civic groups, wove the fabric of a communal way of life that was good and has lasted. Though she died of overwork at the young age of forty-one—probably with little time for the piano and books that her parents moved up Sawdust Road at the beginning of her marriage—her public-spiritedness is something that we ought to remember. Her diaries, published in an edition by Patricia Drury and Ron Bloomfield in 2001, provide a valuable record of her life.

Mary Henderson, who grew up in Newton, Massachusetts, met the Chippewa man, Joseph Cabay, from Saganing (just north of Pinconning on the county line), at the Bromfield Church in Boston (he was attending Harvard) and fell in love with him. She married him against the advice of parents, although he was dying of tuberculosis, and the couple returned to Michigan in 1863. On the trip through Ontario, Mary saw a "funny little house" and asked about them. She was told that she would be seeing more and more log cabins the further west she went. Joseph knew he was coming home to die, and on his deathbed, made Mary promise to stay in Saganing to help his people. She was formally adopted by the tribe and given the name Wah-Sash-Kah-Moqua. After two years as a widow, she reluctantly accepted a second marriage, worked to raise money for the construction of the church, and taught in the school. Wah-Sash-Kah-Moqua lived in the Indian village for most of her long life despite the prejudices of the white community and took it as a compliment when, on occasion, she was identified as a "squaw." Mary Sagatoo's memoir, *Wah Sash Kah Moqua: Or Thirty-Three Years Among the Indians* (1897), is a unique account of the Saganing community.

Midwestern Poetics

Charles Baxter

The unpromising meets the unexotic,
and we are home again, alone,
with this image of the possible:
these hills that anyone can climb,
the lowlands, reeds perched with red-wing
blackbirds, leading painlessly
to cemeteries and small towns
where voices are subdued and have no
region.
A man paints enormous replicas
Of Rembrandt's middle period on the sides
Of barns. He is mad. He leaves.
Without elevations, hurricanes, or
earthquakes, without geological alarms,
we learn to count the angles
in the sky and to admire four-barrel carbu-
retors
in the muscle cars that combine with roadside
trees in the six-pack dark of Saturday.
It's not that something has to happen.
A man writes a letter to himself
and excludes the absolute: he is four seasons,
paths in third-growth woods, nature
that is endlessly familiar.
He is a silo: he stores, he feeds.
No horsemen raging down the mountains
flying banners, no vipers, just this and that
That could be anywhere but happens to be
here.
The children grow up calm: they learn
about psychotic tantrums like tornados.
They plan. There is time, and more time
and more time after that to learn to love
the mild gifts—these apple trees, these
sparrows—in this marriage with a woman
who knows you, but will not kiss you back.

MIDLAND

Profile

Midland (pop. 42,518) is a prosperous, one-industry city dominated through its history by the Dow Chemical Company. Once known as "Chemical City," welcome signs now proclaim it "City of Modern Explorers." Traveling on Midland Road from Saginaw will give you one of few industrial views, but from any other direction, especially coming from the northwest, the city appears to be an island of Mid-Century Modern structures in an otherwise rural, semiforested region. Main Street is built on a rise overlooking the river, spanned by a three-legged bridge, called the "Tridge," which lifts pedestrians up over the confluence of the Chippewa and Tittabawassee Rivers. The parks behind downtown on both banks of the river are frequented by walkers and family groups: You see more kids and dogs here than in any other downtown in the region. East is the factory, west is the Midland Country Club, and north is Dow Gardens, surrounded by architectural gems created by Alden B. Dow, son of Herbert Henry Dow. While father made the city an industrial giant, son redrew the template, turning it into an architectural mecca. As early as 1939, reporters called Midland a model city. But unlike Flint—the other company town—Midland is primarily a white-collar place of chemists and engineers, grateful for high-paying jobs and opportunities to invent. Midland never had a labor movement or a tradition of popular protest, which helps explain the eerie complicity of people here who have been taught to just trust Dow.

History

Midland County, organized in 1850, already had a settled community, which incorporated as the village of Midland City in 1869 and as a city in 1887, lying on the Tittabawassee River that extends northwest for one hundred miles. The pine boom reached Midland County about that time, as lumbermen like Ammi W. Wright and others bought up pine lands and shipped out logs to mills on the Saginaw River. Once cleared, the lumber companies sold their lands to people, many of them Civil War veterans, who developed farms.

In Midland, the big Larkin and Patrick mill at the foot of McDonald Street turned out millions of feet of lumber, millions of shingles, and thousands of staves and barrels every year. Other enterprises produced wood products, such as door hangers and butter tubs, shingles, and wagons. Next to the Larkin and Patrick sawmill was the brine well. As at other mills in the Saginaw Valley, salt was created through evaporation, using sawdust as fuel.

After the salt was separated from the brine, the bittern, rich in bromides, was pumped to the Dickey bromine works. By 1888 Midland had become the bromine capital of the world. Vapors from the bromine works were thought to purify the air and be healthy. Midland was attracting interest as a resort because of the mineral springs and sanitarium established by Lewis and J. S. Eastman in 1876. As the pine era ended, a new industry, based on brine extraction, came to town.

Dow Chemical Company

Herbert Henry Dow (1866–1930), a recent graduate of Case School of Applied Science in Cleveland and a professor of chemistry and toxicology at a nursing school there, experimented in extracting bromine from brine. After a business failure in Canton, Ohio, Dow looked toward Midland and its brine. With backing from a Cleveland sewing machine manufacturer, Dow organized the Midland Chemical Company in 1890 and in 1891 produced the first bromine through electrolysis. At the time, bromine was used mainly in pharmaceuticals, and production was controlled by a German cartel. The Midland Chemical Company agreed to participate in the cartel, but Dow worked on extracting chlorine, magnesium, and other elements from the brine. After some early explosions at his shed factory where he began work before Midland even had electricity, he was soon producing bromine through electrolysis.

With more financial backing, Dow organized in 1897 the Dow Chemical Company. Bleach (bleaching powder), mainly sold to paper mills, was the company's main product until 1909. The company had the cheapest method of producing bromides, thereby undercutting European manufacturers, and successfully broke the cartel by selling in Europe in 1907.

Herbert Henry Dow's success increased his influence on the community. He supported Prohibition, and Midland County became dry in 1908, remaining so for many years thereafter. When pine was in its heyday, numerous saloons lined the north side of Main Street. Dow's lawyer believed that the numerous lawsuits against Dow blaming the loss of shrubs on chlorine was caused by "liquor interests." An Irish settlement across the railroad tracks, known as "Paddy Hollow," was subjected to airborne chlorine pollution.

Although it is possible that Yankee-Irish tensions lay behind the early chlorine lawsuits, the problem of chemical wastes plagued Dow from the start. In fact, by the

1930s, the problem of waste disposal around Midland was one of the reasons Willard Dow (the eldest son who became president of Dow after Herbert died in 1930) became convinced it was time to go to the ocean to extract bromine and magnesium. Brine wells leaked wastes into the ground, contaminating wells; brine holding ponds overflowed, leading to suits from local farmers for ruining land, taking the hair off livestock, and eating through the treads of caterpillar tractors; and injection wells that used hydraulic pressure to pump wastes into the deep layers of the earth altered the underlying geology and hydrology. By the 1980s, the Michigan Department of Natural Resources told Dow that it had to update its whole system of brine waste disposal, so the company chose to "exit the brine business in Michigan," admitting that they didn't know where their wastes were going once they entered disposal wells.

A man of principle and a Sunday school teacher, Dow stood by his total belief in science and technology as the path to a better life and pursued, undeterred, his fascination with new processes and products. The downside of Dow's energetic invention was that the effects of the chemicals produced were investigated only after they were on the market or in the river—in short, when Dow was sued.

World War I proved to be an economic boom for Dow and Midland. Chemical warfare led to the demand for tear gas and mustard gas. The military needed bromides used for medicines, photography, and mining. Its chlorine provided chloroform, carbon tetrachloride and sulfur chloride (for smokescreens), and monochlorobenzene (for explosives), all based on Dow's foundational building blocks—chlorine, bromine, and caustic soda (cheap, almost limitless natural resources). During the war, Dow synthesized indigo (a blue dyestuff) and produced Epsom salts and other products, but judging from the vantage of *Fortune*'s wartime coverage, magnesium extraction was Dow Chemical's "most portentous development," which would be used to make a metal alloy, patented as DowMetal.

At the close of the war, Dow's workforce amounted to 2,300. Midland faced a major housing shortage, with people living in shanties and various temporary housing, and Dow began housing projects. In 1920, Midland's population reached 5,483, more than double its population ten years earlier. The company continued to prosper, and the city grew steadily, even through the Depression of the 1930s. Much of the company's activity was devoted to producing phenols (used to synthesize plastics), including picric acid, and ethylene (a fuel additive).

In 1916—one year into production—local fishermen complained that the fish they caught downstream from the Dow plant tasted bad. Phenol and chlorinated phenol dissolve in water and do not settle out by force of gravity. Once they knew that the phenol was getting into the river and its fish, their solution was simply "ponding"—running wastes into large holding ponds that were later opened to the river at flood stage or high water, allowing dilution by the larger water volumes to "solve" the problem. A dike had also been built around the plant to hold the phenol waste until it was diverted to one of the ponds. But the dike broke one July night, dumping the entire stock of phenol waste into the river. Saginaw was alerted to turn off water intake until the waste phenol had floated by and gone into Lake Huron. In the morning, Herbert Henry Dow was reported to have said that there was really no problem since he saw no dead fish. He was informed that four boats had followed the spill downstream picking up all the dead fish it left in its wake.

World War II increased the demand for styrene, a key ingredient in the making of liquid rubber, which Dow had been manufacturing since 1935, and the government's need for a lightweight structural metal, which led Willard Dow to build a plant in Freeport, Texas, for the extraction of magnesium from sea water. During the years 1937–1941, Dow was by far the fastest growing of the nation's large chemical firms, averaging 26 percent in annual growth. In the postwar period, the company expanded, both within the United States and in other countries. In a joint venture with Corning Glass, Dow created the Dow Corning Corporation in 1943 to research and develop silicones. Dow's Midland Division, created in 1955, manufactured a variety of products, including Saran Wrap and Handi Wrap, but most of its products were intended for industrial, rather than consumer, use.

During the 1950s, the city's population almost doubled, reaching 27,779 in 1960. The company brought in people with advanced chemistry degrees and also employed people (many of them part-time farmers) in such blue-collar jobs as pipefitters. Dow also sold land to Northwood Institute for the relocation of its business college, which would become a university advancing the cause of free enterprise and unfettered capitalism. Philanthropy, largely from the Herbert H. and Grace A. Dow Foundation, but also from foundations established by other Dow executives, went toward projects such as a community center and a library, as well as cultural activities.

Dow has been admired in Mid-Michigan as a symbol of economic prosperity and new products, and Midland residents generally have trusted the company to safely dispose of waste and monitor pollution. But the generally positive reputation was disrupted during the Vietnam War of the 1960s, when Dow became a household name nationally. Its manufacture of napalm, a gelatinous, fire-causing weapon used during the war, led to numerous demonstrations in 1967 and 1968 at universities when it attempted to recruit graduates. The toxic herbicide Agent Orange was the other chemical weapon sprayed in quantity on the highlands and jungles of Vietnam that caused cancers, birth defects, and many other health problems in returning veterans. By 1982, there were more than twelve thousand vets who had filed Agent Orange claims with the Veterans Administration, and eventually thousands filed lawsuits against Dow and other Agent Orange producers, seeking $44 billion in damages. When the cases were consolidated, they made up the first mass tort class-action in U.S. history. Of course, there is no accountability for the damage done to generations of Vietnamese children and their families whose suffering has been documented.

War crimes may be overlooked, but Dow's record of toxic trespass at the local level includes scares so numerous that it is baffling how residents remain unfazed.

Interviewed in 1983 for a piece by Ward Sinclair in the *Washington Post*, John Palen, editor of the *Midland Daily News*, talked up the city as "unusually educated," with "a lot of PhDs, lawyers, and brain surgeons." He added that it lacked the diverse disciplines of a true university town: "This is not a hotbed of humanistic studies. The attitude here is that science and technology constitute a kind of truth and we have it." The article came out in the midst of controversies surrounding dioxin that have occupied Dow's spin wizards, lobbyists, and lawyers for the last forty years.

Dioxin, a byproduct of the production of 2,4,5-T (a main ingredient of Agent Orange), widely thought to be one of the most cancer-causing agents made by man, became cause for public concern in the 1980s—the age of Superfund legislation and its outgrowth, the Natural Resource Damage Assessment laws. Dow officials continued to insist that dioxin is benign and has no harmful impact on human health. A Dow study, much debated and rejected by many scientists, asserted that dioxin is a product of combustion and is found wherever man uses fire. Nevertheless, in 1983, internal documents surfaced suggesting that company scientists had been concerned for years about the potential hazards of dioxin. One 1967 memo detailed the sensitivity of dioxin and outlined how the company disposed of thousands of gallons of dioxin-contaminated water in old wells. Local environmentalists who raised questions and tried to mount protests became outcasts. Others signed petitions expressing undying faith in the company.

Meanwhile, journalists like Michael Brown visited outlying towns, like Hemlock and Alma, and heard anecdotal evidence of increased birth defects in humans and animals, specifically in the period of 1970–1974, following the production of Agent Orange. Around the time the Environmental Protection Agency announced restrictions on 2,4,5-T, there were fifteen cleft palates among Midlanders, when only five would normally be expected. There were also thirty-four urogenetical defects, when only seven should have occurred. Brown asked scientists if a one-shot exposure to dioxin could result in birth defects, and the answer, based on tests with mice, was a strong affirmative. But the emissions continued. There was a dangerous toxic cloud that hung over the city in 1997 when people were told to shelter in place and remain indoors. Dow did everything in its power to get permits for a new incinerator in 1989 to burn PCBs and dioxin. There were seven thousand drums of dioxin-laden wastes in storage at the Midland plant that had been left over from the Agent Orange period. Pushback from Greenpeace and other environmental groups prevented Dow from incinerating this waste in Midland, but it solved the problem by trucking the wastes to an incinerator in Kansas.

By the year 2000, enough dioxin was found to have poisoned the Tittabawassee floodplain that Dow could no longer evade accountability. The discovery that the entire river corridor was heavily polluted with dioxin was made by General Motors, during soil tests on a wetland near Saginaw. Years of testing, tracking, documenting, and litigating ensued. In 2011, the Department of Justice and the Environmental

Protection Agency had Dow pay a $2.5 million civil penalty as a result of violations of the Clean Air Act, Clean Water Act, and the Resource Conservation and Recovery Act at its facilities in Midland. The company was required to repair cracks, limit emissions, and reduce air pollutants. Under a further settlement, reached in 2019 with the federal government, the State of Michigan, and the Saginaw Chippewa Indian Tribe, Dow created a $77 million fund toward projects intended to restore natural habitats in Midland, Bay, and Saginaw Counties.

Dow Corning, after a period of success promoting its silicone breast implants, began to face lawsuits from women, spurred by popular television investigations, which suggested that implants might be carcinogenic. This led the company to pledge $2 billion toward a global settlement fund. The company filed for bankruptcy protection in 1995 but emerged from it in 2004. Although studies exonerated silicone breast implants as a cause of cancer, the damage to the company was already done. In 2015 it merged with Dow Chemical.

Stagnation in the chemical industry and commodity prices led the Dow Chemical Company to merge in 2017 with DuPont, the new corporation being called DowDuPont. The merger streamlined the two companies' operations into three divisions, each responsible for agriculture, materials science, and specialty products. But DowDuPont dissolved in 2019, creating three companies: www.dow.com (materials science), www.dupont.com, and www.corteva.com (agriscience).

Dow's operations in the Midland area consist of its original 2,600-acre site on the Tittabawassee River, where it manufactures silicones and houses research and development; a corporate center, consisting of three office buildings; the East End facility in downtown Midland; two facilities in Auburn, including Dow Central Campus and Auburn Operations; and an office building in the Uptown development in Bay City. Tours that had been given through the 1950s and 1960s were abruptly halted in 1970, and in 2017, Dow bought a mile-section of Saginaw Road to increase, presumably, its privacy.

Alden B. Dow the Architect

Visitors are, however, welcome to view the Mid-Century Modern architecture found throughout Midland. Alden B. Dow (1904–1983), the younger of Herbert Henry Dow's two sons, decided early that he would not follow into the family business and chose instead to study architecture, and he did so at the University of Michigan and Columbia and, later, on a fellowship with Frank Lloyd Wright. Wright's floating Imperial Hotel, which the Dows visited in 1923 on a trip to Japan, made a lasting impression. Herbert Henry Dow had a more than amateur interest in horticulture and garden design, and his son also became fascinated by Japanese aesthetic principles of organicism, dynamism, and humility.

The Alden B. Dow Home and Studio—a must visit (315 Post St.)—was where the young architect worked out his architectural ideas. Influences are clear, but what is exceptional (especially for this region) is the way the building works with nature. Sited on a five-acre parcel carved out of his parents' property with a stream that runs through it, Dow built the studio first, starting with a sealed concrete "boat" which he sunk into a manmade pond. The building demonstrated Alden's patented "unit block" construction system of rhomboid cubes made from the coal cinders of Dow furnaces.

The son's multi-hyphenate creativity (architect, urban planner, filmmaker, photographer) resembles the elder Dow's wizardry, and proximity to the family firm provided inspiration, global reach, and ample opportunity to use his talent. Midland's population of educated professionals could afford modern houses, and its rapid growth between the wars meant that, in addition to homes, the city needed institutional buildings. Alden's resume grew with a country club, ten churches, eleven schools, eight civic buildings, and two residential complexes, in addition to the sixty-three houses. Download the Mid-Century Modern Midland app for driving tours that showcase the vernacular "language" that is his legacy to Midland.

"Playfulness" is a word often used to describe Dow's designs, but there are other fun structures around the city. The Tudoresque Midland County Courthouse (301 W. Main St.), striking for its use of color on exterior murals, was built in 1925. The building was Herbert Henry Dow's idea, designed by Bloodgood Tuttle of Cleveland. The outer walls, constructed of field stone and stucco, are inlaid with designs of pine trees in natural colors and panels portraying the history of the county. These panels, created in a Dow-developed medium, magnesite stucco, colored with pigment and ground glass, were designed by Paul Honore, a Detroit artist who spent months with Dow scientists developing this fresco technique. Next to the courthouse is the Santa School, a fanciful and brightly colored building used once a year in October when the three-day school is in session. Driving through neighborhoods around the country club, you'll see houses made with Alden Dow's unit blocks here and there, and if you are near Cook and Sugnet Roads, look for Robert Schwartz's dome house (private), designed using Dow materials (Styrofoam and paint) as well as a new Dow method of constructing functional structures, called "spiral generation." It was the first home in the United States to be programmed and built by a machine.

The Home and Studio circles around itself like the ouroboros: The shape symbolizes the way Alden Dow's signature building heals the split he observed in his father's life between work and play, facts and feelings. He thought his buildings could be machines for living and utterly organic, part of the environment in which they lived. Each visitor will decide if Dow got that balance right. The attempt, even if not quite achieved, is admirable, as is his desire to create building materials and even art with recycled wastes (cinders and plastic extrusions displayed as sculptures). The Home and Studio can overwhelm with its riot of fun colors, shapes, shadows, and dimensional shifts, with an electric train running above it all. The serpentine layout of linked, open-floor-plan rooms with no center can also feel disorienting. According to the tour guide, Dow hated focal points (too old-fashioned); he wanted everything to be dynamic, giving the individual ever new feelings and ideas. Toward the end of his life, however, he confessed to a friend: "It's lonely here. . . . I did not set out to make it this way, but it's like the Englishman looking out of his house and seeing nothing that isn't his." After forty years of looking at the views he'd composed, perhaps they'd lost their freshness for the creator. But they are ready and waiting for new visitors in this masterpiece of eclectic design. Park at the restored Post Street School, where Grace A. Dow taught for a year before her marriage. Your tour guide will usher you into a house that will either strike you as a Japanese water serpent or a carnival ride.

Midland is certainly a one-industry town, but unlike Flint or Saginaw and most other Michigan cities, its industry is not automotive. The downturns that have affected the automobile industry thus have had little influence on Midland. It is a prosperous place; in 2022, the median household income was $71,911 and the city's poverty rate was 9.3 percent. People are well educated, with 44.1 percent of the population having a bachelor's, graduate, or professional terminal degree. The foreign-born population, at 3.4 percent, is higher than those of Bay and Saginaw Counties, indicating Midland's economic health, while its Black population makes up 2.3 percent of the city's population.

Points of Interest

Dow Gardens (1809 Eastman Ave.), consisting of 110 landscaped acres, once Herbert Henry and Grace A. Dow's home, is a pleasant place for a casual walk. It includes The Pines (the original Dow home, built in 1899), which is open for tours; the Alden B. Dow Home and Studio (315 Post St.), available for tours, containing the noted architect's drawings; the Whiting Forest canopy walk; a café; and visitors' center.

Midland Center for the Arts (1801 W. Saint Andrews) is a multiple-use facility, designed by Alden Dow, that includes art, science, and historical exhibits (from the Midland County Historical Society) and a venue for theatrical and musical performances.

Herbert D. Doan Midland County History Center (3417 W. Main St.) includes exhibits, a research library, and archives, and is the gateway to Heritage Park.

Charles W. Howard Santa Claus School (2408 Pinehurst Ct.), which traces its origins to a school started in 1937 by long-time Macy's Santa Claus, was brought to Bay City in 1968 and then to Midland in 1987, offering an annual three-day "school" for department store Santas.

Northwood University (4000 Whiting Dr.) was founded as Northwood Institute in 1959 at Alma, Michigan. Its original concept was a two-year business college with a campus and competitive sports. The Alden B. Dow–designed campus sits among the pines west of Midland. Dow executives brought the school to Midland in 1962, when the family sold 186 acres to the school and provided a grant the following year. Since its beginning, the school has been a strong advocate of a conservative, free-market economic and political philosophy. A gift by Richard DeVos established a graduate business school and resulted in the school's change in 1993 to Northwood University.

Chippewa Nature Center (400 S. Badour Rd.), located at the confluence of Pine and Chippewa Rivers, was established in 1963 on a 198-acre parcel Dow leased and eventually gave to the center. The Nature Center has grown since to over 1,500 acres with nineteen miles of trails, a visitors' center with displays about local habitats and interesting artifacts (like the replica of the giant beaver skull, clay pottery, and trade goods, as well as items from early logging), and a brand-new nature education center.

Whiting Overlook Park (Poseyville Road, south of Midland) is the best location to view the sprawling Dow complex.

Overlook Park: At the Depocenter

In 1972, Hugh Starks hopped into a boatswain's chair. His men lifted him high up above Midland on the undeveloped edge of the city. Had he faced west, he would have seen Bullock Creek, a rural town filled with rows of corn, family-owned party stores, and modest churches. In the late 1800s, Bullock Creek was the first high ground settlers could find. It soon became a community populated largely by dairy farmers, many of them Mennonites who had moved in from nearby Larkin Township, having exhausted the farmland to the north. They disassembled an unused grange hall and brought it with them, placing it just west of the creek.

In the 1970s, Bullock Creek still retained its rural idylls. It was a community that disclosed itself to you slowly but earnestly. Long driveways and cul-de-sacs hid modest ranch houses in spearmint, pale pink, brown. Some buildings, shrouded by tall birches and pine, revealed themselves only in parallax to passing motorists. Inside these houses were beige tartan couches and wood paneling, heirloom glassware and upright pianos. Men in Bullock Creek wore orange camo, teenage boys drove tractors to school, and everybody gathered on Sundays for supper. Everybody called them Creekers. The sun seemed to set earlier here than elsewhere, reaching down to swaddle its residents and tell the visitor: You've seen enough for today.

But Hugh wasn't interested in Bullock Creek. He looked east toward the rising sun. He wanted to see the Dow Chemical Company.

Hugh was an executive of the company. He wanted to build a park on this spot, and he wanted to be sure the location would afford a pleasing view of the plant. He was concerned that people had grown to dislike the smokestacks, the plumes of smog. But, from thirty feet up, he gazed out over the cooling ponds and treatment facilities, and he liked what he saw. No doubt he came back down to earth beaming.

He wanted people to see this.

Helen Dow Whiting and her husband, Macaulay Whiting were willing to help realize the vision. Helen was the granddaughter of Dow Chemical founder Herbert Henry Dow and Macaulay was a Dow employee. They paid for the park through their private fund, the Whiting Foundation. They would build a hill at the same height Hugh had risen so that everyone could see what he saw. It would be named "Whiting Overlook Park," but nobody calls it that. Everybody drops the name of the financiers.

Construction on Overlook Park would soon begin. But over six hundred million years earlier, a slow but insidious rhythm had begun over Michigan that would make things a bit more difficult. At this time the state was submerged beneath a massive basin of sea water and surrounded by towering coral reefs, some as high as two hundred meters or more. Gaps in the reefs permitted a slow supply of sea water into the basin, water that was steadily evaporated by the heat of the sun. As the water evaporated, its concentration of salt increased until it was completely saturated. At this point, the salt precipitated. Crystals fell to the seabed like snow and formed a solid layer of salt. The water, no longer saturated, was then again salinated by the gentle flow of sea water through the coral gaps. In time, the water became saturated once more, and the crystals fell again.

Over time this rhythm produced a layer of salt that weighed trillions of tons and was up to 1,600 feet thick. The basin, in this slow and steady way, was breathing seawater and exhaling it back into the ocean. This is called the salt cycle.

Life tends to seek out salt. You can predict the locations of mastodon and musk ox skeletons in Michigan by looking for salt "seeps"—locations where the brine forced itself to the surface, much to the delight of the animals, who lapped at the waters. The Chippewa sought out these springs and traded their salts with other tribes. They called it "magic white sand." When the first white settlers came to Michigan, they came to the salt springs in the southeast. Salt was so valuable that a fist of it could buy you a twenty-pound ham. It was not just used as a seasoning—it was a preservative, crucial to survival. It attracted life and it allowed it to flourish.

In the late 1800s, Herbert Henry Dow, like the musk oxen and mammoths, like the Chippewa and white settlers, was drawn to the salt springs. By the late 1960s, the Dow Chemical Company was the world's largest producer of not only bromine, but also chlorine, styrene, phenol, and several other important chemicals. The salt cycle, with its slow, ancient labors, its saturations and yieldings, its pure white crystalline precipitants that fell slowly, mesmerizingly to a gleaming sea floor, had brought first life, then industry to Midland, Michigan.

But the brine that attracted life to Michigan also suffocated it. Grass wouldn't grow on Overlook Park. It took much longer than expected, nearly two years, to develop the hill and coax the turf that blanketed it to take root and overcome the salt that leached its precious water.

The soil, too, seemed to reject any form imposed upon it. The Michigan basin was a depocenter, a location of extraordinary deposition for many minerals. In the Cambrian, period the waves brought in quartz, heavy and pulverized. In the Upper Devonian, period erosion brought muddy black shale from northern Appalachia. This combination of quartz sand and muddy silt made for ground that was intractable. Machinery at Overlook Park often became stuck in piles of mud, and, while

View from Overlook Park of Dow Chemical complex along the Tittabawassee River.
PHOTOGRAPH BY AUTHOR.

construction was finally finished in 1975, it became clear that the soil was unworkable. In some ways it almost seemed hostile to life.

It's a searing blue winter day as I make my way to the park in 2023, exactly fifty years after construction on the park began. To visit the site, you cross the Tittabawassee River. The name of this river has been corrupted many times: The earliest known incantation is *thaw-tippe-a-waso-ach*, a Chippewa phrase that means "what place is the light." For Chippewa peoples, the *thaw-tippe-a-waso-ach* was a light in a dark woods, a path carved through the dense pines and hardwoods that dominated the area. When white settlers arrived, they adapted the name to their tongue: Tittabawassee. Teenagers growing up in the area, though, have distilled this name down to its maternal essence: the Titt. A fitting name for a river that once provided a protective safe haven for the Chippewa and that has run polluted with the byproducts of silicone production—the main component of Dow Corning breast implants.

To cross the Titt, take the Poseyville Road Bridge on the southeast edge of town. As you crest the bridge you see only sky, and when you descend you enter another world entirely, a place that is comfortable, warm, inert. Poseyville Road is named for the Canada thistles that grow along the road. These wildflowers were brought by immigrants who scattered the seeds they brought with them, hoping to grow oats to feed their horses. But the Canada thistle grew taller than any other plant, proud with wild violet crests. A tenacious and spiny weed, it is sometimes called cursed thistle and is often controlled and destroyed. But the early residents of the Bullock Creek area called them posies, and they still flower there today.

Right now in Midland, it's four below zero (we'll have to imagine the flowers), as I visit the park with my mom, my brother, and Hillary, a friend who was also raised in Midland. Sitting in my car at the top of Overlook Park, I'm trying to see what Hugh Starks saw. And trying not to get the police called on me.

Hugh couldn't have predicted that looking at the Dow Chemical plant would one day be considered a suspicious act. "We all play a role in keeping our community safe," said Community Relations Officer Chris Wenzell in 2011. "If you see something that doesn't look right, call it in." In the 1970s, those who looked out across the pond were proud industrialists. In the 1980s, maybe they were resentful environmentalists, dogged but outnumbered. In a post-9/11 world, though, they had become potential terrorists. On Monday, April 18, 2011, a deputy arrived at Overlook Park to investigate reports of an individual taking photographs of the chemical company. Three years later, a "suspicious person" was once again reported observing the plant, this time with binoculars. By the time the deputy arrived, the person had already left.

It's a simple park: A paved drive takes you up the hill, around a loop, and back down. Walking trails, a somewhat recent addition, meander about the park's outer edges. There are a few picnic tables and informational signs, but none of them tell you much about the park and its construction. None of them mention old Hugh. In some photographs, you can see a marble landmark, inscribed with the park's dedication date: June 8, 1985. But now it's nowhere to be seen. Maybe it sank long ago.

Every year, when I was young, my family would drive out to Overlook Park to go sledding. Today, I've brought with me a bright-orange saucer and a blue toboggan. Before I have a chance to say anything, my mom has snatched the saucer and thrown herself down the hill. My brother, never fearing death, is trying to sled standing up. But my thirtieth birthday is in a couple of months, and I'm not about to be outdone by them. I grab the blue sled and push off the hard-packed snow.

For some reason we've always sledded on the east side of the hill, despite its obvious dangers. This side of the hill is steeper and quickly terminated by a barbed wire fence. The hay bales placed there now are a somewhat recent addition—as kids we would sled again and again, carving a slightly deeper and slicker path each time, until we smashed into the fence. I remember hitting the fence and picking myself up, taking the opportunity to poke my nose through the chain link and stare at the brine pond, my body now warmed by pain. I would walk up the hill slowly, the shouts of worried parents echoing from the top of the hill, and only when I reached the top would I notice the tears in my eyes.

As I walk back up the hill, I see two police cars making their rounds. The little park is apparently still heavily patrolled. They spot us with our bright plastic sleds, though, and ascertain little threat.

Most Midlanders couldn't tell you what this body of water is called here at the park. I know only through research that its name is "Tertiary Pond." It is surrounded by many other brine ponds, each with a name that is clinically unsentimental: "Rectangular Pond," "Pentagonal Pond," "Brine Pond Number 6." I imagine the man who named them did so in order, until at last he came to Brine Pond Number 6 and, feeling a bit self-conscious, gave into his natural restraint. He had had his fun.

A manmade peninsula stretches across Tertiary Pond like a feeble hand, blocked by a barbed wire fence. As a child I imagined the men privileged enough to walk this strip. What did they see when they gazed down? I pictured a murky green pulsation, a muddy staircase that wound down to a secret lounge full of aliens. My uncle, a Bullock Creek native who worked in an automobile parts factory in Saginaw, once gave me an oblong metal bearing he had taken from his workplace. "This," he said, "is a UFO." It was shaped like Saturn and gleamed in my hand. I held onto that bearing for years. I imagined the employees who walked the peninsula were like my uncle. Gruff, cynical, precise, and a little bit unreal.

Eventually my uncle suffered from kidney failure. He blamed his stressful life in the auto parts factory for his ailments and grew more and more depressed. His doctor told him he was no longer able to eat salt. He called it white gold. Each week he would lie on a bed and undergo dialysis. His blood circulated through a machine that drew out toxins with a solution of dextrose. Potassium, phosphorus, and sodium were drawn out and the healthy blood recirculated. Drawn out, recirculated, drawn out, recirculated. The salt cycle.

If only he could have some salt. He ate bland meals and grimaced. Injection site wounds on his right arm grew worse and worse, looking as if a spider was spinning a purple-blue web beneath his skin. I could never tell him that I lost the UFO long ago. I felt so guilty. Would he remember?

We're eating cold pizza from Pizza Sam's, a downtown Midland classic, as the sun begins to set. I'm mesmerized by the massive pink cloud of steam that hangs over the center of the plant. It emanates from the Midland Cogeneration Venture, a gas-powered steam and electrical plant that was originally intended to be the site of the Midland Nuclear Power Plant. When Hugh looked over the horizon, he must have imagined it would soon be dominated by nuclear cooling towers. Though it would be heavily criticized by environmentalists, the nuclear power plant was represented by the Midland Nuclear Power Committee, a group that claimed "special awareness of the necessity and urgency of limiting and reducing all sources of environmental pollution." By the late 1960s, Dow Chemical's coal power plants were declining, and the soot and ash they produced covered the town with thick black dust. To make matters worse, Dow executives had discovered that energy production was much cheaper in Texas, where natural gas was so common it was often burned as a waste product in the oil industry. Executives began moving much of the company's energy jobs to Texas, and Midlanders began fearing for their livelihood. The Midland Nuclear Power Plant, though, would keep them employed, and it would eliminate the ghastly smog that hung over the city.

But decades passed with little progress. What was a staunchly prowar and pronuclear American public became disillusioned and angry as the media presented them with images of children burning alive, covered in napalm produced by the Dow Chemical Company. The Three Mile Island incident in 1979 was proof for many that regulatory oversight was ineffective and could not guarantee the safety of nuclear power, and that the Nuclear Regulatory Committee had proven themselves incompetent. Disinformation was rampant, reports conflicted, and Americans developed a deep mistrust of nuclear energy and the agencies that supported it. Local activist Mary Sinclair spoke out against the construction of the nuclear plant, and while many Midlanders despised her, seeing to it that she was ostracized, her children bullied at school, even going so far as to throw their trash on her lawn, it became more and more difficult to deny that her concerns were well-founded.

The Consumers Power Company, a Michigan utility company that had partnered with Dow to build the plant, was suffering from the long-term effects of inflation brought on by the Vietnam War and the high costs of construction and litigation. Dow sued them for millions, claiming the company had misrepresented the costs of construction and its many delays. And once again, structures built in the Michigan basin began to sink. Dirt trucked in to raise the plant above flood levels was improperly compacted, causing the plant's concrete generator building to sink into the earth at an alarming rate. This issue would be costly to address, and it was only one of many quality control problems. By 1984, Consumers Power had run out of money, and on July 16 of that year, the project was canceled.

Maybe it's for the best, as those cooling towers would have obscured the view. Winter sunsets at Overlook Park are unearthly. No doubt owing to the pollutants suspended in the air, the colors in the sky are dazzling, almost overwhelming. Reds, oranges, even greens spill across the sky like oil in water. It's a vaguely unsettling feeling to watch the darkness assert itself over the plant, but somehow the slow rhythms of the smokestack lights are comforting. And at first, when the light leaves, and you look across the horizon, it can be hard to tell what are simple factory bulbs and what are stars.

I asked my grandma, who retired after working at a printing company in Midland for many years, what she knew about the Dow Chemical Company. "I don't know anything about Dow," she said. What would she see when she looked out across the brine ponds?

My father, also a child of Bullock Creek, loved Overlook Park. Born into an engineering family, he became a draftsman, then a CAD designer. He designed steering columns until it became clear in 2008 that the auto industry had failed him. There was no way he could get a job at Dow. He was eventually laid off and could find little work. During this time, he would drive us out to the park, try to talk about chemistry, chain smoke, and scowl. My father knew that Midland was a city for chemical engineers and encouraged my brother and I to get chemistry degrees. Neither of us did. A few years later, angry and resentful toward almost everyone, he died of alcoholism. There was no funeral service.

It was only after my father's death that my aunt told me he had always pressed us into chemical engineering so that we had a reason to stay, a reason he himself could not find. If it had been up to me, I would have had him buried at the very top of this park. That way, he could lie outside the city and look out over it—really get a good look at the place.

Recently, bald eagles have been spotted above Brine Pond Number 6. They have nested in nearby trees. There has been talk of moving the yearly fireworks show to avoid disturbing them. Some people are afraid that they might leave. But I really think they're here to stay. I don't think they mind the fireworks, the pollution, the shouts. Over ten years ago, I left Midland to go to school and start a career. I've lived in Flint, Detroit, Ann Arbor, and various small cities scattered about Michigan. But nothing has really felt quite right.

Sledding today has renewed some part of me. The brine seems to have that effect. But as I warm up in the car, I feel like I'm mourning. Even as an outsider, somebody who has viewed Dow with resentment, the soft red glow of the lights over Tertiary

Pond is hard to leave. The geese have gathered in the pond where the warm brine bubbles to the surface and are sleeping, their bills tucked into their feathers. I finish eating my cold pizza and give everybody a hug. It's dark now, and time for us to go our separate ways.

I'd like the eagles to stay.

Up the Tittabawassee

West of Midland on US-10 is the village of Sanford (pop. 763), essentially a suburb. Named for Charles S. Sanford, who purchased and developed pinelands in this area, it was originally the site of a mill. The dam built here in 1924 on the Tittabawassee River, creating Sanford Lake, overtopped in 2020 due to inadequate maintenance and increased water flow caused by climate change, flooding Midland downstream and creating a disaster of historic proportions. Plans are underway to restore the dams and lakes upstream.

The land north of Sanford is forest and swampy until you reach an agricultural area in the north of the county, centered at Edenville (township pop. 2,493). Some might consider this area to be where "up north" begins—cottages and recreational activities like off-road vehicle racing through woods (especially toward the ghost towns of Billings and Estey) dominate the scene. The dam built here in 1925 also failed and had formed another reservoir, Lake Wixom. This lake carries the name of Frank I. Wixom (1863–1943), an entrepreneur whose vision created the dams and lakes and, in doing so, looked both backward and forward.

Wixom was drawn to magic shows as a young man and later toured Michigan with a minstrel show and a circus. He visited lumber camps along the Tittabawassee in their heyday, amazed by the skill of the "river hogs" who, with long pikes and peaveys, cleared log jams and sorted them. We should recall that these men, employed by the Tittabawassee River Boom Company at Midland, sorted and rafted over ten billion feet of logs between 1864 and 1894. After a successful stint in the oil business, Wixom turned his thoughts toward electrical power. He purchased land, studied the Tittabawassee's flow, and created the Wolverine Power Company, which built dams at Sanford in 1924 and at Edenville in 1925 (as well as two others further upstream in Gladwin County). Wixom understood the area's future potential as a recreational area, having the state stocking the lakes with fish and selling lots for cottages. From 1932 to 1940, he sponsored an annual Lumberjack Homecoming, drawing up to sixty thousand visitors, that featured log "birling" competitions, entertainment, and other special events. His private park, where this was held, contained museums, an old schoolhouse, dining halls, and statues depicting the old "river hogs." All was abandoned after his death, and Lake Wixom remained until 2020 as a recreational and retirement area.

PORT HURON

Profile

People traveling between Chicago and Toronto frequently bypass this pleasant city, but when they do, they miss its charms. The Black River bisects the main artery, Military Street (south of the bridge), and Pine Grove Avenue and Huron Street (north of the bridge). Large Queen Anne–style houses grace the view of the river, while the Black River, which flows from the northwest, hosts a marina and leads residential development inland.

Located sixty-three nautical miles from Detroit, Port Huron (pop. 28,826) sits at the head of the St. Clair River. North is the route across Lake Huron to the Straits of Mackinac and beyond and to Lake Superior. Situated at a crossroads between upper and lower lakes and between two nations, it is no wonder that people have always congregated here. Archaeological evidence suggests there were mound-building Indigenous cultures at the river's mouth (at the location of Pine Grove Park, 1204 Pine Grove Ave.). Fort St. Joseph, the second fortified post established in lower Michigan, was built here in 1686 to protect the French fur trade against English aggression, and Fort Gratiot was built on the site of Fort St. Joseph in 1814 to protect the area from British encroachment and hostile Indians (historical marker at the Edison Parkway–Edison Drive intersection). During the land boom years of 1835–1837, capitalists from Detroit, New York, and Boston purchased land and platted seven different villages with distinct names like Peru, Desmond, Gratiot, Huron, and Montgat. The developers aggregated the plats in 1837 and named it Port Huron.

A Border Town

Although the War of 1812 was settled by treaty in December 1814, anxiety persisted along the border, since Britain still held Canada. When Upper Canadians rebelled against Britain in 1837, Americans in the border region were quick to support their brothers and the cause of republican democracy against what they perceived as British tyranny. They joined "Hunters' Lodges" (branches of a secret society that, at its height, claimed to have two hundred thousand members) and prepared to invade and liberate Canada. To that end, a group of Michigan men attempted to seize the arms in Fort Gratiot early in the winter of 1837–1838 but were foiled by a detachment of Brady Guards. The official position was neutrality with Canada, so the United States deployed soldiers against its own people. Though the Patriots failed, their attempt to put the brakes on unrestrained capitalism, which they feared would lead to wage slavery, penury, and idleness, was bold if not prescient. Hunters or Patriots were farmers and mechanics who stood up for what they felt were values of cooperation, honest labor, and happiness, apart from the alienating world of capitalist commodity markets, paper money, credit, and artificially created scarcity.

Anyone who has ever driven across the Blue Water Bridge knows how sublime the view is. The lapis-blue Lake Huron flows into the channel of the turquoise St. Clair River to create a profusion of life, with boats of all sizes, fishermen, gulls, and black piles of coal, and smokestacks belching fire. Imagine adding to the mix ferry boats and log rafts. In the background, the fairy lights of Canada's Chemical Alley twinkle deceptively. Forty percent of that country's petroleum industry is squeezed into six miles of shoreline, around which are reservations for First Nations. The St. Clair River flows forty miles south, and as the river shallows into the largest freshwater delta in the world, there is another extraordinary waterscape called the St. Clair Flats, made up of nine islands and three major channels with hundreds of smaller cuts. Constance Fenimore Woolson, grandniece of the famous writer James Fenimore Cooper, visited in 1855 and wrote a poem about the delta, in which a Detroiter on a fishing trip searches for words to compose his idea of the Flats: "wild," "boundless," "an ocean full of land, a prairie full of water, a desert full of verdure." What makes it magical is that it is a habitable world made by the river's action of slowing down, dropping its sediment load, and shaping those deposits by a continuous flow.

To live by a large river is to be kept in the heart of things. We become involved in its life, and its constant movement enlivens us. No wonder many who lived here were innovators—they heard the river's song and channeled their own expansive ideas into the effort of making new kinds of boats, machines, technologies, network connections, and even social visions.

Geographers say that rivers create civilization, because they facilitate the movement of peoples, who trade goods, ideas, and even cultural practices, and this happens most profoundly through intermarriage. Coral beads and other implements suggest that the Indians in this region had distant trading partners; some settlers, especially the French, married Native women to produce a Métis group sometimes called the "Muskrat" French. Samuel Ward, who developed a shipbuilding empire in Newport (now Marine City), started small but made a fortune using the waterways to trade. A native of Vermont, he traveled to Salem (now Conneaut), Ohio, on Lake Erie, where he built and operated a packet boat—Ward's "floating bazaar"—that traveled the lakes and rivers selling necessities and some urban luxuries to the pioneers. Eventually, Ward settled in Newport and began building schooners, which he sailed regularly to Green Bay and Chicago.

Lumbering reached its peak at Port Huron in the 1870s, but its decline did not affect the city as adversely as it did many other Michigan lumbering towns. By that time, Port Huron had an array of industries that developed in response to its location as a border city on a major shipping lane and the commercial hub for the agricultural towns of the Thumb. Because the Grand Trunk Western Railroad brought people from Canada, the city was the second-largest point of entry after New York City for new immigrants during the 1880s and 1890s. The Michigan Sulphite Fibre Company began operation in 1888, using a new German process to manufacture fiber pulp, most of its employees being German as well. It became the Port Huron Paper Company in 1910 and later Domstar, until it closed in 2021. Another substantial industry, Mueller Brass Company, built a factory in 1917. Shipwrights, tinkerers, and engineers in and around Port Huron were on the cutting edge of revolutions in transportation that occurred between 1820 and 1920.

Shipbuilding may seem obsolete to us now, but steamships were built on the Black River in Port Huron. The opening of the Erie Canal in 1824 was, for innovative men like Samuel Ward, a boon. Ward sailed and towed his schooner—the *St. Clair*, loaded with walnut and potash—all the way to New York City, opening a route to the sea for Michigan farmers and manufacturers. Technology always moves fast, and Ward adapted to each shift, building steamships in the middle of the nineteenth century, advocating for a federal weather bureau, and, when it was clear that railroads were the future, investing in rolling mills, the Bessemer steel-making process, as well as iron mines. Sam's nephew, Eber Brock Ward, grew up helping his father man the Fort Gratiot lighthouse and went on to become Michigan's first millionaire.

Negotiating crossings effectively and efficiently was crucial to trade between Port Huron and Sarnia, as ferries morphed from rowboats to horse-powered catamarans to steam-powered "swing ferries" that ran on a cable and used the river's current. There were even specially made ferries for trains until the St. Clair Railroad Tunnel was completed and opened in 1891 and electrified in 1908. It was the first subaqueous tunnel in the world, and despite a workers' strike midway through the difficult dig, the tunnel was touted as a symbol of international peace and was opened for pedestrians, temporarily, so all could appreciate how technology helped the cause of international cooperation.

The Motor City (Detroit) and Vehicle City (Flint) claim to be *the* car capitals of Michigan, but the first self-propelled vehicle in Michigan and perhaps in the country was built in a machine shop in Memphis (on the St. Clair–Macomb County line)

Fort Gratiot Light Station, Port Huron.
COURTESY OF THE LIBRARY OF CONGRESS, CAROL M. HIGHSMITH ARCHIVE.

during the winter of 1884–1885. Large chunks of soft coal powered the four-seated vehicle to its maximum speed of twelve miles per hour. Thomas Clegg (1863–1939) and his English-born father, John, drove "The Thing" in the Fourth of July parade in Emmett in 1885, but the car had nowhere to go, literally, because it was unable to cope with the incredibly bad roads of the day. Roads would improve significantly, thanks in part to the Port Huron Engine and Thresher Company that, with its three plants and two foundries, manufactured the enormous machine rollers and dump cars needed for road building. Furthermore, the first International Good Roads Conference was held in the city in 1900. Something else that is not widely known is that gas-powered engines were first developed for boats before they were tried out in Ford and GM vehicles. By the early twentieth century, Port Huron had five car companies manufacturing vehicles.

Edison

Today, we hear a lot about "technology crossover," and we can learn the basics from studying the kinds of innovation that happened early in a city like Port Huron that straddles so many boundaries—between nations, between water and land, between town and country. Thomas Alva Edison (1847–1931), Port Huron's boy wonder and most famous innovator, took up the challenge of connecting over long distance to the next level.

Edison, who was called "Al" by family and friends, spent his formative years in Port Huron. He lived close to the railroad station and was fascinated by the steam engines and equipment there. Al worked as a newsboy on the Grand Trunk train that ran daily to and from Detroit, starting in 1859. With a whole workday to pass in the city before the return trip, he wandered the streets, talked to workmen and mechanics, and experimented in the chemical laboratory he had set up in the back of a baggage car. He even printed his own paper on a printing press he made. When a stick of phosphorus set fire to the car, railroad officials tossed his lab off the train, but by that time, his father had come to accept his son's determination.

Edison had over 1,200 patents—and while he created the incandescent lightbulb and the phonograph and developed early motion picture technology in his New Jersey lab, his proclivities to experiment, to solve practical problems, especially ones related to communication, were shaped by the place in which he grew up. Is it far-fetched to see the materials that would become his stock in trade as somehow connected to the blue river? After a severe winter storm in 1863–1864, large ice flows in the St. Clair River severed the submarine telegraph cable between Port Huron and Sarnia. All communication was cut off until young Edison thought of using the locomotive whistle to toot in the rhythmic cadence of Morse code to the other side. Edison made a career of perfecting methods for communicating information, sound, and rhythm across distances through wires and cables.

Other People with Ideas

Because Port Huron was just upriver from Detroit, it offered men with creative ideas the space and freedom to do their own thing. C. Harold Wills was the chief designer and engineer on every car that Ford manufactured from 1903 to 1912, the pinnacle being the Model T. Other major innovations include planetary transmission and the assembly line. Wills parted company with Henry Ford after World War I because he wanted to experiment with other car designs and Ford notoriously preferred the simplicity of the Model T. Wills discovered nearby Marysville when, sailing on his yacht, he had to seek shelter from a storm in a cove nearby. In March 1919, with the ice barely off the river, he bought 4,200 acres and 4.5 miles of shoreline for his planned automobile factory and utopian community, which he called "the city of contented living" or the "dream city." Wills bet that well-paid and housed men would take pride in their work and build superior cars. He also had to create a market for his luxury cars, which he tried to do with colorful advertisements that featured women drivers for the first time and even made a film, *A Free Trip to Marysville—by Motion Picture*. Despite his marketing strategies and help from investors like the Edison Company, which built a power plant for the fledgling town, the company closed shop in 1927—due to a major economic downturn that bankrupted many.

Women, minorities, and young political activists have also found Port Huron a city that helped them grow their ideas. Bina West Miller, from the small St. Clair County town of Capac, started the Women's Benefit Association that sold life insurance to women and also employed women. By the close of 1894, 5,503 members were enrolled. Mary Frances Doner (1893–1985) was a celebrated pulp fiction author with novel scenarios grounded in local places and the lives of men involved in shipping and salvaging. There is also a long-standing African American community here that dates from the late nineteenth century. Port Huron was a stop on the Underground Railroad, and, after the Civil War, some Black people who had crossed the river to freedom returned. Proximity to the border likely made them feel safe.

The Black Community

Initially, Black people settled in the First Ward, just a few blocks from the St. Clair River, in an area many remember as "one of the most integrated in Michigan," with Mexicans, Italians, Polish, and Irish living in close proximity. When industrialists needed waterfront property, the most Black people moved to South Park—five streets in the southwest section of the city, with Dove and Moak as the north and south borders. South Park grew in the 1920s, when businesses like the Holmes foundry recruited both Black and later Mexican American workers. Also in South Park was Moak Machine and Foundry, which made shell noses in World War I. Following the war, it turned out woodworking machinery, hand saws, and gray iron projects. From 1902, the South Park community sought to organize a church, and that finally happened in 1918 when Shiloh Missionary Baptist Church was officially founded.

Shiloh Missionary Baptist still anchors Port Huron's Black community, and those living in other parts of the city return for Sunday service. The church bell used to ring out every death in the community and warn of inclement weather. "Do you still ring the bell?" I asked when visiting. "Ring it and the whole place would fall down," joked Anita Ashford, one of eight children born to Mandel and Johnnie Mae Ashford from

Mississippi and Alabama. “Naw, she’s in good shape,” insisted Helen, a parishioner who had been vacuuming the sanctuary, readying it for Easter. South Park has suffered in the same ways that historically Black neighborhoods across the state and nation have. Houses have been torn down to make room for a huge industrial park and low-income housing projects. Streets have been dead-ended to further isolate the community, yet folks are proud of this place, even if they’ve left it behind. At the spot on the St. Clair River where Shiloh did baptisms in the early years—at the scenic turnaround at the end of Lincoln Park—the Ashford kids erected benches to honor each parent and themselves. “It is a way of making our presence felt, of saying that Black families were and are here to stay.”

As proud as Anita is of her community, she thinks that people could have “been so much more.” She uses her Daddy, who everyone called “Big Ash,” as an example. He was a poet at heart but spent most of his time just surviving like everyone else did and teaching his kids how to navigate the white world: Pick your battles and don’t get caught up in the “I thing”—“What you do, you do for other people.” Anita, who served on the city council for twenty-one years, won the mayoral election in 2024.

There were never a lot of businesses in South Park, but there was a hotel, a few groceries and restaurants along with hair salons and barber shops, but there was no shortage of blind pigs. They were all over Port Huron, especially during Prohibition, when rum running across the St. Clair River was a lucrative trade from which even young Black men profited—if they could hold their breath and dive for bottles on the river bottom. Most Black people worked for United Brass and Aluminum and the Holmes Foundry, but other companies, like Portland Cement, also employed them. There were, however, some Black men who became very successful. Isaac Lang, for example, started his own tool and die company, Sombur Machine and Tool, that is still in business.

Native Americans called the St. Clair River the *otis-sippi* (“blue river”), and it has always drawn people like a magnet. Men and women fish for walleye up and down the boardwalks, using the rod holders mounted on the guardrails. If it’s too cold, they set their lines, and sit in their trucks, listening for tinkling of bells that means they’ve got a bite. People walk, walk dogs, sit and watch, read and write, or just relax in the presence of an eternal force that takes them to new places.

The place we grow up in shapes our ideas and the possibilities we can imagine for our individual and community lives. Take James O’Sullivan, born in 1876 to an Irish father and English mother, who was ten years old when workers from the United States and Canada began boring and digging the St. Clair River tunnel, which was completed and opened in 1891. An enormous river, a massive engineering project, connections across a border, and, on top of that, the example of Edison as an inventive genius, all the natural and human elements in Port Huron's turn of the century ecosystem, prepared O'Sullivan for his life's mission. He imagined and directed the building of the Grand Coulee Dam—the apogee of the Works Progress Administration infrastructure projects during Franklin D. Roosevelt's New Deal; when completed in 1941, it was called the Eighth Wonder of the World.

O'Sullivan was definitely not a dam builder at the start of his career. He studied literature in college and earned a law degree at the University of Michigan while working at his father's construction company. He drew on all these areas of expertise once he moved west to Seattle and opened a law office in the small town of Ephrata that dealt with land claims and land reclamation. Deeply affected by the hardscrabble life of farmers in a land of sage brush and dust storms without adequate water and perhaps remembering his childhood on Lake Huron and the St. Clair River, he became obsessed with the idea of damming the Columbia River to make electricity available and cheap and, most importantly, to irrigate six hundred thousand acres of land. At the same time, he began studying to make himself a dam engineer, reading all the available literature on the subject.

O'Sullivan returned to Port Huron after his father's death to run the company and supervised the construction of electrical substations, sewers, dams, canals, high schools, churches, steam electrical installation, and grain elevators. But he never let go of his idea for a dam on the Columbia—a river comparable to the St. Clair in terms of size and speed—both rivers discharging more than fifteen thousand cubic feet of water per second. If men of the former generation could tunnel under the St. Clair, then a massive concrete dam (one mile wide and 550 feet high) was not impossible for men of his generation to accomplish. He had begun working on the dam idea in 1919 by writing articles to work out his ideas. His law background served him well during his twenty-year fight with private power interests to reclaim lands to be used for the common good, and he would eventually serve as secretary for the Columbia River Basin Commission that successfully gained federal backing and funds.

The story of Jim O'Sullivan is not just about him but about you and what you are going to do as humanity is faced with environmental crises that threaten our very existence as a species. What ideas and skills has your home place given you that will enable you to imagine a better world and inspire others to build it with you?

Fast forward to the radical movements of the 1960s. Members of the newly formed organization, Students for a Democratic Society, met in June of 1962 at the Franklin D. Roosevelt AFL-CIO Labor Center (in operation from 1946 to 1966; now the site of Lakeport State Park, twelve miles north of Port Huron) where they drafted a manifesto that became their founding document, called the "Port Huron Statement." This organization flourished on campuses in the latter part of the decade, virtually defining the "New Left." The statement, written by Tom Hayden, called for more participatory democracy and critiqued the military-industrial complex while avoiding Marxist theory. These students also wanted work that was about something more than money or survival but educative, not stultifying; creative, not mechanical; self-directed, not manipulated. Many young people today want the same things but must get out from under the dizzying amounts of data, technology, and now artificial intelligence to think and act experimentally. This is why we need to visit and revisit small cities like Port Huron and remember the visions dreamed up here and tried—where the inland sea becomes a blue river that makes a world. The view is open for dreaming. What will you see on the horizon?

Points of Interest

St. Clair Railroad Tunnel (entrance west side of tenth St., just south of the junction of Johnstone and 10th Sts.) is two miles long, with 6,025 feet under the St. Clair River, and connects Port Huron with Sarnia, Ontario. There are two separate rail tunnels: the first opened in 1891 and was the first subaqueous tunnel in the nation. The bigger second tunnel, completed in 1995, needed to accommodate double-stacked shipping containers on railcars. It was one of the largest construction projects in North America, designed and built by an international team.

Great Lakes Maritime Center (51 Court St.), located at the junction of the Black River and the St. Clair River, is a great place to relax and watch the river traffic, freighters, pleasure boats, and sailboats. There are opportunities for learning from the collection of maritime artifacts, underwater camera, and displays that cover the history of the Great Lakes.

Blue Water River Walk is a one-mile walkway beginning at the Maritime Center parking lot and ending at the Seaway Terminal. The entire St. Clair River is a binational Area of Concern, identified as such in 1985 due to contamination of the river and its sediment with heavy metals, toxic organics, and *E. coli* bacteria. All the original objectives have been met and all restrictions on river usage have been removed. Because the St. Clair is home to the largest remaining Great Lakes spawning population of lake sturgeon, much has been done to recreate spawning grounds that creation of the shipping channel damaged.

Carnegie Center, built as a Carnegie library in 1902, is part of the Port Huron Museums group. It showcases the history of the region with a maritime focus, with a whole floor devoted to diving and shipwrecks as well as local history.

Harrington Hotel dominates the corner of Military and Fourth Streets. Built in 1896 in the Richardsonian Romanesque style, President Harry S. Truman and his wife Bess stayed here for part of their honeymoon in 1919. According to their daughter, whenever Truman wanted to regain the radiance of those first days with Bess, he simply wrote, "Port Huron." For him it was a code word for happiness.

Ladies of the Maccabees Temple (901 Huron Ave.) was designed and built in 1906 as the headquarters of the sister organization to the Knights of the Maccabees. Initially, the Knights did not want to recognize the Ladies, but the efforts of the women paid off, particularly those of Bina West Miller, who thought that women also needed a sororal organization that offered them the same social and self-improvement activities as well as insurance. The two separate Maccabees organizations merged and moved headquarters to Detroit in 1928.

Experience Center, a STEM-based center housed in the Clara E. Mackenzie Building on the campus of SC4 (the alternate name of St. Clair Community College) (323 Erie St.), includes Nasr Natural Science Museum—which houses artifacts that document the natural history of the region, including mammoth and mastodon bones as well as a complete skeleton of a woolly rhinoceros—and the Challenger Learning Center, an immersive space-themed simulation experience.

Edison Depot Museum (510 Thomas Edison Parkway), part of the Port Huron Museums group, is former station built by the Grand Trunk Railway Company in 1858. It served as a major entry point for immigrants passing from Canada to the United States, and by 1869, approximately forty-two thousand immigrants had passed through the station. The station is now a museum that showcases Thomas Edison's life in Port Huron. There is a restored baggage car that holds a reconstruction of Edison's chemistry lab.

The Huron Lightship (riverfront at Pine Grove Park), part of the Port Huron Museums group and decommissioned in 1970, was the last functioning lightship (a floating lighthouse) on the Great Lakes.

Blue Water International Bridge (approach at Pine Grove Ave., south of Elmwood St.) is an 871-foot cantilever span completed in 1938 and maintained by the United States and Canada. The original bridge had two lanes for vehicle traffic and a sidewalk until the 1980s, when a third lane was added and the sidewalk removed. The bridge saw so much traffic that a second bridge, the eastbound span, was opened in 1997.

Tuskegee Airmen Memorial, Flag Plaza (riverfront near the Depot Museum), is a memorial that was installed in 2021 to recognize the accomplishments of the Tuskegee Airmen, who trained at Selfridge Field in Mount Clemens, and the two pilots whose planes went down in nearby waters in 1944.

Fort Gratiot Museum and Lighthouse (2802 Omar St.) is part of the Port Huron Museum group and consists of a fort, built in 1814, and a lighthouse (a conical stone tower), completed in 1825 and rebuilt in 1829. The fort hospital is the only piece of the fort that remains. The lighthouse is still an active light—with a green signal to differentiate it from train headlights in the nearby railyard. Visitors may climb to an observation platform.

Wills Sainte Claire Museum (2408 Wills St., Marysville) has a unique collection of classic Wills St. Claire cars, manufactured in Marysville from 1921 to 1926, as well as artifacts from Childe Harold Wills's career that illuminate his vision of a utopian workers' city on the shores of the St. Clair River.

The Black River Greenway

The Black River flows seventy-three miles through the eastern Thumb, from northern Sanilac County to northern St. Clair County. It begins as agricultural drains in the wetlands of Minden Bog, a large peatland near Minden City, and then flows almost due south along the western edge of the Port Huron moraine through rural Sanilac County. High bluffs, near the confluence of Silver Creek with the Black River near Jeddo, expose the moraine to view. The agricultural reach has been channelized, straightened, and the river's banks deforested to facilitate rapid runoff from the fields; the added sediments and fertilizers create potential problems for the river. From Applegate, the river flows and meanders freely. South of Croswell its valley becomes more pronounced as it moves through the pine and hardwood forests of the Beards Hills in the State Game Area. After the river turns east, it flows through the suburban and urban sections of Port Huron until it joins its brown waters with the St. Clair's blue. A hidden gem of the eastern Thumb, the Black River flows through some truly unusual ecosystems.

Minden Bog

The headwaters of the Black River are in Minden Bog, a dome-shaped peat bog, formed after the retreat of the glaciers ten thousand years ago by an extensive buildup of peat over a glacial drainage channel. Minden is one of just a few raised bogs in North America and the only one remaining in Michigan.

Access to the Minden City State Game Area is at the end of Palms Road, just west of Palms in Minden Township. At this location, the Black River is a ditch with black water from the tannins in the decaying plant matter. Cross the river over a small bridge and proceed through a field of tall grass along a ditch lined with birch trees, and you will enter a large peatland. Leatherleaf (*Chamaedaphne calyculata*) shrubs and tamarack trees dot the landscape of the bog, along with several species of blueberries and cranberries. Bog laurel (*Kalmia polifolia*), a small, pink-blooming shrub in the heath family, grows sporadically throughout the bog, along with the strange carnivorous plants known as round leaf sundews (*Drosera rotundifolia*) that grow in the sphagnum moss. Due to low nutrient levels in the boggy soil, these plants obtain nutrients by trapping insects in their sticky tentacle-covered leaves and digesting them with enzymes. Other interesting and elusive plant species here are the ladies' tresses orchid (*Spiranthes sp.*), which forms twisting stems of white blooms in late summer and early fall; the Eastern tamarack (*Larix laricina*), Michigan's only deciduous conifer; and the jack pine (*Pinus banksiana*), a rarity in the Thumb.

In undisturbed areas like the Minden Bog, it is not that surprising that unusual species turn up. The bog was recently home to Michigan's only known wild wolverine. How she got here is something of a mystery. Mostly likely she migrated from northern Canada or crossed Lake Huron on an iceberg. Originally spotted by and later studied extensively by a local hunter and biology teacher, Jeff Ford, the wolverine died in 2010 and is now on display in Bay City State Recreation Area's Saginaw Bay Visitor Center.

Visitors are advised to check in with the Michigan Department of Natural Resources regarding hunting seasons and rules prior to visiting the bog, and it is good to wear orange, especially in autumn.

Near Carsonville

From Minden City State Game Area, the Black River is channelized for the most part until reaching the Carsonville, Applegate, and Croswell areas. Depending on water levels, the river may be navigable for canoes and kayaks starting around Carsonville. Just west of Carsonville, the river flows past the Hi-Way Drive-In Theater, on the south side of M-46. Open seasonally, this outdoor drive-in movie theater from 1948 is still a local favorite. Past the drive-in, the river continues further south to Washington Road. The Washington Road bridge over the Black River, south of Carsonville, offers a rare scenic view. Little additional public river access exists in the Carsonville-Applegate area.

Croswell

As the river winds toward Croswell, it passes the P. L. Graham Park and Campground, about a mile north of the city. The sixteen-acre former Boy Scout campground features walking paths and views of the Black River as it slowly meanders through forests of hardwoods and hemlock trees. The river continues south from the park and passes through Croswell, a town west of the Lake Huron beach town of Lexington, in southern Sanilac County. Croswell began as the community of Black River in 1845, when lumber was being moved down the river.

In Croswell's town center, the river enters Riverbend Park, home to a local attraction, the "Be Good to Your Mother-In-Law Swinging Bridge." This wooden plank bridge spans the Black River, held together by suspension cords and chain fencing. The bridge was originally constructed in 1905 for workers of the Michigan Sugar Company, located just east of downtown Croswell, to cross the Black River, although what this has to do with mothers-in-law is unclear.

A walking trail that begins at the swing bridge and takes you through business district of Croswell to Gingersnap Park, a small pocket park with playground equipment and a massive old-growth bur oak (*Quercus macrocarpa*) likely to be hundreds of years old. Walkers may use Howard and Maple streets to return to the swinging bridge and the river.

Beards Hills and Port Huron State Game Area

Beyond Croswell, the Black River enters northern St. Clair County and the Beards Hills area. As part of the Port Huron State Game Area (PHSGA), this area is much more wooded, making it popular for canoeing and kayaking as well as hunting and hiking. The portion of the river that runs from roughly Comstock Road to Norman Road makes up St. Clair County's designated blueway, the "Black River Experience." The Comstock Road access to the Black River is a small parking space on the north side of the road west of the river. A trail leads downhill to the river's edge and is a rustic access point in the PHSGA. The Norman Road access point offers more parking spaces along the roadside and scenic views of the forest and river valley. Along the east side of the river, north of Norman Road, rustic campsites, complete with fire pits and some grills, nestle in the game area's pine-birch-hardwood forest.

Additional points of interest include an informal overlook of Mill Creek from the clay bluffs on the south side of Beard Road (M-136), west of the Black River, and the PHSGA access off Abbottsford Road (just below the Mill Creek–Black River confluence, east of the small town of Ruby). Stands of oak and pine and a beautiful view of the river valley greet the eyes from the rustic Abbottsford Road parking area, with a pathway leading to the Black River. Dense stands of eastern hemlock (*Tsuga canadensis*) create a sense of being much further north than the Thumb.

In addition, west-southwest of Port Huron State Game Area and the Beards Hills is the twelve-mile Wadhams to Avoca Trail. Formerly a CSX rail line, the trail is now a nonmotorized pathway for biking, hiking, and horseback riding. The highlight of this trail is, without doubt, the Mill Creek trestle bridge. This century-old, 640-foot-long bridge is high (60 feet) and offers a spectacular view of the surrounding land and Mill Creek. The trestle is best accessed by a one-mile walk north from the Wadhams to Avoca trailhead parking on Imlay City Road.

From the Port Huron State Game Area, the river continues south to Woodsong County Park, part of the St. Clair County Parks system. This park was once a Girl Scout camp until St. Clair County purchased the property in 2008. Interesting native plants in this hilly area include horse gentian (*Triosteum aurentiacum*), with its bright-orange fruits, and maidenhair fern (*Adiantum pedatum*), with its feather-like foliage.

Terminus at Port Huron

The section of the Black River that flows through the city of Port Huron has historically suffered the most damage. By 1881, it had already become "a toxic smelly sponge," and this only got worse when Michigan Sulphite Fibre Company, a paper mill established on its banks in 1888, started dumping wastes directly into the river. The river had to be cleaned up if Port Huron had any hope of becoming a tourist destination. The city council of 1896 proposed a canal bringing cleansing lake water into the river, and citizens concurred in a local vote. Some citizens did suggest that if polluters would stop dumping, there would be no need for the canal. However, between 1902 and1922 the canal was dug; little did the city know that it would require ongoing dredging and maintenance to clear sand deposits from its mouth. Today, it is used by recreational boaters as a shorter and safer route to Lake Huron.

The Island Loop Route National Water Trail is a ten-mile-long water route, linking the Black River, the Black River Canal, Lake Huron, and the St. Clair River. To try it, begin at North River Road Park or Bakers Field Park, both of which have ADA-accessible kayak launches. Head downriver, and then up the canal to the left, heading east. Enter Lake Huron after passing under the Taintor Gate, and when you clear the sandbars, turn south to paddle under the Blue Water Bridge along the international border with Canada. Enter the mouth of the Black River to the west, paddle through the city of Port Huron, and back to your starting point.

Along the Black River Canal's south bank is a new addition to the Bridge to Bay Trail, a bike route that runs from Anchor Bay on Lake St. Clair to Lake Huron. Access the trail from Lakeside Park or Kraft Road Beach in Port Huron. Both sites offer sandy beaches on the clear, blue waters of Lake Huron. Kraft Road Beach is closest to where the Black River Canal takes in water from Lake Huron. The seaside spurge (*Euphorbia polygonifolia*), a small, ground-level relative of poinsettias with red stems, tiny green flowers, and opposite green leaves, grows here. This plant is quite localized, only found scattered along Great Lakes beaches.

Inland from the Lake Huron beach, there are two parks on the Black River's main channel: North River Road Park and Bakersfield Park. From here, the Black River flows south into downtown Port Huron, where businesses and marinas line the riverfront. The Great Lakes Maritime Center sits at the river's mouth, where the river spills its waters into the deep blue St. Clair River. The Blue Water River Walk, a one-mile pedestrian path along the St. Clair River shoreline is quite scenic, with gardens of native plant species, freighters passing by on the rivers, and anglers lining the railings. The easternmost point in all of Michigan is just above the Black River's mouth.

Northern St. Clair County

Farming in the northern portion of St. Clair County appears to be less active than it once was, though the Department of Agriculture lists 1,077 farms—everybody and their grandmother is selling eggs. Perhaps the closeness to the river and proximity to Port Huron and the Detroit metropolitan region have drawn people off the land to other occupations. The tree-lined rivers and creek break up the flat, sandy-looking fields, and dream houses and home sites stand, as if lost, in the middle of open fields. There appears to be available land here and the growing farm-to-table movement has everything to do with grocery prices and proximity to markets.

Goodells County Park (8345 County Park Dr.) on the site of the former County Farm, established to provide a home for returning Civil War soldiers, is today a spacious park with a Farm Museum, Historical Village, Butterfly Garden, and an extensive playground and splash pad. When operated as a "poor farm," the crops and livestock helped pay operational costs, but farming ended in 1962. Close by is the Pine River Nature Center (2585 Castor Road) with over two miles of hiking trails.

Old Clyde Township Hall (intersection of Wildcat and Beard Roads)—The first pine boom in Michigan began along the Pine and Black Rivers in this area. In 1832, Francis P. Browning of Detroit established the first steam-powered mill on the Black River in Port Huron and lumbermen moved up the rivers. Clyde Township was organized in 1837, and by 1849, St. Clair County led the state in terms of numbers of sawmills (twenty-seven steam- and twenty-eight water-powered mills), employing 344 men and cutting over thirty-three million board feet. Soon afterward, the pinelands of St. Clair County were exhausted and many of the early lumber barons moved to the Saginaw Valley.

The Dorsey House Restaurant (Wildcat and Beard intersection) claims to have started in 1847, feeding lumbermen and farm hands out of a barn. Today, it is a large and very busy restaurant and lounge. Its longevity at this intersection makes it a landmark in an otherwise rural landscape.

PART III

RURAL LOCALES

THE GERMAN BELT

The German "belt" begins roughly in the middle of Bay County and extends through most of Saginaw County, continues to a lesser degree through Tuscola County, and follows along Lake Huron up to the Caseville region. Germans began to settle in Michigan in the early 1830s, forming communities in Detroit and Monroe and Washtenaw Counties. These early immigrants came as individuals, but the settlements in Saginaw and Bay Counties developed as colonies, organized and led by Lutheran pastors. A settlement at Sebewaing, in southwestern Huron County, also grew from

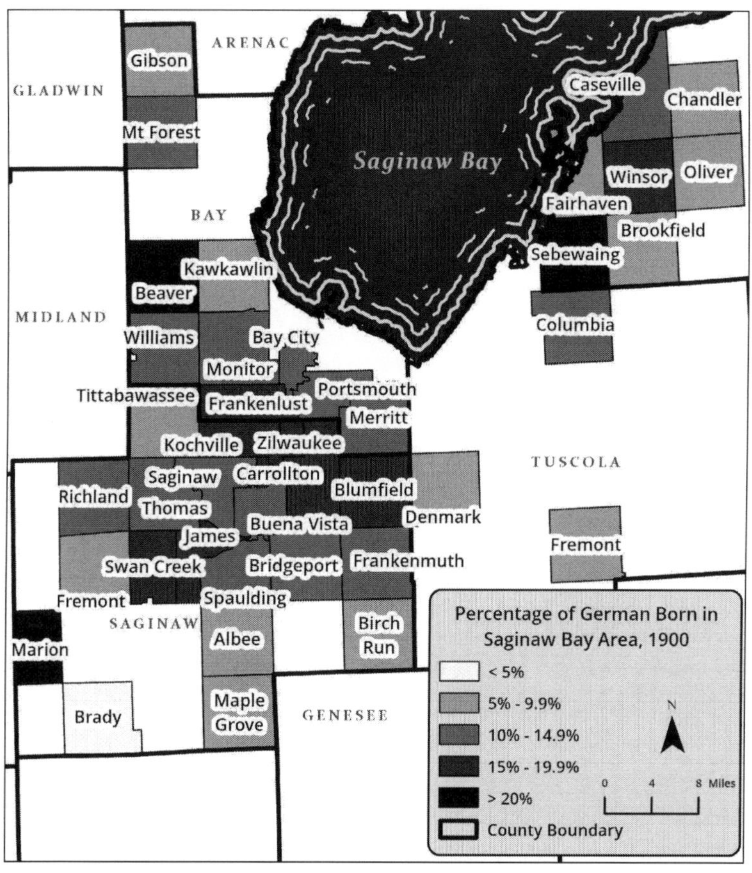

Percentage of German-born residents in Saginaw Bay Area (1900). UNIVERSITY OF MICHIGAN–FLINT GIS CENTER.

a Lutheran mission, and a little further north in Huron County, a utopian religious agricultural colony drew working-class Germans from cities around the Midwest.

By 1900, when the lumber boom and German immigration were largely over, German natives made up 7 to 22 percent of the population of many of the townships and cities in this belt. In Saginaw and Bay City, the number of German-born and second-generation Germans was substantial, although still a minority. In our region, the biggest legacy of German settlement is the network of urban and rural Lutheran schools. Germans also contributed to high culture and trade unionism (see the Saginaw profile) and, of course, Christmas. Decorated trees came to the English-speaking world through a picture in the popular *Godey's Lady's Book*, published in 1850, of Queen Victoria and Prince Albert's lit Christmas tree. The Saginaw Valley had such a tree in December 1846, when Chief Pay-mos-e-gay's Pine River band gathered around one with Edward Baierlein and his wife. "Forty Indians came," noted Baierlein in his memoir, none of whom had accepted Christ, but "a loud 'ah' came from all sides, as they saw the brightly lighted tree before them, full of fruit, in the middle of the winter." The chief exclaimed that he had never found a tree like that in all his forests. Baierlein came to Frankenmuth to assist Pastor Craemer but found he disagreed with the Franconians' approach to mission work, preferring to share life with the Indians their way, in the middle of the woods. He learned their language, legends, beliefs, and never forced his on them, but he practiced Christianity and invited them to share his feast days as he shared theirs.

Frankenmuth

Frankenmuth (pop. 5,193) means "the courage of the Franconians"—a name that gestures to its roots as a colony. Bavarian branding has made it the biggest tourist attraction in Michigan with the highest per capita income of any community in the region. For Thumb folks, if you move to Frankenmuth, you've "made it." With its thirteen hotels, the largest Christmas store in the world, "famous" chicken dinners, white carriages pulled by circus horses that circle the downtown streets to the tune of the "Beer Barrel Polka," faux Bavarian architecture, covered bridge, boat tours on the Cass River, arcades, and shopping on streets that wind up a fake hill by an artificial stream in the "little German village" of River Place Shops, it is no wonder people regularly call the Chamber of Commerce to ask the admission price. A theme-park atmosphere beckons the millions of tourists that drive under the "Willkommen" arches every year.

It is something of an irony that this insular colony, which kept the outside world at bay with an 1848 community constitution that required residents to be German-speaking Lutherans, is now the number one tourist attraction in Michigan. Tourism began after World War I, when Sunday drivers would stop to eat at one of two hotel-restaurants that served "famous" chicken dinners. Zehnder's of Frankenmuth and the Bavarian Inn are still going strong one hundred years later, serving the same menu of generic Thanksgiving-like food with hunks of deep-fried chicken instead of turkey. The restaurants face each other across the main street and display different appearances: Zehnder's redid its facade in the 1920s to resemble Mount Vernon, home of George Washington, apparently to allay American fears of the "Hun," while the Bavarian Inn's architecture is a bold statement only possible in 1959 after D-Day had defanged Germany, and former GIs were eager to recall the Germany they had experienced. The glockenspiel chimes four times a day, and wooden German characters play out the story of the Pied Piper of Hamelin. It is doubtful that the typical visitor distinguishes the Betsy Ross hats in one restaurant from the dirndl dresses in the other or the colonial breeches from lederhosen. What is the secret to Frankenmuth's success? Is it the mix of ingredients—the synthesis of German heritage and American Thanksgiving—that makes a recipe people come back for again and again? Or could it be that the missionary zeal of its first settlers has been translated into a commercial evangelism that brings visitors to Bronner's Christmas Wonderland (which touts itself

Zehnder's of Frankenmuth staff in colonial-style uniforms. COURTESY OF ZEHNDER'S OF FRANKENMUTH.

as "The World's Largest CHRISTmas Store") annually for more than just ornaments or replacement bulbs but for the experience of "CHRISTmas"? Digging into the history of the place should help us all—believers and nonbelievers—to get more out of a visit to "Michigan's Little Bavaria."

The idea for the Frankenmuth mission colony was that of Wilhelm Loehe (Löhe), a clergyman from the small town of Neuendettelsau, in Middle Franconia, who preached the importance of establishing German colonists in Michigan towns for the dual purpose of gathering the German settlers back into the Lutheran fold (they had become godless or too influenced by Methodist circuit riders) and civilizing the Indians. Loehe was a visionary, deeply affected by the Romantic reaction to Enlightenment rationalism. For Loehe, Lutheranism was not a faith based on "me and my God" but a faith lived out and nourished by the community. Once established in Neuendettelsau, Loehe focused on reviving the spirit of his congregation, but rather quickly he began to imagine both North America and the Indian subcontinent as ground for establishing Lutheran communities that would model "how beautiful it is to live with Jesus."

Loehe sent Pastor August Craemer to lead a group of fifteen colonists to Michigan. They left on April 20, 1845, and, following a difficult voyage across the Atlantic that included a train crash en route between Albany and Buffalo, they arrived in Saginaw County. Disagreements among them followed. Craemer wanted to pattern the town on the Bavarian model, with houses built along the same road as the church, but the colonists wanted to build on their own farms in the American way. Later colonists sent by Loehe settled nearby, creating Frankentrost ("Consolation of the Franconians"), Frankenhilf ("Help of the Franconians"), and Frankenlust ("Joy of the Franconians") between 1846 and 1854. Loehe believed that separate settlements would be more effective for the missionary purpose, and Frankentrost was platted on the Bavarian model with houses stretching down the main road from the church.

Disagreements with the colonists, as well as frequent bouts of sickness (probably malaria), set Craemer back, but in the first year he traveled along the Cass and Shiawassee Rivers with a French Catholic interpreter, visiting Indian bands. "Prospects appear to be good," Craemer wrote to Loehe, "only the Ottawa band seems to be totally in the hands of the Methodists." It is important to note that the Saginaw Valley was a competitive religious environment. The Methodists were content to spread the gospel and forgo the civilizing mission, but the Franconian missionaries were intent on recruiting Indian children for their school, where they would wash, dress, and educate them in the English but also the German language (Loehe's preference). According to Pastor Richard Latterner (a Native American Lutheran), the Franconians had a "nationalistic mindset that was common in their day." Craemer had some success, however. By 1847 Frankenmuth had a population of 153. The German school had twenty-five children in attendance, while the Indian school had twenty-one students enrolled. Church records for this year show that eleven German and twelve Indian children were baptized.

The Hubinger brothers, John G. and John Matthew, built much of the village, since they dammed the river and built a sawmill (1848) and a water-powered flouring mill that was replaced by steam power (1857; now being repurposed as a hotel-restaurant, called The Mill at Zehnder Park). Local men established two breweries (the Cass River Brewery, later the Geyer Brothers Brewery, in 1862, and Frankenmuth Brewing Company, in 1899). Other businesses grew, much as other non-German communities in the region did.

However, the society and culture of Frankenmuth, following the design of its original settlers, remained distinctively different. The first constitutions (valid until 1858) specified that residents must be German and members of the Lutheran Church, with all proceedings in German. In a 1927 book, *The Germanic Influence in the Making of Michigan*, John Andrew Russell describes the society as a "theocracy" and "a story out of a picture book." Every family owned its own farm, and the community looked out for its own, including poor, infirm, and disabled people. There were no lawsuits, no banks; differences were adjudicated by the pastor, and the community supplied its own funds for any necessary public works projects. Careful decisions were made about the placement of orphans, roads and fences were repaired by the collective, and farmers used three horses in a plow team instead of two, which reflects an early sensitivity to animal rights. The German language remained universal. The one concession to the outside world was to allow English to be taught in the public schools. German churches, services, religious instruction, and Lutheran school classes were all conducted in German. The biggest festival of the year was the annual *Kirchweih* (*Kaerwa*), or church dedication festival, held in the summer. The community's theological orientation discouraged secular institutions of the sort found in Saginaw, including Masonic lodges, the only exception being a local branch of the Arbeiter-Unterstützungs-Verein (German Workingmen's Mutual Benefit Association). Unlike the rest of Michigan's agricultural communities, Frankenmuth voted almost entirely for the Democratic Party. Around 1900, city fathers rejected a proposal for a railroad track to be laid down through the settlement; keeping out undesirable characters was worth the extra effort of hauling freight to the station in Gera, four miles north of town.

Frankenmuthers drank beer regularly but in moderation, yet as the temperance movement gathered steam during the nineteenth century, Frankenmuth beer drinking became a problem. In April 1909, people in neighboring Genesee County voted to make the county dry. Then in June, an annual outing of the teamsters of Saginaw County, held at the church grove in Frankenmuth, resulted in hundreds of young men coming from Flint. A reporter commented that customers waited in line at Frankenmuth's five hotels and three saloons, and many returned to Flint with "laundry" in their suitcases. Two years later, voters revoked the law, but in 1916, the state voted to enact prohibition, which went into effect the next year. Frankenmuth's indifference or opposition to the prohibition of liquor was one reason to draw outsiders.

The other draw was Frankenmuth's chicken dinners. Katharina, wife of hotel owner Theodore Fischer, was the first to cook meals that became locally popular, but the restaurant business really got its start in the town when one of the Zehnder girls married an Italian-born restaurateur, John Ardussi, who came to Frankenmuth in 1899 to operate a restaurant. His restaurant attracted prominent people driving by carriage from Saginaw. In 1906, a reporter remarked that "since the day when one of its enterprising hotel keepers discovered how to broil a chicken its future has been settled." This may have been Fischer, who had sold his business to Ardussi and shortly afterward bought it back. Fischer's Hotel (later operated by his son Herman) and his dinners became a destination in the 1910s for people out for Sunday drives in their new automobiles. With statewide and then nationwide prohibition from 1917 to 1933, Frankenmuth's numerous "blind pigs" also attracted others.

William Zehnder purchased the Exchange Hotel in 1928 and renamed it Zehnder's Hotel, now called Zehnder's of Frankenmuth (730 S. Main St.). Two years later, Federal agents arrested Zehnder and Herman Fischer for selling alcohol. After pleading guilty, a judge fined them $3,800 (Zehnder) and $8,800 (Fischer), absurdly high amounts, evidently to make examples of them, even though they served beer discreetly in private rooms. Fischer and Zehnder, who had sold Liberty Bonds during World War I, both had witnessed the anti-German hysteria apparent during World War I. Nevertheless, with the end of prohibition and some economic improvement, the two hotels remained popular as Sunday destinations and as weekday stops for truck drivers traveling from Detroit toward Bay City and points north.

Postwar prosperity improved the restaurant business. Zehnder purchased Fischer's Hotel in 1950 but retained the name. Sometime after his death in 1955, his older son, Edwin, purchased Zehnder's Hotel, while his younger son, William "Tiny", became the owner of Fischer's Hotel. Tiny and his family went to Europe on vacation in 1956 and was impressed by the architecture he saw in Munich. This led to his decision to rebrand Fischer's Hotel as the Bavarian Inn Restaurant (713 S. Main St.). The "Bavarianization" began in 1959 with an addition and a remodeling of the facade and later the construction of the glockenspiel in 1965. The town organized its first Bavarian festival in 1959. Zehnder convinced the town to require "Alpine" architecture on the facades of businesses as well.

As Frankenmuth attracted business and opened itself up to outside influence, its Franconian distinctiveness inevitably declined. A reporter in a 1906 story noted that English was understood in the hotels only—everyone spoke the German dialect, but by 1995, the few remaining dialect speakers lived on farms. However, Zehnder's rebranding of Frankenmuth as "Michigan's Little Bavaria," despite using stereotypes, turned out to be a smart business decision, and the pace of Bavarianization quickened, with more locals getting into the act.

Accordionist Marv Herzog began playing at the Bavarian festival in 1960, having learned German tunes (in addition to the ones he recalled from the Frankenmuth Kinderfests of his childhood) to supplement his repertoire of American standards and polkas. In order to increase available parking space, Tiny Zehnder had a Holz-Brücke (a German-style covered bridge) built over the Cass River in 1980. Further developments to attract tourists continued, including hotels, a golf course, the Bavarian Belle Riverboat, and River Place Shops (a faux German village with boutiques and shops) on the site of the old Geyer brewery. The tourist district of the city runs along Main Street from Jefferson Street north to Genesee Street.

Most visitors like to wander up and down the street, which is dotted with various businesses, selling everything from fudge and ice cream to wall crosses and embroidered table linens. Sites include Frankenmuth Historical Museum (613 S. Main St.), with eleven galleries that tell the story of the community. Next door is Fischer's Hall, built in 1894 by Theodore Fischer, a native of Saxony and a Mason and thus an outsider to the community. It was used for dances and other social events outside the watchful eyes of the Lutheran church. Tiny Zehnder donated it to the Frankenmuth Historical Association and moved it in 1986 to its present location on Main Street. The Frankenmuth Woolen Mill (570 S. Main St.) was begun in 1894, when Western sheep raisers were forcing the numerous mills in our area out of business; this locally owned mill produces pillows, bedding, and other goods.

Bronner's Christmas Wonderland draws over two million visitors per year from out of state on bus tours and people from around the Midwest and Michigan. But Bronner's is especially important to the people who drive an hour from one of the darker towns in the valley. They come for the novelty lights and the Christmas spirit, but they get pamphlet reminders of Christian values with every purchase.

On the "Memories of Flint" Facebook site, people refer to Bronner's as a tradition, calling it "world-renowned," "magical," "beautiful," "amazing," "friendly," "special." Several had met proprietor Wally Bronner, described as being "down to earth" and "the last of a dying breed," who followed up their conversations with thank-you notes on company stationery. A St. Lorenz parishioner concurs: "He was down on the floor greeting as many people as he could, joking, quipping, talking about his faith. Not many are born with that kind of ability. He's an example to us all."

Bronner's autobiography, for sale in the store, describes how his upbringing in a village of eight hundred people exposed him to "lifelong habits in which home, school and church were focal points of a good life." He understood that the gathered church and scattered church were connected by the vocation to serve others, which Wally believed must be lived "every hour of every day." Inside the Christmas store is a museum tucked away in a little auditorium (section 2 of the store) where the Wally Bronner story plays regularly. There are also relics from his life: the first signs he painted, the first nativity scene he made, and the first cash register he touched. It isn't self-aggrandizement so much as a testimonial. Another must-see is the Silent Night Memorial Chapel (1992)—a replica of the one in Oberndorf, Austria, where "Silent Night" was first sung in 1818.

Outside the downtown area, points of interest include St. Lorenz Lutheran Church. Nestled in the southwestern corner of the city on West Tuscola Street overlooking the Cass River, the Gothic brick building dates from 1880, having replaced the frame building built in 1852. Services were held exclusively in German until 1933 but today are in English, with services in German once a month. Across the road is the cemetery and a nearby grove. This includes "Church Bells in the Forest," a structure holding two bells cast in Nuremberg and brought here in 1845. Nearby is the Log Cabin Church, a replica (built in 1985) of the first blockhouse on the Cass River built in 1846.

Agritourism probably had its beginnings in Michigan by 1920, when Detroiters drove on Sundays to cider mills outside the city. More recently, some farmers have promoted you-pick fruit during harvest season, and hayrides, pumpkin patches, and corn mazes, to draw groups of children during the ever longer Halloween season. These include Grandpa Tiny's Farm (7775 Weiss St.), which was founded in 1938 by William "Tiny" Zehnder, a working farm with crops and livestock but used for education and agritourism, with a petting barn, flower festival, pumpkin patch, and Santa's reindeer, and Weiss Centennial Farm (5450 Weiss Rd.), established in 1852, still owned and operated by fifth-generation descendant, Roger Weiss and his wife, Joanmarie. The highlight of any tour will probably be the Lely milking robot.

American visitors to Frankenmuth may think it is a real German town, but German visitors hardly recognize it as such. Uwe Siemon-Netto described the town as having a "special charisma" but also noted that "the clock seems to have stopped . . . [in] the 19th century." St. Lorenz services are packed; in contrast to church services in his native Germany, the "r's" of the Franconian dialect are still being rolled, and even those that don't speak the Bayrisch of their ancestors speak High German. Baerbel Stuermer, a new German teacher at St. Lorenz school, thinks the culture is very distinct—neither German nor American: "The older people use 150-year-old words that I've only seen in books." The people hold tightly to their heritage and traditions, and consequently, the town can feel homogeneous, conservative, and "a bit rigid," but "what else can they do?" asks Baerbel. "If they are too open to mainstream American culture, they lose what they have."

What they have seems to be something many Michiganders and tourists from other states want to experience: the feeling of being among an emplaced people in a world that is fundamentally the same after almost two hundred years.

The Other Franconian Colonies

Although Frankenmuth is by far the best known, Loehe encouraged others from Franconia to establish settlements in the region. Frankentrost, an unincorporated town within Blumfield Township (pop. 1,845), was the second colony of Franconians in the Saginaw Valley. Founded in 1847, it never grew much beyond a cheese house, general store, and a few businesses. In contrast to Frankenmuth, where settlers chose to build houses on larger sections of land, settlers here attempted to recreate the European settlement pattern with narrower sections of land that would allow houses to be placed closer together. The settlement pattern is still visible along the two-mile stretch of Holland Road (M-46) between Beyer and Reimer Roads in Blumfield Township that forms Frankentrost. As in the other settlements, the chief site is Immanuel Lutheran Church, built in 1952 to replace the original church, which burned in 1951.

German life is not screamingly obvious here but quiet and deeply rooted. Small farming is alive and well, unlike other areas of Michigan. Farmers can make a living with three hundred acres. Township regulations preserve this way of life by controlling the sale of lots and forbidding commercial strips. As in so many places in Michigan, music is the way culture is carried forward. The Frankentrost Band, organized in 1895, meets in the spring to rehearse in the Immanuel School cafeteria. Brass bands were very popular at the end of the nineteenth century, and every community had one, but few have kept them going. The Frankentrost Band plays German marches for church festivals as well as secular festivals like the Bologna Festival in Yale and, of course, the Bavarian Festival in Frankenmuth.

Frankenlust, west of Bay City and north of University Center, is the name of a township (pop. 3,672) in Bay County and a settlement instigated by the Reverend Ferdinand Sievers, a disciple of Loehe. His father-in-law, Friedrich Koch, a well-to-do glass manufacturer in Hannover, purchased two thousand acres of the former Saginaw Bay Chippewa reserve. The township was organized and named Kochville Township for him in 1855. The northern third was reorganized as Frankenlust Township and made part of Bay County in 1877. The immigrants drained the wetlands and made the land arable. Today there are only two sites that remind us of Frankenlust, both Lutheran parishes with nearby schools and cemeteries. The first, St. Paul's Lutheran Church, at West Side Saginaw Road and Ziegler Roads, was formed in June 1848. The Franconians built log houses along the south side of the Squaconning Creek and cleared the land for farming. They built a log church in 1849 and replaced it with a frame one in 1857. The other, St. John's Lutheran Church is the site of Amelith, named for the town in Germany where Carolina Koch Sievers was born. It also has a school and cemetery. The steeple of the church in Amelith is visible across the farm fields, but the Frankenlust settlement is nearly obscured by sprawl close to the I-75 corridor.

Meeting a "Troster"

We needed rain to meet, because a sunny day would have meant field work for this Frankentrost farmer. A tall man comes through the door of the Beer Works in Richville and peers around the dark room. I wave him over, and he jokes, "Do I look lost?" He sits and we begin to visit. His reddish complexion and sky-blue eyes are familiar (my father was German), but his accent—lilting, with broad flat vowels and rolled Rs, is like nothing I've heard. "We speak a dead language," he quips. "Ya." Wes says "Ya" a lot. He's frank about being conservative and has only good things to say about fellow Franconians like Wally Bronner, and, on the subject of a local farmer who has branched out into agritourism, "Roger's got a good thing going, you know?"

Wes Reinbold is the historian of his Frankentrost church, Immanuel Lutheran, founded in 1847—the second missionary colony sent by Pastor Wilhelm Loehe. I think he thought the purpose of meeting was a history lesson, but I'd read enough. I was out for living history, to see, if I could, how the Franconian DNA shows up after four generations in America.

"Farmer" is how I answer two questions: "What are you?" and "Who are you?" "Farming is my occupation and my identity." Beyond growing sugar beets, soybeans, corn, and wheat in rotation, today's farmer must track the commodities market, keep machines running and tools repaired, pay farm insurance, family health insurance, and taxes. None of this is simple, and Wes is a small farmer with no employees, yet farming has cultivated in him an accepting and optimistic spirit. "My father didn't give much advice, but he did tell me that you can never worry about the weather. You are not always going to have a good year, but you see it through and must always look forward to the next growing season."

In winter, Wes worked other jobs, delivering heating oil and assembling steering wheel columns at the GM plant in Saginaw, where, he said, you had to "check your brain at the door." What was it like for you there? I ask. "Aw—it was like a soap opera." He was talking about the mix of people in the shop: "Some good, some not so good, some cheating on their wives, husbands, boyfriends and girlfriends and a lot just scamming the corporation. I concluded that the company and the union deserve each other." He understands why GM wanted to hire farmers: "Because farmers are goal-oriented and hard working. Every day, you set out to accomplish a big task—like today I'm gonna till the north forty. But what makes factory work different is that it never ends. There was no way to feel you'd accomplished something, no completion, so I worked for the next break or for Friday or for retirement. I hated it. But I was a good employee."

Frankentrost to Saginaw is a mere 8.7 miles, but in Wes's stories, it looms like a foreign land—a place of factories and violent street shootouts that forced a new martini bar downtown to close. But there are opportunities within his small community for diversion. Wes, like his father, grandfather, great-grandfather, and currently, his son, plays in the Frankentrost Band, that has existed since 1895. At fourteen years of age, Wes's grandson is the youngest member, and the oldest is a ninety-year-old trumpet player. The group has over a thousand pieces of German sheet music, and there is also a men's singing club. Wes's definite voice softens when he speaks about his need to sing those old German songs.

My mind wanders to Johann Sebastian Bach (there's a town in the Thumb named Bach, by the way), whose repetitive motifs remind me of seasonal cycles and manual labor. English conductor John Eliot Gardiner describes the texture of certain Bach cantatas as being like "warm topsoil, fertile and well irrigated." With Bach on my brain, I wonder aloud, "Why are the German composers so good?" The men look at me funny, and my husband suggests that maybe it's because of the number of aristocratic courts that existed in the German states. Maybe, I think, but if any music suggests what belief in God feels like, it is Bach's, and he was a devout Lutheran. The subject turns to the trip Wes took with grandkids to the Ark Experience and Creation Museum in Kentucky, and he tells us that he believes in a literal reading of the Bible.

Reflecting on my own question later, I decide that what moves me about Bach is the way a tight structure enables the passionate swells, the counterpoint and delicate modulations. Wes planted sugar beets last week with a mechanical planter that uses computer technology to put the seed in at even depths in perfectly spaced rows. But this week, he was off his tractor and on intimate terms with dirt. Pushing the grains away with his fingers to see seeds splitting open and green life coming forth.

As the conversation wound down, I mentioned that we were headed to the Pheasant Pen in Reese. "Ah, well, that's a niche market." He begins to relate his own attempt at developing a niche. For eight years, he set about raising organic chickens with partners and, just when they were getting their feet on the ground, the banks pulled out. "It was not a happy time. . . . And, you know, it was one of those moments when I had to decide how to handle it. Some men might decide to end it all, but I decided that I was going to show my kids how a Christian man gets through something like this. I held my head high through it, and we came back slowly. I am still coming back from that."

I would not call Wes Reinbold old-fashioned. He manages farm business using the latest technological devices and even took a risk on a new venture. He is, however, conservative in the decisions he makes about new equipment purchases, making do with older tractors and taking care of what he already has instead of expanding his holdings. In his public role on the township board, he has fought the incursion of wind, solar, and shopping centers, knowing that drawing a firm line is the way to preserve a way of life: allowing Frankentrost to be filled with shopping center sprawl would compromise this community of traditional small farms. "It's been a good life," he says to round off the visit, "and I'm looking forward to being that ninety-year-old man still driving a tractor—though my wife tells me I already am."

Richville began as Frankenhilf, the fourth Loehe colony, created in 1851 by Franconan immigrants led by Reverend Herman Kuehn, on over 1,500 acres in Denmark Township, Tuscola County, that had been purchased by Reverend Sievers. Locals today laugh about the 1862 name change to Richville, reflecting the hope of the early colonists. Theological disagreements caused some to move with their pastor to Iowa. The focus here, as in the other Franconian settlements, is the church, St. Michael's Lutheran Church, on South Van Buren Road, with a cemetery on the opposite side of the road and a school on Saginaw Road, but there is also a renovated tavern that serves craft beer, keeping that other German tradition going.

Beyond the Franconian Settlements Proper

Both Saginaw and Bay City, which were close to the rural Franconian colonies, attracted large communities of Germans. These were formed in part by Franconians moving into the cities and in part by immigrants from other parts of Germany. The results were communities more diverse and secular than those in the rural colonies. The Franconian Lutherans rejected secular organizations, but these flourished in the cities. A German wrote in 1859 that near the Cheboyganing River in nearby Buena Vista Township, several educated immigrants from Westphalia and Rheinland had purchased land and become farmers, creating what some called the "Latin" settlement, named for their ability in that language. The tradition of the church dedication festival continued, however, and Germans from Saginaw and Bay City ventured out to Frankenmuth and the other communities on those occasions. In 1866, a visiting German complained to Loehe about a large crowd of people from East Saginaw degrading the observance of the festival by their "drinking, dancing,

The Germania Club Maennerchor (men's chorus), Saginaw, 1905.
GERMANIA CLUB RECORDS, HOYT LIBRARY.

and loud behavior." Clearly in these years tension existed between the pious behavior of Frankenmuth and the Germans in the cities.

On the east side of Saginaw, the German neighborhood was concentrated around Lapeer and Third Streets. On Saginaw's west side, the community was located near the intersection of Court and Fayette Streets. Secular social organizations as well as churches abounded in both Saginaw City and East Saginaw.

Beaver Township was created in 1867 and settled relatively quickly by Germans, who worked in Bay City sawmills, saved money, and bought farms as the lumber boom was ending. In 1880 the township's population was 271 but increased to 1,195 by 1900 (of which 19.3 percent was German-born). Zion Lutheran Church in Auburn has been at the center of the community since 1885 and was easily as important as the four corners of Willard (formerly Ittner's Corners) that had a general store, a cheese factory, and a German beer garden.

In his memoir *The Last Farmer* (1988), Howard Kohn describes German American farmers like his father, Frederick, as "more emotionally driven, fueled by persistence, hard work, commitment, conservative fiscal management and close family participation." Without sons who wanted to farm, Frederick Kohn held on as long as he could, witnessing root and branch changes in American farming. When he finally decided to sell, the decision didn't kill him, because, as his son implies, he knew that "character is all that any of us have at the end, the sole property that is ours."

Hemlock, an unincorporated settlement on M-46 in Richland Township, in western Saginaw County, had a substantial number of Germans settlers, although, like other communities, it was not exclusively German. Lumbering began in the 1850s and, as the forest cleared, farms dotted the area. The Farmers Home Tavern, built in 1869, stands as a survivor from this era and is worth a visit. St. Peter's Lutheran Church, founded in 1880, along with a school, remains important; it had German services for about a hundred years. The Hemlock Area Historical Society and Museum (301–363 N. Hemlock Rd.) contains artifacts and material concerning local history.

Marion Township, in the southwestern part of the county, had in 1900 the highest percentage of German-born in the region. Charles Fowler, Saginaw real estate speculator, developed a sawmill and store at Marion Springs in 1882 and sold cutover land mainly to German immigrants, who developed farms. They organized St. John's Lutheran Church, with a school, soon afterward.

Sebewaing began in 1845, when Friedrich Schmid, pioneer Lutheran pastor in Ann Arbor, sent three recently arrived missionaries from Wurttemberg (the source region for most of the German immigrants to the Ann Arbor area) to attempt to convert a band of Ojibwe living in the region. Johann Jacob Friedrich Auch persevered, while the others left, and built a frame mission house at Shebahyonk (north of Sebewaing) in 1849 that served as a school until 1854, when the band suddenly rejected their teachings and left. The mission house was later moved to Sebewaing in 1954 and restored. Today it is the Luckhard Museum (590 E. Bay St.), housing exhibits relating

Sebewaing Beer label.
AUTHOR'S COLLECTION.

to the mission as well as German books and musical instruments. Liken quickly came to dominate lumbering in Huron County, operating two sawmills and stave mills in Sebewaing and one each at Unionville, Akron, and Fairgrove, besides a creamery, two grain elevators, and more.

Somewhere north of Bay Port between M-25 and Saginaw Bay—a half mile from shore—is the site of the former socialist community of Ora et Labora. Emil Baur, who immigrated from Germany in 1848, converted to Methodism and became a preacher. He launched a utopian German colony in 1862, influenced and partially supported by Johann Rapp's Harmony Society. Baur purchased three thousand acres of wooded, swampy federal land along Wild Fowl Bay—an isolated location (thirty-five miles from East Saginaw) that put distance between colonists and the temptations of city life. The economic structure of the colony was a compromise between complete communal ownership and private enterprise. Colonists who signed a constitution were given a half-acre plot, two cows, two pigs, and two chickens, and they were expected to plant fruit trees and grapevines. On Saturdays, they were permitted to work on their own plots, while Sundays were for worship, but the rest of the week they labored together, digging ditches, logging, setting up a sawmill, and constructing a dock and the buildings necessary for a town, such as a store, post office, tannery, workshops, church, and school.

There were dispiriting early setbacks. The mosquitoes gave them ague and the land proved very difficult to drain. Although industries were established—the colony

Sketch of Ora et Labora. GERMAN CHRISTIAN AGRICULTURAL AND BENEVOLENT SOCIETY OF ORA LABORA RECORDS, 1862–1894, BENTLEY HISTORICAL LIBRARY, UNIVERSITY OF MICHIGAN.

sold logs for telegraph poles and quarried limestone—Baur had to constantly solicit supporters for extra funds and attempt to recruit new colonists, as many returned to the cities or established settlements nearby without the strict religious requirements. In the end, it was the Civil War that broke up the community, which disbanded in 1871. Colonists who had worked the land for a year were given forty-acre homesteads, and many stayed in the area. Baur moved to Ann Arbor, where he taught German in the high school. Upon returning to Ora et Labora in 1871, he found Indians occupying the cabins, having been driven out of the forest by fire. He left money with local people and instructed them to provide potatoes and other foodstuffs. Some think that if Baur had chosen land behind the sand ridge, the colony may have had a better chance of succeeding, but descendants of Baur and families of the original colonists still live locally. They feel the experiment was successful enough—it was the way they wound up on Saginaw Bay.

Pigeon (pop. 1,208) was established by some of the colonists who left Ora et Labora. In fact, Pigeon's first church, the First United Methodist, was a frame building that was moved to the banks of the Pigeon River in 1872. Services were held under trees where flocks of now extinct passenger pigeons nested.

Before incorporation as a village in 1903, Pigeon had the good fortune to be the site where two railroad lines crossed: the Pontiac, Oxford and Port Austin and the

Saginaw, Tuscola and Huron. Farm goods were the main export in the early days, and today the only commodities transported by rail are from the Cooperative Elevator and the nearby Wallace Stone Quarry. The depot is part of the Pigeon Historical Museum with its main location at 59 South Main Street.

The Cooperative Elevator started in Pigeon in 1915 and now has multiple locations around the Thumb. There are other major industries in the village at present. Huron Castings—with two spinoff operations in the village, Blue Diamond Steel and Axis Machining, along with a factory in Shanghai—grew out of a drain tile manufacturing company and family foundry that made parts for trenching equipment. Huron Castings, though it has global reach, continues to meet local needs, busing Black workers with foundry experience from Saginaw to the jobs in Pigeon.

For people like Nancy Schuette and her sons, whose family has had a dairy farm for almost one hundred years, vitality comes from staying where their roots are and continuing the tradition, persisting despite difficulties. Three small dairy farms closed in the past year in smaller German American towns near Bach, and Nancy hopes they can keep going because "Tim [her eldest son], will never sell the cows." Knowing what a herd needs and providing it are deeply satisfying to her three sons, who cannot imagine doing anything else. Wood steps lead from a side entrance to the big kitchen table past a porch that smells like cows and has buckets of lily bulbs and walnut shells. When the walnut trees yield a bumper crop, Nancy keeps busy shelling them in the evenings. When apples ripen in fall, she dries them for winter eating. Side doors open onto small beds covered with quilts, and there are crucifixes hanging on the walls over the beds, the faces of ancestors and descendants surround us as we talk; to visit this homestead is to feel the calm and security of being in a good place where people are, above all, kind.

SHIAWASSEE COUNTY

Owosso

Created in 1837, Shiawassee County's land is slightly rolling, originally covered with maple-beech and oak-hickory forests. It takes its name from the Shiawassee River, which flows into the Saginaw River, but the Looking Glass River and Maple River in the western part of the county flow into the Grand River. Most of the county is agricultural, except its largest city, Owosso (pop. 14,714), and the nearby county seat, Corunna (pop. 3,046).

Bands of Ojibwe lived along these rivers, moving up and down the rivers according to the season. The earliest fur trader to operate in the county was Jean-Baptiste Brillant dit Beaulieu (d. 1781), whose post's remains were thought by Benjamin O. Williams in 1880 to still be standing. Other traders, like Whitmore Knaggs and Richard Godfroy, fluent in French and Ojibwe, followed suit until about 1830, when Yankee traders first came, opening the way for settlers. The traditional way of life ended in 1837, when a smallpox epidemic destroyed and scattered the Native population.

The first people with the intention of clearing the land and settling here came in 1833, although large numbers did not begin settling until late in the decade. They bought land in the southeastern part of the county, along Grand River Road, near Byron. Benjamin O. Williams and his brother Alfred L. Williams purchased land in 1833 on the Shiawassee River at what was then known as Che-boe-wa-ting ("Big Rapids") and Elias Comstock bought land nearby in 1835, becoming the founders of Owosso. Daniel Ball, who brought a colony of settlers from Rochester, New York, built a sawmill and gristmill at the site. Three county commissioners located the site of the county seat, which became Corunna. In 1850, the county's population reached 5,280. The city of Owosso was incorporated in 1859 and named for Wasso, the chief of the Shiawassee band living there in the 1830s.

In 1856, the Detroit and Milwaukee Railroad (later succeeded by the Grand Trunk Western Railroad) laid its first tracks in Owosso, connecting the city to Detroit. Further rail links by 1862 connected Owosso to Saginaw and Lansing. The county continued to grow until 1880, when it reached a population of 27,056 and its land was cleared and agricultural. Most of the growth after 1880 was in Owosso, but the population there stabilized by 1920.

Industries in Owosso developed from sawmills and planing mills cutting hardwood lumber, since the county lacked commercial stands of pine. The Woodard brothers established a planing mill in the 1860s, evolving into the Woodard Furniture Company and, in 1885, the Owosso Casket Company. The Estey Manufacturing Company, established in 1875, made furniture in two factories and by 1905 was the city's largest employer. The Owosso Manufacturing Company, organized in 1881, produced window screens, doors, and snow shovels.

Investors from the Pittsburgh Plate Glass Company organized the Owosso Sugar Company in 1902 and the following year purchased the Prairie Farm tract in Saginaw County. Laborers for the farms were mainly Moravian Czech immigrants, recruited from other states, like Wisconsin and Nebraska, accounting for the Czech population in Shiawassee County (in 1920 there were 475) as well as in the Bannister and Swartz Creek areas. Michigan Sugar Company bought the Owosso company in 1924 but the plant became idle in 1928. Some farmers continued to grow beets through the 1930s, but production declined, and in 1948, the company sold most of its property. The company recruited Mexican Americans from Texas as beet workers and some got jobs in Owosso factories where, despite discrimination, they purchased houses.

The Depression hit Owosso hard, ending its furniture manufacturing. By this time, many county residents were commuting to the factories in Flint. Owosso had begun to develop steel and iron-based industries (such as the Independent Stove Company) but largely escaped the automotive boom. Owosso interests enticed A. G. Redmond, a manufacturer of small motors in Flint and an opponent of labor unions, to move there. He did so in 1938 and continued in business until the 1970s, having later accepted his employees' organizing. In the postwar period, other small manufacturers operated in Owosso. The Ann Arbor Railroad was another major employer.

The city's population peaked in the decade of the 1960s at about seventeen thousand. Since 1970, Owosso has lost population, while Shiawassee County's population has remained fairly stable since 1980.

Flint Writer Kelsey Ronan Visits Owosso

In his memoir and spiritual treatise *God's Country: The Trail to Happiness*, Owosso native James Oliver Curwood (1878–1927) describes taking a friend, a fellow writer grieving the death of his wife, on a drive into the country. Whether they were starting in Owosso or elsewhere, Curwood doesn't specify. A conservationist and gamesmen whose novels were influenced by his time in the wild, Curwood believed in the curative power of nature. Certain of where he was guiding his friend, he remembers a visit to Michigan State Penitentiary, "where a canarybird and a red geranium saved a man from madness and eventually gained him a pardon, sending him out into the world a living being with a new and better religion than he had ever dreamed of before." Reaching the woods, Curwood beckons his friend to follow him out of the car, to sit with him under a tree in silence. The sounds of birds, a distant creek, and a fox settle around the two writers. "This is one of the most wonderful cities in the world," Curwood whispered to his bereaved friend, "and there are hundreds and thousands of such cities, some of them within the reach of all."

Nearly one hundred years after his death, one wonders where Owosso's most celebrated son might direct a traveler—the wonderful cities within the city, perhaps, or the journeys to and away. Say you were starting out in Flint, taking Corunna Road west—he might have you stop along those twenty-five miles of farmland. You might spend another journey entirely listening to deer through the fields, seeing the sky expand over the flatness of the landscape, punctuated by church steeples, barn roofs, and the gold dome of the Flint Islamic Center. In certain seasons, you might stop and explore the farms in Corunna and New Lothrop, their signs pointing you away from Corunna Road. The area is rich in corn, wheat, and soybeans.

Once that farmland gives way to big-box stores, you'll find yourself crossing into Owosso proper. Its twentieth-century notoriety as a "sundown town" came from a reference in *The Autobiography of Malcolm X*, in which he remembered going with his father to a meeting of Marcus Garvey's Universal Negro Improvement Association held there during the day, because, he claimed, "no Negroes were allowed on the streets there after dark." Today, Owosso is working-class, largely conservative, and 93 percent white. Continuing into the city down Corunna Road, visitors will note the prevalence of right-wing sloganeering, the residue of Trump's Make America Great Again campaigns. Flags wave from the flea market parking lot—including one with Trump's face photoshopped onto Rambo's machine gun-toting body. In 2020, Shiawassee County lost its longtime bellwether status when Trump received four thousand more votes than he did in 2016, taking nearly 60 percent of the county. Through the COVID-19 pandemic, Owosso was defiantly vaccine-resistant and vocal against Democratic governor Gretchen Whitmer and her lockdown measures.

These voices aren't without counterpoint, however. In the summer of 2020, hundreds gathered downtown at Owosso City Hall in support of Black Lives Matter, with an eight-minute, forty-six-second "die-in" on the lawn in honor of George Floyd. Mayor Chris Eleveth addressed the crowd. Owosso native Megan Giddings, whose celebrated 2020 novel *Lakewood* explored medical experimentation on Black people, set her novel in an unnamed small Michigan town.

The destination on any day trip ought to be the Shiawassee River at Curwood Castle Park. Here you'll find Owosso's first permanent dwelling, the Elias Comstock Cabin. Built in 1836, this one-room log cabin was the home of Comstock and his wife Lucy, who arrived by ox-drawn wagon with a party of other settlers. Comstock held various public offices during Owosso's early years and the city's first Baptist service was held in the cabin. Over the years, the Comstocks made frame additions and added a long front porch to the cabin. The cabin itself became the living room. The Comstocks sold the land around them for $25 a lot and offered guests a place to sleep while their home was under construction. When Standard Oil Company bought the land in 1920, they found the original cabin preserved, encased by the house constructed around it. All the pieces within the cabin are authentic, including a rope bed with straw filling and nineteenth-century cookware and tools mounted to the wall.

Beside the Comstock cabin sits a more modern structure, brick with a wide porch rounding toward the river. This is the Shiawassee Arts Center, where you can visit the works of Owosso native Frederick Carl Frieseke (1874–1939), who studied painting at the Art Institute of Chicago, went to Paris to study Impressionism, and never came back. Frieske originals—including the late landscape painting "Along the Shiawassee," where the almost ghostly figures of children stand across the river, with spring-skinny trees and frothy blossoms—hang in the front gallery flanked by reproductions of other paintings and biographical information. In the adjoining galleries, the work of regional artists, including paintings, prints, mixed media, and jewelry, is displayed for sale.

It is, however, Curwood Castle, the writing studio of author James Oliver Curwood, sitting on the riverbanks like a fairy tale, that immediately draws the eye as you turn into the park; if you can resist, it's rewarding to leave as your last stop on the winding trail along the riverside. Constructed of creamy yellow stucco and fieldstones, the structure was modeled on an eighteenth-century French château and is on the National Register of Historic Places. In 1923, Curwood completed construction of the castle, although he only had four years in his castle before his death, thought to have resulted from an infected wound after being bitten through his waders on a Florida fishing trip.

A hunter who had extensively traveled in Alaska and the Yukon, Curwood wrote adventure stories with romance plotlines that made them appealing for the burgeoning film industry. With thirty-three books published in his short life, some years publishing two or three books in addition to short stories, Curwood was a best-selling author through the 1910s and 1920s. Many of his novels and short stories served as the source material for over 180 films made around the world. Produced in the early years of cinema, many have been lost. Some more contemporary examples include a French production of *The Bear* (1988), about an orphaned grizzly cub who befriends another bear wounded by hunters. Inside, for $5, you can climb the turrets and see Curwood's first desk, made by his father out of an old sewing table, and follow the story of his life and work along the walls.

At the castle, there are remnants of 1920s glamour and of Curwood's hunting prowess: A massive bear rug howls soundlessly from the library floor, taxidermy is

Curwood Castle, Owosso. PHOTOGRAPH BY AUTHOR.

mounted over the plush purple sofas and glass bookcases where Curwood's work is arranged. On the lower level, there's a portrait gallery of other famed men of Owosso, including Frieske, Thomas Dewey, and designer of the nickel, Felix Oscar Schlag. Those with accessibility concerns (and claustrophobes) should take note that the castle is navigable by tight, winding staircases through which the visitor will walk single file.

Should you wish to pick up one of Curwood's many books on your way out, you'll be disappointed. While you can buy Curwood's name on teddy bears and coffee mugs and postcards of him working at his desk, when I asked where I might find one of his novels, I was told to check eBay. Owosso is a town that honors a writer no one seems to read. Most visitors, I'm told, have never heard of James Oliver Curwood. Rather, they are drawn to the inexplicability of a castle in Mid-Michigan. Still, Curwood's name appears all over town. The annual Curwood Festival started on the occasion of the author's one-hundredth birthday and is held each June. It includes a parade, a carnival, vendors, a 5K and a 10K race, and the coronation of Miss Curwood Festival.

Cross the river on the pedestrian rope bridge and follow the footpath around the Armory. Here you'll find yourself in downtown Owosso, where Owosso's troubled economy and changing generations can be felt along the streets that ring with an early twentieth-century nostalgia. Empty brick storefronts sit beside the boutiques of the new cannabis industry. Oliver's Restaurant is closed, but you can get sushi at Sosumi, stop for dessert at Cupcakes and Kisses, or browse for books at Fable Lane on Main Street (a fine secondhand selection, but no James Oliver Curwood titles, when I stopped in.) At Lebowsky Theater on Main Street you can catch the Owosso Community Players put on musicals and family friendly comedies.

Southwest of the main downtown intersection is the Woodward Building on Elm Street, restored and subdivided into loft apartments. Death was a thriving industry in Owosso. After the Civil War, the region's abundance of timber, waterpower, and land attracted men looking to make their fortune. Among them were Lyman Elnathan Woodard, who arrived from New York with $10,000 and plans to purchase a lumber mill. Joined by his three brothers, Lyman founded Woodard Furniture Company. The company's catalog soon expanded beyond doors and window sashes to pine caskets. A separate business, the Owosso Casket Company, was founded just as death became a booming business. By 1913, the Owosso Casket Company was turning out 150 caskets per day, making it the world's largest casket maker. Thomas E. Dewey didn't defeat Harry S. Truman, but Owosso built caskets for presidents William McKinley and Benjamin Harrison. The factory stood on Main Street, where Owosso City Hall stands today. By the 1930s, the hardship of the Great Depression and depleted natural resources ended the casket company. The Woodard Furniture Company switched from wood furniture to wrought iron and continues to make patio furniture in Owosso. In her 1962 widowhood, Jackie Kennedy purchased the Mayfield collection. The Sculptura chair is in the Smithsonian's permanent collection.

A few blocks north of downtown is a lovely neighborhood of nineteenth-century houses and churches. At 515 N. Washington Street, you'll find the Amos Gould House, currently under renovation. Gould was Owosso's first mayor and a prominent businessman, who founded the city's first bank and organized the Michigan Central Railroad. The house is a mansion modeled on an Italian villa, with a mansard roof and ornate designs.

At the corner of Oliver and Pine is the boyhood home of Thomas E. Dewey, also marked by a Michigan Historic Site plaque. Born 1902 above his father's general store (now demolished), Dewey left Owosso to study at University of Michigan, and from there launched a law career that led to him serving as governor of New York and securing the 1944 and 1948 Republican presidential nominations. Dewey is arguably the most famous man not to win the election; though polls predicted a landslide victory and at least one newspaper prematurely printed its headline, Harry Truman defeated him. The house is now a private residence.

According to the reigning Curwood Festival Queen Alayna Best-Cetrone, a psychology major at University of Michigan–Flint, it's that commitment to history, community, and nature that makes Owosso special. Asked about the legacy of Curwood, Best-Cetrone spoke of her sense of connection to the long-dead writer, of their shared love of nature and the rural landscape. Curwood's books may be hard to come by, but his spirit is very much present. "James Oliver Curwood and I are tight right now," she said.

A Sundown Town

There were never any laws forbidding Black people from being on the streets of Owosso after dark, yet the place impressed itself on Malcolm X's imagination as a sundown town, risky for Black people. How did Owosso get that reputation and has it changed?

Census records show no Black people in Owosso in 1930, but there were 1,375 foreign-born white residents and 69 residents of "other races." These others could have been Mexicans or mixed-race individuals trying to pass, living muted lives, hiding in plain sight. Earl Little—a Baptist preacher and Garveyite activist—had a strong sense of mission and wasn't afraid of standing out. He and his Grenadian wife, Louise, had been selected and sent out as field organizers for Marcus Garvey's United Negro Improvement Association. After Louise—pregnant with Malcolm—was confronted by Klansmen at the door of their house in Omaha, Nebraska, Earl (called Early) moved the family in 1927 to a white neighborhood in Lansing. Their house was burned in 1929 and Earl was temporarily jailed on a baseless suspicion of arson; undeterred, the couple moved east, buying six acres of land to build on where they could grow their own food. Before his murder, Earl apparently traveled to Owosso (by then the state headquarters of the KKK) to encourage what brothers were there to dream of a Black utopia.

In recent years, Owosso's civic leaders have made many efforts to undo the city's racist reputation. After George Floyd's murder by police in May 2020 and the Capitol attack on January 6, 2021, the city's Chamber of Commerce and other leaders decided to present the darker side of the city's history to exorcise any lingering demons. An exhibit at the Shiawassee Arts Center in 2022 featured enlarged pictures of KKK rallies that may have held the mirror up to today's concerned Americans—butcher, baker, tool and die maker—who wear MAGA merch and military camouflage. In November 2021, the Owosso Rotary Club honored Black Civil War veteran Alexander Johnson (1838–1907) in a ceremony at Oak Hill Cemetery. Congresswoman Elissa Slotkin entered Johnson's story into the *Congressional Record.*

The story, based on a brief mention in Johnson's 1907 obituary, developed into one in which the Ku Klux Klan was active in 1871 when it drove out all the Black people in town except Johnson and two others. At that time, we should note, the Ku Klux Klan was a secret society of Confederate veterans terrorizing former slaves in an attempt to undo Reconstruction. To suggest that the KKK was active in Shiawassee County then, however, is absurd, because the organization was confined to the old Confederacy and especially because many Shiawassee County residents had fought and died for the Union and politically supported the Radical Republicans. The 1871 event, as reported in the Owosso *Weekly Press* of October 11, 1871, describes how a mob of forty exacted revenge a day after two white people had been pummeled at a drinking party involving an itinerant Italian band (likely three or four teenage harpists and fiddlers) and a group of Black people. The mob declared that every Black person in town—except for three named individuals (including Johnson, whose wife, incidentally, was white)—had to "to get up and get," and they beat up two Black men in retaliation. The lone justice of the peace was unable to stop the crowd, causing the newspaper to criticize the city administration for failing to quell the incident, commenting "few of the . . . *southern* Ku Klux outrages have been more atrocious than that which took place in this city on Wednesday night last week." As reprehensible as this action was, we should not conflate the racism and xenophobia of an angry mob with the political agenda of the contemporary Ku Klux Klan.

Xenophobia triggered another incident on May 23, 1893, when an angry mob in Corunna lynched William Sullivan, an Irish-born drifter. He had been apprehended for brutally murdering a local farmer who had employed him months earlier, and, as news spread, friends and neighbors gathered "to take an active part in what they termed a duty they owed to themselves and to the community." His origins may have had something to do with the savagery of the mob, but Sullivan expected the "lynching bee" and begged to be sent to Jackson prison quickly to avoid it. Rural people were used to relying on themselves and one another rather than institutions; the few police were negligible and the law an abstraction. Sullivan cut his own throat with a piece of glass so as not to be conscious when the crowd of one thousand broke into his cell and lynched and desecrated his dead body. The vigilante mob was tried in the public press, convicted by some writers and excused by others as harsh but meting out exact justice. The Owosso newspaper, for what it's worth, reminded readers that the law should never be overridden.

Owosso's connection to the 1920s iteration of the Ku Klux Klan resulted from the fact that the head of the state organization, George E. Carr, resided in Owosso, so the state office was located there in the late 1920s. The organization in this period was a reactionary response to white fears about World War I and demographic change, as eastern and southern Europeans and Black people arrived in Flint, Pontiac, and Detroit. Its nonviolent, if intimidating, nature distinguished itself from earlier and later versions of the organization. Its "100 percent Americanism" slogan and its robes, rallies, and marches attracted members, who influenced the 1924 elections, but internal divisions led to its decline.

Owosso made headlines in the Black press during World War II. In 1940, a white mob intimidated a Black contractor from Detroit in 1940, forcing him off a job in Owosso. A few years later, Black attendees at a postal workers convention were Jim Crowed out of town. In 1944, a Black reporter for the *Chicago Defender* arrived by bus to interview the mother of Governor Thomas Dewey, then running for president; he said he felt as welcome in the city "as a case of smallpox." Mrs. Dewey was aware of the town's anti-Negro record but had a lot more to say about the "greedy, rich, and egotistical Jews."

Owosso's leaders want people to experience hospitality in their city. To that end, they have publicized the checkered social history of Owosso, suggesting that it is high time to turn the page on that and be a more inviting place.

Points of Interest

Steam Railroading Institute (405 S. Washington St.) began when a group of Michigan State University engineering students started tinkering with Pere Marquette #1225, a forty-ton steam locomotive that was retired in 1951. University administrators didn't want the old train on campus, so it was moved to this six-acre site on the south bank of the Shiawassee. The mission of the Steam Railroading Institute is to pass on older technologies and educate the public. The institute also sponsors excursions throughout the year, the most popular being the "North Pole Express" available in November and December.

Shiawassee County Historical Museum (1997 N. M-52) offers collections of written and historical material and artifacts related to the history of the Shiawassee County area.

Shiawassee Conservation Association (4247 N. M-52), founded in 1907, is the country's oldest documented conservation group. The building was erected in 1926 on land donated by James Oliver Curwood, who played a role in founding the Michigan United Conservation Clubs, headquartered here.

DeVries Nature Conservancy and Carriage and Sleigh Museum (2635 N. M-52) is a 135-acre riverside farm and field parcel with home and outbuildings, given to the public by Owosso veterinarian Jack DeVries and his wife Frances. The conservancy is developing a historical farm and rural living program to foster learning about Michigan's history and rural past. The museum on the property has one of the best collections of carriages, buggies, surreys, sleighs, and cutters in the Midwest. Owosso's manufacturing past is well represented.

Corunna

A quiet town dominated by its enormous courthouse, Corunna was established as the seat of Shiawassee County in 1840 and incorporated as a village in 1869. Andrew Mack, a businessman and politician who served as Detroit's eleventh mayor, named the village after Coruña, Spain. In 1804, Mack, who had sailed around the world three times, drove a herd of merino sheep that he had purchased in Spain west to Cincinnati, Ohio, where he established a wool factory. A possible link to Mack's woolen interests was Corunna's U.S. Robe Company, which made buffalo robes and hand muffs from quality wool that may have been produced in Owosso, where a woolen mill preceded the casket company. Other than the gristmill, powered by a dam on the Shiawassee—a dam deemed hazardous but still used as a fishing spot—there were coal mines north of town along the river, as well as a manufacturer of radio and phonograph cabinets that employed one thousand people between 1937 and 1942. Historic houses grace the downtown streets, including the home of governor and state representative Andrew Parsons at 318 Shiawassee Street.

The county courthouse is the central feature of the town. Its cornerstone was laid in 1904 to great fanfare and many speeches before the largest crowd in the county's history. The building, designed by Claire Allen, has an elegant clock tower and column facade. It may mix styles, but its size and attention to detail symbolically anchors the community and gives its rural residents a feeling of belonging to a place that was and is significant despite the loss of industry and population.

Another reason to visit Corunna is McCurdy Park, on the Shiawassee River, just a few blocks west of the downtown, which offers an ideal spot to enjoy the river. Hugh McCurdy, a lawyer, politician, and banker, gave the forty-acre plot to the city in 1899. The park originally included a casino, rustic shelters, evergreen-lined walks, lagoons, an island, and even a small zoo. Launch a kayak here for a quick paddle to Owosso. Corunna Historical Village, on Governor Parsons Lane in the park, is a collection of historical buildings from around the area, including a rustic cabin rented by James Oliver Curwood at Houghton Lake, and the Webster Davis-Kribs home, a gracious white house attached to a log cabin.

Durand

The whistle of trains is as much a part of the soundscape of Mid-Michigan as the rush of water in ditches after a heavy rain or guns being fired in Flint and Saginaw on New Year's Eve and the Fourth of July. Wheels on steel rails, the whistle of the locomotive, and the ringing of crossing bells is the sound of transit, of things grown or made locally headed to market; and these lines of metal loaded down with coal, grain, and chemicals (from Dow) enabled Mid-Michigan's farmers and foundries to prosper and built small cities like Durand.

Durand lies in Vernon Township, settled by migrants from New York State in 1833 and organized in 1837. The village of Vernon, lying on the Shiawassee River, slowly developed as a market town and township center and was organized in 1871. Today Vernon is a bedroom community, with a quaint appearance and architecturally significant Gothic Revival buildings. James Van Auken operated a brickyard and built the first brick house in the county in 1846 (the house was demolished in 1961, but a memorial stands on the hillside overlooking the river at western edge of Greenwood Cemetery. This spot is said to have been the location of an Indian trading post.

The Detroit and Milwaukee Railroad laid the first tracks through the township in 1856. Three miles southeast of the village was Vernon Center, a flag stop on the railroad. James C. Brand moved his barrel manufacturing operation to Vernon Center in 1872. He built a steam-powered sawmill at the present site of Oak Street and Mill Street (later renamed Brand Street) and gradually purchased nearby land. The mill closed in 1889 but not before the railroads were firmly established. Much of this development had to do with William H. Putnam, who worked for Brand as his main mill foreman. In 1876, Putnam and Brand, with the help of U.S. congressman George H. Durand, established the first post office and settled on the name Durand.

That same year the Chicago and Lake Huron Railroad (later part of the Grand Trunk Western Railroad), when building a line from Flint to Lansing, modified its route through Vernon after Putnam and other residents persuaded the company, with a gift of $500, to go through Durand. In 1886, the Toledo, Saginaw and Mackinaw Railroad built a line through Durand, and in 1888, the Cincinnati, Saginaw and Mackinaw Railroad (subsequently the Ann Arbor Railroad) connected Durand with Bay City. Durand's central position now allowed railroad customers to transfer between lines, enabling passengers and freight to travel throughout the country.

Incorporated as a village in 1887, Durand's main growth came during the 1890s, the population in 1900 (2,134) being eight times what it was ten years earlier. The railroad brought in a population more diverse than what had existed, including Catholics, who organized St. Mary's parish in 1899. Grand Trunk built a new roundhouse in 1908, the largest in the state, to service its locomotives. Until the Great Depression, the Grand Trunk and the Ann Arbor Railroad companies created a prosperous small city, which incorporated itself as such in 1932.

By this time, economic depression had caused freight traffic to decline and companies to go bankrupt. Although rail traffic boomed during World War II, the decline in passenger traffic continued afterward. None of the companies in Michigan found it profitable, and during the 1960s, they discontinued most of it. The change from steam to diesel locomotives was completed in 1961, rendering the roundhouse obsolete. Finally, the Grand Trunk decommissioned its last passenger train on April 30, 1971, and in 1974, the company closed the depot.

After a period of neglect, Durand rallied to save the depot. This was one of many such efforts around the country during the period leading up to the Bicentennial, as railroad stations large and small, no longer needed for their original purpose, became important symbols of their communities. In Durand, however, the depot was more than a symbol. When Senator Walter Mondale came through in 1976 on a stop in his campaign for vice president, he learned of the depot's plight and the local campaign to save it. Mondale talked with Grand Trunk officials, and in 1979, the company, following an agreement to close the road that crossed the mainline, transferred ownership to the City of Durand.

Michigan railfans make Durand a regular destination, and the Durand Union Station is their focus. Located at the intersection of tracks that form a diamond, or a "union," as it is called, it is a great place to photograph trains as they arrive and depart. The architectural firm of Spires and Rohns of Detroit designed it in a Château Romanesque style, sporting conical spires, built of granite brick and cut limestone and completed in 1903. Restoration, following a 1905 fire, modified the dormers and used red tile instead of slate for the roof. When the depot was dedicated, as many as thirty-five passenger trains and one hundred freight trains passed it daily.

Durand Union Station, 1903. COURTESY OF THE LIBRARY OF CONGRESS.

Durand Union Station houses the Michigan Railroad History Museum, with memorable displays about African American rail workers and train wrecks like the Wallace Brothers Circus train disaster of 1903, as well as the Knights Templar train wreck of 1923. A memorial for twenty-three individuals, several camels, and Maude, the tricycle-riding elephant, stands in Lovejoy Cemetery (8000 E. Prior Rd.). Also in the depot is a model railroad exhibit constructed by the Durand Union Station Model Railroad Engineers, a group run by and for rail buffs. Durand hosts it annual Railroad Days festival in May.

Come enjoy the historical downtown ornamented by the Sandula Clocktower. Working from memory, Hungarian immigrant John Sandula created a copy of a cathedral clock from his native city with an important difference: Abraham Lincoln and George Washington are the figures who strike the bells. The bronze sculpture of a railroad worker was created by another immigrant, El Salvadorean Robert R. Cañas, who practiced medicine in Durand and developed his art through mural commissions. His wonderful paintings are displayed in the grand ballroom on the station's second floor and around town. He also cast the bronze railroad worker who stands in front of the clocktower.

Byways and Ghost Towns

The back roads of Shiawassee County are ideal for pleasure drives: farm fields and vistas but lots of shady woods along the rivers, which offer nice places to stop and cool off on a hot day. Shiatown Park (Bennington Rd. just east of Shiawassee River) is idyllic; just west of it lies what exists of Shiawasseetown, originally platted in 1837 and briefly considered as a site for the state capitol. Juddville (corner of Juddville and Durand Rds.) still retains its Methodist church and a few houses. A drive west on Juddville Road is one of the best ways to experience Fourth of July festivities: You will see the rockets and the starbursts, marking those towns big enough to afford a show, but the percussion will be muted so you can still hear crickets while marveling at fireflies, rising and falling like the bubbles in champagne. For country drives in daylight, there are a number of mostly forgotten spots that make nice stops. Maple River (near the intersection of East Bennington and Colby Rds., five miles south of Owosso) is an early settlement with a former Methodist church (now a private residence) facing a cemetery that is marked "Maple River / 1833." Pioneers came from Oakland County and built several Greek Revival farmhouses as well as an octagon schoolhouse still standing further west on Bennington Road. West Haven (close to what modern maps identify as New Haven) sits in a valley at the confluence of the Shiawassee River and the Six Mile Creek. David Estey operated a water-powered furniture factory here from 1865 until he moved to Owosso in 1875, lured by the $3,000 offered by city fathers. Coal was mined in West Haven early in the twentieth century and shipped out on a railroad spur. Today West Haven's landmark is an iron truss bridge. The bridge is closed to all traffic since 2011, but it can be viewed from East Six Mile Creek Road. A former resident created an aggregation of sheds and outbuildings decorated with old tools and industrial equipment that gives an old-time feel to this picturesque locale.

Although most of the county is rural and agricultural, the size of farms has expanded and their number has decreased lessening the need for local market towns. Those that survive tend to have little more than a dollar store and a gas station and convenience store, located near busy state road intersections. Old downtown commercial buildings are mainly deserted. Nevertheless, people are moving to these towns to experience country living while commuting to distant jobs in places like Ann Arbor, Fenton, Flint, Pontiac, and Lansing.

Byron (pop. 533, incorporated in 1873) lies at the fork of the Shiawassee River and the South Branch of the same river. Five partners in a company platted the community in 1837, dammed the river, and built a sawmill and grist mill. Byron has several early Greek Revival buildings, but most of its brick commercial section was destroyed by an arsonist in 2012. The development of Bancroft (pop. 477, incorporated in 1883) was spurred by the construction in 1877 of the rail line from Flint to Lansing, with mills and grain elevators following. Although the old commercial section is largely gone, its location near I-69 assures that residents can commute to jobs elsewhere. New Lothrop (pop. 588, incorporated in 1946) gained a post office in 1878 and thrived for a time as a local center for the surrounding agricultural region. It was close enough to Flint, however, to allow it to become an outer suburb, and ranch houses dating from the 1960s and later fill parts of the town.

With the chains and box stores covering peoples' basic needs for groceries, fast food, and auto parts, and with Walnut Hills Family Campground (7685 Lehring Rd.) providing family fun, the old main street storefronts still remind us that Bancroft once had an opera house, cigar factory, and a social club hall for dances. The Bancroft Bar remains, and if you come through during hunting season, you may notice a "buck pole" where hunters display their prizes.

In Shiawassee County, there are backroads waiting to be driven and deep pools of time that offer opportunities for full immersion in cemeteries, surviving structures, small lakes, and refreshing rivers. Best of all, you will not see any tourists out here.

LAPEER COUNTY

Statisticians predict that by 2050, two-thirds of the world's population (and 89 percent of that of the United States) will live in urban areas. Urbanization, or even ex-urbanization, will reach a limit, because the earth can bear only so much. Within our region, there has been an influx of people moving out of the Detroit Metro region into Lapeer County and Thumb towns, hungry for Arcadia and community. The influx of newcomers can be tricky for old-timers who know that volunteerism and shared values are what made rural communities work; they see the importance of saving agrarian culture and don't want their towns to become bedroom communities

Two shanty boys in Page and Benson's camp near Otter Lake, c. 1870. CRAPO COLLECTION, GENESEE HISTORICAL COLLECTIONS CENTER, UNIVERSITY OF MICHIGAN–FLINT LIBRARY.

or, worse, suburban enclaves. Historically, small towns in the Midwest produced inventors and industrialists, governors and Supreme Court justices, because of the commitment to schools and nurturance of the young. The feeling of belonging and connection to physical and social environments is harder to come by these days as places feel homogenized and society is dominated by consumption activities. But a visit to the towns of Lapeer County will remind you of the many things you might do in a day other than get a lavender latte or brown sugar oat milk shaken espresso. Well, you can do that too, while checking out lots of other options.

Lapeer County is a rectangle that contains eighteen townships in a regular grid. Its name is derived from *la pierre* (French: "the stone"), which, according to oral tradition, derived from the stones found along the banks of the Flint River that runs through the northwest section of the county, joined by Farmer's Creek. The topography of the county is rolling. A belt of white pine across northern Lapeer County attracted early entrepreneurs, who made fortunes logging: men like Henry Howland Crapo from New Bedford, Massachusetts, and William Peters, a German immigrant who settled in Columbiaville, where his mansion is now a bed and breakfast. Below that are rolling hills, created by glacial movement that has left a landscape of kettle lakes and hogback formations, enjoyed by nature and walking enthusiasts. In the southernmost section of the county, rolling land spreads out into farms and green hills near the villages of Metamora and Dryden. This is horse country, where Detroiters came to play polo and hunt foxes on horseback.

Lapeer

Lapeer (pop. 8,806) is the county seat. Alvin N. Hart, the first settler, came from Connecticut and platted it in 1831, and once the Detroit–Bay City railroad line (later the Michigan Central) was laid down, Lapeer grew quickly. It didn't become the industrial center Flint was probably due to location. Flint was on the Saginaw Trail, and on a potentially navigable section of the Flint River. Lapeer had tracts of pine but lacked a navigable river to export lumber readily. As a result, it retained its original character as the center of rich farm country, where the pace of life is driven by the seasons rather than by industries and by care for a group of individuals, most of whom were not going to progress anywhere. A good way to get a feel for this place is to take a stroll or a slow bike ride along the Lapeer Linear Park, a new 2.2-mile walking-biking trail that begins west of the city and winds all the way to the historic downtown, through the grounds of what was and, in some ways still is, the emblematic institution of this community.

The Oakdale Regional Development Center for Developmental Disabilities, which closed in 1991, was founded in 1895 as the Lapeer State Home for the Feeble-Minded and Epileptic. The town council knew the home would be good for the economy and so promised to provide 160 acres, run a water line to the grounds, and supply free water for the first five years. Built on the cottage plan, at its peak, it was a city unto itself, housing 4,500 residents—815 people more than the city had in 1941—and it was the leading employer in Lapeer County. Patients were enrolled in programs designed to help them reach their greatest potential, which included language arts, crafts, and music. Patients worked on the farm, which raised both dairy and beef cattle and pigs, and its nine hundred acres were planted with alfalfa, oats, and other crops for feed.

The institute was home to mildly, moderately, and severely retarded individuals, some of whom would return to the community; but for many, the woods, hills, and streams of the campus as well as the animals they cared for were the only world they would ever experience. By the 1970s, ideas about how best to care for the mentally disabled were changing, and experts felt that segregating them from society was no longer beneficial. The thinking was that every person, whether disabled or not, was entitled to a normal place in the community. The Michigan Department of Mental Health downsized and eventually closed state institutions and sent people out into the community, housing them in adult foster homes and group homes. Today the facility of one hundred buildings is now just a few ruins, a cemetery, and five buildings that have been repurposed (Roland Warner Middle School, Mott Community College, Chatfield Charter School, and two staff houses).

Though it no longer exists in the physical landscape, the Lapeer Home's impact on the city has been great. Thousands of individuals worked at the facility and even more had friends or family who did, and despite a few blemishes on its record—abuse, runaways, sterilization—locals remember it proudly. When arsonists burned the "Castle," an administration building constructed in part from local fieldstones, the cupolas that crowned its rooftops were salvaged and placed around the city and at both ends of Lapeer's downtown district. They were also incorporated into Lapeer's logo.

Trails for walkers and bikers have been cut through the grounds of what was Oakdale, and there are waymarking signs containing pictures and information about its place in Lapeer's history. "Trails at Oakdale" passes through woods and prairies along Farmer's Creek. The old cemetery grounds are beyond the railroad tracks, where there are still markers but no bodies (most were donated for scientific research). Eventually the paths lead to Cramton Park, stretching for ten blocks along the Flint River, named after U.S. congressman Louis C. Cramton (1875–1944).

It is possible to feel far from industry here, but the city, with its machines, factories, and high tech, is not far away. There is an old lumberjack song about Harry Bahel—who was not shepherding flocks or milking cows but was killed violently in a shingle mill in Arcadia Township. Many Lapeer residents commuted to the factories of Flint for regular work, but today, the direction of their daily drive is south to Lake Orion or Oakland County.

The Lapeer County Historic Court House, the oldest functioning courthouse in Michigan, was built in 1845–1846. The Greek Revival building, with a raised brick foundation, is owned by the Lapeer County Historical Society. It hosts one official hearing a year and opens its doors for tours and other events, such as weddings. A plaque on the front of the building, marks a legal milestone that took place here in 1918, when Lapeer Circuit Court judge William B. Williams upheld a lower court's ruling against a Michigan state law that authorized the sterilization of persons confined to public institutions. Williams's ruling protected individuals from the unjust state law that violated individuals' Fourteenth Amendment rights. It was a major step taken to ensure protections for the most vulnerable members of our society.

The Piety Hill Historic District consists of a 15.5-acre area located in downtown Lapeer. The one-time existence of five churches on the same hill tells you that Christian morality was a binding agent in the community after some initial sectarian tension. In a similar way, the founding fathers, Alvin Hart and Edwin White, had to overcome division between two start-up towns—Lapeer and Whitesville, each with a courthouse of its own—to become one community. This tale of two cities is a theme in our region. Lapeer's early nickname was "Squabble City," and people here, like anywhere, still have their prejudices, but they also have a history of overcoming ideological differences through discussion and debate.

Piety Hill has some of the oldest buildings in the Saginaw Valley; twenty-nine properties still stand along Calhoun, Monroe, Madison, Washington, Main (M-24), Park, Liberty, Church, and Nepessing Streets. The oldest houses are in the Greek Revival style (1830–1860), readily identifiable by its use of a low-pitched roof, eave returns, and sidelights and transom window around the front door, and Gothic Revival (1840–1890), recognizable by the triangular roof line and pointed arch (lancet) windows. There are many examples of Queen Anne architecture that date from the 1880s. Look for steeply pitched roofs, dominant front-facing gable, wood overlays in complex gingerbread patterns, and wrap-around porches. You can also spot examples of Second Empire and Italianate—both styles feature boxy, mansard roofs.

The Eagle Tavern building (237 N. Main St., privately owned) is the oldest structure in the district and probably the most significant. Once called Lapeer Upper Town Hotel, it was the main stagecoach stop in what was formerly called Whitesville. The Eagle Tavern, constructed by Enoch Jay White in 1836 and continuously owned by the White family until 1981, served as a tavern until 1850, when it was converted into a two-family residence and a section of rooms from the original tavern was removed. The current owners were told that it was a stop on the Underground Railroad and have retained and refurbished as many of the original features as possible.

The Marguerite de Angeli Lapeer District Library—the public library, first established in 1880—was located in the courthouse. This structure, called simply the Lapeer County Library, was built in 1923 and is among the newer buildings in the Piety District. It was renamed for Lapeer native Marguerite de Angeli (1887–1987), a prolific children's book author and illustrator. Much of her work explored cultural diversity within America. She is also recognized as the first modern children's author to write a book that featured a Black child. *Bright April*, published in 1946, addresses the problem of racial prejudice and demonstrates how children area able to gain understanding and tolerance through their own natural devices.

Religion is not the centrifugal force that it once was, and churches are closing, consolidating, or being used for new things—like the former Episcopal church in Lapeer's downtown, now the Refuge Homeless Shelter of Lapeer. There is, however, one very successful outgrowth of a Lapeer Methodist Protestant Church: radio station WMPC Gospel 1230 AM. Pastor Frank Hemingway built the station in 1926 after reading a how-to manual. Radio was new technology, and some parishioners thought the gadget was demonic. Today, the station, billed as the longest continuously running Christian radio station in America, is owned and operated by Lapeer's Calvary Bible Church.

The historic downtown is thriving, without a single empty storefront. The city council is working to preserve the small-town atmosphere while providing the conveniences of a larger city. There is a Center for the Arts of Greater Lapeer, developed

Lapeer baseball team, 1904, including Peter Chatfield (*first from left, second row*) and "Chalk" Daniels (*extreme lower left*). LAPEER HISTORICAL SOCIETY.

in a repurposed former department store; the PIX Theater, which dates from 1941 and is the premier performance venue; a new Pocket Park, built in a space left vacant when an apartment complex burned between the PIX Theater and Burke's Flowers. There are many other parks along the Flint River and Farmer's Creek at the eastern end of the downtown: Anrook Park, Rotary Park, and Rowden Park.

If you walk right through town and cross Farmer's Creek, you'll enter a working-class suburb called Birdland, and you'll know it by streets named for birds circling around Audubon Park. The working-class homes here are as old as those on Piety Hill, but no care has been taken to preserve them. When built, most did not have plumbing or electricity. My grandmother still lives here. Walking through streets where I once played as an adult, I feel her waiting for me on her back porch with a pitcher of pink lemonade under the patio awning. Intimacy is what keeps people in small towns and brings them back.

Northern Lapeer County

The landforms of this area tell the story of glacial action that formed morainic hills and lakes, and in other places, swale with alternating rises. Swale lands drain poorly but harbor ecosystems of great diversity. This lovely and relatively unvisited corner of our region was treated as a resource of timber and clean water for the cities.

Holloway Reservoir Regional Park is a 1,975-acre reservoir, formed when the Flint River was dammed in 1955, a million-dollar project built to accommodate Flint's water needs. The city had always drawn its supply of drinking water from the river, upstream of heavy industry, but the postwar population explosion created a need for a reserve supply. By 1968, however, Flint switched to using Detroit water, making the reservoir unnecessary, and it was given to the county for recreational use. Holloway today includes Buttercup Beach, Wolverine Campground, and a canoe launching site at Holloway Dam.

The Hogbacks Area, part of the Holloway Regional Park—straddles the Genesee and Lapeer County line, bordered by Coldwater, Elba, Washburn, McDowell, and Stanley Roads. The area covers 2,000 acres and contains two lakes, a river, creeks, and marshes. The area was on the way to becoming a trailer park development in 1971 when Genesee County Parks acquired a chunk of it. "Hogback" is a geological term that refers to a long, narrow ridge or series of hills with a narrow crest and steep slopes of nearly equal inclination on both flanks. Many of the trails through this exceptional natural area give you the sensation of walking the spine of a very large animal. The area is open year-round—no snowmobiling or off-roading—so it is ideal for walking, horseback riding, snowshoeing, fishing, foraging, and sledding. Entry points to the Hogbacks are at Coldwater Road west to a dead end; Coldwater Road east to a dead end; Washburn Road (Toboggan Hill); and the Elba Equestrian

Fieldstone Houses

Fieldstone gas station, Elba Township, Lapeer County.
PHOTOGRAPH BY AUTHOR.

On a drive through our region, you are likely to see structures made of stones: houses, barns, even outbuildings. As in other parts of the country, many older houses feature stones in the construction of chimneys, porches, and foundations. What is more specific to Michigan and to our area, however, are houses, mostly vernacular in style and built in the late nineteenth and early twentieth centuries, that use fieldstones on the exterior facade. In our region, you see them most often in the Thumb and in counties where there are glacial moraines (eastern Genesee and Lapeer). Farmers plowing fields, even today, turn up a lot of stones. Drive through in the spring, and you'll see rocks sitting on the surface of freshly cultivated soil, and kids are still given the job of rock picking. Notice the stone piles at the edges of fields.

The builders of our region seem to have been influenced by the classic cobblestone style, developed in western New York State in the first half of the nineteenth century using cobblestones from the shores of Lake Ontario. This style may have originally been imported from England. The cobblestones are arranged in clearly delineated rows, and some examples of the style have highly detailed herringbone patterns. Besides regular rows, quoins (heavy pieces of masonry that form the building's corners) are

Bungalow using fieldstones, bricks, and cut stone, Flint.
PHOTOGRAPH BY AUTHOR.

a pronounced feature of the New York–style cobblestone houses.

Michigan pioneers may have been influenced by the cobblestone houses they had seen (and there are several such structures in southern Michigan), but they wrought changes on the earlier style. The stones in their fields were irregular and much rougher, not similarly sized cobbles smoothed by the lapping of lake waves. What is consistent, though, is the attempt to create quoins with masonry, brick, or larger rocks and arranging the irregular stones in rows.

It is less common to see fieldstone houses in cities than in rural areas, but there is a fabulous example on Mabel Avenue off Lewis Street in Flint. The mason used brick to create quoins and bricks and stone in patterns, showing the influence of the earlier New York style. This house is an Arts and Crafts bungalow, common in Flint, but in the rural areas you see buildings incorporating architectural influences from Gothic Revival and Queen Anne as well.

Complex (1875 N. Elba Rd.), where there are hitching posts, porta-johns, and campfire rings.

The Lapeer State Game Area consists of 8,599 acres that includes two trails; one is three miles long and ready for beginners, and the other is a bit more challenging, stretching four miles. While rules vary from location to location, some activities that take place in these areas are camping, hiking, fishing, hunting, foraging, bird-watching, biking, boating, off-roading, and skiing.

Elba and Oregon Townships (each with pop. 5,500) have settlements, some named and others marked only by churches and burial grounds. Elba is a four-corners at the intersection of Elba and Davison Roads. There is a township hall with a library, a bank, a dollar store, gas station, and two ice cream parlors. Head north on nearby German Road and just before Stanley Road is Oregon United Methodist Church, called the "German Church" when it began its life in 1873. There is a pretty cemetery where Native American Peter Chatfield is buried. Chatfield played and coached Lapeer High School baseball and football teams and helped Indian Dave trap turtles in nearby Hemingway Lake that they sent by train to Detroit. Head south to check out the largest body of water in the county, Lake Nepessing, stocked with walleye since 1986 and home to twenty-seven fish species. There is a Department of Natural Resources boat access site off Hunt Road on the north shore. Peter Chatfield's father was part of the band that had a winter camp at Lake Nepessing.

North Branch (pop. 900) is on the site of two Indian encampments, and a few Natives bought lots here but moved to Isabella County after 1855. Originally called Beachville, it took the name of the north branch of the Flint River when it was incorporated in 1881. This busy small town has independent businesses, inspired, perhaps, by the longevity of the Daniel Orr Sons hardware store, which closed in 2025 after 150 years in business. Visit North Branch on the rare day when the Daniel Orr

Sons Museum (6714 Jefferson St.) is open. It houses a massive collection of farm and household tools, as well as wagons, buggies, sleighs, early Fords, a reconstructed post office and a jail cell. Most modern people have one "tool"—the cellphone—but a museum like this one reminds us that these implements are key to making everything you see around you.

Extend your visit to check out any of the tiny towns east or west—Burnside, Clifford, or Silverwood. On the map, they may look like drive-by places, but they'll look different after a visit reveals their character. Take the detour to St. Mary's Burnside (5622 Summers Rd.), a rural Catholic Church with a mixed ethnic population in the cemetery and amazing folk art gravestones, incorporating heart and flower mosaics made with pink and gray granite stones. Clifford has a post office and a branch of the Lapeer District Library in an old brick school building. The brick works in Silverwood supplied the materials for building in the towns around and has some glowing examples itself of Gothic Revival houses and a small warehouse with the inscription "H. C. Bearup 1896" on the stone entablature. A local woman owns both the Silverwood bar and a yard ornament business. She followed her passion for pouring concrete into molds that form geese, penguins, religious figures, gnomes, and deer, which she'll sell to anyone who stops and inquires.

Southern Lapeer County

The country backroads stretching between Elba, Hadley, Metamora, Dryden, Almont, and Imlay City are some of the most scenic paths one might find in all of Michigan. The towns are quaint and villages were named for poets and literary characters. Tocqueville observed that Shakespeare and Milton were at home in log cabins and noted that the typical American had to have passion and intellect in order to persist in realizing his one big idea: settlement. Industries came later, which might surprise you given the rustic appearance of the region. But Champion Homes (later Champion Motor Homes) began manufacturing mobile homes in Dryden in 1953, advertising them as the "ideal lake cottage or hunting lodge," and Sea Ray, one of the earliest boat building firms to use fiberglass, began its long life in Metamora with a sixteen-foot family runabout. There is a lot to take in here, and it can all be done with leisurely drives, meandering walks, and gentle pond paddles at one of the many natural areas.

Hadley Township (pop. 4,547) retains a rural identity despite growing suburban sprawl. On either side of the roads running out of Flint, there are farm fields, some tilled and some fallow. Many old homesteads are bleaching in the sun with decaying barns and topless silos, but newish houses line the roads. Farmers sold one-acre roadside plots while continuing to farm or lease the back fields. These vacated farms are way-markers of the paths restless Americans took out of the boondocks. But there are also intact and architecturally unique barns, some with fieldstone foundations or gate posts made of puddingstones. There is evidence that city people are coming out here to try rural life: There are horse boarding facilities here, dog training "ranches," Christmas tree farms, truck farms, and hobby farms where Scottish Highland cattle graze the slopes of the Hadley Hills. Some of these hills, south of Hegel Road, are high enough to be named and measured—Pinnacle Point at 1,262 feet and Kerr (Cemetery) Hill at 1,258. This morainic topography continues south through Oakland County, the Irish Hills, down into northern Ohio and Indiana, and is full of recreation areas. Ortonville Recreation Area (5,400 acres of woodlands and lakes) straddles Lapeer and Oakland County with all of Big Fish Lake in southern Lapeer. Make sure to visit the stand of oaks at the southern end of the lake where there is also a beach.

The center of Hadley Township, established in 1835, was and still is the Community Church, backed by a cemetery with graves that go back to 1837. The Hadley mill is across the street. At one time, it was a functioning gristmill along a pretty creek with a covered bridge. The Hartwig family gave the whole area to the township for use as a

Ivory family in front of their Greek Revival house in Hadley Township, LAPEER COUNTY, 1888. HADLEY HISTORICAL SOCIETY.

park. There is a town in Massachusetts named Hadley, and the old maple trees lining the road and the Greek Revival houses will remind you of quaint villages back east.

Metamora (pop. 565) has an identity unique to the area. The ride to Metamora is a roller coaster along the ridgelines of a glacier-carved landscape. Baily Lake (north of Brocker Rd. near the intersection with Diehl) is a good example of a kettle formed by a deposited chunk of ice melting in place. Mt. Christie at 1,251 feet (near Davison Lake Road) is one of the Hadley Hills' high peaks. Where the land flattens along Brocker Road, marked as a "Scenic Byway," there are working farms.

Metamora got its name from the very popular play *Metamora; or, The Last of the Wampanoags* (1829), written by John Augustus Stone, as a vehicle for one of the most prominent American actors of the nineteenth century, Edwin Forrest. Metamora is a fictional chief, cast in the "noble Indian" mode, who eventually kills his wife to protect her from the terrors of settler-colonialism and enslavement, before being slain by white pioneers. What were the local settlers thinking when they named this village Metamora? If anything, the name signaled a cultural appropriation of their stories.

Metamora in 2023 feels very upscale, a place where the wealthy have country homes, stables, and clubs. There are at least three real estate offices in this very small town, as well as architects and building contractors. If you drive the back roads, you will see advertisements for exclusive homesites, with names like "Steeplechase."

Metamora Crossroads Historic District is composed of 3.5 acres with fourteen historic structures that were built primarily between 1850 to 1910. In 1850, the first store was built in Barrows Corners, as Metamora was originally called, establishing the settlement founded by Eber Barrows in 1839. The area was dotted with farms, but because much of the land is quite steep and pitched irregularly, the auto boom of the 1920s drew many farmers off the land and into factories. Farms were sold to wealthy Detroiters who wanted to establish horse breeding facilities and hunt clubs. For them, Metamora was ideal, because it was accessible, scenic, and had plenty of natural cover and land that was available.

Metamora Historical Society is in the Old Town Hall and Opera House, built in 1888. The simple space has a small but attractive stage, and cases with historical artifacts. The White Horse Inn (1 E. High St.), originally called the Hoard House, was developed in 1848 by Daniel Ammerman as a general goods store and later run by Lorenzo Hoard as an inn and stagecoach stop equipped with stables. When the railroads were built in 1872, Hoard also gained those passengers as guests. The inn was thoroughly renovated in 2014 and is a very pleasant if pricey place to get a meal.

Metamora Hunt Club on Barber Road is a fox-hunting club, established in 1928 by members of the Bloomfield Open Hunt and the Grosse Pointe Hunt Club. Members purchased eleven thousand acres in "the hills" for stables, riding trails, and training areas. The fox hunts and equestrian competitions and shows regularly made the society page of the Detroit newspapers in the 1930s and 1940s. Today, the area is still known for upper-end hunting. Hunter's Creek Club on Sutton Road is a private club for bird hunting and hunting dog training. Opened in 1958, it was Michigan's first pheasant hunting and game preserve.

Seven Ponds Nature Center (3854 Crawford Rd.), established in 1967, is located in Metamora and Dryden Townships. The center's 486 acres feature deep glacial lakes, marshes, swamps, fields, prairie, and woodlands. Nature Center lands include the nearby Jonathan Woods Nature Preserve, which contains a mature hardwood forest, a leatherleaf bog, and a cold-water brook. There is also a nine-acre reconstructed tallgrass prairie. There are miles of trails, boardwalks, and bridges that give the walker a view across the linked ponds. Paddling is possible, and there is a dock for easy put-ins behind the center.

Dryden (pop. 951) is the largest village in the southern tier of the county. Settlers established the village in 1836, but a state senator named the town Dryden after the English poet. The Ladies Library Association, established in 1870, became prominent due to the energy of the members who collected funds for the library, erected a building, and offered aid to victims of the 1881 Thumb fire. Portraits of the original women in this Library Association hang on the second floor of the village library today. The village retains a small-town feel, but its population grew by 30 percent between 1990 and 2000, indicating that people are moving out of areas of urban sprawl, seeking perhaps a greater sense of community and participation that is available in such places.

Imlay City (pop. 3,703) in eastern Lapeer County exists because of the railroad. It was founded in 1850 by the chief engineer of the Port Huron–Lake Michigan Railroad, who anticipated it being a likely produce depot between the cities of Capac and Lapeer, once the railroad line from Ontario to Chicago was finished in 1870. The population of Imlay City has grown since 1880 and now remains steady, probably because it is on I-69 (midway between Flint and Port Huron) and is an easy drive to the Detroit suburbs down Van Dyke (M-53) through the pleasant towns of Almont and Romeo. These major thoroughfares are very busy, with grocery stores, fast food franchises, and the typical big-box stores and plazas that one finds on every strip in America. The old downtown has yet to find a way to compete with the strip stores.

Farmers of Dutch descent from western Michigan came to the Imlay City area in the 1920s, moving from communities in western Michigan like Zeeland and Hudsonville. They established the Christian Reformed Church on M-53 and muck farms in wet areas that had to be drained to produce vegetables—especially cucumbers. Today, Mexican immigrants, many from the state of Jalisco, provide the field labor and factory work for growing and processing the cucumber crop. They began to move into the area in 1940 and lived in shacks for workers, attending Mexican dances in four-corners like Lesterville—gathering places in the middle of farm fields. Hispanics today make up nearly one-third of the city's population; most work in the Vlasic Pickle (now owned by Pinnacle Foods) plant. The Vlasic family businesses began as a creamery in the Detroit area in the 1920s. After World War II, the first pickle factory was opened in Imlay City, and the company grew to become the largest pickle producer in the country. The Hispanic community is a visible part of Imlay City, with Mexican restaurants, businesses, social services, and a Pentecostal church side by side on Almont Avenue.

The big event every August is the East Michigan State Fair. The fair opened in 1896, and the grandstand is a permanent fixture, though harness racing now shares the space with tractor pulls, daredevil auto stunts, motorcycle racing, and demolition derbies. Michigan fairs began as agricultural expos that stressed participation and education for farmers. Husbandry is still passed down within families and extended families, and agriculture is taught in schools and clubs like Future Farmers of America and 4-H. The annual Eastern Michigan State Fair has been updated with a Woods 'n' Water Outdoor Weekend in September and a Lavender Festival in June. Also worth a visit is the Imlay City Historical Museum (77 Main St.).

Almont (pop. 2,830) sits on the border of suburban and rural universes on M-53, between Imlay City and Romeo. Like other towns in southern Lapeer County, Almont has slowly transformed from an agricultural community to a country haven for those who want to live in a semirural environment and commute to work. It is also a weekend getaway for those keen on visiting orchards and cider mills with corn mazes, petting zoos, and "pick your own" strawberries, raspberries, peaches, and apples.

Almont remains an elegant-looking town with historic houses, notably the F. P. Currier House on St. Clair Street, a modified octagon house, which was the first of its kind in Michigan. But it was a rough and ready place in the past. In 1827, when four intrepid individuals hove a road to access lumber, they tapped a whiskey keg until they were tapped out, only to have wolves serenade them in their camp all night. Whiskey even greased the wheels of justice. In 1833, Daniel Black, from Genesee County, New York, built the first house that included a tavern, with dances that attracted young people from as far as Rochester and Utica. A majority of settlers came west from Saratoga, Genesee, and Erie Counties in New York, but there were also Scottish immigrants who arrived directly from Glasgow beginning in 1841. There is still a Scotch Settlement Road southeast of the village, and in 1846, the Scotch Settlement Almont Society was organized in Bruce Township (Macomb County), directly south of Almont Township. Nineteenth-century Almont had wagon shops, hardware and tin shops, foundries, and a starch factory that caused an outbreak of "potato fever" that killed fifteen people in 1846—at the same time as the Irish potato famine. Late blight pathogen, responsible for the mid-century famine in Ireland, actually originated in North America: Philadelphia and New York City reported cases as early as 1843, and then it crossed the Atlantic, probably with a shipment of seed potatoes for Belgian farmers in 1845.

Don Lierman, a graduate of the University of Michigan–Flint, has lived in Imlay City all his life and calls it his "Emerald City." His phrase conjures images from L. Frank Baum's *The Wizard of Oz*, in which the emerald city of Oz and its political system turn out to be a dystopia—but that is not Don's Imlay City. For him, there still is no place like home. Those who have analyzed the allegory of *The Wizard of Oz* say that Baum's yellow-brick road refers to the gold standard, but he also took his family on vacation to Traverse City, where he was impressed by the yellow-brick Northern Michigan Asylum (1881). So we end where we began, on the grounds of Oakdale, wondering what kind of a "home" it really was—administering therapeutic care or practicing an early form of eugenics—and to what extent is that institution a fitting emblem for life in small-town Michigan.

FARMING THE SAGINAW VALLEY

Our region is essentially rural. When William "Billy" Durant and J. Dallas Dort set out to market "Blue Ribbon" road carts, they relied on their farm connections. Today, as you drive the roads north, west, and east out of Flint, you see rusting cultivators and old steel wheels leaning against trees with petunias planted around them. A country drive gives you a look into agriculture past, present, and future, and it should raise questions. Why are there so many dilapidated barns in one area but functioning barns in another? Why are some fields plowed and others fallow? What is growing in these fields? Why so many grain and dry bean elevators? Where are all the farmers? Where are the dairy cows? There's a farm in the middle of the Thumb where cars headed to Lake Huron stop regularly, surprised by the rare sight of cows. If a girl or boy gets close enough to reach out a hand, a cow may grab it with her rough-like-sandpaper wrap-around tongue, designed to grab and pull grass. Huron County has 145,000 cows—the largest number in any Michigan county, and most are hidden away in concentrated animal feeding operations (CAFOs)—pole barns with eight thousand or even fifteen thousand animals to a facility. We are losing so much in the general drive to overproduce, not least of which is the opportunity to learn about ourselves and our place on earth through interaction with animals. Just this single piece of the farming puzzle should make us curious to travel the rural roads and find out what's happening on our farms.

For quite some time, at least since the farm crisis of the 1980s, when Secretary of Agriculture Earl Butz adjured farmers to "get big or get out," quantity seems to have won out over concerns about quality and human values. Small farmers did get out, leaving the land in record numbers. Between 1950 and 2023, Huron County lost 2,563 farms. The pull of factory jobs, plus the rising costs of land, equipment, fuel, insurance (medical, farm, crop) were partly responsible, but above all it was the policy-driven push to supersize that made it impossible for many small and even mid-sized farmers to compete. Others have kept pace with agrarian structural change, expanding from four hundred to three thousand acres. Though they may regret the shrinking of their communities, most will defend their choice to size up as a necessary adaptation to progress and market demand. "As long as people want to shop at Walmart, farmers have to think in terms of the biggest yields and lowest

Wind turbines and an old barn in the Thumb. PHOTOGRAPH BY JASON SCHNETTLER.

costs," Richard D'Arcy explained. He farms three thousand acres in Sanilac County with his wife, one hired hand, and computerized combines and harvesters.

Still other farmers refuse to succumb to market pressures that would mean incurring huge debt for more land and bigger equipment. Wes Reinbold, a fifth-generation farmer and Blumfield Township supervisor, runs down what things cost: a new planter, $250,000; new tractor, $300,000; new harvester, $600,000. He admits that technology is a temptation, but the decision to go big is not inevitable: "It all depends on what you want to buy." He sticks to what worked for his father, rotates crops, drives older tractors, and misses the days when every farm had a variety of animals and things weren't so specialized. His neighbor over in Frankenmuth, Roger Weiss, paid over $500,000 for a robotic milking system from Denmark. Both men are living more or less traditional lives, farming about three hundred acres each, but have made different decisions about investment in technology.

Learning about the challenges farmers face may help dismantle the wall that divides urban and rural people. We have a lot in common. We are all eaters; we are all threatened by a corporate model that reduces diversity of approach in field, factory, and university; and, finally, we are all at risk of being displaced by machines and robots. We don't have to stereotype one another as "cidiots" and rednecks. All of us need earth and ideas, dirtied hands and educated minds. In Michigan's past, most working people were also farmers, and as Flint and Saginaw became industrial centers in the 1910s and 1920s, "shopworker-farmer" emerged as a new occupational category. Factory work supplemented farm income and helped families make it through the winter months.

The region once supported a variety of truck farms and grazing animals. Dairy cows and sheep were concentrated in Lapeer and the middle Thumb. Farmers raised celery and cucumbers in the rich mucklands of Lapeer and Sanilac Counties, potatoes around Reese, and sugar beets in the lake-plain loams of the basin. Animal agriculture shrank as farmers began planting cash crops—sugar beets, soybeans, dry beans, and wheat—that have reduced variety in the crop palette.

From settlement times, farms were necessarily small (forty to eighty acres), because the land first had to be cleared and because with a single team of horses a farmer could manage only about fifty acres. More acres required a second team. Men spent the winter cutting and clearing trees and the spring digging out stumps. Sheep solved the problem of how to cope with cutover land, because they grazed between stumps, keeping down the second growth. By 1873, there were two woolen mills in Flint, with others in Corunna, Lapeer, Vassar, and Lexington, as well as a large mill in Columbiaville that operated from 1884 to 1949. Much of the land was very wet, so farmers dug drainage ditches until mechanized trenching equipment eased some of that labor, and nineteenth-century legislation enabled groups of proximate farmers to create "drainage districts" that formalized cost sharing. Men, horses, and oxen did the field work; every farm had animals, including cows, pigs, and chickens; and most communities had their own creameries and cheese factories to process milk: The Huron County seat of Bad Axe has had twelve local dairies.

Farm life in the early days was hard but marked by a high degree of cooperation and sociability. Settlers organized work bees for felling trees, building roads, cabins, and barns, always accompanied by a keg of whiskey and plenty of food to make the occasion festive. Summer threshing was a big event, and neighboring farmers would either pool money to buy a threshing machine together or crews would pull one with a steam-powered tractor from farm to farm—a practice that continued into the 1950s. Rural neighborhoods established local organizations, which enhanced social life as well as advocacy for farmers' concerns.

Automation changed the social landscape of rural communities. Henry Ford—a proponent of industrial and agricultural integration—imagined his Model T as a machine for rural use: Not only would it decrease isolation, but the engine and rear-wheel crankshafts could be used to grind feed, saw wood, churn butter, pump water, shear sheep, elevate grain, and shell corn. When horses were needed by the army in World War I, Ford came out with attachment kits that turned Model Ts into field tractors. Frugal farmers loved the idea, but it proved impractical. Ford responded by building an affordable tractor that revolutionized farm life—the Fordson, manufactured in Dearborn from 1917 to 1920. If you are curious about heirloom tractors and old farm machinery—or even if you're just curious about rural life and attitudes—you should plan to visit the annual Oakley Steam and Antique Tractor Show in mid-August (17180 Ferden Rd., Oakley).

To pay for tractors, farmers had to cultivate more land and spend time traveling between fields. This required bigger, faster, and more powerful machines with rubber wheels. The Allis-Chalmers Model WC became the first tractor to come with standard pneumatic rubber tires, the result of a collaboration between the Wisconsin firm and Harvey Firestone, a farmer-industrialist who oversaw the research, development, and experimentation on his Ohio farm. Ginny Knag, whose family has farmed in Grand Blanc since 1831, commented that her father bought an Allis-Chalmers in 1940 and never looked back: "He did not have warm, fuzzy feelings for horses; they get sick, and you have to grow the food to feed them."

It is hard to argue against the need for some agricultural mechanization. Rural labor was back-breaking, literally. If you visit the Thumb Octagon Barn (6948 Richie Rd., Gagetown), you will see a wide range of inventions and labor-saving devices, including a portable treadmill for a horse to walk that powered small engines. All of the larger towns had foundries and factories that made farm tools. Factories that made drain tile from glacial clays appeared at the end of the nineteenth century in places like Akron, Sebewaing, and Ruth. Today, there are seven companies in the region that manufacture drain tile from plastics.

Industry entered the field in other ways, too. At the end of the nineteenth century, the federal government, following Napoleon, encouraged domestic sugar production to reduce the nation's dependence on Caribbean suppliers. Robert C. Kedzie, chemist at the Michigan Agricultural Experiment Station, saw that Mid-Michigan's climate was similar to those of the beet-growing areas of Germany and France, and he experimented with growing seeds. Local farmers, too, were willing to grow them but needed processing plants and a market. National and state government initiatives in 1897 were a spur. The federal government provided Michigan farmers with seed for a second trial cultivation, and the state legislature passed a law offering a bounty of one cent per pound to any farmer who would grow sugar beets. The trial was successful enough to inspire three Bay City investors to visit the processing plants in Colorado and Nebraska. The trip convinced them to build the first sugar factory in Michigan in Essexville in 1898. Within ten years there were fourteen different sugar companies in the state and thirteen factories in our region.

Sugar beet agriculture and processing arrived in the Saginaw Valley just after lumber, and many barons used their excess capital to build processing plants. The mills contracted with farmers to supply the seed, fertilizer, and transport, and they paid well. If a struggling farmer could manage to put in a field or two of sugar beets he could make a decent living. Sociologists of agriculture suggest that contract production began the process of turning an independent farmer into just another laborer, but locals don't see it that way. Beets have always been just one of the crops farmers grow because "you can't plant beets in the same field year after year . . . depletes the soil." Grown in rotation, however, they worked well, providing roughage for grazing animals and aerating the soil with their dense root mass.

Sugar plants, piling stations, festivals, and the distinctive smell of beet processing are as much a part of local culture in the Saginaw Valley as cars. Mountains of softball-sized brown-red tubers dot the landscape in September at eight piling stations; and there are four sugar mills—in Bay City, Caro, Sebewaing, and Croswell—where you can watch trucks unloading beets onto conveyor belts for processing into sucrose that looks and tastes no different from the cane variety. The opening of Michigan Sugar's new molasses desugarization facility in Bay City, able to capture 90 to 95 percent of the sugar in beets, keeps it on the cutting edge.

If you think soy and tofu are new, think again. First cultivated by a Kent County farmer in 1853, Seventh-Day Adventists at Dr. John Harvey Kellogg's Battle Creek health resort developed it as a health food. Henry Ford initiated its industrial crossover, when he used soybean oil to make paint enamels and car parts. Market demand for soybeans was fortuitous: Farmers needed a new plant to fill out their rotation since they didn't need the quantity of forage crops (oats, alfalfa, clover, and hay) to feed horses. Because the soybean plant fixes nitrogen in the soil, it also improved soil quality. Today, Michigan manufactures over two hundred commercial soy products, almost all of them food.

Dried or "dry" beans—mature seeds that have dried in the pod on the plant—became a regional specialty crop during the Depression. Michigan farmers grow eight commercial classes of dry beans: navy, small white, black turtle, pinto, light red kidney, dark red kidney, cranberry, and yellow eye. Thumb "navies" fed our troops and our British and Russian allies during World War II, and black beans emerged as a new regional crop in 1980 with farmers growing them on contract for shipment to Mexico. Let's not forget pickles! Though Berrien Springs, Michigan, called dibs on the Pickle Festival, the Thumb is still a major producer. Watch for the special harvesters gathering pickling cucumbers from area fields in August and September, delivering to Vlasic Pickles in Imlay City; Hausbeck Pickles & Peppers in Saginaw; or Mr. Chips, Inc., in Pinconning for processing.

You will notice other farm-related businesses and industries as you drive around the region. Elevators—those concrete and metal "cathedrals" standing in the midst of fields, on waterways, and next to railroad tracks—enable farmers to stockpile and store grain and dry beans, giving them the option of waiting for prices to increase before they sell. Elevators are a big business with many employees, but the biggest, Cooperative Elevator Company, which began its life as the Pigeon Co-Op in 1903, has been a grower-owned cooperative since 2004. There are two livestock markets in Marlette and Cass City that hold weekly auctions, six US Department of

Cooperative Elevator, in Pigeon, dates to 1903. PHOTOGRAPH BY AUTHOR.

Agriculture–approved slaughterhouses—three in Thumb towns of Minden City, Peck, and Pigeon—and a Dairy Farmers of America plant that condenses milk in Cass City. There are also feed and fertilizer suppliers as well as micronutrient manufacturers. A facility in Reese, for example, collects and processes old batteries, removing the zinc and manganese and preparing them for field use. There are elevators, milling companies, and soybean processing plants.

One of the bigger changes to the agricultural picture has happened in dairy farming. Small dairy farmers have been selling out for decades as the CAFO model became the dominant one. There are holdouts—like Nancy Schuette and her three sons, who run a small dairy farm near Pigeon. They milk fifty-five cows twice a day and grow food for the animals, along with some beets and navies for extra income. Nancy tells her sons that when they get tired of milking they can go, but Tim, who wanted to farm from the age of six, doesn't think he will ever be able to leave. He milks, doctors, delivers calves, and takes care of the crops with breaks for meals and church on Sunday. Farming is who he is. The problem for small dairy farmers in the current economic landscape is that the big operations produce so much that

A new CAFO with manure lagoon in foreground, near Clifford. PHOTOGRAPH BY AUTHOR.

they drive down milk prices and outbid the small farms for land to lease. "You need land to grow food for your animals, and we just lost a forty-acre piece this week," she remarks. Local gossip says Coca-Cola owns a nearby farm, and so does a doctor who lives in California.

Since 2000, European immigrant farmers (mainly Dutch but some Irish) have been moving into the Thumb, as well as Ontario, Ohio, Indiana, and Iowa, buying up whole square miles of land for CAFOs. A foreigner with $800,000 to invest can get an EB-5 visa and green card. Most of these new immigrants say that they come for the chance to operate a larger farm (just as in the days of old). But there's nothing old-school about a CAFO, which by definition is a facility with one thousand or more "animal units." They are coming here because the European Union has imposed strict regulations on herd size and manure output to control the "nitrogen crisis." Instead of paying tax on excessive nitrate and phosphate (chemicals in animal manure), Dutch farmers with lots of cash come to Huron County where they operate multiple CAFOs, ruffling the feathers of locals, who, to get in on the action, sell all their hay and forage crops to the factory farm, becoming, in effect, employees. "Employees who may be screwed over," added a local man—"after investing in cutting and baling equipment, the big boss could very well decide it's cheaper to do it himself." Meanwhile, U.S. agribusinesses and the Farm Bureau lobby against all regulation and defend the

"Right to Farm" for every farmer, making no distinctions between one with fifty-five animals and one with three thousand. In doing so, they put the economic gains of the few before the health of the environment, rural communities, the viability of small farms, and the rights of animals, forced to live short, tortured lives.

Once a farmer has more than one hundred milking cows to a herd, the logistics of them going outside becomes untenable. Because disease spreads rapidly in CAFO environments, the animals are kept alive with prophylactic antibiotics and vaccines; bovine growth hormones are often used to increase milk production. These practices are illegal in the Netherlands. The animals on Nancy Schuettes's farm are social, vocal, and curious. Their lives have variety: While some are being milked, others are hanging out in a paddock with the bull, while many others wander and graze a pasture.

A growing number of Amish farmers in the region support families on the income from forty acres. They can do it because they don't have utility bills, don't participate in consumer culture, and rely on preindustrial farming practices: horses instead of tractors, manure instead of fertilizers, and no pesticides. There's a long-standing community in Caro and newer communities in Millington and Maple Valley Township (between Marlette and Brown City). The Amish are good neighbors and use their carpentry skills to develop rapport with the larger community. By contrast, the Dutch farmers contribute to the community with cash donations and deliver their animals to county fairs, where rural children who have never seen a cow give birth watch "the miracle of life" in wonder without knowing that the cow and calf will be immediately separated after the show and sent to the assembly line.

The next generation of environmentally aware and digitally savvy farmers are inclining toward regenerative practices like no- and low-till methods, organic farming, and growing heirloom varieties. Some are developing side businesses, like Noah Dutcher, of Shiawassee County, who uses drones to seed, spray, and fertilize in targeted ways to reduce in-field damage to crops and lessen the amount of chemicals and fertilizers put onto fields. Others are developing value-added products like germination blankets made from the straw they grow and mixing pet foods and bird seed in repurposed grain elevators. There has been a trend toward interacting directly with customers, because young farmers, like Ashley Kennedy of Bad Axe, see that the public "wants to support the local and they want sustainable." Hanna Campbell of Owosso is opening a farm market that sells, directly to the public, vegetables, eggs, chicken and beef, along with her homemade baked goods. Community-supported agriculture has potential for bridging the urban-rural divide, with customers buying shares of the harvest each season. The success of such initiatives varies, but Thread Creek Farm (3305 E. Hill Rd.) in Grand Blanc, in partnership with the Local Grocer in Flint, has had as many as 120 people buy weekly shares of their harvest. Experiments with agritourism like Pinni Mini Farm (735 East Townline 16 Rd., Pinconning) hope to waylay suburban families headed up north to a farm that doubles as petting zoo and animal sanctuary. A majority of their animals (cows, pigs, horses, a donkey, and emus) were rehomed or rescued.

Although factories have been in the garden since the first sugar mill, the General Motors mindset—take more, sell more, waste more—has never dominated as noticeably as it does in today's CAFO environments, where animals and migrant workers are pushed to their bodily limits. The average heifer lives through two or three cycles of pregnancy and lactation before she is "spent" (sold for meat). At the slaughterhouse, the speed of the line, both in the killing and the disassembling animal bodies into parts, forces the workers to focus on keeping up, rather than thinking or feeling. Animals may resist but cannot go on strike and, realistically, neither can the Hispanic workforce, both legal and undocumented. Change can only come from rural people speaking up in defense of their traditional economies and way of life against corporate interests and farming on an industrial scale. Because many young farmers are making thoughtful investments in technologies and methods that preserve land, water, and local communities, there is hope that what Wendell Berry calls "the necessary mosaic of local agrarian cultures" may be restored.

Mosaic implies variety, and if today's farms had more of that, they might look more like the truck farms of the past that had a little bit of everything. An agrarian mosaic also speaks to a range of farms sizes, breeds of animals, crops grown, marketing strategies, and even the fraternal organizations farmers can join. In the not too distant past, there were a whole range of farmers' organizations in our region, all of which provided agricultural advocacy and education as well as social activity: the Patrons of Husbandry (Grange) had eighty-two locals in our ten-county study area as of 1919, just a few of which still meet, notably the Burns Grange #160; Ancient Order of Gleaners, started by Caro printer Grant Slocum in 1894 to provide fellowship and insurance; and Farmers' Clubs. Today, there is one organization that dominates: the Farm Bureau. The overlapping of rural and urban worlds in our region's past may, partially, account for the success of the 1936–1937 Sit-Down Strike. Many of the Flint Sit-Down strikers were farmers, shocked into joining the fledgling United Auto Workers by the effect the fast-moving assembly line had on their bodies. These men came from rural areas where the Grange advocated for farmers' interests against monopolistic tendencies of big industries like the railroads. Whether or not Granger militancy made it easier for some Republican farmers to join the leftist United Auto Workers has never been researched. We do know, however, that the Flint Sit-Down Strike of 1936–1937 rippled back into agrarian worlds. The Black farmer and vice president of the Southern Tenant Farmer's Union, Owen Whitfield, took inspiration from it to plan and carry out the sharecroppers' strike in the Missouri Boot Heel—a reservoir of labor for GM. In January, 1939, hundreds of sharecroppers' families camped by the road to bring public attention to their evictions. Franklin D. Roosevelt's Agricultural Adjustment Act paid farmers not to grow corn in an effort to stabilize prices, but instead of sharing the windfall, the landowners put the tenant farmers off the land.

Thousands of small farmers in our region have been put off the land by economic policies and powerful interest groups. Wendell Berry calls this "cultural genocide," and, save for a brief period in the late 1970s and early 1980s, farmers haven't been able to mount effective protests. In the Saginaw Valley, the farm crisis came hard on the heels of a contamination event that traumatized farmers and nonfarmers alike. A chemical company in St. Louis, Michigan, in the west edge of our watershed, shipped flame retardants—polybrominated biphenyl (PBB)—instead of a nutritional supplement to be mixed into livestock feed. An epidemic of health problems followed that ended with herds having to be shot into mass graves as well as contaminated dairy and meat entering the food supply. One dairy farmer with 125 head noted the whole "mix-up" took the heart out of farming for him, and it wasn't just the money but the devotional labor of twenty years: "Building a good herd of cows is artwork."

As more and more small farmers were forced to sell out, they organized the American Agricultural Movement in 1977. "Tractorcade" protests happened on a national and local scale. At the Washington, DC, event in 1977, farmers broke into and trashed the Farm Bureau office, deriding it as nothing but an insurance company that works against small farmers. Locally, farmers drove their tractors to Lansing and Owosso in 1981 to pressure President Ronald Reagan to end the Soviet grain embargo. What farmers wanted then and still want is parity—to live on par with the rest of the economy. Just as industrial workers must organize to insist upon a living wage, farmers—for a brief window of time—felt they had to organize to insist upon commodity prices that covered the cost of production and guaranteed a decent standard of living.

Today the Farm Bureau advertises itself as "the voice of Michigan farmers" and acknowledges that it is "a family of companies" offering insurance, legal aid, and business and accounting assistance. It is hard to imagine how one corporation can advocate for the interests of all farmers when they work at such different and conflicting scales. In private conversations, farmers will gossip and vent their frustrations. While they know that the Darwinian logic of capitalist enterprise puts them in competition with their own neighbors, most are mum about the structures of inequality that give some families an advantage over others. It's safer to make outsiders—"cidiots" and elites—the enemy, and it is also understandable when urbanites are so uncaring and uncurious about rural problems.

Working to rebuild urban-rural connections may, however, open up mutually beneficial opportunities and lead to greater understanding. Why wouldn't a local creamery help solve Flint's food desert problem? The Weiss Farm is considering the idea, and the Cook Farm in Ortonville, which does this already, is prospering. Meanwhile, demolition is just being completed on a Flint landmark—the McDonald

Dairy, started in 1931 by two brothers, John and William, originally from Sanilac County. The McDonalds were true innovators, introducing homogenization (1932) and square milk bottles for easy refrigerator storage; they even reorganized the dairy to run as a cooperative, owned by the milk producers themselves. The McDonald name changed to Country Fresh, a Grand Rapids dairy firm that ran it until 2009, when it closed the Flint plant and moved south to Livonia. The engraved entablature over the entrance was demolished with the building, but it read: "The farm is still the enduring base on which the whole economy of the nation rests."

William McDonald had a 120-acre farm on Perry Road, which he donated to the Grand Blanc Community Foundation. Two barns—one with a faded sign saying "W. A. McDonald"—still stand as "placemakers," but the land was sold for expensive subdivisions where immigrant doctors now live. That barn reminds us that by sprawling all over the distinction between city and country, we kill diversity (bio- and geo-). Places matter; the best way to honor their integrity is to do what good farmers (and doctors) have done and still do: make the rounds.

Dining Out, wood block print by Laura DeLind.

PART IV

TOURS

THE THUMB

The Thumb is a geographically distinct extension of land that makes Michigan a mitten. It was explored and settled early by merchants and migrants plying the rivers and lakes in canoes and schooners and slogging through swamps on foot long before there were roads or railroads. Most residents have ancestors who migrated from or through Ontario. It can be easy to forget that the Thumb is a U.S. border region until political tensions extend wait times at the Blue Water Bridge in Port Huron or excite immigration checks.

The Thumb region has had some historical events that made the micro-region significant nationally. For instance, among the earliest to settle here were those fleeing from the so-called Patriots War of 1837. American "Patriots," organized in "hunters' lodges," unsuccessfully planned to invade Canada and end British tyranny on the North American continent. The Thumb was in the national spotlight again when the fire of 1881 swept across the peninsula. The Thumb fire was the first disaster to which the newly formed Red Cross responded.

The landscapes of the Thumb are varied. Moraines, sand ridges, pine forests, coastal marshes, wet prairies, and kettle lakes are more characteristic of the western Thumb (Tuscola and Lapeer Counties), while Huron, Sanilac, and St. Clair Counties tend to be more level and are heavily farmed. Rail tourism dates from the 1890s, when private resorts like Pointe Aux Barques developed. Cottage tourism began in the 1920s, and by 1939, the American Automobile Association was advertising the Thumb as an ideal touring destination, with "rolling hills, blue water, the best fishing in the country, pheasants galore, ducks to darken the sky, and miles of snowy beaches." Today, cottages—three or four rows deep—crowd the coast from Caseville to Port Austin, but they are medium-sized homes, not mansions. Compared to other parts of our state, the Thumb feels more remote and less commercial. That may change, however, if the "Forgotten Coast" campaign catches on.

We have broken the Thumb into several drives or routes: the M-25 coastal tour, the Cass River tour from the Petroglyphs to the Otter Lake area, the mid-Thumb drive, and a visit to Shay Lake that explains how a resort for Black families developed there in the 1950s and 1960s.

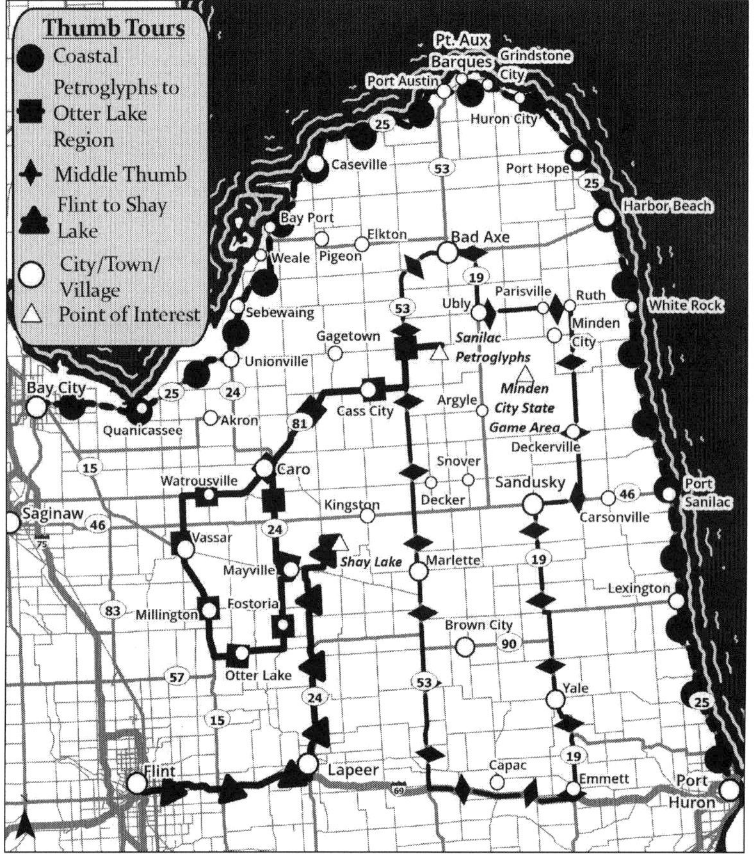

Thumb Driving Tours. UNIVERSITY OF MICHIGAN–FLINT GIS CENTER.

Coastal Tour

If there is a drive that enables us to grasp Michigan's Thumb, it is the 140-mile-long M-25 coastal road that traces the peninsula's outline. The character of each coast is different: sand and marsh on the west side, forests and rocky shoreline on the east. Along this coastline were utopian communities and some of Michigan's earliest resorts. Since I-75 opened a direct route to Mackinac, downstate tourists bypass the Thumb, leaving it "forgotten" to all but locals who enjoy the white sand at Caseville and Port Austin without crowds.

Before the interstate or even M-25, there were Indian trails—paths, really; and paths are made by people with habitual or ritual knowledge of a place. Landform maps of the Thumb mark old shorelines, and the main Indian path ran atop the sand ridge that is closest to the coast. It's called "Sand Road," on modern maps and is broken up into three sections. The M-25 drive is a study in green and blue and all shades of gray when summer storms roll in off Wildfowl Bay. But don't be content with the view through the windshield. Stop, get out, walk for an hour here and another hour there. That's the way space becomes a place.

West Side: Bay City to Port Austin, Following M-25

As you drive out of Bay City on Center Avenue, you pass the mansions built with the money made and the wood cut from the forests of the Thumb. The road veers south and inland to meet the southernmost tip of Saginaw Bay.

Quanicassee (from *kewan-a-ka-see*, "lone tree") is a small community on Saginaw Bay near the Quanicassee River's mouth, at the edge of what was impassable swamp, an ideal hunting and fishing ground. Today, there are bait and tackle shops and marine suppliers. Look for the statue of a beer-drinking bear in a field on Old State Road near the river, marking the place where Frank Vanderbilt had a hotel around 1910, where he had such a bear to perform for tourists. Prohibition ended his operation, and he sold the bear to a hunting club. Take Finn Road to Quanicassee Wildlife Area or, for better bay access, Quanicassee Road to Vanderbilt Park.

The highway proceeds inland from the lake to Wisner (pop. 648), a township with no village center. A historical marker at the Wisner Cemetery here describes the legendary Indian Dave, buried here in an unmarked grave.

Unionville (pop. 486), established by settlers on Wessacagen Creek, is known today as Wiscoggin Drain. The village grew slowly after 1856, when two men brought supplies stored in their homes to meet the settlers' needs, including a liberal stock of mosquito netting. Lack of a port meant slow growth, but after the Civil War, the Unionville area became a destination for members of the Moravian Church from Ohio, Pennsylvania, and Germany. The Moravian Church on Cass Avenue, built in 1870, is well kept and remains active.

The land around Unionville and Akron (a short detour south) was, for many centuries, an endless sea of cattails and swamp grass that ran west farther than the eye could see. Settlers were drawn to the area by cheap land ($1.25 per acre) purchased from the State of Michigan that had been transferred from the federal government as a result of the Swamp Land Acts of 1849 and 1850. Settlers had two years to improve it, which meant digging drainage ditches and then smaller trenches to place ceramic drainage tiles that removed excess water. As early as the 1870s, German farmers got the latest ditching machines that could be pulled with horses, and two factories made tile in Akron. Along Vassar Road (west of Akron) there was a six-mile drainage ditch, completed in 1917, that drained water into Saginaw Bay. After the fields were drained, farmers intentionally ignited them to help burn away the muck of the marsh. These fires would burn for months and sometimes years, some through the winter, giving off an unpleasant odor. When crops were finally planted in these fields, the soil proved to be excellent for raising grain, corn, and sugar beets. Found on the western end of Tuscola County and the east end of Bay County, these soils are superior for growing potatoes and truck farming. Drain tile technology was and is central to the region's productivity. In Bay and Huron Counties, 48 to 65 percent of the land has subsurface drainage. In Tuscola and Sanilac Counties 27 to 47 percent of the land is tiled.

Fish Point State Wildlife Area lies within the most heavily hunted shoreline of Saginaw Bay, which is the area northeast from the Quanicassee River extending to the town of Bay Port. The area contains 3,700 acres of excellent waterfowl habitat along seven miles of shoreline. A managed hunt unit surrounds a permanent marsh and water area that acts as a refuge. This is an ideal location to experience the unique ecosystem that is the Great Lakes coastal marsh, with submerged plants like wild celery and wet prairie with bluestem grasses and blazing star. This wetland supports over three million waterfowl, making it ideal for birdwatchers at any time other than duck hunting season.

Pioneer Sugar plant, Sebewaing. PHOTOGRAPH BY AUTHOR.

Sebewaing (pop. 1,725) is situated at the mouth of the Sebewaing River, where the biggest and most notable structure is the Pioneer Sugar mill, originally built in 1901. The mill was the brainchild of German-born John C. Liken, who came to Sebewaing in 1866. Liken quickly came to dominate lumbering in Huron County, operating two sawmills and stave mills in Sebewaing and one each at Unionville, Akron, and Fairgrove, besides a creamery, two grain elevators, and more. Today, Michigan Sugar Company is owned by a grower cooperative. October means muddy roads, trails of beets, and fleets of semitrucks going from fields to mill and back again long into the night. The sugar beet harvest and duck hunting season—both in mid to late fall—are ritual activities that have hung on. The town once had a brewery (E. O. Braendle Brewery, in operation from 1880 to 1965) and an auto parts manufacturing company (which closed in 2008). Locals thought that would be the end of the town, but Sebewaing persists, still hosting the annual Sugar Festival, with a marina, county park, and campground, awaiting young people with new ideas.

Don't leave Sebewaing without visiting Sportsman's Haven Museum (Center St. at Main), a private museum, ice cream parlor, and antique shop filled with artifacts that will give you a feel for the heyday of waterfowl hunting and commercial fishing on Saginaw Bay. Doug Deming bought Fish Point hunting club from his grandfather and moved his collection of decoys, duck boats, specialty lures, and even a Russian camelback ice fishing shelter to this antique shop when he closed the lodge. The Charles W. Liken House (324 N. Center St.) is a community attic with artifacts of seafaring, fishing, farming, and town life. Old Sebewaing Township Hall (92 S. Center St.) is the former Arbeiter Hall, which hosted concerts, plays, dances, and, of course, drinking. Upstairs is a bar and old bottles of Sebewaing beer, as well as relics and photos of Indigenous life, hunting decoys, and even a piece of the old post office.

Beyond Sebewaing, M-25 swings away from the coast, and you may want to take a detour further inland to visit one of the many four-corner villages that once dotted the Thumb, supplying necessities and pleasure to hardworking farmers. In Kilmanagh (via Kilmanagh Rd.), the Rummel and Woldt general store is being restored. There is an old bank building that is now a successful bar and motorcycle club at Colwood (a four-corners) and an older bar across the street with a mural of a mermaid in a martini glass.

Weale is no longer marked on maps, but Weale Road is. This area was called Shebayonk when Nau-qua-chic-a-ming's band lived here near Lutheran missionaries between 1845 and 1854. Weale was known as the "Carvers' Village," since so many duck hunters who were also skilled decoy carvers and duck-boat makers built cottages here and worked at their crafts. Several, including Otto Misch (1886–1978), were from Port Huron. Decoys are considered folk art; the older ones are very collectible and the newer ones beautifully detailed.

From Bay Port north along M-25 the landscape changes. Instead of farm fields, there are hardwood forests with sections of pine, and the road stays close to the lake.

Bay Port (pop. 582), on Wild Fowl Bay, is notable chiefly for its scenic surroundings. Dense pine forests attracted the early settlers; lumber and fishing were the two early industries. Bay Port Fish Company is the last commercial fishery on Saginaw Bay, and the William Wallace Quarry (8785 Ribble Road) has the distinction of being the oldest business in Huron County, still producing aggregates and stone products.

Bay Port was developed early as a summer resort. When the Bay Port Hotel opened in 1886, its electric lighting made it the showplace of the upper Thumb. The Saginaw, Tuscola and Huron Railroad brought Saginaw residents here so they could swim, boat, hunt, and enjoy natural springs. All that remains of the hotel is a worn steppingstone (find the historical marker) where the stagecoach stopped.

The view of the bay from this spot is breathtaking, especially in stormy weather, so it's surprising Bay Port has few visitors, except those who come for the annual Fish Sandwich Festival in August. The Bay Port Inn is the only restaurant, and the Bay Port History Museum (836 Second St.) occupies a former Methodist Church.

Northeast of Bay Port is the Old Bay Port Cemetery (Sand Road off M-25 to where it dead-ends). The earliest graves date from the 1880s, but the most striking monument is a pedestal atop two twenty-foot columns, marking the grave of William H. Doerfner (1899–1997), general manager of Saginaw Steering.

Sand Point is a spit of land jutting into Saginaw Bay with patches of forest: The mansions of summer people crowd together where there were once just fishing cottages. Caseville (pop. 648) commands a sweeping view of sand beaches and blue waters. The first white settler Reuben Dodge was in the neighborhood with a wife and family as early as 1836, and they knew the place as the "mouth" (of the Pigeon River). He shared the area with Chippewa Indians, who camped above where the cemetery is today, and early sources speak of an "arrow factory" and a place where they made pottery. Leonard Case, a wealthy Cleveland capitalist for whom Case Western Reserve University as well as the town is named, purchased twenty thousand acres in 1852. His son-in-law Francis Crawford later bought the land, cutting and shipping lumber and platting the town, which became an industrial center with iron works, a rail connection, and a shipbuilding industry. Crawford's home, one of few remaining artifacts of early Caseville, stood on the bluff overlooking the harbor but was moved to the main road in 1996.

Tourism began in the 1890s when a group of men from Cass City came, saw the sand beaches with oak trees, and formed the Cass City Club, buying property on the bluff. Cottage tourism developed slowly in the 1910s and 1920s, slumped during the Depression, but boomed after World War II. Today the village is one of the most popular summer beach destinations. On the bay is Caseville County Park for swimming and camping. Every August, the Cheeseburger Festival brings up to two hundred thousand people into the town. Thumb towns specialize in festivals, and food is the focus of many—potato (Munger), bean (Fairgrove), fish sandwich (Bay Port), sugar beet (Sebewaing), blueberry (Montrose), and bologna (Yale). The Caseville Historical Museum (6733 Prospect St.), in the former Maccabees Hall, displays artifacts from the area.

Further along M-25 is Albert E. Sleeper State Park, between Caseville and Port Austin, a half mile of sandy shoreline with forested dunes. Nature trails through the dunes as well as canvas tents on the shore that can be rented by the night are special features. Huron County Nature Center (Loosemore Rd., before Port Crescent State Park) is a wilderness arboretum with an interpretive center and reproductions of art from the Detroit Institute of Arts standing in the woods around an amphitheater. Rush Lake State Game Area is a large preserve around a cattail-filled lake, managed by the Department of Natural Resources. There are bogs near the eastern dunes and "holes" at the end of Quarry Road, which used to be the former Babbit Sandstone Company, which hoped, in the 1880s, to compete with Grindstone City. The game area can be traversed via the unimproved Sand Road. Port Crescent Cemetery (Port Crescent Rd.) is the only evidence that there was once a bustling lumber town here between 1864 and 1881. Port Crescent State Park, day access or campground access, off M-25, was established in 1959 on the site of an early trading post and industrial community that harvested lumber and later sand. If you walk the trails through the dunes, you may discover faint footprints of the early community in old foundations. There are three miles of coastline, ten overnight camping facilities, a dark sky park, as well as a canoe and kayak livery on the Pinnebog River. Hugh Loosemore, who first emigrated from England to Canada, bought 162 acres of land along this coast and called his grounds "Titania Park" (Hugh knew his Shakespeare!). A chunk of exposed limestone marked the location of his driftwood castle. Hugh lived like a hermit and put notices in local papers, warning visitors away from cranberry and hay marshes on the Lord's Day.

East Side: Port Austin to Port Huron, Following M-25

Port Austin (pop. 662), a village at the tip of the Thumb, was originally named Bird's Creek for the first settler, Jeduthan Bird. A fugitive of the Patriots' War, he fled Canada in a small sailboat with his wife and two sons and found an excellent hiding place in a cove on this stretch of shore. Other refugees from this failed rebellion followed and took up land in the hideaway, making it a permanent settlement. Bird built a mill and a dam on the creek that bears his name and set about lumbering and establishing a fishing business. Born in Massachusetts about 1798, Bird grew up in New York before moving to Canada, a not uncommon story that calls attention to the cultural and socioeconomic ties of peoples along the border zone. In 1815, one hundred thousand residents of Lower and Upper Canada (Quebec and Ontario) were American-born, and much of the Thumb was settled by Canadians.

Though the township was not organized until 1862, the founders of Port Austin were men who imagined themselves advancing the revolutionary spirit of America's origins. All along the Michigan-Ontario border in 1837 and 1838, the Patriots' War was big news, and many regarded the Ohioans and Michiganders involved in the Battles of Windsor, Pelee Island, and Fighting Island as heroes who sought to eradicate tyranny. In Canada, tyranny meant the discriminatory land practices that favored the Church of England as well as old gentry families, and in America, tyranny was the banking system and the paper money economy that was beginning to marginalize the small farmer, household production, and the system of barter. Very significant in its time, the Patriots' War has been written out of American history, yet its animating attitudes are felt across the Thumb in the "Don't Tread on Me" flags and opposition to "elites."

Port Austin lacks the concentration of downstate wealth that Traverse City or Petoskey have, but it is equally scenic and more of a true getaway. Wander through town, watch sunsets, beachcomb, swim at Bird Creek Park, or kayak to Turnip Rock, a turnip or flower-pot-shaped seastack formed by wave erosion. The water surrounding the rock is shallow and allows people to get out of their kayaks to take a break and explore. Because Turnip Rock is privately owned, it can only be accessed by water. It is a seven-mile round-trip paddle from the put-ins in Port Austin.

Pointe Aux Barques is a private resort at the very tip of the Thumb, founded by Stanford Crapo, Henry Crapo's grandson, in 1896. Crapo was involved with Portland

Turnip Rock, off Pointe Aux Barques. PHOTOGRAPH BY JASON SCHNETTLER.

Cement in Alpena and often took the boat between there and Detroit, passing the rocky point. He saw the potential for development. Some of the better-known summer residents included tire manufacturer Harvey Firestone and newspaper poet Edgar Guest. The community guards its shoreline with "No Trespassing" signs, aimed at the kayakers paddling from Port Austin to check out Turnip Rock and the sea caves east of it.

Port Austin Reef Lighthouse sits 2.5 miles north of Port Austin in Lake Huron. Construction of the lighthouse began in 1877, unique for its octagonal base with stone locally quarried for the foundation. The U.S. Coast Guard decommissioned it in 1979, but a Port Austin man obtained a license to restore the structure, and work is ongoing, with the goal of starting a lighthouse keepers' program.

Grindstone City was a thriving business center for one hundred years. The industrial potential of the stone in the area was first discovered by Captain Aaron Peer when his schooner used the harbor as a haven during a storm. After shipping some of the rock to Detroit for use as paving, he bought four hundred acres of land in 1836 and began quarrying sandstone to make milling grindstones, whetstones, and scythe stones. The products were of such superior quality that they were marketed not only in the United States but also in Europe. Two factories operated until World War I, when carborundum made quarrying unprofitable.

Workers at Grindstone City, c. 1905. PIGEON HISTORICAL SOCIETY.

Once past Port Austin and Grindstone City, the tourist cottages thin to nothing. Farms and fields come down to the edge of Huron, and the people collect into towns rather than stringing out along the lake. Lake Huron was and, to some extent, still is an important shipping lane with freighters carrying ore, stone, wheat, grain, and other raw materials to the factories of Detroit and cities of the upper Midwest.

Most Thumb towns and all on the eastern side of the peninsula began as lumber towns. The first sawmill in what would become Sanilac County was built on the Black

Survivors of the devastating 1881 forest fire. FRANK LESLIE'S ILLUSTRATED NEWSPAPER, OCTOBER 1, 1881, 73.

River in 1836, and more sawmills appeared along the Thumb coastline by the early 1850s. The coastal areas were logged first because of the ease of transporting logs by ship. With logging came devastating fires. Pioneers themselves used fire to clear land, as the Indians had done, and locomotive sparks added another hazard. There were two catastrophic fires, one in 1871 and another in 1881. Some evidence suggests that meteorites from the burned-out Biela Comet landed in the Thumb, but both fires were most likely caused by the slash left behind in frenzied resource exploitation. *The New York Times* declared the 1881 fire a "national catastrophe"—the first crisis to which the new American Red Cross, founded in May 1881, responded. The fire left 1,500 families destitute and homeless, hundreds of people dead, and thousands of charred animal carcasses along the roads. Those in coastal communities were luckier than inlanders, because they could flee to the lake. Huron's waters saved the lives of hundreds of people and many thousands of animals, wild and tame.

The counties most seriously impacted bounced back most quickly. The population in Huron, Sanilac, and Tuscola Counties grew at a faster rate than other areas of Michigan in the 1880s. Tradesmen and businessmen saw opportunities to prosper from the rebuilding, and the fire saved farmers and townsmen the hard labor of clearing the land. But it also annihilated elk, deer, black bear, and beaver, and it forced the Indians to leave. Charitable organizations distributed seeds, and settlers were determined to rebuild and prosper.

Huron City is a privately owned ghost town that looks like a village museum. Langdon Hubbard, a lumberman from Connecticut, platted the town in 1854 and rebuilt it twice after both fires. Hubbard's son-in-law William Lyon Phelps, a Yale professor, literary critic, and minister, summered here and drew large crowds to his Sunday talks and sermons at the Methodist Church from 1922 to 1937. Today, Huron City consists of a string of original buildings and ones that have been relocated to form the Huron City Museum—on a hillside overlooking the lake. "It's a gold mine," remarked a local; but for now, it remains blessedly empty of McMansions, with just an inn, general store, a few houses, and the famous pink church.

Pointe Aux Barques Lighthouse (7320 Lighthouse Rd., Port Hope) is among the ten oldest lighthouses in Michigan, built by the U.S. Lighthouse Service in 1847 to mark the turning point of Lake Huron into Saginaw Bay and to warn of shallow waters and rocky shoals. The Lighthouse Museum preserves the memory of epic storms (the 1913 White Hurricane), shipwrecks (*Daniel J. Morrell*, on November 29, 1966), survivors, and Michigan's first female light keeper, Catherine Shook, who took over for her husband, Peter, after he drowned in 1849.

The Thumb Bottomlands Preserve, located offshore and north of Port Austin, is one of two areas in the Great Lakes with eighty or more shipwrecks concentrated on the nearby lake bottom. Twenty of those are well preserved. The 120-acre Lighthouse County Park has a campground with a boat launch for those who want to explore the water, as well as a small pier for those who prefer to stay on land. Kernan Memorial Nature Sanctuary is forty-five acres on a natural inlet that was never developed, called Whiskey Harbor. The Michigan Nature Association obtained the site for the sanctuary as a bequest from William Kernan. Much of the habitat is wetlands, and the harbor is rocky and shallow, perfect for migrating gulls and ducks. This is a great place for spotting shore birds, such as black-bellied plovers and sanderlings, and seeing rare wildflowers, like the burr marigold and the cardinal flower.

Port Hope (pop. 278) was, according to local legend, named in 1855 by William Southard, a New Hampshire native, who backed William Stafford's lumber venture. Caught in a storm on a visit, he insisted on being put off in a small rowboat and, if he made it to shore, declared the place would be his port of hope. Stafford built a sawmill on Diamond Creek in 1858, and a town grew up around it but was twice destroyed in the great fires. The Stafford Lumber Mill chimney (1853) is all that remains of the mill and the effort of pioneers, but tools and artifacts, displays and dioramas, gathered at the Lumberyard Museum of the Thumb (8016 Portland Ave.) help visitors picture the past. Today Port Hope feels like a resort town with gift shops and festivals. A lighthouse offers a view of the rocky lakeshore.

Harbor Beach (pop. 1,596) was called Sand Beach until 1900, when the town changed its name to reflect the completion of a massive anchorage, by some measurements still the largest freshwater harbor in the world. The U.S. government adopted the harbor in 1873 and completed it in 1894, which, for native son Frank Murphy, was proof that the federal government could be a force for good.

Two lumbermen, John Allen and Alanson Daggett, arrived first, in 1838. The sawmill they built on what is now Rock Falls Creek operated for many years and was purchased by Jeremiah Jenks Jr., who installed the equipment for a steam-powered mill. Jenks, called the "Father of Harbor Beach" for his enterprising nature, also bought a flour mill that would become the Huron Milling Company and developed a diversified line of wheat and protein products, wheat starches, adhesives, wallpaper pastes, and the seasoning monosodium glutamate, which was the company's claim to fame. In 1956, it became Hercules Powder Company and exists today as Sensient Flavors. Jenks also bought land, platted streets, and built the long dock used by steamships for loading and unloading. John Murphy, Irish immigrant and lawyer in town, insisted his son Frank work in this local factory, where, before he left for college in Ann Arbor, he supervised three hundred Polish workers.

Harbor Beach has had a big Coast Guard presence since 1881. The History Walking Trail provides a good orientation with ideas for museums to visit, like the Grice House Museum (864 N. Lakeshore Rd.), the only house to survive the fire, partly built of local stone, with a "Marine Room" and a two-story pavilion on the grounds that held a range of community events from square dances to civic meetings. Other points of interest include the Harbor Beach Lighthouse, constructed on the breakwall to guide ships into the harbor of refuge, completed in 1885. Today it can be visited through boat tours on Saturdays in the summer. Frank Murphy Memorial Museum (142 S. Huron Ave.) is a Michigan historical site that includes his father John Murphy's law office and the original family home, as well as the larger Victorian Gothic Revival home they bought next door. This is no ordinary house museum but a tribute to an American public figure who supported the poor, the worker, and the marginal in his capacities as mayor of Detroit, governor of Michigan, U.S. attorney general, and Supreme Court justice. Franklin D. Roosevelt named him governor general of the Philippines, where he served from 1933 to 1935, and as a result, the museum contains a world-class Philippine collection, including carvings, fabric, woven grass mats, and paintings by Fernando Amorsolo. Of major significance to labor history is the desk where General Motors executives signed the agreement to recognize the United Auto Workers. The Resort, founded in 1896, is a private summer community consisting of forty historic summer cottages, where meals are taken at a clubhouse in semiformal attire. Henry Ford had a summer home here, and local legends remember he liked to call square dances but was "really bad" at recalling the figures.

Shipwrecks off Harbor Beach, which can be viewed from kayaks or boats, include the *George H. Waud*, a schooner built in 1866 and stranded in 1902, and the *John Wesley*, built in 1872 and run aground in 1901, are well preserved and can be viewed from kayaks or boats.

White Rock is an unincorporated community named for the large white limestone boulder offshore in Lake Huron, where Ojibwe Indians left offerings for the *manidoo* under the water that would protect them as they moved along the coast in their canoes. When white settlers began to hold novelty dances on the rock (with musicians playing from boats nearby), the Indians believed the Great Spirit became angry, summoning a storm and killing the dancers with lightening. The rock was used to mark the boundary of Indian lands unceded in the 1807 Treaty of Detroit, and during World War II it was used for target practice. Today, the community has only a few houses, a bait shop, and the White Rock School Museum (White Rock Rd., half mile west of M-25).

Forestville (pop. 104) is the smallest incorporated village in Michigan—a quiet refuge for vacationers, with lake access for swimming and boating, a marina, and campground. Named for its dense surrounding woods, it quickly grew around the lumber industry. Eber Ward, who owned local timberlands, lived in Forestville for a year to supervise mill operations and the shipping of timber from a famously long dock. Battered by storms and crushed by winter ice, this had to be repaired and rebuilt frequently, but through its long life, it was an economic hub, a fishing pier for the community, and a social center, when sailors returned home to their families. West of town is the site of Colonie Saxonia, a large cooperative of families from Saxony recruited by Saginaw native Max Allardt. An original settler's cabin is still visible along the Bay City Forestville Road.

Forester Township runs along the coast north of Port Sanilac. Sanilac County Forester Park, with a beach, playground, and RV campground is a popular destination in the summer. Port Sanilac (pop. 567) was called Bark Shanty Point by the first settlers in 1844, who found upon the site a shack that had been occupied four years earlier by a group of Detroit tanners. Today, Port Sanilac has the biggest marina, with the most services of any port on the Thumb coast. Congress appropriated money to construct a lighthouse in 1884 and it was first lit in 1886. Though now a private residence, tours are given at select times throughout the summer, enabling visitors to climb the fifty-step tower to view Lake Huron and the shoreline. Sanilac County Historic Village and Museum (228 S. Ridge St.) contains buildings from around the region, notably the Loop-Harrison Mansion, built in the 1870s with yellow brick imported from Ontario and shipped across the lake and the Dairy Museum, which recognizes Huron County as a longtime leader in Michigan milk production. Sanilac County Lexington Park on the coast has a lovely campground and a private beach with steps down the bluff.

Lexington (pop. 924) was originally Greenbush, which became Lexington in 1845 and an official village in 1855. Fishing followed lumber as the main livelihood of the residents, but farming was also significant because of the ease of marketing produce and animals on ships that plied the coast to small towns and Port Huron just twenty miles south. Today the village is very much a summer destination, advertised as "The First Resort North," just an hour north from Metro Detroit. Historic buildings you may want to visit include the Moore Public Library, originally the law office of John Devine, the first attorney in Sanilac County, and the H. R. Noble Building, which houses the current library. The Lexington General Store, dating from the 1850s, with its squeaky wood floors, keeps alive the old-time feel and historic presence. The Lexington Village Theatre, a brick building that stands out on the corner of a main street in town, is still a popular draw. Other points of interest include the Cadillac House (5502 Main St.), first opened in 1859, when guests came from Detroit via steamship. Though it was not damaged during the Thumb fires, the great winter storm of 1913 killed the shipping business and led industries to relocate south to Port Huron. For years, it was a restaurant-bar, but after restoration in the 1970s, it accommodates guests. The Maltese Castle, or Stone House (7345 Elms Rd.), was designed and constructed by Valentine Falzon, a Maltese immigrant, while unemployed during the Great Depression.

Petroglyphs to Otter Lake Tour

Any large feature in the landscape creates its own world—Ayers Rock, Stonehenge, the Barabar hills with their famous caves. The Sanilac Petroglyphs might not be as big or famous, but this sandstone outcropping was the center of the world for the Indigenous people of this region. The graffitied stone (between three hundred and one thousand years old) was first exposed at the time of the Thumb fires. Today, gas stations, not outcroppings, are the gathering places. They sprout at major intersections and grow into community hubs, surrounded by miles of windswept fields. We begin at the rock, follow along the Cass River—a corridor of trees and green—that marked a boundary, presettlement, between hardwoods and conifers. South of the Cass, the land was originally heavily forested with white pine and hemlock, and even today there remains a large tract of white pine south of Caro between the river and M-46.

As we head down into the woods and wetlands that extend to the outside edge of greater Flint, you'll see agriculture scaled from acres to backyard gardens. You'll see deer that appear to eat what locals plant, and, if you're lucky, you'll see turkeys, pheasant, sandhill cranes, bald eagles, ducks, geese, swans, muskrats, ground hogs, and the occasional fox. This is the region Indian Dave, or Ishdonquit, made home by walking, camping, fishing, collecting wild ginseng to dry and sell, and cutting reeds for basket making or small branches for whittling bows and toys. Each swamp had a name and each settlement familiar faces. From Otisville and Otter Lake, to Fostoria, Vassar, Watrousville, Wahjamega, all the way up to the sand ridge south of the bay and as far east as Minden City where he often traded, Ishdonquit walked. His spirit is out there somewhere. Let's see if we can catch up to it.

Sanilac Petroglyphs State Historic Park (8251 Germania Rd., Cass City) is a unique sandstone outcropping covered in carvings of animals, birds, and geometric and humanoid shapes, including the famous (and iconic) archer. These carvings are the only known prehistoric petroglyphs in the state. The 240-acre park is jointly managed by the Department of Natural Resources and the Saginaw Chippewa Indian Tribe, who consider the site sacred. In the Anishinaabe language, the petroglyphs are *Ezhibiigaadek Asin* (written on stone), recording teachings, myths, and even history: the archer who shoots knowledge into the future; the Eagle Man; the Great Lakes water panther. The carvings may also record vision quests or seasonal events, and document aspects of daily life.

Cass City (pop. 2,493). A traveler from Britain joked about calling this place a "city" in 1886. It was, in his view, a type of thousands of other places struggling to exist within the primeval forest. Evidence of a successful struggle is the State Reward Road No. 1 (see historical marker east of town on M-81). If it's Tuesday, drive east to the Michigan Livestock Market (6425 E. Cass City Rd.). On auction day, the lot is full of livestock transport trucks and pickups. There's a small restaurant on-site—also a community gathering place—with lots of meat on the menu, as well as a selection of homemade pies. At the entrance to the city park, there is a memorial to astronaut Brewster Shaw as well as a big painted quilt square—part of the Thumb Quilt Trail, a way to draw attention to the old barns still standing that represent a whole way of life and the lost art of barn raising. Cass River access is south of town, where a pedestrian bridge crosses on River Road, west of Cemetery Road, with a modest parking area, making for either a quick scenic stop or a longer river expedition. The bridge is part of the Cass City Railway Walking Trail, which continues north toward town. The Dairy Farmers of America Co-Operative plant (4105 Division St.) is where most of the milk produced in the Thumb is condensed. Dairy Farmers of America has 239 farmer-members in Michigan, and in 2020, they produced 3.54 million pounds of milk from cows laboring in CAFOs mainly. The days when cows wandered the streets of Cass City are long gone; now, only the few family dairies and Amish farms let cows eat out on grass. Huron is the top milk-producing county in the state, and the facility is looking to expand.

Other Cass City features include a drive-thru party store (common in Ohio but unusual for this area), the historic single-screen Cass City Theatre, Rolling Hills golf course, and Elkland Cemetery, home to many different and unusual styles of headstones, including stone tree stumps and at least one that includes a morel mushroom. North of East Cass City Road is wild land, dubbed the Sanilac Flats, where the north and south branches of the Cass River meet.

Gagetown began as a mill and a store built by Joseph Gage, a Canadian immigrant, in 1869. The railroad came to town in the 1880s, causing a great deal of growth, including an opera house with seating for over three hundred people. With the closing of the railroad, however, things began to slow down, and today Gagetown's population could almost squeeze into the now-demolished opera house. The village is home to some historic buildings. There are homes built with yellow brick in the Canadian Queen Anne style; barns with red-tiled silos (the tile was fireproof and covered bricks, specially designed to prevent moisture seepage); and St. Agatha's Church with two red-brick towers, built in 1917, which served as the first Catholic parish in Tuscola County. Gagetown's biggest employer is Vita Plus Feeds. The area's biggest tourist attraction is the Thumb Octagon Barn & Agricultural Museum (6948 Richie Rd., Gagetown). The unusual (and very large—14,300 sq. ft.) octagon-shaped barn and accompanying house were built by Gagetown banker James Purdy. The fifteen-room house was begun in 1919. The barn followed in 1923 and was inspired by round and octagonal barns Purdy may have seen when traveling in Iowa. The shape is supposed to make the building more wind-resistant in tornado-prone areas.

Caro (pop. 4,285), first called Centerville when it started as a logging camp in 1847, became Tuscola's county seat when, according to legend, Indian Dave and a local man confiscated county records in Vassar and paddled them upstream to Caro. The village was incorporated in 1871 under that name (a shortened form of Egypt's Cairo), and today it is the most bustling center in the western Thumb, with restaurants, shops, the Tuscola County Fair every July and the Pumpkin Festival every October. It is also home to the Depression-era county courthouse and post office (210 Lincoln

St.), completed in 1939. Inside the latter building see the wall mural *Mail on the Farm*, painted by David Fredenthal as part of the Works Progress Administration's Federal Art Project in 1941. Notice the massive arms, legs, and hands of the farm couple, and the affection of two draft horses for one another. Connections between humans and animals and to the land are emphasized in this special work.

Caro's street layout is unique: Not platted on a grid, streets shoot out from the center like the spokes of a wagon wheel. Frank, Almer, and State are main roads, but the oddly angled intersections make each visit a surprising exploration. So do the houses. From the steps of the post office, an interesting roof shingled to look like thatch is visible. On closer inspection, this is the Moore mansion (123 Almer St.), built in the 1920s. Peak in the grounds and see stone pathways, a curious inground pool, and that roof and carriage house! Next door is Himelhoch Bed & Breakfast. Stone houses are all over the region, not surprising to locals who have tried to garden, farm, or just dig a hole; rocks are an abundant local building material. Builder ingenuity shows in the many vernacular house designs and ornamental features using cobble, rubble, field, and pudding stones.

That sweet smell in Caro's air, ranging from a yeasty, beer-like aroma to the difficult to describe but entirely unmistakable scent of sugar beets cooking, comes from the two factories on the south side of town: the ethanol plant and the sugar factory. Caro's sugar factory began life as Peninsular Sugar Refining Company in 1898 and is now part of Michigan Sugar, a grower-owned cooperative. It is the oldest sugar mill still in operation.

Nearby parks include Chippewa Landing City Park (800–902 Ellington St.), a sixteen-acre park with boat launch, dog park, sledding hill, playground, and a paved pedestrian trail. A recent project extended the trail by connecting it to the Exchange Club Forest walking trails on the other side of M-24, which meander through a forty-five-acre section of woods. Several different loops are available, some including sections of boardwalk. Indianfields Township Park (2220 W. Caro Rd.) is a one-hundred-acre park, bordered on the east by the Cass River and the abandoned Wahjamega facility. Founded as an epileptic hospital in 1914, its Mission Revival–style buildings, even in disuse, had a unique flair that encouraged generations of ghost stories and dares. In 2024, however, these historic local landmarks were demolished, leaving nothing but an open field.

North of the city of Caro, at Ellington, there is a stately brick building from 1901 with a wheat sheaf in a circular medallion as well as the words "Ellington. Arbor. No. 1" (2791 East Caro Rd.). This was a local hall for the Gleaners, a rural organization started by Caro newspaper publisher Grant H. Slocum in 1894, taking ideas from other fraternal orders, the Book of Ruth, and his experiences growing up on a nearby farm. The Gleaners sold life insurance and ran an old age home. Today, the group still exists as a service club.

Watrousville (pop. 549) is a worthwhile stop with its not-to-be-missed Lincoln pole, originally placed there by supporters during the campaign of 1864, in front of the former general store that now houses the Watrousville-Caro Area Historical Society (4607 W. Caro Rd.). The museum has many curious artifacts, including a bow made by Indian Dave, antlers from an elk shot nearby, as well as old county maps and ephemera. A plank road to Saginaw was begun in 1852 and, through the lumber era, the village grew to have seventy buildings, six stores, four hotels, and the usual doctors, dentist, blacksmiths, and livery stables. The town was platted by Aaron Watrous, who arrived in 1853 to cut pine on the Cass River. Decline set in after the trees were gone and the railroad bypassed the town, and all that remains is a church and a single store.

The exquisite Second Empire Richard C. Burtis House (2010–2283 S. Ringle Rd.), locally known as the "wedding cake house," was built by a merchant and shoemaker, who had also moved from New York State, first coming to the area in 1855, like other wealthy men such as Oliver Hazard Perry of Cleveland, to hunt elk. He bought forty acres of land nearby and built this unique house for his bride, fitted out with an emerald marble fireplace, parquet wood floors, and a winding staircase.

Vassar (pop. 2,705), still identified with its lumber-era moniker, "Cork Pine City," was founded in 1849 by James Edmunds and Townsend North but named for Matthew Vassar (founder of Vassar College), a relative of Edmunds, who bankrolled the settlement venture but never set foot in the town. Incorporated as a village in 1871 and a city in 1944, Vassar was a lumber town straddling the Cass River that was known for its cork pine forests—"cork pine" was a phrase first coined in Michigan that described its soft, light, and easy-to-work texture. City Hall (287 E. Huron Ave.) has an Indian Dave mural, painted by Detroit artist Warren W. Simpson in 1952. The central figures are Dave and a young boy in the midst of exchanging stories, while the work of logging and developing the wilderness progresses around them.

Vassar is famous locally for the M-15 hill—a notable landscape feature in what is otherwise a very flat area. The city makes use of the hill every October for the Pumpkin Roll, when pumpkins are available for purchase to roll down the road at buckets for prizes. In February, weather permitting, the hill is the site of Chill on the Hill, when M-15 is temporarily shut down for sledding.

Vassar has also been locally famous for its floods. Since 1900, the city has flooded at least twenty-eight times. The worst during that time was the flood of 1904; the worst in recent memory is the flood of 1986, when residents in flooded areas were able to canoe from their second-story windows. Flood damage is less severe in recent years, thanks to mitigation efforts by the Army Corps of Engineers, and building policies that have limited building and rebuilding in the Cass's floodplains. This has protected the historic brick buildings of downtown, including Vassar's Art Deco single-screen movie theater, first opened in 1937.

Wood products industries and foundries that made farm equipment have been replaced by indoor grow facilities since marijuana was legalized in 2018. Other local attractions include the Vassar Historical Museum (450 S. Main St.); North House, founder Townsend North's Victorian home that today houses a bed and breakfast; the Vassar Rail Trail, a two-mile paved recreation trail that runs along the river and through wooded areas and fields; and many local parks.

Millington (pop. 1,025) was incorporated as a village in 1877. Like many of the towns in the area, it began as a lumber town with a sawmill built in 1859. In something of a nod to the village's early logging history, in 2018, Dyna Products, which manufactures firewood processors, relocated to Millington—along with the Amish community that runs it. Antique stores line the main drag and points of interest include the Millington-Arbela Museum (8534 State Rd.), housed in a former bank building made of heavy local stone, which has a pair of elk antlers found at the bottom of a local lake and artifacts related to Indian Dave. Southern Links Trailway (Millington Elementary School) is the start of a ten-mile paved recreational trail (non-motorized only) that connects Millington in the north with Otter Lake and Columbiaville in the south. The trail runs along farm fields, woods, and several small ponds, and includes multiple sections of boardwalk. For a wilder exploration, head to Murphy Lake State Game Area, east of Millington, for the 2,700-plus acres of woodland (hardwood, hemlock, and some pine), marsh, and swamp. The northernmost parking area at Swaffer Road is also the access point to a trail that runs over five miles through the game area. It is also a walk-in access to Murphy Lake, a 209-acre multiuse lake. Public boating access is available via Murphy Lake Road.

Otter Lake (pop. 426) was an important lumber town in Lapeer County during its early years. The waters of the lake were used to help power the steam locomotives that hauled local timber away, and ice from the lake was carried to neighboring communities to stock their ice houses. Otter Lake was officially incorporated in 1883. The main attraction is the sixty-eight-acre multiuse spring-fed lake itself. Fishing on the lake is considered to be generally good, with bass, pike, panfish, and bullhead being most prevalent. The village operates a park on the southern lakeshore that includes a public swimming beach, boat launch, playground, and camping area. Access to the park is paid, even for foot traffic, but prices are reasonable. The village is also the halfway point of the ten-mile Southern Links Trailway.

Fostoria (pop. 1,081) is situated in a rolling landscape of pine ridges and cedar swamps. It was named for Thomas Foster, a Canadian-born lumberman, who came to Saginaw in 1858 and cut pine in Tuscola and Genesee counties until the trees were gone. After that, he worked his 320-acre farm and became a large-scale stock breeder (Hereford cattle and purebred sheep).

Fostoria was a busy place in its heyday, with a grain elevator and a single gauge railroad line, the Flint River Railroad, nicknamed "Huckleberry." At one time, the Pere

The Thoreau of Murphy Lake

Myles Willard is the acknowledged expert on the flora and fauna of Murphy Lake, having made the study of it his life's work. He has photographed and written self-published field guides to the birds, waterfowl, amphibians, butterflies, and moths of the area, and he is finishing up a book on orchids and another on mammals. He isn't the only one of his kind hiding in the pockets of Tuscola County. Many countrymen and women retire out here, but that verb doesn't suit these experts on everything from migrating birds to heritage seeds. They traffic knowledge and experiences among themselves in a sort of intervillage commerce: "Ernie saw a hybrid of dog and fox along the Murphy Lake Road" or "Sadie noticed a nest of great horned owlets at eye level in the tree near so-and-so's house on Barnes Road." They volunteer at the community "Share Shop" in Mayville, buy hardware and groceries at Neiman's (formerly Wingert's), in business for almost one hundred years, none of them miss the rat race.

Myles Willard's house is set down in pine woods along a stream. Out back, there are bird feeders, a single chair facing the woods, and a canoe leaning against a small barn. Deer paths lead into thickets, but there is nothing here to frighten wildlife away from this dwelling.

In his living room, there are two chairs, and I can see that he spends his time in the big one next to a table with an open Bible, bookmarked with a fiddle bow. That spot gives him a view of the bird feeders and the wood line. While we visit, he sits in an equally big rocker and rocks back and forth, listening intently and lecturing but not before asking if I wanted to hear a story or a lecture before he begins.

His people came from Missouri to Flint for factory jobs, but his own parents moved out to Frankenmuth, where he was born and schooled as one of the few non-Lutheran outsiders. "I still remember them speaking German on the streets." When it was time for him to buy his own house, Myles knew he wanted to be as close to Murphy Lake as he could get and found a rundown old place on twenty-four acres—a former farm—that only cost $9,000 (in 1976). He knew it was meant to be when he saw two ruffed grouse perched on the mailbox and the wide stream flowing right through the property.

"Why," I ask, "are there so many unusual things around here?" Diversity of habitat, is the short answer, elaborated with explanation of the way the forest type changes from southern trees like sassafras, hickory, and white oaks to more characteristically northern trees—hemlocks and red oaks. The only uncut stand of virgin oaks in the entire Thumb is here at Murphy Lake. He knows the bog where showy lady slippers grow and the patches of pine needles where pink slippers have turned up in years past. He has seen and expects to see hybrid varieties of warblers, rare lizards, and salamanders. Hybridity is the engine of evolution. But you have to slow down, wait on life, lift up logs. Surprise! Beholding something new, you change, too. He wonders at all the people walking so fast, concerned only with exercise, not with seeing.

Myles Willard isn't sorry he quit teaching fifth grade before he was old enough to retire. New state requirements devalued what teachers were trying to do, so he brought his classroom specimens home and they fill the room with outstretched wings: "Most of them were given to me, so I didn't have to shoot them," he says and explains how he taught himself taxidermy from a mail order booklet so his students could see every species of local waterfowl at close range. After leaving the classroom, he turned avocations into paying work so he and his wife would not have to move into a trailer and has, for many years, sold books and photographs at local craft fairs and festivals.

Not teaching also gave him more time for the serious study of things like glaciation. He has concluded that the experts are wrong in the number and dating of the Michigan glaciers. Instead of fifteen thousand years ago, Myles thinks there was just a single glacier that moved in and out of the area much more recently—maybe just five thousand years ago. Evidence for his theory is everywhere: in the newness of the creeks, the many dry and wet kettles, the striations that show direction in the exposed sand bank where cliff swallows nest. He spent a year coloring in soil maps that show the exact locations of bands of sand, clay, gravel, and morainic outwash. The unfolded maps cover his entire living room floor and look like a musical score, a symphony of flowing earth that maps the glacier's movement.

After lunch, we head out for a drive, during which Myles points out a half-albino robin, two trumpeter swans on the pond at Kowitz's farm, a pheasant pecking in a corn field, the moss-covered footings of a pioneer's cabin, red trillium, new sedges, and a tree engraved with a bear's claw marks. Along the way, I learn that skunk cabbages use the muscles in their roots to retract new growth if March temperatures dip too far below freezing and that blackbirds mate for life but migrate separately. "So they return to the same mates?" A story follows about his buddy, Ron, a Flint cop, who had lost his wife. Myles and other friends were trying to encourage him by taking him out. "We were driving along but had to stop. A male red-wing was trying to pull the body of a dead female out of the road. Roger had to watch that. Tells you a lot about pair loyalty." Myles's wife, Marilyn, had passed away a few weeks before I met him in April 2023, yet the house was full of her—portraits on the walls, the "I LOVE YOU" banner hanging in the living room, and the overflowing basket of sympathy cards on the couch.

Myles and Marilyn went to Alaska camping many times, to Newfoundland in search of the elusive ivory gull that, believe it or not, turned up on the river in downtown Flint, where it died after three days from starvation, pollution, or just too many people. "Truthfully, I have never found one place that is as varied and interesting as Murphy Lake State Game Area," Myles confided. When you find that kind of biodiversity, you sell everything you have and buy that field.

Marquette, operators of the Huckleberry Railroad, tried to buy the Fostoria Hotel, still visible from Goodrich Road near the intersection of Fostoria, perhaps to bring shop workers out of Flint for weekends of square dancing, berry picking, hunting, and fishing. On the main drag, an elegant brick hall, marked with the name Briggs (former supervisor and postmaster of Watertown Township), stands as a witness the passing of time, enterprise, and people. With the fraternal orders of Oddfellows and Rebekahs gone, gathering places of today are the newly renovated Buck Wild saloon and the still-active Tribesmen motorcycle club, founded in 1970. The club's emblem, an Indian in full headdress, stands prominently on the main entrance looking at the quiet street. In the 1980s, the Tribesmen funded WKRP (Watertown Kids Recreation Program) and hosted an annual bikers' rally. Only once did the rally cause problems, when a Detroit gang came up. A fight ensued, and before its members left, the gang threatened to burn all of Fostoria down.

The marsh on both sides of Goodrich Road is likely the same one that original settlers struggled through to arrive on sections of choice farmland, predominantly covered in maple trees and reasonably level. Early farmers found plenty of rocks when they plowed as well as Indian artifacts. Dig into the hills today, and you will see visible veins of gravel and pure "potter's sand." Gravel and sand businesses—a large one visible on North Lake and Goodrich Roads—are still digging and trucking, still making pits deep enough for kids to swim in. This glacial hill country is dotted with lakes, some developed (North Lake) but others mostly free of houses (Cedar and Spruce Lakes). Second- and third-growth pine is visible on the ridges, but the stumps that pioneers once lined up to fence in cows and horses are gone. Pleasures in this neck of the woods have always involved nature—watching stars through leafless trees during the spring sugar bush—but lots of locals also took inspiration from books. Arthur Spencer, not yet twenty but inspired by Henry David Thoreau's *Walden*, built his own cabin on the edge of the Goodrich Road swamp, which became the base of operations for plundering the local muskrat population. "How blissful just to find the spot is real—That it is not a dream," wrote his wife, Helen Schott. The swamps, the stars, the frisking calves, and the heavy springtime grass are all still here in this gently rugged pocket of Tuscola County, waiting to be rediscovered.

Mayville (pop. 950) is a centerless but tight-knit community. Clinton and Marion Manwell, a local farm family, hosted a threshing day, beginning in 1965, that became an annual festival and ran for eighteen years. Thousands would come to socialize, watch the men working with old farm equipment, and partake of free coffee and beans. Today, locals meet at independent stores like Neiman's (formerly Wingert's)—groceries, hardware, and Subway—along with the Community Share Shop, as well as the Mayville Museum (2124 E. Ohmer Rd.). The museum has a bow and large amphora-shaped basket said to be made by Indian Dave and folk art, including rag rugs, pictures made from family members' hair, and memorials crafted from wheat sheaves. Lucile Bauer painted local landmarks and sold postcards of her work to benefit the Teen Ranch Camps in Marlette, Kingston, and North Branch. The museum has files full of letters from neighbors with reminiscences about Ishdonquit's "tee pee," his herbal cures, and his costume. Local white women sung him to rest at his wigwam after he died in May, 1909. Carp were thrashing the shorelines, riverways, and cuts along Saginaw Bay during the "Dandelion Moon," and spring was in full bloom, when Tchi-bay-kon, the road that all spirits of Chippewa-Ottawa travel, called to Indian Dave.

Middle Thumb Tour

Driving to the interior means leaving the interstate behind along with any "cidiot" attitudes. "'Cidiot' is a portmanteau word," explains Ubly native Jacqui Gilbert, "that combines the meanings of 'city' and 'idiot.' It is used a lot around here to criticize people from urban or suburban areas who might look down their noses at the conservative values and humble lifestyles of people out here."

In rural Michigan, kids take hunting safety classes as early as age ten, work the sugar beet harvest for a first job, and gather on fall weekends to process a deer and have a few beers. Or they go for a drive—which is a good way to experience how mind-emptying open trees and open sky can be.

Think worn dirt roads, bright green fields of winter wheat, sticky air and the drone of cicadas, beans and sugar beets, the odd roadside stand where you can pick up a warm tomato, bumpy gourd, six ears of corn for a dollar, jar of jam, and a dozen eggs. Drop your money in the labeled shoebox on the table. Think of wind stirring everything from roadside chicory and Queen Anne's lace to the lace curtains still hanging in an empty schoolhouse window at a long-forgotten four-corners. Think of people who lived here, far from Lake Huron, with no escape, when the 1881 fire tore through, hunkering down in open fields, ditches, and swampy places, sharing "safety" with wild animals. They must have known every nook and cranny, every rise and depression, of this land. They must have been forever grateful to a well or a ditch that saved them. Think about a different way of life.

Dale Edgington, who works for an agricultural business and has a small truck farm, moved his family to the Thumb for distance from a dispirited world. "Too many people believe that the world is getting worse and worse, which is why I envy the Amish. By avoiding at least some of that external influence, they have better reason to hope." Jacqui Gilbert tried hard to leave Ubly, attending college in Flint, but she couldn't get the land out of her senses: the sweet herbaceous corn, drone of cicadas, yeasty smells of sugar beets cooking, and beets dropped from trucks, making a trail to the mills. Even if you are just a visitor, it's rejuvenating to feel a different life rhythm, one more in sync with the seasons and the weather.

This interior loop takes you from I-69, north on M-19 to Bad Axe, where you pick up M-53, heading west and then south. Watch for some pretty unusual barn art, created by Detroit muralists, part of the 53 North Project, who painted ten barns in ten years, designed to lure tourists toward "the forgotten coast."

Emmett is the first town you come to after exiting I-69 and it's as good an introduction to life in the slow lane as you'll get. Most businesses, open or closed, identify as Irish with a shamrock or bit o' green. Note the elevator east of town and the fieldstone houses, and be sure to visit Bob's roadside stand.

Capac (pop. 1,983), a village in western St. Clair County, serves as a market community for the area, whose agriculture has declined as more of its population looks toward greater Detroit for work. The Capac Community Historical Society, responsible for acquiring and moving the local train depot, runs the Capac 1914 Grand Trunk Depot Museum. Its prize feature is the miniature "Model City," constructed by Bruce and Irving Kempf in 1916, which drew wide-eyed audiences at fairs and department stores before World War II. A circus train accident destroyed the original model city along with Fred and Blanche Kempf, who saved their little girl Hazel by passing her out of the train window to an injured circus roustabout. The museum holds many other local artifacts, notably its collection of Thumb-area milk bottles, which speaks volumes about the negative impact on local communities of industrial dairy production.

Yale (pop. 1,910) is a busy town almost on the St. Clair–Sanilac County line, presided over by the imposing Yale Hotel, now functioning as an apartment building. C. Roy & Sons (444 Roy Dr.), which began its one-hundred-year life as a butcher shop and became locally famous for making bologna, runs a slaughterhouse and a store that has more than bologna. The annual Bologna Festival (since 1991) is a big event. An even older business is the Yale Expositor (21 Main St.), that has printed a weekly newspaper since 1882. The front room of the office is a community museum of sorts, and you can take a peep at a linotype printer that arrived in town on a train from California in 1919. Plans are afoot to create a historical society. Be sure to stop by the town park that skirts the edge of Mill Creek, a tributary of the Black River.

Sandusky (pop. 2,678) is the Sanilac County seat. Businesses that serve townspeople—doctors, dentists, retail stores—are up and down M-19 through the old town that includes a Presbyterian fieldstone church, a new microbrewery, and a community mental health center. Sandusky's strip along M-46 lacks for nothing: West of town is Vibracoustic, a shop making parts to remedy noise, vibration, and harshness in car and truck rides; east of town is the unmarked Michigan Peat—a Texas-based company that sued the Michigan Department of Natural Resources to block its attempt to curtail peat harvesting in Minden Bog north of town. The United States has relatively little buried peat (a nonrenewable energy source that's received a lot of recent attention because of global carbon dynamics); and Michigan is one of three peat-rich states. There's a smaller bog in the Sandusky Game Area, with access via Stringer Road. See a green-yellow birch forest or hear frogs, geese, and sandhill cranes, and you'll know you are there. If you want to explore the towns east of Sandusky that edge the Minden Bog, continue on M-46.

Carsonville (pop. 502) is named for Arthur Carson, a native of Ireland, who moved here from Ohio in 1864 and built a store, then a hotel, and finally a grain elevator. Though the town remains a town, it is not thriving. Coming from the west, you pass a big thrift warehouse and a trucking company. Semis next to trailers provide contrast to the old double-gable Canadian-style yellow-brick house (on Main Street), suggesting life may have been easier in the past.

There are a number of small towns and unincorporated settlements surrounding the Minden Peat Bog. Deckerville (pop. 878), Minden City (pop. 181), Palms (pop. 550), and Argyle (township pop. 716) were communities with small farms and farm businesses, fortunate if the railroad line came through. Different national groups were concentrated in these places: Deckerville had Canadians and Scots, while Minden and Palms had Irish. But Deckerville also had the lumber baron, Charles Decker, who established the sawmill and platted the town, a flax mill, five factories, and five hotels. Old photos show streets jammed with carriages, and William Phillip had a "ten cent barn," where you could leave your horse to be watered and fed while when you came to town. The Deckerville Museum (2485 Black River St.) has collections of local items, such as a hat and other belongings of Dr. G. C. Vincent—a local homeopathic physician who won a fiddling contest at Port Huron in 1925, a time when Henry Ford had instigated a nationwide craze for old-time music—a German immigrant's steamer trunk and archaeological finds like a mastodon tooth and Native arrowheads and pottery. Today the village is down to one factory, if you don't count the factory farms that employ local people. Despite the shifting economic fortunes of the village, population has remained stable: Smokestack chasers retire home and suburbanites are moving there, searching for a hometown ambiance they miss.

Minden City, along with Palms and Argyle, both on the edge of the bog, have large convenience stores with fishing tackle and hardware, but not much else. The people in these places stay connected through a public library and community hospital (Deckerville) or the weekly published newspaper (*Minden City Herald*). Hillside Cemetery (Wheatland Rd.) has one of the few memorials to the Great Thumb Fire of 1881. After the fire, John M. Cole buried six of his neighbors, including a young mother who had a two-day old infant, on his farm and planted a cherry tree over their graves.

Ruth (township pop. 624) contains vestiges of the township's German Catholic origins, namely the Holy Apostle parish and an old Knights of Columbus Hall. Its industries, too, are longstanding: There is a massive sugar beet receiving station on the tracks, and the former Ruth Drain Tile Company has been making concrete blocks since 1976. Farmer's Tavern has a Harley-Davidson sign on the front to welcome bikers, who are a big part of Thumb tourism.

Head west toward Parisville and you'll pass a Shrine at the intersection of Atwater and Minden Roads. At just this point, flames of the great fire that swept through the region in 1881 divided, sparing the Albert Lemanski family and farm. In gratitude Lemanski erected a wooden crucifix. There were once many wayside shrines like this one, and there were other Polish towns like Cracow that no longer exist.

Parisville was the first Polish settlement in Michigan, dating from 1856, and one of the first in the United States. Most of the Poles who settled here came from Ontario. By the 1860s, there were one hundred families. The village has had four different Catholic churches in its history, beginning with St. Mary's, a log structure that was destroyed, as was the entire settlement, in the 1871 fire. Joseph Mindak, in an 1875 letter to a Catholic paper, recalled that it was "not so easy to pick ourselves up." He attributed the resurrection to the encouragement of their priest, Father Joseph Musielewicz. The Parisville Hotel is still standing, as well as a monument that encourages us to recall the history of the area that included New Parisville (one mile north) and Cracow (northwest).

Ubly (pop. 843) is named in a doggerel verse by popular newspaper poet (and summer resident of Point Aux Barques) Edgar Guest: "On the road to Pointe Aux Barques, / Situated in the Thumb, / Is a narrow sign which marks / Roads to Ubly and to Lum." The success of this ditty depends on his claim that bypassed places stimulate our imaginations. Ubly, "bubbly Ubly," started life as Sidon, then Paggett's Corners, and finally was named for a city in England. Poles and Germans were the dominant nationalities, but there was also a group of Scottish Gaelic-speaking refugees evicted by landlords from the Hebrides island of Uist. Arriving in Huron County in 1856 via Canada, they settled around M-53 and Atwater Road and built a Catholic church, named St. Columbkille, for Scotland's patron saint. Ubly schools never served meat on Fridays during Lent and Jacqui Gilbert says her classmates had *babcias* (Polish for "grandmother") who taught them to play euchre and dance the polka.

Ubly is promisingly situated on the Cass River and had, in the past, a milk condenser, an overall factory (where women were paid $1 for a ten-hour day), and electricity in 1937–1938 through a New Deal program, the Rural Electrification Administration. The federal government gave low-interest loans for local cooperatives to build lines in remote areas. Six hundred area farmers attended the organizational meeting in Bad Axe, and within ten months, 1,400 miles of lines, three substations, and a generating plant in Ubly were completed. Governor Frank Murphy threw the switch that sent the electric current to 752 farms. Today, that plant houses Gemini Plastics, a manufacturer of plastic parts that provides jobs to locals and makes Ubly more prosperous than other towns nearby. Restaurants and a brew pub cater to vacationers, and the country club restaurant is the local choice for big event dinners.

At its 1896 incorporation, town fathers established ordinances to provide shelter for the homeless and medical care for the needy. Today we would call this "liberal," but then it was just what decent folks did. Not everyone was decent though, and Ubly had its own true crime story. Dr. John MacGregor fell in love with the wife of local farmer John Wesley Sparling, and proceeded to poison John and his three sons with arsenic. A 2008 historical novel, *The Thumb Pointed Fingers*, written by Sparling descendant Jacki Howard, gave her the chance to follow up on stories relatives told about the "dying Sparlings." MacGregor, though convicted and sentenced, was inexplicably pardoned by Governor Woodbridge Ferris in 1916 and appointed prison doctor at Jackson State Prison, where he had been incarcerated. The Sparlings are buried in the nearby Tyre Cemetery.

Bad Axe (pop. 3,025) is the Huron County seat—a place where elk trails crossed and men prospecting for a state road route in 1861 found a broken axe used to dehorn elk and named their camp Bad Axe. The now iconic name that predated any community by ten years stuck. Fast forward to 2023: David Siev, son of Cambodian and Mexican immigrants, used it as the title of his documentary—*Bad Axe*—which tells a family story of the struggle to call this white, rural county seat their home, where they run a successful business. Like all small towns, Bad Axe had differences.

As one local woman noted, when she was young, "it was more about the Catholics versus the Protestants or the East End (the other side of the tracks) versus the rest of town." Protestant Canadians who came to Michigan joined the Loyal Order of Orange and bonded through shared anti-Catholic feeling, and, as was true across rural Michigan, the KKK had a strong presence here in the 1920s. When a couple of young men showed up at a Black Lives Matter parade in 2020 carrying AK-47s, it surprised no one. Huron County is a Republican stronghold, and a diehard Democrat resident related hearing constant rumbling about the "stolen" election. A visit to the Bad Axe Museum of Local History (303 N. Port Crescent) will provide context for present-day observations. It is well stocked with photos, artifacts, ephemera, and stories its hosts will be glad to share.

Though no longer towering over the low-lying town, residents remember the old courthouse, built by a Bay City firm in 1875. During the 1881 fire, when darkness fell midday and a gale-force wind created moving walls of fire, the town packed into its only brick building for safety. The courthouse was demolished in 1998. Residents regret the loss but will remind you to see *the* bad axe on display in the public library. When you visit the Pioneer Log Cabin Village (206 S. Hanselman St.)—with six authentic cabins moved from points around the county—remember that you are entering buildings that survived the general holocaust. Step inside and feel how different the scale of life was.

Today's Bad Axe residents are survivors, too. Some survived decades working at Detroit factories before they came back. But a different home greeted them: million-dollar homes instead of lakeshore cottages; confined animal feeding operations (CAFOs), instead of small dairy farms; and Thumb Plastics, Inc., instead of the Bloch and Guggenheimer pickle plant that was the largest in the Thumb for forty years. Although Walmart and Meijer have eliminated economic diversity, there are a couple of factories, Gemini and Talco, that make plastic car parts and plastic drain tile. Bad Axe also has three hotels with an easy drive to the coast that hope to woo tourists, since accommodation in Caseville and Port Austin can be hard to find. If you stay the night, check out the new walking trail (3/4 mi. paved) that begins north of the city maintenance garage.

In Verona Township, northeast of Bad Axe, a group of Russian Jews from Bay City created in 1891 a Zionist utopian agricultural colony called the Palestine Colony. The land was still burned over from the 1881 fire, and the colonists were peddlers without farming experience. They received financial assistance from Baron de Hirsch and the help of a retired farmer from the Utica area, but as failing years outnumbered successful ones, most of the colonists returned to the city. In 1900 the land was sold to other European immigrants for homesteads.

Elkton (pop. 796) was named by a Port Austin butcher who processed three enormous elk from what was the Bagley Camp (now Elkton Center). The town is surrounded by fields planted with beans, sugar beets, and hay, but also a one-hundred-turbine wind park operated by DTE Energy that locals feel disturbs the evening peace with constant whirring and flashing red lights. Elkton's downtown is faded: An old elevator stands stolidly by railroad tracks and the former hotel-church-brothel combo—now a bar—has few customers. Places up against years of persistent poverty are target locations for CAFOs, and a family of Dutch immigrants own and operate three nearby. Locals talk about the pros and cons to this new way of dairying, but feelings leak out when they remember how joyful the cows were when put out to pasture in spring: "They seemed to know exactly the spot of meadow they wanted to revisit."

The Historical Society (4910 York St.) is a community closet museum, and the Log Cabin Museum, just a few hundred feet away, built in the Pinnebog area in 1865, is perhaps more interesting. Like its near neighbors, Sebewaing and Pigeon, Elkton had a heavily German population and a metal stamping factory, part of German-born Henry Drettman's Active Industries.

Snover (pop. 300), named after 1895–1898 U.S. congressman Horace G. Snover, began in the late nineteenth century as a post office in the middle of the Thumb, along with a church. Most of the local businesses are long gone, although Snover still has some great old storefronts. Snover's big draw presently is Country View Bulk Foods (Germania Road), owned and run by a Mennonite family who started selling foodstuffs out of a shed on their property. Word has spread all the way to Flint, and there is even a café on the premises.

Lamotte Township (Sanilac County) (pop. 764), named for an early French family, received an influx of Mennonite immigrants from Ontario, who belonged to a new sect called the Brethren, founded in 1883. The Brethren broke away from the Mennonite mother ship because of the belief that a river baptism had to have three total immersions, one for each member of the Trinity. In Lamotte Township today there are still three churches that were originally Mennonite Brethren: Mooretown Brethren in Christ, Cherith Mennonite Church, and Lamotte Missionary Church. Brethren and Missionary Churches had week-long summer camp meetings in Brown City, and many congregants built semipermanent cabins.

Decker is an unincorporated community in Lamotte Township located at the intersection of Snover and Decker Roads. The settlement still retains a hint of infamy as the site of the farm where Timothy McVeigh stayed intermittently before committing the 1995 Oklahoma City bombing. That year, a national television audience focused on Decker, as it watched Ted Koppel host a "town meeting" at the Methodist Church that attempted to explore the recent phenomenon of right-wing militias and antigovernment terrorism.

In Marlette (pop. 1,848), established in 1856, townsfolk solved their flooding problem by burying the river that once ran through town. Marlette, at the southern edge of the burned region in the 1881 fire, was the center of relief efforts. Town fathers wanted industry beyond the usual lumber, dairy, and farm machine businesses, and in 1939 persuaded Gurdon Wolfe of Snover, who had begun to build mobile homes, to set up shop in Marlette. In twenty years, due in large part to the labor force of small farmers from all the nearby towns, there were four trailer manufacturers in the village: Marlette Coach Company, General Coach Works, and two firms owned by Guerdon Industries, which had subsidiaries in four other states. City leaders worried about the impact of suburbanization on the industry, but mobile home manufacture was still Michigan's fifth largest industry in 1960; and the trailer and trailer court are alternatives for the working poor, giving them some freedom to choose their land and lifestyle. Out here, you are likely to notice lone mobile homes on land that is poorer and wetter. In the abandoned trailer courts of Flint, you often see trailers with the Marlette label on them.

Another surprising facet of life in Marlette were the teen "ranch camps" that brought inner-city boys and racial diversity into the village. They lived family-style in cottages (three in Marlette and two in Kingston) with local adults; some of the boys were adopted by local families. The iconic center of town today is tripartite: the restored train depot and Marlette History Museum, an old grain elevator, and Moore's ice cream shop. Visit all three.

Kingston (pop. 395), sat in a low spot, so the settlers built on swamp and lumbered, which meant a sawmill, roads, store, churches, and eventually a grain elevator. In the case of Kingston, there was also a brick kiln and shingle mill. "Wild Bob" Burman, raised in Kingston, was one of the pioneers of open-wheel racing in the United States. He left the farm and began working for Durant-Dort carriage works in Jackson, Michigan, where he test-drove the earliest Buicks. At Durant's request he, with Louis Chevrolet, formed the Buick racing team. His fame peaked in August 1911, when at the wheel of the Blitzen Benz, he covered a mile at an average speed of 142 mph. Wild Bob died in a crash at the young age of thirty-two.

The town grew when the Pontiac, Oxford and Port Austin Railroad, later known as the Pontiac, Oxford and Northern, was completed in 1883, and locals nicknamed the steam engine the Polly Ann or "the Poor, Old, and Neglected." The Polly Ann Trail is part of the Rails-to-Trails system; it's a 16.9-mile nonmotorized biking and walking path that extends north from Orion Township in Oakland County on the former railroad bed.

Brown City (pop. 1,300) is home of the Missionary Church Campground (8700 Wilcox Rd.). Since 1929, thousands of people converge on this spot for ten days for fellowship, prayer, conversion, or just to revive their faith. Camp meetings were a fixture across the American frontier, and Michigan's Thumb has many. The privately owned Bruce mansion (5977 N. Van Dyke Rd.) is a notable example of Second Empire–style architecture.

Shiloh

June Wollstonecraft

At the crossroads of Bailey and Stimson Roads (near Brown City), my family home stood as a testament to modern life. The big white house with blue shutters stood out against the fields of crops, making my home look like a skyscraper compared to the smaller Amish farmhouses.

What made my childhood unique was our proximity to the Amish community that lived just beyond the hedgerow separating our properties. From a young age, I was captivated by my neighbors' way of life. The Amish children were dressed in simple clothes and wide-brimmed hats, a stark contrast to my jeans and band T-shirts, and the ever-present glow of the TV lit up our living room while the Amish homes blended into the blackness of night. Their world moved at a different pace, one dictated by the sun and the seasons rather than the ticking of clocks and daylight savings. Though we lived side by side, our interactions, when there were any, were minimal. The space between our properties was more like a boundary between worlds, and I was left curious about their lives.

In the early morning, I would hear the clip-clop of horse hooves against the hardened dirt road as their buggies passed by our house. It was a comforting sound that became part of my daily rhythm, marking time in a way no clock could. Their lives were focused on building a community and raising enough food for their families to survive between harvest seasons (though the local grocery store would provide during the coldest parts of winter).

School was another realm where our lives ran parallel yet never intersected. My classmates and I would chatter about the latest TV shows, our favorite young-adult books, and after-school plans, while the Amish children attended their own one-room schoolhouse, learning lessons that were as much about survival and community as they were about reading and arithmetic. I often wondered what their school day was like, picturing them in the same style of clothes they will spend their entire lives in. The contrast between our lives was stark, yet I felt a strange connection, as if we were part of the same story told in different languages. When I made eye contact with a group of Amish girls, the few times our school schedules aligned, it was as if my eyes were a time machine and I was watching my great-grandparents walking to school.

The only relationship I had with the Amish community was with their animals. They trained their horses to not be afraid of cars by tying them to posts along the dirt roads, while donkeys wore wooden brindles to pull steel plows. What seemed barbaric to me growing up was pretty normal for all farmers before they came to rely on tractors and other machines. On an Amish farm, animals are tools, discarded when they are no longer useful.

My favorite memory is of a brown and white Shetland pony that I named Shiloh. His owners left him at an abandoned farmhouse across the road from my home. Shiloh was there to eat away the overgrown grass of the lawn that hadn't been cut in three years. The first thing I would do when I got home from school was visit Shiloh. I gave him the scraps of vegetables and fruit that I had. It didn't take long for me to see myself in Shiloh, and we became friends very quickly.

Looking back, I remember how the colors of his brown and white coat melded together though the hairs were separate. Each color stood strong beside the other. If I had to summarize my relationship growing up with the

Amish, I would compare it to Shiloh's coat. While we lived a life of coexistence—shopping at the same grocery store, visiting the smalltown cafe, and enjoying the soybean festival that was held every August—our lives were still distinctly separate.

Flint to Shay Lake: History of a Black Resort in the Middle of White Michigan

Just a dot on the map, tucked away in the southeastern corner of Tuscola County in Michigan's Thumb, Shay Lake would go on to punch above its diminutive size on the social and cultural register in the latter half of the twentieth century. The time was right. The state's industrial centers in southeastern Michigan were thriving in the postwar era, providing greater opportunities for ordinary, working-class people to buy vacation homes in secluded regions up north. Black families in the industrial cities also benefited from the economic prosperity of the period. However, the opportunity for Black folks to buy cottages around the state's eleven-thousand-plus lakes was as restricted—by custom or deed—as it was in the segregated neighborhoods downstate.

Idlewild was one exception. Located in a rural part of northwestern lower Michigan about 225 miles from Detroit, it was one of the few resorts in the country where Black people could vacation and buy property before *legal* segregation was outlawed by the 1964 Civil Rights Act. While Idlewild was nearing the end of its heyday and on the decline, Shay Lake emerged to fill the void. For a half-century, beginning in the late 1950s, it was the spot for many Black blue- and white-collar workers (many of whom were employed in the booming automotive industry), as well as Black professionals who fled Detroit, Flint, and Saginaw from late spring through mid-autumn for a weekend getaway at their modest cottages.

Shay Lake—whose forty-five acres was filled with bluegills, perch, crayfish, clams, and tiny shells—was at the center of many Black Baby Boomers' childhoods and upbringing. It had become the new "Black Eden of Michigan."

Sometime in 1957, Clarence Campbell Sr. and his wife Rose loaded up their three young children in the family's 1956 pink Buick to go for a ride. "We often took rides in the country for entertainment back in those days. But this ride was different, as it seemed we were going someplace special," said the father's oldest son, Clarence Jr., or Chuck, as he's known in the family. He was just seven or eight years old at the time. "Of course, as usual, we got lost, mostly because the directions on this business card Dad had obtained from Lafayette [a family friend] weren't clear."

Clarence Sr., born in April 1921, was a decorated combat veteran of World War II who had served with the all-Black 92nd Infantry Division in Italy. After the war, he returned to his factory job at AC Spark Plug in Flint, while Rose worked as an elevator operator for Citizens Bank. The couple, who both grew up in Flint and recalled hearing stories about the summer homes of some of their white high school classmates, had longed for a retreat of their own up north. Then, during a golf outing with friends, Clarence learned about the availability of some waterfront property on a small lake north of Lapeer in the Thumb.

"Eventually, as we rounded this circular road, I could see we were at a lake," said Chuck. "We stopped at what looked like some type of meeting hall. It was the clubhouse, and upstairs was where Fred Matthews and his family lived. Except for a few lots that had been sold to other individuals, there were just few cottages on the lake at that time; Mr. Matthews owned property surrounding the lake."

According to property records on file with the Tuscola County Register of Deeds, there were two large parcels on the northeast shoreline owned by a group of three investors—Matthews, Kane, and the People's Bank of Caro—that in 1949 had been platted into 328 lots in Shay Lake Subdivision No. 1 and No. 2. The rest of the lakeshore was undeveloped.

By the summer of 1958, the Campbells had scraped and saved up enough money to secure a sliver of waterfront property in Subdivision No. 2. There they began building a mid-century modern flat-roof cottage with a wraparound deck on Lot 334, down a gentle slope near the clubhouse. "I remember the folks spent a lot of time clearing the lot before they could build," said Gail Williams, their oldest child. "It was pretty crude and rustic. There were just a few little, small cottages. Maybe one or two bedrooms. Daddy went in 50–50 with Mr. [Quimby] Rosemond on the land and later bought out Mr. Rosemond. He bought another place at the lake." Clarence and Rose, along with fellow Flint families Rosemond and Brackins, whose cottage was just up the road on lot 324, were among the original "settlers" who transformed the sleepy, largely undeveloped area into a lively recreational retreat for Black families.

How Shay Lake became a magnet for urban Black families seeking resort property in such a secluded, rural locale is not clear. Dayton Township's Black population is today still less than 2 percent. We do know that Shay Lake was a site of fishing, boating, and picnicking by the time of World War I, according to reports in the *Tuscola County Advertiser*.

People from the Flint and Detroit areas also frequented the area to visit friends and relatives and watch local ball teams cross bats at Shay Lake Park (on the lake's east side) that by 1930 included horseshoe courts, boating, fishing, swimming, swings, teeter-totter, merry-go-rounds, and a maypole. Festivities on Decoration Day, May 30, 1930, included a ball game between a team from the nearby community of Mayville and the "Buick Stars Colored Team."

In 1923–1924, Buick sponsored a team in Southern California called the Buick All-Stars that "boasted of 'colored stars' from the Negro Leagues," according to *Baseball Team Names: A Worldwide Dictionary, 1869–2011*. It is unknown whether the same team visited Shay Lake or if any players from Flint were on the roster for that May 30, 1930, game. Other "colored" ball teams, from Saginaw and elsewhere, barnstormed across the Thumb to play games against local teams during the period. Early forays into Thumb towns by the Buick Stars and other teams helped put Shay Lake on the map as an imagined recreational destination for the Black men and their fans who traveled there. Then, as now, ideas and information often traveled by word of mouth.

But another generation would pass and the Second World War would be fought and won in the interim before that dream would come to fruition for Black people seeking resort property at Shay Lake. Meanwhile, the Shay Stone Ballroom (aka Shaystone Gardens)—a building that would later be known as "the clubhouse"—at Shay Lake Park would through the intervening years host weddings and dance parties on the weekends, with music provided by live orchestras. By the mid-1940s, the same newspaper advertisements also included "cottages for rent."

Shay Lake Park opened under new management for the season in May 1946, the same year Fred G. Matthews and wife Judy moved to Kingston after purchasing Shay Lake Park. Williams recalls playing with the Matthewses' daughter Arlene and her sisters and being shown around the lake. "The other side of the lake was undeveloped, just a few pathways," Williams said. She continued: "The Matthewses weren't well off. They didn't have much. Mr. Matthews had like a sportsman club." However, she thinks Matthewses may have "sunk money into the lake without getting the return. It was mostly poor whites in the area (at the time), but he wasn't making any money. Mr. Matthews decided to start selling to black folks."

Mary Drier, a reporter for the *Tuscola County Advertiser* from the mid-1980s to 2015, said in a 2021 interview that "the land wasn't considered very desirable. The area around the lake was quite swampy and dirt had to be brought in to make it suitable for building." Drier speculated that because Shay Lake was remote, isolated, and relatively unoccupied, an influx of Black people from the cities would not be a cause for alarm for some white residents.

Still, the transition to a Black enclave was fraught with the same racial baggage of the era. Williams recalled how her father endured racial epithets while the family cottage was under construction. "Some white guys would get in the boat and drive back and forth in front of the cottage, threatening to destroy the place and calling him 'niggers' and stuff like that." Norman Brackins, a son of one of the original Black families, recalled an incident when his parents first traveled to Shay Lake in 1955. "As we were driving over on the old side of the lake (east of the clubhouse), a lady came out. She had an accent. More of a foreign accent, it seemed, but it could have been Southern. As we were going by, she said, 'You niggers go home. We don't want you here.' My father told us not to worry about it. That was the only incident I remember."

Williams added that white neighbors next door provided the Campbells with water before they were able to install a well on the property. A different neighbor would allow Clarence Campbell to bunk at their place while he was building the family cottage. By 1959, the two-bedroom cottage, with its massive cinderblock fireplace and wraparound deck, was finished.

Beginning in August 1958 and continuing through December 1962, land on the north and west sides of the lake was platted and named Shay Lake Heights Subdivision, Nos. 1–6. Truckloads of dirt were brought in to prepare the land for future development. Chuck Campbell remembers himself and a playmate named Philip Thompson playing on those hills of fresh dirt in Shay Lake Heights. The parcels, which contained several hundred lots, came under the control of Select Land Development Company, whose copartners were William Fisher, Edmund Wozniak, and Arden Thompson. Frank and Mary Chantney also were listed as proprietors of the land.

But it was Arden Thompson, whose oldest son was Philip, who came to be most closely associated with the development and marketing of Shay Lake Heights Subdivision. He had originally owned a place on the lake's east side a few doors north of the Campbells' new cottage. Thompson later built a contemporary split-level house on Shay Lake Road at Sucker Creek Drain from the proceeds of the many property sales. In subsequent years, there would be a large sign in front of his split-level ranch that read "Select Land Development Company."

Thompson started Select Land Development Company in 1956 and, according to his 1993 obituary, was the founder of Shay Lake Heights and the person responsible for most of the development of Shay Lake. While working for Ford Motor Company, Thompson learned that there were few if any places where Black people could buy resort property, except for Idlewild, said Bert Slater, who has lived at Shay Lake for two decades. "The white guy supposedly befriended a Black woman who also worked at the plant," said Slater, a real estate agent and retired corporate manager from Southfield.

Bob Adams, who moved to the lake in 2009 after retiring from Chrysler, said he "heard the story that a lot of other people heard" about the origins of the lake's draw for Black people. Adams had been visiting Shay Lake since he was nine years old and eventually bought property in 1978. "This was half the distance compared to going to Idlewild," Adams said. "People really didn't want to go that far. My aunt had a place at Idlewild, so it gave me a perspective on the two places." By the early 1960s, Select Land Development Company was advertising lots and cottages for sale in the *Michigan Chronicle*, a Black newspaper based in Detroit. A review of property transactions suggests many of the properties were sold and acquired via land contract, and the lake's popularity took off.

Brackins remembers fondly the early days of being at the lake. He and his siblings spent countless hours exploring and hanging out with friends whose parents also had cottages there. "We would be at each other's cottages way into the night," he said. "The nights here would be really dark because there weren't any streetlights. But we didn't worry about that at all. And then there was the clubhouse."

Williams recalled that Judy Matthews sold the clubhouse and some property to Emmitt Jenkins of Flint. Jenkins and his wife Rose had already purchased property on Sucker Creek along the canal in 1960. "He was a big numbers man and drove a big Lincoln. His wife had a beauty shop on the North Side (in Flint)," said Williams.

For entertainment at the clubhouse, Williams recalls a group called "The Flints," as well as Mary Wells, one of the early stars of Motown Records. Brackins remembers Saginaw native Stevie Wonder performing at the clubhouse around the time that his hit single "Fingertips" was released in 1962. "A lot of groups from Detroit played here," he said. Others included Flint saxophonist Sherwood Pea, who played with the Motown house band and toured with jazz legends Sonny Stitt and the Court Basie Orchestra. The Temptations and Diana Ross are also rumored to have passed through Shay Lake in those early days before hitting it big. "I do remember Brook Benton playing (at the clubhouse) one Sunday as we were leaving," Chuck Campbell added.

However, Shay Lake never achieved the level of fame as a Black entertainment venue that Idlewild enjoyed during its heyday. Although musicians, mostly from the Detroit area, still played there occasionally, by the early to mid-1970s the lake had become better known as a more family-oriented recreation spot. Boating, swimming, waterskiing, dirt bikes, teenage parties, and family gatherings assumed center stage as the chief form of weekend fun and entertainment.

By this time, the first wave of Black Baby Boomers who had seen military service in Vietnam or in other parts of Southeast Asia had returned and were ready to unwind. Meanwhile, more property owners began docking speedboats at their lakefront cottages in place of the rowboats of earlier years.

Darryl Buchanan called Shay Lake the setting for his "coming-of-age" story. "It was a carefree time. For me, it was like the *Wonder Years*," said Buchanan, referring to the popular ABC series that was reprised in 2021 with a Black family in the title role. "A magical place for me. And everybody had a motorcycle," said Buchanan, although he did not. His only worry at the lake, he said, were the "drop-offs," a transition area where the lake's shallow bottom suddenly drops into the deeper water. A Detroit native, Buchanan grew up near the epicenter of the 1967 riot and witnessed it unfold. But his father and stepmother owned a waterfront cottage from 1967 to 1975, located on the point, a soft peninsula on the lake's west side—Shay Lakes Heights, the so-called new side. It provided an escape from the city and the neighborhood, he said. "I can remember standing in the front room and seeing the lake on all three sides. It was pretty awesome." He also remembers "meeting the most beautiful girl I can ever remember seeing at Shay Lake. She was visiting a neighbor that had a cottage."

Once at the lake, Buchanan said, "I hung out with Jesse Stephens and his crew. Jesse was 'Mr. Shay Lake' to me. He was just the man." Stephens, whose parents owned and operated the Shay Lake Grocery, a small general store and gas station, was also well known for his waterskiing exploits. "Mr. Shay Lake," who hailed from Highland Park, often joined with Derrick Williamson, another outstanding waterskier, and his family

A cottager in boat on Shay Lake, late 1960s. COURTESY OF BOB CAMPBELL.

in showing off their dazzling slalom work on the lake. Williamson's father, a graduate of Howard University Medical School, was a successful physician in Detroit; his mother, a one-time civil servant at the Pentagon, worked extensively with Dr. Charles H. Wright and the original Museum of African American History in Detroit. The Williamsons owned a blue-and-white, 140-horsepower inboard-outboard, flat-bottomed boat, and their ranch-style lakefront cottage was among the finest at Shay Lake.

Learning how to waterski is how Carole Williams, Clarence Campbell's third daughter, began to connect with other teenagers at the lake. From a social standpoint, things began to change when her older brother Chuck came back from the Army in 1972. "Me learning how to ski got people on the new side to say: 'Hey, there are people over there (on the east side) our age,'" said Williams. "The first time I slalomed, Addison and Marnell (two Detroit teenagers her age) stopped by to say 'Great job.' It took me forever to get up and, of course, Daddy drove the boat crazy." The seventeen-foot aluminum Duratech Neptune was powered by a 115-horsepower Mercury and considered one of the fastest boats on the lake.

For a Flint native, connecting with the Detroit crowd also brought new experiences. "During that time, we found out they were doing progressives," she said. "The Detroit people were doing these parties, going house to house. I got to go, which was a big deal. So, the time from about [age] thirteen to seventeen (the early to mid-1970s), that was a pretty cool time. We got bikes, too." Williams recalled how the simple act of installing a light in front of the lake-facing cottage was also a big deal. "Seeing the front porch lights lit up across the lake at night would give us an idea of how many people were at the lake for the weekend. So, we were big-time now." Looking back, she added, holiday weekends were extra. "Daddy would buy extra stuff, extra pop, hot dog buns, one can of cinnamon rolls. We'd each get one cinnamon roll. He would try to make it extra special for us. Periodically, we would go into Kingston for ice cream." However, the clubhouse did not factor into her *Wonder Years* at the lake. "The clubhouse was rickety, old and scary at that point," she said.

By the end of the 1970s and into the early 1980s, the social climate at Shay Lake had cooled. In some cases, family situations changed, as the children and teens moved into adulthood and went away to college. In others, couples divorced and the property sold. There were also economic jolts of the 1979 oil crisis, fueled by the Iranian revolution, and the deep recession of 1980–1983. "Most of my friends left the state in the early '80s, as GM and the auto industry was slumping," said Williams. "My age group that would have repopulated the lake started pulling out for places like Texas."

The economy rebounded in the mid-1980s, and Shay Lake experienced something of a second act—a modest revival (at least compared to the go-go 1970s) that would last another decade or so. However, much of the second generation of the original owners had moved onto other recreational and vacation venues that were either out of reach or unavailable to the first-generation, such as exotic locales like Jamaica. The transition was in full motion by end of the 1990s and into the early 2000s, as indicated by the various property transactions on the record at the Tuscola County Register of Deeds. Further decline and changes in the U.S. auto industry, and the broader economy, throughout the period were factors, too, Buchanan said. "Not having the same level of disposable income, that obviously impacted what happened at Shay Lake, as it did at other resort communities in Michigan," he said.

Clarence and Rose Campbell sold their property finally in November 2002, after forty-four years. Nearly a half-century of the ground heaving from the annual freeze-and-thaw cycles had taken its toll on the lakefront structure that rested on a foundation too shallow for the terrain. "One day around 2002, Pops called me to say he sold the cottage," Chuck Campbell said. "It was time; she had served us well." The Campbells' cottage was demolished soon after Rick and Cindy Kinel, who lived next door year-round, bought the property and expanded their lot. Clarence died six years later in 2008 and Rose in 2012.

Today, Shay Lake is more of a residential community of year-round residents—70 percent white instead of overwhelmingly Black, according to Henry Harris Jr., the lone Black member of the six-member association board, who retired from the Detroit Police Department after thirty-five years.

The association has about eighty-five members who pay $150 annually, primarily to maintain the roads, Harris said. The public lake is monitored by the Michigan Department of Natural Resources but to get on the water requires access through someone's private land. When traveling along the dirt roads that ring the lake, "private property" and "no trespassing" signs are a common sight as well as fenced-in, gated lots. There are even signs along the access roads to alert visitors that they have entered a private area. To be sure, it is a different vibe from the days of yore when "we would roam from yard to yard," according to Carole Williams.

In 2014, a "KKK picnic" sign was posted on a vacant lot in the Shay Lake Heights Subdivision at Shay Lake Road and Arden Park Drive. "When the sign was found, people tried to pass it off that it was private property," said Harris, who told the Tuscola County prosecutor that it was ethnic intimidation. "Nothing ever happened to the man [considered to be responsible]." About three dozen residents attended a neighborhood watch meeting held at the clubhouse; everybody was angered by the racist incident, he said. There haven't been any such incidents since.

Overall, Shay Lake is "quiet, laid back," said Bob Adams. "It's a neighborly environment." And there is hope for a third act, in which it becomes a spot for weekend getaways. "People are trying to move here," said Adams. "I've run into a number of Black people [whose parents owned property there] who are trying to move back." Adams, along with co-organizers Harris and Bert Slater, have hosted the Shay Lake Fishing Derby for fourteen years for children from the Flint, Detroit, and Saginaw areas. Some local children have participated, too. Slater also operates Camp A.R.T.I.S. at the clubhouse, which hosts youth groups from grades five through twelve for a weekend of camping, fishing, and water sports. It has drawn youth from about a seventy-mile radius. "We also share some of the history of the lake," he said. "We would work with church groups, family groups and youth organizations. We're working to add more programming."

The clubhouse and several lakefront cottages are advertised on vacation rental sites, such as Vrbo and AirBnb, and reviews are good. That too spells the end of the era when Shay Lake was an exclusively Black enclave. It remains to be seen whether a new and younger generation of urban Black families will seek refuge and invest in the area their foreparents pioneered. A spot that provided the kind of lived experiences one might read about or see on television, such as a boy, age twelve, finding a stone arrowhead artifact that had been left behind by a Native American inhabitant long ago; digging in the sand at the water's edge only to be amazed by the unearthing of a recently hatched baby turtle; or witnessing the natural process of a small frog being devoured slowly by a snake that had slithered up beside it on a partially submerged log in front of the family's cottage. Time will tell. Of greater certainty is the lake itself. Shay Lake will live on, regardless.

RESTORING OUR WATERLAND

Water is the great shapeshifter. In its solid form as glacier, it sculpted and scoured channels and basins and, when it turned to liquid, filled them with itself, creating rivers, lakes, and ground water aquifers that move through mineral-rich bedrock to nourish swamps: peat-making wetlands that were originally thick with shrubs, hardwoods, and conifers. Just as the Great Black Swamp across northern Ohio was anathema to settlers moving west, the area where the major rivers of the Saginaw Valley converge, being about seventy miles in breadth, was a mire even after the cities of Flint, Saginaw, and Bay City began to grow and after the first federal Swamp Act, passed in 1849, turned wetlands over to the states, hoping to promote drainage of these water-sodden acres.

But $1.50-per-acre swamp-bottom land prices were just not enough to attract families to an area deemed "unhealthy" due to mosquitoes, and the mire remained a blank spot on the map until men with money and big equipment devised new social configurations—agribusiness and a collective farm. The great drying was part of the settlement process across our region, but in this microregion of "considerable" rivers, it proved much more difficult. After years of increasingly damaging floods, the Army Corps of Engineers concluded that the region's rivers needed more room.

In the decades since the Shiawassee National Wildlife Refuge and the Shiawassee River State Game Area were formed, state and federal laws have protected these regional wetland treasures because they are both extensive and contiguous with the Great Lakes. A 1972 amendment to the Clean Water Act (1970) extended federal oversight to navigable rivers, which included the Saginaw and tributaries in its watershed. With the climate changing rapidly, scientists are now more than ever stressing the importance of peat-making swamps, fens, and bogs that filter polluted water, hold carbon, and provide habitat for wildlife. Sometimes they are called the kidneys of the land and sometimes the planet's green lungs.

Saginaw industrialist and avid hunter William B. Mershon (1856–1943) lamented species loss in his 1923 memoir, *Recollections of My Fifty Years Hunting and Fishing*. He witnessed firsthand the extinction of the passenger pigeon, blaming market hunters but also habitat destruction. Hunters like Mershon were the first conservationists—a tradition that organizations like Ducks Unlimited continues. Unlike other great

Midwest swamps and marshes, enough of the Saginaw Mire remained for it to be restored to an expansive twenty-thousand-acre-plus tract of wetlands. The region is now beginning to be used for serious study by the scientific community and the general public.

Archaeologists have identified over thirty early Woodland sites here at these important river confluences. Understanding the more fluid lives of Indigenous peoples who depended on wetlands, paddling up and down the rivers according to the season, may help see homelands in new ways. The great American naturalist Henry David Thoreau said famously that he would rather have a swamp in his front yard than a lawn, and his love of desolate wild mixtures could, if embraced more widely, check the American obsession with development (if you call parking lots with box stores and factories development). If we position ourselves in the midst, sunk in the mire and contentedly stuck, we may design more sustainable forms of life.

Shiawassee Flats

Today, the heart of the Saginaw River Valley is a vast network of marshes and swampland south of the city of Saginaw, formed by the confluence of six tributary rivers (Flint, Cass, Shiawassee, Tittabawassee, Chippewa, and Bad) that flow together to form the twenty-two-mile Saginaw River. The whole area, known locally as the Shiawassee Flats, is an inland delta of latticed waterways that extends into Crow Island, north of Saginaw, east to Quanicassee and west to Tobico marsh. The earliest settlers described the land as wet prairie, with bluejoint grass as high as a horse's back, that held ten inches of water normally and was prone to flash flooding. They used the word "muskeg" to describe the peaty lands adjoining these marshes, dotted with ponds, stunted trees, and covered in grassy hummocks. The St. Clair Flats, where the St. Clair River enters Lake St. Clair, is the only other delta in the Great Lakes system, once known as the "Venice of America," when Detroit weekenders arrived to stay in hotels around 1900. By contrast, the Shiawassee Flats is an untouristed wonderland—a refuge for migrating waterfowl and songbirds, home to wildlife, with a full record of Indigenous life preserved in fashioned stones and artifacts being excavated and studied by archaeologists.

Part prairie farm, part wildlife refuge, part state game area, the Saginaw Flats began as a glacial lake bottom in the last ice age, then existed for millennia as an estuary or delta, endured a great drying after settlement, and is now regaining its integrity as a coastal wetland. Naturalists consider the area "coastal" because seiches in the bay (akin to tidal movements) are felt as far inland as St. Charles.

If you are out in the middle of the old Prairie Farm tract, standing somewhere south of the Flint River on Townline Road east of St. Charles, you might think you are

Saginaw River looking east at the Shiawassee Flats. PHOTOGRAPH BY TIMOTHY H. KAUFMAN.

hallucinating when you look out across the endless acres of plowed furrows and feel you are at sea. This land holds the memory of water, intensified if sandhill cranes with their bubbly calls are migrating in the skies above or picking the stubbled fields below. North of this prairie is the Refuge, a watery paradise, sometimes called Michigan's Everglades—where a 6.5-mile Wildlife Drive (access at 6000 Bishop Rd.) meanders past forest, grasslands, and marshes, along open water pools and the Shiawassee River.

White settlers who came to the Saginaw Basin worked hard to ditch and dike the area so they could farm, but in doing so, they exacerbated the flooding problem. Regional planning studies in the 1940s, followed by an Army Corps of Engineers report in the mid-1950s, concluded that rivers needed floodplains. U.S. Fish and Wildlife Department recommendations led to the creation of the Shiawassee State Game Area and the Shiawassee National Wildlife Refuge, established in 1951 and 1953, respectively, to store flood water as well as to provide habitat for migrating birds and waterfowl. The recognition that the vast marsh was actually necessary for flood control and water filtration was a watershed moment that interrupted decades of settler practice. Yet that history too is important, because it was through the difficult interactions with this marsh landscape that new kinds of farming and social organization emerged. The land of big skies fed big dreams.

Agribusiness

When the first settlers arrived in Albee and Spaulding Townships, they found it too wet and too full of mosquitoes to farm. Floods from spring freshets and northeasters from Georgian Bay piled the sluggish river waters back on themselves to the height of ten or fifteen feet, leaving mud and debris when they retreated. The first to experiment with "improvements" were a group of Saginaw land dealers and lawyers, who cobbled together a ten-thousand-acre parcel that they called "Prairie Farm" and proceeded to dig the first ditch across the northern section of their prairie land to the Flint River, a distance of about two miles, enclosing three or four hundred acres. Their early efforts demonstrated the potential of the region for agriculture, but they had trouble keeping workmen on the job in this out-of-the-way place. Eventually they sold out to the Saginaw Realty Company, who tried to build dikes, but mud swallowed teams of horses. It wasn't until 1903, when members of the Pitcairn family, owners of the Pittsburgh Plate Glass Company, with controlling interests in the Owosso Sugar Company, bought Prairie Farm and excavated a network of drainage ditches and enclosed the land with a thirty-six-mile-long dike. They constructed a pump house on an embankment next to the Flint River that could lift 160,000 gallons of water an hour from the ditches and laid a rail spur that connected the farm to the Grand Trunk line at Taymouth. Prairie Farm was said to be the largest active farm east of the Mississippi, and its success was due largely to the skill and energy of its manager, Jacob DeGeus, a native of Holland, who assumed managerial control in 1904 and began to breed Belgian draft horses.

The few roads through the area, indicated on today's atlases, run atop the old dikes, and you can still visit Alicia, once the center of peppermint oil manufacture and a thriving farm community that grew sugar beets, beans, corn, oats, hay, and peppermint and housed a small army of laborers in eighty frame cottages and two dormitories. Prairie Farm even had its own electric plant and water system, making it an island of light and activity when communities beyond its dikes were submerged in annual floodwaters. In many ways, it was a precursor to the industrial agriculture of today. The main difference is that Prairie Farm relied on an army of workers whereas the almost total mechanization of twenty-first-century farming has left Alicia a ghost town with a couple of houses, two closed stores, and an abandoned church.

Utopian Community

Owosso Sugar was sold to Michigan Sugar in 1924, but the Pitcairns kept the deed to Prairie Farm, until, nine years later, the John Pitcairn estate sold it to Joseph Cohen, a Russian Jewish anarchist living in Brooklyn, who dreamed of starting a utopian community for destitute urbanites. Cohen and his fellow "libertarian anarchists" believed society should peacefully reconstitute into cooperative communities.

Self-sustaining networks of these communities would eventually develop, eliminating the need for national governments. Recruits for the new Sunrise Cooperative Farm Community would have to pay a $500 admission fee, be under the age of forty-five without large numbers of children, and not be "conservatives and religious people . . . nor professed Communists." Hundreds of applications for membership flooded into Cohen's office for membership in his agrarian utopia that took inspiration from several nineteenth-century intentional communities in New York and the Midwest.

Construction at Sunrise began in July 1933 to upgrade the shanties Owosso Sugar had used to house Czech and Mexican workers. The first year was successful, with much enthusiasm about "the great things [they] were going to accomplish under such glorious skies," but the community quickly broke into factions. With people coming from eighteen states and twelve countries, it was impossible to keep political and cultural differences out of the picture. Even the food served in the common dining rooms became a source of contention, when people began to remember and long for what they cooked and ate back home. More fundamentally, residents' lack of farming and mechanical experience and Cohen's idealism, which made him reluctant to assign work tasks, led to failure. In his memoir, *In Quest of Heaven*, Cohen addresses the need people have for affirmation, especially in a social experiment when family structure was loosened, everyone was fumbling to learn new skills, and there were few opportunities to enjoy social life.

By 1936, Cohen realized he couldn't boost morale enough to battle the rate of attrition, and sold the farm to the Federal Rural Rehabilitation Corporation and Resettlement Administration. The *Detroit Free Press* made much of Uncle Sam bailing out a "failed . . . Communist enterprise" and noted in the same derisive tone that this would be the largest of the three hundred New Deal communal farms. Three hundred families moved to the Saginaw Valley from unproductive lands in Allegan and Washtenaw Counties to join the fifteen who stayed on from the Sunrise colony. Each family was given forty- or eighty-acre pieces on which to raise vegetables, sheep, and dairy cattle and would be permitted to buy their farms on sixty-year mortgages. President Harry S. Truman abolished these programs in 1946, because critics thought them to be inspired by Soviet collective farms, and the federal government sold off the land. Today, about twenty farmers work the land, operating a cooperative to jointly purchase supplies and market their crops.

Restoration

It took a village to turn the vast Saginaw marsh into productive farmland and it requires another "village," made up of naturalists, engineers, farmers, sportsman's groups, toxicologists, and environmental lawyers, to secure the funds, identify point source polluters, and plan and carry out projects to restore the estuarine character of the basin and safeguard the marsh. Joseph Cohen learned about the peaty composition of Prairie Farm's soils when he tried to extinguish a field fire; and scientists are only now coming to understand that plant matter built up over centuries and compressed into peat plays a very important role in the filtering and carbon-storing processes. This is especially important in our region, where the rivers drain heavily farmed areas and so carry high levels of nitrogen and phosphorus that can turn into algae blooms if not sucked up by the plants. Without its magnificent marshes, Saginaw Bay could become as clotted with algae as Lake Erie.

The ultimate goal of wetland restoration is to incorporate the old farmed and diked areas back into the maze of rivers and get closer to original flow patterns. Laser photography that can identify a river's "paleo-channel" helps engineers decide which levees to break, where to introduce new water, and where to place water control mechanisms. Rewilding is hard on farmers, especially those with deep roots in this place. When the Shiawassee National Wildlife Refuge was created, 25 percent of the land was owned by unwilling sellers that had to be taken by the federal government through Michigan's eminent domain laws. Farmers were given, in exchange, sharecropping agreements that took decades to work through, so croplands could be removed from production and wetland restoration could begin in 2011. Farmers and environmentalists will be, for the foreseeable future, figuring out how to live on the land in mutually beneficial ways.

Walk the Ferguson Bayou Trail at the refuge, and you will experience bottomland hardwood forests, lakeplain prairies, and emergent marshes. You may spot a river otter or a beaver, see native trumpeter swans, or hear sandhill cranes. Ducks, snowy egrets, geese, and raptors are abundant, as are deer and river otters. Even rare species like the Blanding's turtle are coming back. Muskrats, which have declined across their range, are also thriving, making use of the heavy reeds for building their huts. Without them, the work of removing the nonnative species would be exponentially harder.

Recreating the diversity of marshland plants that once existed here—bulrush, aster, goldenrod, willow, and native cattails—requires breaking into the wild monoculture of phragmites and invasive cattails. Phragmites is that tough, tall, reed grass with the grayish-purple feathery flower head. It adapts to degraded conditions and proliferates along highway edges, construction sites, lowlands and ditches. Low water levels in the Great Lakes from 1998 to 2013 opened new shoreline area for this aggressive colonizer, and now a dense band of reeds trims Saginaw Bay and backs right up to farm fields with acre after acre of planted monocultures. The nutrient-rich runoff from these fields makes it difficult to contain the phragmites, which are mowed, burned, and sprayed heavily with chemicals. In other countries, people use phragmites for thatch, mats, baskets, and even musical instruments, and, while Michiganders don't live under thatch or sit on reed mats, scientists are looking for more sustainable ways to manage them through biocontrol methods or even harvesting them as feedstock for cellulosic ethanol or other kinds of biofuels.

Refuge biologists have been harvesting the invasive cattails, shredding and selling them to farmers as recycled fertilizer.

Refuge lands are also expanding because of reparations environmental warriors have forced Dow Chemical to make. Beginning as early as the late 1890s, the Dow plant in Midland released pollutants into the Tittabawassee River that have infiltrated and damaged the entire watershed: phenol, brine wastes, pesticides, and, later, the byproducts of various chemical processes, commonly referred to as dioxins. Federal, state, and tribal governments conducted a Natural Resource Damage Assessment to determine what would compensate the public for resources lost over time. The first Natural Resource Damage Assessment in our watershed began in 1980, related to the Saginaw River and GM's release of PCBs into the river and the wastewater of Saginaw and Bay City. Settlement of that claim came in 1998. The later dioxin claim, settled in 2019, caused Dow to turn over much more land, including the former Germania Club golf course north of the Tittabawassee, as well as lands along that river's bank up into Midland County and along the Saginaw River.

Saginaw Bay

Dr. Thomas A. Palmer was paddling a birchbark canoe with an Indian guide between Pinconning and Point Au Gres one day in 1867, intending to vaccinate Indians during a smallpox outbreak, and commented on rough water caused by "a school of sturgeon fish, averaging in weight between 50–125 pounds." Today, native places, as well as Native peoples, still suffer the aftershocks of settlement, resource extraction, and massive industrialization that left the waters troubled. You can still enjoy a morning like the one Palmer enjoyed on Saginaw Bay, shore fishing or paddling a kayak, but you will not find yourself in a school of sturgeon—not yet.

The Saginaw Bay is the fifty-one-mile-long inlet of Lake Huron that makes lower Michigan a mitten. It was formed by a probing glacial lobe that may have been struck by a comet hitting the ice sheet. An imaginary line through the waves from Sand Point to Lookout Point bisects the bay into inner and outer sections, with mean depths of fifteen feet and forty-eight feet, respectively. Because it is so shallow, the waters of the inner bay respond rapidly to wind changes. Storms can rise suddenly, with piled waves curling to white caps underneath climbing cumulonimbus clouds that darken from gray to green and violet in storms. In the outer bay, the water follows the larger circulation patterns of Lake Huron. Clashing flow patterns produce storms for which the bay is notorious. There are shallower protected bays along both east and west shores, as well as a sand and gravel bar called the Coryeon Reef off the eastern shoreline, that provide spawning habitat for species that do not go up the rivers to deposit eggs. The Quanicassee, Saginaw, Tittabawassee, Pinconning, Rifle, and Au Gres Rivers have been and still are popular spawning locations.

Fishermen at Bay Port, c. 1945. DRAWING BY CONNOR TINNIN.

In its pristine state, Saginaw Bay was a natural hatchery for a range of fish species, from sturgeon and arctic grayling to walleye, yellow perch, herring, channel catfish, lake trout, and whitefish. But, because it catches the nutrient and chemical loads of all the rivers that flow through formerly industrial and still heavily farmed lands, it's far from "pure." The cry to preserve the bay and its fish sounded as soon as the first state Fisheries Commission was formed and began to issue annual reports in 1871. The expressed concerns of this period were pound nets, the introduction of sport fish like brook trout in the 1850s, pollution caused by logging, and overfishing. In 1880 alone, more than four million pounds of sturgeon were processed in Michigan, taken from Lake Huron and Lake St. Clair.

Those concerns did not stop the development of commercial fishing, which was robust and relatively stable until the 1930s. Lake herring was the predominant species, with annual catches of one to eight million pounds, but walleye, yellow perch, and suckers were also abundant, each providing annual catches of one million pounds. Whitefish and lake trout, though not as plentiful in the bay as Lake Huron, were still important. The early fisheries, located near shore and on major rivers tributary to the bay, used spears, seines, and gill nets. Pound nets, hooks, and trap nets followed, as fishers became mechanically equipped and moved to deeper offshore waters. Fish production increased rapidly in the late nineteenth century and peaked in 1902 at 14.2 million pounds. Since then, production has gradually declined, to a low of 1.4 million pounds in 1974. At present, commercial fishery targets only lake trout and yellow perch, and production remains below historical levels. Many feel the industry is dying because of overregulation. Certain fish species, like walleye and yellow perch, are protected, the fishing season is shortened, and net depths tightly controlled. There are even laws that regulate by-catch (fish netted unintentionally); and fishermen must spend time returning them to the waters of the bay. At present, there are only fifty commercial licenses issued statewide, compared to more than three hundred in 1968, and only about thirty-five of them are fished annually. A proposed bill could bar net fishing in Saginaw Bay by 2027, leaving hook and line as the only legal method.

In 1966, the Michigan Department of Natural Resources broke from tradition and established a Great Lakes fishery policy that made recreational fishery management its primary goal and relegated commercial fishing to a secondary role. They did this because of the alarming shrinkage of fish populations due to natural and manmade invasive species. The sea lamprey came into the Great Lakes in the 1940s, probably through the new and enlarged Welland Canal, which opened in 1932, enabling ships from the Atlantic to move around Niagara Falls and access the inner lakes. In the ocean, sea lampreys no longer kill fish. The slow and steady process of natural selection rewarded those that survived until fish and lamprey made accommodations and are now able to coexist. This is not the case in the Great Lakes. During the time of highest lamprey abundance, up to 85 percent of fish not killed by them were marked with attack wounds. The problem is now being addressed with lampricides and gates that block their access to tributary rivers and streams.

Other invasives that trouble the bay are zebra and quagga mussels, which have devastated whitefish populations by depleting the underwater food web, as has manmade chemicals and byproducts of industrial processes—PCBs, phenol, mercury, dioxins, and more—that are harder to see and possibly harder to address. These chemicals create anoxic conditions and contaminate the bottom sediments, which benthic feeders like sturgeon and catfish ingest and where walleye eggs lay incubating for three weeks before they hatch.

The Saginaw Basin has the longest contiguous coastal marshes in the United States. They provide the essential ecosystem service of filtering water. There are a number of ideal access points: The Wildfowl Bay State Wildlife and Game Area, northeast of Sebewaing and Bayport, is a large wetland with open water that is dotted with many tiny islands: Heisterman, Duck, Maisou, Middle Ground, Defoe, and Lone Tree. Sandspit embayments here, as well as at Pinconning and Nayangquing Point, create sheltered aquatic environments that support marsh plant growth. Submerged vegetation is a good thing, but too much of it is not, which is why the Department of Environment, Great Lakes, and Energy has created a nutrient load budget that helps farmers manage runoff and avoid algae blooms. The Saginaw Bay was listed as an area of concern in 1987 by the International Joint Commission, which shares responsibility for Great Lakes stewardship.

Since then, there have been steady improvements, thanks to the monitoring and legislative work that has been done by biologists and toxicologists. Dredging and projects connected to habitat restoration along the bay's shoreline and across its coastal marshes have helped immensely. The restoration plan that followed the 2019 settlement with Dow Chemical includes restoration of 415 acres of shoreline habitat near the Saginaw River's mouth, construction of rock reefs in the bay as a fish spawning area, and several projects to encourage community use of the bay, including a docking facility and education center to expand the programming at Bay Sail—a nonprofit that operates the schooner *Appledore* and provides sail training and environmental education for youth. The Saginaw River Rear Range Lighthouse is still being renovated for public access.

If you've never explored a marsh, do yourself a favor and stop at Quanicassee State Wildlife Area (2300 N. Finn Road, Essexville) or Vanderbilt County Park (8078–8462 Vanderbilt Rd., Fairgrove). The park provides Bay access to fishermen in all seasons, whether they are launching boats or loading ATVs with ice fishing equipment for a drive across windswept ice. Push through the windbreak of trees and phragmites, and you'll see bright green marsh against the blue water of the lake and the different blue of the sky. If you're lucky, there will be lots of snowy egrets high stepping in shallows or perched in dead trees, sunning and preening. In the distance is the ominous boxy shape of a power plant mentioned in the signage about warmer waters and thinning ice in areas near the plant.

The muck you may sink into—made of reeds and marsh grass—is related to "nuisance" muck—the icky, sometimes smelly, masses that wash up on bay beaches. Although nutrient pollution and eutrophication contribute to muck making, Saginaw Bay is a naturally florid environment with a lot of vegetation, caused by its shallows and fluctuating water levels.

Walleye have always done well in Saginaw Bay and are still the big sport fish in these waters. Their vacant ghost eyes are light sensitive, causing them to prefer muddy waters, cloudy days, and working the night shift. Sturgeon reintroduction began in 2017 after local communities had made enough progress improving the health of tributary riparian zones, removing dams and dredging rivers of toxins. Since then, every fall, 250 eight-inch fish are imprinted with the waters of the Shiawassee, Cass, Flint, and Tittabawassee and begin their long lives in upstream places to which they will return annually. This initiative is supported by Michigan State University, Michigan Department of Natural Resources, and the U.S. Fish and Wildlife Service and by local funds raised through the Adopt a Sturgeon Program. The plush toy fish,

Student in the Flint River Ecology Study holds a large pike. PHOTOGRAPH BY HEATHER DAWSON.

given to each person who adopts, encourages identification with the ultimate survivor, a fish left over from the Jurassic period. Having them back in our waters is a redo of sorts, a reminder that if time, like water, flows in a cycle, then it may be time for all of us to regain paradise, which in mythology is the place where the rivers meet the sea—or the inland sea for Mid-Michiganders.

Saginaw Valley Field Trips

Paul Yelensky, who lived with his parents at the Sunrise Cooperative Farm, said in a 1988 interview that their Saginaw marsh years were the "best part of his parents' lives" and very important to his own. The work there made them what Yelensky calls "earthy people." Since that time, the basin has lost wetlands, wild rice beds, bluejoint grass prairies, sturgeon, herring, and the safe fresh water flowing through

Mating dance of two egrets at the Shiawassee National Wildlife Refuge. PHOTOGRAPH BY BRADLEY ARY.

the veins of the land. But damage means there is a bigger role for land stewards to play and more urgency for them to stay and tend to the process of rewilding. "I never found so much peace until I started wildlife photography," writes Bradley Ary, who spends as much time as possible in the National Wildlife Refuge observing nesting eagles, egrets, and dancing cranes; the rich mix of life here, "has made me a better person."

Points of Interest

Shiawassee National Wildlife Refuge includes the main part of the refuge (at the end of Curtis Road, off M-13) with access to the Ferguson Bayou Trail. The Wildlife Drive (access only by automobile from June to September) begins at 6000 Bishop Road. Green Point (access from Swan Creek Rd.) is a seventy-six-acre floodplain tract north of the Shiawassee River, within the City of Saginaw. It includes footpaths and the Green Point Environmental Learning Center (3010 Maple St.). Refuge lands along the Cass River (access from M-13) can be explored from the kayak launch near the bridge.

Shiawassee River State Game Area (access from Wahl and Prior Roads east from M-52) consists of fifteen square miles of wetlands and bayous segmented by forty miles of dikes and levees. Biking the dike roads gives you a great view of the array of wildlife present here throughout the year.

Crow Island State Game Area (3580 State Park Dr., Bay City) features 3500 acres on the Saginaw River, intersected by M-13. The area includes emergent wetlands, managed wetland impoundments, grasslands, and agricultural uplands. White pelicans use the area in the summer, and trumpeter swans nest here. Cheboyganing Creek joins the Saginaw River at the northern edge of this marsh complex.

Quanicassee State Wildlife Area (access and parking on North Finn Road and on East Nebobish Road) consists of two tracts on Saginaw Bay east of Bay City. There are miles of marshes and open water shallows with intermittently exposed marsh and mudflats and a boat launch.

Nayanquing Point State Wildlife Area (three miles north of Linwood, take Kitchen Road east from M-13, then north on North Tower Beach Road), a 1,505-acre wildlife area with an observation tower, provides a high-quality and diverse coastal habitat for a variety of recreational opportunities. Despite its small size, tens of thousands of ducks, swans, geese, wading birds, shorebirds, raptors, and songbirds migrate through each fall and spring.

Saginaw River Headwaters Recreation Area (77 W. Center St., Saginaw) is a 334-acre slice of riverside land that was the location of a former GM factory and the Saginaw Malleable Iron foundry. Given to Saginaw County for public use and opened in 2023, it is a place that needs time and careful stewards to regain its health.

Saginaw Basin Land Conservancy

The Saginaw Basin Land Conservancy, serving the entire Saginaw Bay watershed, has restored and rehabilitated hundreds of acres of partner landscapes, helped municipalities improve and maintain parks, and offered critical programming centered on conservation and the environment. Projects like the Saginaw Bay Birding Trail mapped a 142-mile trail from Port Crescent State Park that follows the shoreline of Saginaw Bay, linking all of the natural areas birders are likely to enjoy. The conservancy-managed lands, both urban and rural, are open to the public from dawn until dusk.

Here is a sampling of them.

Points of Interest

The Pinconning Trailhead of the Saginaw Bay Coastal Wildlands network (east of the Pinconning River on the south side of Pinconning Road near Maloney Road) comprises thirty-nine acres that are home to a variety of wetland types, including lowland deciduous forests, scrub and shrub, and emergent marsh. The property is part of a larger conservancy project to link contiguous open spaces, extending from the Saganing River Delta south to the Pinconning River outlets.

Wah Sash Kah Moqua Trailheads of the Saginaw Bay Coastal Wildlands (parking on Bay-Arenac Line Road, four miles east of M-13) is a network in a 123-acre area of former farmland restored to wooded wetlands and grasslands, comprising three separate parcels.

Discovery Preserve at Euclid Park (1701 S. Euclid Ave., Bay City) contains a nature playground with a small play cabin for kids and families.

Michigan Sugar Trails, situated on Middlegrounds Island in Bay City, are located on the west side of Evergreen Road south of the large open field immediately south of the Lafayette Bridge.

Riverbend West Nature Area (480 Marquette St.) in West Bay City is an 8.5-acre rustic site along the Saginaw River with native vegetation near the old Defoe shipyard.

Janet H. Hash Riverfront Preserve in downtown Saginaw sits at the corner of Genesee and Niagara Streets across from the Saginaw United High School (1903 N. Niagara St.).

Rivers of the Saginaw Valley

The rivers of the Saginaw Valley have beautiful Ojibwe names: Shiawassee, Tittabawassee, Cheboyganing, as well as the original name of the Flint River, Pewanogowink, "river of fire stones." The poets of every nation sing their lands and waterways, and the Saginaw Valley had its own river poet in Albert Miller, one of its earliest pioneers. He worked as a trader in Flint, eventually becoming a Bay County judge, and was elected president of the Pioneer Society of the Saginaw Valley when it formed in 1874. He wrote "The Rivers of the Saginaw Valley" (fifteen pages of rhyming verse) in 1889 and read it at that group's annual meeting.

The poem recounts stories of trips taken sixty years before in boats on the Saginaw River and canoes up the Tittabawassee, Shiawassee, Flint, and Cass. Along the way, Miller points out tributaries, explains the meaning of their Indian names, and notes landmarks that he had learned by heart: the old Indian apple tree, the perch of the white owl, a particularly tall butternut tree, a swamp that hid the mouth of Misteguay, and the big lake-river of the inland delta. These functioned as way markers in a watery world of frequent floods. Springtime inundations were predictable and even helpful to the land. But the other kind, the "one-hundred-year" floods—the ones that impacted the entire region—continue to be so memorable that people still mark time by them: 1871, 1904, 1947, 1986, 2020. In 1904, local papers in Saginaw sold postcards with "excellent views" of flooded city streets, but on May 19, 2020, when the Tittabawassee powered through the Edenville and Sanford earthen dams, no one was snapping pictures. The more factories, highways, shopping centers, and housing tracts that covered the landscape, the more residents dreaded floods.

Miller's poem gives us an idea of what these rivers were like in their natural state: messy and full of impassable driftwood blockages that forced men to get out of the river and haul boats and baggage around them. The upstream reaches of the Cass and the South Branch of the Flint are still much as they were in 1830, but the downstream sections of the rivers through urban areas have been dredged and contained by concrete walls and levees.

Stay on the highways and everything is a grid; even farmlands are ditched and diked in monotonous straight lines. Paddle a river, and it will take you into a curved world of refuge, where progress matters less than staying in the stream of things. Fish scull, kingfishers dive, the paddler strokes the water in a heightened state of awareness, making quick judgments, feeling the heart catch at a quickening current or the sight of small rapids. Most paddlers use their canoes and kayaks for escape—a way to vanish or check out for an indeterminate period of unavailability.

While no one would call our rivers wild or pristine, they actually are (save in their urban sections); and because they are so flashy (responsive to rainfall), they provide just the right degree of stimulating frisson for paddlers.

Mistakes Have Been Made River

Amanda Seney

On the day before Thanksgiving, my dear husband and I set out for Cass City, the traditional start of the navigable portion of the Cass. We were armed with a borrowed inflatable two-seater kayak, electric pump with appropriate nozzle adapter, route knowledge pieced together from our own experience and Jerry Dennis and Craig Date's 1986 classic *Canoeing Michigan Rivers*, and a sense of purpose and optimism that was, it turns out, horribly misplaced. But it was unseasonably sunny, and we were pleased with ourselves for playing hooky from holiday preparations and doing something ill-advised instead.

We parked at the pedestrian bridge on River Road, just west of the intersection with Cemetery, and scrambled down the bank with our newly inflated vessel, doing our best to wind between the trees, not into them. (Were we dubious about the kayak? Yes. Did we let that stop us? No. No, we did not.) It was not the easiest river access we've ever managed, but it wasn't the worst, either. In a relatively short time, we were bobbing along with the current.

But it wasn't long before we realized mistakes had been made.

First: The river, often shallow at the best of times, was not at the best of times. The week before it was running high after fall rains, and we hoped to take advantage of the increased flow. By the time we made our trip, however, the river was no longer swollen. We dragged bottom and got hung up several times, each necessitating fraught minutes of scooting, inadvisable use of kayak paddles as poles to push ourselves along, and debate over whether we might actually need to get out and carry the kayak. If we weren't doing our best to avoid getting stuck, or getting ourselves unstuck, we were dodging the boulders that, after an initial uneventful stretch, were large and frequent.

Have I mentioned we are leisure paddlers, at best? Dennis and Craig classify the Cass as a Skill Level I river, and this is mostly true; but this section was turning out to be rather beyond our enjoyment level.

Then it started raining. Cold, end-of-November rain spattered us as the wind roared enthusiastically up the river in the exact opposite direction we wanted to go. We struggled along, getting wetter and wetter. I lost feeling in my hands somewhere around the two-hour mark. It was also around this point that bumping the rough outer fabric of the kayak with each paddle stroke began rubbing the skin off my knuckles. Fortunately, the numbness meant I didn't feel a thing and had no idea there was an issue until I noticed the blood everywhere. I turned to show my dear husband my injury, but he was leaning at a forty-five-degree angle, face to the sky.

"Hey, I think if you pull those straps you can adjust your seat so you're not leaning back so far," I offered.

"I did. This is as tight as they go," he answered, with grim fatalism.

And so it went. The rain rained, the wind blew, the current was nonexistent, and several cold, damp hours later we were only halfway to where we thought we'd be.

"So . . . I'm thinking we should get out here and call my mom for a ride. What do you think?"

"Already planning on it." My dear husband paddled for shore like it was a long-lost relative.

We clambered up the bank, hauling the kayak after us and dumping out the water that had accumulated and in which we had been sitting for the entire journey, the seats not being raised to allow for such unforeseen eventualities. While we waited, soaked and shivering, for our rescuer, we disassembled and deflated the kayak, lurching like Frankenstein on limbs that refused to bend properly.

My hands were stiff for days afterward. One of my knuckles scarred from the hours of abrasion. When we returned the kayak to its owners, we advised them to burn it for closure, and to prevent its evil from spreading.

And that's how the Cass became "Mistakes have been made, and I said I was sorry" River.

The good news is that it isn't always "Mistakes have been made, and I said I was sorry" River. Sometimes it's "Look at the bald eagles!" River, or "Was that a beaver?" River, or "What an excellent way to spend an afternoon" River.

All four of the Saginaw's major tributaries offer excellent paddling, and three (Shiawassee, Cass, and Flint) are nationally designated "Water Trails," along with the Saginaw Bay Blueways Trails, that take you along sections of the bay, enabling access to the Au Gres, Rifle, and Kawkawlin Rivers. There is also a water trail that covers the length of the Saginaw River from Wickes Park to the river's mouth. To access the bay, use the Department of Natural Resources launch (1 Shady Shore Rd., Bay City). To paddle the Saginaw River, launch at Wickes Park (3500 Wickespark Dr.) and be ready for big boat traffic.

Dams were built on all of the tributary rivers to run mills, generate power, create recreational opportunities, and provide flood control; most of the dams have been removed or removal is in process. Portages are required at the Hamilton and Grand Traverse dams (Flint), Frankenmuth and Caro dams (Cass), and Corunna and Chesaning dams (Shiawassee). Michigan law allows you to use private property when necessary to navigate a block in a public waterway, as long as you are minimally invasive while doing so. Your best course is to consult Water Trail maps online to plan your paddle.

Multiday camping excursions are possible on the Shiawassee and the Cass. Walnut Hills (Durand) is the best bet for overnight camping on the Shiawassee; on the Cass, check out either Wesleyan Woods or Riverside Park, both in Vassar.

Cass River

The Cass River, formed by the joining of the north, south, and middle branches north of Cass City in a wetland called the Sanilac Flats, flows southwest through the Thumb until it joins the Shiawassee at M-13. The terrain was once full of pine, elk, and bear; today, its fifty-nine-plus miles meander through farms, woods, and towns, including Frankenmuth, picking up sediment from the fields after rain, branches and trees from the woods after windy days, and the occasional tire from the bridges. The river carries the name of territorial governor Lewis Cass, but the Natives knew it as O-not-o-way-see-bee ("river of the Hurons"). Paddling the Cass can be lovely, serene, and relaxing. A few popular trips on the Cass Water Trail (from M-46 to Wickes Park) include:

- River Road Pedestrian Bridge (Cass City) to Chippewa Landing (Caro)—17 miles, 5–7 hours.
- M-46 Bridge Access to Vassar Canoe and Kayak Launch—6.3 miles, 2–3 hours.
- Vassar Canoe-Kayak Launch to Tuscola Township Park—5.7 miles, 2–3 hours.
- Vassar Canoe-Kayak Launch to Frankenmuth (Heritage Park or Memorial Park)—10.7 miles, 4–6 hours.

Flint River

The Flint River is not mentioned in any of the paddling guides to the rivers of lower Michigan because its reputation was poisoned by GM and the Flint Water Crisis. Truth be told, the seventy-eight-mile Flint offers a range of great trips through varied ecosystems. Its north and south branches, not for the faint of heart, flow through pine and hemlock forests in Lapeer County and converge near Columbiaville. There is a lake and a reservoir, both of which make for excellent fishing; and below the Holloway dam, the river flows through hardwood forests with plentiful wildlife and a range of water birds and raptors. Even the urban section is full of interest. In the 1960s, the Army Corps of Engineers encased the two-mile city section in concrete to prevent flood damage to the city and factory complex. Despite having been manipulated and damaged, the Flint's comeback is something to celebrate. Below Flushing, the current quickens as you paddle, the smell of the water falling over rapids is remarkably fresh, and walleye are once again spawning in the river's middle reach. Once in the Shiawassee Wildlife Refuge, you can follow the natural channel or take the artificial cut that's a straight shot into the "lake." One of the objectives of the wetland restoration, in progress, is to allow the Flint to flow in its historic channel.

To wet your feet in the River of Fire Stones, try these two trips:

- Irish Road to Stanley Road Fishing Site (Mott Lake)—8 miles, 3 hours. The river in this stretch is clean, clear brown water with sandy shorelines, willowed islands, and cattail marshes in the approach to Mott Lake. Takeout is at the fishing pavilion, clearly visible on your left.
- Flushing Park to Barber Park in Montrose—6 miles, 2–3 hours. A gradient drop creates small rapids, and rock bluffs on both banks evoke wilder landscapes. A sandstone monolith standing still in the current is all that remains of Thomas L. L. Brent's dam. Barber Park on your left has a kayak landing and makes for an easy pull out. Just beyond Barber Park is Pewanogowink (now in Taymouth

Township), where the largest band of Natives in our region lived after the Treaty of Saginaw.

Shiawassee River

The Shiawassee River originates in Springfield Township (Oakland County) and flows northwest 110 miles through smaller cities that were once more industrial—Fenton, Owosso, Chesaning—as well as through scenic farm fields, forested floodplains, and embankments. The Shiawassee County segment, from Byron to Chesaning, is picturesque, with plenty of wildlife, welcoming mature forest stands, and good smallmouth bass fishing. Beyond the "country scenic" experience of paddling the Shiawassee, the five river towns (Byron, Vernon, Corunna, Owosso, and Chesaning) have amenities and historical interest to boot.

Three popular trips on the Shiawassee include:

- Geeck Road County Park to Shiatown County Park, 6 miles—2 hours. For the first three miles the river is curving, with a moderate flow, forested, shady, and sparsely settled, with steep embankments rising around the midpoint of the journey. It passes three bridges and a few islands. The last half mile or so is the fast-moving current where the reservoir was drawn down in 2012. There is a noticeable increase in kingfishers upstream from the old reservoir that cackle away while sweeping the shoreline, then perching, and then sweeping again. Historical note: Shiawassee Town was Shig-e-mas-king ("soft maple place") to the Indians and one of the earliest settlements in the county. For a single day, it was Michigan's state capital. A paper town was platted with room for three thousand people, and once the river was dammed, three mills were constructed. Despite these efforts, the town did not develop. Today, Shiatown County Park is a beautiful spot. The river runs swift and splits to flow around an island. On the opposite bank is floodplain prairie with tall grasses—backlit with setting sunlight in the evening, wildflowers, and songbirds. It's an ideal place to finish or start a paddle or spend a few peaceful hours fishing, reading, or just watching the river flow.
- Shiatown County Park to Vernon, then Lytle Road County Park, 7.6 miles—3 hours. The river trip is entertaining, with riffles, rocks, river bends, and occasional tree falls to navigate around. The grade of the river between Shiatown and the Vernon landing is 7.5 feet per mile, which makes for a lively current. The landscapes vary, from tree-lined farm fields and deep forest in floodplains, with the option to stay in the shade for most of the trip.
- Harmon Partridge Park landing to Henderson Road County Park, 7.6 miles—2 hours. A favorite section with paddlers, due to the riffles, turns, fishing "holes,"

faster current, large islands with alternate routes, and steep embankments. Harmon Partridge Park is north of Owosso and accessible via Chippewa Trail, and Henderson Park has two kayak launches on the left bank of the river.

Tittabawassee River

"Pine grew on every valley stream / On Tittabawassee the most was seen," writes Albert Miller; the 72.4-mile Tittabawassee River was the last of these rivers to be lumbered. Once the trees were cut and boom companies dismantled, Green Point, located at the confluence of the Tittabawassee, Shiawassee, and Cass Rivers, was rechristened as a pleasure ground for Saginawians. In 1894, the Union Street Railway built Riverside Park to encourage people to ride the trolley on weekends. The Saginaw Canoe Club, organized in 1904, had their Adirondack-style lodge at the west end of the park. One of its purposes was to promote canoeing as a leisure time activity. There was also a colony of summertime houseboats and a tent city for "camping," all just a stone's throw from a city that was in the process of reinventing itself.

The "Titt," as locals playfully call it, widens significantly below the Tridge—a three- legged pedestrian bridge opened in 1981—which gives walkers an escape from the bustle of everyday, putting them in the place where two rivers converge: Chippewa and Tittabawassee. Above the Dow dam, there is no cause to worry about contamination; below the dam, there is minimal cause for concern since paddlers have limited contact with sediments that hold dioxin contaminants.

There are a number of developed kayak launches on the Tittabawassee, including

- Tridge launch at Chippewassee Park (110 Ashman St.) on the north side of the river in Midland
- The Chippewa Nature Center launch (141 W. Chippewa River Rd.)
- Freeland Launch at Festival Park (10000 Freeland Rd.) on the northwest side of the Tittabawassee by the Freeland Rd. bridge

For other spots to put in, check out the Tittabawassee River Water Trail maps, which can be found readily online. There are also many upstream trips on the Chippewa River. For information, check out the website of Buckley's Mountainside Canoes.

The Tittabawassee experienced a five-hundred-year flood on May 19, 2020. Two upstream earthen dams at Sanford and Edenville, built in 1925 to generate hydroelectric power, gave way after six inches of rainfall. Federal authorities rated the Edenville dam's condition unsatisfactory in 2018, but Boyce Hydro Power, a private company whose out of state owners used the dams as a tax shelter, had failed to make the necessary repairs. When the Tittabawassee burst through her impoundments, she rose thirty-four feet (six feet above the marker for a major flood event) and washed over towns and cities down to Midland, pouring into libraries, museums, and archives.

This flood event, like so many natural disasters in our watershed, brought out the best in the community. "Everybody helped everybody," local businesswoman Connie Methner told Detroit's WXYZ days after the disaster. "Everybody had a smile on their face for everybody. This town has changed!" Sanford started a community bulletin board on Facebook called "Sanford Strong." Water in its ugliest manifestation did what water does: It made a mess and, in doing so, brought people together. Everyone lost all they had, and everyone's houses were full of mud and muck. Amazingly, not a single human life was lost. The dams are being reconstructed to restore the lakes, but the catastrophe reminds us to make room for the rivers, which was the advice Army Corps of Engineers gave Michigan in their 1970 report on the valley's flood problem.

In an age when we are all aware of our carbon footprints, a canoe or kayak is one of the few things in the material world that costs almost nothing to maintain and run. And nothing takes you so far. Speeding along the dark tongues of a current or floating by turtles sunning and herons and egrets fishing, letting yourself be mesmerized by rippling light waves on the undersides of leaves, you can forget every negative thing you've read about Flint and this valley. It's wonderful world when seen from the river—so *carpe diem* and pick a trip.

Hunting and Conservation

The first peoples to occupy our region were hunters and fishers. Their way of life gave them a thorough knowledge of the fish and other fauna that were so plentiful in our waters and on our lands. As late as 1855, the men of Kinne-woop's band in Indianfields Township, Tuscola County, hunted deer and elk. However, by this time, settlers were already clearing farms in the area. Their needs conflicted with those of the Natives, but the settlers were more numerous and powerful, and in any case the Treaty of Saginaw settled what was to be the course of the future. Certain species of wild animals had to be dealt with for settlers to have any chance of establishing farms and raising livestock. In 1837, the state legislature passed an act setting a bounty of $10 on adult wolves and $5 for each whelp under three months. The state payout for wolf bounties between 1840 and 1849 was $9,496, and the state only paid half the fee. Other animals had bounties on their heads, as well, including bobcats, lynx, coyotes, and even rats.

Over time, hunters' techniques and targets have changed, as has the landscape. The French Canadians who settled in the Detroit area in the eighteenth century lived near marshes along the Detroit River and Lake St. Clair. Although some farmed, others relied on hunting ducks and trapping muskrats. By 1820, the land along Lake St. Clair and the St. Clair River was taken, and rather than moving to interior farmland that was sought by migrants from New York, some of these Detroit French moved to the familiar marshland along the western shore of Saginaw Bay, where they continued to hunt and trap. When Alexis de Tocqueville visited Saginaw in 1831, he described the typical Frenchman living there as having adopted the habits, customs, and manners of the Indians: "He wears moccasins, otterskin cap, and woollen cloak. He is an unwearying hunter, sleeps in the open, and lives on wild honey and bison flesh." Because the French preferred to live close to the water, they were dubbed "Muskrat" French in nineteenth-century vernacular and derided by British and Anglo-American officials for being a "lazy idle people, depending chiefly on the savages for their subsistence." Until quite recently, muskrat dinners were served during Lent in Monroe, downriver Detroit, Algonac, and Bay City. The story was that the bishop had given Catholics in downriver Detroit special permission to eat the meat of this aquatic (fish-like) animal during the Lenten fast. Although Monroe and Lake St. Clair are known centers of Muskrat French culture, many think the muskrat belt extends along any regional river that flows into a larger body of water. It most certainly includes the Saginaw and Bay City marshes.

Although the first permanent resident of Bay City, Leon Trombley, came from Detroit in 1831 as a farmer for the Indian band living there, others came to the area as hunters and trappers. Louis DuPraw (DuPrat) came from Detroit around 1830 and found the land so attractive near the Squaconning Creek in Kochville Township, Saginaw County, that he sold his land in Detroit and came north. He grew some crops but mainly hunted and trapped. He had a reputation for courage (killing a bear with a hand axe in a marsh) and endurance (starting over after being flooded out), and his two sons, Louis Jr. and Jacques, were the main market hunters of their time.

Market hunting in nineteenth-century Michigan typically involved hunting for deer or ducks. Using dogs, the hunter would force deer into water, where they became easy targets. They processed the skins for the buckskin trade, saved the antlers, and shipped out the venison to lumber camps and cities. State laws made it illegal in the 1880s, but it was a way of life for Muskrat Frenchmen, who continued shooting ducks and taking them to Detroit restaurants into the 1950s, when agents made many arrests of the Sears and LaParl families in the St. Clair Flats. Some Bay City men started the "Muskrat Club" in the 1970s to keep alive the tradition of eating muskrat, and "marsh rabbit" was also on the menu at a diner on McGraw Street, last known as the List Lounge.

As late as the 1850s, the Thumb's population of the now extinct eastern subspecies of elk attracted hunters, like Oliver Hazard Perry of Cleveland. Elkton, in Huron County, and Elk Township, in Sanilac County, were named for the animal. Museums in Millington and Otisville have elk horns found at the bottom of local lakes, and the Watrousville museum possesses a mounted trophy set. This majestic animal, however, was last seen in the area in 1880 in Huron County, and the subspecies went extinct a few years later.

The laws prohibiting market hunting resulted from efforts by another category of hunter. These men were generally wealthy city residents who formed clubs in part to preserve land for hunting and fishing. Some of the key hunting grounds along the Saginaw Bay, where private and some public hunters' lodges were established, were Bay Port and Wildfowl Bay, Weale and the Middle Grounds, Rose Island and Shook Island, the Sebewaing area, Fish Point, the Quanicassee River and shoreline area, Breezy Point, Saginaw River and Crow Island, the Nayanquing Point area, and Wigwam Bay and the Rifle River. In this period, from roughly 1870 to 1950, duck hunting reigned supreme.

William B. Mershon personifies the elite hunter of this era. His 1923 memoir describes the Saginaw-area marshes, like Mishtegay, Ferguson Bayou, Crow Island, Cheboyganing, and Squaconning, as his favorite hunting grounds. However, he also valued the low and wet "swamp" found in hardwood forests once frequented by native wild turkeys; prairies stalked for bobwhite quail and partridge; wood bayous and lagoons along the Tittabawassee, where woodcock lurked in shadowy places; and the dense forests skirting West Saginaw that drew flocks of passenger pigeons from nesting grounds around Sebewaing.

Having lived through the clear-cutting of both white pine and later oak forests to make way for settlement and urbanization, Mershon saw how such processes damaged the landscape he loved, rendering it smooth as a billiard table with interurban rail lines rattling, slappety-bang, through the very heart of duck country. Once waterlogged, too much had been drained, diked, and crisscrossed with wire fencing. Loss of trees meant loss of food. Passenger pigeons that thrived on hardwood mast eventually became extinct. Birds, waterfowl, and animals lost cover and nesting sites. Some species were overhunted and others, like bears, moved on in search of wilderness. Mershon remembers seeing bears coming into the city in the fall of 1871, when fires raged through the Thumb and the smoke was fog thick. If the extinction of mammals and birds wasn't bad enough, wealthy men began introducing invasive fish. Mershon's father planted trout that cannibalized the grayling, his son's favorite food and game fish.

Draining swamps and marshland caused waterfowl to diminish in number, and market hunting depleted the region's deer. Deer might have increased after the fire of 1881, as new browse became available, but it did not happen. Around 1885, no whitetail deer were left in the southern half of the Lower Peninsula. By 1900, one needed to mount an expedition to remote parts of the Upper Peninsula to hunt deer, something limited to those with means.

The frontispiece of Mershon's memoir is a photograph of a wild turkey he killed in 1886, captioned "The Last of His Race." Mershon was no fool; though he blamed species extinction on habitat loss, he could see what he and his cronies had done to native species and had the courage to own up to it. "Future generations should have hunting and fishing. . . . These incentives to the life out of doors should be perpetuated," he writes. "It is late, very late—but not altogether too late to make the start."

The Migratory Bird Treaty Act of 1916 helped. Bans on deer hunting by county started in 1893 for various periods of time, and in 1933, it was outlawed in all the counties in our region. These bans allowed the deer population to increase, so that in 1948, the entire state of Michigan was opened for deer hunting. In the 1940s, the state created refuges (which Mershon had recommended) and game areas. The eighteen in our region gained importance as both waterfowl and deer hunting grew in popularity in postwar Michigan.

Game birds were severely reduced in number during the nineteenth century. Heath hens became extinct and bobwhite quail nearly so. Today we have turkeys, ring-necked pheasants, and ruffed grouse. Federal law allows snipe, rails, and woodcock to be hunted, but few hunt them anymore. Ring-necked pheasants were imported from China in 1895, and the state began a breeding facility in 1917 near Mason that distributed eggs to farmers, who in turn hatched and released them. Family farms proved to be ideal for these birds, which were a hybrid variety of English and Chinese pheasants. Orville Chapin of Pigeon, a teacher, farmer, and surveyor, received three hundred eggs from the Michigan Department of Conservation in 1918, which he hatched and nurtured until mature enough to be released. Other Thumb locals remember hearing that pheasants were released from trains. Hunting them was allowed in 1925, and by the 1950s, they were so common and hunting them so popular that the local schools closed on opening day of pheasant season. Then a decline set in due to habitat depletion caused by urbanization and sprawl along with scaled-up farming, with large fields planted almost road to road, instead of small fields with fence rows and pastures with brushy wetlands. Attempts by the state to introduce other varieties of pheasants, like the Sichuan, have yet to reach success.

Deer hunting, meanwhile, increased from 1948 to 1982, evidenced by state hunting license applications. In our region it was so popular that planning for vacations during the annual deer season (November 15–30) became a priority for auto factory management. A national contract negotiated by the United Auto Workers in 1999 included a paid Veterans Day holiday on a Monday (the first day of firearms deer season), rather than on Thursday, the official national holiday. By the postwar era, Michigan autoworkers had developed a collective consciousness about their rights to the land. In 1957, when a Republican legislature was preparing to get Governor G. Mennen Williams to sign a bill for the creation of private game preserves with longer hunting seasons and virtually no restrictions, the Michigan CIO asked Williams to veto the bill. The president of the Michigan CIO Council criticized the bill as "classist" and expressed rank-and-file worries that the best bird areas would be gobbled up by preserves for the elite.

Increasing wages and prosperity, as well as the completion of I-75, led to the recreational development of areas in northern Michigan during this period. People

Waterfowling's Final Frontier

Tom Huggler

The late Al Davis, of Columbiaville, Michigan, lived to hunt ducks. Davis worked the second shift at an auto factory in Flint so he could be in the marsh on Saginaw Bay or on the flats of Lake St. Clair a hundred miles from home before dawn the next morning. When sleep deprivation took over—as it always does with rabid waterfowlers—Davis would float rivers close to home in his aluminum canoe, but he never fell asleep at the paddle. He left that task to me.

One such trip occurred years ago on a day deep into October when Davis and I floated the Flint River from his sixteen-foot Smokercraft. I sat cross-legged in the bow, a 20-gauge double barrel across my knees, and tried to keep a wary eye open for ducks, as Davis kept the canoe on course with deft paddle flicks from the stern.

But I found it hard to concentrate on duck hunting that morning. Five minutes from the parking lot was time enough to drown out road noise, and soon I had put telephones and typewriters out of my mind. Adding to my reverie were gold and red maple leaves that swirled in the brown current and pockets of fog that curled like campfire smoke above the bubbling stream. The patchy fog, in particular, rendered a dreamlike atmosphere to the morning, and it was fitting to think back to earlier times when this same river had borne me along as a schoolboy trapper and fisherman.

I thought about the wood ducks, herons and deer that were in such short supply here when I was a kid but that were much more plentiful now. I thought about the sandbars where we camped, the bonfires that sputtered all night, the bullheads and mud puppies we snaked from the dark stream. I got so wrapped up in remembering things of the past that it seemed entirely possible that the man in the stern, moving us along with silent, steady strokes, was not my friend at all but rather my dad. I was thirteen again, legs shivering in hip boots, eyes watering from the November wind in my face, the mug of cocoa (now coffee) cradled between my hands and growing tepid too fast.

A beaver swimming nearby cracked the water with its tail like a pistol shot and then dived. Al's ninety-pound yellow Lab, John, leaped from the canoe as though fired from a slingshot, and my heart jumped into my throat. Somehow Davis kept the canoe from flipping and then ordered John back into the boat.

Five minutes later, I missed the first pair of wood ducks—a colorful drake and a hen with white eye patch. They scuttled down the bank, leaped into the river and were aloft before I could react.

"You gotta be quick," Al reminded me. "Keep your gun halfway up on the turns. Pretend you're a kid playing with marbles, hunching over the ring. Steady and ready—that's the key to float hunting."

When we switched places, the edgy birds seemed to become more concentrated. Singles and pairs that we spooked rocketed downstream to join other ducks, and during the last mile of our float we were putting as many as a dozen woodies in the air at once. I had never before experienced such a spectacle of color—the autumn sun bouncing off the drake's burnished colors of red, white, and purple. Al shot his two-bird limit, and then I scored twice, too.

"Rivers are the final frontier for duck and goose hunters," he used to say, "because nobody hunts 'em."

That experience and others opened my eyes to the enormous potential awaiting waterfowlers. Rivers are the earth's arteries, and the blood supply seems inexhaustible. Michigan has thirty-six thousand miles of navigable waterways. Many of these are ideal for float hunting, because ducks and geese use them for migratory corridors and to rest and feed in spring and fall. Geese often nest on islands and along points, and puddle ducks in particular like the bayous and pool areas formed by oxbows and switchbacks. Heavy rainfall that sends rivers over their banks floods the timbered bottom lands that wood ducks and mallards find so attractive. Thousands of local puddlers, including teal, pintails and black ducks, raise their families on these waterways and sometimes never see a human being until they migrate south in the fall.

I like a canoe for negotiating the smaller streams I favor, because the craft are light, quiet, and easy to handle in tight spots. A fourteen- or fifteen-foot canoe is large enough for one hunter; for two, use a canoe at least sixteen feet long. Only the bow hunter should shoot. The stern paddler should keep his gun unloaded and his mind on keeping the canoe upright.

Puddle ducks that use rivers all season long—and even unsophisticated diving ducks in the late season—are usually smart, and getting close enough for flushes within range requires patience and stealth. By early fall, waterfowl that have survived the dangers associated with growing up on a river—snapping turtles, eagles, coyotes, and large owls—are plenty wary. The area where they live probably contributes to their vigilance, because field of vision is limited along a heavily wooded waterway. I don't think I've ever encountered a stupid small stream duck.

"I swear I heard a duck stretch his wings," whispered Al Davis, as he hunched lower in the bow. Dense fog wafted from the mud-colored water as our canoe sliced quietly downstream, while I corrected course with a paddle turn here and there from my seat in the stern.

On another morning in October, sunshine fought to penetrate three feet of dense fog that blanketed the stream like wet wool. This time we were floating the Shiawassee River for puddlers and hoping the fog would allow us to creep close to resting ducks. Suddenly I heard the sound of a duck running on water, trying to get airborne. The wet smacks of webbed feet gave way to frantic quacking, and then a drake mallard, emerald head as polished as a billiard ball, punched up for the open sky. Al dropped him, cleanly, with a single shot from his 12-gauge pump.

"A river never sleeps," wrote Roderick Haig-Brown, but I often do, especially when I'm carried along by water that passes this way once. The way I look at it, nothing out there is more graceful than a river, and fluidity is everything. But on this dreamlike morning sleep was impossible. After all, it was my turn in the bow.

---

bought cabins and lakeside cottages to which they retired on weekends and vacations to get as far away as possible from the clanking din of factories. Hunting and fishing were the working man's response to blue-collar blues. Union newspapers from this period were full of advertisements offering cabins and tracts of land, snowmobiles, fishing boats, and off-road vehicles. One only needs to see the traffic on I-75 on the first or third day of three-day weekends to see what people intend to do on their short breaks from work.

Hunting and fishing remain popular, even ritualized, pastimes for many in our region. Local writer Tom Huggler, who grew up hunting pheasants after school in the fields in Genesee Township and trapping mink on the Flint River, thinks most hunters come to care about being "out there" more than the number of points on a buck's antlers. Even so, Michiganders are in no hurry to trade in their rods and guns for notebooks and cameras. The year 2020 was a banner year in the sale of hunting licenses—about 2.5 million, third highest in the nation, although participation numbers are falling again, most likely due to the aging of Boomers and the prevalence of technology. With fewer hunters in the field, the deer population has exploded, and that has created serious problems for local farmers. This reality confirms Huggler's point that participation in the life and death of "wild things" is one of the ways human beings help preserve balance in the vast ecosystem of parts that mesh together.

Oak Openings

The quotation I have held onto longest and put into a tiny frame was typed onto a scrap of paper, covered with laminate, and tacked under the cedar eaves of The Nature House (an oft-visited interpretive center in the Jersey Pine Barrens): "Conservation is Not Enough; the Thing that is Missing is Love." By the time I discovered that this was truth and pulled out the loose nail to claim it as my own, the naturalist who wanted these words remembered had left the world. But the door into nature that The Nature House opened never closed. Its artifacts, specimens, and words, assembled to demonstrate the dependence of each living thing in an ecosystem on every other, were among many inspirations for this guide. Places speak through the harmony of their features; but, in a Rust Belt landscape, ecosystem harmonies have been disrupted for over a century. Recovery requires discovery and preservation of remnants from which we can imagine, extrapolate, and then recreate an *oikos* (the Greek word meaning "home," which is the root of "ecosystem").

I arrived in Flint in 1996 when factory whistles still blew shift changes and LeSabres still rolled off the Buick City assembly line. My husband and I, both transplants, drank at Bottom Street across from Chevy in the Hole and took long walks through all sections of the city. As we learned about Flint by walking and reading, we were behaving like "cultural cowbirds," making other birds' nests our own. When the factories closed, Flint citizens, even those of us not affected directly, could think and talk of little else but GM, unemployment, arson, blight, and problems, nothing but problems. Scrambling to understand the new postindustrial reality, some of us forgot the sky and lost track of the ground. But because, sooner or later, all of us must go to ground and because we need not only see differently but find different things to see, let this, our last tour, be one where you meet some grand arboreal survivors, remnants of an original landscape type called "oak openings" or, in modern terminology, "oak savanna."

Oak openings were clusters of bur and white oak, spaced wide enough apart that they allowed horse-drawn wagons of immigrants to move between the trees with ease.

The title of James Fenimore Cooper's Michigan novel *Oak Openings: Or the Bee Hunter* (1847) is curious for the way it makes the human protagonist secondary to the book's true hero—the landscape. "These openings," explains the novel's narrator, "had not the character of ordinary forests. The air circulates freely beneath their oaks, the sun penetrates in a thousand places, and grass grows, wild but verdant." Natives planted crops in the openings and settlers followed their lead, rejoicing that they had less work to do clearing land for farms. In the novel, the openings serve as meeting places for disparate characters of the Northwest Territory—Frenchman, Yankee, Chippewa and Potawatomi—who, as they exchange knowledge (of beelining and shifting tribal allegiances) and cooperate to harvest wild honey, develop frontier community. Cooper set the book in Kalamazoo County where he owned land, but travelers to and through Genesee County said similar things about the openings in our area (specifically around Fenton, extending north into Mundy Township): "Through the oak openings . . . the ground was really beautiful with flowers, filling the air with fragrance."

Even in the City of Flint today, there are remnants of oak openings. An obvious one is on the grounds of the Flint Institute of Arts and Gloria Coles Flint Public Library, former site of the Oak Grove Sanitarium, and another on the wide lawns of the former Michigan School for the Deaf (now Powers Catholic High School). Glenwood Cemetery is thick with oaks, as are three amazing parks in the North End: Max Brandon, Bassett, and Oak Knoll. The north bluff of the Flint River (behind Atwood Stadium) is populated by a community of oaks that was named Mus-cu-ta-wa-ningh ("burned-over plain") by the Indigenous people who once used fire to clear a place to grow corn and other crops.

Wherever the search for openings takes you, make a point to visit the two bur oaks standing in the bottomland along Gilkey Creek on either side of the Court Street bridge (Burroughs Park near the road and next to the ruins of the Apprentice Building behind Whittier Junior High School). Bur oaks are easily recognized by their irregular waxy leaves and thick crusts of corky bark—an adaptation to the fires used to clear land. Trunk circumferences of 184 and 154 inches tells us that these two trees are 280 and 245 years old. "One of the remarkable things about wood," writes Eric Sloane, "is its self-expression. . . . It is always telling something about itself." The branches of these two comrades twist and contort as if occasions of weather over the centuries forced each to grow in new directions, and yet the tree on the north appears to lean toward its fellow, pulled, perhaps, by interconnected roots.

As you spend time in these groves of trees that stand together and apart, it is an easy metaphorical leap to see in them the people of Flint who have also survived many five-alarm fires. I am thinking about the water activists who camped in Kearsley Park for a six-month period during the Water Crisis under a homemade sign made of tree limbs that said "Pure Michigan, Pure Bullshit." They were inspired by the nonviolent protest of the Sit-Down strikers of 1936–1937. Communities are forged in struggle, they grow up in groves, and more than a few college students have noticed that Flint

"Tent city" at Oak Park, Flint, c. 1912. THE SLOAN MUSEUM ARCHIVES PHOTOGRAPH COLLECTION, SMOD_1970.103.196_001, SLOAN MUSEUM ARCHIVES.

has more openings than other places to participate in community-building. More openings because more need to reach out to those neglected figures, marginalized by color, poverty, old age, or mental illness. Elizabeth—troubled and unhoused, who may have served in Afghanistan but took a bullet through a breast on Dort Highway ("My boob job saved me!")—still believes she is the Holy Spirit on a mission to teach Flint how to make everything they need from leaves. Clara B's ninety-some year-old Aunt Mary, when asked why she would not go to an old age home, replied, "Because living in a place with only one kind of people is unnatural." Eric, from the group home on Avon, wrote his "girl" a daily love letter and panhandled for enough change to buy her a pop—everyday. Learning to see such virtuous souls who, "like seasoned timber never give," leads to affection and stewardship. Not knowing guarantees loss.

Case in point is Oak Park, Flint's first city park, an opening on the edge of the Buick City brownfield, cut down in March 2025. Imagine: A whole grove of trees fell in a city and no one heard them. It is possible because we live in silos and have no local journalism, no reporters to wake us up like the town criers of old. A few families who had once lived in the Oak Park neighborhood (cleared during 1980s urban renewal), spoke out about their attachment to these trees and to this park. Had more people known enough to care, public outcry might have prevented the decommissioning of the park fourteen years ago, its sale to Ashley Capital, and its destruction for no good reason. "It was like grief when over twenty trees were turned into wood chips," said one resident, who condemned city hall for selling a public asset and a piece of Flint's history. Those trees witnessed an industry's rise and fall, provided shelter for workers who lived in tents while houses were being built, gave people a place to recreate, and, later when the neighborhood was erased, kept vigil and continued to provide visual pleasure. Now there is just a metal box on a parking lot that tires the eyes and seems to go on for miles and miles of unrelieved desolation. You can visit the three trees that remain at the top of North Street off Hamilton (turn across from the Lear Corporation).

I will always remember Oak Park as a respite on a pilgrimage made with a class of University of Michigan–Flint freshmen. They wandered on the paths between the trees and, looking out over the 413-acre brownfield and spoke about the feeling of being at sea. There were even seagulls swooping and diving down into the waves of mud, looking for scraps. The trees felt like a sacred grove that day, and they encouraged me to read out bits and pieces from Isaiah 61, because the passage fit the place so well: "Those who mourn in Zion," you are "oaks of righteousness, the planting of the Lord." It is you who will build up the ancient ruins, raise up the former devastations, and repair the ruined cities—the devastations of many generations.

Deforestation was the original sin against the land of lower Michigan: trees were cut to clear it for settlement, then for farming, and finally for big business, but the lumber boom lasted forty years. The auto boom in the Flint and Saginaw area lasted barely one hundred. These days, urban renewal continues fast and furious under the new name of blight clearance, which amounts to developers working tirelessly to return much of Flint to Mus-cu-ta-wa-ningh. To keep clients and students feeling safe, Hurley Hospital and Kettering University took out a neat row of nineteenth-century workers' houses associated with the old Stone woolen mill. Ridged like clam shells, they stood along Stone Street near Atwood Stadium. There might be one left.

As the work of redevelopment makes Flint in places feel more rural than much of rural America, farmland—finite and precious—continues to be paved over. Once transformed for industry, it can never be cultivated again. The public was up in arms for over a year about the land grab in Mundy Township: two square miles of farm fields, hardwoods, wetlands, homes and a school have already been ruined to develop a megasite for a high-tech production facility. Progress was halted, temporarily, due to wetlands violations in the spring of 2025 and just a month or so later, the company backed out of the deal, even though they were getting the site for free and billions in incentive money from the State of Michigan. The Flint and Genesee Group is moving forward to market the site to another industrial firm, despite the trauma residents feel whether impacted directly (forced out of homes by eminent domain) or indirectly (losing the peace and quiet of a rural area).

Local people, struggling to stay informed in the post-newspaper-era, have good ideas. "I'm not against the megasite," said a Genesee Township resident in a doctor's office waiting room, "I'm against where they are placing it. Why not tear down the dead mall a mile away and build it there?" Or why not develop the former AC Spark Plug site on Dort Highway in Flint? The explanation generally given is cost: a fresh build on cleared land is better for the bottom line. But with rural land prices skyrocketing in Michigan largely due to economic development initiatives like the Mundy Township megasite and the hyperscale data center in Saline Township, developers ought to reconsider the possibilities of urban brownfields. If new industrial ventures could occupy old industrial sites, it would save productive farmland and bring people and businesses back to Flint and Saginaw. The green energy land rush for wind- and solar-farm sites threatens farmers in all our counties, and even puts the wild lands of the eastern Thumb at risk. Local people in and around the town of Minden are upset about Detroit Edison's plans to put a solar farm in the middle of Minden Bog, which will ruin five hundred acres of a unique bog ecosystem. They know it makes no sense and are dismayed by neighbors eager to sell out but angry at the Democratic state government who are not being good stewards of protected state lands. "When a hail storm wrecks the solar panels like one just did in Saginaw County, they'll never get them out of the bog," said a Deckerville man.

Corporate behavior is all too predictable. General Motors, the Flint and Genesee Group, DTE—they will go on doing what growth machines do: increase the modular footprint, build on and fill in every opening. But dwellers in the land must do what human beings evolved to do: activate the seeking systems in our brains to find life and understand the conditions and connections that breed and support it. Discovery begins by noticing, appreciating, learning, valuing. Then, regeneration will begin to happen from the ground up, as it must. This guide points out oaks and artifacts, people and occupations, folk heroes, poets, and their songs; but it also leaves space for you, dear reader, to discover your own openings, explore the avenues, cast out a baited line, walk in a new direction, grab a paddle or your car keys. Do it without overthinking, do it to learn and grow in a new direction, do it so that it can never be said of our region in fifty years or one hundred that "the thing that was missing was love."

EPILOGUE

I heard the bank foreclosed on Harmony Manor and was worried about the residents of this group home, who were my friends. My dog pulled me toward the dead end, following a scent, and I dreaded seeing nobody smoking on the porch or sitting in the circle of lawn chairs. There was somebody though, not at the manor but in front of the abandoned house, colored like wet earth, dropping clothes from a trash bag into a fire. She eyed me through the flames. Elizabeth? Is that you? I've looked for you everywhere. She is downcast—sullen—although the blue hat she wears, standing up with a pompom, makes her look like a clown.

"You're the teacher. Don't you care that your neighbors are disappearing? All these houses are empty. Someone is taking all the people. Gone. Gone. Gone. What *do* you care about? I discovered I'm the Holy Spirit, but I need crack to do my work, and they want to take that away from me, too."

She palms a small, blackened pipe, unzips a dirty pouch, and pulls out a small rock that looks like a petrified tear.

"Sit down and smoke with me."

I wish I could but I'm afraid.

"Afraid of what?—of being happy?" She asks and answers her question because she knows I don't know. The know-nothing white teacher.

"Got a lighter?"

I fished one out of my pocket and offered to hold her Bible, noticing the annotations, while she holds the flame to the end of the pipe. The crack did what it does. I flipped pages and wound up in the Book of Job. Then I started talking out loud like I do when I'm teaching, "My favorite part is—the animals—because they live outside all orders but God loves them because they are wild and he can't control them." "The animals!" she echoes, eyes shining.

Behemoth. Leviathan. How do you picture that one? I ask.

"Like a panther."

Hm. I see it more like a dragon.

"I saw a dragon last week on Welch Boulevard near the garden of Eden."

I invite her to Sister Christina's women's group, thinking a Black sister might be able to speak to her troubles better than I could, but she snaps back, "If you really want to help me, buy me some more crack." But I can't do that, so I go home and think of something I can do. I scribble her a note, reminding her she's loved, tuck it into Mr. Rogers's *Friends*, a thin paperback perpetually sliding off the pile of kids' books leftover from when my daughter was little, and leave it on the porch with a hot cross bun on top in case the Holy Spirit gets hungry. As usual I have no idea what I'm doing.

"I found you"—she says when our paths cross later that night, towering over me, close, aglow with expectation. "I got your note; thank you for the cake. If you give me just a few dollars, I'll have enough." To buy crack? "Yeah." Meeting no resistance, she smiles big, "I can tell you the truth!" She holds Panda's leash, while I slip inside to get a few bills, and fold them into her hand. Not bothering to count, she grabs my arm and together we skip down the street like school friends. "One day, I am going to rent Raspberries and Rhythm, and we'll have gatherings where people can rap the Bible. You'll smoke crack with me. I'll write five articles for the New York Times. Sure, I can do it. Are you crazy? Even a monkey can do it." Her happy talk rises over the street, while somewhere down below and back in time, I recall her saying, "Faith is stepping out into nothing. That's where Jesus met his best friend, Peter."

"Come back and sit with me!," she hollers, crossing the street to her connection.

After I finish the dog walk and carry Panda up the porch steps, I head down to the spooky house expecting ebullience though the rain is falling harder. She's there, but the fire is out and she has dumped her backpack looking for cigarettes. I kneel down to collect her things and put it all back in her pack: the two Bibles, the mallet, wire, screwdriver, cards for reading the ground, the red ball, the packages of crushed Girl Scout cookies. Mr. Rogers's *Friends*. But no cigarettes. I bum one from Cindy Jo, the last person left in the Group Home, who stands in the cracked doorway concerned. It doesn't matter that she never makes sense; she is kind. I go back to Elizabeth's porch and sit down to watch the puddles on Court Street flash yellow, red, green, while she smokes and talks about rapes and dog rapes and a video that went all around the North End, and God's "issues"—how the job he gave her is too big. I rub her back. "I am always alone. I don't have any friends." My hand becomes my mother's hand or the hands of Montessori women who put the children down for naps by rubbing backs.

You can take a break, Holy Spirit, and just be Elizabeth.

Although I remember saying that, what I felt was something entirely different, something like awe that a woman who has nothing believes she is everything. She prays for the spirits in the empty houses, tells people there is more to life than "pursuing comfortability," and sings loudly her version of the Flintstones jingle, changing "modern stone-age family" to "modern kind of family"—Crayola crayons in the same box, "cuz the forty acres and a mule they promised us was bullshit. There is so much work, and we can do it, but first we gotta learn how to be neighbors again."

APPENDIX

AUTHORSHIP CREDITS

Part I. The General Background

Natural Setting .... *Martin M. Kaufman*
An Archaeological Journey .... *Beverley A. Smith*
The Indigenous People After Settlement .... *Paul M. Gifford*
Migration and Immigration .... *Paul M. Gifford*
The Automobile Industry .... *Ted McClelland*
The Rise and Fall of Buick City .... *Thomas F. Adams*
Race and Flint's Water Crisis .... *Katrinell Davis*
Regional Literature .... *William David Barillas*

Part II. Cities

Flint and Genesee County

Profile .... *Mary Jo Kietzman and Paul M. Gifford*
Politics .... *Paul Rozycki*

Neighborhoods

The North End .... *Mary Jo Kietzman*
The East Side .... *Mary Jo Kietzman*
The West Side .... *Mary Jo Kietzman*
The South Side .... *Connor Coyne, Bob Campbell, and Paul M. Gifford*
Little Missouri .... *Mary Jo Kietzman*
Flint's Suburbs .... *Mary Jo Kietzman and Paul M. Gifford*

Saginaw

Profile .... *Mary Jo Kietzman and Samuel Fitzpatrick*
Shaping Their Community: Black Americans in East Saginaw .... *Jennifer Vannette*

The Look for America Tour on STARS Route 7 .... *William Wright*
The Theodore Roethke Home Museum ..... *Jeff Vande Zande and Mary Jo Kietzman*
Backwater Burbs .... *Mary Jo Kietzman and Paul M. Gifford*

Bay City

Profile .... *Samuel Fitzpatrick, Mary Jo Kietzman, and Paul M. Gifford*
St. Stanislaus Kostka Church .... *Tony Groulx and Mary Jo Kietzman*
Tobico Marsh .... *Tony Groulx*
Kawkawlin, Linwood, Pinconning .... *Mary Jo Kietzman and Paul M. Gifford*
Women's Work .... *Mary Jo Kietzman*

Midland

Profile .... *Mary Jo Kietzman and Paul M. Gifford*
Overlook Park: At the Depocenter .... *Zachary Scott*
Up the Tittabawassee .... *Paul M. Gifford*

Port Huron

Profile .... *Mary Jo Kietzman and Bre Moore*
The Black River Greenway .... *Eric J. Girgenti*
Northern St. Clair County .... *Mary Jo Kietzman*

Part III. Rural Locales

The German Belt .... *Mary Jo Kietzman and Paul M. Gifford*

Shiawassee County

Owosso .... *Paul M. Gifford and Mary Jo Kietzman*
Flint Writer Kelsey Ronan Visits Owosso .... *Kelsey Ronan*
Corunna .... *Mary Jo Kietzman*
Durand .... *Paul M. Gifford and Mary Jo Kietzman*
Byways and Ghost Towns .... *Mary Jo Kietzman and Paul M. Gifford*

Lapeer County

Lapeer .... *Brittany Grabetz*
Northern Lapeer County .... *Mary Jo Kietzman and Paul M. Gifford*
Southern Lapeer County .... *Mary Jo Kietzman*

Farming the Saginaw Valley .... *Mary Jo Kietzman*

Part IV. Tours

The Thumb

Coastal Tour .... *Mary Jo Kietzman and Bre Moore*
Petroglyphs to Otter Lake Tour .... *Amanda Seney and Mary Jo Kietzman*
Middle Thumb Tour .... *Mary Jo Kietzman*
Flint to Shay Lake: History of a Black Resort in the Middle of
White Michigan .... *Bob Campbell*

Restoring Our Waterland

Shiawassee Flats .... *Mary Jo Kietzman*
Saginaw Bay .... *Mary Jo Kietzman*
Saginaw Valley Field Trips .... *Mary Jo Kietzman*
Saginaw Basin Land Conservancy .... *Trevor Edmunds*
Rivers of the Saginaw Valley .. *Mary Jo Kietzman, Amanda Seney, and Phil Hathaway*
Hunting and Conservation .... *Mary Jo Kietzman and Paul M. Gifford*
Oak Openings .... *Mary Jo Kietzman*

Epilogue .... *Mary Jo Kietzman*

Sidebars

Harry Dunn .... *Public Domain*
Flint Cultural Center .... *Paul M. Gifford and Mary Jo Kietzman*
The Crim .... *Paul M. Gifford*
Statue City .... *Paul M. Gifford*
Among Children .... *Philip Levine*
Feed Five Thousand .... *Artist Relford*
Mother Flint .... *Jina Bhagat*
Shanty Boy Monroe .... *Public Domain*
The Saginaw Song .... *Theodore Roethke*
Midwestern Poetics .... *Charles Baxter*
Meeting a "Troster" .... *Mary Jo Kietzman*
Fieldstone Houses .... *Paul M. Gifford and Mary Jo Kietzman*
The Thoreau of Murphy Lake .... *Mary Jo Kietzman*
Shiloh .... *June Wollstonecraft*
Mistakes Have Been Made River .... *Amanda Seney*
Waterfowling's Final Frontier .... *Tom Huggler*

BIBLIOGRAPHY

"Der Abfall der Gemeinde Shebahyongk." *Kirchliche Mittheilungen aus und über Nord-Amerika* 9 (1854): 65–70.

Aiyer, Ananthakrishnan. *Telling Our Stories: Legacy of the Civil Rights Movement in Flint.* N.p.: The Flint ColorLine Project, 2007.

Anderson, William. *Michigan's Marguerite de Angeli: The Story of Lapeer's Native Author-Illustrator.* Lapeer, MI: Marguerite de Angeli Library, 1987.

Alvi, Irfan A., and Isabelle S. Alvi. "Why Dams Fail: A Systems Perspective and Case Study." *Civil Engineering and Environmental Systems*, 40, no. 3 (2023): 150–75. https://doi.org/10.1080/10286608.2023.2283704.

Anderson, Michelle. "The New Minimal Cities." *Yale Law Journal* 123, no. 5 (2014): 1118–227.

Appelbaum, Yoni. *Stuck: How the Privileged and the Propertied Broke the Engine of American Opportunity.* New York: Random House, 2025.

Arbogast, Alan F., and T. P. Jameson. "Age Estimates of Inland Dunes in East-Central Lower Michigan Using Soils Data." *Physical Geography* 19, no. 6 (1998): 485–501.

Arndt, Leslie E. *The Bay County Story: Memoirs of the County's 125 Years.* Linwood, MI: Published by the author, 1982.

Atkinson, Scott, ed. *Happy Anyway: A Flint Anthology.* Cleveland: Belt Publishing, 2016.

Atlas of Genesee Co. Michigan. New York: F. W. Beers, 1873.

Atlas of Saginaw Co. Michigan. New York: F. W. Beers, 1877.

Baierlein, E. R. *In the Wilderness with the Red Indians.* Translated by Anita Z. Boldt. Detroit: Wayne State University Press, 1996.

Banner, Melvin. *The Black Pioneer in Michigan.* Midland, MI: Pendell Publishing, 1973.

Barillas, William. "Michigan's Pioneers and the Destruction of the Hardwood Forest." *Michigan Historical Review* 15 (Fall 1989): 1–22.

———. *The Midwestern Pastoral: Place and Landscape in Literature of the American Heartland.* Athens: Ohio University Press, 2006.

Barnett, LeRoy. "Michigan War with Mammals: Bounties, Hunters, and Trappers Against Unwanted Species." *Michigan Historical Review* 37, no. 1 (2011): 77–117.

Bennett, C. L., Lawrence Atwell Ryel, and Louis J. Hawn. *A History of Michigan Deer Hunting.* N.p.: Michigan Department of Conservation, 1966.

Berry, Wendell. *The Unsettling of America: Culture & Agriculture.* San Francisco: Sierra Club Books, 1977.

———. "What Liberal Elites Don't Know About Rural Americans Can Hurt Us: The *New York*

Review of Books Strikes Out, Again." *Barn Raiser*, https://barnraisingmedia.com/wendell-berry-new-york-review-of-books-rural-america/.

Beynon, Erdman Doane. "Assyrians and Druses and Their Antecedents." *Geographical Review* 34, no. 2 (1944): 259–74.

———. "The Southern White Laborer Migrates to Michigan." *American Sociological Review* 3 (1938): 333–43.

Blois, John T. *1838 Gazetteer of the State of Michigan*. 1838. Facsimile. Knightstown, IN: The Bookmark, 1979.

Boggs, Brian J., and M. Jean Sloan. *Depot Dreams: A Compilation of Stories, Life, and History of Durand Union Station*. N.p.: n.d.

Bowes, John P. *Land Too Good for Indians: Northern Indian Removal*. Norman: University of Oklahoma Press, 2016.

Brainerd, Alvah. *A Pioneer History of the Township of Grand Blanc, Genesee County, Michigan*. 1878. Repr., Mount Pleasant: Central Michigan University by the University Press, n.d.

Brakefield, Catherine Ulrich. *Images of America: The Lapeer Area*. Charleston, SC: Arcadia Publishing, 2006.

Brandt, E. N. *Growth Company: Dow Chemical's First Century*. East Lansing: Michigan State University Press, 1997.

Brashler, Janet G., and Margaret B. Holman. "Late Woodland Continuity and Change in the Saginaw Valley of Michigan." *Arctic Anthropology* 22 (1985): 141–52.

Bridging the Years: A Bicentennial Project. Port Huron, MI: Michigan American Revolution Bicentennial Commission, Port Huron Area Bicentennial Committee, [1976?].

Bronner, Wally. *Sharing Joy: An Autobiography*. Coauthored by William Anderson. Frankenmuth, MI: Bronner's Christmas Wonderland, 2006.

Brooky, Kyle. *Abandoned Flint*. N.p.: Arcadia Publishing, 2020.

Brown, Michael R. "The Parish of Mt. Morris St. Mary's: An Examination of an Irish-Catholic Community, 1860–1900." Master's thesis, University of Michigan–Flint, 1981.

Buchanan, Janet, Seta Chorbajian, Andrea Dominguez, Brandon Hartleben, Brianna Knoppow, Joshua Miller, Caitlin Schulze, and Cecelia Seiter. "Restoring the Shiawassee Flats: Estuarine Gateway to Saginaw Bay." Project for MS, School of Natural Resources & Environment, University of Michigan.

Bullard, Catherine Crapo. *Crapo Farm*. New Bedford, MA: Published by the author, 1961.

Burnell, Mary C., and Amy Marcaccio. *Blue Water Reflections: A Pictorial History of Port Huron and the St. Clair River District*. Norfolk, VA: The Donning Company, 1983.

Byrds, The (Bernice and Debby). *Shall I Tell You? (From the Heart)*. Ypsilanti, MI: Pathway, [196-?], 33⅓ rpm.

Celebrating 90 Years, 1917 to 2007: GM Powertrain Saginaw Malleable Iron Plant. Saginaw, MI: Saginaw News, 2007.

Celebrating 150 Years: Huron County, Michigan, 1859–2009. Bad Axe, MI: Huron County Historical Society, 2009.

Chariton, Jordan. *We the Poisoned: Exposing the Flint Water Crisis Cover-Up and the Poisoning of 100,000*

Americans. Lanham, MD: Rowman & Littlefield, 2024.

Charles Stewart Mott Foundation. Annual Reports, 1970–2022. https://www.mott.org/about/annual-reports/.

Cherishing Today . . . Dreaming Tomorrow, 1891–1991: St. Anne Parish, Linwood, Michigan. N.p., 1991.

Clark, Anna. *The Poisoned City: Flint's Water and the American Urban Tragedy*. New York: Metropolitan Books, 2018.

Cleland, Charles E. *Faith in Paper: The Ethnohistory and Litigation of Upper Great Lakes Indian Treaties*. Ann Arbor: University of Michigan Press, 2011.

———. *Rites of Conquest: The History and Culture of Michigan's Native Americans*. Ann Arbor: University of Michigan Press, 1992.

Cohen, Joseph Jacob. *In Quest of Heaven: The Story of the Sunrise Co-operative Farm Community*. Philadelphia: Porcupine Press, 1975.

A Comprehensive Assessment of America's Infrastructure. Reston, VA: American Society of Civil Engineers, 2021.

Conway, James. *Little MO*. Philadelphia: Xlibris, 2000.

Crapo, Henry Howland, II. *The Story of Henry Howland Crapo 1804–1869*. Boston: The Todd, 1933.

Crawford, Kim. *The Daring Trader: Jacob Smith in the Michigan Territory, 1802–1825*. East Lansing: Michigan State University Press, 2012.

Cumming, John. *The Lynching at Corunna*. Mount Pleasant, MI: Private press of John Cumming, 1980.

Dandaneau, Steven P. *A Town Abandoned: Flint, Michigan, Confronts Deindustrialization*. Albany: State University of New York Press, 1996.

Davis, Katrinell M. *Tainted Tap: Flint's Journey from Crisis to Recovery*. Chapel Hill: University of North Carolina Press, 2021.

———. "Too Close to Home: The Incidence and Health Effects of Neighborhood Neglect in Flint, Michigan." In *Urban Emergency (Mis)Management and the Crisis of Neoliberalism*, edited by Terressa A. Benz and Graham Cassano, 120–59. Leiden: Brill, 2021.

DeLind, Laura B. "Place, Work, and Civic Agriculture: Common Fields for Cultivation." *Agriculture and Human Values* 19 (2002): 217–24.

———. "The State, Hog Hotels, and the 'Right to Farm': A Curious Relationship." *Agriculture and Human Values* (Summer 1995): 34–44.

———. "Sustainable Agriculture in Michigan: Some Missing Dimensions." *Agriculture and Human Values* 8, no. 4 (Fall 1991): 38–45.

Dennis, Jerry, and Craig Date. *Canoeing Michigan Rivers: A Comprehensive Guide to 45 Rivers*. [Petoskey, MI]: Friede Publications, 1986.

Deterding, John G. *Living with Jesus: A History of the Evangelical Lutheran Church of Saint Lorenz, Frankenmuth, Michigan*. N.p., [1995].

Dewhurst, C. Kurt, and Yvonne R. Lockwood, eds. *Michigan Folklife Reader*. East Lansing: Michigan State University Press, 1987.

Diba Jimooyung: Telling Our Story; A History of the Saginaw Ojibwe Anishinabek. Mount Pleasant, MI: Saginaw Chippewa Indian Tribe of Michigan, 2003.

Dinsmore, Dorothy Stott, and Anne M. Hallock. *Indian Dave's Travels: A Colorful Character.* N.p.: Published by the authors, 1987.

Dorr, John A., and Donald F. Eschman. *Geology of Michigan.* Ann Arbor: University of Michigan Press, 1970.

Doyle, Jack. *Trespass Against Us: Dow Chemical & the Toxic Century.* Monroe, ME: Common Courage Press, 2004.

Drury, Patricia, and Ron Bloomfield. *Recipe for a Community: The Historical and Culinary Growth of 19th Century Linwood, Michigan.* Bay City, MI: Bay County Historical Society, 2001.

Dudley, Kathryn Marie. *Debt and Dispossession: Farm Loss in America's Heartland.* Chicago: University of Chicago Press, 2000.

———. *The End of the Line: Lost Jobs, New Lives in Postindustrial America.* Chicago: University of Chicago Press, 1994.

Dunnigan, Brian Leigh. *Frontier Metropolis: Picturing Early Detroit, 1701–1838.* Detroit: Wayne State University Press, 2001.

Dustin, Fred. "The Treaty of Saginaw, 1819." *Michigan History Magazine* 4 (1920): 243–78.

Ederer, Roselynn. *Forever Young at Heart.* Building a Michigan Lumber Town 5. Saginaw, MI: Thomastown Publishing, 2003.

———. *Indiantown: An Ojibwe Village Becomes a Farm Community.* Saginaw, MI: Thomastown Publishing, 2011.

Editor of the Western Gazette. *Three Months in the United States and Canada.* Yeovil: Office of the Western Gazette, [1886].

Edsforth, Ronald. *Class Conflict and Cultural Consensus: The Making of a Mass Consumer Society in Flint, Michigan.* New Brunswick, NJ: Rutgers University Press, 1987.

Edmunds, David, and Joseph L. Peyser. *The Fox Wars: Mesquakie Challenge to New France.* Norman: University of Oklahoma Press, 1993.

Elder, Jane E. *Wilderness, Water, and Rust: A Journey toward Great Lakes Resilience.* East Lansing, MI: Michigan State University Press, 2024.

Ellis, Anthony R. *Running the Crim: Stories from the Coolest Race in Michigan.* Flint Township, MI: Running Brain, 2005.

Ellis, Franklin. *History of Genesee County, Michigan: With Illustrations and Biographical Sketches.* Philadelphia: Everts & Abbott, 1879.

———. *History of Shiawassee and Clinton Counties, Michigan.* Philadelphia: D. W. Ensign, 1880.

Erickson, Robert E. *History of the Evangelical Lutheran Church of the Following Counties of Michigan: Wayne, Oakland, Bay, Midland, Monroe, Macomb, St. Clair, Saginaw, Gladwin, Clare, Huron, Sanilac, Tuscola, Lapeer, Ingham, Jackson, Shiawasee, Genesee, Calhoun, Lenawee, Hillsdale, Branch, and Presque Isle.* Detroit: Robert E. Erickson, 1924.

Fainstein, Susan S. *The Just City.* Ithaca: Cornell University Press, 2010.

Farrand, William R., and Robert W. Kelley. *The Glacial Lakes Around Michigan.* Bulletin 4, Michigan Department of Environmental Quality. [Lansing: Department of Conservation,] 1988.

Fine, Lisa M. *The Story of REO Joe: Work, Kin, and Community in Autotown, U.S.A.* Philadelphia: Temple University Press, 2004.

Fine, Sidney. *Sit-Down: The General Motors Strike of 1936–1937*. Ann Arbor: University of Michigan Press, 1969.

Firey, Walter. *Social Aspects to Land Use Planning in the Country-City Fringe: The Case of Flint, Michigan*. East Lansing: Michigan State College, 1946.

Fitting, James E. *Archaeology of Michigan: A Guide to the Prehistory of the Great Lakes Region*. Garden City, NY: The Natural History Press for the American Museum of Natural History, 1970.

Flinn, Gary. *Hidden History of Flint*. Charleston, SC.: History Press, 2017.

———. *Remembering Flint, Michigan: Stories from the Vehicle City*. American Chronicles: A History Press. Charleston, SC: History Press, 2010.

Form, William H., and Sigmund Nosow. *Community in Disaster*. New York: Harper, 1958.

Fox, Truman B. *History of Saginaw County, from the Year 1819 down to the Present Time*. East Saginaw, MI: Enterprise Printing, 1858.

Frazier, LaToya Ruby. *Flint is Family in Three Acts*. Göttingen, Germany: Steidl; Pleasantville, NY: The Gordon Parks Foundation, 2022.

Frelich, L. E. *Forest Dynamics and Disturbance Regimes: Studies from Temperate Evergreen-Deciduous Forests*. Cambridge: Cambridge University Press, 2002.

Fromwiller, Laura, and Jan Gillis. *Oakdale: The Lapeer State Home*. Images of America. Charleston, SC: Arcadia Publishing, 2014.

Fuller, Burns. *Burns Fuller Remembers: Fenton, My Home Town*. Fenton, MI: Independent Printing, 1966.

Fünfzig Jahre deutschen Strebens: Gedenkblätter zum fünfzigjährigen Jubiläum der "Germania" von Saginaw, Michigan, U.S.A. N.p., 1906.

Gansser, Augustus H. *History of Bay County and Representative Citizens*. Chicago: Richmond & Arnold, 1905.

Gault, Edgar H., and C. N. Davisson. *The Saginaw Valley Problem: A Preliminary Report Prepared for the Michigan Planning Commission for the Use of Its Organization Committee on Saginaw Valley Regional Planning*. N.p., 1945.

Ghimire, S. N., and J. W. Schulenberg. "Impacts of Climate Change on the Environment, Increase in Reservoir Levels, and Safety Threats to Earthen Dams: Post Failure Case Study of Two Cascading Dams in Michigan." *Civil and Environmental Engineering* 18, no. 2 (2022): 551–64. https://doi.org/10.2478/cee-2022-0053.

Goodstein, Anita Shafer. "Labor Relations in the Saginaw Valley Lumber Industry, 1865–1885." *Bulletin of the Business Historical Society* 22, no. 4 (1953): 193–221.

Griswold, Wendy. *American Guides*. Chicago: University of Chicago Press, 2016.

———. *Regionalism and the Reading Class*. Chicago: University of Chicago Press, 2008.

Gulig, Anthony. *An Historical Analysis of the Saginaw, Black River, and Swan Creek Chippewa Treaties of 1855 and 1864*. N.p.: State of Michigan, 2007. https://turtletalk.blog/wp-content/uploads/2008/05/gulig-report.pdf.

Gustin, Lawrence R., ed. *Picture History of Flint*. Grand Rapids, MI: William B. Eerdmans, 1976.

Gwinn, Florence McKinnon. *Pioneer History of Huron County, Michigan*. N.p.: Huron County Pioneer and Historical Society, 1932.

Haddex, Diane. *Alden B. Dow: Midwestern Modern*. Midland, MI: Alden B. Dow Home and Studio, 2007.

Hamilton, Ian. "Theodore Roethke." *Agenda* (London, UK) 3, no. 4 (1964): 5–10.

Hanna-Attisha, Mona, Jenny LaChance, Richard Casey Sadler, and Allison Champney Schnepp. "Elevated Blood Lead Levels in Children Associated with the Flint Drinking Water Crisis: A Spatial Analysis of Risk and Public Health Response." *American Journal of Public Health* 106, no. 2 (2016): 283–90.

Hansen, Marcus Lee. *The Mingling of the Canadian and American Peoples*. Vol. 1, *Historical*. Edited by John Bartlet Brebner. New York: Russell & Russell, 1940.

Hargreaves, Irene M., and Harold M. Foehl. *The Story of Logging the White Pine in the Saginaw Valley*. Bay City: Red Keg Press, 1964.

Harrington, Michael. "No 'Half-Baked Bacchus' from Saginaw." *Commonweal* 89, no. 20 (February 21, 1969): 656–57.

Hathaway, Phil. *History of the Shiawassee River: A 123-Mile Long Tale about Geology, Native Americans, Pioneers, Water Power, Water Users, Resource Degradation and Recovery*. 3rd ed. N.p.: Friends of the Shiawassee River, 2021.

Hayes, Yutha. *Going Up the Swartz: History of Swartz Creek Area, 1836–1976*. Linden, MI: Creative Communications, 1976.

Hazelton, George H. "Reminiscences of Seventeen Years Residence in Michigan, 1836–1853." *Michigan Pioneer Collections*, 1st ser., vol. 21 (1892): 370–418.

Heitmeyer, Mickey E., Cary M. Aloia, Eric M. Dunton, Brian J. Newman, and Josh D. Eash. *Hydrogeomorphic Evaluation of Ecosystem Restoration and Management Options for Shiawassee National Wildlife Refuge*. Bloomfield, MO: Blue Heron Conservation Design and Printing, 2013.

Henthorn, Thomas. "A Catholic Dilemma: White Flight in Northwest Flint." *Michigan Historical Review* 31, no. 2 (2005): 1–42.

———. "The Civic Park Story." *Michigan Historical Review* 47, no. 2 (2021): 1–29.

Hey, Chester. *Stories of the Upper Thumb: Huron County; Prose, Poems and Pictures*. N.p., 1932.

Hickey, M. "Reminiscences of Rev. M. Hickey, Clergyman of the Methodist Episcopal Church, Residing at Detroit, Michigan." *Michigan Pioneer Collections*, 1st ser., vol. 4 (1881): 23–33.

Highsmith, Andrew R. *Demolition Means Progress: Flint, Michigan, and the Fate of the American Metropolis*. Chicago: University of Chicago Press, 2015.

The History, Commercial Advantages and Future Prospects of Bay City, Michigan. Bay City, MI: Henry S. Dow, 1875.

History of Lapeer County, Michigan. Chicago: H. R. Page, 1884.

History of Saginaw County, Michigan. Chicago: Chas. C. Chapman, 1881.

History of Tuscola and Bay Counties, Michigan. Chicago: H. R. Page, 1883.

Hollander, Gail M. "Raising Cane in the Glades: Regional Development and Agroenvironmental Conflict in South Florida." PhD diss., University of Iowa, 1999. ProQuest (9945417).

———. "'Subject to Control': Shifting Geographies of Race and Labour in US Sugar Agroindustry, 1930–1950." *Cultural Geographies* 13 (2006): 266–92.

Houdek, John T., and Charles F. Heller, Jr. "Part-Owner Farm Operators in Nineteenth-Century

Michigan: Forerunners of Today's Commercial Farmers." *Agricultural History* 76, no. 3 (2002): 546–77.

Huggler, Thomas E. *Westwind Woods*. Lansing, MI: Michigan United Conservation Clubs, 1978.

Huggler, Thomas E., and Avery Color Studios. *Midwest Meanders*. Otisville, MI: Avery Color Studios, 1984.

"Huron County: Tip of Michigan's Thumb." Special issue, *Michigan Tradesman*, no. 3325 (October 28, 1953).

Ihlder, John. "Flint: When Men Build Automobiles Who Builds Their City?" *The Survey* 36, no. 23 (1916): 549–57.

Images: Millennium Edition. Marlette, MI: Marlette History Society, [2000?].

Industries of the Saginaws. East Saginaw, MI: J. M. Elstner, 1887.

Jackson, Douglas R., and Ione M. Korff. *Early Tales of Akron, Michigan*. Midland, MI: Published by the authors, 2008.

Jackson, Kenneth T. *Crabgrass Frontier: The Suburbanization of the United States*. New York: Oxford University Press, 1985.

Jacobs, Jane. *The Death and Life of Great American Cities*. 1961. New York: Modern Library, 2011.

———. *Vital Little Plans: The Short Works of Jane Jacobs*. Edited by Samuel Zipp and Nathan Storring. New York: Random House, 2016.

Jezierski, John Vincent. *Enterprising Images: The Goodridge Brothers, African American Photographers, 1847–1922*. Detroit: Wayne State University Press, 2000.

Johnston, Basil. *Ojibway Heritage*. Lincoln: University of Nebraska Press, 1976.

Jordan, Laura. "Neoliberalism Writ Large and Small." *Anthropology Matters* 15, no. 1 (2014): 18–62.

Judd, Richard W. *Socialist Cities: Municipal Politics and the Grass Roots of American Socialism*. Albany: State University of New York Press, 1989.

Kaiser, James M. "Wilhelm Loehe and the Chippewa Outreach at Frankenmuth." *Missio Apostolica* 22, no. 1 (2014): 73–82.

Kanter, Deborah E. "Mexican Priests and Migrant Ministry in the Midwest, 1953–1961." *U.S. Catholic Historian* 39, no. 1 (2021): 93–112.

Karpiuk, Robert S. *Dow Research Pioneers: Recollections*. Midland, MI: Pendell Publishing, 1984.

Kilar, Jeremy W. *Germans in Michigan*. Discovering the Peoples of Michigan. East Lansing: Michigan State University Press, 2002.

———. *Michigan's Lumbertowns: Lumbermen and Laborers in Saginaw, Bay City, and Muskegon, 1870–1905*. Detroit: Wayne State University Press, 1990.

Kilar, Jeremy W., with Sandy L. Schwan. *Saginaw's Changeable Past: An Illustrated History*. St. Louis: G. Bradley Publishing, 1994.

Kingston, MI: 1857–1982. Kingston, MI: Kingston Historical Society, 1982.

Knott, John R. *Imagining the Forest: Narratives of Michigan and the Upper Midwest*. Ann Arbor: University of Michigan Press, 2012.

Kohn, Howard. *The Last Farmer: An American Memoir*. Lincoln: University of Nebraska Press, 2004.

Krafft, Norman A. *Beloved Brother: Bootleg and Bounty; Frankenmuth and the 1930s*. N.p.: Published by the author, 1994.

LaForest, James. "'Muskrat French': Origins of a Culture, a Language, and a People." *Michigan Historical Review* 40, no. 2 (2014): 87–100.

Lamarre, Jean. *The French Canadians of Michigan: Their Contribution to the Development of the Saginaw Valley and the Keweenaw Peninsula, 1840–1914*. Detroit: Wayne State University Press, 2003.

Lamb, Brooks. *Love for the Land: Lessons from Farmers Who Persist in Place*. New Haven: Yale University Press, 2023.

Lamotte Missionary Church: The First One Hundred Years, 1887–1987. N.p., [1987?].

Larsen, Vickie, John Pendell, and Lloyd Witt. "Father Norman DuKette: The Beginnings of an Archival History, Christ the King 90th Anniversary, Nov. 23, 2019." Unpublished.

Lehmann, Dirk. "German in Every Particular? From Historic Settlement to Theme Towns: Examples of 'Little Germanies' in America." PhD diss., Pennsylvania State University, 2007. ProQuest (3380607).

Lemieux, Christina M. "Michigan Utopia: The Sunrise Cooperative Farm Community." *Chronicle* 23, no. 6 (1988): 4–8.

Lewis, Martin D. *Lumberman from Flint: The Michigan Career of Henry H. Crapo, 1855–1869*. Detroit: Wayne State University Press, 1958.

Lewis, Peirce F. "Impact of Negro Migration on the Electoral Geography of Flint, Michigan, 1932–1962: A Cartographic Analysis." *Annals of the Association of American Geographers* 55, no. 1 (1965): 1–25.

Lincoln, James H., and James L. Donahue. *Fiery Trial*. New ed. Lansing: Historical Society of Michigan, 2022.

Lord, George, and Albert Price. "Growth Ideology in a Period of Decline: Deindustrialization and Restructuring, Flint Style." *Social Problems* 39, no. 2 (1992): 155–69.

Love, Edmund G. *The Situation in Flushing*. New York: Harper & Row, 1965.

Luckhard, Charles F. *Faith in the Forest: A True Story of Pioneer Lutheran Missionaries; Laboring Among the Chippewa Indians in Michigan, 1833–1868*. Repr., Red Flannel Underwear Press, n.d.

Lusch, David P., Kristy E. Stanley, Randall J. Schaetzl, Anthony D. Kendall, Remke L. Van Dam, Asger Nielsen, Bradley E. Blumer, et al. "Characterization and Mapping of Patterned Ground in the Saginaw Lowlands, Michigan: Possible Evidence for Late-Wisconsin Permafrost." *Annals of the Association of American Geographers* 99, no. 3 (2009): 445–66.

Madden, Michael. "You'd Never Know It Existed: Abram Peer, Forgotten Amusements, & a Hidden Lakeshore." *The Historian: A Publication of the Genesee County Historical Society* (Fall–Winter 2023): 40–41.

Mapes, Kathleen. *Sweet Tyranny: Migrant Labor, Industrial Agriculture, and Imperial Politics*. Urbana: University of Illinois Press, 2009.

Marsh, William M. *Landscape Planning: Environmental Applications*. 3rd ed. New York: Wiley, 1998.

McClelland, Edward. *Midnight in Vehicle City: General Motors, Flint, and the Strike That Created the Middle Class*. Boston: Beacon Press, 2021.

———. *Nothin' But Blue Skies: The Heyday, Hard Times, and Hopes of America's Industrial Heartland*. New York: Bloomsbury Press, 2013.

McCormick, William R. "Sketch by W. R. McCormick." *Michigan Pioneer Collections*, 1st ser., vol. 4

(1881): 364–73.

McEwen, Jerry. *Room at the Inn: The Tiny Zehnder Story*. Chelsea, MI: Bookcrafters, 1999.

McKether, Willie. "Roots of Civil Rights Politics in Northern Churches: Black Migrants to Saginaw, Michigan, 1915 to 1960." *Critical Sociology* 37, no. 5 (2011): 689–707.

———. "Voices in Transition: African American Migration to Saginaw, Michigan, 1920–1960." PhD diss., Wayne State University, 2005. ProQuest (3196218).

Mershon, William B. *Recollections of My Fifty Years Hunting and Fishing*. Boston: The Stratford Company, 1923.

Methodist Episcopal Church. Missionary Society. *Thirty-fifth Annual Report of the Missionary Society of the Methodist Episcopal Church*. New York: Conference Office, 1854.

Michigan: A Guide to the Wolverine State. American Guide. New York: Oxford University Press, 1941.

Michigan Supreme Court. *Reports of Cases Heard and Decided in the Supreme Court of Michigan from November 14, 1860, to the end of January Term, 1862*. Vol. 5. Ann Arbor: Thomas M. Cooley, 1862.

Miller, Albert. "Incidents in the Early History of the Saginaw Valley." *Michigan Pioneer Collections*, 1st ser., vol. 13 (1889): 351–83.

———. "Michigan Pioneer Lumbermen." *Lumberman's Gazette* 1, no. 3 (1872): 18; 1, no. 4 (1872): 19; 1, no. 6 (1872): 9.

———. "Pioneer Sketches." *Michigan Pioneer Collections*, 1st ser., vol. 7 (1884): 223–62.

———. "The Rivers of the Saginaw Valley Sixty Years Ago." *Michigan Pioneer Collections*, 1st ser., vol. 14 (1889): 495–510.

Mills, James Cooke. *History of Saginaw County, Michigan*. Saginaw: Seemann & Peters, 1918.

Mitsch, William J., and James G. Gosselink. *Wetlands*. 3rd ed. New York: John Wiley & Sons, 2000.

Mitts, Dorothy Marie. *That Noble Country: The Romance of the St. Clair River Country*. Philadelphia: Dorrance and Company, 1968.

Moore, Michael. *Here Comes Trouble: Stories from My Life*. New York: Grand Central Publishing, 2011.

Nelb, Tawny Ryan. "The Tittabawassee Boom Company: A Mixed Blessing of the Lumbering Industry." *The Midland Log: A Journal of the Midland County Historical Society* (Summer/Fall 2023): 3–56.

Neumann, Tracy. *Remaking the Rust Belt: The Postindustrial Transformation of North America*. Philadelphia: University of Pennsylvania Press, 2016.

Nickels, Ashley E. Power, *Participation, and Protest in Flint, Michigan: Unpacking the Policy Paradox of Municipal Takeovers*. Philadelphia: Temple University Press, 2019.

Nielsen, Waldemar A. *The Big Foundations*. New York: Columbia University Press, 1972.

O'Gieblyn, Megan. *Interior States: Essays*. New York: Anchor Books, 2018.

The Past and Present of Shiawassee County, Michigan. Lansing: Michigan Historical Publishing Association [1906?].

Pauli, Benjamin J. *Flint Fights Back: Environmental Justice and Democracy in the Flint Water Crisis*. Cambridge, MA: MIT Press, 2019.

Perry, Oliver Hazard. *Hunting Expeditions of Oliver Hazard Perry, of Cleveland, Verbatim from his Diaries*. Cleveland: Private distribution, 1899.

Pickelhaupt, Bill. *The Right Place at the Right Time: The Volga-Germans of Michigan's Thumb*. N.p.:

Flylister Press, 2009.

Pielack, Leslie K. *The Saginaw Trail: From Native American Path to Woodward Avenue*. Charleston, SC: History Press, 2018.

Pierce, James. "Notice of the Peninsula of Michigan, in relation to its Topography, Scenery, Agriculture, Population, Resources, &c." *American Journal of Science* 10, no. 2 (1826): 304–19.

Planning & Zone Center, Inc. *Frankenmuth and Frankenmuth Township: 2015 Joint Growth Management Plan*. City of Frankenmuth and Frankenmuth Planning Commissions, 2015. https://cms6.revize.com/revize/frankenmuth/2015_Master_Plan_Final.pdf.

Plemmons, Michael. *Fianna: A Story Every Canadian Learns, But One Conveniently Forgotten in America*. Chicago: 3A Publishing, 2009.

Ponder, C. S. "Spatializing the Municipal Bond Market: Urban Resilience under Racial Capitalism." *Annals of the American Association of Geographers* 111, no. 7 (2021): 2112–29.

Pound, Arthur. *The Turning Wheel: The Story of General Motors Through Twenty-five Years, 1908–1933*. Garden City, NY: Doubleday, Doran, 1934.

Quastler, I. E. *Where the Rails Cross: A Railroad History of Durand, Michigan*. Coronado, CA: R & I Enterprises, 2005.

Quentin, Karl Quentin. *Reisebilder und Studien aus dem Norden der Vereinigten Staaten von Amerika*. Arnsberg, H. F. Grote, 1851.

Rabin, R. "The Lead Industry and Lead Water Pipes: 'A Modest Campaign.'" *American Journal of Public Health* 98, no. 9 (2008): 1584–92.

Rebanks, James. *Pastoral Song: A Farmer's Journey*. New York: Mariner Books, 2020.

Renehan, Edward. *The Life of Charles Stewart Mott: Industrialist, Philanthropist, Mr. Flint*. Ann Arbor: University of Michigan Press, 2019.

Reuter, Dorothy. *Methodist Indian Ministries in Michigan, 1830–1990*. N.p.: United Methodist Historical Society, 1990.

Rhoads, Roxanne, and Joe Schipani. *Haunted Flint*. Charleston, SC: Haunted Press, 2019.

Robinson, Sidney K. *The Architecture of Alden B. Dow*. Detroit: Wayne State University Press, 1983.

Rogers, D. Laurence. *Paul Bunyan: How a Terrible Timber Feller Became a Legend*. Bay City, MI: Historical Press, 1993.

Rosales, Steven. "'This Street is Essentially Mexican': An Oral History of the Mexican American Community of Saginaw, Michigan, 1920–1980." *Michigan Historical Review* 40, no. 2 (2014): 33–62.

Ruffin, Roosevelt Samuel. *Black Presence in Saginaw, Mich: 1855–1900*. N.p., 1978.

Russell, John Andrew. *The Germanic Influence in the Making of Michigan*. Detroit: University of Detroit, 1927.

Sagatoo, Mary. *Wah Sash Kah Moqua: Or Thirty-three Years Among the Indians*. Boston: Charles A. White, 1897.

"Das Saginaw-Thal." *Hamburger Auswanderungs-Zeitung: Organ für Auswanderung und Colonisation*, June 4, 1859, 5.

Salamon, Sonya. *Newcomers to Old Towns: Suburbanization of the Heartland*. Chicago: University of Chicago Press, 2003.

Sanders, Rhonda. *Bronze Pillars: An Oral History of African-Americans in Flint.* Flint, MI: Flint Journal and Alfred P. Sloan Museum, 1995.

Salamon, Sonya. "From Hometown to Nontown: Rural Community Effects of Suburbanization." *Rural Sociology* 68, no. 1 (2003): 1–24.

Schmidt, Utz H. *Michigan's Thumb, a Paradise for Saxonia Settlers: Conflict and Hardship while Forming Colonie Saxonia in Delaware Township, Sanilac County, Michigan 1850s-1930s.* Palms, MI: Published by the author, 2019.

Schramm, Jack E., William H. Henning, and Richard R. Andrews. *When Eastern Michigan Rode the Rails.* Rev. ed. Glendale, CA: Interurban Press, 1984.

Schultz, Gerard. *The New History of Michigan's Thumb.* N.p., 1964.

Schutter, Kara and Taylor Bruce. *Detroit.* Austin, TX: Wildsam Field Guides, 2021.

Schweitzer, Robert, and Michael W. R. Davis. *America's Favorite Homes: Mail-Order Catalogues as a Guide to Popular Early 20th-Century Houses.* Detroit: Wayne State University Press, 1990.

Sebewaing 150: Sebewaing Township 1853–2003. Sebewaing, MI: Walter J. Rummel, 2003.

Seager, Allan. *The Glass House: The Life of Theodore Roethke.* Ann Arbor: University of Michigan Press, 1991.

Seger, Donna, and Kenneth Seger, for the Fenton Historical Society. *Fenton.* Postcard History. Charleston, SC: Arcadia Publishing, 2009.

Seibert, Allie. *Forgotten Fenton: Uncovering the Mysteries of a Michigan Town.* N.p.: Household History, 2023.

Shadbolt, Ryan P., Eleanor A. Waller, Joseph P. Messina, and Julie A. Winkler. "Source Regions of Lower-Tropospheric Airflow Trajectories for the Lower Peninsula of Michigan: A 40-Year Air Mass Climatology." *Journal of Geophysical Research: Atmospheres,* 111, no. D21 (2006).

Shaw, Elizabeth Philips, and Jeff Ford. *The Lone Wolverine: Tracking Michigan's Most Elusive Animal.* Ann Arbor: University of Michigan Press, 2012.

Shelton, Napier. *Man and Wildlife in the Thumb of Michigan Since the Last Ice Age.* N.p., 2022.

Shofner, Jerrell H. "The Legacy of Racial Slavery: Free Enterprise and Forced Labor in Florida in the 1940s." *Journal of Southern History* 47, no. 3 (1981): 411–26.

Shulman, Holly C., ed. "The Dolley Madison Digital Edition." University of Virginia Press, 2004–2024. https://rotunda.upress.virginia.edu/dmde/.

Shurtleff, William, and Akiko Aoyagi. *History of Soybeans and Soyfoods in Michigan (1853–2021): Extensively Annotated Bibliography and Sourcebook.* Lafayette, CA: Soyinfo Center, 2021.

Sloane, Eric. *A Reverence for Wood.* New York: Ballantine Books, 1965.

Sinclair, Ward. "Dioxin Brings Dow Under Fire: Dow Comes Under Attack for Its Pollutants and Its Politics . . . As Company Town on a Poisoned River Enjoys Its Prosperity." *Washington Post,* April 24, 1983, A1.

Smith, Art. "Community in Action: Statement of Purpose." *Saginaw Afro-Herald* 1, no. 1, August 11, 1967, 2.

Spillman, Don. "Shop Committee Report." *Headlight,* January 20, 1982, 2.

Standard Atlas of Saginaw County, Michigan. Chicago: George A. Ogle, 1916.

Stocker, Harry Emilius. *A Home Mission History of the Moravian Church in the United States and*

Canada. N.p.: Special Publication Committee of the Moravian Church, 1924.

Stout, William A. *Saginaw Bay Waterfowl Hunting and Decoy Carvers*. Bloomfield Hills, MI: Published by the author, 2007.

Strieter, Johannes. *Sacred Storytelling: The Autobiography of Johannes Strieter (1829–1920) and Related Sources*. Translated by Nathaniel J. Biebert. Eugene, OR: Resource Publications, 2020.

Sutton, Robert P. *Communal Utopias and the American Experience: Secular Communities, 1824–2000*. Westport, CT: Praeger, 2004.

Tainted Tap Podcast. "Tainted Tap Podcast." 2021. https://www.buzzsprout.com/1743778.

Tanner, Eloise Mitchell. *It Has Been My Privilege*. Atlanta: Published by the author, 1967.

Terkel, Studs. *Hard Times: An Oral History of the Great Depression*. New York: Pantheon Books, 1970.

Thomas, James M., and A. B. Galatian. *Indian and Pioneer History of the Saginaw Valley*. East Saginaw, MI: Lewis and Lyon, 1866.

Thoreau, Henry David. *Walden, Civil Disobedience, and Other Writings*. Edited by William Rossi. New York: W. W. Norton, 2008.

The Thumb Region of Michigan: As Seen by the Old AAA Traveler. N.p.: Automobile Club of Michigan, [1939?].

Thumb's Up! A Collection of Historical Essays on Huron County and the Thumb. Repr., Sebewaing, MI: Red Flannel Underwear Press, 1999.

Tocqueville, Alexis de. *A Fortnight in the Wilderness*. Delray Beach, FL: Levenger Press, 2003.

———. *Journey to America*. Translated by George Lawrence. Edited by J. P. Mayer. New Haven, CT: Yale University Press, 1960.

Toft, Larry G. *Downtown Saginaw: Heart of a Historic City*. Brookfield, MO: Donning Company Publishers, 2018.

Valdes, Dennis Nodin. *Al Norte: Agricultural Workers in the Great Lakes Region, 1917–1970*. Mexican American Monographs 13. Austin: University of Texas Press, 1991.

Vinyard, JoEllen McNergney. *Right in Michigan's Grassroots: From the KKK to the Michigan Militia*. Ann Arbor: University of Michigan Press, 2011.

Wainwright, Loudon. "The Man in the Middle." *Life*, July 21, 1972.

Wakefield, Francis. "The Elusive Mascoutens." *Michigan History* 50 (September 1966): 228–34.

Warren, Francis Herbert. *Michigan Manual of Freedman's Progress*. [Detroit]: The Commission, 1915.

Weesner, Theodore. *The Car Thief*. 1967. New York: Astor + Blue Editions, 2012.

———. *Winning the City*. New York: Avon Books, 1991.

Weiss, Joanmarie Hofmann. *Fischer Hall: Frankenmuth's Gathering Place*. Frankenmuth, MI: Frankenmuth Historical Association, 1988.

Weitschat, Arthur Alfred. "Bavarianism in Frankenmuth: The Geography of an Ethnic Idea in a Small Town." Master's thesis, Wayne State University, 1976.

West, Kenneth B. "Standard Cotton Products and the General Motors Sit-Down Strike: Some 'Forgotten Men' Remembered." *Michigan Historical Review* 14 (Spring 1988): 57–73.

White, Richard. *The Middle Ground: Indians, Empires, and Republics in the Great Lakes Region, 1650–1815*. Cambridge: Cambridge University Press, 1991.

Whitlock, Annie McMahon. *Place-Based Social Studies Education: Learning from Flint, Michigan*.

Research and Practice in Social Studies. New York: Teachers College Press, 2024.

Wik, Reynold Millard. "Henry Ford's Science and Technology for Rural America." *Technology and Culture* 3, no. 3 (1962): 247–58.

Wilkinson, Alec. *Big Sugar: Seasons in the Cane Fields in Florida*. New York: Vintage Books, 1989.

Willard, Myles. *Birds of the Murphy Lake State Game Area*. Mayville, MI: Published by the author, 2019.

Williams, B. O. "First Settlement of Shiawassee County." *Michigan Pioneer Collections*, 1st ser., vol. 2 (1878): 477–79.

Williams, Ephraim S. "Legends of Indian History in Saginaw Valley." *Michigan Pioneer Collections*, 1st ser., vol. 10 (1886): 134–36.

———. "Remembrances of Early Days in Saginaw in 1833." *Michigan Pioneer Collections*, 1st ser., vol. 10 (1886): 142–47.

———. "The Treaty of Saginaw in the Year 1819." *Michigan Pioneer Collections*, 1st ser., vol. 7 (1886): 262–70.

Williams, Isaac D. *Sunshine and Shadow of Slave Life*. East Saginaw, MI: Evening News Printing and Binding House, 1885.

Wolicki, Dale Patrick, and Bay County Historical Society. *The Historic Architecture of Bay City, Michigan*. Bay City, MI: Bay County Historical Society, 1998.

Wood, Edwin O. *History of Genesee County, Michigan, Her People, Industries and Institutions*. Indianapolis: Federal Publishing Company, 1916.

Woolcock, James E. "The History of Genesee County Parks and Recreation Commission," 2021. Unpublished.

Woolson, Constance Fenimore. *The St. Clair Flats*. [Detroit]: James R. Osgood, 1897.

Worth, Richard. *Baseball Team Names: A Worldwide Dictionary, 1869–2011*. Jefferson, NC: McFarland & Company, 2013.

Wyckoff, Larry M. "1854 Annuity Payment Roll and the Location of the Saginaw Chippewa Bands." 2019. https://www.academia.edu/40021896/1854_Annuity_Payment_Roll_and_the_Location_of_the_Saginaw_Chippewa_Bands.

———. "1864 Chippewas of Saginaw Annuity Payment Roll." 2020. https://www.academia.edu/30802800/1864_Chippewas_of_Saginaw_Annuity_Payment_Roll.

Yates, Dorothy Langdon. *Salt of the Earth: A History of Midland County Michigan*. Midland, MI: Midland County Historical Society, 1987.

Young, Clarence H., and William A. Quinn. *Foundation for Living: The Story of Charles Stewart Mott and Flint*. New York: McGraw-Hill, 1963.

Young, Gordon. *Teardown: Memoir of a Vanishing City*. Berkeley: University of California Press, 2013.

Zehnder, Herman F. *Teach My People the Truth: The Story of Frankenmuth, Michigan*. Bay City, MI: Published by the author, 1970.

Zipes, Greg. *Justice and Faith: The Frank Murphy Story*. Ann Arbor: University of Michigan Press, 2021.

Government Documents

City of Flint. *Capital Investment Plan*. Approved March 1, 2017. https://app.box.com/s/571hyuuk3uh08gkr5gx8uwr0le1m7k3e.

Department of Environment, Great Lakes, and Energy. "Areas of Concern." 2021. https://www.michigan.gov/egle/0,9429,7-135-3313_3677_95060--,00.html.

National Oceanic and Atmospheric Administration. "Longwaves and Shortwaves." https://www.weather.gov/jetstream/longshort.

Office of the Governor. *Flint Water Advisory Task Force: Final Report*. Lansing, MI: Office of the Governor, State of Michigan, 2016. https://www.michigan.gov/documents/snyder/ FWATF_FINAL_REPORT_21March2016_517805_7.pdf.

U.S. White House, "Fact Sheet: The Biden-Harris Lead Pipe and Paint Action Plan." December 16, 2021. https://bidenwhitehouse.archives.gov/briefing-room/statements-releases/2021/12/16/fact-sheet-the-biden-harris-lead-pipe-and-paint-action-plan/.

U.S. Department of Agriculture. "Food Waste FAQs." https://www.usda.gov/foodwaste/faqs.

Newspapers

Bay City Times
Detroit Free Press
Flint Journal
The Headlight
Midland News
Owosso Times
Port Huron Times Herald
Saginaw Afro-Herald
Saginaw News
Tuscola County Advertiser

Manuscript Collections

Bentley Historical Library, University of Michigan–Ann Arbor.

Chatfield, Peter. Paper, c. 1937.

Genesee Historical Collections Center, University of Michigan–Flint Library.

Beasley, Olive. Papers, 1942–1995.

Meister, Richard. Papers, 1970–1980.

University of Michigan-Flint Labor History Project. Interviews available at: https://digitalarchives.umflint.edu/digital/collection/p16210coll3.

CONTRIBUTORS

Thomas F. Adams, a retired General Motors auto worker and labor activist, received the degrees of MA and PhD from Michigan State University.

William David Barillas, author of *The Midwestern Pastoral: Place and Landscape in Literature of the American Heartland* (2006) and editor of *A Field Guide to the Poetry of Theodore Roethke* (2021), has published essays, nonfiction, poems, and interviews. A native of Flint, Michigan, he currently lives in Connecticut.

Jina Bhagat is the daughter of Indian immigrants who moved to Flint in her childhood. Having grown up working and living in a local motel in the city, she thanks her parents, the city of Flint, and its people for being her biggest sources of hope and inspiration.

Bob Campbell, a Flint native, worked at AC Spark Plug and wrote for the *Flint Journal*. His debut novel *Motown Man* was published in 2020.

Connor Coyne, of Flint, has published a serial novel, *Urbantasm*, and a novella, *Hollywood*. He is the director of the Flint-based Gothic Funk Press and facilitates writing workshops for the Gloria Coles Flint Public Library.

Katrinell Davis, Ph.D., a Flint native, is professor of sociology and director of African American Studies at Florida State University. She is the author of *Hard Work Is Not Enough* and *Tainted Tap*, which examine workplace inequalities and the Flint water crisis, respectively.

Trevor Edmunds has worked for the Saginaw Basin Land Conservancy for over twelve years. He is a Michigan master naturalist, International Society of Arboriculture-certified arborist, and holds a bachelor's degree from Northern Michigan University in environmental conservation.

Samuel Fitzpatrick, a Saginaw native now residing in Bay City, is the former education coordinator of the Historical Museum of Bay County and is now the corporate social media coordinator for Xcel Ortho Consulting.

Paul M. Gifford, a Detroit native, is senior associate archivist emeritus at the University of Michigan–Flint, where he worked from 1987 to 2018, and has written books and articles on folk music and genealogy.

Eric J. Girgenti, a Detroit native, graduated from the University of Michigan–Dearborn.

Brittany Grabetz, a University of Michigan–Flint alumna, loves the great outdoors, small towns, and Michigan history.

Tony Groulx, poet and writer, spent his formative years in Bay City, Michigan.

Phil Hathaway is a retired community development director for the City of Owosso, where he regularly interfaced with the Shiawassee River to develop riverside parks. Upon retirement, he authored a water trail plan and secured that designation for the Shiawassee River through the National Park Service's National Water Trail Plan program.

Tom Huggler, a Flint-area native and graduate of University of Michigan–Flint, is a freelance writer and novelist who lives in Mid-Michigan.

Martin M. Kaufman, professor emeritus of geography, planning, and environment at the University of Michigan–Flint, has published widely on environment-related issues and led the effort to map the water pipes during the Flint Water Crisis.

Mary Jo Kietzman, associate professor of English literature at the University of Michigan–Flint, has written books on literature and pedagogy. The needs of Flint students led her to develop courses that involved walking the city and exploring local rivers. This guidebook grew out of these teaching experiences.

Ted McClelland is the author of *Midnight in Vehicle City: General Motors, Flint, and the Strike that Created the Middle Class* and *Chorus of the Union: How Abraham Lincoln and Stephen Douglas Set Aside Their Rivalry to Save the Nation.*

Bre Moore was born and raised in a rural town close to the Thumb and is a graduate of the University of Michigan–Flint.

Artist Relford, raised in Flint, is a paralegal, screenwriter, actor, film producer and director, CEO of the Hip Hop Fraternity Flint Chapter, and founder of the Feed 5000 movement.

Kelsey Ronan grew up in Flint, Michigan, and published *Chevy in the Hole* in 2022, which was a New York Times Book Review Editor's Choice and a Michigan Notable Book. She lives in the Detroit area.

Paul Rozycki is a retired professor of political science at Mott Community College. He planned a career as a journalist but began a teaching career after earning degrees at Northern Illinois University and Indiana University. He retains an interest in journalism, and he has been a political commentator for several local media outlets and writes a monthly column for the *East Village Magazine*.

Zachary Scott is a software engineer currently retraining as a psychotherapist. He was born and raised in Midland, Michigan, and now lives in the Detroit area.

Amanda Seney lives and writes on the edge of the Thumb. Her work is featured in *The MacGuffin*, *Club Plum*, *Qua*, and *Rabble Review*.

Beverley A. Smith is associate professor emeritus of anthropology at the University of Michigan–Flint. Her archaeological work includes projects for Michigan tribes, Parks Canada, and several Michigan universities as a collaborative researcher.

Jeff Vande Zande is a novelist who teaches fiction writing, screenwriting, and film production at Delta College. His novels include *Into the Desperate Country*, *Landscape with Fragmented Figures*, *American Poet*, *Detroit Muscle*, *Rules of Order*, and *The Dance of Rotten Sticks*.

Jennifer Vannette, outreach coordinator for the Castle Museum of Saginaw County History, holds a PhD in history from Central Michigan University, where her research interests centered on human and civil rights.

June Wollstonecraft grew up in Brown City and is a graduate of University of Michigan–Flint. She now lives and works in Flint with her three cats.

William Wright, a Bay City native and resident, worked in planning, economic development, and environmental protection in the Saginaw Valley for more than fifty years.

INDEX

A

B

E

F

I

J

M

P

Q

R

S

T

U

V

W

Y

Z